Eminent Mainers

Royal Bird Bradford

Eminent Mainers

Succinct Biographies of
THOUSANDS OF AMAZING MAINERS,
Mostly Dead,
and a Few People from Away
Who Have Done Something Useful
Within the State of Maine

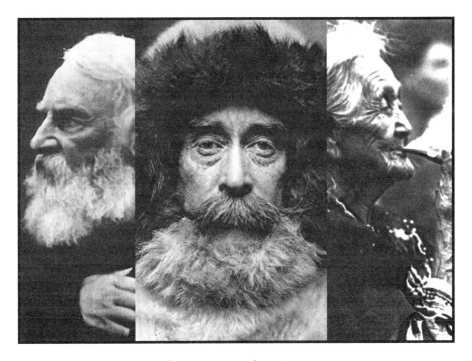

Arthur Douglas Stover

Tilbury House 📖 Publishers
Gardiner, Maine

Tilbury House, Publishers
2 Mechanic Street
Gardiner, Maine 04345
800-582-1899
www.tilburyhouse.com

First Edition: November 2006 • 10 9 8 7 6 5 4 3 2 1

Library of Congress Cataloging-in-Publication Data
Stover, Arthur Douglas, 1947-
Eminent Mainers : succinct biographies of thousands of amazing Mainers mostly dead
and a few people from away who have done something useful within the state of Maine /
compiled by Arthur Douglas Stover. -- 1st ed.
p. cm.
Includes index.
ISBN-13: 978-0-88448-285-7 (pbk. : alk. paper)
ISBN-10: 0-88448-285-5 (pbk. : alk. paper)
1. Maine--Biography--Directories. 2. Maine--History. I. Title.
CT238.S76 2006
920.0741--dc22
                                              2006024301

Designed on Crummett Mountain by Edith Allard, Somerville, Maine
Copyediting by Regina Knox, Readfield, Maine
Printed and bound at Maple Vail, Kirkwood, New York.
Covers printed by the John P. Pow Company

Photographs on pages 121 and 369 courtesy of of the author; photographs on pages 46, 55, 64, 65,
163, 171, 188, 271, 282, 320, 357, 385, 399, 403, 501, and 504 courtesy of Maine Historic
Preservation Commission; all others courtesy of Maine State Museum.

For my friend William David "Bill" Barry,
who also cares deeply for this peculiar tribe

Another damned fat, thick, square book!
Scribble, scribble, scribble! Eh! Mr. Gibbon?

—WILLIAM HENRY, DUKE OF GLOUCESTER 1743–1805
Upon being presented the second volume of The Decline and Fall of the Roman Empire by the
author, Edward Gibbon.

When you steal from one author,
it's plagiarism,
if you steal from many,
its research

—WILSON MIZNER 1876-1933

Yet everybody says I'm such a disagreeable man!
And I can't think why!

—PRINCESS IDA 1884
Sir William Schwenk Gilbert 1836-1911

Take, therefor, no thought unto the morrow
For the morrow shall that thought unto itself.
Sufficient unto the day
Is the evil thereof

MATTHEW VI, 34

Introduction

In 1934 Arnold Toynbee, in his multi-volume *A Study in History*, proposed a theory of "optimum climate" for the development of civilizations. One of his supporting examples was the difference between Massachusetts and Maine: "Massachusetts has always been one of the leading English-speaking communities on the North American continent...on the other hand, Maine has always been unimportant and obscure...[surviving] as a kind of 'museum-piece'—a relic of seventeenth-century New England, a land of woods and lakes which is still inhabited by woodsmen and watermen and hunters.... Maine today is at once one of the longest-settled regions within the frontiers of the Union and one of the least urbanized and least sophisticated."

What follows is, among other things, a refutation of Dr. Toynbee's thesis.

I began this compilation as an adjunct to a proposal for the placement of historical markers and plaques through the state. In time, the growing list took on a life of its own, although the original intent remains a valid one. As I made additions, some patterns emerged, for example, certain towns or groups of towns seem, despite their rural and isolated nature, to be unusually productive: how odd that of the five Mainers accorded British knighthoods, two (Sir Hiram Maxim and Sir Harry Oakes) were born in Sangerville. Another characteristic is mobility: being from a maritime culture, Mainers weren't deterred by great distances or the perils of travel from departing for the gold fields of California or the alien cultures of Hawaii or Japan, Ethiopia, or Japan. Mainers also have a well-known penchant for invention, be it the microwave oven or the doughnut, the machine gun or the micrometer. The list is long. Mainers have a talent for the publication of books and magazines: the publishing houses of George Putnam, Cyrus H. K. Curtis, Frank Munsey, William Howard Gannett, Alden Blethen, and Liberty Holden, among others, attest to that assertion. Several Mainers have become household names: Eben Jordan of Jordan Marsh, Amos Whitney of Pratt & Whitney, James Sanborn of Chase & Sanborn, F. E. & F. O. Stanley of Stanley Steamer fame. Other Mainers founded well-known companies, such as General Mills, International Harvester, IBM, Standard & Poor's, the Cadillac Motorcar Co., the A & P, United Artists, and others.

I began my search with a fairly compulsive reading of sundry volumes of *Who Was Who* followed by a search of the *Dictionary of American Biography*, *Appleton's Cyclopedia*, *Grove's Dictionary of Music*, and a host of other specialized biographical dictionaries. A close reading of Kenneth Thompson's *Civil War Maine Hall of Fame* and Jeff Hollinsworth's *Magnificent Mainers* proved very useful, as did the two volumes of William Bunting's *A Day's Work*. The Maine State Library has a fairly complete collection of Maine biographies, as does the Maine Historical Society.

My original manuscript, extracted with some difficulty from my computer, contained some 4,000 names. My editor insisted on paring it down so that it would not assume the proportions of a doorstop. Certainly there are many interesting, accomplished individuals who are not included herein, but my lists continue to grow. Once begun, how can one stop?

My thanks go to—

At the Maine Historical Society: William D. Barry, Matthew Jude Barker, John Mayer, Stephanie Philbrick, and Nicholas Noyes; at the Maine State Library: Cathryn Wilson, Susan McCarthy, Emil Schoeder, Melanie Mohney, Susan Quirion-Lord, Marie Pierce, and Ben Keating; at the Maine State Museum: Bruce Bourque, Edwin Churchill, Deanna Bonner-Ganter (who was particularly helpful in selecting photos from the MSM archives), Marian Smith, and Joseph R. Phillips; at the Maine Historic Preservation Commission: Earle G. Shuttleworth, Jr., and Elizabeth Trautman; patient friends: Brooks and Jeff Randolph, Roby and Candace O'Brien, Sandra Hodge, Joe Barth and Doreen Conboy, Peter Green, Kathy Bardford, Pam Burr, Tom Chapin, Lucia Robinson, Bill Bunting, Fred and Marge Blonder, Chris and Olga Hasty, Les Fossel, Chris Cooper, Millaine Wooley, Mike Herz, Nigel Calder, Dane Anderson, Chace Anderson (who provided useful information about Liberty Holden), Eleanor Everson, Jay Robbins, Martha Frink, Robert and Carol Lenna, Joe Muir; my editor/publisher, Jennifer Bunting, who patiently nudged me through the ups and downs of turning my lists into a book; especial thanks go to Noel Coulantes, who simply gave me a new computer system when he saw the antique I was using, and also to his ever-lovely (and knowledgble) sidekick, Heidemarie Nyhuis, who has had to extract me, more than once, from Computer Hell, by my big toe.

Arthur Douglas Stover
Damariscotta, Maine

Suggestions for the lists welcome at
PO Box 36, Alna, ME 04535, or
stoverdouglas@hotmail.com

A Tantalizing List of Some Probable Firsts

Invented and sold a can opener at age thirteen, later invented the buttonholder for
  Singer—Edward Beecher Allen

Built first oil pipeline in the world, invented first practical elevator, the modern,
  geared fishing reel and the metal tape measure—Leonard Atwood

First person to traverse the entire Appalachian Trail—Myron Haliburton Avery

First man to catch a salmon on the Penotscot with a fly—Fred Wellington Ayer

First American physician to use the hypodermic syringe—Benjamin Fordyce Barker

Intented the wave antenna, made studies of the behavior of radio waves in the upper
  atmosphere, oversaw the construction of RCA's first television, designed and
  installed the television antenna atop the Empire State Building—Harold Henry
  Beverage

Discovered Hyperion, the eighth moon of Saturn, discovered the crêpe ring of Saturn,
  discovered the first moon of Neptune, discovered many comets, made the first
  photograph of the moon, first photograph of a star (Vega), and invented the
  chronograph—William Cranch Bond

Inventor of the fish hatching trap and fish ladder—Edward Augustus Brackett

Made first archaeological investigation in Crete—Champlin Burrage

First woman to sing a Wagnerian role in the U.S.—Annie Louise Cary

First floating power plant—Hugh Chisholm

Developed the first commercial chewing gum—John Curtis

Invented a vacuum-operated cotton picker—Woodbury Kidder Dana

First to use traction in orthopedic treatment—Henry Gasslett Davis

First self-propelled farm machine—William Deering

First inexpensive, factory-made watches—Aaron Lufkin Dennison

First to traverse North Africa by motorcycle—Frank A. Elwell

Inventor of circular and band saws with removable teeth—James Ezekiel Emerson

Invented the first electrical fire alarm system in the world and developed the
  aluminum electroplating process—Moses Gerrish Farmer

First woman to complete a round-the-world journey in a Locomobile—Harriet White
  Fisher

First photograph of the spectrum of starlight—John Henry Freese

Inventor of the modern sanitary napkin—Lillian Gilbreth

Opened first kindergarten in the U.S.—Mary J. Garland

Created first intelligence test in the U.S.—Henry Herbert Goddard

Constructed first mechanical calculating machine—George Bernard Grant

Invented the earmuff—Chester Greenwood

Invented the doughnut—Hansen Crockett Gregory

First successful removal of a goiter—Charles Lyman Greene

Produced first breech-loading firearms with interchangeable parts—John Hancock
  Hall

First to sell tea by mail—George Huntington Hartford

Invented the electric tachometer—Neville Monroe Hopkins
Established the first ostrich farm in the U.S.—Charles Fitz Abner Johnson
Invented the first visible writing typewriter (and then the first noiseless typewriter) and a consecutive numbering machine—Wellington Parker Kidder
Invented machinery to make a square-bottomed bag—Margaret Knight
First practical use of caterpillar tread—Alvin Lombard
First clipping service in the U.S.—Robert Luce
First transcriptions of traditional koto music in Western notation—Luther Whiting Mason
Built first tricycle with the front wheel spokes in compression, develped first fully automatic machine gun, invented cordite, the modern aerial bomb, and a steam inhaler for asthmatics—Sir Hiram Stevens Maxim
Invented smokeless cannon powder, maximite, and stabillite—Hudson Maxim
Devised the first rubber drive belt and the first cylinder printing machine—Thomas Jefferson Mayall
Constructed the first sand filter for water purification—Hiram Francis Mills
First American to be decorated by the emperor of Japan—Edward Sylvester Morse
Invented a rubber diving suit with a tightly fitting helmet and leaden shoes—Leonard Norcross
Invented the flat-slab form of reinforced concrete construction—Orlando Whitney Norcross
First symphony and first oratorio composed by an American—John Knowles Paine
Invented first self-recording electrical target for the army—Francis Jarvis Patten
First white woman to winter with an arctic expedition, mother of the most northerly born white child—Josephine Diebitsch Peary
First man to reach the North Pole—Robert Edwin Peary
Invented an essential logging tool, the peavey or cant-dog—Joseph Peavey
Organized first excursion trains in the U.S.—Josiah Perham
First female cabinet member—Francis Perkins
First dietician to use "calories" to calculate diet intake for weight loss—Lulu Hunt Peters
First American to be knighted—Sir William Phips
Invented the radio direction finder—Greenleaf Whittier Pickard
Invented the centrifugal wringer and the wet-wash system still in use—John Carroll Poland
First to climb Mount Washington—Jedidiah Preble
First female graduate of M.I.T. and first professional female scientist in the U.S. —Ellen Henriette Swallow Richards
Inventor of modern gymnastic equipment, such as the horse, parallel bars, rings, &c.—Dudley Allen Sargent
Invented the pile driver—Samuel Sewall
Designed the first complete high-voltage substation—Arthur Elmer Silver

First woman to serve in both houses of Congress—Margaret Chase Smith
Noticed while standing next to a magnetron that the chocolate bar in his pocket had melted without heat, and realized the cooking potential of microwaves—Percy LeBaron Spencer
Invented the air brush, produced the first successful steam-operated automobile in New England, drove the first motorized vehicle to reach the top of Mount Washington—Francis Edgar Stanley and Freelan Oscar Stanley
Red Sox leader in saves and games pitched—Robert William "Bigfoot" Stanley
First physician to administer oxygen—George R. Starkey
Invented combination square and ruler with sliding head, a center tri-square, a bevelling instrument, a surface gauge, a micrometer caliper square, and a number of other unique instruments—Laroy S. Starrett
Chief constructor of the Empire State Building—William Starrett
Invented the duplex system of telegraphy—Joseph Barke Stearns
First photograph of the earth's curvature, first nonstop flight across the U.S.—Albert William Stevens
Author of the first lesbian love story—Margaret Jane Mussey Sweat
Started the first cult in California—Luther Calvin Tibbetts
Invented the Very pistol flare gun—Edward Wilson Very
Invented a machine for winding thread, the spooler—Amos Whitney
Invented a multiplying camera—Simon Wing
First female Unitarian minister—Eliza Tupper Wilkes
Made first scales capable of weighing coal-filled railroad cars—Marlon Hamblen Winslow

Signers of the Declaration of Independence
Matthew Thornton, William Whipple

Signers of the United States Constitution
Rufus King

Vice Presidents of the United States
Hannibal Hamlin, Nelson Aldrich Rockefeller

Members of the Cabinet
Secretary of State: Elihu Benjamin Washburne, James Gillespie Blaine, Edmund Sixtus Muskie
Secretary of the Treasury: William Pitt Fessenden, Hugh McCulloch, Lot Myrick Morrill
Secretary of the Navy: John Davis Long
Attorney General: Nathan Clifford
Postmaster General: Horatio King, Timothy Otis Howe

Secretary of Labor: Frances Perkins

Ministers, Envoys Extraordinary, Ministers Plenipotentiary, and Ambassadors

Bolivia: John Winchester Dana
Bulgaria: Charles Stetson Wilson
Canada: Kenneth M. Curtis
Chile: John O'Leary
China: Frederick Ferdinand Low
Columbia: Luther Franklin McKinney
France: Elihu Washburne
Great Britain: Rufus King, John Hay Whitney
Hawaii: George W. Merrill, Harold Marsh Sewall, John Leavitt Stevens
Ireland: William Howard Taft III
Japan: Alfred Eliab Buck
Netherlands: William Emory Quinby, John Shepard Pike, William Pitt Preble
Norway: Margaret Joy Tibbetts
Pakistan: Horace Augustus Hildreth
Paraguay: Charles Ames Washburn
Portugal: Henry Dearborn, Edward Kavanaugh
Rumania: Charles Stetson Wilson
Spain: Hannibal Hamlin
Sri Lanka and the Maldives: John Hathaway Reed
Sweden and Norway: John Leavitt Stevens, William Widgery Thomas, Jr.
United Nations: James Russell Wiggins
Uruguay and Paraguay: John Curtis Caldwell, John Leavitt Stevens

Representing Countries Other than The United States

Elisha Hunt Allen: Hawaiian Minister to the United States
Everett Andrews son: Ethiopian Minister to the League of Nations

Members of the Supreme Court of the United States

Associate Justice William Cushing, Associate Justice Nathan Clifford, Chief Justice Melville Weston Fuller

Presidents Pro Tempore of the United States Senate

Henry Styles Bridges, William Pierce Frye, George Higgins Moses

Members of the United States Senate

Arizona: Ralph Henry Cameron
California: George Clement Perkins, Abram Pease Williams
Florida: Edward John Gurney

Illinois: Paul Howard Douglas

Indiana: Daniel Darwin Pratt

Maine: James Gillespie Blaine, James Ware Bradbury, Ralph Owen Brewster, Edwin Chick Burleigh, John Chandler, Judah Dana, George Evans, John Fairfield, Nathan Allen Farwell, Bert Manfred Fernald, William Pitt Fessenden, William Pierce Frye, Obidiah Gardner, Arthur Robinson Gould, Eugene Hale, Frederick Hale, Hannibal Hamlin, John Holmes, Charles Fletcher Johnson, Wyman Bradbury Seavey Moor, Lott Myrick Morrill, Edmund Sixtus Muskie, Amos Nourse, Albion Keith Parris, Frederick George Payne, John Ruggles, Ether Shepley, Margaret Chase Smith, Peleg Sprague, Wallace Humphrey White, Jr., Reuel Williams

Massachusetts: Prentiss Mellen

Michigan: Alpheus Felch, Francis Brown Stockbridge

Minnesota: William Drew Washburn

Mississippi: Adelbert Ames

Missouri: Daniel Tarbox Jewett

Montana: Paris Gibson

New Hampshire: Henry Styles Bridges, George Higgins Moses

New Jersey: John Fairfield Dryden

New York: Rufus King, William North

North Dakota: Edwin Fremont Ladd

Oregon: Lafayette Grover, James Willis Nesmith

Wisconsin: Timothy Otis Howe

Speakers of the United States House of Representatives
James Gillespie Blaine, Thomas Brackett Reed

Members of the United States House of Representatives
Alabama: Alfred Eliab Buck, Benjamin White Norris

Arizona: Ralph Henry Cameron, John Noble Goodwin (also represented Maine), Nathan Oakes Murphy

California: Samuel Greeley Hilborn, Frederick Ferdinand Low, Donald Campbell McRuer

Colorado: Hiram Pitt Bennet, Allen Alexander Bradford

Dakota Territory: Walter Atwood Burleigh

Florida: Edward John Guerney

Georgia: Charles Henry Prince

Illinois: Owen Lovejoy, Abner Taylor, Elihu Washburne

Indiana: Daniel Darwin Pratt

Iowa: Thomas Bowman, Nathaniel Cobb Deering, Henry Otis Pratt

Kansas: Stephen Alonzo Cobb, Orrin Larrabee Miller, Edmund Needham Morrill

Louisiana: James Mann, Eleazer Wheelock Ripley

Maine: Nehemiah Abbott, Amos Lawrence Alexander, Elisha Hunt Allen, Hugh Johnston Anderson, John Anderson, Charles Andrews, John Appleton, Jeremiah Bailey, James Bates, Carroll Lynwood Beedy, Hiram Belcher, Samuel Page Benson, James Gillespie Blaine, Charles Addison Boutelle, George Bradbury, Ralph Owen Brewster, Daniel Bronson, Benjamin Brown, Edwin Chick Burleigh, John Holmes Burleigh, William Burleigh, Samuel Butman, Frederic Carr, James Carr, Timothy Jarvis Carter, Shepard Cary, John Chandler, Jonathan Cilley, Asa William Henry Clapp, Franklin Clark, Nathan Clifford, Stephen Coburn, Frank Morey Coffin, Samuel Shepard Connor, Orchard Cook, Joshua Cushman, Richard Cutts, Joseph Dane, Thams Davee, Samuel Davis, Henry Dearborn, Nelson Dingley, Jr., Robert Pinckney Dunlap, George Evans, John Fairfield, Ephraim Wilder Farley, Frank Fellows, Thomas Amory Deblois Fessenden, William Pitt Fessenden, Edwin Flye, Stephen Clark Foster, Ezra Bartlett French, William Pierce Frye, Joshua Gage, Barzillai Gannett, Elbridge Gerry, Charles Jervis Gilman, Louis Bertrand Goodall, Robert Goodenow, Rufus King Goodenow, Forrest Goodwin, John Noble Goodwin (also represented Arizona Territory), Samuel Wadsworth Gould, Frank Edward Guernsey, Eugene Hale, Robert Hale, Joseph Hall, Hannibal Hamlin, Simon Moulton Hamlin, David Hammons, Mark Harris, Ebenezer Herrick, Joshua Herrick, Ira Greenlief Hersey, Samuel Fessenden Hersey, Mark Langdon Hill, Asher Crosby Hinds, Cornelius Holland, John Holmes, Levi Hubbard, Daniel Ilsley, Leonard Jarvis, Edward Kavanagh, David Kidder, Cyrus King, Ebenezer Knowlton, George Washington Ladd, Silas Lee, Enoch Lincoln, Stephen Decatur Lindsey, Charles Edgar Littlefield, Nathaniel Sweat Littlefield, Stephen Longfellow, Joshua Adams Lowell, John Lynch, Moses MacDonald, Alfred Marshall, Moses Mason, Samuel Mayall, Jr., John Dennis McCrate, Daniel John McGillicuddy, Clifford Guy McIntyre, Rufus McIntyre, Seth Llewellyn Milliken, Edward Carleton Moran, Anson Peaslee Morrill, Samuel Plummer Morrill, Freeman Harlow Morse, Thompson Henry Murch, Charles Pembroke Nelson, John Edward Nelson, Joseph Cobham Noyes, Jeremiah OBrien, James Churchill Oliver, Benjamin Orr, John Otis, Isaac Parker, James Parker, Gorham Parks, Albion Keith Parris, Virgil Delphini Parris, Donald Barrows Partridge, Sidney Perham, John Jasiel Perry, John Andrew Peters I, John Andrew Peters II, Frederick Augustus Pike, Harris Merrill Plaisted, Llewellyn Powers, Benjamin Randall, Nathan Reed, Isaac Reed, Thomas Brackett Reed, John Hovey Rice, Thomas Rice, James Wheelock Ripley, Ernest William Roberts, Edward Robinson, Cullen Sawtelle, John Fairfield Scammon, Luther Severance, Ephraim Knight Smart, Albert Smith, Clyde Harold Smith, Francis Ormand Jonathan Smith, Margaret Chase Smith, Donald Francis Snow, Donald Eton Somes, Peleg Sprague, John Philip Swasey, Lorenzo De Medici Sweat, Peleg Tallman, George Thatcher, Samuel Thatcher, Stanley Roger Tupper, John Gregg Utterbeck, Peleg Wadsworth, Charles Wesley Walton, Israel Washburn, Jr., Benjamin White, Wallace Humphrey White, Ezekiel Whitman, William

Widgery, James Sullivan Wiley, Hezekiah Williams, William Durkee Williamson, John Wilson, Joseph Ferdinand Wingate, Abiel Wood, John M. Wood

Massachusetts: Charles Russell Clason, Frank Herbert Foss, Daniel Wheelwright Gooch, Angier Louis Goodwin, John Walter Heselton, John Davis Long, Robert Luce, Edith Nourse Rogers, Lorenzo Sabine, William Henry Wilder

Michigan: Alvin Morrill Bentley

Minnesota: John Thomas Averill, Solomon Gilman Comstock, Mark Hill Dunnell, Loren Fletcher, Frank Mellen Nye, William Drew Washburn

Mississippi: Seargent Smith Prentiss

Missouri: William Augustus Hall, Joseph Hammons, Joseph Morrill Harper

New Hampshire: Fletcher Hale, Luther Franklin McKinney, William Bradbury Small, Amos Tuck

New York: DeAlva Stanwood Alexander, Charles Swan Benton, Frank Swett Black, David Augustus Boody, James Brooks, Luther Cullen Carter, Anson Herrick, Mark Trafton

Ohio: William Doan, Henry Ivory Emerson, Bellamy Storers

Oregon: Lafayette Grover, James Willis Nesmith, Isaac Ingalls Stevens

Pennsylvania: Abraham Andrews Barker, John W. Howe, Daniel Johnson Morrell

South Dakota: Freeman Tulley Knowles

Texas: Volney Erskine Howard

Virginia: Richard Small Ayer, Charles Horace Upton

Washington: Charles West Kimball

Wisconsin: John Sproat Brown, Ben C. Eastman, John Fox Potter, Cadwallader Washburn, Daniel Wells

Governors of States, Commonwealths, or Territories

Arizona: John Noble Goodwin, Nathan Oakes Murphy

California: Frederick Ferdinand Low, George Clement Perkins

Connecticut: Charles Wilbert Snow

Florida: Marcellus Lovejoy Stearns

Guam: George Leland Dyer

Hawaii: Wallace Rider Farrington

Iowa: Samuel Merrill

Kansas: Edmund Needham Morrill

Louisiana: George Foster Shepley (military)

Maine: Benjamin Ames, Hugh Johnston Anderson, Lewis Orin Barrows, Percival Proctor Baxter, Joseph Robinson Bodwell, Louis Jefferson Brann, Ralph Owen Brewster, Edwin Chick Burleigh, Joshua Lawrence Chamberlain, Clinton Ames Clauson, Henry Bradstreet Cleaves, William Titcomb Cobb, Abner Coburn, Selden Connor, Samuel Cony, William George Crosby, Burton Melvin Cross, Kenneth M. Curtis, Nathan Cutler, John Winchester Dana, Daniel Franklin Davis, Nelson Dingley, Jr., Robert Pinckney Dunlap, David Dunn, John Fairfield,

Bert Manfred Fernald, Alonzo Garcelon, William Tudor Gardiner, William
Thomas Haines, Joshua Hall, Hannibal Hamlin, Robert M. Haskell, Horace
Augustus Hildreth, John Fremont Hill, John Hubbard, Jonathan Glidden
Hunton, Edward Kavanagh, Edward Kent, Enoch Lincoln, James Bernard
Longley, Sebastian Streeter Marble, Carl E. Milliken, Anson Peaslee Morrill,
Lot Myrick Morrill, Edmund Sixtus Muskie, Frederick Hale Parkhurst, Albion
Keith Parris, Frederick George Payne, Sidney Perham, Fererick William Plaisted,
Harris Merrill Plaisted, Llewellyn Powers, Henry Brewer Quinby, John H. Reed,
Frederick Robie, Daniel Rose, Sumner Sewall, Samuel Emerson Smith, Richard
Hampton Vose, Israel Washburn, Jr., Samuel Wells, Joseph Hartwell Williams,
William Durkee Williamson
Massachusetts: John Albion Andrew, John Davis Long, Sir William Pepperrell,
    Sir William Phips, James Sullivan
Michigan: Alpheus Felch, Hazen Stuart Pingree, Francis Brown Stockbridge
Mississippi: Adelbert Ames
Nevada: Roswell Keyes Cord
New Hampshire: Nathaniel Springer Berry, Henry Styles Bridges, Ichabod Goodwin,
    Joseph Morrill Harper, John Sullivan
New Mexico: James Henry Carleton (military)
New York: Frank Sweat Black, Nelson Aldrich Rockefeller
Oregon: Lafayette Grover
Rhode Island: Emery John San Souci
Washington: John Harte McGraw, John Rankin Rogers, Isaac Ingalls Stevens
Wisconsin: Cadwallader Colden Washburn

Chiefs of Naval Operations

Charles Frederick Hughes, William Veazie Pratt

Commandant of the Marine Corps

Charles Heywood

Commandant of the Coast Guard

Harry Gabriel Hamlet

Recipients of the Medal of Honor

Adelbert Ames, John Anglin, James Bailey, Thomas Belcher, Charles J. Bibber,
John F. Bickford, Robert M. Blair, Robert M. Boody, Alonzo Bowman, Edward R.
Bowman, Lloyd Milton Brett, Brian L. Buker, Robert Goldthwaite Carter, Joshua
Lawrence Chamberlain, David B. Champagne, John Chapman, John F. Chase,
Charles Amory Clark, Clarence Milville Condon, Edward C. Dahlgren, Samuel W.
Davis, Thomas M. Doherty, Adam Duncan, William Dunn, Llewellyn G. Estes,
William Farley, Albert E. Fernald, Herbert Louis Foss, William G. Fournier, John B.

Frisbee, Charles Giddings, Clair Goodblood, Gary Ivan Gordon, Marcus Aurelius Hanna, Moses C. Hanscom, Ephraim W. Harrington, Frank W. Haskell, Cyrus Hayden, Asbury F. Haynes, Francis Snow Hesseltine, William Bliss Hincks, Oliver Otis Howard, Henry J. Hyde, Thomas Worcester Hyde, Thomas Kendrick, Horatio Collins King, Abaither J. Knowles, George D. Libby, George H. Littlefield, Charles Joseph Loring, Alphonso M. Lunt, John Mack, Charles Potter Mattocks, Adam McCullock, Thomas Joseph McMahon, Henry Clay Morrison, Augustus Morrill, Lewis Lee Red Millett, Daniel Milliken, Walter Goodale Morrill, Henry D. OBrien, Henry Brown Osgood (later rescinded), Edward M. Pike, Horace L. Piper (later rescinded), William B. Poole, Everett Parker Pope, Axel Hayford Reed, James Richmond, Otis O. Roberts, John Robinson, Auzella Savage, Herbert Emery Schonland, Richard Henry Sewall, Donald S. Skidgel, Charles H. Smith, Charles Henry Smith, Joseph Sewall Smith, William Smith, Andrew Barclay Spurling, Hazard Stevens, Thomas Taylor, Wilbur Taylor, John Darling Terry, Sidney Warren Thaxter, Edward Parsons Tobie, Andrew Jackson Tozier, Amasa Sawyer Tracy, Othniel Tripp, James W. Verney, Robert T. Waugh, Henry W. Wheeler, Frank Mellen Whitman, Edward Newton Whittier, Henry Clay Wood, Horatio Nelson Young, Jay Zeamer, Jr.

Recipients of the Victoria Cross
William Henry Metcalf, William Henry Seeley

Recipients of a Pulitzer Prize
James Phinney Baxter (for history), Robert Peter Tristram Coffin (for poetry), Owen Gould Davis (for drama), Edna St. Vincent Millay (for poetry), Walter Hamor Piston (two awards, both for music), Laura Elizabeth Howe Richards (for biography), Edwin Arlington Robinson (three awards, all for poetry), E. B. White (special citation)

Recipients of an Academy Award
Harry Peter McNab Brown, Jr.(for the screen play for *A Place in the Sun*), Frank Edwin Churchill (for the music for *Dumbo*), John Ford (six awards, all for best director)

A Listing by Birthplace
Addison: William Henry Plumer
Albion: Elijah Parish Lovejoy, Owen Lovejoy
Alfred: John Holmes Goodenow, Usher Parsons
Alna: Fred Houdlette Albee, John Thomas Averill, Edwin Arlington Robinson, Florence Donnell White
Alton: Charles Hildreth Lewis
Andover: Henry Varnum Poor, Henry William Poor, John Alfred Poor
Anson: Ben Foster, Edward Bruce Moore, Auzella Savage, Nathan Weston Spaulding
Appleton: Adelphus Bartlett Keith
Argyle: Solomon Gilman Comstock

Athens: Alonzo Boothby

Auburn: Forest Orville Additon, Edwin Franklin Brown, Erwin Dain Canham, Windsor Pratt Daggett, Edward Nelson Dingley, Anson Morrill Goddard, George Milbury Gould, Robert Luce, Elmer Drew Merrill, John Carroll Perkins, Lewis H. Ross, Leon Eugene Seltzer, Chauncey Brewster Tinker

Augusta: Edward Francis Adams, Horatio Bridge, Granville Wellington Carter, Samuel Cony, Burton Melvin Cross, Charles Densmore Curtis, Harlow Morrell Davis, William Herbert Dunton, Melville Weston Fuller, Guy Patterson Gannett, William Howard Gannett, Ursula Newell Gestefeld, George Huntington Hartford, Charles Henry Lamson, William Sidney Perham, John Fox Potter, Thomas Sewall, Frederick Percival Small, Daniel Caldwell Stanwood, Edward Stanwood, Isaac Augustus Stanwood, George Leonard Vose, Joseph Hartwell Williams, Seth Williams, Edward Francis Winslow, Willard Gordon Wyman

Avon: Zebulon York

Baileyville: Francis William Pettygrove

Baldwin: Alonzo Benjamin Bowers, Henry Francis Brown

Bangor: Gardner Weld Allen, Fred Wellington Ayer, Francis Edward Barbour, Thomas Belcher, Karl Worth Bigelow, Harold Sherburne Boardman, Frank Augustus Bourne, George Adams Bright, James Carr, Francis Hector Clerque, Franklin Webster Cram, William Robert Crowley, Edward Matthew Curran, Elliott Carr Cutler, William Hammett Davis, Carl Pullen Dennett, John Henry Freese, Richard Golden, Robert Winslow Gordon, William McCrillis Griswold, Francis Snow Hesseltine, Carl Frederick Holden, John Irwin Hutchison, Edward Austin Kent, Guy Whitman Leadbetter, Frederick Taylor Lord, Hiram Francis Mills, William Herbert Murphy, Hayford Peirce, Waldo Peirce, John Wing Prentiss, Louis Ross, Eugene Francis Sanger, Boutelle Savage, William Otis Sawtelle, Thomas Taylor, Frederick Porter Vinton, Charles Stetson Wilson

Bar Harbor: Doris Hodgkins Monteux, Esther Ralston, Nelson Aldrich Rockefeller

Barker Plantation: John Harte McGraw

Bath: Maurice Westcott Avery, Nathaniel Springer Berry, Elizabeth Chamberlain Burgess, Georgia Eva Cayvan, McDonald Clarke, Alice May Douglas, James William Elwell, Francis Henry Fassett, Henry Gannett, Joseph Foster Green, Frank Warren Hawthorne, Thomas Sumner Hayes, Charles Frederick Hughes, Francis Haynes Jenks, George Frederic Magoun, Henry Albert Magoun, Charles Wyman Morse, George W. Percy, Thomas Gustave Plant, Samuel Worcester Rowse, Sarah Smith Sampson, Fred Clark Scribner, Arthur Sewall, Frank Sewall, Harold Marsh Sewall, Samuel Swanton Sewall, Sumner Sewall, William Bacon Stevens, Francis Brown Stockbridge, Joseph William Torrey

Belfast: George Eli Burd, William George Crosby, Herbert Louis Foss, Clara Savage Littledale, Edward Palmer, William Veazie Pratt, John Alexander Ross, Dudley Allen Sergent, Albert William Stevens, Edward Wilson Very

Belgrade: George William Knox, Everett Parker Pope, John Franklin Spaulding,

Greenleaf Thurlow Stevens

Belmont: Josephine Bicknell Neal

Benton: Brian L. Buker, Albert Weston Grant, Asher Crosby Hinds, Carroll Atwood Wilson

Berwick: Hannah Tobey Shapleigh Farmer, Samuel Plaisted, James Sullivan, John Sullivan

Bethel: Henry D. Bean, Luther Cullen Carter, Cuvier Grover, Lafayette Grover, Bion Freeman Kendall, Margaret Joy Tibbetts

Biddeford: Alton Dermot Adams, Carlos Heard Baker, Arthur Jean Baptiste Cartier, Charles Deane, Joseph Stanislaus Galland, Frank Alpine Hill, Lucian Obed Hooper, Samuel Jordan, John Lyman, Thomas Bird Mosher, Walter Eugene Perkins, Edward Staples Cousens Smith, Amos Whitney, Joseph Willard

Bingham: Obed J. Wilson

Blue Hill: Samuel Peters Brown, Mary Ellen Chase

Boothbay: Mabel Viola Harris Conkling

Bowdoinham: Gardner Colby, Robert Browne Hall, Orrington Lunt, Francis Jarvis Patten

Bradford: John Curtis

Bradley: Temple Emery Dorr

Brewer: Joshua Lawrence Chamberlain, Samuel Davis, Roscoe Gilkey Dickinson, Charles Fletcher Dole, Fannie Hardy Eckstorm, Edward Holyoke Farrington, Oliver Cummings Farrington, William Emery Quinby, Elizabeth Burr Thelberg

Bridgewater: Frank M. Hume, Rose Tapley

Bridgton: Robert Goldthwaite Carter, Henry Bradstreet Cleaves, John Ripley Freeman, George D. Libby, Thomas Reginald Skelton, Jr.

Bristol: William Osgood Blaney, Weston Percival Chamberlain, Samuel P. Dinsmore, Thomas Drummond, Harvey Farrin Gamage, Marcus Aurelius Hanna, William North, Samoset, Joshua Soule

Brooklin: Victor Alonzo Friend

Brooksville: Clarence Milville Condon, David Atwood Wasson

Brownfield: Paris Gibson

Brownville: George Edward Reed

Brunswick: Gorham Dummer Abbot, John Stevens Abbott, Martin Brewer Anderson, Robert Peter Tristram Coffin, James Greenleaf Croswell, Robert Pinckney Dunlap, Seth Eastman, Jeremiah Hacker, Moses Emery Merrill, Alpheus Spring Packard, George Palmer Putnam, John Rankin Rogers, Sol George Lincoln Sands, Egbert Coffin Smyth, Samuel Phillips Newman Smyth, Samuel Thompson, Cadwallader A. Washburn

Buckfield: Hermon Carey Bumpus, John Davis Long, Virgil Delphini Parris, Thomas Stowell Phelps, Albion Woodbury Small, Seba Smith

Bucksport: John Augustus Darling, Edward Winslow Hincks, Edward Young Hincks, William Bliss Hincks

Buxton: James Crockett Bradbury, Mark Hill Dunnell, Grace Mabel Sherwood, Charles Henry Smith

Byron: Augustus Merrill

Calais: William Wallace Bates, Albert William Bradbury, Charles Townsend Copeland, Bernice Brown Cronkhite, George Leland Dyer, Henry D. O'Brien, James Shepard Pike, Mary Newmarch Prescott, Thomas Pendelton Robinson, Lloyd Raymond Sorenson, Harriet Prescott Spofford, Frederic Pike Stearns, Amos Parker Wilder

Camden: Enos Cobb, William Conway

Canaan: Isaac Sparrow Bangs, Abner Coburn (in that part that is now Skowhegan)

Canton: Horatio Bisbee, Dexter Arnold Hawkins, Donald Barrows Partridge

Cape Elizabeth: John Ford, William Clarke Larrabee, William B. Poole, Stewart Munn Taylor

Caribou: Wallace L. Hardison, Florence Collins Porter, Donald S. Skidgel, Charles Collins Teague

Carmel: Lucius Alonzo Emery, Myrna Fahey

Carthage: Hiram Pitt Bennet

Castine: Boyd Wheeler Bartlett, Noah Brooks, Bernard-Anselm d'Abbadie, Baron de Castin, Edward Patterson Williams

Charlotte: Ebenezer Fisher

Chelsea: John F. Chase

Cherryfield: Hiram Burnham

Chesterville: Laura Drake Gill

China: Augustine Jones, Eli Jones, Rufus Jones, Stephen Alfred Jones, Laroy S. Starrett

Clinton: Henry Leland Haskell, Orlando Whitney Norcross

Columbia Falls: Augustus Choate Hamlin

Corinna: Jesse Hawes, Marshall Ora Leighton, Gilbert Patten

Corinth: Arthur Robinson Gould, Ora Haley, Frank Mason Robinson

Cornish: Sherman Grant Bonney, David Dunn

Cranberry: Andrew Barclay Spurling

Cumberland: Charles Gould Morton

Damariscotta: Charles Addison Boutelle, Samuel Walter Woodward

Danville: Eben Dyer Jordan

Dead River: Lloyd Milton Brett

Dearborn: Anson Peaslee Morrill, Lot Myrick Morrill (both in that portion that is now Belgrade)

Deer Isle: James Henry Walton

Denmark: Rufus Ingalls, Hazen Stuart Pingree

Detroit: Henry Clay Whitney

Dexter: Ralph Owen Brewster, Fred Francis Proctor, Arthur Elmer Silver, Charles Gould Treat

Dixmont: Benjamin F. Upton

Dover-Foxcroft: Edmund Burke Delabarre, Lillian Marian Nancy Ames Stevens, James Everett Stuart

Dresden: Benjamin Fiske Barrett

Durham: Nelson Dingley, Jr., Samuel Newell, Frederick Morris Warren

East Machias: Edwin Gardner Ames, Arlo Bates, Austin Cary, George Harris, Samuel Harris, Roswell Dwight Hitchcock, Frederick Augustus Pike

Eastport: Israel DeWolfe Andrews, Henry Russell Beatty, Edward R. Bowman, Nathaniel Butler, Joseph Saville Cony, Napolean Jackson Tecumseh Dana, Robert Thaxter Edes, Harry Gabriel Hamlet, Otis Tufton Mason, Carol Norton, Frank Hutchison Peavey, Mary Hayden Green Pike, Helen Ring Robinson, Amos Smith, George Bruce Upton, Frank E. Wallis

Edgecomb: John Brown Emerson, John Fairfield Merry, Rufus King Sewall

Eliot: John Forsyth Hanscom, John Fremont Hill, Nellie Mathes Horne, Simon Frost

Ellsworth: Anne Crosby Emery Allinson, Henry Crosby Emery, Eugene Griffen, Bryant Edward Moore, Hoyt Augustus Moore, John Andrew Peters, John Hay Whitney

Embden: Perley Walker, James Leon Williams

Fairfield: Seldon Connor, Frank Bunker Gilbreth, Walter L. Hustus

Falmouth: Joseph Cummings

Farmingdale: George Bernard Grant

Farmington: Edward Abbott, Leonard Atwood, George Fordyce Blake, Micah S. Croswell, Chester Greenwood, Ira Vaughn Hiscock, Lillian Norton, Harrie Webster, Frank Nathaniel Whittier, Solomon Adams Woods

Fayette: Frank Everett Wing

Fort Kent: Claire Goodblood

Foxcroft: Alfred Eliab Buck

Frankfort: Lemuel Pratt Grant

Freedom: Daniel Franklin Davis, Benjamin Franklin Smith

Freeport: Cyrus Augustus Bartol, Raymond Franklin Bennett, Aaron Lufkin Dennison, Gideon Lane Soule

Friendship: Allen Alexander Bradford

Fryeburg: Charles Swan Benton, Alexander Stuart Bradley, Wilbur Fisk Crafts, John Winchester Dana, Clinton Buswell Evans, Samuel Fessenden, John Locke, Nescumbiout, James Ripley Osgood, Kate Putnam Osgood, Clement Adams Walker

Gardiner: Orison Blunt, Charles Russell Clason, Richard Stevens Danforth, Augustus Plummer Davis, Horace Augustus Hildreth, George Warren Lawrence, George Everett MacDonald, William Clark Noble, John Pope, Henry Richards, Robert Hallowell Richards, Vivian Blanche Small, Frank Parker Stockbridge, John Reed Swanton, Letitia Katherine Vannah

Georgetown: Daniel Malcolm, Walter E. Reid

Glenburn: Winfield Scott Chapin

Gorham: James Phinney Baxter, Edgar Blake, Raymond Earl Davis, Dana Estes, Arthur Leighton Guptill, Edward Herbert Hall, Helen Gertrude Russell, Orland

Francis Smith, Ellen Gould Harmon White

Gouldsboro: Robert Gould Shaw

Gray: Harwood Lawrence Childs, Jedediah Cobb, Melvin Porter Frank, Charles Lyman Greene, Samuel Mayall, Jr.

Great Pond: Gleason Leonard Archer

Greene: James Bates, Aaron Simon Daggett, William Wallace Stetson

Greenwood: Leon Leonwood Bean, Atherton Bernard Furlong, Addison Emery Verrill

Hallowell: Jacob Abbott, Hiram Belcher, Elias Bond, William Thomas Chase, George Barrell Cheever, Henry Theodore Cheever, Charles Albert Curtis, George Evans, Almon Gunnison, Carroll Rede Harding, Holmes Hinkley, Timothy Hopkins, Thomas Hamlin Hubbard, Horatio Oliver Ladd, Robert Benjamin Lewis, Samuel Vaughan Merrick, Howard Madison Parshley, Osbourne Russell, Theodate Louise Smith, Reuel Williams

Hampden: John Sproat Brown, Philip Marshall Brown, John Bacon Crosby, John Bacon Curtis, Dorothea Lynde Dix, Charles Hamlin

Hancock: Edville Gerhardt Abbott

Harmony: James Hutchings Baker, Clyde Harold Smith, Bartlett Tripp

Harrison: Melville Ezra Ingalls

Hartford: Phillips H. Lord, Axel Hayford Reed

Hartland: George Gore

Hebron: Oscar Dana Allen, Albion Keith Parris, Alexander Parris

Highland: Herbert Carl Crow

Hodgdon: Ira Greenlief Hersey, George Otis Smith

Hope: George Adelbert Alden, Raymond Henry Fogler

Houlton: Charles Cotesworth Beaman, William Warren Haskin, George Joseph Keegan, Henry Clay Merriam, Samantha Reed Smith, Louis Robert Sullivan, Ashley Horace Thorndike, Eliza Tupper Wilkes

Howland: Percy Lebaron Spencer

Island Falls: Willard Linwood Chase, George Foster Robinson

Jackson: Ezra Abbot, David Augustus Boody

Jay: John Lewis Childs, Joseph Foxcroft Cole, Franklin Winslow Johnson, Preston Kyes, Millard Mayhew Parker

Jefferson: Oliver Crosby Gray, Frank Morrill Murphy, Nathan Oakes Murphy

Jonesport: Carroll Edward Dobbin

Kennebunk: William E. Barry, George Folsom, John Frost, Benjamin Franklin Hardy, Francis H. Kimball, Charles Coffin Little, Kenneth Roberts

Kennebunkport: Dorothy Walker Bush, William Lyman Greene, Hugh McCulloch, George Clement Perkins

Kingfield: Chansonetta Stanley Emmons, Francis Edgar Stanley, Freelan Oscar Stanley

Kittery: Willis Boyd Allen, John Pascal Brooks, Calvin Hayes Cobb, Tunis Augustus McDonough Craven, Samuel Cutts, Frank Lysander Fernald, Walter Elmore Fernald, John Frost, Simon Frost, James Hill, Andrew Pepperrell, Sir William

Pepperrell, Richard Henry Seward, William Whipple

Knox: Alden Joseph Blethen, Frank Asbury Sherman

Lamoine: David Bartlett

Lebanon: Ralph Farnum, Claudius Buchanan Grant, Charles Coffin Jewett, John Punchard Jewett, Sumner Increase Kimball, Charles Edgar Littlefield, Charles Cogswell Rollins, Frederick Hill Wood

Leeds: Kenneth M. Curtis, Oliver Otis Howard, Danville Leadbetter, Ruggles Sylvester Morse

Levant: Clark Fisher, Merrit Caldwell Fernald, Sewell Ford, Luthene Claremont Gilman

Lexington: Elijah Hedding Gammon

Lewiston: Henry Livermore Abbott, George Robert Acheson, Alice Mary Baldwin, George Ellsworth Boomer, Edward Burgess Butler, George Millet Chase, Ernest Arthur Coombs, Charles Sumner Frost, William Pierce Frye, Alonzo Garcelon, Pliny Earle Goddard, Leland Matthew Goodrich, Edmund Marsden Hartley, Anson Herrick, Wayne C. Jordan, James Bernard Longley, Bernard Mayo, Clarence J. White, Wallace Humphrey White, Jr.

Liberty: Harry Alvin Brown, John Hamilton Brown

Limerick: Alpheus Felch, Joseph Morrill Harper, Anne Carroll Moore

Limington: Frank Swett Black, Robert M. Boody, Charles Edward Garman, Edward Thomas Sumner Lord

Lincoln: Gary Ivan Gordon, Ernest Shurtliff Holmes, Fenwicke Lindsay Holmes

Linneus: Clarence Blenden Burleigh, Albion Gustavus Young

Lisbon: Delbert Dana Coombs, William Dunn, Charles Lewis Potter, Franklin Simmons

Livermore: George Dana Boardman, Clement Caldwell Haskell, Edwin Bradbury Haskell, Timothy Otis Howe, Henry Arthur Sanders,Cadwallader Colden Washburn, Charles Ames Washburn, Israel Washburn, Jr., Stanley Washburn, William Drew Washburn, Elihu Benjamin Washburne

Livermore Falls: Louise Bogan, Oscar Cargill, Marshman Edward Wadsworth

Lovell: Jonathan Eastman Johnson, Philip Carrigan Johnson, Jr., John Carroll Poland, Frederick Albert Pottle, Marcellus Lovejoy Stearns

Lubec: Myron Halliburton Avery, James Henry Carleton, George Higgins Moses, Sumner Tucker Pike

Machias: Edward Franklin Albee, Henry Bruce, Charles Austin Cary, Stephen Clark Foster, Mary J. Garland, George Stillman Hilliard, John Daniel McDonald, Henry H. Porter, Joseph Adams Smith

Machiasport: Samuel Valentine Cole

Madawaska: Clement Theophilus Blanchet, Elizabeth Winona Leclerque Joy

Madison: Robert Amie Bearor, Nathan Weston Blanchard, Louis Jefferson Brann, Albert Moore Spear, Cyrus Walker, Samuel Burns Weston

Manchester: William Henry Allen

Marshfield: Lura Beam
Mattawamkeag: Ernest Wilder Bradford
Mechanic Falls: Lewis Lee Millett
Medford: Frank Elwyn Weymouth
Mercer: Frank Andrew Munsey
Mexico: Frank Edwin Churchill
Milford: Lulu Hunt Peters
Milo: Wilder Stevens Metcalf, Ezra Kimball Sprague
Minot: Samuel Greeley Hilborn, Crosby Stuart Noyes
Monmouth: Joseph William Fowler, Andrew Jackson Tozier
Monson: George Pullen Jackson
Montville: Richard Small Ayer
Mount Desert: Davis Wasgate Clark, Harold Eugene Donnell, Charles Henry Fernald, George Ward Nichols
Mount Vernon: Loren Fletcher, John Leavitt Stevens
Naples: Edward Beecher Allen, Daniel Chaplin
New Canada Plantation: Mattie Pinette
New Gloucester: Peleg Whitman Chandler, Llewellyn Solomon Haskell, Hannah Chandler Ropes
New Sharon: Charles Franklin Thwing
Newcastle: Henry Clifford, Joseph Tarr Copeland, Edward Kavanagh, John Smith Sewall, Jacob Sleeper
Newfield: Charles Wesley Tuttle, Horace Parnell Tuttle
Newport: Lewis Orin Barrows, Benjamin Franklin Clarke, Merle Crowell
Nobleboro: Nathaniel Cushing Bryant
Norridgewock: Charles Frederick Allen, Jotham Bixby, Rebecca Sophia Clarke, Pitt Dillingham, James Ezekiel Emerson, Volney Erskine Howard, Wellington Parker Kidder, Minot Judson Savage, Charles Greene Sawtelle, Cullen Sawtelle, Franklin H. Sawtelle, Sarah Perry Smith, Frederic Henry Spaulding
North Berwick: Paul Ansel Chadbourne, Howard Merrill Clute, Daniel Raynes Goodwin, Ichabod Goodwin, Ichabod Goodwin Hobbs, Thomas Jefferson Mayall, Daniel Johnson Morrell
North Haven: Harold Henry Beverage, Alexis Everett Frye
North Yarmouth: Rufus Anderson, Rufus William Bailey, Peter Chardon Brooks, Samuel Gilman Brown, Charles Collins, Ammi Ruhamah Cutter, Elizabeth Oakes Prince Smith
Norway: George Lafayette Beal, Nathaniel Cobb Deering, Alanson Mellen Dunham, Zora Klain, John Albert Sanborn, Sidney Irving Smith, Charles Asbury Stephens
Oakland: John Ayer, Walter Scott Wyman
Old Town: Priscilla Ann Attean, Taber Davis Bailey, "Molly Spotted Elk," Bernard Langlais, Clara Neptune Joseph Nicolar, Joseph Peavey, Joseph Wingate Sewall, Louis Sockelexis, Eugene Hanes Smith, Louise Averill Svedsen

Orland: Carl Darling Buck, Walter Van Tilburg Clark, Edward Ginn

Orneville: Hudson Maxim

Orono: Wallace Rider Farrington, Merritt Lyndon Fernald, Ard Godfrey, Jonathan Norcross, Luther Tracy Townsend, Eva McDonald Valesh

Orrington: Benjamin Franklin Mudge, Edward Allen Pierce, Franklin Clement Robinson, Calvin Ryder

Otisfield: Llewellyn Nathaniel Edwards, Joseph W. Holden

Palermo: Jonathan Clark Greeley

Paris: Charles Andrews, Mary Deering Caswell, Augustus Luther Crocker, Charles Deering, James Deering, George Lura Donham, Stephen Albert Emery, Hannibal Hamlin, Obed Hussey, William Wallace Kimball, William Wirt Kimball, Horatio King, Reta Shaw

Parkman: Charles Alton Ellis, Harold Brown Harvey, Victor Almon McKusick, Vincent McKusick, George Russell Shaw

Parsonsfield: Cyrus Fogg Brackett, James Ware Bradbury, Luther Orlando Emerson, John Usher Parsons, Alzina Ann Parsons Stevens, Lorenzo De Medici Sweat, Amos Tuck

Patten: Gladys Anne Clare

Pembroke: Charles Herbert Best, Henry Stiles Bridges, Ronald Bridges, William Robinson Pattangall,

Penobscot: Herbert Wood Leach

Perham: Edward C. Dahlgren

Perkins (Swan Island): Jacob Barker

Perry: Annie Louise Leslie

Phillips: Carroll Lynwood Beedy, Cornelia Thurza Crosby, Richard Hinckley Field, Weston Earle Fuller, Augustus White Stinchfield

Phippsburg: John Cutting Berry, John B. Frisbee, John Abel Lord

Pittsfield: Carl E. Milliken, Hugh Pendexter, Llewellyn Powers

Pittston: Edwin Warren Marble Bailey, William Dearborn Clark, Elizabeth A. Follansbee, Albert Gallatin Jewett, Daniel Tarbox Jewett, John Hildreth McCollum, Charles Melville Scammon, William Smyth, Charles Augustus Stilphen

Poland: Bert Manfred Fernald, Seth Mellen Milliken, Hiram Weston Ricker

Portland: Hiram Abrams, James Alden, Frank Leonard Allen, John Anglin, John Howard Appleton, James Phinney Baxter, Percival Proctor Baxter, Henry Adams Bellows, Alvin Morrell Bentley, Charles J. Bibber, Helen Augusta Blanchard, Clarence Bretton Blethen, William Cranch Bond, George Bradbury, George Pond Brockway, Erastus Brooks, James Brooks, Harry B. Brown, Harry Peter McNab Brown, Jr., William Robinson Brown, Champlin Burrage, Alfred Edgar Burton, Edward Pierce Casey, Charles Augustus Chambers, Charles Henry Chase, George Chase, Charles Lorenzo Clarke, Nathan Clifford, Josephine Cobb, Charles Codman, Nathaniel Coffin, Samuel Colman, Oscar Sidney Cox, Charles

Henderson Craven, Cyrus Herman Kotzschmar Curtis, Oakley Chester Curtis, Samuel Trask Dana, Woodbury Kidder Dana, Owen Gould Davis, Nathaniel Deering, Winfred Thaxter Dennison, George Herman Derry, Edmund Lawrence Dorman, Neal Dow, Esther Clousman Dunn, Frank A. Elwell, Charles Henry Emery, Willy Ferrero, Francis Fessenden, James Flavin, Francis Ford, Samuel Freeman, Edward Sanborn French, Charles Wellington Furlong, George Grant Gatley, Edward Thaxter Gignoux, Mildred Elizabeth Sisk Gillars, Charles William Goddard I, Charles William Goddard II, Morrill Goddard, Nathaniel Gordon, James Bradstreet Greenough, Walter Griffin, Edward John Gurney, Arthur Hackett, John Hancock Hall, William Augustus Hall, Frederick William Hamilton, James Clarence Hamlen, James Augustine Healy, Neville Monroe Hopkins, Pauline Elizabeth Hopkins, Joseph Holt Ingraham, Alnah James Johnston, Charles Jones, Chester Jones, Richard Edwin Jostberg, Elijah Kellogg, Horatio Collins King, Margaret Center Klingelsmith, Alexander Wadsworth Longfellow, Henry Wadsworth Longfellow, Samuel Longfellow, Stephen Long-fellow, William Pitt Preble Longfellow, Charles Joseph Loring, Charles Morgridge Loring, Harold Amasa Loring, John Franklin MacVane, Shailer Mathews, Isaac McLellan, Grenville Moody, James Appleton Morgan, Edward Sylvester Morse, Eliza Happy Morton, John Neal, James Edward Oliver, John Knowles Paine, Lizzie Pitts Merrill Palmer, Sara Payson Willis Parton, George Perley Phenix, Greenleaf Whittier Pickard, Edward Preble, George Henry Preble, Elizabeth Payson Prentiss, Seargent Smith Prentiss, Elisabeth Cavazza Jones Pullen, Thomas Brackett Reed, Robert Edwin Ricker, Weld Allen Rollins, Morrill Ross, Merrill Burr Sands, Herbert Emery Schonland, Harriet Winslow List Sewall, Philip Burdette Sharpe, George Foster Shepley, Manley Hale Simons, Mathew Hale Smith, Peter Thacher Smith, Frederic Maxwell Somers, Horatio Southgate, Robert William Stanley, Bellamy Storer, David Humphreys Storer, Margaret Jane Mussey Sweat, William Henry Thomas, William Widgery Thomas, John Sidney Thrasher, Jane Plummer Thurston, Samuel Veazie, Alexander Scammel Wadsworth, Henry Wadsworth, Francis Waldo, Samuel Waldo, Royal Whitman, Nathaniel Parker Willis

Presque Isle: Frank Holmes Cushman
Prospect: Freeman McGilvery
Randolph: Harry Eugene Andrews
Raymond: Liberty Emery Holden
Readfield: Robert Bishop, Mary Ann Berry Brown, Joseph Cummings Chase, John Hubbard, Horace M. Lane, Leonard Norcross
Richmond: DeAlva Stanwood Alexander, Charles Henry Clarke, Winterton Conway Curtis
Robbinston: Gail Laughlin, Grace Harriet Macurdy
Rockland: Adelbert Ames, Hiram Gregory Berry, William Partridge Burpee, Effie Carlton Crockett Canning, William Titcomb Cobb, Maxine Elliott, Isaac Smith

Kalloch, Herbert Mayhew Lord, Edna St. Vincent Millay, Kathleen Kalloch Millay, Edward Carleton Moran, Mary Brown Patten, Albert Freeman Pillsbury, Walter Hamor Piston, Richard Henry Rice, Albert Sydney Snow, Elias Steever Stover, Davis Tilson

Rockport: Herbert Thorndike Clough, Hansen Crockett Gregory

Rumford: John Milton Adams, Edmund Sixtus Muskie

Saco: Frank Arthur Banks, Waldo Elias Boardman, Samuel Brannan, James Madison Cutts, Richard Cutts, Arthur Philip Fairfield, John Fairfield, George Lincoln Goodale, Elizabeth Deering Hanscom, Kenneth Fuller Maxcy, Edith Nourse Rogers, Emery John San Souci, Nathaniel Sargent, George Foster Shepley, John Rutledge Shepley, Lyman Beecher Stowe, John Langdon Sullivan, Clarence Eugene Woodman

Saint Albans: Simon Wing

Saint George: Charles Wilbert Snow

Salem: Daniel Collamore Heath

Sanford: Samuel Longley Bickford

Sangerville: Charles Amory Clark, Sir Hiram Stevens Maxim, Sir Harry Oakes

Scarborough: Cyrus King, Rufus King, William King, Jeremiah O'Brien, John O'Brien, Joseph Addison Sewall, Winford Henry Smith

Searsmont: Charles West Kendall

Searsport: Clifford Nickels Carver, Roswell Keyes Colcord, Frederic E. Manson

Sedgwick: Frederick Allen Gower

Shapleigh: Frank Abbott, Albert Sumner Bradford, Joshua Moody Young

Shirley: Edgar Wilson "Bill" Nye

Sidney: Nehemiah Abbott, Earle Emerson Bessey, Lewis Nathaniel Chase

Skowhegan: Abner Coburn, Charles Albert Coffin, Daniel Dole, Edmund Pearson Dole, John Edward French, George H. Littlefield, Margaret Chase Smith, William Henry Wildes

South Berwick: John Holmes Burleigh, Stephen Lincoln Goodale, John Noble Goodwin, John Lord Hayes, Joseph Hayes, John Hubbard, Sarah Orne Jewett, Nathan Lord, Luther Calvin Tibbetts, Fred Allan Walker

South Portland: Alvah Randall Small, Frances Laurens Vinton

South Thomaston: Sumner Waldron Jackson

Southport: Ralph Henry Cameron

Springfield: Alvin Lombard

Springvale: Edawrd Swift Dunster

Standish: Milton Prince Higgins, Albion Parris Howe, Lucien Howe, Charles H. Smith

Starks: Edwin Fremont Ladd

Stetson: Mark Leslie Hersey

Steuben: Martha Gallison Moore Avery, Henry Dyer Moore, John Godfrey Moore, William Tuckerman Shaw

Strong: Elizabeth Chase Akers, Aurelia Mace
Sullivan: Charles Fitz Abner Johnson, Marcus Libby Urann
Sumner: George Ricker Berry, Lorenzo Dow, Samuel Freeman Hersey
Surry: Archelaus L. Hamblen, Everett William Lord
Temple: Dorcas Doyen, John Fairfield Dryden, Harvey D. Parker
Thomaston: Fred Lowry Andrews, William Henry Andrews, Charles Grandison
    Bryant, Greenleaf Cilley, Jonathan Prince Cilley, Charles Copeland, Charles
    Rundlett Flint, Jeremiah Howard Gilman, Charles Copeland Morse, Henry Knox
    Thatcher
Topsham: William Henry Sealey, Earl Baldwin Smith
Tremont: John F. Bickford, Merle Elliott Tracy
Trenton: James Gillpatrick Blunt
Turner: Royal Bird Bradford, Ethan Allen Chase, Solon Chase, Albert Field Gilmore,
    Eugene Hale, Luther Whiting Mason, George W. Merrill, Samuel Merrill,
    Leonard Swett, Royal Emerson Whitman
Union: Lysander Hill, John Langdon Sibley, Augustin Thompson, Francis Edward
    Thompson, Richard Edward Thompson
Unity: Gustavus Benson Brackett, Walter M. Brackett, George Colby Chase
Vassalboro: Theophilus Capen Abbot, Edward Augustus Brackett, Amy Morris
    Bradley, Holman Francis Day, Henry Herbert Goddard, Amy Morris Homans,
    Albert Prescott Marble, Charles Henry Nichols, Albert Keith Smiley, Daniel
    Smiley, Edward Henry Weeks
Vienna: Milton Bradley
Vinalhaven: Harold Vinal
Waite: William Henry Metcalf
Waldoboro: Augusta Simmons Stetson
Wales: James Solomon Sanborn
Warren: Everett Andrews Colson, Benjamin Flint Buxton, Charles Clark Hanley,
    Ella Maude Moore, Edward O'Brien, Ellis Spear, Benjamin Bussey Thatcher
Washington: Alonzo Bowman, George Washington McNear, Clyde L. Sukeforth
Waterboro: Amos Lawrence Allen
Waterford: Charles Farrar Browne, Cyrus Hamlin, Thomas Treadwell Stone
Waterville: Walter Atwood Burleigh, David B. Champagne, Samuel Stillman Conant,
    Arthur Ulderic DesJardins, Henry Wesley Dunn, Charles Heywood, Frederick
    Thayer Hill, Edson Fobes Hitchings, William Hume, Clarence Earle Lovejoy,
    Harold Marston Morse, Frederick Craig Mortimer, Antonia Savage Sawyer,
    Edward Stevens Sheldon, Daniel Appleton White Smith, Alexander Sullivan,
    Carroll Atwood Tyler, Daniel Wells
Wayne: Thomas Brigham Bishop, John Emory Bryant, Annie Louise Cary, Hiram
    Robert Nickerson
Webster: William Eugene Berry, John Lincoln Dearing, Franklin Simmons
Weld: Joseph Barker Stearns

Wells: Lebbeus Brooks, Albert Day, George Barrell Emerson, Rufus Hatch, David Kinnison, John Fairfield Scammon, Seth Storer, Esther Wheelwright

Westbrook: Benjamin Paul Akers, Edward Pennell Brooks, James Deering Fessenden, Edmund Needham Morrill, Appleton Oaksmith, Carl Leo Stearns, Joseph Peter Vachon, Marlon Hamblen Winslow

West Gardiner: John Frank Stevens

West Paris: Edwin Jonathan Mann

Westport: William May Garland, James Richard Jewett

Whitefield: William Farley, Eliakim Parker Scammon, Jonathan Young Scammon

Williamsburg: Walter Goodale Morrill

Wilton: Benjamin Fordyce Barker, Guy Goodwin Fernald, Sylvia Hardy, Josiah Perham

Windham: John Anderson, John Albion Andrew, Harrison Bray Moore, Abba Louisa Goold Woolson

Windsor: Simon Jones Murphy

Winslow: Howard Burton Shaw

Winterport: Albert E. Fernald, James Otis Kaler, Frederick Ferdinand Low

Winthrop: William Gerrish Beale, Samuel Page Benson, Delphia Louis Bissonette, Charles Bowdoin Fillebrown, Thomas Fillebrown, Hiram Avery Pitts, John Abiel Pitts, Emily Fairbaks Talbot, William Everett Waters, Fremont Wood, Henry Clay Wood

Wiscasset: Hugh Johnston Anderson, John Francis Anderson, Thomas Bowman, Benjamin Patterson Browne, William Elisha Chenery, John Huntington Crane Coffin, Edmund Flagg, Patience Tucker Stapleton, Richard Hawley Tucker

Woodstock: Sidney Perham, Charles Otis Whitman

Woolwich: Sir William Phips

Yarmouth: Timothy Alden, Horatio Willis Dresser

York: William Batchelder Bradbury, Cyrus Hayden, William Hutchings, Margaret Knight, Amos Main, Rufus McIntyre, Joseph Moody, Samuel Moody, Jeremiah Moulton, Jedidiah Preble, William Pitt Preble, David Sewall, Dummer Sewall, Jotham Sewall, Samuel Sewall, Stephen Sewall, Sarah Barrell Keating Wood

Abbot, Ezra 1819–84, born: Jackson; graduate: Phillips Academy, Exeter, A.B. Bowdoin College 1840, A.M. 1843, L.L.D. (Hon.) Yale University 1869, D.D. Harvard University 1872; taught high school at Cambridgeport, Massachusetts, 1847; member: American Oriental Society 1852; library staff, Harvard University, later resident librarian 1856; American Academy of Arts and Sciences 1861; lecturer on textual criticism of New Testament and Bussey professor: Harvard Divinity School 1872–84; member: New Testament Committee for Revision of English Bible (much of the text is the work of Abbot) 1871–81; editor: *Critical History of the Doctrine of Future Life* 1864, *Church of the First Three Centuries* 1865; author: *The Authorship of the Fourth Gospel* 1880, contributed over 400 articles to Smith's *Dictionary of the Bible* 1867–70.

Abbot, Gorham Dummer 1807–74, born: Brunswick; son of Rev. Jacob Abbot, proprietor of Phillips, brother of John S. C. Abbott and Jacob Abbott; A.B. Bowdoin College 1826, Andover Theological Seminary 1831; L.L.D. (Hon.) Ingham University 1860; principal: Castine Academy; associate principal: Amherst (Massachusetts) Academy; to recover his health, made a long journey, on horseback through the South; joined his brother Jacob in the founding of the Mt. Vernon School for Young Ladies; in Boston ordained Presbyterian ministry; pastor: New Rochelle, New York, 1837–41; undertook to provide the 50,000 public schools in the United States with libraries, text-books, and educational journals; collected and tabulated the educational facilities and institutional methods, systems of instruction, libraries, and publications for use of schools in the United States and in foreign countries, the results were disseminated to various state and territorial governments; founded the Society for the Diffusion of Useful Knowledge 1836, served as secretary for several years; fifty volumes were selected or published to form the nucleus of school libraries, test books were prepared, and an educational journal started; founded the New Seminary for Young Ladies, New York, 1843, the first such school for females in New York, later moved to large building on Union Square, provided for by the heirs of Henry Springler and adopted the name Springler Institute 1848, brought scholars of the highest rank, such as Benjamin Silliman, as lecturers, later moved to the Townsend Mansion, at Fifth Avenue and Thirty-fourth Street, adopted the name of Abbot Collegiate Institution, suffered from the exigencies occasioned by the Civil War; when Abbot retired to South Natick, Massachusetts, in 1870, the school became the Reed School; author: *The Family at Home, or Familiar Illustrations of Various Domestic Duties* 1834, *Mexico and the United States; Their Mutual Relations and Common Interests* 1869; was sought out and gave wise counsel to the founders of Vasser and Wellesley colleges, had an immense impact on the thinking of those who sought to educate females.

Abbot, Theophilus Capen 1826–92, born: Vassalboro; A.B. Waterville College 1845, student: Bangor Theological Seminary; taught school in various academies in Maine; principal: Ann Arbor (Michigan) High School 1856; chairman: Department of English Literature, Michigan Agricultural College (later Michigan State University) 1858–66, chairman, Department of Logic and Mental Philosophy from 1866, treasurer 1858–61, president 1863–85.

Abbott, Berenice 1898–1991, born: Springfield, Ohio; student: Ohio State University 1917–18, *Kunstschule*, Berlin 1923, recipient of honorary doctorates from the University of Maine 1971, Smith College 1973, New School for Social Research 1981, Bowdoin College 1982, Bates College 1981; began career as darkroom assistant to Man Ray in Paris 1923–25, owner of her own photographic studio, Paris, 1926–29, made portraits of James Joyce, Jean Cocteau, Djuna Barnes, André Gide, and others, saved the photographer Eugène Atget's life's work; in New York from 1929, specialized in documentary and portrait photography; photographer: Federal Arts Project, New York, 1930–39; exhibitions include: Museum of Modern Art, Marlborough Gallery, New York, Smithsonian Institution, Washington, Museum of Fine Arts, Boston, Art Institute of Chicago, Museum of Fine Art, Houston, San Francisco Museum of Art, Bibliothèque Nationale, Paris; author: *Changing New York* 1939, *Greenwich Village: Today and Yesterday* 1949, *Portrait of Maine* 1968, *Berenice Abbott Photographs* 1970, *Guide to Better Photography* 1941, *The View Camera Made Simple* 1948, *The World of Atget* 1964, *Berenice Abbott, American Photographer* 1982; recipient: Friends of Photography Award 1983, International Erice Prize for Photography 1987; member: American Academy of Arts and Letters; settled in Monson.

Abbott, Edville Gerhardt 1871–1938, born: Hancock; attended public school in Hancock, graduate: East Maine Conference Seminary, Bucksport, A.B. Bowdoin College 1896, A.M. 1898, Sc.D. (Hon.) 1915, M.D. Medical School of Maine 1898; house surgeon: Maine General Hospital, Portland; made a special study of orthopedic surgery in Boston, New York and the Friedrich Wilhelm University, Berlin 1900–01; practiced in Portland, instrumental in the founding of the Children's Hospital 1908, surgeon in chief, devoted entirely to the free treatment of deformities and lameness of children; orthopedic surgeon to Maine General Hospital, visiting surgeon to Sisters Hospital and the Webber Hospital, consultant to the Maine State Sanitarium and the Maine Central Railroad; clinical instructor: Medical School of Maine 1902, professor from 1914; author of numerous articles for medical journals; originated the Abbott method (a gradual straightening of a scoliosis by use of a succession of plaster casts).

Abbott, Edward 1841–1908, born: Farmington; son of Jacob Abbott; A.B. New York University 1860, D.D. 1890, student at Andover Theological Seminary 1860–62; in the Civil War: served in the U.S. Sanitary Commission in Washington and with the Army of the Potomac; ordained Congregational minister, founding pastor, Pilgrim Congregational Church, Cambridge, Massachusetts, 1865–69; editor: *The Congregationalist* 1869–78, editor in chief: *Literary World* 1878–88, ordained Protestant Episcopal minister, rector: Saint James Church, Cambridge 1879–1906, declined election as missionary bishop of Japan; member: Cambridge School Committee; Board of Visitors: Wellesley College; author: *The Babys Things, A Parable* 1871, *The Conversations of Jesus* 1875, *A Paragraph History of the United States* 1875, *A Paragraph History of the American Revolution* (2 volumes) 1876, *Revolutionary Times* 1876, *The Long-Look Books* (3 volumes) 1874, *History of Cambridge* 1880, *Memoir of Jacob Abbott* 1882, *Phillips Brooks* 1900.

Abbott, Frank 1836–97, born: Shapleigh; studied dentistry with Dr. J. E. Ostrander, Oneida, New York, 1855; practiced in Johnstown, New York; in the Civil War: commissioned first lieutenant, USV, 1862, assigned to Co. E, 115th New York INF, USV, captured at Harper's Ferry 1862, after he was exchanged, returned to Johnstown, later removed to New York; M.D. New York University medical department 1871; clinical lecturer: New York College of Dentistry 1866, professor of operative dentistry 1868, dean 1869–97; president: U.S. Dental Association 1888, president: National Association of Dental Faculties 1895; Abbott enjoyed a worldwide reputation as a dental educator, under his administration, the New York College of Dentistry came to be regarded as the most progressive in the country, inventor of numerous dental tools, some of which are still in use; author: *Alveolar Abscess, Its Causes, Prognosis and Treatment* 1872, *Caries of Human Teeth* 1879, *The Mouth and Teeth*, written for Woods *Household Practice of Medicine* 1880, *Absorption of the Roots of Temporary Teeth* 1884, *Studies of the Pathology of Enamel of Human Teeth, with Special Reference to the Etiology of Caries* 1885, *Hyperostosis of Roots of Teeth* 1886, *Teeth of Rabbits* 1887, *Contributions to the Knowledge of Tumors of the Jaw* 1888, *Growth of Enamel* 1889, *Diseases of the Antrum Due to Dental Complications, and Its Treatment* 1889, *Dental Pathology and Practice* 1896.

Abbott, Henry Livermore 1892–1969, born: Lewiston; grandson of Charles Francis Adams, Jr., great grandson of John Quincy Adams, Peter Chardon Brooks; graduate: Groton Academy, B.S. U.S. Naval Academy, obtained the rank of captain, USN; senior naval member: Joint and Combined Intelligence Staff of the Joint Chiefs of Staff, awarded the Navy Cross (1918) and the Green Commendation Ribbon (1946); died in Washington, D.C.

Abbott, Jacob 1803–79, born: Hallowell; son of Jacob Abbot, proprietor of Phillips, brother of Gorham Dummer Abbot and John S. C. Abbott; graduate: Hallowell Academy, A.B. Bowdoin College 1820, Andover Theological Seminary 1824; teacher at Portland Academy; tutor, later professor of mathematics and natural philosophy: Amherst College to 1829, removed to Boston, where he founded the Mount Vernon School 1828, an early secondary school for girls; his *The Teacher* published 1833, was an appeal for student honor and conscience rather than traditional discipline, which became widely used in normal schools, set up a student court, where students were tried in a court of their peers, the first of its kind in America;

removed to Roxbury 1833, later to Farmington, where he established the Abbott Family School (Little Blue); Bowdoin College overseer 1841–47; author of over 180 volumes including 28 in the *Rollo* series, a teacher's guide to the series, entitled *The Rollo Code of Morals, or the Rules of Duty of Children, Arranged with Questions for the Use of Schools* 1841, also twenty volumes of biographical histories and the *Franconia Series* in ten volumes; son-in-law of Benjamin Vaughan, father of Edward Abbott, Lyman Abbott, editor of *Outlook* for fifty years and a leading proponent of the Social Gospel, Austin Abbott, author of numerous legal digests and reports, and Benjamin Vaughan Abbott, also the author of numerous legal digests and reports.

Abbott, John Stevens Cabot 1805–77, born: Brunswick; son of Rev. Jacob Abbot, proprietor of Phillips, brother of Jacob Abbott and Gorham Dummer Abbot; A.B. Bowdoin College 1825, graduate: Andover Theological Seminary; ordained Congregational minister 1830; pastor in Worcester, Massachusetts, later Roxbury and Nantucket, Massachusetts, and Fair Haven, Connecticut; his first book *The Mother at Home...*, grew out of lectures given before a small group of ladies in Worcester, although Abbott was unknown, the book achieved a phenomenal success, both here and abroad, being translated into every European language and into various dialects of Africa and India; became a lifelong friend of Louis Napoleon, subsequent to a visit to France; Bowdoin College overseer 1851–62; author: *The Mother at Home, or, The Principles of Maternal Duty Familiarly Illustrated* 1833, *The Child at Home, or, the Principles of Filial Duty Familiarly Illustrated* 1834, *The Path of Peace: or, A Practical Guide to Duty and Happiness* 1836, *Kings and Queens; or, Life in the Palace, consisting of Historical Sketches of Josephine and Maria Louisa, Louis Philippe, Ferdinand of Austria, Nicholas, Isabella II, Leopold and Victoria* 1848, *History of Marie Antoinette* 1849, *History of Josephine* 1851, *History of Napoleon Bonaparte* 1855, *Confidential Correspondence of the Emperor Napoleon and the Empress Josephine; including Letters from the Time of Their Marriage until the Death of Josephine, also Several Private Letters from the Emperor to his Brother Joseph, and Other Important Personages* 1856, *The French Revolution of 1789: As Viewed in the Light of Republican Institutions* 1859, *South and North, or, Impressions Received During a Trip to Cuba and the South* 1860, *The History of Napoleon III: Emperor of the French, Including a Brief Narrative of All the Most Important Events which have Occurred in Europe Since the Fall of Napoleon I Until the Present Time* 1868, *The History of the Civil War in America: Comprising a Full and Impartial Account of the Origin and Progress of the Rebellion of the Various Naval and Military Engagements, of the Heroic Deeds Performed by the Armies and Individuals, and of Touching Scenes in the Field, the Camp, the Hospital and the Cabin* 1864–67, *The Life of Ulysses S. Grant, Containing a Brief but Faithful Narrative of Those Military and Diplomatic Achievements which have Entitled Him to the Confidence and Gratitude of his Countrymen* 1868, *History of Joseph Bonaparte: King of Naples and of Italy* 1869, *Prussia and the Franco-Prussian War; Containing a Brief Narrative of the Origin of the Kingdom, Its Past History and a Detailed Account of the Causes and Results of the Late War with Austria; with an Account of the*

Origin of the Present War with France and of the Extraordinary Campaign into the Heart of the Empire: Including Biographical Sketches of King William and Count von Bismarck 1871, *Daniel Boone: Pioneer of Kentucky* 1872, *Ferdinand de Soto: The Discoverer of the Mississippi* 1873, *Peter Stuyvesant, the Last Dutch Governor of New Amsterdam* 1873, *Christopher Carson, Known as Kit Carson* 1873, *The Life and Adventures of Rear Admiral John Paul Jones, Commonly called Paul Jones* 1874, *Captain William Kidd: and Others of the Pirates or Buccaneers Who Ravaged the Seas, the Islands and the Continents of America Two Hundred Years Ago* 1874, *David Crockett: Pioneer of Kentucky* 1874, *The Adventures of the Chévalier de la Salle and His Companions: In Their Explorations of the Prairies, Forests, Lakes and Rivers of the New World, and Their Interviews with the Savage Tribes, Two Hundred Years Ago* 1875, *Miles Standish, the Puritan Captain* 1875, *The Life of Christopher Columbus* 1875, *The History of the State of Ohio: From the Discovery of the Great Valley, to the Present Time; Including Narratives of Early Explorations* 1875, *The History of Christianity: Consisting of the Life and Teachings of Jesus of Nazareth: The Adventures of Paul and the Apostles; From the Earliest Period to the Present Time* 1875, *George Washington, or, Life in America One Hundred Years Ago* 1875, *The History of Maine* 1875, *Benjamin Franklin: A Picture of the Struggles of Our Infant Nation, One Hundred Years Ago* 1876, *History of Madame Roland* 1878, *Henry IV, King of France and Navarre* 1884, *Hernando Cortez* 1884, *The History of Hortense, Daughter of Josephine, Queen of Holland, Mother of Napoleon III* 1898, *Austria: Its Rise and Present Power* 1898, *History of King Philip: Sovereign Chief of the Wampanoags* 1899, *History of Louis Philippe: King of the French* 1899. Lincoln once remarked that most of the history that he knew was by Abbott.

Abbott, Nehemiah 1804–77, born: Sidney; studied law at the Litchfield (Connecticut) law school, member: Maine bar 1836, practiced in Calais, removed to Columbus, Mississippi, 1839, removed to Belfast 1840; member: Maine House of Representatives 1842, 1843, 1845, member from the Third District: U.S. House of Representatives (Republican) 1857–59, mayor of Belfast 1865–76; buried in Grove Cemetery, Belfast.

Abrams, Hiram 1878–1926, born: Portland; son of a Russian immigrant real estate broker; attended public schools in Portland, left school at age sixteen, sold newspapers, bought a cow and started a dairy at age fifteen; collector for an install-ment house; traveling salesman for ladies' garments, salesman for Victor Talking Machine Co., salesman: Steinert & Sons, sheet music publishers, became interested in providing lantern slides for theatres, made arrangements with a New York pro-ducer, began doing business with Walter E. Greene, president of the film exchange in Portland and former president of Artcraft Pictures Corporation and vice president of Famous Players-Lasky Corp., with whom he was associated from 1907; silent movie distributor in Portland, Boston, and New Haven, providing motion pictures to several thousand theatres; with the formation of Paramount Pictures Corp. 1914, the principal film exchanges in the country were consolidated; assumed control of New England distribution; removed to Hollywood, president: Paramount Pictures Corp. 1916, founder and president of United Artists Corp. from 1919, established to distribute the motion pictures of Charlie Chaplin, Mary Pickford, Douglas Fairbanks, and D. W. Griffith; an important figure in the development of the motion picture industry; purchased the Portland franchise of the Eastern Baseball League so that Portland could have a professional baseball team 1917.

Acheson, George Robert 1904–89, born: Lewiston; enlisted in the U.S. Army Air Corps 24th Pursuit Squadron 1925, commissioned second lieutenant, USA, 1929; commanding officer: 67th Bombardment Squadron 1941, with 1st Air Support Service Command 1941–42, commanding officer: 55th Bomber Wing 1943–45, promoted to brigadier general, USA, 1944; commanding officer: Alaskan Air Command 1953–56, retired as major general, USA, 1959; decorations include: Distinguished Service Medal, Legion of Merit, Distinguished Flying Cross, two Air Medals, and the Commendation Ribbon.

Adams, Alton Dermont 1864–1943, born: Biddeford; son of a music teacher; attended Wesleyan University, Lehigh University, Cornell University, B.S. Harvard University 1897, A.M. 1901, L.L.B. Harvard University Law School 1904; testing engineer: Brush Electric Co., Cleveland, Ohio, 1884, electrical engineer: Thomson-Houston Electric Co., Lynn, Massachusetts, 1885–87; Jenney Electric Co., Indianapolis, Indiana, 1891–93, Commercial Electric Co., Indianapolis, 1893–94; independent electrical engineer, Boston, designing electrical machinery 1894–1904, public service engineer and accountant, with offices in Worcester, Boston, and Wellesley, Massachusetts, 1904–43, engaged in the investigation and valuation of public utilities, appeared for cities and states in over fifty court cases involving rates or valuation of public service plants, including suppliers of electricity, water, and gas, and railway companies; his extensive testimony, before the U.S. Industrial Commission in 1901 attracted national attention; with his unparalleled knowledge of earnings of municipal and corporate electrical plants, often cited by progressive leaders in their battles against unregulated utilities, came to be regarded as the leading authority in the country on utility valuation.

Adams, Edward Francis 1839–1929, born: Augusta; A.B. Western Reserve College 1860; in the Civil War: private 41st Ohio USV; editorial writer: *San Francisco Chronicle* from 1865; president: Commonwealth Club, for its first ten years; author: *The Modern Farmer* 1899, *Critique of Socialism* 1905, *Inhumanity of Socialism* 1913.

Adams, George Eliashib 1801–75, born: Worthington, Massachusetts; cousin of President John Adams; A.B. Yale College ΦBK 1821, D.D. Bowdoin College 1819, student: Andover Theological Seminary 1826; professor of sacred literature: Bangor

Theological Seminary 1827–29, pastor: First Parish Church (Congregational), Brunswick, 1829–70. It was here during one of his sermons, when one of his parishioners, Harriet Beecher Stowe, conceived of *Uncle Tom's Cabin*; pastor: Orange, New Jersey; father-in-law of Joshua Lawrence Chamberlain.

Adams, John Milton 1819–97, born: Rumford; attended local public school, Turner High School, Goulds Academy, graduate: Gorham Seminary 1842; spent a year at St. Hyacinthe College, Canada, perfecting his French, began to teach at age seventeen, studied law in the office of Fessenden & Deblois, Portland; member: Maine bar 1846, associated with John A. Poor and Nathan Clifford; became editor of the *Eastern Argus* from 1857, sole owner from 1866, served as an orderly sergeant in the Aroostook War, held the rank of colonel on Governor Hubbard's staff; member: Portland School Committee, Cumberland County superintendent of schools; reporter of decisions of the Maine Supreme Judicial Court, compiling volumes forty and forty-one; appointed by President Cleveland to the Board of Visitors: U.S. Military Academy.

Additon, Forrest Orville 1879–1958, born: Auburn, son of a school superintendent; graduate: Port Byron (Illinois) Academy, student: Dixon College, Port Byron, Rush Medical College, Chicago; associated with the Chattahootchie Furniture Co., Flowery Branch, Georgia, from 1898, owner from 1900, principal stockholder when the company was incorporated in 1946, chairman of the board to 1956; by the time of his death, the company was shipping to every state in the Union, Canada, Mexico, and various countries in the West Indies; Additon held patents on various items, including a folding safe, a furniture device sold under the name of Vanirobe, a wardrobe, a warning signal, an invalid walker, a bathtub, a beverage Spoon Tang; founded the Georgia Chair Co., Gainesville, Georgia, 1910; member of advisory board: Works Progress Administration; mayor of Flowery Branch 1922–32; possessed a fine singing voice and was a proficient performer on the harmonica and several stringed instruments, composed several songs, including *Heart of the U.S.A.* 1940, which was adopted as the official Illinois state song; author of several books, including *A Girl in Every Port*, which contained many of his poems and drawings; named poet laureate of Fort Lauderdale, Florida, 1948; won the Better Homes and Gardens National Cooking Award for lacing and cooking bacon; invented a card game known as El Diablo.

Akers, Benjamin Paul 1825–61, born: Saccarappa (later Westbrook); son of a wood turner; nicknamed St. Paul for his serious cast of mind, later added the name Paul to his own, attended local public school, apprenticed to his father, whereby he demonstrated a talent for designing ornamental woodwork, worked as a printer at the *Portland Transcript*, engaged in serious study of art and literature at the Mechanics Institute, removed to Boston 1849, learned plaster casting from Joseph Carew, opened a studio in Portland, made busts of H. W. Longfellow, Samuel Appleton, John Neal, and others; spent two years in Florence, Italy, where he executed two bas-reliefs *Night* and *Morning* for Samuel Appleton, modeled his first statue *Benjamin in Egypt*, which was destroyed when the New York Crystal Palace burned in 1854; in Washington, D.C., 1854, made busts of Franklin Pierce, Edward Everett, a medallion head of Sam Houston, and others; removed to Rome 1855, where he produced his best work, including *Una and the Lion, St. Elizabeth of Hungary, The Dead Pearl Diver* (described by Hawthorne in his *Marble Faun*, now in the Portland Museum of Art), and a colossal head of John Milton, which received particular praise from Robert Browning; returned to New York, where he completed a statue of Commodore Matthew C. Perry for Central Park 1858; returned to Portland 1860, married Elizabeth Chase, died in Philadelphia 1861.

Akers, Elizabeth Chase 1832–1911, born: Strong; daughter of a Methodist clergyman; at age fourteen, began to work as a bookbinder and teacher, began writing for publication at age fifteen, assistant editor: *Portland Transcript* 1855–61, became a contributor to the *Atlantic Monthly* 1858, wrote her famous poem *Rock Me to Sleep, Mother*, which, set to music, was popular with both sides in the Civil War (1859); after the death of Paul Akers, secured a position as copyist with the chief quartermaster in Washington; literary editor: *Portland Advertiser* 1874–81, author: *Forest Buds from the Woods of Maine* 1855, *Poems by Elizabeth Akers* 1866, 1868-69, *Queen Catharines Rose* 1885, *The Silver Bridge* 1885, *The Triangular Society* 1887, *Two Saints* 1888, *The High, Top Sweeting* 1891, *The Proud Lady of Stavaren* 1897, *Ballad of the Bronx* 1901, *The Sunset Song* 1903; wife of Paul Akers 1860–61, later married E. M. Allen, a merchant in New York; asked, near the end of her life to epitomize her life and work, she replied "I believe in labor as a saving grace, in equal rights and equal morals for men and women, in the right of women to decline marriage without being killed or ridiculed for it, in the abolition of wife beating, drunkenness, political corruption, gambling, and custom houses, and in the prevention of cruelty to all creatures, dumb or otherwise."

Albee, Edward Franklin 1857–1930, born: Machias; left home at age nineteen to join the business department of Barnum's Circus; for seven years led the life of an itinerant showman; associated with B. F. Keith from the beginning of vaudeville; manager: Gaiety Theatre and Museum, Boston (chiefly a dime museum of freaks of nature), having received his training under the tutelage of Barnum, proved an apt student of the dynamics of theatricals and quickly mastered the fundamentals of their application, sought to create an improved form of entertainment based on the highest artistic and moral standards, adopting the watchwords cleanliness, courtesy, and comfort, the Gaiety soon ranked as Boston's chief place of amusement; soon opened theatres in Providence, Philadelphia, New York, general manager 1885, formed an association of vaudeville managers 1906, which became the United Booking Office, name changed to B. F. Keith Vaudeville Exchange 1918; in his will, Keith left to

8

Albee most of his holdings 1918, president: Keith-Albee Vaudeville Exchange 1925, effected the consolidation of Keith-Albee and Orpheum circuits, president of the new corporation with assets of over $100 million, in 1928, the Radio Corporation of America joined the organization to form the Radio-Keith-Orpheum circuit, a number of smaller organizations were brought into the consolidation, including the Film Booking Office Productions, Pathé, which produced newsreels, Cecil De Mille Pictures Corp., the Producers Distributing Corp., the Metropolitan Distributing Corp., the resulting organization controlled more than 1,000 theatres, employed an average of 2,000 vaudeville artists and 10,000 managers and employees; provided $15 million to finish the Cathedral of St. John the Divine; during World War I: chairman of a committee which sold more than $27 million of Liberty bonds; chairman of the committee that bought and began the restoration of Jefferson's home Monticello; built a hospital in Saranac Lake, New York, for tubercular vaudeville performers; awarded an honorary A.B. degree by St. Stephens (later Bard) College, of which he was a trustee; credited with the phrase "never give a sucker an even break"; grandfather of playwright of same name; interred in a mausoleum overlooking the steps of the National Vaudeville Association plot in the Kensico Cemetery, Valhalla, New York.

Albee, Fred Houdlette 1876–1945, born: Alna; graduate: Lincoln Academy, A.B. Bowdoin College 1899, M.D. Harvard University Medical School 1903, Sc.D. (Hon.) University of Vermont 1916, Bowdoin College 1917, Rutgers University 1940, L.L.D. Colby College 1930; instructor in orthopedic surgery: Columbia University College of Physicians and Surgeons 1903-11; assistant professor: Cornell University Medical School; professor of orthopedic surgery: University of Vermont; professor and head of department: New York University Medical School; consulting surgeon to twenty-four hospitals, consultant to the Byrd Antarctic Expedition; founder and director: Florida Medical Center, Venice, Florida; director: U.S. Army General Hospital, No. 3; author: *Bone Grafting Surgery* 1915; *Orthopedic and Reconstructive Surgery* 1919, *Injuries and Diseases of the Hip* 1937, *Bone Graft Surgery in Disease, Injury and Deformity* 1940, *A Surgeon's Fight to Rebuild Men* 1943; demonstrated bone grafting in Germany, England, France 1914; founding member and first governor: American College of Surgeons; decorated by Romania, Cuba, Spain, Hungary, France, Italy, &c.

Alden, George Adelbert 1838–1907, born: Hope; grandson of Ebenezer Alden; created Geo. A. Alden Company, in its day, accounted for half of the rubber, gutta-percha, and shellac imports to United States, largest importer of cocoa; his son Adelbert was an organizer of U.S. Rubber Company.

Alden, James 1810–77, born: Portland; nephew of Admiral George Tate, of the Russian Imperial Navy; appointed midshipman, USN, 1828, attached to the Boston Navy Yard to 1830, served aboard USS *John Adams*, in the Mediterranean squadron to 1833; promoted to passed midshipman, USN, 1834, with Wilkes in South Seas Expedition 1838–42, while in the Fiji Islands, a detachment under his command, was attacked by irate natives, which he repulsed and managed to recover the bodies of those men killed; promoted to lieutenant, USN, 1841, aboard USS *Constitution* for her around-the-world cruise, under Captain John (Mad Jack) Percival; commanding officer: of an expedition to cut out Chinese war junks lying under the fort at Zuron Bay, Cochin, China, this was the first military action taken by the United States in what was to become Vietnam; in the war with Mexico: officer in the home squadron, participated in the battles of Vera Cruz, Tuspan, Tabasco; attached to the coast survey 1848–60, commanded the *John Y. Mason* and *Walker*, in survey duty on the eastern seaboard, promoted to commander, USN, 1855, commanding officer: USS *Active*, participated in the Indian war on Puget Sound 1856, his timely arrival at San Juan Island prevented the Pig War from getting out of hand 1859; during the Civil War: commanding officer: USS *South Carolina*, aided in the reenforcement of Fort Pickens; while on blockade duty off Galveston, captured thirteen merchant craft; dispatched to the Gosport Naval Yard by the secretary of the navy to take command of the USS *Merrimac* and save her from falling into Confederate hands, the commander of the navy yard would not let him sail, and *Merrimac* had to be burned; commanding officer: USS *Richmond* at New Orleans, Vicksburg; promoted to captain, USN, 1863; commanding officer: USS *Brooklyn* at Mobile Bay, as such, led the attack; when Alden saw the USS *Tecumseh*, commanded by his childhood friend, Tunis Craven, strike a mine (or torpedo, as they were then known) and rapidly sink, he backed the *Brooklyn* down and threw the line out of order, it was in response to this action that caused Farragut to issue his order, "Damn the torpedoes, four bells, Jouett go ahead," later took part in the assault on Fort Fisher, promoted to commodore, USN, 1866; after war: commanding officer: flagship USS *Susquehanna*, commanding officer: USS *Minnesota*, promoted to rear admiral, USN, 1871, commandant: Navy Yard, Mare Island, California, chief of Bureau of Navigation 1869–71, promoted to vice admiral, USN, commanding officer: European squadron, flagship USS *Wabash*, retired to San Francisco, buried in the Eastern Cemetery, Portland; a destroyer USS *Alden* (DD-211), named in his honor, was launched 1919, and received three battle stars in World War II.

Alden, Timothy 1771–1839, born: Yarmouth; A.B. Harvard College 1794; ordained Congregational minister, pastor: South Congregational Church, Portsmouth, New Hampshire, 1793–1805; president and professor: Allegheny College 1817–31; organizer of American Antiquarian Society; librarian: Massachusetts Historical Society; prepared library catalogue for New York Historical Society; author: *Missions Among the Senecas* 1827.

Alexander, DeAlva Stanwood 1846–1925, born: Richmond; removed with his mother to Ohio 1859; in the Civil War: Pvt. 128th Ohio Infantry, USV, 1862–65; graduate: Edward Little Institute, Auburn, A.B. Bowdoin College 1870, A.M. 1873,

L.L.D. 1907; editor: *Daily Gazette*, Fort Wayne, Indiana 1871–74; delegate: Republican National Convention, Philadelphia, 1872; removed to Indianapolis, Indiana, 1874, correspondent: *Cincinnati Gazette*; secretary: Republican State Committee (Indiana) 1874–78; practiced law in Indianapolis 1881–85; commander of the Department of the Potomac: Grand Army of the Republic; removed to Buffalo, New York; 5th auditor, U.S. Treasury Department 1881–85, U.S. district attorney, Northern District of New York 1889–93; member: U.S. House of Representatives (Republican) 1897–1911, chairman: Committee on Rivers and Harbors; unsuccessful candidate for reelection 1910; Bowdoin College overseer 1905–25, vice president of the Board of Overseers 1915–19; author: *Political History of New York* (THREE volumes) 1906-09, *History and Procedure of the House of Representatives* 1916, *Four Famous New Yorkers*; close friend and political ally of Theodore Roosevelt; buried in Forest Lawn Cemetery, Buffalo.

Allen, Amos Lawrence 1837–1911, born: Waterboro; A.B. Bowdoin College 1860, L.L.B. George Washington University 1866; member: Maine bar 1866, clerk: U.S. Treasury Department 1867–70, York County clerk of courts 1870–84, special examiner, Pension Bureau 1884–85; member: Maine House of Representatives 1886–87; delegate: Republican National Convention 1896; private secretary to Thomas B. Reed 1893–96, appointed to fill Reed's unexpired term 1899, elected member from the 1st District: U.S. House of Representatives (Republican) 1901–11; died in office, buried in Evergreen Cemetery, Alfred.

Allen, Charles Frederick 1816–99, born: Norridgewock; son of a surveyor and Somerset County register of probate; graduate: Bloomfield Academy, A.B. Bowdoin College 1839, D.D. 1872, Wesleyan University 1872; after teaching at Maine Wesleyan Seminary, Kents Hill, for four years, ordained minister in the Methodist Episcopal church, presided over various churches in the Maine conference for nearly fifty years, secretary of the conference for seven years, delegate to the general conference 1864, 1868, 1880; first president: Maine State College of Agriculture and Mechanic Arts (later University of Maine) 1871–79; when Allen became president, the school had two faculty and thirteen students; returned to the Methodist ministry 1879, presiding elder for three years; Bowdoin College overseer 1889–99.

Allen, Edward Beecher 1882–1935, born: Naples; displayed mechanical genius at an early age; invented and sold a can opener at age thirteen; at fourteen, invented a loom shuttle; dropped out of school at age fifteen, apprenticed in the Portland Co. locomotive works; went to work in a shoe factory in Portland owned by his father 1877; perfected his third major invention, a machine for heeling shoes, sold this device to the McKay Heel Co., Lawrence, Massachusetts, which he joined and in which he became a partner; sold out and established a machine repair shop in Portland 1888, here he invented an improved buttonhole clamp which trimmed the sewing machine thread automatically, which he sold to the Singer Manufacturing Co., which he joined and became their inventor of buttonhole machinery, stationed in Elizabethport, New Jersey, to 1906, when he transferred to the company's main plant in Bridgeport, Connecticut, as assistant works manager, later resigned to concentrate on invention; Singer set aside a portion of the factory for his work, possessed over 200 patents on sewing machine improvements; in response to an appeal from the W. & J. Sloane Co., dealers in furniture and floor covering, Allen devised a machine that would sew strips of carpet together automatically, a task that had previously been performed by hand, the first carpet so sewn was laid in the Metropolitan Opera House, New York, in one day.

Allen, Elisha Hunt 1804–83, born New Salem, Massachusetts; A.B. Williams College 1823; studied law with his father, member: Vermont bar 1825, practiced in Brattleboro, Vermont, 1825-27; removed to Portland, associated with John Appleton in the firm of Allen & Appleton; member: Maine House of Representatives 1835–40, 1846, speaker 1838–41, took a conspicuous part in the boundary dispute with New Brunswick, finally settled by the Webster-Ashburton Treaty; member: U.S. House of Representatives (Whig) 1841–43, member: Committee on Foreign Affairs; removed to Boston, member: Massachusetts House of Representatives 1848; appointe, by President Taylor U.S. consul in Hawaii 1849–57, quickly appreciated the importance of the Hawaiian Islands and began a campaign to have them annexed to the United States, secured the assent of King Kamehameha III to a plan that would have the U.S. government pay $300,000 to the Hawaiian royal family; appointed Hawaiian minister of finance 1854, took the potential treaty to Washington where it was being considered by Congress, when the king died and was succeeded by Kamehameha IV, who was partial to the British, the treaty was withdrawn, later, having convinced the new king of the advantages of a treaty of reciprocity, was commissioned Hawaiian envoy extraordinaire and minister plenipotentiary to the United States; failed in his mission due to politics surrounding the tensions that would lead to the Civil War 1856–57; upon his return to Hawaii, he was appointed chancellor, chief justice, and member of the privy council, making him the most influential figure in the government 1857–75; returned once again to Washington as minister in 1864 to negotiate a treaty of reciprocity but failed because of the Civil War; he was successful in his third attempt in 1869, once again minister 1876–83, became dean of the diplomatic corps in Washington, the only American to hold this position, died at the White House New Year's Day levée, buried in Evergreen Cemetery, Portland.

Allen, Frank Leonard 1884–1966, born: Portland; student: Massachusetts School of Art, School of Museum of Fine Art, Boston, Art Students League, New York, student at Harvard University and the Sorbonne, Paris; director of art, public schools of Saugus, Massachusetts, 1907–09, professor of English: Imperial Higher Normal School, Peking, China, 1909–12, instructor in fine arts: Pratt Institute, Brooklyn,

New York, 1912–30, director of art education: Cranbrook Academy, Bloomfield Hills, Michigan, 1930–32, director: Yonkers (New York) Evening School of Design 1915–26, director of art: Boothbay Studios Summer School of Art 1920–42, director: Allen School of Painting, Rockport, Massachusetts, from 1943; director: School of Individual in Art, New York, 1932–34; head, department of design: Massachusetts School of Art, Boston, and supervisor of vocational art education in industry and business, Commonwealth of Massachusetts, from 1934; president: Eastern Arts Association 1938–39.

Allen, Gardner Weld 1856–1944, born: Bangor; A.B. Harvard College 1877, M.D. Harvard University Medical School 1883; practiced in Boston 1884–1922; surgeon, genitourinary department: Boston Dispensary 1886–1905, visiting physician: Home for Aged Women, Boston 1889–98, surgeon: Massachusetts Naval Militia 1893–1901, instructor in genito-urinary surgery: Tufts University Medical School 1897–1906; member: Massachusetts Naval Brigade 1890–1901, in the Spanish-American War: passed assistant surgeon with the rank of lieutenant, USN, aboard USS *Prairie* on blockade duty in the West Indies 1898; in World War I: ship's surgeon, U.S. Shipping Board 1918, aboard transport *Shoshone*, on convoy duty to France; author: *Our Navy and the Barbary Corsairs* 1905, *Our Naval War with France* 1909, *A Naval History of the American Revolution* 1913, *Papers of Francis Gregory Dallas, USN* 1917, *Massachusetts Privateers of the Revolution* 1927, *Papers of Isaac Hull, Commodore USN* 1929, *Our Navy and the West Indian Pirates* 1929, *Papers of John D. Long, Secretary of the Navy 1897–1902* 1939, contributed chapter on Massachusetts in the War of 1812 to *Commonwealth History of Massachusetts*, eleven naval biographies for *Dictionary of American Biography*; concerned for the welfare and education of colored people, was president of the trustees of Donations for Education in Liberia 1919–44, also completed a history of the organization 1923.

Allen, Oscar Dana 1836–1913, born: Hebron; A.B. Sheffield Scientific School, Yale University 1861, Ph.D. 1871; assistant professor of chemistry: Yale University 1861–71, professor of metallurgy and assaying from 1871, chair of department from 1873; made early and notable investigations of the properties of cesium and rubidium; published in *American Journal of Science*; editor and reviser of *Freseniuss Quantitative Analysis* 1881.

Allen, William 1784–1868, born: Pittsfield, Massachusetts; son of Congregational minister; A.B. Harvard College ΦBK 1802; licensed to preach 1804, preached, for a time, in western New York; regent, assistant librarian: Harvard College, prepared the first edition of *American Biographical and Historical Dictionary* 1809, contributed notices of the lives of American clergyman to Bogue's *History of the Dissenters* 1807, succeeded to his father's pastorate in Pittsfield 1810–17, chosen president of the short-lived Dartmouth University 1817; elected third president of Bowdoin College

1820–39, during his administration, the Medical School of Maine was founded, Winthrop and Commons halls erected; as a result of the interference of the Maine legislature in the governing board of Bowdoin College, Allen failed to achieve re-election in 1831, appealing to the U.S. District Court, Allen was reinstated by Judge Story 1833; after his resignation in 1839, compiled a supplement to *Webster's Dictionary*, with 10,000 words not found in any dictionary of the time, author of various hymns, religious poems, lectures, and biographical articles; died in Northampton, Massachusetts.

Allen, William Henry 1808–82, born: Manchester; student: Maine Wesleyan Seminary, Kents Hill, A.B. Bowdoin College 1833; professor of Greek and Latin: Methodist Conference Seminary, Cazenovia, New York; principal: Augusta High School; professor of chemistry and natural history: Dickinson College 1836–46, professor of philosophy and English literature: Dickinson College 1846–49, acting president 1848–49, second and fourth president of Girard College 1849–62, 1867–82; president: Pennsylvania Agricultural College (later Pennsylvania State University) 1865-67; president: American Bible Society 1872–80.

Allen, Willis Boyd 1855–1938, born: Kittery Point; son of a lawyer and partner of John D. Long; graduate: Boston Latin School, A.B. Harvard College 1878, L.L.B. Boston University 1881; member: Massachusetts bar, practiced in Boston, associated with the law firm of Allen, Hemenway & Savage to 1887; editor: *The Cottage Hearth*, *Our Sunday Afternoon*, both weeklies published in Boston, author: *Pine Cones* 1885, *Silver Rags* 1886, *Christmas at Surf Point* 1886, *Northern Cross* 1887, *Mountaineering* series (five volumes) 1887, *Kelp* 1889, *Cloud and Cliff* 1889, *The Red Mountain of Alaska* 1889, *Forest Home* series (five volumes) 1889, *The Lion City of Africa* 1890, *In The Morning* 1890, *John Brownlow's Folks* 1891, *The Boyhood of John Kent* 1891, *Lost on Umbagog* 1894, *Snowed In* 1894, *The Mammoth Hunters* 1895, *Son of Liberty* 1896, *Called to the Front* 1897, *Great Island* 1897, *Around the Yule Log* 1898, *Cleared for Action* 1898, *Navy Blue* 1898, *Pineboro Quartette* 1898, *The Head of Pasht* 1900, *Play Away* 1902, *Under the Pine Tree Flag* 1902, *Sword and Plowshare* 1904, *The North Pacific* 1905, *Gold Hunter of Alaska* 1909, *The Violet Book* 1909.

Allinson, Anne Crosby Emery 1871–1932, born: Ellsworth; sister of Henry Crosby Emery; A.B. Bryn Mawr College 1892, Ph.D. 1896, Litt.D. (Hon.) Bowdoin College 1916, Brown University 1916; dean of women and assistant professor of classical philology: University of Wisconsin 1897–1900, dean: Women's College, Brown University 1900–05, acting dean 1920–21; author of daily column "Distaff," *Providence Evening Bulletin* from 1926, alumnae director: Bryn Mawr College 1901–10, author: *Greek Lands and Letters* 1909, *Roads from Rome* 1913, *Children of the Way* 1923, *Friends with Life* 1925.

Ames, Adelbert 1835–1933, born: East Thomaston (later Rockland); went to sea as a young man, mate on a clipper ship; graduate: U.S. Military Academy 1861, commissioned first lieutenant, USA, assigned to the 5th Artillery, 1st Bull Run, brevetted major, USA, and received the Medal of Honor: remained upon the field in command of a section of Griffen's battery, directing its fire after being severely wounded and refusing to leave the field until too weak to sit upon the caisson where he had been placed by men of his command, took part in the siege of Yorktown, the battles of Gainess Mill and Malvern Hill, for which he was brevetted lieutenant colonel, USA, organized the 20th Maine, USV, which he lead at Antietam and Fredericksburg, commissioned brigadier general, USV, 1863, commanded a brigade at Gettysburg, took temporary command of the X Corps, brevetted colonel, USA, assisted in the siege of Charleston, the battle of Cold Harbor, the siege of Petersburg, commanding officer: Amess Division 2nd Div. XXIV Corps, Fort Fisher, brevetted brigadier general, USA; after the war: military governor of Mississippi 1868–70, elected civilian governor of Mississippi 1874–76, resigned rather than face impeachment by the newly all-white legislature; member: U.S. Senate from Mississippi (Republican) 1870–74, chairman: Committee on Enrolled Bills; engaged in flour milling in Minneapolis; in the Spanish American War: brigadier general, USV, siege of Santiago; retired to Lowell, Massachusetts, and Ormond Beach, Florida, where he died, last surviving full general officer from the American Civil War, buried in Hildreth Family Cemetery, Lowell, Massachusetts; son-in-law of Benjamin Butler, father of Butler Ames, member: U.S. House of Representatives 1903–13.

Ames, Benjamin 1778–1835, born: Andover, Massachusetts; A.B. Harvard College ΦBK 1803; read law, member: Massachusetts bar 1806, practiced in Bath, appointed Lincoln County attorney by Governor James Sullivan 1807–11, judge of the circuit court of common pleas 1811–14; Bowdoin College overseer 1818–28; delegate: Maine Constitutional Convention 1819, member: Maine House of Representatives 1820–23, first speaker 1820–23; with the resignation of Governor William Durkee Williamson, 25 December 1821, assumed office to 2 January 1822, when he resigned; member, president: Maine Senate 1824; member: Maine House of Representatives 1827; became involved with William King in a particularly vicious squabble, wherein each accused the other of trading with the enemy during the War of 1812, among other charges and counter charges; removed to Cincinnati 1827 and practiced law for two years; upon his return to Maine, suffered a stroke and subsequently died at the home of his brother-in-law in Houlton.

Ames, Edwin Gardner 1856–1935, born: East Machias; from an early age, assisted his father in his lumber business, removed to San Francisco 1879; collector for Pope & Talbot, a lumber company, which came to be the largest in the Pacific Northwest, founded by two Mainers from Machias, appointed assistant manager of their mill in Port Gamble, Washington, 1881; resident manager: Puget Mill Co., headquartered in Seattle 1911, made general manager 1914; vice president, director: Seattle National Bank, director: Metropolitan Bank of Seattle, trustee: Washington Savings Institution, a founder: Pacific Coast Lumber Manufacturers Association; Pacific lumber inspection bureau; Kitsap County commissioner 1882–93; a major benefactor of the University of Washington, donating to it his home to be used as the president's residence, his extensive library, including a portion of a Gutenberg Bible, and several valuable tracts of land.

Anderson, Hugh Johnston 1801–81, born: Wiscasset; son of an Irish immigrant, after the death of his father in 1810, removed to Belfast, where he worked in his uncle's store, eventually becoming partner; clerk of Waldo County courts 1824–36; member from the 1st District: U.Ss House of Representatives (Democrat) 1837–41; fourteenth governor of Maine 1844–47; unsuccessful candidate for U.S. Senate 1847; appointed by President Pierce commissioner of U.S. Customs 1853–57, appointed by President Buchanan chairman of the committee to re-organize the San Francisco mint 1857–59; appointed by President Andrew Johnson sixth auditor of the U.S. Treasury 1866–69; removed to Portland, Oregon, 1880; buried in Grove Cemetery, Belfast; his portrait is in the Maine Statehouse collection.

Anderson, John 1792–1883, born: Windham; A.B. Bowdoin College 1813; member: Maine bar 1816, practiced in Portland; member: Maine Senate 1823; member from the 2nd District: U.S. House of Representatives (Jacksonian) 1825–33, chairman of Committee on Elections, Naval Affairs Committee; mayor of Portland 1833, 1842; collector of U.S. customs, Portland 1833–36, 1837–41, 1843–48; Bowdoin College overseer 1821–32; buried in Windham Town Cemetery.

Anderson, Martin Brewer 1815–90, born: Brunswick; son of a shipwright; attended public schools in Brunswick and Bath; A.B. Waterville College 1840, L.L.D. 1853, University of New York 1882, student at Newton Theological Institution 1840; ordained Baptist minister, instructor in Latin, Greek, and mathematics: Waterville College 1841, professor of rhetoric 1843–50; member: Ethnological Society of New York; owner and editor: *New York Recorder* 1850–53; founding president: University of Rochester 1853–88; refused the presidencies of Brown University, Union College, and the University of Michigan, nominations for Congress from both parties; president: American Baptist Missionary Union; member: Niagara Falls Park Commission; associate editor and contributor to Johnson's *Cyclopedia*, contributor of a vast number of papers and articles for newspapers and professional journals; retired to Lake Helen, Florida.

Anderson, Rufus 1796–1880, born: North Yarmouth; son of a Congregational minister and Bowdoin College overseer; A.B. Bowdoin College 1818, graduate: Andover Theological Seminary 1822, D.D. Dartmouth College 1836, L.L.D. Bowdoin

College 1866; editor: *Missionary Herald* (organ of the American Board of Foreign Missions) 1822, chief assistant to secretary: American Board of Foreign Missions 1822–24, assistant secretary 1824–32, corresponding secretary 1832–66, in that capacity, visited the Mediterranean missions in 1843, the Indian missions in 1854, and those of the Sandwich Islands in 1863; lecturer at Andover Theological Seminary 1867–69; a founder: Mount Holyoke College 1837, American Oriental Society 1842; an organizer of the Hanover Street Church, Boston; author: *Memoir of Catherine Brown* 1825, *Observations on Peloponnesus and the Greek Islands* 1828, *Irish Missions in the Early Ages* 1839, *Bartimeus* 1857, *Missions in the Levant* 1860, *The Hawaiian Islands, Their Progress and Condition* 1864, *Foreign Missions, Their Relations and Claims* 1869, *A Heathen Nation Civilized* 1870, *A History of the Missions of the American Board of Foreign Missions* (five volumes) 1872.

Andrew, John Albion 1818–67, born: Windham; son of a merchant; attended the academies in Portland, Yarmouth, Bridgton, and Gorham; A.B. Bowdoin College 1837; studied law in Boston, with Henry Fuller; member: Massachusetts bar 1840; associated with the cases of fugitive slaves Burns and Sims, became an ardent abolitionist; a founder of the Free Soil Party, raised money for John Brown's defense; member: Massachusetts House of Representatives 1858, delegate: Republican National Convention 1860; vigorous Civil War governor of Massachusetts (Republican) 1861–66, reelected annually, with large majorities; one of his first official acts was to put the Massachusetts militia on a war footing, in case hostilities were to break out, communicated with the governors of Maine and New Hampshire to reorganize the provisioning of their respective militias, thus prepared, it was possible for Andrew to send five regiments of Massachusetts militia to Washington, immediately after President Lincoln's proclamation of 15 April 1861, one of which, the 6th Massachusetts Volunteers, was attacked in the streets of Baltimore; was able, through moral suasion, to persuade the normally parsimonious Massachusetts legislature to fund the nearly unlimited creation and equipping of Massachusetts regiments for the war effort, advocated emancipation of slaves and the equipping of Negro regiments, personally saw to the creation of the famous 54th Massachusetts Volunteers, resisted federal authorities in their efforts to arrest Southern sympathizers residing in Massachusetts, liberalized the Commonwealth's divorce laws, advocated the elimination of the death penalty; declined the offer of the presidency of Antioch College; presided over the first national Unitarian convention; buried in Hingham (Massachusetts) Cemetery.

Andrews, Charles 1814–52, born: Paris; graduate: Hebron Academy; member: Maine bar 1837; practiced in Turner; member: Maine House of Representatives 1839–43, speaker 1842; clerk of Oxford County courts 1845-48; member from the 4th District: U.S. House of Representatives (Democrat) 1851–52, died in office; cenotaph in Congressional Cemetery, Washington, buried in Hillside Cemetery, Paris.

Andrews, Fred Lowry 1873–1967, born: Thomaston, son of a ship captain; attended public schools in Thomaston, studied bookkeeping at a business school in Boston 1893, worked as a janitor and delivery boy while in high school, later was a clothing salesman in a general furnishing and clothing store in Thomaston; bookkeeper: Curtis & Co., a commercial produce company in Boston 1893–99, removed to Denver, Colorado, employed as bookkeeper and credit manager for the Bridaham-Quereau Drug Co., later the Davis-Bridaham Drug Co., an incorporator and secretary of the new company, later, as Davis Brothers, Inc., director and treasurer 1933, general manager 1943, president 1945, chairman of the board from 1953; under his leadership, the company became one of the most successful independent wholesale drug houses in the country; president: National Wholesale Druggists Association 1950.

Andrews, Harry Eugene 1861–1926, born: Pittston (that part that is now Randolph); entered newspaper business at seventeen, with *Lewiston Journal* 1878–98, last eight years as part owner; with the *Los Angeles Times* from 1898, managing editor and part owner from 1906; was present when the Times Building was blown up by an anarchist's bomb, with twenty killed; director: *Times-Mirror*; president: Big Conduit Land Co., vice president: Van Nuys Boulevard Land Co..

Andrews, Israel DeWolf 1813–71, born: Eastport; as U.S. consul in New Brunswick 1847, was detailed by U.S. Secretary of State Clayton to investigate trade in British North America and the ramifications of reciprocity; completing his exhaustive report, became the chief lobbyist for the passage of the treaty in United States and Great Britain; planting articles in periodicals, dispensing bribes, confronting Southerners who believed that reciprocity was a first step in annexing a large, generally abolitionist population, working out the details of inshore fishing conflicts; with the passage of the Clayton-Bulwer treaty, came in for intense criticism of his methods, but few criticized the results.

Andrews, William Henry 1860–1923, born: Thomaston; graduate: Thomaston High School, Bryant and Stratton Business College, Boston; began business career in Boston with Wadsworth, Howland. and Co., manufacturers of varnish 1879–91; purchased an interest in Pratt and Lambert, Inc., treasurer 1895, general manager 1896, president 1907, chairman of the board 1917; expanded Pratt & Lambert from a manufacturer of varnish into a modern paint, oil, and varnish company, largest in the United States and Canada.

Anglin, John 1850–1905, born: Portland; cabin boy, USN, recipient: Medal of Honor, served on board the USS *Pontoosuc* during the capture of Fort Fisher and Wilmington, 24 December 1864 to 22 January, 1865. "Carrying out his duties faithfully during this period, Anglin was recommended for gallantry and for his cool courage while under fire of the enemy throughout these various actions." At age fourteen, Anglin was the second youngest recipient of the Medal of Honor; buried in Calvary Cemetery, South Portland.

Appleton, James 1786–1862, born: Ipswich, Massachusetts; member: Massachusetts House of Representatives; in the War of 1812: brigadier general, Massachusetts militia; removed to Portland, member: Maine House of Representatives 1836; became interested in the subject of Prohibition, made speeches throughout the state, contributed articles to sundry publications about total abstinence and the suppression of the liquor trade, first to advance the principle of statutory prohibition of the manufacture and sale of liquors, made a report to the legislature to that effect which had a profound impact on that body and culminated, eventually, in the passage of the Maine liquor law; known as the father of Prohibition.

Appleton, Jesse 1772–1819, born: New Ipswich, New Hampshire; A.B. Dartmouth College φBK 1792, D.D. 1810, Harvard College 1810; ordained Congregational minister, Hampton, New Hampshire, 1797, second president: Bowdoin College 1807–19, trustee and overseer *ex officio* 1807–19; trustee: Phillips Academy, Exeter; member: American Academy of Arts and Sciences; *The Works of Jesse Appleton, D.D.* was published posthumously in 1836; father-in-law of President Franklin Pierce and Alpheus Spring Packard.

Appleton, John 1804–91, born: New Ipswich, New Hampshire; nephew of Jesse Appleton; graduate: New Ipswich Academy, A.B. Bowdoin College 1822, studied law with George Farley, Groton, Massachusetts, and with his kinsman, Nathan Dane Appleton, Alfred; member: New Hampshire bar 1826, practiced in Dixmont for six months, removed to Sebec, where he remained for six years, removed to Bangor 1832, partner with Elisha Allen, styled Allen & Appleton, to 1840, after Allen's election to Congress, reporter of decisions, Penobscot County 1841, partner with John Hill and Moses Appleton to 1852, when John Appleton was appointed associate justice: Maine Supreme Judicial Court 1852, chief justice 1862, reappointed 1869, 1876, 1883; Appleton's long tenure on the bench resulted in his having an immense influence on the development of the Maine law; his *Treatise on Evidence* 1860 was considered a radical departure from the norm on that subject, but the underlying principles contained were generally adopted nationwide; Bowdoin College overseer 1868–70, trustee 1870–91; his portrait is in the Maine Statehouse collection.

Appleton, John 1815–64, born: Beverly, Massachusetts; A.B. Bowdoin College 1834; settled in Portland, member: Cumberland County bar 1837; editor: *Eastern Argus* 1839–44; chief clerk: Department of the Navy 1845–48; keeper of the official journal of President Polk's procession through New England 1847; chargé d'affairs: Bolivia 1848–49; law partner of Nathan Clifford; member from the 2nd District: U.S. House of Representatives (Democrat) 1851–53; secretary of legation: London

1855–56; assistant secretary of state 1857–60; minister to Russia 1860–61; buried in Evergreen Cemetery, Portland.

Appleton, John Howard 1844–1930, born: Portland; brother of William Hyde Appleton; Ph.B. Brown University 1863, A.M. 1869, Sc.D. 1900; assistant instructor, instructor analytical chemistry: Brown University 1863–68, professor of chemistry applied to arts 1868–72, professor of chemistry 1872–1914; Rhode Island state sealer of weights and measures; author: *The Young Chemist* 1878, *Short Course in Qualitative Analysis* 1878, *Qualitative Analysis* 1881, *Laboratory Yearbook* 1883–92, *Beginners Handbook of Chemistry* 1884, *Advanced Qualitative Analysis* 1889, *Lessons in Chemical Philosophy* 1890, *Metals of the Chemist* 1891, *Report Book for Chemical Work* 1891, *Carbon Compounds* 1892, *Easy Experiments in Organic Chemistry* 1898.

Appleton, William Hyde 1843–1926, born: Portland; brother of John Howard Appleton; A.B. Harvard College ΦBK 1864, A.M. 1867, Ph.D. Swarthmore College 1888, L.L.D. 1912, student of Greek and philology: universities of Berlin and Bonn 1870–71, Athens 1871-72; tutor in Greek: Harvard College 1868–70, professor of Greek and German: Swarthmore College 1872–88, president 1889–91, 1891–95, professor of Greek language and literature 1905–09; author: *Greek Poets in English Verse* 1873.

Archer, Gleason Leonard 1880–1966, born: Great Pond; student at Boston University 1902–04, L.L.B. 1906, L.L.D. Atlanta Law School 1926, L.L.M. John Marshall Law School, Chicago 1944; member: Massachusetts bar 1906, founded Suffolk Law School, which is now Suffolk University (and which was the largest law school in the country during the 1920s) 1906, president 1937–48; founder, director: Archer Blueberry Nursery 1948–63; by appointment: chief arbitrator in dispute between Springfield Street Railroad and its employees 1914; special assistant to Massachusetts Commissioners on Uniform State Laws 1926–28; vice chairman: General Commission for the Boston Tercentenary 1930; national chairman: Democratic National Committee 1944–45; author: *Pilgrim Pioneers, New England Colonies 1630–1692, Pioneers of the Rockbound Coast, Robert Duke of Kragcastle, The Giant of Eagle Mountain, More Than a Man, I Dont Believe It, Building a School: Hi-Jacking a University*, books on law, history, radio.

Attean, Pricilla Ann 1941–95, born: Old Town; student: University of Maine; assistant manager: Pompei Restaurant, Bridgeport, Connecticut 1970–81; consultant: Penobscot Nation, Old Town 1982–84, tribal, state relations officer 1984–95; member: Maine House of Representatives 1984–95, chairman: Joint Select Committee on Indian Affairs 1984–95; member, Census Committee: Penobscot Nation, Old Town 1982–84, Adult Vocational Training Committee 1985–95, Museum Committee 1985–95.

Atwood, Leonard 1845–1930, born: Farmington Falls; after service in the U.S. Navy, during the Civil War, removed to Titusville, Pennsylvania, where he drilled an oil well and built the first oil pipeline in the world, selling out, he removed to New York where he invented the first practical elevator (vertical railway) and installed several, including one in the Metropolitan Hotel, built a factory in New London, Connecticut, to supply demand, sold out to Otis; invented the Yankee Hod Carrier, a mechanical, labor-saving device, widely used; returned to Farmington Falls, where he constructed the Franklin Pulp Mill, later, one of the earliest components of International Paper; removed to Canada, where he built the Halifax & Southwestern Railroad, later a part of the Grand Trunk Railroad; returning to Maine, he purchased controlling interest in and became president of the Wiscasset & Québec Railroad and reorganized it as the Wiscasset, Waterville & Farmington Railroad Co. 1898; invented the modern, geared fishing reel, the metal tape measure, and a compound, articulated steam locomotive.

Averill, John Thomas 1825–89, born: Alna; removed with his family to Montville 1838; graduate: Maine Wesleyan Seminary, Kents Hill, Readfield 1846; taught school for a year, removed to Winthrop, where he engaged in mercantile interests for three years; migrated to Pennsylvania as a lumberman 1852, then to Lake City, Minnesota, as grain merchant, member: Minnesota Senate 1858–60; in the Civil War rose to brevetted. brigadier general, USV; after the war, in paper business in Saint Paul; member U.S. House of Representatives (Republican) 1871–75, chairman: Committee on Indian Affairs, member: Republican National Committee 1868–80; buried in Oakland Cemetery, St. Paul.

Avery, Martha Gallison Moore 1851–1929, born: Steuben; daughter of a shipwright, sister of Henry Dyer Moore and John Godfrey Moore; operated a millinery business in Ellsworth; member: First Nationalist Club of Boston; author of articles for *The Nationalist*; member: Socialist-Labor party, lecturer, Socialist-Labor candidate for Massachusetts Commmonwealth Treasurer (first female candidate for statewide office in Massachusetts) 1897; founded: Karl Marx Club, a weekly lecture and discussion series dedicated to exploring Marxist thought and word, director and chief lecturer, named changed to Boston School of Political Economy 1901; baptized Roman Catholic 1900, attempted to purge the Socialist-Labor party of those who attacked the church, espoused violence and free love, suspended by central committee 1903; author: *The Nation of Fatherless Children* 1903, which received the praise of Theodore Roosevelt; a founder: Common Cause Society, Boston 1912, contributor of articles to *Common Cause*, president 1922-29; founded Catholic Truth Guild 1917, distributors of Catholic antisocialist propaganda; outspoken opponent of female suffrage.

Avery, Maurice Westcott 1896–1973, born: Bath, son of the owner of a livery stable; attended public schools in Bath, A.B. Bowdoin College φBK 1919, A.M. 1922,

Ph.D. Harvard University 1928; principal: Rockport High School 1920–21, instructor in Latin: Williams College 1923, assistant professor 1927, associate professor 1935, professor 1954, Massachusetts Professor of Latin Language and Literature 1960–65; designed a course in Greek and classical civilization for students who had received little or no education in this discipline, feeling that modern political, social and cultural forms were originally created by Greek and Roman civilizations, some familiarity with these civilizations was necessary for an appreciation of modern society; editor: *Latin Prose Literature* 1931; a proficient violinist and pianist.

Avery, Myron Haliburton 1899–1952, born: North Lubec; attended local public schools in Lubec, A.B. Bowdoin College ΦBK 1920, L.L.B. Harvard University Law School 1923; admiralty attorney for the U.S. Shipping Board (later U.S. Maritime Commission), Washington 1928–42; in World War II: lieutenant, USNR, advanced up the ranks to captain, USN, 1947, while on duty with the naval reserve, reorganized the admiralty division of the Judge Advocate General's Office and established and coordinated its field offices; admiralty counsel and director of the admiralty division: Department of U.S. Navy 1948–52, awarded the Legion of Merit; chairman: Appalachian Trail Conference 1931–52, during that time, he perfected that organization from a loose group of interested individuals into an incorporated body and coordinated the work of individuals and organizations until there came into being a continuous trail of over 2,000 miles in length from Georgia to Maine; covered the entire trail, on foot, prior to 1936, thus becoming the first person to traverse the entire Appalachian Trail; organized and president: Potomac Appalachian Trail 1927–41; organized the Maine Appalachian Trail Club, overseer of trails 1935–49, president 1949–52; recognized authority on the Katahdin region, coauthor: *An Annotated Bibliography of Katahdin* 1936, author: *Guide to the Appalachian Trail in Maine* 1942; his extensive research on Royalist Americans who left for Nova Scotia during the Revolutionary War remained unpublished at the time of his early death in Annapolis Royal, Nova Scotia; Avery Peak on Bigelow Mountain is named in his honor.

Ayer, Fred Wellington 1855–1936, born: Bangor; graduate: Phillips Academy, Andover; Farmington State Normal School; established F. W. Ayer & Co., Bangor 1876, manufacturer and dealer in lumber, acquired mills in Palmer and Orono; founder, president: Eastern Manufacturing Co., manufacturers of pulp and paper 1897; president: Second National Bank of Bangor 1902–07; member: Queen City Dramatic Association (later the Buskin Club) which produced plays and brought in leading actors and actresses to Bangor; a founder of the Tarrantine Club; noted authority on Oriental rugs; built up a collection of postal stamps that he later sold to the Duke of York (later King George VI); he was the first man to catch a salmon on the Penobscot with a fly; a devoted baseball player, he built up the Bangor team to the point that it won the New England league championship.

Ayer, John 1883–1961, born: Oakland; B.S. Massachusetts Institute of Technology 1905, graduate student: Technical High School, Charlottenburg, Berlin 1906–07; assistant engineer: Charles River Basin Commission 1907–13, engineer and designer of concrete dams and power houses 1910–13, assistant engineer and director of the Port of Boston 1913–17, assistant engineer: Fay, Spofford & Thorndike 1917–18, executive engineer 1918–19, division engineer 1920–22, vice president to 1961, director of construction: Fay, Spofford & Thorndike, specializing in design and construction of waterfront projects, such as shipbuilding and graving docks for the Bureau of Yards and Dock, U.S. Navy, Commonwealth Dry Dock and Pier, Boston, Hampden County Memorial Bridge, Springfield, Massachusetts, Bethlehem Ship Building Corporation, Victory Plant, Quincy, Massachusetts; associated with three other firms in design and construction of dry docks and other improvements for the U.Ss Navy; work for the v Army in northern Canada, Newfoundland, and Alaska.

Ayer, Richard Small 1829–1896, born: Montville; in the Civil War: private Co. A, 4th Maine Volunteers, promoted to captain, USV, mustered out for injuries 1863; removed to Warsaw, Virginia 1865, delegate: Virginia Constitutional Convention 1867; member from Virginia's 1st District: U.S. House of Representatives (Republican) 1870–71; moved back to Montville, member: Maine House of Representatives 1888; buried in Mt. Repose Cemetery, Montville.

Ayer, Winslow B. 1860–1935, born: Bangor; B.S. Massachusetts Institute of Technology 1881; removed to Oregon 1883, president: Eastern and Western Lumber Company, Portland, Oregon; member: Commission on Minimum Wages and Industrial Conditions in the State of Oregon, Commission for Commission Government of Portland, Federal Food Administrator for Portland 1917, founding president of the Portland Art Museum, to which he donated Renoir's *Sailboats at Argenteuil*.

Babson, Seth 1831–1907, born: Maine; made an overland journey to Sacramento, California, 1850, established his reputation as one of the first practicing architects in California; designed the home of Governor Stanford, the Crocker Art Gallery, &c.; president of the San Francisco chapter of the American Institute of Architects, member: California State Board of Architects.

Bailey, Edwin Warren Marble 1863–1940, born: East Pittston; son of a carriage maker; removed to Amesbury, Massachusetts, with his father, Samuel Robinson Bailey, established the S. R. Bailey Co. 1882, which ultimately became one of the most important carriage builders in the country, began the production of the Bailey Electric, one of the first electric automobiles, associated with Thomas A. Edison in the application of the Edison battery to automobiles, superintendent: Biddle and Smart Co., Amesbury 1915, manufacturers of automobile bodies, established the Bailey Manufacturing Co. 1920, later the Bailey Co., manufacturers of rolled metal shapes, occupied a factory of one hundred and twenty thousand square feet, manufactured glass run channel for automobile windows; member and president: National Carriage Builder's Association, member: National Association of Manufacturers, Ancient and Honorable Artillery Company; died in Barbados, buried in East Pittston.

Bailey, Hannah Clark Johnston 1839–1923, born: Cornwall-on-Hudson, New York; daughter of a tanner, who later farmed and was a Society of Friends minister; attended public school and a Quaker boarding school; taught in upstate New York 1858–67; accompanied a female Quaker preacher on a tour of New England churches, poorhouses, and jails; met and married Moses Bailey, a member of the Bailey family of Winthrop Center, famous for their manufacture of oil cloth 1868; on a trip to North Carolina 1879, they founded a mission for the establishment of schools for poor people; after her husband's death, she compiled his memoir *Reminiscences of a Christian Life* 1884; served as treasurer of the Women's Foreign Missionary Society for ten years; joined the Woman's Christian Temperance Union 1883; appointed superintendent: Department of Peace and International Arbitration of the Universal Peace Union 1887, as such, organized peace bands among school children, encouraged their teachers to promote international goodwill, circulated petitions, Bible readings, leaflets, and illustrated calendars, published two newspapers: *Pacific Banner* for adults and *Acorns* for children, two books: *Voices of Peace* and *Gleanings on the Subject of Peace and Arbitration*; through her leadership, the WCTU Department of Peace and International Arbitration was represented in fourteen countries and twenty-six states; appointed world superintendent of peace of the World's Woman's Christian Temperance Union 1888; personally lobbied President Benjamin Harrison to opt for arbitration, rather than war, with Chile 1892; lectured extensively in Europe, Asia, and Africa; president: Maine Woman Suffrage Association 1891–97, treasurer: National Council of Women 1895–99; an outspoken critic of the Spanish-American War and subsequent American actions in the Philippine Insurrection, her pleas for arbitration found fertile ground in the establishment of the World Court 1901; represented Maine on the National Board of Charities and Correction; lobbied for the establishment of a Maine women's reformatory; soon after her retirement in 1916, the WCTU abandoned its antiwar stance and supported the entrance of the United States into World War I.

Bailey, Jacob 1731–1818, born: Rowley, Massachusetts; son of a farmer, as a child, began his lifelong mania for recording his thoughts, often sharp and bitter; A.B. Harvard College 1755, A.M. 1758; as an undergraduate, was a charity student, waited on tables, and held a Hollis Scholarship and during winter vacations, kept school in Rowely; became an itinerant Congregational preacher; approached by the Society for the Propagation of the Gospel in Foreign Parts in Portsmouth and, acquiring the patronage of Silvester Gardiner, removed to England where he was ordained Anglican priest 1760; removed to Pownalborough (that part that is now Dresden), at the invitation of residents concerned about the activities of French Jesuit priests (an appeal probably concocted by Silvester Gardiner); conducted services in the courthouse, as well as on an itinerant basis in many scattered settlements, until Saint John's Church was completed; an adamant Tory, despite threats and intimidation, refused to delete prayers for the king after the outbreak of revolution, came into severe conflict with his Harvard classmates Jonathan Bowman and Charles Cushing; subsequent to his petition to the general court, he was allowed to depart for Annapolis, Nova Scotia, 1778, where he served as rector of St. Luke's Church and chaplain to the garrison; his *The Frontier Missionary* was published, posthumously, in 1853.

Bailey, Jeremiah 1773–1853, born: Little Compton, Rhode Island; A.B. Brown College 1794; member: Massachusetts bar, practiced in Wiscasset from 1798; presidential elector 1808, member: Massachusetts General Court 1811–14, judge of probate 1816–34; member from the 1st District: U.S. House of Representatives (Whig) 1835–37; collector of U.S. customs, Wiscasset 1849–53; Bowdoin College overseer 1801–30, vice president of the board of overseers 1817–19, president 1819–29, Bowdoin College trustee 1830-38; buried in Evergreen Cemetery, Wiscasset.

Bailey, Rufus William 1793–1863, born: North Yarmouth; A.B. Dartmouth College 1813, taught at the academies at Salisbury, New Hampshire, and Blue Hill; studied law with Daniel Webster; student: Andover Theological Seminary; pastor: Congregational Church, Norwich, Vermont, teacher of moral philosophy: Norwich Military School; editor: *The Patriarch* 1841, professor of languages: Austin (predecessor of University of Texas) College 1854, president 1858–63; author: *The Mother's Request, The Family Preacher, A Primary Grammar, The Scholar's Companion*, a series of letters on slavery published as *The Issue*.

Bailey, Taber Davis 1874–1938; born: Old Town; son of an attorney and member of the Maine House of Representatives; graduate: Bangor High School 1892, A.B. Bowdoin College 1896, studied law in the office of Davis & Bailey, Bangor, member: Maine bar 1898, practiced in Bangor, member: Bangor City Council 1897–1900, president 1901, Bangor city solicitor 1902–03, member: Maine Senate (Republican) 1913–21, president 1917-18, led the fight for interstate transmission of hydroelectric power; owned the Eastman Car Co., owners of potato-carrying railroad cars.

Baker, Carlos Heard 1909–1987, born: Biddeford; A.B. Dartmouth College ΦBK 1932, A.M. Harvard University 1933, Ph.D. Princeton University 1940; teacher: Thornton Academy 1933–34, Nichols School, Buffalo 1934–36, instructor in English: Princeton University; editor: *American Issues* 1941; assistant professor of English, Princeton University 1942, associate professor 1946, professor 1952, Woodrow Wilson professor of English from 1953, chairman: department of English from 1952; author: *Shadows in Stone* 1930, *The American Looks at the World* 1944, *Shelley's Major Poetry:*

The Fabric of a Vision 1948, *The Prelude with a Selection from the Shorter Poems and Sonnets and the 1800 Preface to Lyrical Ballads* 1948, *Hemingway: The Writer as Artist* 1956, *A Friend in Power: A Novel* 1958, *Hemingway and His Critics, an International Anthology* 1961, *Ernest Hemingway: Critiques of Four Major Novels* 1962, *The Land of Rumbelow, A Fable in the Form of a Novel* 1963, *A Year and a Day, Poems* 1963, *Ernest Hemingway: A Life Story* 1969, *The Gay Head Conspiracy: A Novel of Suspense* 1973, *The Talisman: and other Stories* 1976, *Ernest Hemingway: Selected Letters 1917-1961*, 1981, *The Echoing Green: Romanticism, Modernism and the Phenomena of Transference in Poetry* 1984, *Emerson Amongst the Eccentrics: A Group Portrait* 1996; member: Century Association.

Baker, James Hutchings 1848–1925, born: Harmony; attended local district schools, graduate: Nichols Latin School, Lewiston, A.B. Bates College 1873, L.L.D. 1892; principal: Yarmouth Academy 1873–75, principal: Denver (Colorado) High School 1875–92, during which time the enrollment increased from fifty to seven hundred, the most progressive methods were employed; declined the offer of the presidency of the Colorado State Agricultural College 1882; president: Colorado State Teachers' Association 1880, elected member of the National Council of Education 1886, chairman of the committee on the relations of high schools to colleges 1890; president: National Educational Association 1891; elected third president: University of Colorado 1892–1914, originated the plan which led to the renown report of the National Committee of Ten, author: *Elementary Psychology* 1890, *Education and Life* 1900, *American Problems* 1917, *Educational Aims and Civic Needs* 1913, *American University Progress and College Reform, Relation to School and Society* 1916, *After the War—What?* 1918, *Of Himself and Other Things* 1922.

Baldwin, Alice Mary 1875–1960, born: Lewiston, student: Bates College, A.B. Cornell University 1903, A.M. 1902, graduate study at Columbia University 1903–04, the Sorbonne 1903, Bryn Mawr College 1907–08, University of Pennsylvania 1914–19, fellow: University of Chicago 1921–23, Ph.D. 1926; dean of women and instructor in history: Fargo (North Dakota) College, 1904–06, instructor in history and head of department: Baldwin School 1906–21, assistant professor: University of Chicago 1923–24, associate professor 1928–39, professor 1939–47, dean of women 1924–30; author: *The New England Clergy and the American Revolution* 1928, *The Clergy of Connecticut in Revolutionary Days* 1936, *The Development and Place of the Coordinate College*, editor.

Ballard, Martha Moore 1735–1812, born: Sudbury, Massachusetts; in Hallowell, employed as a midwife; diarist.

Bangs, Isaac Sparrow 1831–1903, born: Canaan; left his position as cashier at Waterville Bank to enter the Union army as a private 1861, captain Co A, 20th

Maine USV, 1862: Antietam, Shepardstown Ford, Fredericksburg; lieutenant colonel U.S. Colored Troops 1863, commanding officer: 4th Regiment, Ullman's Brigade (later: 81st Colored Infantry), siege of Port Hudson; colonel 10th U.S. Colored Heavy Artillery 1863, commanding officer: forts Jackson, Saint Phillip, Livingston, and Pike and the defenses of New Orleans; mustered out 1864, Bvt. brigadier general, USV, for gallant and meritorious service during war.

Banks, Frank Arthur 1883–1957, born: Saco; B.S. in Civil Engineering, University of Maine 1906, Eng.D. 1940, L.L.D. Washington State College 1944; engineer: U.S. Reclamation Service, Lower Yellowstone Project, Montana 1906–09, designing engineer: Boise, Idaho 1909–13, construction engineer: Jackson Lake Dam, Wyoming, 1913–16, Minidoka Project 1916–20, American Falls Dam 1920–26, Owyhee Dam and Project 1926–33, supervising engineer: Grand Coulee Dam 1933–43, acting administrator: Bonneville Power project 1939, regional director: Region 1, U.S. Bureau of Reclamation 1943–45, district manager: Columbia River project from 1945.

Barbour, Francis Edward 1870–1948, born: Bangor; son of a minister and a professor of theology at Yale University; graduate: Phillips Academy, Exeter, Ph.D. Sheffield School, Yale University 1892, played varsity football as an under graduate, removed to Ann Arbor, Michigan, where he served as the first football coach at the University of Michigan 1892–94; traffic clerk: New York Central Railroad Co., Montréal; traveling passenger agent, Albany, New York; division passenger agent, Montréal; general passenger agent, Rutland, Vermont, to 1909; secretary: Beech-Nut Packing Co., Canajoharie, New York, vice president 1921, chairman of the board of directors 1946–48; vice president, director: Utica Mutual Insurance Co., Allied Fire Insurance Co., Utica, director: Up-State Telephone Corp., Grocery Manufacturers of America, president: Canajoharie Library-Art Gallery Association 1925–48, supervised the operation of the gallery.

Barker, Benjamin Fordyce 1818–91, born: Wilton, grandson of Jacob Abbott, great grandson of Benjamin Vaughn; son of a physician; A.B. Bowdoin College 1837, M.D. Medical School of Maine 1841, student: École de Médicine de Paris 1843–45; practiced in Norwich, Connecticut briefly, professor of obstetrics: Medical School of Maine 1846, president: Connecticut Medical Society 1848, an incorporator and professor of obstetrics: New York Medical College 1849; president: New York Medical Society 1856; founder and president: American Gynecological Society; president: New York Academy of Medicine, first American physician to use the hypodermic syringe, excise a fibroid tumor; attended General Ulysses S. Grant, in his final illness; author: *Puerperal Diseases* 1872, standard text, translated into many languages, *On Sea-Sickness* 1870.

Barker, Jacob 1779–1871, born: Swan Island (Perkins Township); cousin of Benjamin Franklin; removed to New York at age seventeen, entered the counting house of Isaac Hicks, sent to Nantucket by several merchants to purchase several vessels on commission, became the owner of three ships and a brig, controlled a large credit in the United States branch bank before the age of twenty-one, commission merchant and maritime trader from 1801, opened a large oil trade with Russia, established a branch house in Liverpool, became one of the largest ship owners in the country, a founder of the Tammany Society of New York, a founder, along with Alexander Hamilton and DeWitt Clinton, of the Exchange Bank, Wall Street, New York, 1815, supplied the steam engine for and was a principal backer of the building of the *Clermont*, the first successful steamboat, built by Robert Fulton 1806; founder: *New York Union*, a newspaper in support of Governor Clinton; an intimate of President Madison, helped remove the portrait of Washington and state papers from the White House, at direction of Dolley Madison, in anticipation of the burning of Washington by British troops 1814; member: New York Senate 1816, became a vocal advocate of the construction of the Erie Canal; member: New Orleans bar 1834, an opponent of slavery, manager of the New Orleans terminus of the underground railroad; president: Bank of Commerce, New Orleans, to 1869; removed to Philadelphia, where he died; father of Anna Hazard Barker Ward, known for her extraordinary beauty and her marriage to Samuel Gray Ward, an important transcendentalist writer; author: *Incidents in the Life of Jacob Barker of New Orleans; With Historical Facts; His Financial Transactions with the Government and His Course on Important Political Questions from 1800–1855* 1855.

Barker, Jeremiah 1752–1835, born: Scituate, Massachusetts; attended common school, studied medicine with Dr. Bela Lincoln at Harvard and in Aberdeen, Scotland; early in his career, compiled a *Vade Mecum* from several medical textbooks and anatomical drawings of his own devising; first practiced in Gorham, Maine, but finding the field already covered by Dr. Stephen Swett, removed to Barnstable, Massachusetts 1772–79; during the revolution, served aboard a privateer as surgeon, was captured and released, also served in the ill-fated attack against Castine 1779; returned to Gorham, where he practiced until building a house in Stroudwater, from which his practice extended far up and down the coast; compiled a large store of accounts of epidemics of scarlatina, measles, malignant fever, and putrid sore throat that he encountered in the district 1790–1810; also published careful meteorological records; experimented with alkalies as a sovereign treatment for sundry aliments; maintained an active correspondence with numerous medical experts of the day, including Dr. Benjamin Rush, Dr. Benjamin Waterhouse, Samuel Latham Mitchell, Lyman Spaulding, Dr. Benjamin Vaughan, and Henry Dearborn; visited many fellow physicians in New England and wrote up their most interesting cases, later published in the *Proceedings* of the Massachusetts Medical Society; was one of the original Sixty-niners that met in the Friends Chapel in Portland to discuss temperance in the district 1818.

Barrett, Benjamin Fiske 1808–92, born: Dresden; A.B. Bowdoin College 1832, graduate: Harvard Divinity School 1838; ordained New Church (Swedenborgian) Society, New York 1840, pastor in New York 1840–48, Cincinnati 1848–50, itinerant preacher 1854–60, editor: *New Church Monthly*, took charge of the first Swedenborgian church in Philadelphia; author: *Lectures on the Doctrines of the New Jerusalem Church* 1842, *Letters on the Divine Trinity, The Golden Reed* 1855, *Catholicity of the New Church, The Visible Church, Beauty for Ashes* 1856, *Report of the Inquiry into the Allegations against B. F. Barrett* 1867, *Episcopalianism* 1871, *On Future Life* 1872, *The Golden City, The New Church, Its Nature and Whereabouts, Swedenborg and Channing, A New View of Hell* 1872, *Life of Emanuel Swedenborg and Channing* 1877, *Footprints of the New Age* 1890, editor: *Swedenborg Periodical, New Christianity.*

Barrows, Lewis Orin 1893–1967, born: Newport; son of a druggist; attended public school in Newport and Hebron Academy, A.B. University of Maine 1916; pharmacist: Barrows Drug Store, Newport, insurance agent; Newport town treasurer; member: executive council 1926, Republican state committeeman; unsuccessful candidate for the Republican nomination for governor 1932; Maine secretary of state 1935; governor of Maine 1937–41; assistant to the president of the Liberty Mutual Insurance Companies 1942–57.

Bartlett, Boyd Wheeler 1897–1965, born: Castine; son of a schoolteacher, nephew of Percy Bartlett; attended public schools in Castine and Chelsea, Massachusetts; A.B. Bowdoin College ΦΒΚ 1917, lettered in football and tennis, captain of the hockey team, Sc.D. 1949, B.S. U.S. Military Academy 1919, B.S. Massachusetts Institute of Technology 1921, A.M. Columbia University 1926, Ph.D. 1932, his doctoral research was on the magnetic susceptibilities of paramagnetic crystals; graduate research in atomic physics: University of Munich 1934–35; commissioned first lieutenant, USA, Corps of Engineers 1919–22, physicist: Bell Telephone Laboratories, New York 1922–27, assistant professor of physics: Bowdoin College 1927–29, associate professor 1929–31, professor 1931–42, coordinator: civilian pilot training 1940–42, major, USA, promoted to colonel, USA, 1942-44, assistant professor of physics: U.S. Military Academy, professor, head of department of electricity, member: academic board 1945–61, brigadier general, USA; Bartlett initiated the study of atomic and nuclear physics at West Point, established the nuclear engineering program, arranged for annual visits of cadets to the Brookhaven National Laboratories and Columbia University's Nevis Cyclotron, instrumental in bringing about the installation of a nuclear laboratory at West Point, including a subcritical reactor, a student-built cyclotron, introduced such topics as: transitors, color television, servomechanisms, and analog computers, acquired a digital computer in his last teaching year; member:

board of overseers, trustee: Bowdoin College; chairman: U.S. Military Academy athletic board, Admissions Committee; decorated: Legion of Merit with oak leaf cluster; fellow: American Academy of Arts and Sciences; buried in Castine.

Bartlett, David 1855–1913, born: Lamoine; student: Castine Normal School, A.B. University of Michigan 1877, student: University of Michigan Law School; practiced in Boulder, Colorado, removed to Cooperstown, North Dakota; chairman: North Dakota University Board of Regents, president: Cooperstown School Board, president: Griggs County Telephone Company; Griggs County attorney, ; energetic supporter of statehood for North Dakota; member: North Dakota Constitutional Convention 1889, North Dakota Senate, North Dakota lieutenant-governor 1901–07.

Bartlett, Washington Allen 1820–1871, born: Maine; appointed midshipman, U.S. Navy 1833, passed midshipman 1839, lieutenant 1844, because of his knowledge of Spanish, appointed *alcade* of Yerba Buena, California, after the American conquest 1846, issued an ordinance changing the name of the settlement and port of entry to San Francisco, presided over the first jury trial in California, which happened to involve a suit against Samuel Brannan 1847, captured by a party of native Californians, in rebellion, on being released, he was ordered to his ship and spent several years as a serving officer in the navy, settled in New York 1855; his daughter, Frances Aurelia, married a wealthy Cuban in such splendor that it became known as the Diamond Wedding 1859, lampooned as such in a poem by Edmund C. Stedman, which nearly led to a duel between the author and Bartlett.

Bartol, Cyrus Augustus 1813–1900, born: Freeport; A.B. Bowdoin College 1832, graduate: Harvard Divinity School 1835; preached in Cincinnati, where he was a contributor to *The Western Messenger* 1835–36, pastor: West Unitarian Church, Boston 1837–89; a friend of Ralph Waldo Emerson and Theodore Parker (although he did not share some of their then-radical views), he was a member of the Transcendental Club, his home became a central gathering point of transcendentalist thinkers in Boston; last of the original transcendentalists to die; contributor: *The Christian Examiner, The Radical, The Index, The Unitarian Review*, author: *Discourses on the Christian Spirit and Life* 1850, *Discourses on Christian Body and Form* 1854, *Pictures of Europe Framed in Ideas* 1855, *History of the West Church and Its Ministers* 1858, *Church and Congregation* 1858, *Word of the Spirit to the Church* 1859, *Radical Problems* 1872, *The Rising Faith* 1874, *Principles and Portraits* 1880.

Bates, Arlo 1850–1918, born: East Machias; son of a surgeon; B.S. Bowdoin College 1876, A.M. 1879, Litt. D. 1894; while an undergraduate, editor: *Bowdoin Orient*; editor: *Broadside*, a newspaper devoted to Civil Service reform, Boston 1878, editor in chief: *Boston Sunday Courier* 1880–93; professor of English literature: Massachusetts Institute of Technology 1893–1915; fellow: American Academy of Arts and Sciences;

author: *Patty's Perversities* 1881, *Mr. F. Seymour Hayden and Engraving* 1882, *Mr. Jacobs* 1883, *The Pagans* 1884, *A Wheel of Fire* 1885, *Berries of the Brier* 1886, *Sonnets in the Shadow* 1887, *A Lad's Love* 1887, *The Philistine* 1889, *Albrecht: The Poet and His Self* 1891, *A Book O Nine Tales* 1891, *Told in the Gate* 1892, *In the Bundle of Time* 1893, *The Torch Bearers* 1894, *Talks on Writing English* 1897, *Talks on the Study of Literature* 1898, *The Puritans* 1899, *Under the Beech Tree* 1899, *Love in a Cloud* 1900, *The Diary of a Saint* 1902; son-in-law of George Vose.

Bates, Benjamin E. 1808–78, born: Mansfield, Massachusetts; attended Wrentham Academy; partner: Davis, Bates, and Turner, wholesale merchants in Boston; removed to Lewiston 1847; organized the Lewiston Water Power Co., founded Bates Mill, organized First National Bank of Lewiston, the first bank in that city; a prime mover in the filling of Back Bay, Boston, as president: National Bank of Commerce, Boston, served as an important early investor and director of the Union Pacific Railroad Co.; Bates College was renamed in his honor.

Bates, James 1789–1862, born: Greene; removed to Fayette with parents 1796, studied medicine in Fayette with Dr. Charles Smith and in Hallowell with Dr. Ariel Mann; M.D. Harvard University Medical School 1813, appointed surgeon's mate: Colonel Denny McCobbs volunteer infantry, served throughout the War of 1812, surgeon's mate in General Winfield Scott's brigade on the Niagara frontier, present at the surrender of Fort Erie and at the battles of Chippewa and Bridgewater, chief medical officer of a military hospital near Buffalo, having charge of nearly 700 wounded and sick; practiced in Hallowell 1815–19, Norridgewock from 1819; member from the 7th District: U.S. House of Representatives 1831–33 (Democrat); superintendent: Maine Insane Hospital, until that institution was destroyed by fire 1845–51, made an extensive study of heating and ventilation systems for the reconstruction of that hospital, later practiced in Gardiner, Fairfield, and Yarmouth; buried in Old Oak Cemetery, Norridgewock.

Bates, William Wallace 1827–1912, born: Calais; son of a shipwright, himself a shipwright from 1839; wrote tracts and lectured on temperance, removed to Manitowoc, Wisconsin, 1849, which became known as Clipper City, for the extreme schooners he built there, campaigned for a reform of tonnage admeasurement by Congress, drew up the bill that became law on the subject 1858; editor: *Nautical Magazine and Naval Journal*, New York 1854–58; returned to Wisconsin, where he built lake steamers for the Goodrich line; in the Civil War: captain USV, served with the 56th Illinois and 19th Wisconsin Volunteers 1861–63; in shipbuilding and dry docking in Chicago 1864–81; his pamphlet disapproving of the free-ship concept had considerable effect on legislation 1870, member of the Council of Lake Shipbuilders for improving rules, chairman of the Committee on Publication, his work contained a new system of marine inspection and freeboard rules that later became law; constructed and operated a large dry dock in Portland, Oregon, 1881–85; conducted experiments on the design of American merchant sailing vessels; manager: Inland Lloyd, Buffalo 1885–88; an organizer: Shipping League 1887; U.S. commissioner of navigation, Washington, D.C. 1889–92; author: *Rules for Shipbuilding* 1876, 1894 (2nd ed.), *American Marine* 1892, *American Navigation* 1902, *The Shipping Question Investigated.*

Baxter, James Phinney 1831–1921, born: Gorham; son of a physician; attended  public school in Portland and Lynn, Massachusetts and studied privately with tutors; A.M. Bowdoin College 1881, D.Litt. 1904; made his initial fortune canning provisions for the Union Army in the Civil War, elected to six terms mayor of Portland 1893–97, 1904–05; organized the Portland Society of Art 1883; built, donated, and endowed Baxter Public Library 1888; Bowdoin College overseer 1894–1921; president: Maine Historical Society, Merchants National Bank, Portland Publishing Co., fellow: American Academy of Arts and Sciences; author: *The Great Seal of New England* 1884, *Idyls of the Year, The Trelawney Papers, George Cleeve and His Times, The British Invasion from the North, Early Voyages to America, Sir Fernando Gorges and His Province of Maine, Reminiscences of a Great Enterprise* 1890, *The Campaign Against the Pequakets; Its Causes and Its Results* 1890, *The Beginning of Maine* 1891, *A Lost Manuscript* 1891, *Isaac Jogues, A.D. 1636* 1891, *The Abnakis and Their Ethnic Relations* 1892, *The Pioneers of New France in New England* 1893, *Christopher Levett and His Voyage to Casco Bay, in 1623* 1894, editor: *Documentary History of Maine* in twenty volumes; maintained a model farm on Mackworth Island, with a famous herd of St. Lambert Jersey cows; father of James Phinney Baxter and Percival Proctor Baxter.

Baxter, James Phinney 1893–1975, born: Portland; A.B. Williams College 1917, A.M. 1921, A.M. Harvard University 1923, Ph.D. 1926; L.L.D. (Hon.) Harvard and Amherst 1938, University of Maine and Wesleyan 1939, Hobart College 1942, Bowdoin College 1944, Litt.D. Syracuse University 1949, Columbia University 1954, Brown University 1956, University of Rochester 1960; instructor in history: Harvard University 1925–27, assistant professor 1927–31, associate professor 1931–36, professor 1936–37; master of Adams House 1931–37; president: Williams College 1937–1961; educational adviser: U.S. Military Academy, lecturer: Lowell Institute, Naval War College, Cambridge University; Harvard University overseer; president: American Association of Colleges and Universities; author: *The Introduction of the Ironclad Warship* 1933, *Scientists Against Time* 1946; translator; recipient: Pulitzer Prize for history 1947.

Baxter, Joseph 1676–1745, born: Braintree (that portion that is now Quincy), Massachusetts; A.B. Harvard College 1693, A.M. 1696; preached his first sermon in Braintree 1694, accepted the call from Medfield and was ordained 1697; also engaged in investments, owned a portion of the iron works in Stoughton and Walpole, purchased an island in Merrymeeting Bay, later purchased Mustard's Island, near Topsham, and agreed to settle two families on it; purchased a neck of land between the Kennebunk and Black rivers, attended the meetings of the Brunswick and Topsham proprietors; also received land in Sturbridge and Charlton, Massachusetts; after the Peace of Utrecht of 1713 ended the Indian warfare that had troubled Maine for forty years, it was decided by the general court to send a missionary to counteract the influence of Father Sébastien Râle, a position that Baxter accepted 1717; accompanied by Governor Shute and a large delegation of gentry, proceeded to Georgetown, where he was presented to a large body of Indians by the Governor who commanded them to obey and love him; Baxter was the first Congregational minister on the Kennebeck, using Georgetown as his base of operations, traveled to Augusta, Brunswick, Topsham and other places with a scattering of settlers; carried with him a supply of toys so as to entice Indian children to his lessons in reading; engaged in a friendly debate with Father Râle, by letter, over the superiority of their respective disciplines; journeyed to Nantucket to baptize thirty-five persons 1728; opposed the preachings of George Whitefield and the excesses of the Great Awakening; advocated the prohibition of alcohol; ancestor of James Phinney Baxter.

Baxter, Percival Proctor 1876–1969, born: Portland; son of James Phinney

Baxter; graduate: Portland High School 1894, A.B. Bowdoin College φBK 1898, L.L.B. Harvard University Law School 1901; never practiced but assisted his father in various business and real estate matters; member: Maine House of Representatives 1905–06, 1917–18, 1919–20; member: Maine Senate 1909–10, 1921, president 1921, as president, subsequent to the death of Governor Frederick Hale Parkhurst, became acting governor of Maine (Republican) 1921–25, vigorous opponent of special interests, in particular, Central Maine Power, initiated major educational improvements and penal reforms, made the first female appointments to public office; not a candidate for renomination 1924, unsuccessful candidate for the Republican nomination for U.S. Senate 1926; devoted himself to assembling of what became Baxter State Park, made major contributions to the Maine School for the Deaf, later renamed Governor Baxter School for the Deaf, in his honor; after his death, his corpse was cremated and the remains dropped on Mount Katahdin from an airplane.

Beal, George Lafayette 1825–1896, born: Norway; removed with his family to Portland, as a small boy, attended Westbrook Seminary; apprenticed to a Boston bookbinder 1840, returned to Norway to practice his trade 1850; agent of the Canadian Express Co. 1853, enlisted in the Norway Light Infantry as a private 1855, rose to captain of militia by the time of the Civil War; in the Civil War, he and his unit were the first militia unit to be activated, mustered in as Company G, 1st Maine Volunteers, put on guard duty in Washington, reorganized as the 10th Maine Volunteers, with Beal as colonel October, 1861; at Sharpsburg, the 10th Maine suffered very heavy casualties, Beal was wounded and his horse killed; promoted to colonel, USV, recruited the 29th Maine, December 1863, took part in the Red River campaign, as 2nd BRI, 1st DIV, XIX Corps, transferred to the Shenandoah Valley, fought well at Winchester and Fishers Hill, brigadier general, USV, November 1864; Bvt. major general USV, 1865, after service in western North Carolina, mustered out 1866; Maine adjutant general 1880–85, Maine state treasurer 1888–94; buried in South Paris.

Beale, William Gerrish 1854–1923, born: Winthrop; A.B. Bowdoin College 1877, L.L.D. 1912; studied in law office of Williams and Thompson, Chicago, while principal of Hyde Park (Illinois) High School, member: Illinois bar 1881, partner: Isham, Lincoln, and Beale; president: board of education, Chicago 1891–92; corporation counsel: city of Chicago 1895–97, one of three trustees of will of Joseph Medill with majority control of *Chicago Tribune*, drew up the famous, much contested, but never overturned will of Marshall Field; trustee: Chicago Elevated Railways, director: Chicago & Alton Railroad.

Beam, Lura 1887–1978, born: Marshfield; student: University of California 1904–06, A.B. Columbia University 1908, A.M. 1917; instructor in psychology: Gregory Normal School, Wilmington, North Carolina 1908–10, instructor in education: Le Moyne Normal School, Memphis, Tennessee 1910–11, assistant superintendent of education: American Missionary Association 1911–19, with department of education: Interchurch World Movement 1919, associate secretary of research in education: Council of Church Boards of Education, with intermittent studies for the Association of American Colleges 1919–26, research in education: National Commission on Maternal Health, Inc. 1927–33, chairman, Committee on Fine Arts, American Association of University Women from 1926; coauthor: *A Thousand Marriages* 1931, author: *The Single Woman* 1933, *A Maine Hamlet* 1955, numerous pamphlets and articles in magazines giving results of educational surveys; retired to Bronxville, New York.

Beaman, Charles Cotesworth 1840–1900, born: Houlton; son of a Congregational minister; graduate: Smithfield Seminary, Scituate, Rhode Island, A.B. Harvard College 1861; principal: Marblehead (Massachusetts) Academy 1861–64, L.L.B. Harvard University Law School 1865; his freshman thesis *The Rights and Duties of Belliger-*

ent Vessels in Neutral Waters won the Bowdoin Prize, later reprinted in *North American Review* 1866, which attracted the attention of Senator Charles Sumner, who made him his private secretary and clerk of Senate Foreign Relations Committee; practiced in New York 1867, examiner of claims in the U.S. Department of State 1871–72, v solicitor: Geneva Tribunal-*Alabama* Claims, where his great skill in disposing of various new and important questions of maritime and international law was widely noted and resulted in his book *National and Private Alabama Claims and Their Amicable Settlement* 1871; formed a partnership in New York with Edward Dickerson, an able patent attorney 1873, member of the firm of Evarts, Southmayd & Choate 1879, partner: Evarts, Choate & Beaman 1884; appointed by Governor Theodore Roosevelt to the commission to revise the charter of New York City 1900; son-in-law and partner of U.S. Secretary of State William Evarts, brother-in-law of Charles Harrison Tweed.

Bean, Henry D. 1853–1941, born: Bethel; studied law with Hon. Enoch Foster, Bethel, member: Oregon bar 1881, city attorney: Pendelton, Oregon, 1883–84, recorder 1885–86, member: Oregon House of Representatives 1883, district attorney: Sixth District of Oregon 1896–1900, county judge: Unadilla County 1904-06, judge: Circuit Court 1906–10, justice: Oregon Supreme Court from 1911, chief justice 1930–32, 1937–38.

Bean, Leon Leonwood 1872–1967, born: Greenwood; orphaned at age thirteen, sold soap to finance his last year (eighth grade) at Maine Wesleyan Seminary, Kents Hill; in Yarmouth from 1893, worked in clothing store; employee: W. H. Moody's shoe store in Augusta 1902–09; invented the Maine Hunting Shoe 1911; opened store in Freeport 1914; added hunting apparel 1917; buried in Webster Road Cemetery, Freeport.

Bearor, Robert Amie 1922–70, born: Madison, son of a carpenter; student: University of Maine, University of Wisconsin 1941–44, M.D. Boston University 1948, interned at Central Maine Hospital, Lewiston 1948–49, resident in internal medicine: Pratt Diagnostic Clinic, Boston 1949–50, general practitioner: North Haven; in World War II: captain, USA Medical Corps 1941–53, stationed at Fort Bliss, Texas, and in Korea 1951–53, medical resident: Veterans Administration Hospital, Memphis, Tennessee, 1953–55, resident in radiology: Beckley (West Virginia) Memorial Hospital 1957–60; fellow: American Cancer Society, University of Pennsylvania 1960–62, member of medical staff: Maine Medical Center, Portland, assistant radiologist, with charge of the department of radiology, instructor: Maine Medical Center School of Radiologic Technology, a specialist in the daily care of cancer patients, was himself diagnosed with cancer, while hospitalized and receiving treatment visited other cancer patients that he had treated to show them that a reasonable and useful life was still possible; consultant to the Merck Hospital, Portland, Sisters of

Mercy and Central Maine General hospitals; president: Maine Radiological Society 1969–70.

Beatty, Henry Russell 1906–72, born: Eastport; son of a tinsmith; attended public schools in Dorchester and Boston, Massachusetts, B.S. University of Maine 1927, M.S Administrative Engineering: New York University 1945, D.Eng. Stevens University, Northeastern University 1962, University of Maine 1963; superintendent of engineering: General Electric Co. 1927–33, salesman: Remington Rand Co. 1933–34, production superintendent: Holtzer Cabot Electric Co. 1934–37; professor, dean of engineering, assistant to president: Pratt Institute 1937–53; founding president: Wentworth Institute 1953–71, president: Wentworth College of Technology 1970–72; consultant: College of Petroleum Minerals, Saudi Arabia 1968–72; trustee: National Science Foundation, Gordon College, American Nuclear Society; member: American Academy of Arts and Sciences; revised: *Principles of Industrial Management* 1951.

Beedy, Carroll Lynwood 1880–1947, born: Phillips; A.B. Bates College 1903, L.L.B. Yale University Law School 1906; member: Maine bar 1907, practiced in Portland, Cumberland County prosecuting attorney 1917–21; member from the First District: U.S. House of Representatives 1921–35 (Republican); buried in Evergreen Cemetery, Portland.

Belcher, Hiram 1790–1857, born: Hallowell; member: Maine bar 1812, practiced law in Farmington from 1812, Farmington town clerk 1814–19; member: Maine House of Representatives 1822, 1829, 1832, member: Maine Senate 1838, 1839; member from the Third District: U.S. House of Representatives 1847–49 (Whig); buried in Center Meeting House Cemetery, Farmington.

Belcher, Supply 1752–1836, born: Stoughton, Massachusetts; kept a tavern, member: Stoughton Musical Society, where he possibly came into contact with William Billings; a minuteman, served in the battle of Lexington, later commissioned captain in the Continental Army; removed to Hallowell 1785, was among the first settlers in Farmington 1791; served as justice of the peace, selectman, schoolteacher, first town clerk, first representative to the Massachusetts General Court; organizer of the first town choir, composer: *The Harmony of Maine: Being an Original Composition of Psalm and Hymn Tunes, of Various Metres, Suitable for Divine Worship: With a Number of Fuging Pieces and Anthems: Together with a Concise Introduction to the Grounds of Musick, and Rules for Learners: For the Use of Singing Schools and Musical Societies* 1794; came to be known as the Handel of Maine.

Belcher, Thomas 1834–98, born: Bangor; private, Co. I, 9th Maine Infantry, recipient: Medal of Honor, Chapin's Farm, Virginia, took a guidon from the hands of the bearer, mortally wounded, and advanced with it nearer to the battery than any other man; buried at National Veterans Home, Togus.

Bellows, Henry Adams 1885–1939, born: Portland; A.B. Harvard College 1905, Ph.D. 1910; assistant in English: Harvard University 1906–09, acting editor: *Harvard Graduate Magazine* 1906–07, assistant professor of rhetoric: University of Minnesota 1910–12; managing editor: *The Bellman*, Minneapolis 1912–19, *The Northwestern Miller* 1914–25, manager: radio station WCCO 1925–27, 1928–29, president: Northwestern Broadcasting, Inc. 1929–34, vice president: Columbia Broadcasting System 1930–34, director of public relations: General Mills, Inc. from 1936; member: Federal Radio Commission 1927; music critic: *Minneapolis Daily News* 1920–23; author: *Manual for Local Defense* 1918, *A Treatise of Riot Duty for the National Guard* 1920, *Highland Light and Other Poems* 1921, *The Poetic Edda* 1923, translator: Abelards *Historia Calamitatus* 1922.

Bennet, Hiram Pitt 1826–1914, born: Carthage; removed with his parents to Richland County, Ohio, 1831; attended Ohio Wesleyan University, taught school in Missouri 1850, studied law, admitted to Iowa bar 1851, practiced in Glenwood, judge of the circuit court of Iowa 1852, removed to Nebraska Territory 1854, settled in Nebraska City, unsuccessfully contested the election of Bird Chapman to the Thirty-Fourth Congress 1855; member: Nebraska Territorial Council 1856, member, speaker: Nebraska Territorial House of Representatives 1858, removed to Denver, Colorado, 1859, first territorial delegate from Colorado to the U.S. House of Representatives 1861–65, Colorado secretary of state 1867, postmaster of Denver 1869–74, member: first Colorado Senate 1876; appointed state land agent 1888–95, primarily responsible for recovering state lands improperly alienated; buried in Riverside Cemetery.

Bennett, Raymond Franklin 1875–1949, born: Freeport; B.S. Massachusetts Institute of Technology 1899, his senior thesis "An Experimental Investigation of the Efficiency of Tackles" was regarded as notable for its pioneering in that field; employed briefly in the construction of the Wachusetts Reservoir, Clinton, Massachusetts, and in the drafting department of the New York, New Haven & Hartford Railroad Co.; returned to Portland 1900, employed in his father's waterfront construction business, William F. Bennett & Son Co., incorporated 1909, as Bennett Contracting Corp., treasurer, president 1911–43, built wharf buildings, pile driving and submarine pipe laying, notably: installation of a 3,000-foot, 8-inch steel pipe across White Head Passage from Peaks Island to Cushing Island 1940–41, his then-unique controlled buoyancy method of deepwater pipe laying attracted considerable attention, used to advantage in the laying of the 7,100-foot, 12-inch wrought iron pipe from Great Diamond Island to Mackworth Island 1942–43 and a pipe of similar dimension from Falmouth Neck to Martin's Point; granted a number of patents for his inventions, including: boom points for derricks 1907, a pile-driving machine 1908, a load-handling apparatus 1912, methods and apparatus for forming trenches 1929, methods of and apparatus for leveling work 1930, methods of laying underwater pipes and apparatus 1932, coin racks for quick and accurate handling and checking of assorted specie 1940; organized, president: Bennett McClearn Corp. 1922–45; member: Portland School Committee 1911–15, member: Portland High School Building Committee 1915–18; deeply interested in astronomy, maintained a private observatory in West Falmouth, vice president, director, auditor: Maine Astronomical Society.

Benson, Samuel Page 1804–76, born: Winthrop; A.B. Bowdoin College 1825; member: Kennebec County bar 1828, practiced in Unity, then Winthrop; railroad builder, secretary: Androscoggin & Kennebec Railroad (later part of Maine Central Railroad); member: Maine House of Representatives 1833, 1834, member: Maine Senate 1836, Maine secretary of state 1838–41; member from the Fourth District: U.S. House of Representatives (Democrat) 1853–57; president: board of overseers, Bowdoin College 1860–76; buried in Maple Cemetery, Winthrop.

Bentley, Alvin Morrell 1918–69, born: Portland; graduate: Southern Pines (North Carolina) High School 1934, Asheville (North Carolina) Preparatory School 1936, A.B. University of Michigan 1940, A.M. (Hon.) 1963, D.Sc. Cleary College, Michigan 1955, Nazareth College, Michigan, 1965, D.Hum. Lawrence Institute of Technology, Michigan 1966; attended the Turner Diplomatic School, Washington 1940–42, U.S. foreign service officer: Mexico City 1942–44, Bogota 1945–46, Budapest 1947–9, Rome 1949–50; resigned from the State Department out of dissatisfaction with U.S. foreign policy, wrote a number of newspaper articles and delivered several addresses on the threat of communism; vice president: Lake Huron Broadcasting Co., Saginaw, Michigan, from 1952; director: Owosso Manufacturing Company, a company started by his grandfather which manufactured scythe handles, grain cradles, rakes, snow shovels, door and window screens, later turned to making automobile trim; member: v House of Representatives 1952–60 (Republican); Bentley was one of the four members of the House of Representatives wounded when Puerto Rican nationalists opened fire in the House chamber 1954; established Alvin M. Bentley Foundation, which awarded scholarships to students in most of Michigan's private and public universities and colleges; member: board of regents, University of Michigan 1966–69, endowed the A. M. and H. P. Bentley Chair of History at the University of Michigan, in memory of his parents, gave 720 acres of land in Shiawassee County for the erection of a community college; buried in Oak Hill Cemetery, Owosso.

Benton, Charles Swan 1810–82, born: Fryeburg; removed to Herkimer County, New York, to live with an older brother 1824; student: Lowville (New York) Academy, studied law, learned tanner's trade, editor: *Mohawk Courier* and *Little Falls Gazette* 1830–32; member: New York bar 1835, practiced in Little Falls; surrogate of Herkimer County 1837; judge advocate: New York state militia; member: U.S. House of Representatives (Democrat) 1843–47; clerk of the court of appeals 1847–49; removed to

Milwaukee, Wisconsin, 1855, editor: *Milwaukee News*, register: U.S. Land Office, La Crosse, Wisconsin 1856–61; unsuccessful candidate for U.S. House of Representatives 1862; judge: La Crosse County 1874–81; buried in Oak Grove Cemetery, La Crosse.

Berry, George Ricker 1865–1945, born: Sumner; A.B. Colby College 1885, D.D. 1904, graduate: Newton Theological Institution 1889, Ph.D. University of Chicago 1895; ordained Baptist minister 1887, pastor: Liberty 1887–92, fellow in Semitics: University of Chicago 1893–94, assistant 1895–96, instructor in Semitic languages, Colgate University 1898–1916, professor of hermeneutics and Old Testament history and theology 1916–18, professor of Old Testament interpretation and Semitic languages 1918–28, professor of Semitic languages and literature: Colgate-Rochester Divinity School 1928–34; author: *The Letters of the Room 2 Collection in the British Museum* 1896, *New Old Testament* 1897, *New Lexicon of the Old Testament* 1897, *New Lexicon of the New Testament* 1897, *The Book of Proverbs* 1904, *The Old Testament Among the Semitic Religious* 1910, *Premillennialism and Old Testament Prediction* 1929, *The Books of Psalms* 1934, *The Classic Greek Dictionary: Greek-English and English-Greek* 1934, *Higher Criticism and the Old Testament* 1937, *Old and New in Palestine* 1939, *The Old Testament—A Liability or Asset* 1941.

Berry, Hiram Gregory 1824–1863, born: East Thomaston (later Rockland); son of a veteran of the War of 1812, grandson of a veteran of the Revolution; carpenter, navigator aboard coasting vessels, bank president, member: Maine House of Representatives, mayor of Rockland, founded and commanded the Rockland Guard, a militia unit with a high reputation for drill and discipline; in the Civil War: colonel, USV, commanding officer: 4th Maine Volunteer Infantry 1861, present at the first battle of Bull Run, served on the Peninsula as brigadier general, USV, 1862, where he was mentioned very favorably in dispatches by Generals Kearny, Hooker, Heintzelman, and McClellan, conspicuous in the fighting at the siege of Williamsburg, Fair Oaks, the Seven Days; at Fredericksburg, commanded the 3rd Brigade, III Corps, promoted to major general, USV, 1862; at Chancellorsville, commanded General Hooker's old division of the III Corps, killed leading a bayonet charge, subsequent to Jackson's flanking maneuver; buried in Achorn Cemetery, Rockland, his grave is marked by an heroic-sized statue.

Berry, John Cutting 1847–1936, born: Phippsburg; graduate: Monmouth Academy, M.D. Jefferson Medical College, Philadelphia, 1871; medical missionary in Kobe, Japan, 1872–93, medical director: Kobe International Hospital, Hyogo prefectural hospital, regularly attended four district dispensaries, conducted the first dissections in Japan; he was called upon to treat prisoners in Kobe prisons and, as a result, he sought permission from the government to study and report on general prison conditions in Japan, this led to reforms that made Japan's prison system one of the best in the world; established the first Sunday school in Japan taught in Japanese for the Japanese

1873; translated and published the first Christian hymnal in Japan 1873; transferred to Kyoto where he established the Doshisha University hospital and the first training school for nurses 1886, medical director for ten years and professor of physiology and hygiene for six years; Berry and his crew of assistants and nurses were the first medical group to reach the area of the great Gifu earthquake 1891; decorated, by the emperor: Imperial Order of the Sacred Treasure 1912, after his return to the United States in 1893, settled in Worcester, Massachusetts, where he practiced, specializing in diseases of the eye and ear; in 1930, a biography of him was compiled by the Marquis Okubo and published in Japanese, the first foreigner so honored 1930; on his eighty-eighth birthday, a commemorative banner was sent to him by Japanese nurses and social workers; at the eighth national convention of Japanese social workers, he was extended special honors and hailed as the father of social work in Japan 1935.

Berry, Nathaniel Springer 1796–1894, born: Bath; son of a shipwright; named for his maternal grandfather, a captain of artillery, killed in the American Revolution; orphaned at age six, at age nine, chore-boy in a tavern, apprenticed to a tanner and currier in Bath, New Hampshire, removed to Bristol, New Hampshire, at age twenty-one, managed a tannery, which he later owned, introduced the process of tanning leathers in hot liquid, removed, with his tannery, to Hebron, New Hampshire, 1840; Colonel, New Hampshire militia, justice of the peace, and quorum for twenty-three years, judge of the court of common pleas 1841–50, judge of probate 1856–61, member: New Hampshire House of Representatives 1828, 1833, 1834, 1837, 1854, member: New Hampshire Senate 1835–36, delegate: Democratic National Convention 1840, left the Democratic party, due to its stance on slavery, helped found the Free Soil party, was its first candidate for governor of New Hampshire 1854, received the nomination in four succeeding conventions; as Republican nominee 1861, elected thirtieth governor 1861–63, armed and equipped fourteen regiments of infantry, three companies of sharpshooters, four companies of cavalry, and one company of heavy artillery, in all, over 15,000 men for service in the Civil War; visited Washington, at his own expense, five times on business concerning the troops; one of twenty-two governors who met at Altoona, Pennsylvania, 1862, and prepared an address to President Lincoln pledging their continuing support, chosen to deliver the address to Lincoln; after his retirement removed to Andover, Massachusetts, 1864–78, removed to Milwaukee, Wisconsin, 1878–83, where he lived with his daughter, returned to Bristol, New Hampshire; a man of strong piety, represented New Hampshire at the Methodist general conference 1872, member of the board of trustees: Northfield Conference Seminary, founding president: Grafton County Bible Society, founded several Sunday schools and the first temperance society in New Hampshire, among the men in his own tannery.

Berry, William E. 1846–1932, born: Kennebunk; after attending local schools, apprenticed, as a draughtsman, to his distant relation, William Ralph Emerson 1864, also took architecture courses at the Lowell Institute, began documenting historic architecture in southern Maine; eventually joined the Boston firm of Peabody & Stearns, where his command of early American domestic architecture in Peabody & Stearns numerous designs in Colonial Revival is evident; in 1883, he removed from Boston to Kennebunk, took up residence in Wallingford Hall, which had been built by his wife's grandfather, and began an architectural career that continued for nearly fifty years, during which time he designed cottages, homes, churches, libraries, and hotels; author: *Sketch of the Old River* 1888, *A Stroll by a Familiar River* 1909, *Chronicles of Kennebunk* 1923, *A Stroll Thro the Past* 1933

Berry, William Eugene 1879–1960, born: Webster; son of a farmer and teacher, subsequent to his father's death, his mother became an itinerant minister in the Society of Friends; attended the Friends Academy, West Branch, Iowa, Worcester (Massachusetts) High School, A.B. William Penn College, Okaloosa, Iowa, 1900, graduate student: Harvard Divinity School, A.B. Harvard College 1903, A.M. 1904, Ph.D. University of Chicago 1922; registrar, instructor in Hebrew, Latin, and Greek: William Penn College 1908–36, professor of Greek and religion: Earlham College, Richmond, Indiana, 1936–49; author: *Greek Word-Order Based Upon the Laws of Plato* 1922, *The Society of Friends* [Quakers] *in America* chapters for *American Church of the Protestant Heritage* 1952; frequently wrote Bible notes for the lesson quarterlies of the Society of Friends; member, advisory board: Five Year Meeting of Friends in America for the Revised Standard Version of the New Testament; chairman: Peace Association of Friends in America 1926–30.

Bessey, Earle Emerson 1871–1931, born: Sidney; graduate: Coburn Classical Institute, M.D. Dartmouth College School of Medicine 1901; assistant: Dr. Channing's sanitarium, Brookline, Massachusetts, specialized in treatment of nervous and mental disorders, attached to the staff of the Danvers State Insane Hospital for six years, founded Bessey Hospital, Boston, a private surgical and medical institution 1908; established the Knollwood Sanitarium, Waban, Massachusetts, 1911.

Best, Charles Herbert 1899–1978, born: West Pembroke; A.B. University of Toronto 1921, A.M. 1922, M.D. 1925, recipient of honorary degrees from University of London, University of Chicago, University of Paris, Cambridge University, Oxford University, University of Maine, &c.; research associate: Banting-Best research department, University of Toronto 1923–41, director 1941–67; co-discover of insulin with Banting 1921 (did not, however, share the Nobel Prize with Banting, who did split the prize money with Best); author: *The Internal Secretion of the Pancreas* 1922, *The Physiological Basis of Medical Practice* (nine editions) 1933, *The Human Body* (four editions), numerous papers on insulin, histamines, choline, heparin, shock, carbohydrate, and fat metabolism.

Beston, Henry 1888–1968, born: Quincy, Massachusetts; A.B. Harvard College 1909; member: editorial staff, *Atlantic Monthly*, editor: *The Living Age* 1919–23; with American Field Service, attached to French army 1915–16, enlisted man: U.S. Navy 1918, settled in Nobleboro; author: *Full Speed Ahead* 1919, *Firelight Fairy Book* 1919 (same with preface by Theodore Roosevelt 1921), *Starlight Wonder Book* 1923, *The Book of Gallant Vagabonds* 1925, *The Sons of Kai* 1926, *The Outermost House* 1928, *London* 1929, *Herbs and the Earth* 1935, *American Memory* 1937, *The Runaway Tree* 1941, *The St. Lawrence River* (in the *Rivers of America* series) 1942, *Northern Farm* 1948, *White Pine and Blue Water* 1950, editor: *The St. Lawrence* 1951; husband of Elizabeth Coatsworth.

Beverage, Harold Henry 1893–1993, born: North Haven; as a young man, picked up the distress call of RMS *Titanic*, and subsequent telegraphic communications of various rescue ships; B.S. in electrical engineering: University of Maine 1915, D.Eng. 1938; associated with General Electric Co. 1915–20, assistant to Dr. E. F. W. Alexanderson; in World War I, divided his time between the U.S. Navy transatlantic radio communications station at New Brunswick, New Jersey, and the navy receiving station at Otter Cliffs, Maine, where he installed an Alexanderson barrage receiver; in the course of this work made the very important discovery that long wires were directive, this led to the invention of the wave antenna; in 1919 made two trips to Europe to prepare long-distance radio telephone apparatus for the use of President Wilson while attending the Versailles Peace Conference; in 1920 became the chief engineer in charge of communication receiver research for the Radio Corporation of America, a position he held to 1929; most of his twenty-five patents were for antenna design, made studies of the behavior of radio waves in the upper atmosphere, oversaw the construction of RCA's first television, designed and installed the television antenna atop the Empire State Building; awarded the Morris Lieberman Memorial Prize by the Institute of Radio Engineers for the directive radio antenna 1923; director, president: Institute of Radio Engineers 1937; competent on the trombone, clarinet, and saxophone.

Bibber, Charles J. 1837-1883, born: Portland; gunner's mate, USN, recipient: Medal of Honor, "Bibber served on board the USS *Agawam*, as one of a volunteer crew of a powder boat which was exploded near Fort Fisher, 23 December 1864. The powder boat, towed in by the USS *Wilderness* to prevent detection by the enemy, cast off and slowly steamed to within three hundred yards of the beach. After fuses and fires had been lit and a second anchor with short scope let go to assure the boats tailing inshore, the crew again boarded the USS *Wilderness* and proceeded a distance of twelve miles from shore. Less than two hours later the explosion took place, and the following day fires were observed still burning at the forts." Buried in Woodlawn Cemetery, Everett, Massachusetts.

Bickford, John F. 1843–1927, born: Tremont; captain of the top, USN, recipient: Medal of Honor, served on board the USS *Kearsarge* when she destroyed the CSS *Alabama* off Cherbourg, France, 19 June 1864. "Acting as the first loader of the pivot gun during this bitter engagement, Bickford exhibited marked coolness and good conduct and was highly recommended for his gallantry under fire by his divisional officer." Buried in Mt. Pleasant Cemetery, Gloucester, Massachusetts.

Bickford, Samuel Longley 1885–1959, born: Sanford, son of a Baptist minister; attended public schools in Maine, Vermont, and New Hampshire; went to work at age fifteen as an operative of the Smith & Wesson Co., Springfield, Massachusetts, also employed by the Waldorf restaurant in Springfield, later worked for the Waldorf restaurants in Boston and Providence, manager of the two Waldorf restaurants in Buffalo, New York, 1906, purchased a half-interest in the White House restaurant in Washington 1909, became part owner of six area restaurants by 1911, sold his one-third interest in this chain for $25,000 and removed to Philadelphia 1912, operated the Waldorf restaurant for six months, removed to Boston, invested in the Waldorf system, with which he was associated to 1921, founded Bickford's, Inc. 1921, with headquarters in Brooklyn, New York; absorbed Traveler's Lunch, Paterson, New Jersey, 1924; purchased the White Lunch system, later the Foster Lunch system, Ltd., with restaurants in San Francisco and Oakland, California, Portland, Oregon, Seattle and Tacoma, Washington, 1924; purchased the Hayes Lunch system chain, later the Hayes-Bickford system, in Boston, 1924; by the time of his death, Bickford's, Inc., operated some eighty-five restaurants, forty-eight of which were in New York City, with subsidiaries in Boston, San Francisco, Pittsburgh, Baltimore, and Miami, as well as other major cities throughout the country; entered the institutional food service field, formed Bickford's Catering, Inc., later the National Food Management Service 1952, which served various airlines, hospitals, schools, factories, and banks; director: M & M Cafeterias, Inc., Thomson Court Realty, Inc., Bickford's Realty, John R. Thompson, Inc.; operated a 300-acre dairy farm, Alasta Farm, in Newton, Connecticut.

Bickmore, Albert Smith 1839–1914, born: Tenants Harbor; son of a ship captain and shipwright, accompanied his father on several voyages; A.B. Dartmouth College 1860, B.S. Harvard College 1864; student of Agassiz, visited Bermuda 1863, for the purpose of collecting for the Museum of Comparative Zoology, Cambridge; in the Civil War: enlisted in the 44th Massachusetts Volunteer Infantry and served for nine months, mostly in North Carolina; sailed from Boston, via the Cape of Good Hope for Java, traveled for a year in the Celebes, Sumatra, the Spice Islands, Singapore, Saigon, Cochin, China, Hong Kong, made another year's journey through the interior of China, from Canton to Yungting Lake, down the Yangtse River to Shanghai, and northward to Peking and Korea, a third year was spent along the coasts of China and Japan, across Siberia to Moscow, St. Petersburg, Berlin, and London; the significance of his expedition to the East Indies has been compared to that of Darwin's aboard the *Beagle*; author: *Travels in the East Indian Archipelago* 1868; made a life fellow of the Royal Geographical Society, London; professor of natural history: Madison (later Colgate) University 1868–69; with the support of Theodore Roosevelt, Sr., J. P. Morgan, Sr., and others, organized the American Museum of Natural History, New York, superintendent 1869–84; known as the father of the museum.

Bigelow, Karl Worth 1898–1980, born: Bangor; A.B. Clark University ΦBK 1920, L.H.D. 1938, student: Cornell University 1920–21, Ph.D. Harvard University 1929, L.L.D. (Hon.) Parsons College 1941, Moravian College 1963, D.Litt. University of East Africa 1970; instructor in economics: Cornell University 1920–21, tutor, instructor in economics and sociology: Harvard and Radcliffe colleges 1921–30, assistant professor of economics: University of Buffalo 1930–31, professor 1931–37; headmaster: Park School, Buffalo 1933–35; visiting professor of education: Columbia University Teachers College 1936–37, professor 1937–63; director: Institute for Education in Africa 1962–66, director: Afro-Anglo-American Program in Teacher Education 1960–69, visiting lecturer: University of London, Institute of Education 1958, Inglis lecturer: Harvard University Graduate School of Education 1964, consultant: Association for Teaching Education in Africa 1969–78; member, Overseas Liaison Committee: American Council of Education 1963–73, vice chairman 1965–69, chairman: commission sent by the State Department to study relations of American volunteer agencies with Germany and Austria 1950; lecturer, consultant: UNESCO seminar on education for international understanding, France 1947; member: U.S. national commission, UNESCO 1948–54, United States member, governing body: Institute for Education, Germany 1957–61; student of higher education and teacher training in British Africa under auspices of the British Colonial Office, University of London Institute for Education and Inter-university Council for Higher Education in the Colonies 1952; delegate: American Association of College Teacher Education to American Council of Education 1951–56, member of council: University of Zambia 1964–73; recipient: Distinguished Service Medal, Columbia University Teachers College 1970; coauthor: *The Improvement of Teacher Education* 1952, *Education and Foreign Affairs* 1965, member, editorial board: *International Review of Education* 1955–61, *Teacher Education in New Countries* 1962–72; contributor of numerous articles for professional journals.

Bisbee, Horatio 1839–1916, born: Canton; son of a farmer; student: Auburn Academy, Westbrook Seminary, Tufts College, withdrew in his sophomore year; enlisted in the 5th Massachusetts Volunteers, April 1861, rose from private to colonel 5th Massachusetts Infantry and Ninth Maine Infantry, USV, served at the battles of Bull Run, engagements along the Carolina coast, Florida, and Georgia, mustered out 1863; A.B. Tufts College 1863, A.M. 1892; member: Illinois bar 1864, removed to Florida, practiced in Jacksonville, U.S. attorney for Northern Florida 1869–73, Florida attorney general 1872; member: U.S. House of Representatives 1877–79, 1881, 1882–85 (Republican); buried in Green-Wood Cemetery, Dixfield.

Bishop, Robert 1938–91, born: Readfield; Ph.D. in American Culture: University of Michigan 1975; publicity manager: Greenfield Village and Henry Ford Museum, Dearborn, Michigan 1966–74, museum editor 1974–76; professor of art history: University of Michigan at Dearborn 1977, Ann Arbor 1975–77; director: Museum of American Folk Art, New York, from 1976, adjutant professor of art and art education: New York University from 1980; author, designer: *Centuries and Styles of the American Chair 1640–1970* 1973, *How to Know American Antique Furniture* 1973, *Guide to American Antique Furniture* 1973, *American Folk Sculpture* 1974, *New Discoveries in American Quilts* 1975, *The Borden Limner and His Contemporaries* 1976, *Treasurers of American Folk Art* 1979, coauthor, designer: *Americas Quilts and Coverlets* 1972, *American Painted and Decorated Furniture* 1972, *The American Clock* 1976, *A Gallery of Amish Quilts* 1976, coauthor: *World Furniture* 1979, *The World of Antiques, Art and Architecture in Victorian America* 1979, *Folk Painters of America* 1979, *A Gallery of American Weathervanes and Whirligigs* 1980, *Young America: A Folk Art History* 1986, *All Flags Flying* 1986, editor, picture editor of other books; director: New York County Museum from 1978; Koreshan Unity, Estero, Florida, from 1978, Pioneer Educational Foundation, Estero, Florida, from 1978, Grove House, Coconut Grove, Florida, from 1977; chairman of the board: ISALTA, New York from 1980; recipient: Impresario Award for creative writing, International Cultural Society 1975, Silver Medal: International Film and Television Festival 1978; buried in Readfield.

Bishop, Thomas Brigham 1835–1905, born: Wayne; at age fifteen, constructed a machine for the manufacture of friction matches, independently formulated ignition dip, later duplicated and scaled up in Dover; at age sixteen decided to make music his career, studied harp and guitar, became a blackface minstrel; during this period, credited by some, with the composition of the tunes for *When Johnny Comes Marching Home*, *Battle Hymn of the Republic*, and numerous other familiar songs of the period; taking up photography, introduced the tin type to New York, drastically reducing the cost of being photographed; during the Civil War, employed by the federal government as a photographer, after war, turned his attention to speculation and introduced a system of dealing fractional lots of grain, eventually having offices in some eighty cities, commonly known as bucket shops.

Bissonnette, Delphia Louis Del 1899–1972, born: Winthrop; displayed a talent for baseball while attending Maine Wesleyan Academy, Kents Hill, and Westbrook Seminary; played in the Portland *Telegram* semiprofessional league where he batted .600; selected to play in an all-star match with the Boston *Red Sox*, his superlative pitching kept the Portland team in the lead for eight innings until Babe Ruth scored; played for the New York *Yankees* for one year but was dropped for injuries;

later played for the Brooklyn *Dodgers*, his best year being 1930 when he scored 192 hits and batted .336; became famous for having been walked, with the bases loaded; coached the Boston *Braves* in 1947; buried in Glenside Cemetery, Winthrop.

Bixby, Jotham 1831–1917, born: Norridgewock; sailed to California, around the Horn, to mine gold 1852, acquired enough capital to become a sheep farmer in San Luis Obispo County 1856, accumulated 50,000 acres of land in the Long Beach area; his 30,000 sheep produced 200,000 pounds of wool per annum; founder and president: Bixby Land Company, which continues in family hands, to this day, vice president: National Bank of Long Beach; associated with Nathan Blanchard and Wallace Hardison in the creation of Union Oil Company of California.

Black, Frank Swett 1853–1913, born: Limington; son of a farmer and keeper of the York County jail, Alfred; attended public schools in Alfred (Maine) and Lebanon Academy (Massachusetts), A.B. Dartmouth College 1875; associated with the *Johnstown* (New York) *Journal* 1876, entered the law office of Robertson & Foster, Troy, New York, 1877, reporter for the *Troy Whig*; member: New York bar 1879, partner: Smith-Wellington & Black, became one of the leading lawyers in Rensselaer County, counsel for the Committee of Safety created after the murder of Robert Ross 1893; member: U.S. House of Representatives from New York (Republican) 1895–97; member of committees on Pacific railways and private land claims; governor of New York 1897–99; began the work of reclaiming the Adirondack forests and the establishment of a state school of forestry, completed the state capitol building, which had been under construction for a quarter of a century and was the source of egregious waste and jobbery; was implicated in the scandal revolving around the rebuilding of the New York Sate Barge Canal and was not renominated; the nomination went to Theodore Roosevelt; removed to New York, member: Black, Olcutt & Gruber 1899, later Black & Peck; placed Theodore Roosevelt's name into nomination at the Republican National Convention 1904; editor: *New York and the War with Spain: The History of the Empire State Regiments* 1903; buried on his farm in Freedom, New Hampshire.

Blaine, James Gillespie 1830–1893, born: West Brownsville, Pennsylvania;  grandson of Colonel Ephraim Blaine, commissary general of the northern department of the Revolutionary army 1778–83; son of a farmer, justice of the peace, and noted bird-watcher; attended local district school, sent to board with a distant relation, Hon. Thomas Ewing, and to attend a school in Lancaster, Ohio, run by an Oxford University graduate, William Lyon, uncle of Lord Lyon, future minister of Great Britain to the United States, became closely associated with Ewing's sons and stepsons, notably the future General William Tecumseh Sherman and his younger brother, future U.S. Secretary of State John Sherman; A.B. Washington College 1847, graduated with first honors, teacher at Western Military Institute, Blue Lick Springs, Kentucky, for three years; while there, met and married Harriet Stanwood of Augusta, cousin of Isaac Augustus and Edward Stanwood; teacher of mathematics: Pennsylvania Institution for the Blind 1852–54; removed to Augusta, editor and half-owner of *Kennebec Journal* 1854–60; delegate: first Republican National Convention 1856; appointed by Governor Lot Morrill as commissioner to examine prisons and reformatories, within Maine and elsewhere, and to recommend improvements, therein, traveled to fifteen states and made an elaborate report to the governor of his findings, many of his recommendations were adopted by the legislature; member: Maine House of Representatives 1858–62, speaker 1860–62, member: U.S. House of Representatives (Republican) 1863–76, speaker 1869–76, instrumental in muting the harsher aspects of reconstruction, the language of 14th Amendment to the United States Constitution was largely of his devising; unsuccessful candidate for the Republican nomination for president of the United States 1876, 1880; member: U.S. Senate 1876–81; United States secretary of state 1881 (his approach to Latin America formalized as the Pan-American Union), 1889–92; was walking, arm-in-arm with President Garfield, when Garfield was shot in the back 1881; Republican nominee for president of the United States 1884; author: *Life of Hon. Luther Severance, Twenty Years of Congress* 1884; father-in-law of Walter Damrosch, conductor of the New York Philharmonic Society; originally buried in Oak Hill Cemetery, Washington, reinterred in Blaine Memorial Park, Augusta, 1920. Counties in Idaho, Montana, Nebraska, and Oklahoma are named in his honor.

Blake, Edgar 1869–1943, born: Gorham; B.S. Boston University School of Theology ΦBK 1898, D.D. (Hon.) Nebraska Wesleyan 1909, Wesleyan University 1915, DePauw University 1929; ordained Methodist minister 1899, pastor: Salem, New Hampshire, 1895–99, Lebanon, New Hampshire, 1899-1903, Manchester, New Hampshire 1903–08; associated with the Board of Sunday Schools of the Methodist Episcopal Church 1908–12, corresponding secretary: Board of Sunday Schools 1912–20, president from 1920, having general supervision of the Sunday school work of the church in America and in foreign countries, elected bishop 1920, assigned to the Episcopal supervision of the Mediterranean area, including: France, Italy, Spain, and North Africa, reelected 1924, upon his reelection in 1928, was reassigned to the Indianapolis area; in 1932, this area was discontinued, Indiana and Michigan were combined in the Detroit area, to which Blake was assigned, where he remained to his retirement in 1940; considered a liberal, campaigned against war, liquor, privilege, and social injustice; while in Europe in 1920–28, supervising the distribution of a million dollars for reconstruction of war areas by the Methodist church, he urged the cancellation of Allied war debt and recognition of the Soviet government of Russia; on a visit to the Soviet Union in 1923, praised the governments social and educational objectives, though denouncing its methods, pledged $50,000 to the Russian Orthodox church for the education of clergymen, this was repudiated by Methodist authorities, but Blake was able to raise the funds through private subscription; advocated a planned economy 1936, joined a citizens' committee for civil rights in the automobile industry, sponsored by the American Civil Liberties Union 1937; signed a petition by the American Friends of Spanish Democracy, urging help of the Loyalist cause in Spain 1938.

Blake, George Fordyce 1819– ?, born: Farmington Falls; son of a physician; engaged by a brick manufacturer of Cambridge and Medford, Massachusetts, as a mechanical engineer, taking general charge of the works 1846; in order to work recalcitrant Medford clay, he invented a machine that could pulverize clay of any consistency, patented 1861; his principal inventions were a water meter, patented in 1852 and a steam pump, patented in 1864; organized the firm of George F. Blake & Co. 1864, incorporated as Blake Manufacturing Co. 1874, for the manufacture of water meters and steam pumps in Boston, devoted himself to improving his pumps, so that they might be able to pump liquids, from the lightest to the heaviest in gravity, absorbed the Knowles Pump Works, Warren, Massachusetts, 1879, the company had agencies in all principal cities in the country, with headquarters in New York, the company's factory was relocated to East Cambridge, Massachusetts, 1890, a manufactory was set up in London, England, 1876, to expeditiously supply foreign orders, the company was merged with International Pump Co. 1899.

Blanchard, Helen Augusta 1839–1922, born: Portland; daughter of Nathaniel Blanchard, noted shipwright; held at least twenty-eight patented inventions, including overseam of the long-stitch machine 1873, sewing and trimming gig and zig-zag stitchmaker 1880, crocheting machine (very popular) 1882, Blanchard machine for hat lining, and a new overseam machine; she also invented a self-taking needle and a surgical needle, her overseam machine is on display at the Smithsonian Museum of American History.

Blanchard, Nathan Weston 1831–1917, born: Madison; grandson of Nathan Weston, cousin of Melville Weston Fuller; graduate: Ricker Classical Institute, A.B. Waterville College 1855, A.M. 1877; removed to California 1855, engaged in mining; founder: Santa Paula in Ventura County 1872; part owner of Limoneira, the largest lemon grove in the world, associated with Charles Collins Teague; president: Nathan W. Blanchard Investment Co., Limoneira Co., Thermal Belt Water Co., Santa Paula Water Works, founder: Union Oil Co., became associated with Simon Jones and William Herbert Murphy; member: California House of Representatives 1862–63; founder and trustee: Pomona College 1887.

Blaney, William Osgood 1841–1910, born: Bristol; student: Lincoln Academy, Newcastle; clerk in Boston 1864–69; partner: Crosby and Blaney, flour and grain merchants, Boston 1869–79; Blaney, Brown and Co. 1879–1905, director 1897–1900, president from 1900; president: Commercial National Bank, Boston, Boston Commercial Exchange 1883–84; vice president: John Hancock Mutual Life Insurance Co.; president: Boston Chamber of Commerce; president: American Congregational Association.

Blethen, Alden Joseph 1846–1915, born: Knox, graduate: Maine Wesleyan Seminary and College, Kents Hill 1868, A.M. Bowdoin College 1872; leasee and principal: Abbott Family School 1869–73; member: Maine bar 1873, practiced law in Portland 1873–80; manager: *Kansas City Journal* 1880–84; half-owner, manager, and editor: *Minneapolis Tribune* and *Minneapolis Journal* 1888–89; editor and publisher: *Seattle Times*; colonel on staff of governors Nelson and Clough of Minnesota; regent: University of Washington.

Blethen, Clarence Bretton 1879–1941, born: Portland; son of Alden Blethen; attended public schools in Minneapolis, student: University of Washington 1896–99, University of Chicago 1899–1900; with *Seattle Times* from 1900, managing editor 1901, set up a picture beat in San Francisco 1906, subsequent to the earthquake, engaged the first telegraph line available and kept it open to the *Seattle Times* for hours, offered fifty dollars apiece for all photographs, sight unseen, of the catastrophe; subsequent to the death of his father became editor and publisher from 1915, president: Seattle Times Co. from 1921, president: Blethen Corp.; noted for his high journalistic standards and as an inventor and pioneer in the use of wire photographs, photogravure, teletype machines, natural color photography; in World War I: colonel, USA Coastal Artillery, defense commander in the North Pacific Coast Artillery District, ordered to Washington, D.C., to serve as officer in charge of interior liaison, after the war, continued on in the Washington National Guard until he became its commanding general, promoted to brigadier general, USA Reserve Corps 1924, the governor of Washington promoted him to major general on the retired list 1940; member: Bohemian Club, San Francisco.

Blunt, James Gillpatrick 1826–81, born: Trenton; merchant seaman 1841–46; M.D. Sterling Medical College, Columbus, Ohio, 1849, practiced medicine in New Madison, Ohio, 1849–56, removed to Kansas 1856, practiced medicine in Leavenworth; ally of John Brown in Bleeding Kansas, assisted slaves in escaping to Canada, member: antislavery convention which framed the Kansas constitution 1859; with the outbreak of the Civil War, commissioned lieutenant colonel, USV, commanding officer: 3rd Kansas Cavalry, July 1861, promoted to brigadier general, USV, commanding officer: Kansas Brigade, commanding officer: department of Kansas 1862, defeated Confederate forces and their Cherokee allies at Old Fort Wayne 22 July 1862, defeated Confederate forces and Cherokee allies at Maysville, on the western border of Arkansas 22 October 1862, defeated Confederate General Marmaduke at Cane Hill 28 November 1862, defeated General Thomas Hindman and his large force at Prairie Grove 7 December 1862, preventing Confederate incursion into Missouri, captured Fort Van Buren, on the Arkansas River 28 December 1862; promoted to major general, USV, commanding officer: Army of the Frontier: a combination of regular army, Jayhawkers, and Cherokees, defeated General Sterling Price near Kansas City, 28 October 1864, driving him out of Missouri, commanding officer: district of South Kansas; known as "Fat Boy" behind his back, raised first Indian regiments in U.S. Army; after the war, practiced medicine in Leavenworth for four years, removed to Washington, where he was a claims agent for many years, died insane at St. Elizabeth's Hospital, Washington, D.C.; buried in Mount Muncie Cemetery, Leavenworth, Kansas.

Blunt, Orison 1816–1879, born: Gardiner; went to sea at age fourteen, later settled in New York, where he apprenticed to a gunsmith; later, became a gunsmith on his own account, in time, became a very prosperous gunmaker and importer of foreign arms; invented a breech-loading cannon and a type of gun known as a pepperbox, which could discharge seventy rounds, per minute, a model was forwarded to President Lincoln, who sought to have it tested at the front, but it was captured by the Confederates before its utility could be determined; elected alderman, representing the Third Ward of New York city 1853, reelected 1856, elected to a seat on the Manhattan County Board of Supervisors 1858–61, by special act of the New York legislature, his term was fixed at six years 1860, reelected for the term of 1862–68, thus becoming a dissident member of the famous ring led by William Marcie Tweed; unsuccessful Union party nominee for mayor 1864; dedicated opponent of inflated city contracts and outright swindles, took an active part in promoting Belgian-block pavement for the city, introduced the use of steam fire engines, recommended the lighting of piers, recommended the use of iron pipes to bring Croton water to the city, battled Fernando Woods and his friends for control of the city's police force, so great was the admiration of the police for Blunt that the entire force serenaded him; in the Civil War: devoted himself to the raising of troops, their equipping and training, and finding the funds to hire substitutes for firemen and policemen.

Boardman, George Dana 1801–31, born: Livermore; son of a Baptist minister; A.B. Waterville College 1822, student: Andover Theological Seminary; ordained Baptist minister in West Yarmouth 1825, sailed for Calcutta, learned the Burmese language, planted a mission which became the center of all Baptist missions in Burma at Maulmain 1827, established a mission at Tavoy, baptized Ko-mah-byn, a Karen convert, who became the chief native Baptist proselytizer, began a series of progressions about the country, which had an enormous impact; died of tuberculosis; his work was memorialized in at least two works: *Memoir of George Dana Boardman* by

Rev. A. King 1875, and *G.D. Boardman and the Burman Mission.*

Boardman, Harold Sherburne 1874– ?, born: Bangor; B.C.E. Maine State College ΦBK 1895, graduate student: Massachusetts Institute of Technology 1896, M.Civil Engineering: University of Maine 1898, D.Engineering 1922, L.L.D. Colby College 1927, D.Engineering Rhode Island College 1928, L.L.D. Bates College 1929; tutor in drawing: University of Maine 1896–99, draftsman: Union Bridge Co. 1899–1900, American Bridge Co. 1900–01, instructor in civil engineering: University of Maine 1901–03, associate professor 1903–04, professor and head of department 1904–26, dean: College of Technology 1910–26, acting president 1925–26, president 1926–34; while member of faculty also actively engaged in many important hydrographic, structural, hydraulic and highway projects; chairman: engineering section, Association of Land Grant Colleges 1922–23; chairman: Maine Liquor Commission 1937–41.

Boardman, Waldo Elias 1851–1922, born: Saco; son of a bootmaker; assisted his father in bootmaking, removed to Boston; patent solicitor and counsel in patent cases, associated with a weekly trade journal in New York; entered the drug and confectionary business; D.M.D. Harvard University Dental School 1886, instructor in operative dentistry: Harvard University 1890-1900; curator: Dental Museum, Harvard University from 1891; editor: *Quinquesimal Catalogue* Dental Department, Harvard University from 1896; librarian: Dental Library, Harvard University from 1897; honorary president: Fourth International Dental Congress, St. Louis 1904; president: Massachusetts Dental Society 1906–07, Northwestern Dental Association 1904–05, National Dental Association 1904–05.

Bodwell, Joseph Robinson 1818–87, born: Methuen (that part which is now Lawrence, Massachusetts); son of a poor farmer; bound out, at an early age, to another farmer, became a hired hand, at six dollars a month; at age sixteen, purchased a farm, in company with his father, in West Methuen 1838; contracted to haul granite from the quarry in Pelham, New Hampshire, to the construction site of the dam in Lawrence 1848; in conjunction with Moses Webster, engaged in quarrying; on his own account, purchased a quarry site on Fox Island, near Vinalhaven, with one yoke of oxen, which he drove and shod himself 1852, business was so good that a corporation was formed, with Bodwell as president and general manager, became the largest quarrier of granite in the country, removed to Hallowell, where he purchased the Hallowell quarry 1866, also engaged in farming, stock breeding; Bodwell was one of the original importers of Hereford cattle into the United States, also engaged in ice and lumber operations on the Kennebec; founder and president: Bodwell Water Power Co., Old Town; mayor of Hallowell 1869–71; member: Maine House of Representatives; delegate: Republican National Convention 1880; elected thirty-fourth governor of Maine 1886, died in office before his program of amelioration of working conditions and kindness to animals could be legislated; buried in Hallowell Cemetery.

Bogan, Louise 1897–1970, born: Livermore Falls; daughter of a clerk in a paper mill, grew up in a series of boarding houses; student: Mount Saint Mary's Academy, Manchester, New Hampshire, 1907–09, Girls Latin School, Boston 1910–15; rather than attend Radcliffe College, she married a soldier home from the Great War, after this marriage was quickly dissolved, she lived in Greenwich Village, where she began publishing her poems, joined a band of bohemians and occasionally drove the getaway car for a fur thief; Edmund Wilson deduced her great abilities and locked her in a room until she produced her first critical essay; she became the poetry critic for *The New Yorker* magazine, where she remained for the rest of her life; fellow: John Simon Guggenheim Memorial Foundation 1933, 1937; fellow, American Letters: Library of Congress 1944; chairman of poetry, Library of Congress 1945–46; essayist for *The New Yorker* magazine; recipient: Bollingen Prize 1955; member: American Academy of Arts and Sciences; author: *Body of this Death* 1923, *Dark Summer* 1929, *The Sleeping Fury* 1937, *Poems and New Poems* 1941, *Collected Poems 1923–54*, *Selected Criticism* 1955, *The Blue Estuaries, Poems 1923–68*, 1968, *A Poet's Alphabet* 1970.

Bond, Elias 1813–1896, born: Hallowell; apprentice: Bent & Bush mill, Chelmsford, Massachusetts, 1829, hatter, operated a company store, Lowell, returned to Hallowell, student: Hallowell Academy, prepared for the ministry; A.B. Bowdoin College 1837, D.D. 1890, B.D. Bangor Theological Seminary 1840; sent by the Board of Foreign Missions to Hawaii (in company with Daniel Dole), established mission at Kohala, Hawaii, established school 1842, established Kohala Girls' School 1874, established Kohala Teachers' School 1841, established a series of churches, established Kohala Sugar Plantation in order to give employment to his parishioners 1860, established Kohala Chinese Church for Chinese immigrants 1883, composed an Hawaiian language primer, hymnal, and a dictionary, endowed a lecture series at Bangor Theological Seminary; buried in Waianaia Cemetery, North Kohala.

Bond, William Cranch 1789–1859, born: Portland; son of a clockmaker and silver smith; removed, with his family, to Boston 1793; apprenticed to his father at an early age; before age fifteen, had constructed a chronometer after a description by La Perouse, the first in the United States; made observations of a total eclipse of the sun 1806, made crude astronomical instruments of his own devising; received encouragement from Josiah Quincy, president of Harvard College; discovered and made observations of a comet, his findings published by the American Academy of Arts and Sciences 1811; at the request of Harvard College, made a journey to England to study the construction and mechanical equipment of the Royal Observatory at Greenwich 1818; built his own observatory in Dorchester; assisted the Wilkes Expedition to the South Pacific by making observations to be repeated in the South Pacific and constructed magnetic instruments to record data to be compared to data from other locations 1838; urged by Josiah Quincy to return to Cambridge and Harvard College, as first director: Harvard University Observatory and Astronomical Observer to Harvard College, fitted an observatory at his university residence at Dana House 1839, for the construction of a new observatory, Bond devised the, now-standard, rotating dome 1844; declined an offer to run the U.S. Naval Observatory in Washington 1845; constructed an eighteen-inch equatorial telescope, then equaled by only one other, in the world 1847, discovered Hyperion, the eighth moon of Saturn 1848, discovered the crêpe ring of Saturn, also discovered the first moon of Neptune, discovered many comets, made elaborate studies of the Orion Nebula, sunspots, &c.; in cooperation with the U.S. Coast Survey, conducted a large number of chronometer expeditions; first to apply photography to astronomy, made the first photograph of the moon 1849, first photograph of a star (Vega) 1850; invented the chronograph, used to transmit true time, by telegraph, to all parts of New England 1850; conducted experiments, with Captain Charles Wilkes, USN, to determine the velocity of sound caused by the discharge of a cannon under different atmospheric conditions 1852; member: American Academy of Arts and Sciences; first American to be elected to the Royal Astronomical Society; recipient: honorary A.M., Harvard University 1842.

Bonney, Sherman Grant 1864–1942, born: Cornish; A.B. Bates College 1886, A.M. 1889, M.D. Harvard University Medical School 1889; practiced in Lewiston 1889, removed to Denver 1891, professor of medicine and dean: University of Denver Medical School; president, board of trustees: University of Denver and Goss College of Medicine; author: *Pulmonary Tuberculosis and Its Complications* 1908; donor of Bonney Memorial Library, Cornish.

Boody, David Augustus 1837–1930, born: Jackson; attended public school in Jackson, graduate: Phillips Academy, Andover; while engaged as a school teacher, began to study law in the office of Charles Brown, Bangor, later, in the office of Samuel Abbott, Belfast; member: Maine bar 1860, practiced in Belfast; removed to Brooklyn, New York, 1862, entered the banking business of his uncle, Henry Boody, displayed such acumen as to be made partner 1864, senior partner: Boody, McLellan and Co., bankers and brokers in New York; founder and president: Berkeley Institute, Brooklyn 1886–92 (now the Berkeley Carroll School); member: U.S. House of Representatives (Democrat) 1891, resigned to serve as mayor of Brooklyn, New York, 1892–94; president: board of trustees, Brooklyn Public Library 1897–1930; member: New York Stock Exchange to 1926; president: Louisiana & Northwestern Railroad Co., Sprague National Bank, City Savings Bank (both of Brooklyn), United States Title Guaranty Co.; at the age of ninety-two gave as his formula for a long, happy existence: "keep cool, confident, cheerful—and marry young, whether you can afford it or not." Buried in Green-Wood Cemetery, Brooklyn.

Boody, Robert M. 1836–1913, born: Limington; sergeant (highest rank: second lieutenant), Company B, 40th New York Infantry, recipient: Medal of Honor, Williamsburg and Chancellorsville, "This soldier at Williamsburg, Virginia, then a corporal, at great personal risk, voluntarily saved the lives of and brought from the battlefield two wounded comrades. A year later, at Chancellorsville, he voluntarily, and at great personal risk, brought from the field of battle and saved the life of Captain George B. Carse, Company C, 40th New York Volunteer Infantry." Buried in Green-Wood Cemetery, Haverhill, Massachusetts.

Boomer, George Ellsworth 1862– ?, born: Lewiston; cotton mill operative, later learned printer's trade; founded: *Providence* (Rhode Island) *Justice*, first socialist newspaper in New England 1893; Socialist party candidate for governor of Rhode Island 1895; publisher and editor: *Spirit of 76*, Tacoma, Washington, Socialist party candidate for governor of Washington 1908.

Boothby, Alonzo 1840–1902, born: Athens; attended Athens Academy, Maine Wesleyan Seminary, Kents Hill; studied medicine with Dr. Kinsman of Athens, attended medical courses at Medical School of Maine, continued his studies with Dr. David Constant of New York; in the Civil War: served in the Union army as a surgical dresser, while pursuing medical studies at Georgetown University Medical School, from which he received a diploma in 1863; contract surgeon, assigned to the Patent Office and Armory Square hospitals; commissioned first assistant surgeon to the 2nd U.S. Colored Regiment 1864, returned to Maine and practiced in Wilton for two years, removed to Boston; visiting physician to the Homeopathic Dispensary; lecturer: Boston University Medical School from 1873, spent the year 1883 observing in hospitals in London, Vienna, and Berlin; opened a private hospital on Worcester Square 1889, which came to be one of the largest in Boston; president: Massachusetts Homeopathic Medical Society, Boston Homeopathic Society, Massachusetts Surgical and Gynecological Society.

Bourne, Frank Augustus 1871–1936, born: Bangor; student at University of Maine 1889–91, B.S. Massachusetts Institute of Technology 1895, M.S. 1896, student at Harvard University 1898–99; in general architectural practice in Boston from 1899; principal works include Congregational Church, Winchester, Massachusetts, Congregational Church, Bangor, Congregational Church, Chelsea, Massachusetts, Saint John's Church, Franklin, Massachusetts, Mission of the Epiphany, Dorchester, Massachusetts, Church of All Nations, Boston, numerous residences, including some fifty in Back Bay, in charge of moving the Charles Street Church and restoring the historic edifice, designed the Morgan Memorial Buildings; member: American Institute of Architects; author: *Study of the Orders of Architecture* 1906, *Architectural Drawing* 1914.

Boutelle, Charles Addison 1839–1901, born: Damariscotta; shipmaster, acting  master, USN, 1862, blockade of Charleston and Wilmington, promoted to lieutenant, USN, for gallantry, while serving as navigator aboard USS *Sassacus*, in the engagement with rebel ironclad CSS *Albemarle*, commanding officer: USS *Nyanza*, capture of Mobile; managing editor and proprietor: *Bangor Whig and Courier* from 1870, member (at-large 1883–85, Fourth District 1879–83): U.S. House of Representatives 1883–99 (Republican), chairman: House Naval Affairs Committee; son-in-law of Maine Adjutant General John Littlefield Hodsdon; buried in Mount Hope Cemetery, Bangor.

Bowers, Alonzo Benjamin 1830–1909, born: West Baldwin; son of a farmer and miller; student: Bridgton Academy, Maine Wesleyan Seminary, Kents Hill, Bridgewater (Connecticut) State Normal School, Phillips Academy, Andover, Massachusetts; built first dam at sixteen, removed to California 1853, taught at Benecia Collegiate Institute 1853–54, principal: male department, San Francisco Classical High School, an organizer of the public school system of Petaluma; chief clerk: Office of California Surveyor General 1863, deputy surveyor general 1864, established disputed county boundaries, prepared a topographical map of Sonoma County, said to be the largest of its kind, based upon actual surveys, to be produced in the United States, to that time, published with legislative authority 1866; in charge of state land sales 1863–67; engaged in mining, lecturing; invented transport of earth with flumes 1853, invented flexibly connected discharge pipes, a method of building levees; his hydraulic dredge, which came to be known as the Bowers Dredge, along with his rotary excavator, secured by 12 patents and 389 claims, was quickly adopted worldwide and worked a revolution in dredging; president of several large dredging companies; had very bright idea of moving logs in a flume, constructed some immense flumes for this purpose; a founder: California Society of Civil Engineers; member: Parliament of International Association of Navigation Congresses.

Bowman, Alonzo 1848–98, born: Washington; sergeant, Company M, 6th U.S. Cavalry, recipient: Medal of Honor, at Cibicu Creek, Arizona, 30 August 1881, "exhibited conspicuous and extraordinary bravery in attacking mutinous scouts." Buried at Fort Bayard National Cemetery, Fort Bayard, New Mexico.

Bowman, Edward R. 1826–98, born: Eastport; quartermaster, USN, recipient: Medal of Honor, "On board the USS *Ticonderoga* during the attack on Fort Fisher, 13 to 15 January 1865. Despite severe wounds sustained during action, Bowman displayed outstanding courage in the performance of duty as his ship maintained its well-placed fire upon batteries on shore, and thereafter, as these materially lessened the power of the guns on the mound which had been turned upon our assaulting columns. During this battle the flag was planted on one of the strongest fortifications possessed by the rebels." Buried in Hillside Cemetery, Eastport.

Bowman, Jonathan 1735–1804, born: Dorchester, Massachusetts; son of a Congregational minister; A.B. Harvard College 1755, as an undergraduate, roomed with his cousin John Hancock, held Flynt and Stoughton scholarships; taught school in Dorchester and Hingham; when Lincoln County was organized in 1760, his uncle, Thomas Hancock, and other Plymouth Company proprietors chose him to represent their interests in Pownalborough, appointed collector of excise, register of probate, register of deeds, clerk of the court of sessions and the court of common pleas, justice of the peace; employed Gershom Flagg to construct his house (extant and on the National Register of Historic Places), using prefabricated pieces from his uncle's store in Boston; served as town treasurer, chaired a committee for the erection of a meetinghouse at Wiscasset Point; appointed judge of probate 1772; became involved (along with Charles Cushing) in a long and vituperative dispute with his classmate, Jacob Bailey, that involved a lethal combination of religious and political matters; at one point both Bowman and Cushing hid Bailey's canoe so that he could not carry his message of low Toryism upriver, claimed and seized Bailey's parsonage lot, attempted to revive ancient property qualifications for voting in town meetings; became the target of large rioting mob because of his opposition to the Solemn League and Covenant, eventually came out for the rebellion and was chosen moderator of Pownalborough town meeting, he was also reappointed to his offices by the new government (when one of his black slaves took all the talk of liberty and freedom to heart and departed for the army in Massachusetts, Bowman advertised for his return in the Cambridge newspaper); elected selectman, chairman of the Committee of Correspondence, Inspection, and Safety and delegate to the Lincoln County Congress 1776; with Charles Vaughan, constructed wharves below Bath and in Hallowell, as well as stores and houses in the latter; after the war, served as manager of the Sidley Bridge Lottery, treasurer of Hallowell Academy; appointed judge of the court of common pleas 1800; buried in the family cemetery near his home.

Bowman, Thomas 1848–1917, born: Wiscasset, removed to Council Bluffs, Iowa, 1868; merchant; treasurer: Pottawattomie County 1875–79; mayor 1882, postmaster 1885–99, owner: *Council Bluff Globe* from 1887; member from Iowa's Ninth District: U.S. House of Representatives 1891–93 (Democrat); postmaster 1904–08; buried in Pine Grove Cemetery, Dresden.

Brackett, Cyrus Fogg 1833–1915, born: Parsonfield; A.B. Bowdoin College (put his way through by teaching at various rural schools) 1859, studied medicine at Harvard University, M.D. Medical School of Maine 1863, L.L.D. (Hon.) Lafayette College 1883, Bowdoin College 1892, Princeton University 1910; instructor in chemistry: Bowdoin College 1863, professor of chemistry 1864–73, also taught courses in natural science, geology, zoology, and physics; Joseph Henry professor of chemistry: Princeton University 1873–1906, Brackett was widely regarded as one of the foremost lecturers of his day, with ingenious demonstrations using apparatus of his own devising and a wide reference to philosophy, physics, and literature; closely associated with Thomas A. Edison, who often sought Brackett's counsel, developed a dynamometer to measure the power delivered by Edison's early generators, his classroom was the first in the United States to be lighted by electricity; also closely associated with Alexander Graham Bell, testified in litigation establishing Bell's primacy, rigged the first telephone line in Princeton; founded the Princeton University School of Engineering 1889, which occupies Brackett Hall, named in his honor; member: American Philosophical Society, charter member: American Physical Society, chairman: Princeton University Sanitation Committee, president: New Jersey State Board of Health 1888–1908; Brackett is memorialized by a lectureship and a chair of physics; when Princeton's then-president Woodrow Wilson awarded him with an honorary doctorate of laws, during commencement 1910, he was given a standing ovation; author: *Textbook of Physics* 1884.

Brackett, Edward Augustus 1818–1908, born: Vassalboro; son of a farmer, clockmaker, and nurseryman, brother of Walter and Gustavus Brackett; graduate: Friends School, Philadelphia; began study of art in Cincinnati 1835, removed to Washington, D.C., modeled a bust of Senator Talmadge 1839, William Henry Harrison 1841, built a studio in South Woburn, Massachusetts, 1841, portrait busts of Bryant, Longfellow, Allston, Garrison, Wendell Phillips, Benjamin Butler, John Brown, the latter particularly received praise; represented in the Boston Athenaeum, the United States Capitol, the Metropolitan Museum, New York, the Boston Museum of Fine Arts; commissioner of Land Fisheries, Massachusetts, chairman for twenty-seven years; inventor of the hatching trap now in universal use and the fish ladder; raised quail and grouse for release; author: *Materialized Apparitions: If Not Beings from Another Life, What Are They?* 1886, *Twilight Hours or Leisure Hours of an Artist* 1845, *The World We Live In* 1902, *Chips the Builder Threw Away* 1904.

Brackett, Gustavus Benson 1827–1915, born: Unity; brother of Edward and Walter Brackett; educated at Denmark (Iowa) Academy; in Civil War: captain of engineers for three years; commissioner in charge of Iowa exhibits at Centennial Exposition, Philadelphia, 1876, U.S. commissioner to Paris Exposition 1873, represented pomological division, Department of Agriculture, Chicago Exposition 1893; practical nurseryman and horticulturist; secretary: American Pomological Society; chief of division of pomology, U.S. Department of Agriculture.

Brackett, Joseph 1797–1882, born: Maine; elder, Shaker community, Alfred; composer of the most famous Shaker hymn, *Simple Gifts* 1875, which he maintained had been channeled to him through a black African spirit, Laughing John.

Brackett, Walter M. 1823–1919, born: Unity; brother of Edward and Gustavus Brackett; began painting 1843, first portraits but later turned to fish, especially trout and salmon, exhibited in Boston, New York, work in Crystal Palace, London, many pieces in the Queen's Corridor, Buckingham Palace, War Department, Washington, D.C., &c.; a founding member and president of the Boston Art Club.

Bradbury, Albert William 1840–1909, born: Calais; A.B. Bowdoin College 1860; in the Civil War: first lieutenant, 1st Maine Mounted Artillery 1861, promoted through the ranks to lieutenant colonel, chief of artillery: 19th Corps 1864, chief of artillery under Sheridan, participated in many battles; after the war: member: Maine bar 1867, Bangor city solicitor and U.S. district attorney for Maine 1894–98.

Bradbury, George 1770–1823, born: Falmouth (Portland); A.B. Harvard College 1789; studied law, member: Massachusetts bar, practiced in Portland; member: Massachusetts House of Representatives 1806–10, 1811, 1812, member: U.S. House of Representatives 1813–17 (Federalist); unsuccessful candidate for renomination 1816; associate clerk: Portland court 1817–20; member: Maine Senate 1820; buried in Eastern Cemetery, Portland.

Bradbury, James Crockett 1806–65, born: Buxton; son of a farmer, studied medicine under his brother Samuel in Bangor, M.D. Medical College of Maine 1839, practiced in Howland, later in Orono; in the Civil War: chosen by the governor to oversee a committee of surgeons that examined new recruits, temporarily took charge of a hospital in Augusta, overwhelmed with invalided soldiers from the front and drastically reduced the mortality at that place; was often called upon to treat injured loggers in remote locations; famed in the profession for having saved a patient from amputation of an arm (see "Extensive Laceration of the Muscles of the Forearm," *Boston Medical and Surgical Journal*) and, also, for an amputation at the hip-joint for osteosarcoma, only the fourth time that difficult operation had been performed in the country; on one occasion, was told by a wealthy man to treat his maid servant as cheaply as possible and take it out of someone who was more able to pay, a year later, having treated the wife of the same man, Bradbury added to the charges expenses related to the treatment of the maid; after an attack of paralysis in 1863, he gradually sank into a coma.

Bradbury, James Ware 1802–1901, born: Parsonsfield; student: Gorham Academy; A.B. Bowdoin College 1825; principal: Hallowell Academy; founded first normal school in New England, in Effingham, New Hampshire, 1829; studied law with Ether Shepley and Rufus McIntyre, practiced in Augusta, partner with Lot Morrell; Kennebec County prosecuting attorney 1834–38; delegate: Democratic National Convention 1844; Democratic presidential elector 1844; member: U.S. Senate (Democrat) 1846–52, chairman: Committee on Printing and a special committee on French spoilation claims, prepared the bill for the creation of the U.S. Court of Claims; president: Maine Historical Society 1867–87; in 1896, at age ninety-four, took strong stand against the Democratic platform; buried in Forest Grove Cemetery, Augusta.

Bradbury, Theophilus 1739–1803, born: Newbury, Massachusetts; son of a ship's captain and merchant; A.B. Harvard College 1757, A.M. 1760, as an undergraduate, waited on tables, worked as a scholar of the house and held a Browne Scholarship; originally went to Falmouth to keep school 1757, but with the creation of Cumberland and Lincoln counties 1761, decided for the law, member: Massachusetts bar 1761, practiced in Falmouth (later Portland) 1761–79; known to his contemporaries as a grave and dignified practitioner, an excellent special pleader, and a gentleman of impressive character and manners; built a house on the corner of Middle and Willow Streets, which survived the fire of 1775, only to succumb to the Great Fire of 1866; not being able to make ends meet, served as collector of excise on liquor, tea, coffee, and china for Cumberland County; probably in retaliation for his stance on rioters, he and his wife were indicted for dancing in a tavern; served as clerk of the First Parish; publicly protested the radical nature of the Falmouth town meeting February 1774; became a proprietor of Narragansett No. 1 (later Buxton) and moderated a town meeting there called to protest the Boston Port Act and publicly apologized for his previous stance in February; with his old friend, John Adams, represented one Richard King, who had been plundered by a Whig mob; all doubts of his political leanings vanished when he read aloud to the assembled people of Falmouth Captain Mowat's ultimatum; managed to keep his own house from catching fire, but in the desolation left by Mowat's firing of the town, removed to Windham to 1779, at which point he removed to Newburyport; built a fine mansion, instructed many, including John Quincy Adams, in the law, maintained a flourishing law practice, and made a fortune in shipping; appointed to the Newburyport committee to consider the Massachusetts constitution 1780, served on the town school committee, secretary to the board of trustees of Dummer Academy; appointed justice of the peace and quorum for Essex County 1783; served as aide-de-camp to General Titcomb of the Second Essex Division, Massachusetts Militia; member: Massachusetts Senate 1791–95; member: U.S. House of Representatives (Federalist) 1795–97; judge: Massachusetts Supreme Court from 1797; Federalist presidential elector 1800; member: American Academy of Arts and Sciences; buried in Old Hill Burying Ground, Newbury.

Bradbury, William Batchelder 1816–1868, born: York; studied harmony with Sumner Hill, Lowell Mason's Boston Academy of Music, sang in Mason's Bowdoin Street Church Choir, sent to Saint John, New Brunswick and Machias to conduct singing classes; organist and music director: First Baptist Church, Brooklyn, New York, 1840; music director: Baptist Tabernacle, New York, 1841, annual festivals with children's choirs of up to 1,000 voices, led the fight to include music in public school curriculum; student in Europe, mostly in Leipzig, piano with Wenzel, singing with Boehme, harmony with Hauptman, and composition with Moscheles; wrote letters from Europe published in *New York Observer* and the *New York Evangelist* 1847–49; upon his return, published numerous collections of music and teacher of music to children; his tunebook *The Jubilee* sold over 200,000 copies; for Sunday schools, Bradbury pioneered small collections with cheerful titles, such as *The Golden Chain* and *Fresh Laurels*, which sold 2 million and 1.2 million copies, respectively; his most popular and enduring hymns are *Jesus Loves Me* and *He Leadth Me*, others still in the repertory of evangelical churches are *Just As I Am Without One Plea, Sweet Hour of Prayer*, and *He Leadth Me*; founded the Bradbury Piano Company, which received the endorsements of Theodore Thomas, William Mason, and Louis Moreau Gottschalk, eventually became the Knabe Piano Co.; author of 59 publications, including at least 2 cantatas, 812 hymn tunes, 28 anthems, 10 motets, 9 glees, 78 secular songs, 5 quartets, 10 patriotic choruses and songs, 13 sacred sentences, introits, and responses.

Bradford, Albert Sumner 1860–1933, born: Shapleigh, son of a farmer; attended local schools irregularly, ran away from the farm at age twelve and secured employment in Boston with a market gardener, continued on for several years, learned the gardener's trade, including plant propagation, vegetable cultivation, and hotbed culture; after the death of his employer, went to sea on a whaler, after his return, secured employment as a fireman for the Boston & Lowell Railroad Co., at age eighteen, became an engineer, operating the company's fastest train, the Montréal Express, tiring of the hazards of railroading, returned to market gardening, caretaker of hothouses on an estate in Massachusetts, removed to Santa Ana, California, 1887, ranch foreman for Daniel Halliday, purchased twenty acres in the Placentia district of Orange County 1890, added more acreage and planted them to Navel and Valencia oranges, achieved success as a supplier of nursery stock, with the introduction of refrigerated railroad cars, the demand for nursery stock grew intensely and with it, Bradford's business; an organizer, director: Southern California Fruit Exchange, as such, closely associated with Charles Collins Teague; vice president : Anaheim Union Water Co. 1900–14, chairman of its Ditch Committee; founder, director: First National Bank of Anaheim, American Savings Bank, founder of the town of Placentia, California, organized the Placentia National Bank, president to 1925, when it was sold to the Bank of Italy; founder, president: Placentia Savings Bank; vice president, director: Southern Counties Gas Co. of California 1913–33, president: Republic Petroleum Corp., director: Standard Bond & Mortgage Co., Los Angeles, chairman: Orange County Board of Foresters, for a number of years had charge of the Orange County exhibit at the annual Orange Show at San Bernardino, where he created novel and original designs with oranges that attracted wide attention; his home in Placentia was given to the city and is maintained as an historic site.

Bradford, Allen Alexander 1815–88, born: Friendship; son of a farmer; attended public school in Friendship, studied law with Jonathan Cilley in Thomaston 1833; removed to Missouri 1841, member: Missouri bar 1843, clerk of circuit court: Atchison County (Missouri) 1845–51; removed to Iowa, judge: Sixth District of Iowa 1852–55; removed to Nebraska, member: Nebraska Territorial House of Representatives 1856–58; removed to Central City, Colorado, appointed by President Lincoln as judge, Supreme Court, Colorado Territory 1862, member: U.S. House of Representatives 1865–71 (Republican); engaged in the practice of law in Pueblo; buried in City Cemetery, Pueblo.

Bradford, Ernest Wilder 1862– ?, born: Mattawamkeag; orphaned at age five, raised by his uncle, Charles Cushman, in Winslow; graduate: Oak Grove Seminary 1882, clerk in the law office of his brother, Chester Bradford, in Indianapolis, L.L.B. Central Law School of Indiana 1883; member: Indiana bar; partner: C. & E. W. Bradford 1887; removed to Washington, D.C., 1893; member: U.S. Supreme Court bar; senior member: Bradford & Doolittle, with offices in Washington and Indianapolis; specializing in patent, trademark and corporation law, senior member: Bradford & Harvey, specializing in Federal Trade Commission and federal tax matters; coauthor: *Manual of the Federal Trade Commission* 1916; president: American Patent Law Association; secretary: patent and trademark section, American Bar Association.

Bradford, Royal Bird 1844–1914, born: Turner; graduate: U.S. Naval Academy  1865; commissioned ensign, USN, promoted through the ranks to rear admiral, USN, 1904; while serving as chief of the Bureau of Ordnance, published his *Notes on Movable Torpedoes* 1882, which was the first systematic, American appreciation of a new, and, in his view, profoundly important war machine; formulated and drafted war plans for war with Spain, while attached to the Naval War College, Newport 1896; chief of the bureau of equipment, during the Spanish-American War; naval attaché: Paris Peace Commission 1898, his rigorous and well-thought-out Mahanian views on naval expansion and the need for coaling stations had an enormous impact on the views of the peace commissioners (including Senator William Frye) and the subsequent resolution of the Spanish-American War (*i.e.* the retention of the Philippines, Guam, and Puerto Rico), insisted on the retention of Wake Island, to be used as a cable station; demonstrated the need for these actions, to the civilian population, in his coaling stations for the navy, *Forum* magazine, February 1899; one of the chief planners of the Panama Revolution 1903; at his insistence, the navy installed a large coal-loading plant in Guam 1905; his portrait, by D. D. Coombs, is in the Maine Statehouse Collection.

Bradley, Alexander Stuart 1838– ?, born: Fryeburg; A.B. Bowdoin College 1858; studied law with William Pitt Fessenden, Portland; member: Maine bar 1863; register in bankruptcy, Nashville, Tennessee, 1867–72; removed to Chicago 1872, as attorney, successfully prosecuted case for illegally closing Jackson Park, won license tax cases for city against the three street railways of Chicago in U.S. Circuit Court; an organizer of the Anti-Monopoly League of Illinois to contest grant of legislature to Illinois Central Railroad (1869) of the whole outer harbor and land under water at Chicago 1881; published pamphlet *The Lake Front Steal*; counsel for the *People* v. *Illinois Central Railroad* in U.S. Circuit Court, being decided for the People 1888, upheld by the U.S. Supreme Court 1892.

Bradley, Amy Morris 1823–1904, born: East Vassalboro; teacher in Vassalboro public schools, spent a term at Vassalboro Academy 1842; principal of grammar school in Gardiner 1844–47; assistant: Winthrop School, Boston 1847–50; assistant: Putnam Grammar School, East Cambridge, Massachusetts, 1850; forced to resign, due to ill health, removed to Charleston, South Carolina, where she developed an abiding hatred of slavery; removed to Costa Rica to serve as a governess 1853; removed to San José, opened Costa Rica's first English language school to 1857; translator for New England Glass Co., Boston 1858; in the Civil War: volunteered as a nurse for the 3rd and 5th Maine Volunteers, General H. W. Slocum observed the superior quality of Bradley's hospital, appointed her matron of the brigade hospital, volunteered: U.S. Sanitary Commission, head nurse aboard hospital ships, director: U.S. Sanitary Commission convalescent hospital, Washington 1862–65; published a newspaper: *Soldier's Journal*, providing practical advice to convalescing soldiers on benefits, artificial limbs, labor possibilities, &c.; appointed by American Unitarian Association: special agent, Soldiers Memorial Society; missionary in Wilmington, North Carolina, oversaw the establishment of schools for poor whites as well as emancipated slaves, with the support of Wilmington's citizens, Northern friends, the Peabody Educational Fund, and the Freedmen's Bureau, opened two more schools, which became the public school system of Wilmington; founded the Tileston Normal School to train local teachers 1872.

Bradley, Milton 1836–1911, born: Vienna; son of a country merchant who introduced to Maine the manufacture of potato starch; removed with his family to Lowell, Massachusetts, 1847, graduate: Lowell High School; made drawings in the office of a civil engineer and patent solicitor, later became an independent mechanical engineer; realizing the need of further formal education, entered Harvard University, S.B. Lawrence Scientific School 1856; after graduation, secured a position as draftsman in a locomotive works in Springfield, Massachusetts, 1856; opened his own office in Springfield, practiced as a mechanical engineer and patent solicitor, became interested in lithography, developed a board game *The Checkered Game of Life*, founder: Milton Bradley Co. 1875, manufacturer of board games, school materials, books, early animations; the Bradley system for color instruction established the first color nomenclature based on spectrum standards, definitely located by their wave lengths, roughly corresponding to musical notation; author of *Color in The Classroom*, and others; early proponent of Froebel; publisher of the influential *Kindergarten Review*, father of the American kindergarten; member: Springfield City Council, Springfield school board; buried in Springfield (Massachusetts) Cemetery.

Brann, Louis Jefferson 1876–1948, born: Madison; son of a merchant; attended public schools in Gardiner, A.B. University of Maine 1898; cut ice in Gardiner to pay his tuition, studied law in the office of Daniel McGillicuddy and Frank Morey, Lewiston; member: Maine bar 1901, practiced in Lewiston; clerk, Legal Affairs Committee: Maine House of Representatives 1902; Lewiston city solicitor 1906–07; collector of taxes 1908; register of probate for Androscoggin County 1906–13; municipal court judge 1913–16; mayor of Lewiston for five terms; unsuccessful candidate for the Democratic nomination for governor 1926, governor of Maine (Democrat) 1933–37; unsuccessful Democratic candidate for U.S. Senate 1936, 1940, unsuccessful Democratic candidate for governor 1938, unsuccessful Democratic candidate for U.S. House of Representatives 1942; removed to Boston and practiced law, chairman: Federal Solid Fuel War Council 1942; later became a member of the law firm of Brann & Isaacson, Lewiston.

Brannan, Samuel 1819–89, born: Saco; learned printing trade in Ohio 1836; converted to Church of Jesus Christ of Latter Day Saints; moved to New York City; published *New York Messenger* 1842; Mormon elder, after the murder of Joseph Smith, it became obvious that the Mormons, to survive, must remove to a remote location, Brannan was chosen to lead an expedition to Mexican California 1845, sailed in ship *Brooklyn* with 238 people, a printing press, type, and paper, agricultural implements, and a flour mill, arrived 1846 (first Anglo-American settlers in California after capture in Mexican War), founded the Mormon colony of New Hope, at the junction of the San Joaquin and Stanislaus Rivers; made an extraordinary journey east through the snows of the Sierras, the deserts, and hostile Indians of Nevada and Idaho, to Green River, Wyoming, to convince Brigham Young of the wisdom of pressing on to the West Coast, rebuffed, returned to California; published *California Star*, first newspaper in San Francisco 1847–48; removed to Sutter's Fort, where he operated a store; several of the Mormon immigrants were at work, building a mill for Sutter at Coloma; Brannan, hearing rumors of a gold strike, journeyed to Coloma, filled a glass vial with gold dust, and personally spread the word of the discovery in the streets of San Francisco, walking about crying, "gold, gold, gold, from the American River!"; read out of the Mormon church for failing to tithe; member: first San Francisco City Council; founding president: San Francisco Committee of Vigilance 1851; erected the first flour mill in California; mayor of San Francisco; promoter and investor in banks, railroads, such as the California Northern Railroad Co., which became a part of the

Union Pacific Railroad, shipping, telegraph; became one of the wealthiest men in California; held extensive farmland on Oahu and numerous building lots in Honolulu; member: California State Senate 1851; funded the construction of the first public school in San Francisco; founded and named the town of Calistoga; aided, with money and arms, the Mexicans in rebellion against Maximilian, received a large grant of land in Sonora, but his colonization plan came to naught; drank excessively, died in poverty.

Brett, Lloyd Milton 1856–1927, born: Dead River; B.S. U.S. Military Academy 1879, second lieutenant, 2nd Cavalry, USA; recipient: Medal of Honor, "O'Fallons Creek, Montana, 1 April 1880, fearless exposure and dashing bravery in cutting off the Indians' pony herd, thereby greatly crippling the hostiles," promoted through the ranks to brigadier general, USA, 1917; adjutant general: District of Columbia militia 1903–08; superintendent: Yellowstone National Park 1910–16; commanding officer 160th Infantry Brigade 1917–19, colonel 3rd U.S. Cavalry 1919, recipient: croix de guerre (France); buried in Arlington National Cemetery.

Brewster, Ralph Owen 1888–1961, born: Dexter; son of a farmer; attended

public schools in Dexter, A.B. Bowdoin College 1909, L.L.B. Harvard University Law School 1913, L.L.D. (Hon.) University of Maine 1928; principal: Castine High School 1910; member: Maine bar 1913, practiced in Portland; member: Portland School Committee 1915–23; member: Maine House of Representatives 1917–18; in World War I: rose in rank from private to captain and regimental adjutant, 3rd Infantry, Maine National Guard; member: Maine House of Representatives 1921–22, member: Maine Senate 1922-25; governor of Maine (Republican) 1925–29; member from the Third District: U.S. House of Representatives: 1935–41; member: U.S. Senate 1941–53, member: War Investigating Committee (the so-called Truman Committee) from 1943, chairman from 1944, subsequent to Truman's elevation to vice president, investigated the Southern California wartime aircraft industry, in particular: Howard Hughes, who was prompted by Brewster's caustic comments to fly the Spruce Goose, Hughes also charged that Brewster was in league with Juan Trippe of Pan American Airways to subvert Hughes's Trans World Airways; buried in Mt. Pleasant Cemetery, Dexter.

Bridge, Horatio 1806–93, born: Augusta; A.B. Bowdoin College 1826, student at  Northampton law school, member: Maine bar 1828, practiced in Skowhegan and Augusta; received appointment as purser, USN, 1838, on board USS *Cyane* two-year cruise on the African coast, on board USS *Saratoga*; duty at Portsmouth Naval Shipyard, two-year cruise on USS *United States* in the Mediterranean; duty at Portsmouth 1849–51; assigned to the USS *Portsmouth*, Pacific Squadron; chief of Bureau of Provisions and Clothing, where his idea of comprehensive fleet supply met with conspicuous success 1853–68; paymaster general, retired with rank of commodore 1868, died at Athens, Pennsylvania; close friend and classmate of Nathaniel Hawthorne, underwrote the cost of publishing Hawthorne's *Twice-Told Stories*; author: *Journal of An African Cruiser* 1845, *Personal Reminiscences of Nathaniel Hawthorne* 1893; a supply ship USS *Bridge* (AF-1), named in his honor, was launched 1916, received one battle star for World War II.

Bridges, Henry Styles 1898–1961, born: West Pembroke; brother of Ronald Bridges; B.S. in agricultural science, University of Maine 1918; instructor: Sanderson Academy, Ashfield, Massachusetts, 1918–19; agricultural extension agent: Hancock County; New Hampshire 1921–22; secretary: New Hampshire Farm Bureau Federation 1922–23; editor: *The Granite State Monthly* 1924–26; director and secretary: New Hampshire Investment Co. 1924–29; member: New Hampshire Public Utilities Commission 1930–36; governor of New Hampshire 1934–36; member: U.S. Senate (Republican) 1936–61, Senate minority leader 1952; president *pro tempore* 1953–55; chairman: Appropriations Committee, Joint Committee on Foreign Economic Cooperation, Joint Committee on Inaugural Arrangements; buried in Pine Grove Cemetery, Concord.

Bridges, Ronald 1905–59, born: West Pembroke; brother of Henry Styles Bridges; A.B. Bowdoin College 1930, A.M. Harvard University 1932, L.H.D. (Hon.) Pacific University 1944, University of Maine 1956, Nasson College 1954, D.D. Grinnell College 1950, S.T.D. Bowdoin College 1955, L.L.D. Yankton College 1956; grade school teacher: Cooper 1922–23, Sanford High School 1926–29, Wassookeag School, Dexter 1930–31, Milton (Massachusetts) High School 1932–34; lecturer and writer on politics and religion from 1934; managing editor: *The Republican*, Chicago 1938–40; associate professor: Arizona State College, Tempe 1941–45; president: Pacific School of Religion 1945–50; Carl Patton professor of homiletics: Union Theological Seminary, New York 1949–50; consultant and lecturer 1950–54; religious affairs adviser: U.S. Information Agency from 1955; trustee: Bangor Theological Seminary 1940-46,

Pacific University 1944–48, Pacific School of Religion 1944–46, Mills College 1949–50, Howard University 1951–53; unsuccessful Republican candidate for U.S. House of Representatives, First Maine District 1936; member: Republican National Committee 1937–40; chairman: Congregational Publishing Society 1938–42; moderator: General Council of Congregational and Christian Churches 1944–46; Congregational delegate: World Council of Churches 1948–54; president: American Board of Commissioners for Foreign Missions 1950–55.

Bright, George Adams 1837–1905, born: Bangor; M.D. Harvard University Medical School 1859; acting assistant surgeon, USN, 1861, assistant surgeon 1864, passed assistant surgeon 1874, medical inspector 1893, medical director, retired as rear admiral, USN, 1899; served on board USS *New Ironsides*, USS *Susquehanna*, USS *Tuscarora*, USS *Constellation*, USS *Newark*; on duty at: Naval Hospital Boston, Mare Island, Norfolk, Washington, D.C..

Brockway, George Pond 1916–2001, born: Portland; A.B. Williams College ΦBK 1938, as an undergraduate, served as editor of the Williams College literary magazine *Sketch*; began with McGraw-Hill Book Co. 1938–42; served in France and Germany as an officer in the U.S. Army artillery; joined the publishing house of W. W. Norton & Co. 1946, as copy editor and salesman; president 1958–76, chairman of the board 1976–84; managed to keep Norton an independent company in a period when most large publishing houses became subsidiaries of conglomerates; published Betty Friedan's *Feminine Mystique*, Fawn Brodie's *Thomas Jefferson: An Intimate Portrait*, John Sirica's *To Set the Record Straight*, Norman Cousins's *Anatomy of an Illness*, several of Erik Ericson's works, Robert Kennedy's account of the Cuban missile crisis, *Thirteen Days*, among many others, he also had a penchant for Maine authors, including May Sarton; began the series of Norton Anthologies, including *The Norton Anthology of World Masterpieces*, *The Norton Anthology of English Literature*, and *The Norton Anthology of American Literature*; director: Yale University Press; columnist for *New Leader* magazine, a founder of the journal *Post-Keynesian Economics*.

Brooks, Edward 1734–1811, born: Medford, Massachusetts; A.B. Harvard College 1757, A.M. 1760, his undergraduate diary remains one of the most complete records of college life in that period; his mention of actually studying in the library (rather than merely borrowing books) is the earliest such reference; became a lifelong friend of John Adams; his grand-daughter, the daughter of Peter Chardon Brooks, would eventually marry Adams's grandson, Charles Francis Adams; after college, he kept school in Dedham briefly until recalled to Harvard, where he served as librarian and butler; given a three-year Hopkins Scholarship by the college, so that he might study theology; received an unanimous call to the pulpit in North Yarmouth 1763; married Abigail Brown, sister of Thomas Browne; soon came into conflict with his congregation over his liberality, his introduction of hymn singing, and the reading of scripture in services; a majority of the congregation requested an ecclesiastical council, which reluctantly agreed to his dismissal 1769; returned to Medford, where he kept school, as well as serving as an itinerant preacher; fought in the battle at Lexington; served as chaplain aboard the USS *Hancock*, making him the first United States naval chaplain; *Hancock* was captured and taken to Halifax, where Brooks contracted smallpox 1778; after his return to Medford he kept school until his death; buried in Oak Grove Cemetery, Medford; among his descendants are Philips Brooks, Henry Adams, Brooks Adams, and Francis Parkman.

Brooks, Edward Pennell 1895–1991, born: Westbrook; B.S. Massachusetts Institute of Technology 1917, D.Sc. (Hon.) Drexel Institute of Technology 1958; with Sears, Roebuck & Company 1927–51, vice president of factories 1939–51, director 1941–52; founding dean, School of Industrial Management: Massachusetts Institute of Technology 1951–59; director: Colonial Growth & Energy Fund, Colonial Fund, Inc., Plymouth Cordage Co.; trustee: American Optical Company, Savings and Profit Sharing Pension Fund: Sears, Roebuck & Company Employees; member of the corporation: Massachusetts Institute of Technology; in World War I: first lieutenant, USA, 1917–19, served with the American Expeditionary Forces in France, decorated: Distinguished Service Medal; recipient: Medal of Freedom, fellow: American Academy of Arts and Sciences.

Brooks, Erastus 1815–86, born: Portland; posthumous son of the captain of the privateer *Yankee*, lost with all hands, late in 1814, younger brother of James Brooks; bound out to a Boston grocery, where he worked for board and clothes, apprenticed to a compositor's trade, attended Brown University, started *Yankee* newspaper in Wiscasset, removed to Haverhill, Massachusetts, where he taught school, attracting the attention of John Greenleaf Whittier, member of the Haverhill School Committee, editor and proprietor of the *Haverhill Gazette*, later reporter for the *Portland Advertiser*; traveled from southern Africa to Russia as a correspondent, Washington correspondent for the *New York Express*, later editor: *New York Express*, during a cholera epidemic, when most had fled the city, he remained, editing the paper singlehandedly; availed himself of the offer from Ezra Cornell to use the new telegraph line from Albany to New York, communicated news of the legislature to New York far in advance of any other paper; made a walking tour of Europe, from Queenstown to Moscow, communicated letters to the *Express* that were widely reprinted, on his return, his vessel wrecked off Sandy Hook, Brooks was one of the few survivors; as editor of the *Express*, took an active part in the agitation against the exemption of Catholic church property from taxation, which led him into a vigorous public debate with Archbishop Hughes; elected to the New York Senate as a member of the American or Know Nothing party 1851, 1853, unsuccessful candidate for governor 1856; delegate: Democratic National Convention 1852, 1856, 1860, delegate: New York State Constitutional Convention 1866–67, chairman of the Committee on Charities;

member: New York Assembly 1878, 1879, 1881, 1882, 1883, chairman: Ways and Means Committee 1882; member: New York State Board of Health; trustee: New York Institution for the Instruction of the Deaf and Dumb, Nursery and Child's Hospital; so great was his interest in the cause of Indian rights that he left his sickbed to attend Albert Smiley's Conference on Indian Affairs at Lake Mohonk; an old friend of Ezra Cornell, served as a founding trustee of Cornell University, never missed a trustees' meeting in twenty years.

Brooks, James 1810–73, born: Portland; son of the captain of the privateer *Yankee*, which was lost, with all hands, late in 1814, older brother of Erastus Brooks; attended public school until age eleven, when he was apprenticed to a storekeeper in Lewiston, who was so impressed with his abilities, that he released Brooks from his apprenticeship and assisted him in gaining further education; graduate: Monmouth Academy, A.B. Waterville College 1831, first in his class; taught at a Latin school in Portland, studied law with John Neal, and began to write anonymous letters to the *Portland Advertiser*, although made a member of the Maine bar, an offer to write for the *Advertiser*, settled him into a life in journalism, later editor: *Portland Advertiser*, member: Maine House of Representatives 1831, 1835, introduced the enabling legislation that provided for the building of the St. Lawrence & Atlantic Railroad; unsuccessful candidate for U.S. House of Representatives 1836; removed to Washington, D.C., 1836, where he wrote a number of letters that were printed in Portland and reproduced throughout the country and in Europe; made walking tours of the South and Europe as correspondent for the *Advertiser*; founded, with his brother Erastus, the *New York Daily Express* 1836, editor to 1873, removed to Indiana, where he made speeches for William Henry Harrison, met and married Harrison's cousin, Mary Randolph (whom he required to manumit three slaves before their marriage); member: New York Assembly 1847, member: U.S. House of Representatives (Whig) 1849–53, (Democrat) 1863–73, member: Ways and Means Committee, twice Democratic candidate for speaker; delegate: New York Constitutional Convention 1867; director: Union Pacific Railroad from 1869; died one week after being censured by Congress for attempted bribery in the Crédit Mobilier affair 1873; author: *A Seven Months Run Up and Down and Around the World* 1872; buried in Green-Wood Cemetery, Brooklyn, New York.

Brooks, John Pascal 1861– ?, born: Kittery; graduate: Phillips Academy, Exeter, B.S. Dartmouth College 1885, M.S. 1893, Sc.D. (Hon.) 1915, Sc.D. Clarkson College of Technology, Potsdam, New York, 1931; professor of civil engineering: State University of Kentucky 1897–1906, associate professor of civil engineering: University of Illinois 1906-11; founding president: Clarkson College of Technology, Potsdam, New York, 1911-28; author: *Handbook for Surveyors* 1895, *Handbook of Street Railroad Location* 1897, *Reinforced Concrete* 1911.

Brooks, Lebbeus 1819–58, born: Wells; an inventor and mathematician from an early age; copyrighted a table for 6 percent interest and perpetual almanac 1849, on an average table and 7 percent interest table 1851, patents on an improved spirit level 1854, a machine for sawing marble, and a saw set 1856; at the time of his death in Saco, he had ready for application a mill saw set, a straw cutter, a spring-bed rest, as well as an improved decimal interest table for copyright.

Brooks, Noah 1830–1903, born: Castine; son of a shipbuilder, grandson of John Holmes, cousin of John Holmes Goodenow; attended public schools in Castine, removed to Boston 1848, studied landscape painting, began career as a newspaperman in Boston, with the *Atlas* 1850, removed to Dixon, Illinois, 1855, where he made an unsuccessful attempt at storekeeping, removed to Kansas, where he engaged in farming, associated with the Kansas free-state agitations, removed to California by ox team in a party of immigrants 1859, founded the *Marysville Appeal*, Civil War correspondent for the *Sacramento Union* 1862–65, slated to become private secretary to his close friend, President Lincoln, but the assassination intervened, a bad cold having prevented him from attending the theatre, the night of the assassination; appointed by President Andrew Johnson as naval officer of the port of San Francisco, but was removed after eighteen months for failing to adhere to certain political requirements; editor: *Alta California* 1866–71, regular contributor to the *Overland Monthly* from 1866, on the staff of the *New York Tribune* 1871–75, *New York Times* 1875–84; editor: *Newark Advertiser* 1884–94; author, his works include: *The Boy Immigrant* 1876, *The Fairport Nine* 1880, *Our Baseball Club* 1884, *Abraham Lincoln, a Biography for Young People* 1888, *The Boy Settlers* 1891, *American Statesmen* 1893, *Tales of the Maine Coast* 1894, *Abraham Lincoln and the Downfall of American Slavery* 1894, *Short Studies in American Party Politics* 1895, *How the Republic Is Governed* 1895, *Washington in Lincoln's Time* 1896, *The Mediterranean Trip* 1896, *Scribners History of the United States* 1896, *The Story of Marco Polo* 1896, *General Henry Knox, A Revolutionary Soldier*; retired to Castine.

Brooks, Peter Chardon 1767–1849, born: North Yarmouth; son of Edward Brooks; after his father's death, apprenticed to shoemaker in Boston, started an insurance company at the Bunch of Grapes tavern 1789, through careful attention to detail and careful accounting, grew so wealthy in twelve years, that he was considered the wealthiest man in New England, retired from business 1803, devoted himself, to 1806, to liquidating his business concerns and settlement of risks; president: New England Insurance Company, the first in Massachusetts; member: Massachusetts Senate and House of Representatives, prominent in his stand against the establishment of a state lottery, chairman of a committee to examine generally into the concerns of every lottery now in operation in the commonwealth 1821; member: first Boston City Council; delegate: Massachusetts Constitutional Convention 1820; treasurer: Washington Monument Association; father-in-law of Charles Francis Adams and Edward

Everett, grandfather of Henry Adams, Brooks Adams, among others; his grandson, Peter Chardon Brooks III, commissioned the design and construction of the Montauk Building in Chicago, the first structure to be termed a skyscaper.

Brown, Benjamin 1756–1831, born: Swansea, Massachusetts; studied medicine, practiced in Waldoboro, surgeon aboard frigate *Boston*, commanding officer: Samuel Tucker, on her mission of delivering John Adams to France, aboard *Thorne*, captured and imprisoned on Prince Edward Island, escaped in an open boat to Boston; member: Massachusetts House of Representatives 1809–11, 1812, 1819; member: U.S. House of Representatives (Federalist) 1815–17; buried in Waldoboro Cemetery.

Brown, Edwin Franklin 1862– ?, born: Auburn; son of a manufacturer of prismatic sidewalk lights; attended public schools in Evanston, Illinois, and Illinois State University; began in the repair department of the Hartford Sewing Machine Co., Chicago, 1880; entered the bicycle department of Messrs. John Wilkinson & Co., won the bicycle championship of the Northwest 1881, making a mile in 3.08 minutes, one of the first purchasers of a high-wheeled bicycle in Chicago, conducted a party of forty wheelmen through Canada 1882; as early as 1885, Brown built a steam tricycle, in 1886, built a four-wheeled machine that obtained a speed of 10 mph, in 1889, constructed a three-wheeled automobile that ran at a rate of 20 mph, this machine was exhibited at the first automobile show held in Chicago 1902; associated with his father's iron business from 1882; special bank examiner under Comptroller Dawes 1896, receiver of over twenty national banks with headquarters in Chicago; organizer, president: Manufacturers Bank of Chicago 1903, became Monroe National Bank 1905; charter member: American Motor League, vice president: Chicago Automobile Club.

Brown, Harry Alvin 1879–1949, born: Liberty; A.B. Bates College 1903, A.B. University of Colorado 1907, A.M. 1923, Ph.D. Columbia University 1937, Ed.D. Bates College 1925, Miami University 1925; teacher in Maine rural schools 1899–1902, supervising principal of schools: Liberty 1903–04, district superintendent of schools: Salem and Hudson, New Hampshire, 1904–05, superintendent of schools: Glasgow, Montana, 1907–09, district superintendent of schools: Colebrook and Errol, New Hampshire, 1909–13, deputy superintendent of public instruction; director: Bureau of Educational Research, New Hampshire, 1913–17; president: State Teachers College, Oshkosh, Wisconsin 1917–30; president: Illinois State Normal University 1930–44; chairman: American Association of Teachers Colleges 1925–26; contributor of numerous articles on educational topics, author: *Latin in Secondary Schools* 1919.

Brown, Harry Peter McNab, Jr. 1917–86, born: Portland; student: Harvard University 1940, with *Time* magazine 1939, *The New Yorker* magazine 1939-40, attached to *Yank* army newspaper, New York 1942; author: *The End of a Decade* 1941,

The Poem of Bunker Hill 1941, *The Violent* 1943, *A Walk in the Sun* 1944, *Poems 1941–44* 1945, *Arctic in His Hunger* 1948, *The Stars in their Courses* 1960, *A Quiet Place to Work* 1968, *The Wild Hunt* 1973, *The Gathering* 1977, numerous film scripts including: *Arch of Triumph* 1947, *The Sands of Iwo Jima* 1949, *A Place in the Sun* 1951, *The Sniper* 1952, *Between Heaven and Hell* 1956, *Oceans 11*; recipient: Young Poets' Prize 1935, Lloyd McKim Garrison Award, Harvard University 1939, Shelley Award 1939, Commonwealth Club Award 1949, Academy Award for the screenplay *A Place in the Sun* 1952; member: National Rifle Association; made home in Beverly Hills, California.

Brown, Henry Francis 1837–1912, born: East Baldwin, attended district school in East Baldwin, Fryeburg Academy, Limerick Academy; removed to Wisconsin, later Minnesota, where he became the owner of very large tracts of timber lands, mills, yards, &c., associated with the production of iron ore, acquired several large mines in the Mesabe Range of Minnesota, which he leased to the U.S. Steel Co.; conducted an extensive shorthorn cattle breeding operation on the outskirts of Minneapolis from 1867; president: American Shorthorn Breeders Association 1906–08; a founder: North American Telegraph Co. of Minnesota, a company organized to compete with the Western Union Telegraph Co., built lines connecting Minneapolis and St. Paul with Chicago and points west; president, treasurer: Browndale Farms, Inc.; president: Union National Bank of Minneapolis; Republican presidential elector 1884.

Brown, John Bundy 1805–81, born Lancaster, New Hampshire; son of an operator of a stagecoach tavern in Gray; operated grocery store, opened his first sugar house 1845, devised a revolutionary process for manufacture of sugar from molasses, constructed the largest rum distillery in the world, Portland; built the 240-room Falmouth Hotel, the Lancaster Building, and an opulent mansion on Western Promenade.

Brown, John Hamilton 1837– ?, born: Liberty; removed to Haverhill, Massachusetts; invented steel die for heeling women's shoes; to New York 1863, devised a combination pleating machine, rotary ruching press, and ruffling machine, invented a quilting machine; director: National Rifle Association, captain: New York Rifle Club, member: American rifle team that beat the British team at Wimbledon with rifles of his design 1883; invented a segmented tube, wire-wound gun.

Brown, James Sproat 1824–78, born: Hampden; member: Maine bar 1843; removed to Milwaukee 1846, prosecuting attorney: Milwaukee County 1846; Wisconsin attorney general 1846–49; mayor of Milwaukee 1861; member: U.S. House of Representatives (Democrat) 1863–65; buried in Forest Home Cemetery, Milwaukee.

Brown, Mary Ann Berry 1840–1936, born: Kents Hill, Readfield; at age twenty-one, married Ivory Brown, a Baptist preacher from Parsonsfield; in 1864, they made their way to Augusta, where Ivory Brown enlisted in the 31st Maine Volunteer Regiment; desiring to accompany her husband, Mary Ann performed clerical duties with the regiment before it shipped out for Virginia, continuing her chores as a camp nurse, legend has it that she, on more than one occasion, shouldered a musket and fought alongside the men; when her husband was wounded, she cared for him until he was discharged in 1865, at which point, he returned to his ministry; after his death in 1902, she removed to Portland and acted as preacher and conducted religious meetings; buried in Pine Grove Cemetery, Brownfield.

Brown, Philip Marshall 1875–1966, born: Hampden; A.B. Williams College 1898, L.L.D. 1918, A.M. Harvard University 1912; private secretary to Lloyd C. Griscom 1900–01; second secretary, American Legation, Constantinople 1901-03; secretary to legation: Guatemala and Honduras 1903–07 (various times: chargé d'affaires); secretary: American Embassy, Constantinople; chargé d'affaires 1907–08; envoy extraordinary and minister plenipotentiary to Honduras 1908–10; instructor in international law and diplomacy: Harvard University 1912–13; assistant professor of international law and diplomacy: Princeton University 1913–14, professor 1915–29; trustee: Princeton University, American University; president: American Peace Society 1940–46, Washington Urban League 1942–44, English-Speaking Union of Washington 1944–46; associate editor: *American Journal of International Law*; author: *Foreigners in Turkey, International Realities, International Society, The Venture of Belief, The Science of Peace.*

Brown, Samuel Gilman 1813–85, born: North Yarmouth, son of Rev. Francis Brown, president of Dartmouth College 1815–20; A.B. Dartmouth College 1831, L.L.D. (Hon.) 1868, D.D. Columbia University 1852; taught high school at Ellington, Connecticut, 1832–34, principal: Abbot Academy, Andover, Massachusetts, 1835–38, graduate: Andover Theological Seminary 1837, professor of oratory and belles lettres: Dartmouth College 1840–63, ordained Congregational minister 1852, professor of intellectual philosophy and political economy 1863–67, seventh president: Hamilton College 1867–81, Walcott professor of the evidences of Christianity 1867–81, instructor in intellectual philosophy: Hamilton College, instructor in intellectual and moral philosophy: Dartmouth College, provisional professor of mental and moral philosophy: Bowdoin College 1881–85; trustee: Hamilton College 1867–85, Auburn Theological Seminary 1872–82; member: American Board of Commissioners for Foreign Missions; life director: American Bible Society, American Tract Society; author: *The Studies of an Orator* 1840, *Biographies of Self-Taught Men* 1847, *The Spirit of a Scholar* 1847, *Eulogy on the Life and Character of Henry Clay* 1852, *The Works of Rufus Choate with a Memoir of His Life* (2 volumes) 1862.

Brown, Samuel Peters 1816–98, born: North Blue Hill; attended public school in Blue Hill, taught school in Blue Hill, surveyor, operated the Blue Hill granite quarry, removed to Orland 1847; merchant, shipbuilder, dealer in lumber and ice, supplier of timber for the construction of naval vessels, owned three plantations in Maryland, on Chesapeake Bay; partner in the firm of Warren, Brown & Co., operators of the extensive Repentenay lumber mills in Canada, owned a controlling interest in the Allegheny Land, Lumber and Boom Co., which operated a heavily timbered section, known as the land of Canaan in West Virginia, involved in the Alaska Commercial Co., which secured a lease on the Alaska Seal Islands; member: Maine House of Representatives 1845–46, 1858–59; appointed by President Lincoln as naval agent at Washington and through him, many millions of dollars worth of ships, guns, and naval supplies were purchased during the Civil War; became involved in efforts to reform Washington city government, member of the levy court, founded the village of Mount Pleasant, later incorporated into the city of Washington, author of the bill passed in 1871 that provided for a territorial form of government for the District of Columbia, the bill repealed the charters of Georgetown and Washington City, abolished the levy court, provided for a governor, a board of public works, a secretary of the territory, and a council of eleven members to be appointed by the president and confirmed by the Senate, a legislative assembly of twenty-two members, and a delegate to Congress to be elected by the voters of the district; appointed member of the public works board, which took over complete supervision and control of streets, sewers, roads, and bridges in the district; formulated a comprehensive plan of improvements, secured the charter for the Metropolitan Street Railroad Co. 1864, of which he was president and oversaw construction; formed a partnership with his son, Austin, styled S. P. Brown & Son 1866, for the purpose of carrying on the lumber, coal, building material, and contract business with the government, supplied coal for the entire U.S. Navy, delivering it aboard ships at Port Richmond, Philadelphia, for shipment to all stations, foreign and domestic; obtained the charter for the National Safe Deposit Co. 1867, president, during the Civil War; was much involved in the care for Maine soldiers who were ill or injured.

Brown, William Robinson 1875–1955, born: Portland, graduate: Phillips Academy, Andover, Massachusetts, A.B. Williams College 1897; employed by Berlin Mills, Inc., Portland, manufacturers of pulp and paper, of which his father, William Wentworth Brown, owned a portion, served as general manager of the woods division 1900–43, became Brown Co. 1907, Brown Corp. of Québec organized 1903, responsible for the expansion of wood operations on the St. Maurice River and in various other locations in Québec; Berlin Mills was the first woods organization to employ a private forester, first to employ the Lombard Log Hauler; during the Great Depression, it was necessary to ensure the survival of the company through arrangements with the city of Berlin, New Hampshire; established the first woods safety program and accident cases were hospitalized long before the enactment of a employer's liability law;

established the largest privately operated tree nursery in the country; at its peak, had 5,900 square miles of forest land under his immediate supervision; founded the New Hampshire Timberland Association, primarily for fire protection, founded a similar organization in Vermont; organized and wrote the constitution and by-laws of the St. Maurice Forest Protection Association, the first in Canada 1912; organized the Kennebec Fire Protective Association 1913; founded the Timberland Mutual Fire Insurance Co. 1917, which specialized in forest protection and was the first of its kind in the United States; appointed to the first New Hampshire Forestry Commission 1909, served to 1953, assisted in writing the first forestry law for New Hampshire, chairman of the commission when it conducted its first survey of the states forestry resources 1924; U.S. delegate: World Forestry Conference, Rome 1926; traveled in Finland, Sweden, Czechoslovakia, and Germany to study forest practices there; chairman: North Eastern Forest Research Council, U.S. Forest Service; raised Arabian horses on his farm in Berlin, his horses set records in the U.S. Army endurance contests and retired the Mounted Service Cup by winning three times in the first five tests; member: U.S. Remount Board from 1929; acquired a large collection of prints, paintings, and books on the horse; author: *The Horse of the Desert* 1929, *Our Forest Heritage* 1957, numerous articles on forestry.

Browne, Benjamin Patterson 1893–1976, born: Wiscasset; student: Harvard University, summer of 1924, Boston University, summers of 1926, 1927, School of Theology 1928–30, Andover-Newton Seminary 1930–32, D.D. (Hon.) Eastern Baptist Theological Seminary, Overbrook, Pennsylvania, 1947, William Jewell College 1962, L.H.D. Hillsdale College, Northern Baptist Theological Seminary 1963, Litt.D. Ottawa University 1961, Ed.D. Judson College, Elgin, Illinois, 1967; ordained Baptist minister 1912, pastor: Corliss Street Church, Bath, 1912–16, Essex Street Church, Bangor, 1916–21, First Baptist Church: Rockland, 1921–28; president: Maine United Baptist Ministers Conference 1926; minister: First Baptist Church, Winchester, Massachusetts, 1928–32, 2nd Baptist Church, Holyoke, Massachusetts, 1932–41; president: Northern Baptist Educational Society 1941–42, director of promotion, Massachusetts Baptist Convention, headquartered in the Tremont Temple, Boston 1941–44; executive secretary: Pennsylvania Baptist Convention, Philadelphia 1944–47; editorial executive: Christian publications of Board of Education and Publications: American Baptist Convention, Philadelphia 1947–62; president: Associated Church Press; president: Northern Baptist Theological Seminary 1959–62; founder, first president: Judson College, Elgin, Illinois, 1962–66, chancellor 1967–76; president: Christian Writers' Conference 1948, executive director: National Christian Writers' Guild; trustee: Lincoln Academy, Newcastle; author: *Let There Be Light* 1956, *The Writers' Conference Comes to You* 1956, *Signal Flares* 1960, *Gateway to Morning* 1961, *Tales of Baptist Daring* 1962, *Illustrations for Preaching* 1975, *Meaning of Church Membership* 1944, *Martyrs of Christ* 1945, *Magnificent Men* 1946, compiler and editor: *Christian Journalism for Today* 1952, staff editor: *Massachusetts Baptist Bulletin* 1941–44, editor:

Eminent Mainers

The Pennsylvania Baptist 1944–47, *The Baptist Leader* 1947–62; buried in Bluff City Cemetery, Elgin, Illinois.

Browne, Charles Farrar 1834–67, born: Waterford; son of a surveyor; apprenticed as a printer at the *Skowhegan Clarion*, wrote for the *Norway Advertiser-Democrat*, the *Skowhegan Clarion*, the *Boston Carpet Bag*, the *Toledo Commercial*, and, finally, the *Cleveland Plain Dealer* 1858, where he created the fictional character Artemus Ward, originally meant as filler, but soon achieved immense popularity across the country; contributing editor: *Vanity Fair*, from 1860, traveled to California and Utah collecting information on the Mormons, which became a series of lectures, with panoramic accompaniment, that were considered to the best of their type 1862; author: *Artemus Ward: His Book* 1862, *Artemus Ward: His Travels* 1865, *Artemus Ward in London* 1867; immensely popular on the lecture circuit, both in the United States and in Great Britain, he was a practitioner of the dead pan form of humor; Lincoln often turned to Ward for diversion from his cares; died in Southampton, England, buried in Elm Vale Cemetery, Waterford.

Bruce, Henry 1798– ?, born: Machias; appointed to the U.S. Navy as midshipman 1813, captured, when the USS *Frolic* was taken by HMS *Orpheus*, held prisoner in Halifax for six months; promoted to lieutenant, USN, 1823, attached to USS *Macedonian*, later to USS *Franklin*, when that ship conveyed Minister Richard Rush to Great Britain; served aboard the frigate USS *Brandywine* in the Mediterranean squadron 1837, commissioned commander, USN, 1841, commanding officer: USS *Truxtun*, captured the African slaver *Spitfire* 1845, commanded the naval rendezvous in Boston 1848–50; put on the reserve list 1855, commissioned commodore, USN, 1862, retired 1867.

Bryant, Charles Grandison 1803–50, born: Thomaston; raised in Bangor; member: Independent Volunteers (militia unit) 1827–31; housewright, designed First Baptist Church, Bangor; first person in Maine to designate himself as an architect; member: Bangor Mechanic Association, president 1832; designed and constructed, in Bangor: residences of William Emerson, Samuel Garnsey, Nathaniel Hatch, Elias Aldrich, Kent-Cutting double house, Nicholas Norcross, Samuel Smith, Dwinel double house, Poor-Appleton double house, George W. Brown, commercial structures: City Point Block, two groups of stores for Rufus Dwinel, Mercantile Bank, Mercantile Row, Bangor House, churches: Pine Street Methodist Church, Mount Hope Cemetery, the second garden cemetery in the United States; became deeply involved in the rebellion in Canada, organized the Bangor Cadets 1838, participated in the invasion of Canada from Vermont, probably received support from various lumber magnates to divert British attention from the Aroostook region; with the Canadian invasion repelled, became involved in maneuvers in the Aroostook War, possibly intending to provoke the British in order to draw in the federal government; probably designed the blockhouse in Fort Kent; removed to Galveston, Texas, 1839, designed and constructed a windmill and several bridges; charter member: Galveston Artillery Company 1840, battalion adjutant: Galveston Fusiliers, saw action in the Mexican War; designed Saint Mary's Cathedral and Galveston Prison and Court House; adjutant and commissary of three companies of Texas Rangers; murdered by a party of Lipan Apache Indians.

Bryant, John Emory 1836–1900, born: Wayne; graduate: Maine Wesleyan Seminary, Kents Hill 1859; in the Civil War: captain, 8th Maine Volunteers, served in the Sea Islands, commanded Black troops, led raids on plantations to release slaves, resigned commission 1864; studied law, member: Maine bar 1865; appointed general superintendent: Freedmen's Bureau, Augusta, Georgia, 1865, organized Georgia Equal Rights Association 1866, first president, an organizer of the Republican party in Georgia 1867, member: State Central Committee, Georgia Constitutional Convention 1868, member: Georgia House of Representatives, chairman: Public Education Committee, received much of the credit for exposing Governor Bullock to charges of fraud and corruption; appointed deputy collector of customs: Savannah 1872–77, editor: *Savannah Journal*; Republican candidate for U.S. House of Representatives 1874, 1876, Republican state chairman 1876–80; editor: *Georgia Republican*; secretary: Republican state committee 1882–84; U.S. marshal for Northern Georgia 1884–85; lecturer for the Union League; Methodist minister: Mt. Vernon, New York, 1891–95.

Bryant, Nathaniel Cushing 1823–74, born: Damariscotta Mills, Nobleboro; son of Cushing Bryant, nephew of Admiral Joseph Smith; attended Lincoln Academy; received an appointment as midshipman, USN, through intercession of Jonathan Cilley 1837, made first cruise aboard USS *Erie*, D. G. Farragut: commanding officer; aboard USS *Preble* 1840–42, stationed aboard the naval school ship (predecessor of the U.S. Naval Academy), Philadelphia 1843, commissioned passed midshipman, USN, 1843, cruise of USS *Decatur* off Brazil, detached and ordered to the depot of charts, later, acting commanding officer: sloop USS *Plymouth*, Mediterranean squadron, also officer aboard steam frigate USS *Cumberland* 1844, during the war with Mexico officer: commanding officer: USS *Dale* with the Pacific squadron, participated in the capture of Mulaje 1847, bombardment of Guaymus, participated in land operations about Cochori and Bacochivampo; acting master of the receiving ship at Boston, commissioned lieutenant, USN, aboard USS *Bainbridge* in the Brazil squadron, executive officer: steam frigate USS *San Jacinto* to Siam to negotiate treaty with King Mongkout 1855; at the outbreak of the Civil War, on duty at Navy Yard, Mare Island, California, ordered to duty with the home squadron, later aboard USS *Richmond*, assigned to construction of ironclads on Mississippi, commanding officer: USS *Cairo*, participated in the capture of Forts Henry and Donaldson; commissioned commander, USN, captured CSS *Sumter* and CSS *Bragg*; detached for sick leave, later on special duty with Admiral Gregory 1864, ordered to the West Gulf Squadron and

Pensacola Navy Yard; on duty at the ordnance station, Mound City, Illinois, later in charge of naval stores at Pensacola, retired for disability, removed to Cedar Falls, Iowa.

Buck, Alfred Eliab 1832–1902, born: Foxcroft; son of a Baptist deacon; A.B. Waterville College 1859; school teacher in Hallowell 1860, principal: Lewiston High School 1861; in the Civil War: rejected on his first enlistment, determined to serve, raised a company at his own expense, commissioned captain, USV, assigned to the 13th Maine Volunteers 1861–63, served on Ship Island on the Mississippi coast, lieutenant colonel, USV, organizer and commanding officer: 91st Colored Infantry 1864, lead his troops in the capture of Fort Blakley, Alabama, Bvt. colonel, USV, inspector general for western Louisiana to 1865; after the war, produced turpentine, until he was burned out, on Montgomery Island, Alabama; delegate: Alabama Constitutional Convention 1867, chairman: Committee on Preamble and Bill of Rights; appointed clerk of the Mobile County Court; member, president: Mobile City Council; Republican presidential elector 1868; member: U.S. House of Representatives (Republican) 1869–71; removed to Atlanta 1873; delegate: Republican National Convention 1880, 1884, 1888, chairman of the Georgia delegation 1884, 1888; director, secretary, treasurer: Tecumseh Iron Co., Cherokee County, Alabama, president: Wilson Ridge Ore Co.; clerk: U.S. District Court 1887, U.S. marshal for the Northern District of Georgia 1889–93; appointed envoy extraordinary and pinister plenipotentiary to Japan by President McKinley 1897–1902, died in Tokyo; buried in Arlington National Cemetery.

Buck, Carl Darling 1866–1955, born: Orland; A.B. Yale College ΦBK 1886, Ph.D. 1889, member: American School of Classical Studies, Athens 1887–89, student at University of Leipzig 1889–92, Ph.D. (Hon.) University of Athens 1912, Litt.D. Princeton University 1935; assistant professor of Sanskrit and Indo-European comparative literature: University of Chicago 1892–94, associate professor 1894–1900, professor 1900–03, professor and head of department 1903–33, Martin A. Ryerson distinguished service professor 1930–33; member: American Philosophical Society, American Academy of Arts and Sciences, president: American Philosophical Association 1915–16, president: American Linguistic Society 1927, 1937, a chair named in his honor was established at the University of Chicago Divinity School; author: *Vocalismus der oskischen Sprache* Leipzig 1892, *Hale-Buck Latin Grammar* 1903, *Grammar of Oscan and Umbrian* 1904, *Sketch of Linguistic Conditions in Chicago* 1903, *Introduction to the Study of Greek Dialects* 1909, *Comparative Grammar of Greek and Latin* 1933, *Reserve Index of Greek Nouns and Adjectives* 1945, *Dictionary of Selected Synonyms in the Principal Indo-European Languages* 1949.

Bucknan, Ransford D. 1869–1915, born: Hansport, Nova Scotia, raised in Bucksport, went to sea at fourteen, commanding officer: merchant ships, sail and steam, Great Lakes, Atlantic, and Pacific; superintendent: American Steel Barge Co. of New York, Pacific Mail Steamship Co. in Panama, Cramps Shipyard, Philadelphia, trial captain of USS *Maine* and Imperial Ottoman Naval Vessel *Medjidia*; naval adviser and aide-de-camp to the Sultan in Constantinople from 1904, decorated: Order of Osmanieh.

Buker, Brian L. 1949–70, born: Benton; sergeant, U.S. Army, Detachment B-55, 5th Special Forces Group, 1st Special Forces; recipient: Medal of Honor (posthumous), Chau Doc Province, Republic of Vietnam, 5 April 1970, "for conspicuous gallantry and intrepidity in action at the risk of life, above and beyond the call of duty. SGT Buker, Detachment B-55, distinguished himself while serving as platoon adviser of a Vietnamese mobile strike force company during an offensive mission. SGT Buker personally led the platoon, cleared a strategically located, well guarded pass, and established the first foothold at the top of what had been an impenetrable mountain fortress. When the platoon came under intense fire from a determined enemy located in two heavily fortified bunkers, and realizing that withdrawal would result in heavy casualties, SGT Buker unhesitatingly, and with complete disregard for his personal safety, charged through the hail of enemy fire and destroyed the first bunker with hand grenades. While reorganizing his men for the attack on the second bunker, SGT Buker was seriously wounded. Despite his wounds and the deadly enemy fire, he crawled forward and destroyed the second bunker. SGT Buker refused medical attention and was reorganizing his men to continue the attack when he was mortally wounded. As a direct result of his heroic actions, many casualties were averted, and the assault of the enemy position was successful. SGT Buker's extraordinary heroism at the cost of his life is in the highest traditions of the military service and reflect great credit upon him, his unit and the U.S. Army." Buried in Brown Cemetery, Benton.

Bumpus, Hermon Carey 1862–1942, born: Buckfield; son of a physician; removed with his family, to Dorchester, Massachusetts, where his father taught at Cullin Institution 1868; Ph.B. Brown University ΦBK 1884, Ph.D. Clark University 1891, Sc.D. (Hon.) Tufts University 1905, Brown University 1905, L.L.D. Clark University 1909; professor of biology: Olivet College 1886–89, fellow: Clark University 1889–90, assistant professor of zoology: Brown University 1890–91, associate professor 1891–92, professor of anatomy 1892–1901; assistant director: U.S. Fish Commission Marine Biology Laboratory, Woods Hole, Massachusetts, 1893–95, director 1898–1901; assistant to president and curator of department of invertebrates: American Museum of Natural History 1901–02, director 1902–11; member of faculty: Columbia University 1905–11; business manager: University of Wisconsin 1911–14; president: Tufts University 1914–19; secretary: Brown University Corporation 1924–39; director: Buffalo Museum of Science 1925–30; member: Board of Fellows, Brown University 1905–42; trustee: Woods Hole Marine Biology Laboratory from 1900, Mt. Desert Biology Laboratory from 1924; president: American Society of Zoologists 1903, Fourth International Fisheries Congress, Washington 1908, chairman: Commission on Museums in National Parks, chairman: advisory board: National Park Service 1936–40; author: *A Laboratory Course in Invertebrate Zoology* 1893, numerous articles and monographs on biology.

Burd, George Eli 1857–1924, born: Belfast; B.S. U.S. Naval Academy 1878, commissioned assistant engineer, USN, 1880, passed assistant engineer 1889, chief engineer 1898, transferred to line, lieutenant, USN, 1899, lieutenant commander, USN, 1901, commander, USN, 1906, captain, USN, 1910, rear admiral, USN, 1916; served as chief engineer: USS *Badger*, West Indies campaign, Spanish-American War; engineering officer at sea and navy yards in San Francisco, Boston, New York, Bremerton; in charge of industrial activity, construction and engineering: Navy Yard, New York, from 1914, in charge of all alterations, reconstruction, engineering and repair work on 723 vessels assigned to Third Naval District, including all troop transports used in World War I.

Burgess, Elizabeth Chamberlain 1873–1949, born: Bath; diploma: Roosevelt Hospital Nursing School, New York 1904, B.S. Columbia University 1923, A.M. 1925; assistant director and instructor: nursing schools 1905–12; director of nursing school and superintendent of nurses: Michael Reese Hospital, Chicago 1912–16; inspector of nursing schools, New York 1916–20; secretary: Board of Nurse Examiners, New York State Department of Education 1920–22; lecturer, instructor, assistant professor, associate professor, professor of nursing: Teachers College, Columbia University 1920–43; during World War I: assistant inspector of nursing service, Office of Surgeon general, USA; president: National League of Nursing Education 1929–33.

Burleigh, Edwin Chick 1843–1916, born: Linneus; grandson of a representa-

tive to the Massachusetts general court, son of the Maine state land agent; attended public school in Linneus, graduate: Houlton Academy, teacher, surveyor; in the Civil War: enlisted in the District of Columbia volunteer cavalry, but illness prevented him from joining, accepted an appointment in the office of the Maine adjutant general 1864; Maine state land agent 1865–78; assistant clerk: Maine House of Representatives 1876–78; clerk, office of Maine state treasurer 1880; Maine state treasurer 1885–89; governor of Maine 1889–93; member from the Third District: U.S. House of Representatives (Republican) 1897–1911, member: U.S. Senate 1913–1916, died in office; part owner and publisher: *Kennebec Journal* 1887–1916;

father of Clarence Blendon Burleigh; buried in Forest Grove Cemetery, Augusta.

Burleigh, John Holmes 1823–1877, born: South Berwick; son of William Burleigh; at sixteen went to sea, commanded several vessels 1846–53; woolen manufacturer in South Berwick; banking; member: Maine House of Representatives 1862, 1864, 1866, 1872; member from the First District: U.S. House of Representatives (Republican) 1873–77; buried in Portland Street Cemetery, South Berwick.

Burleigh, Walter Atwood 1820–96, born: Waterville; traveled extensively in Europe and South America, as a youth, studied medicine in New York with Dr. Valentine Mott; served as a private in the Aroostook War 1839; practiced medicine in Richmond, removed to Kittanning, Pennsylvania 1845, having campaigned vigorously for the Republican slate in 1860, was offered but declined a foreign mission but accepted the post of Yankton Sioux Indian agent, Greenwood, Dakota Territory, 1861–65, that post was, at that time, the principal depot of supplies for military posts and Indian agencies of the upper Mississippi region; with the outbreak of major hostilities with the neighboring Santee Sioux, Burleigh managed to avoid a massacre in Greenwood through his personal eloquence, directed at the Yankton Sioux and having secured, in Washington, an appropriation and 3,000 soldiers, who rendezvoused at Sioux City 1863; secured the appointment of fifty Yankton Sioux as scouts for the U.S. Army, and saw to their proper compensation; Dakota territorial delegate: U.S. House of Representatives (Republican) 1865–69, associated with measures beneficial to the development of the West, the building of a northern, transcontinental railroad route and reforms in the treatment of the Indians; member: Dakota Territorial Council 1877–79; removed to Miles City, Montana, 1879, practiced law, member: Montana Territorial Council 1887, delegate: Montana Constitutional Convention 1889, member: first Montana House of Representatives; prosecuting attorney, Custer County 1889–90, returned to South Dakota, member: South Dakota Senate 1893; buried in Yankton (South Dakota) Cemetery.

Burnham, Hiram 1814–64, born: Narraguagus (later Cherryfield); Washington County commissioner, coroner, lumberman; in the Civil War: helped recruit and made colonel of the 6th Maine Volunteers 1861, which suffered heavy casualties in the Peninsula campaign as part of Hancocks brigade in Smiths IV Corps, later, as part of the VI Corps, saw action at Antietam, in the Chancellorsville campaign, lost heavily at Fredericksburg, taking Maryes Heights, in reserve at Gettysburg, fought gallantly in the Overland campaign 1864; commissioned brigadier general, USV, 1864; commanded a brigade in the XVIII Corps; killed leading a probing attack at Fort Harrison, below Chaffin's Bluff, in the Petersburg campaign; buried in Pine Grove Cemetery, Cherryfield.

Eminent Mainers

Burpee, William Partridge 1846–1940, born: Rockland; graduate: Maine Wesleyan Seminary, Kents Hill; exhibited at Pennsylvania Academy of Fine Art, Corcoran Gallery, Washington, D.C., Museum of Fine Arts, St. Louis, Art Institute of Chicago; most notable works include: *Evening at Gloucester, Snow Covered Rocks at Sunset, Forge of Vulcan.*

Burrage, Champlin 1874–1951, born: Portland; son of Henry S. Burrage; A.B. Brown University ΦBK 1896, A.M. 1905, B.D. Newton Theological Institution 1898, student at universities of Berlin and Marburg 1899–1901, Oxford University 1906–15, B.Litt. Oxford University 1909; historical research in English libraries 1901–15, librarian: Manchester College, Oxford University 1912–15; librarian: John Carter Brown library, Brown University and member of faculty 1915–17; historical archaeology and philological research in American libraries and museums 1915–20; author: *A New Year's Guilt by Robert Browne, 1588* 1904, *The Church Covenant Idea* 1904, *The True Story of Robert Browne* 1906, *The Retraction of Robert Browne* 1907, *New Facts Concerning John Robinson* 1910, *The Early English Dissenters in the Light of Recent Research* 1912, *John Penrym the So-Called Martyr of Congregationalism* 1913, *Nazareth and the Beginnings of Christianity* 1914, *John Pory's Lost Description of the Plymouth Colony* 1918, *An Answer to John Robinson of Leyden* 1920, *The Minoan Hieroglyphic Inscriptions, 1; The Phaestos Whorl* (reprinted from *Harvard Studies in Classical Philology*, vol. 32, 1921, this work is believed to contain a considerable number of first readings from the prehistoric Cretan inscriptions), *Studies in the Hieroglyphic Inscriptions and Pictographs of Minoan Crete and Neighboring Countries and Islands*; contributor: *English Historical Review, American Journal of Theology, Harvard Theology Review*, &c.; collector: Henry S. Burrage Collection: Colgate University library (relics of mound builders of Ohio, Muskingum Valley, and Blennerhasset Island regions) and the Burrage Collection of Cretan Antiquities from 1927, compiler and editor: *Seaman's Handbook for Shore Leave* 1919; made Minoan and Hittite investigations in Ashmolean Museum, British Museum, and museums in Athens and Candia; made first archaeological investigation in Crete 1926–27.

Burrage, Henry Sweetser 1837–1926, born: Fitchburg, Massachusetts; A.M. Brown University 1861, graduate: Newton Theological Institution 1867, student: University of Halle 1868–69, D.D. Brown University 1883, L.L.D. (Hon.) University of Maine 1922; served as sergeant major, second lieutenant, first lieutenant, captain, and major: 36th Massachusetts Infantry, USV, 1862–65; ordained Baptist minister 1869, pastor: Waterville 1870–73, editor: *Zion's Advocate* 1873–1905, chaplain: National Home for Disabled Soldiers, Togus 1905–12, Maine state historian from 1907, president: Maine Baptist Educational Society 1893–98; trustee: Colby College, Newton Theological Institution, Brown University; author: *The Act of Baptism in the History of the Christian Church* 1879, *History of the Baptists in New England* 1894, *Gettysburg and Lincoln* 1906, *Early English and French Voyages* 1923, *Thomas Hamlin Hub-*

bard Bvt. Brigadier General, USV 1923, editor: *History of the Thirty Sixth Massachusetts Volunteers* 1884, *Rosier's Relation of Weymouth's Voyage to the Coast of Maine 1605* 1887; father of Champlin Burrage.

Burroughs, George *c.*1650–92, born: possibly either in Scituate or in Salem, Massachusetts; A.B. Harvard College 1670; Congregational minister at the First Parish, Falmouth (that portion that is now Portland) by 1674, escaped, along with other settlers, to Bangs (now Cushing) Island to avoid death and dismemberment by the Indians in their great raid of 1676, wrote of his vicissitudes to Henry Jocelyn, of Black Point, later this most detailed account of the raid was sent to the governor and council in Boston; invited to preach at Salem, Massachusetts, 1680, called by that town, which had been quite unhappy with his predecessor 1681, after falling into a debt, occasioned by the funeral expenses of his wife, being unable to collect his salary and finally having suit brought against him (later dropped), Burroughs, despairing of the spiritual condition of Salem, removed back to Falmouth 1683; relinquished a tract of land that had been granted to him, prior to the raid, to assist the town in its efforts to rebuild itself; preached before the general assembly in York 1686; before having to flee, once more, the destruction wrought by the French and their Indian allies in 1690, Burroughs had become a well-respected and trusted inhabitant of Falmouth; subsequent to the raid, Burroughs removed to Wells, where he preached until he was accused of witchcraft by the authorities in Salem, arrested and returned to that place, where he was put on trial, accused of consorting with the devil, feats of uncanny strength, and other acts of a diabolical nature; after his conviction, he was taken, with four others, to Gallows Hill and hanged, in a ceremony presided over by Cotton Mather.

Burton, Alfred Edgar 1857–1935, born: Portland; son of a banker; B.S. Bowdoin College 1878, C.E. 1881, D.Sci.(Hon.) 1913; draftsman and topographer: U.S. Coast and Geodetic Survey 1879–82; instructor: Massachusetts Institute of Technology 1882–84, assistant and associate professor 1884–96, professor of topographic engineering: Massachusetts Institute of Technology from 1896, dean from 1902; member: Massachusetts Topographic Survey Commission 1895–1900, in conjunction with his classmate at Bowdoin College, Robert E. Peary, in charge of scientific expeditions to Omanak, North Greenland 1896, effected the removal of the 36.5-ton Cape York meteorite to the American Museum of Natural History, New York; organized and led an eclipse expedition to Washington, Georgia, 1900, Sumatra 1901; Bowdoin College overseer from 1905; fellow: American Academy of Arts and Sciences; author of extensive reports on his various expeditions for *Technology Quarterly*, editor: *Pendulum and the Magnetic Observations in Greenland* 1897; in World War I: asked the U.S. Shipping Board to establish and furnish instructors and plan the work of thirty navigation schools on the Atlantic, Pacific, and Gulf coasts and on the Great Lakes; fellow: American Academy of Arts and Sciences.

Bush, Dorothy Walker 1901–92, born: Kennebunkport; daughter of a dry-goods merchant and investment banker; raised in St. Louis, Missouri, married Prescott Bush in Kennebunkport 1921, had five children, the second being George Herbert Walker Bush, forty-first president of the United States; while her husband was a member of the U.S. Senate, she wrote a newspaper column, "Washington Life of a Senator's Wife, "which was distributed to twenty Connecticut newspapers; a versatile athlete, she excelled in baseball, basketball, track, and tennis, she was runner-up in the girls' national tennis championship in Merion, Pennsylvania; moments before she left to give birth to her first child, she hit a homer in a family baseball game.

Butler, Edward Burgess 1853–1927, born: Lewiston; son of a dry-goods merchant; at age sixteen, employed by a wholesale dry-goods merchant in Boston, after six years experience as a bundle boy, packer, and entry clerk and traveling salesman; with brothers George H. Butler and Charles H. Butler, founded Butler Brothers, Boston 1877, later, relocated to Chicago, dealers in notions and small wares, originated, in 1878, the concept of the 5 Cent Store, developed and refined the concept of the department store; rather than send out salesmen, as was then the usual approach, sent out a complete catalogue, entitled *Our Drummer*, supplier to 5 Cent Stores across the country, later had hotels in New York, Chicago, Saint Louis, Minneapolis, Dallas; president: Glenwood (Illinois) Manual Training School; trustee: Hull House Social Settlement, Art Institute of Chicago, Chicago Orphan Asylum, Rockford College, director of the Corn Exchange National Bank; possessed one of the finest private collections of art in Chicago and a remarkable collection of Civil War and Revolutionary War autograph letters and documents, as well as photographs; after his retirement to Pasadena, devoted himself to painting, in the impressionist style, his work was well-regarded and hang in several museums.

Butler, Nathaniel 1853–1927, born: Eastport; son of a Baptist minister; A.B. Colby College 1873, A.M. 1876, D.D. 1895; associate principal: Ferry Hall Female College, Lake Forest, Illinois 1873–76, Highland Hall College for Women 1876–79, principal 1880–84, master: Yale School for Boys, Chicago 1879–80; ordained Baptist minister 1884; professor of rhetoric and English literature: University of Chicago 1884–86, professor of Latin 1886–89, professor of English language and literature: University of Illinois 1889–92; sixth president: Colby College 1895–1901; dean, college of education: University of Chicago 1905–09, dean: University College, University of Chicago 1916–23; author: *The Study of Latin* 1883, *Bellum Helveticum* 1889.

Butman, Samuel 1788–1864, born: Worcester, Massachusetts; son of a soldier in the American Revolution, who removed to Dixmont 1804; farmer; served as a captain of militia in the War of 1812, established several mills in Dixmont Center; delegate: Maine Constitutional Convention 1819, member: Maine House of Representatives 1822, 1826, 1827, member: U.S. House of Representatives (Democrat) 1827–31;

Penobscot County commissioner 1846; member: Maine Senate, president 1853; died in Plymouth.

Buxton, Benjamin Flint 1810–76, born: Warren; son of Edmund Buxton, the first physician to settle in Warren; studied medicine with his father, another physician in Waldoboro, M.D. Medical College of Maine 1830, returned to Warren, known to travel ten miles on snowshoes to attend a birth; removed to California in 1849 to mine for gold; finding the actual labors of mining disagreeable, he sold supplies of all sorts to the miners, returned to Maine to purchase a ship and supplies, on the return, the ship was wrecked on Cape St. Lucas; all aboard were rescued and taken to Acapulco, where he established a floating hospital, which he administered for a year; returning to Maine, via Panama, he contracted Chagres fever, which left him debilitated for some time; in the Civil War: despite his opposition to the war, was appointed surgeon of the 5th Maine Regiment of Volunteers, captured at the first battle of Bull Run, where luck would have it, he was a friend of the Confederate commander General Beauregard, who placed him at his right side at dinner; after tending to federal wounded and conducting them to Richmond, he was paroled; after running a hospital for wounded soldiers in Augusta, he returned to his regiment and served until he, too, was invalided out; president: Maine Medical Association 1871, author of several papers on sundry medical issues.

Cameron, Ralph Henry 1863–1953, born: Southport; son of the owner of a fishing schooner; attended public school in Southport, until the age of thirteen; fisherman on the Grand Banks, &c. 1876–81, clerked in Hovey's Store, Boston 1882, removed to Arizona 1883, employed at Reardon's sawmill, near Flagstaff; partner with Thomas F. McMillon in raising sheep 1884, partner with John Lind in a grocery business, drove cattle to Kansas feeding lots; discovered the Last Chance Copper Mine, located 2,500 feet below the rim of the Grand Canyon, in association with this, located and constructed the Cameron (now Bright Angel) trail into the Grand Canyon; sheriff of Coconino County 1891, 1894–98; associated with Bucky O'Neal in putting through the first rail line to the canyon 1901, the line running from Williams to El Tovar; honorary chief of the Navaho Nation, who greatly esteemed his tracking abilities; member: Coconino County board of supervisors 1904–08, chairman 1906–08; delegate: Republican National Convention, Saint Louis 1896; territorial delegate: U.S. House of Representatives (Republican) 1909–12, as such, led the forces of statehood in the U.S. Congress and spoke eloquently on the floor, in their favor; unsuccessful candidate for U.S. Senate 1911, governor 1914; member: U.S. Senate 1921–27, member: Indian Affairs, Irrigation and Reclamation, and Military Affairs Committees; while in Congress, he was instrumental in obtaining grants of money for the development and reclamation of thousands of acres of desert, secured passage of the Cameron-San Carlos Bill which authorized the construction of the Coolidge Dam on the Gila River, unsuccessful in obtaining authorization of major hydroelectric projects in the Grand Canyon; unsuccessful candidate for reelection 1925, unsuccessful candidate for U.S. Senate 1928; during World War II: engaged in mica mining in California, Georgia, and North Carolina; buried at the head of the Bright Angel trail.

Canham, Erwin Dain 1904–82, born: Auburn; A.B. Bates College 1925, Litt.D. 1946, A.B., A.M. Oxford University (Rhodes scholar), recipient of numerous honorary degrees; reporter: *Christian Science Monitor* 1925, covered annual sessions of the League of Nations 1926–28, chief correspondent for *Christian Science Monitor* at League of Nations naval conference 1930, correspondent: Geneva 1930–32, head of Washington bureau 1932–39, general news editor 1939–41, managing editor 1941–44, editor 1945–64, editor in chief 1964–74; chairman: U.S. delegation, United Nations conference on freedom of information; alternate delegate: United Nations general assembly 1949; chairman: Federal Reserve Bank, Boston 1962–67; president: Boston Public Library from 1968; trustee: Bates College, Wellesley College, Simmons College; commander: Order of the British Empire, officer, French Legion of Honor, Order of George I (Greece); chairman of the board: U.S. Chamber of Commerce 1960; author: *Awakening: The World at Mid-Century* 1951, *New Frontiers for Freedom* 1954, *Commitment to Freedom* 1958, *The Christian Science Way of Life*, *A Christian Scientist's Life* 1962, editor: *Man's Great Future.*

Canning, Effie Carlton Crockett 1856–1940, born: Rockland; at age fifteen composed the music for *Rock-A-Bye-Baby*, an English poem first popular in the 1660s; fearing her father's reaction, it was originally published anonymously; buried in Mount Feake Cemetery, Waltham, Massachusetts.

Cargill, Oscar 1898–1972, born: Livermore Falls; son of a teacher; B.S. Wesleyan University ΦBK 1922, student: Stanford University 1924–25, Ph.D. Columbia University 1930, D.Litt. (Hon.) New York University 1967, L.H.D. Ohio University 1968; instructor in English: Michigan State College 1922–23, Marietta College 1923–25, New York University 1925–30, Cutting traveling fellow: Columbia University 1927–28, associate professor of English: New York University 1930–45, professor 1945–66, chairman: department of English 1949–63, head: graduate department of English 1956–63, originally a medievalist, Cargill was a pioneer in the study of American literature and criticism, drawing many eminent scholars to the department, with the result that it became one of the best known in the country; director: New York University American Civilization Program 1948–65; conducted first class in composition by closed-circuit television 1955–56; director: New York University Press 1957–65; director: Works Progress Administration *Index to American Periodicals* 1932–39; contributing editor, English texts: MacMillan Co. 1935–63; general editor: Gotham Library from 1959; member: poetry jury: National Book Award 1954; author: *Drama and Literature* 1930, *Highways in College Composition* 1930, *Intellectual America* 1942, *New Highways in College Composition* 1943, *Novels of Henry James* 1961, *Toward* *a Pluralistic Criticism* 1965; editor: Walt Whitman's *The Wound Dresser* 1949, Walt Whitman's *Leaves of Grass* 1950, Thoreau's *Selected Writings on Nature and Poetry* 1952, *The Wolfe-Watt Correspondence* 1953, Henry James's *Daisy Miller and Washington Square* 1956, *Studies in the English Renaissance Drama* 1959, *ONeill and His Plays* 1961, *The Ambassadors* 1962, *The Portrait of a Lady* 1963, *The Octopus* 1964.

Carleton, James Henry 1814–73, born: Lubec, his parents having fled the British occupation of Eastport; had literary aspirations as a young man, corresponded with Charles Dickens, among others; served as a lieutenant of militia in the Aroostook War 1839; appointed second lieutenant, USA, assigned to the 1st U.S. Dragoons 1839, with Kearney on the Rocky Mountain Expedition 1846, on General Wool's staff during Mexican War, brevetted for gallantry at Buena Vista, participated in several Indian expeditions, transferred to 1st U.S. Cavalry, 3 August 1861, raised the California Brigade, which he marched across the Yuma and Gila deserts to Mesilla on the Rio Grande in order to thwart a Confederate invasion, clashed with Mangas Coloradas and Cochise in Apache Pass in July 1862, brigadier general USV; relieved Canby as military governor of New Mexico 1862; dealt very harshly with the Navahos, directed his subordinate, Kit Carson, to drive the tribe to their new reservation in Bosque Redondo, New Mexico, where many died, before they were allowed to return to their traditional lands; brevetted to major general, USV, and major general, USA; appointed lieutenant colonel of the 4th Cavalry 1866, on active duty until his death in San Antonio; author: *The Battle of Buena Vista, with the Operations of the Army of Occupation for One Month* 1848; buried in Mt. Auburn Cemetery, Cambridge, Massachusetts; his son, Henry Guy Carleton, became a distinguished playwright in New York.

Carr, James 1777–1818, born: Bangor; son of Francis Carr; student: Phillips Academy, Exeter, Byfield Academy; clerk on board USS *Crescent*; secretary to U.S. consul in Algiers; member: Massachusetts House of Representatives 1806–11, member from the Seventeenth District: U.S. House of Representatives (Federalist) 1815–17; drowned in the Ohio River, body not recovered, cenotaph in Mount Hope Cemetery, Bangor.

Carroll, Gladys Hasty 1904–99, born: Rochester, New York; graduate: Berwick Academy, A.B. Bates College 1925; settled in York; author: *Land Spell* 1930, *As The Earth Turns* (nominated for a Pulitzer Prize, made into a movie) 1933, *A Few Foolish Ones* 1935, *Neighbor to the Sky* 1937, *West of the Hill* 1949, *Christmas Without Johnny* 1950, *Dunnybrook* 1952, *Only Fifty Years Ago* 1962, *To Remember Forever: The Journal of a College Girl 1922-23* 1963, *The Road Grows Strange* 1965, *The Light Here Kindled* 1967, *New England Sees It Through; Mist on the Mirror* 1969, *Christmas Through the Years* 1969, *Years Away from Home* 1972, *Unless You Die Young* 1977, *The Book That Came Alive* 1979, *Come with Me Home* 1980, *Wings of Berwick Academy* 1992.

Carson, Rachel Louise 1907–64, born: Springdale, Pennsylvania; daughter of a real estate and insurance agent; attended public schools in Springvale and Parnassus, Pennsylvania; A.B. Pennsylvania College for Women 1929, D.Litt. (Hon.) 1952, A.M. Johns Hopkins University 1932, D.Litt. Smith College 1953, D.Sc. Oberlin College 1952, D.L. Drexel Institute of Technology 1952; graduate student: Woods Hole Oceanographic Laboratory, Woods Hole Oceanographic Institution various times after 1929; assistant in zoology: Johns Hopkins University, summers of 1930–36; assistant in zoology: University of Maryland 1931–36; aquatic biologist: U.S. Bureau of Fisheries, later the U.S. Fish and Wildlife Service 1936–52; editor in chief: U.S. Fish and Wildlife Service 1949–52; during World War II: participated with the Fish and Wildlife Service in a program calling for an investigation of undersea sounds, life, and terrain to aid the U.S. Navy in developing techniques and equipment for submarine detection, and during the course of the program, she accompanied oceanographic expeditions to the North Atlantic and Florida waters; recipient: Guggenhiem Fellowship 1951–52; author: "Under the Sea," an article for the *Atlantic Monthly* 1937, at the request of the publishing house of Simon & Schuster, she expanded the article to the book *Under the Sea Wind* 1941, *The Sea Around Us* 1951, which reached the bestseller lists, *The Edge of the Sea* 1956, *Silent Spring* 1962, which set off a storm of criticism and spurred President Kennedy to authorize his Science Advisory Committee to investigate her thesis, which they found to be largely correct, many consider this to be the birth of the modern ecology movement; lived, part-time, in Southport, where she did much of her research and writing.

Carter, Granville Wellington 1920–92, born: Augusta; student: Coburn Classical Institute 1938–39, Portland School of Fine Art and Applied Art 1944–45, National Academy of Design 1945–48, *Grand Chaumiere de Paris* 1954; lecturer and sculptor: Washington Cathedral and Hofstra University 1966–92, instructor: National Academy School of Fine Arts 1967–92; important works include: heroic-size limestone Archangels Michael and Gabriel at South Transept, Washington Cathedral, portrait medals for Hall of Fame, New York: Stonewall Jackson, James Fenimore Cooper, Thomas Edison, Jane Addams, George Washington, official sesquicentennial medal for the state of Maine, heroic-size bust of Charles A. Lindbergh, heroic-sized bust of Chaing Kai-shek, monumental bronze bust of Alexander Stewart, heroic-sized equestrian monument of General Casimir Pulaski, Coach John Heisman; recipient first prize: National Academy of Design 1946, Louis Comfort Tiffany fellow 1954.

Carter, Luther Cullen 1805–75, born: Bethel; merchant in New York; member: New York board of education 1853; farmer on Long Island; member: U.S. House of Representatives 1859–61 (Union Republican), chairman: Committee on District of Columbia; unsuccessful candidate for reelection 1860; buried in Green-Wood Cemetery, Brooklyn.

Carter, Robert Goldthwaite 1845–1936, born: Bridgton; in the Civil War: enlisted as a private soldier 1862–64, graduate: U.S. Military Academy 1870; as second lieutenant, USA, 4th Cavalry, USA, recipient: Medal of Honor, Brazos River, Texas, 10 October 1871, "Held the left of the line with a few men during the charge of a large body of Indians, after the right of the line had retreated, and by delivering a rapid fire, succeeded in checking the enemy until other troops came to the rescue." Obtained the rank of brevet captain, USA, before retirement for disability 1876; author: *Col. Thomas Goldthwait—Was He a Tory?* 1895, *Four Brothers in Blue: or, Sunshine and Shadows of the War of Rebellion, The Old Sergeant's Story; Winning the West from the Indians and Bad Men in 1870–76*; buried in Arlington National Cemetery.

Carter, Worrall Reed 1885–1975, born aboard the family clipper ship *Storm King*, in the Pacific Ocean, raised in Yarmouth; B.S. U.S. Naval Academy 1908, A.M. Columbia 1915; commissioned ensign, USN, 1908, advanced through the ranks to commodore 1944; commanding officer: submarines C-5 1911–12, D-3 1912–13, L-11 1915–17; member of the U.S. Navy mission to Brazil 1925-29, commanding officer: USS *Osbourne* 1927–29, USS *Nokomis* 1931–33, USS *Marblehead* 1936–38, commanding officer: U.S. Naval Station, Guantanamo, Cuba 1938–40, commanding officer: Submarine Squadron Four 1940–41, chief of staff of Battleships, Battle Force 1941–42, commanding officer: naval service squadron (Admiral Nimitzs secret floating support of Pacific Fleet in its drive across the Pacific) 1942–45, retired as rear admiral, USN, 1947; decorated: Distinguished Service Medal, Legion of Merit, various area medals.

Cartier, Arthur Jean Baptiste 1886–1953, born: Biddeford; son of an insurance agent; attended public schools in Biddeford, student: Boston Universty 1905–06, L.L.B. University of Maine 1909, L.L.M. 1914; member: Maine bar 1909, practiced in Biddeford to 1912, Biddeford city solicitor 1910-12; member: Massachusetts bar 1911, practiced in Fall River 1912–32, removed to Boston, member: Cartier, Doherty & O'Brien 1932–34; assistant U.S. attorney 1934–47, U.S. marshal 1947–53; president: Belmont Realty Co., gave lectures on how to detect counterfeit currency; unsuccessful Democratic candidate for the U.S. House of Representatives 1916, 1918, 1920, 1922, 1924, unsuccessful candidate for state auditor 1919; delegate-at-large: Democratic National Convention 1924.

Carver, Clifford Nickels 1891–1965, born: Searsport; graduate: Lawrenceville School, Litt.B. Princeton University 1913, research student: Trinity College, Cambridge 1913–14, L.L.D. (Hon.) Bates College 1963; secretary to American ambassador, London 1914–15, aide to Colonel E. M. House on his mission to Europe for Woodrow Wilson 1915–16; assistant to Bernard Baruch in the Council of National Defense 1917; commissioned lieutenant (junior grade) USNR 1917, on duty: Office of Naval Intelligence, Washington 1917–18; aide to Rear Admiral Roger Welles;

attached to USS *Rochester* on convoy duty; chairman: Baker, Carver and Morrell, Inc., shippers and freight forwarders; decorated: chevalier, Order of the Crown (Belgium), commander, Order of St. Olaf (Norway).

Cary, Annie Louise 1841–1921, born: Wayne; daughter of a physician; graduate: Gorham Female Academy 1862, at age eighteen, removed to Boston where she sang contralto and mezzo-soprano in church choirs, began to appear in concerts in various cities in New England; at age twenty-four, removed to Europe to study voice, engaged to sing in an opera company in Copenhagen, toured in Gottenburg, Christiana, and Stockholm, later sang in Brussels, Hamburg, and other cities in Germany, appeared with considerable success with the Italian Opera Company in London, associated with the Italian Opera Company at the New York Academy of Music; first American woman to sing a Wagnerian role in the United States; toured Russia; retired 1882, Maine's first *prima donna*; donor of the Cary Memorial Library, Wayne.

Cary, Austin 1865–1936, born: East Machias, brother of George Foster Cary; A.B. Bowdoin College 1887, A.M. 1890, studied biology at Johns Hopkins University and Princeton University 1888–91, D.Sc. (Hon.) Bowdoin College 1922; instructor of geology and biology: Bowdoin College 1887–88; in the employ of the Maine forest commission and the forestry division of the U.S. Department of Agriculture 1893–96; forester: Berlin Mills Corp., Portland 1898–1904; instructor: Yale University Forestry School 1904–05; assistant professor of forestry: Harvard University 1905–09; New York state forester 1909–10; chief forester: U.S. Forest Service 1910–35; author: *Woodsman's Manual* 1909.

Cary, Charles Austin 1890– ?, born: Machias, son of George Foster Cary, nephew of Austin Cary; student: Washington Academy 1902–06, A.B. *magna cum laude* Bowdoin College φBK 1910, A.M. (Hon.) 1950, L.L.D. (Hon.), S.B. Massachusetts Institute of Technology 1912; member: engineering department: Electric Bond & Share Co., New York 1912–17, assistant to chief engineer 1917–18; with E. I. DuPont de Nemours & Co. 1918–55, assistant manager: nylon division 1940–44, manager 1944–45, assistant general manager: nylon department 1945–46, vice president, member: executive committee 1947–55, director from 1947, retired 1955; chairman of the board: International Freighting Corp. 1948–55; director: Delaware Power & Light Co.; Bowdoin College trustee.

Cary, Shepard 1805–66, born: New Salem, Massachusetts; removed to Houlton 1822; merchant, lumberman, farmer; member: Maine House of Representatives 1832, 1833, 1839–42, 1848–49, 1862; Democratic presidential elector 1836; member: Maine Senate 1843, 1850–53; member: U.S. House of Representatives, 7th District (Democrat) 1844–45, Liberty party candidate for governor 1854; buried in Evergreen Cemetery, Houlton.

Casey, Edward Pearce 1864–1940, born: Portland; son of General Thomas Lincoln Casey, great grandson of Major General Silas Casey; C.E. Columbia University 1886, Ph.B. 1888, student: École des Beaux Arts, Paris for three years, architect for completion of Library of Congress 1892–97, prize winner: New York City Hall competition 1893, joined with William Burr in competing for design of Memorial Bridge, Washington, D.C., on first prize 1900, 1st Prize: Grant memorial 1902, designed Constitution Hall, Connecticut Avenue viaduct, Commodore Barry memorial, New York state monument: Antietam and Gettysburg, several buildings for the American University, Beirut.

Caswell, Mary Deering 1848–1925, born: Paris; orphaned at an early age; student: Bridgton and Fryeburg Academies, Waynflete School; taught at Portland High School; founder and principal: Caswell School, Portland 1883–89, founder and principal: Marlborough School for Girls, Los Angeles, from 1889; an ardent horsewoman, she required her students to be proficient in equitation; she is regarded as the first art historian in Southern California, lecturing both at her school and in public on various art matters, lead art history tours in Europe; an ardent antisuffragist, spoke against the proposed 19th Amendment at legislative hearings and large public meetings and contributed articles to newspapers and periodicals; author: *An Average Boy's Vacation* 1876, *Letters to Hetty Heedless and Others* 1880, *Address in Opposition to Women's Suffrage* 1913, *The Marlborough Course in Art History* 1919.

Cayvan, Georgia Eva 1858–1906, born: Bath; daughter of a merchant sailor, who was lost at sea, and Mother Cayvan, the owner of a small candy store; began giving readings and recitations at age fourteen, appeared as Hebe in an early production of *H.M.S. Pinafore* in Boston 1879, studied elocution with Lewis Monroe, had professional debut as Dolly Dutton in *Hazel Kirke* at Madison Square Theatre 1880, appeared as Daisy Brown, with William Gillette in his *The Professor*, the principal female role in *Oedipus Tyrannus*, played Lisa in *White Stone*, Dara in *Siberia*, Hattie in *Old Shipmates*, Lura in *Romany Rye*, leading lady in California Theatre, San Francisco; leading lady for Daniel Frohman, who created for her, the roles of Hattie, in *Old Shipmates*, Minnie Gilfillin in *Sweet Lavender*, Ann Cruger in *The Charity Ball*, Lady Harding in *The Idler*, Zepher Elaine in *Nerves*, Camilla Brent in *Lady Bountiful*, Katherine Thorpe in *Squire Kate*, Florence Winthrop in *Americans Abroad*, Lady Nollie in *The Amazon* 1887–94; after a failed attempt at creating her own company, with Lionel Barrymore, and being named correspondent in a divorce case 1896, left the stage and descended into madness; died in a sanitarium on Long Island, New York.

Chadbourne, Paul Ansel 1823–83, born: North Berwick; orphaned at age thirteen, worked on a neighbor's farm in the summer and learned the carpenter's trade, when not attending district school, apprenticed to a druggist in Great Falls, New Hampshire, where he acquired knowledge of chemistry; graduate: Phillips Academy, Exeter, supported himself copying legal papers; A.B. Williams College 1848, graduated first in his class, L.L.D. (Hon.) 1868, D.D. Amherst College 1872; taught school in Freehold, New Jersey, principal: Great Falls (New Hampshire) High School 1850, tutor: Williams College 1851, principal: East Windsor (Connecticut) Academy, studied theology at Theological Seminary of Connecticut, licensed to preach 1853, first dean of botany and chemistry: Williams College 1853, professor of chemistry and natural history: Bowdoin College, dean: Medical School of Maine 1852–58, also lectured at Berkshire Medical College, Mount Holyoke Seminary, Smithsonian Institution, Lowell Institute, Western Reserve College; member: Massachusetts Senate 1865, founding president: Massachusetts Agriculture College (later University of Massachusetts) 1866–67, 1882–83, president: University of Wisconsin 1867–70, president: Williams College 1872–81; editor: *The Wealth of the United States* 1882, *Public Service of New York* 1882, author: *Lectures in Natural History, Its Relation to Intellect, Taste, Wealth and Religion* (Smithsonian Institution) 1859, *Lectures on Natural Theology* (Lowell Institution) 1860, *Instinct in Animal and Men* 1872, *Strength of Men and Stability of Nations* 1872, *Hope of Righteousness* 1877; conducted exploring and scientific expeditions to Newfoundland 1855, Florida 1857, and Greenland 1861; delegate: Republican National Convention 1876, Republican presidential elector 1880.

Chamberlain, Joshua Lawrence 1828–1914, born: Brewer; son and grandson

of citizen-soldiers, nephew of Ebenezer Mattoon Chamberlain; attended the military academy of Major Whiting in Ellsworth, A.B. Bowdoin College ΦBK 1852, A.M. 1855, L.L.D. (Hon.) College of Pennsylvania 1866, Bowdoin College 1869; student: Bangor Theological Seminary 1855; instructor in logic and natural theology: Bowdoin College 1855–56, professor of rhetoric and oratory 1856–61, 1865–66; professor of modern language 1861–65; given a leave of absence in order to study in Europe, instead, went to Augusta, met with Gov. Israel Washburn, Jr., and was commissioned lieutenant colonel, USV, assigned to the 20th Maine Infantry, August 1862, colonel, USV, May 1863; participated in the battles of Antietam, Fredericksburg, Chancellorsville, Gettysburg, recipient: Medal of Honor, "daring heroism and great tenacity in holding his position on Little Round Top against repeated assaults and carrying the advance position on Big Round Top," commanding officer: 3rd brigade, V Corps, Spotsylvania, Cold Harbor, brigadier general, USV, June 1864 for meritorious and efficient services and specially gallant conduct, brevetted major general, USV, March 1865 for conspicuous gallantry, this brevet promotion was the only battlefield promotion made by General Grant during the entire war; commanding officer: 1st Division, V Corps; commanding officer: surrender parade, Appomattox, Chamberlain's conduct of the surrender, wherein he had his detail salute the defeated Confederate infantry, elicited a tremendous response and did much to begin the healing process after the war; elected twenty-sixth governor of Maine (Republican) 1866–71; sixth president of Bowdoin College 1871–83; professor of mental and moral philosophy: Bowdoin College 1874–79, lecturer on political science and public law 1879–85; major general of Maine Militia 1876, his wise and, sometime, heroic actions in Augusta during January 1880, averted a possible civil war between Fusionists and Republicans in the absence of a civil government; involved in real estate development in Florida 1888–92; surveyor of the Port of Portland, U.S. Customs 1900–14; trustee: Bowdoin College 1867–1914, overseer ex officio 1871–83, president: General Alumni Association 1867–72; son-in-law of George Eliasheb Adams; author: *Maine, Her Place in History* 1877, *The Passing of the Armies* 1915; buried in Pine Grove Cemetery, Brunswick.

Chamberlain, Weston Percival 1871–1948, born: Bristol, son of a merchant; graduate: Lincoln Academy, A.B. Bowdoin College ΦBK 1893, M.D. Harvard University Medical School 1897; interned: Massachusetts General Hospital, commissioned first lieutenant USA Medical Corps 1898, assistant surgeon: Fortress Monroe, Virginia, promoted through the ranks to colonel 1917, in the Spanish-American War: served in Cuba, then posted to the Philippines 1899, stationed on the hospital ship USS *Relief*, serving as executive officer, stationed at Fort Adams, Newport, Rhode Island, 1901-03, Cabana Barracks, Havana, Cuba, 1903–04, returned to the Philippines for two years, surgeon: Jackson Barracks, New Orleans, made one of the first studies of the incidence of hookworm in Southern recruits, returned to the Philippines 1910, president of the board for the study of tropical disease, investigated the prevention and cure of beri beri, the effects of emetin and ultra-violet light on amoebae, the influence of the tropical climate on white men; detailed to the London School of Tropical Medicine, graduate 1912; surgeon: Plattsburg (New York) Barracks 1912–16, assistant surgeon: Fort Sam Houston, Texas, during the mobilization of troops on the Mexican border, directly involved in initiating and developing an efficient system of border hospitals; in World War I: detailed to Harvard University Medical School where he was instructor in military medicine, later on duty in the office of the surgeon general in Washington 1917–22; chief sanitary officer, USA, given high marks for his conduct during the influenza epidemic; graduate: Army War College 1923, commandant: Army Medical School, Washington, during his administration, the school moved to new quarters on the Walter Reed Hospital reservation; chief health officer, Panama Canal Zone 1924–29, achieved the lowest rates of malaria and yellow fever infection, to date, constructed the Corozal hospital for the insane, Palo Saxo leper colony, many sanitary improvements in Panama City; chief of the professional service division, office of the surgeon general 1929–33.

Chambers, Charles Augustus 1873– ?, born: Portland; student in public schools in Arkansas and Louisiana; trained in horticulture in California with George C. Roeding, with nursery business in Fresno from 1891, with Fancher Creek Nurseries ten years; secretary, treasurer: Fresno Nursery Co. twelve years, later manager: nursery department, Luther Burbank Co. of San Francisco; industrial agent: Memphis, Dallas & Gulf Railway Co.; regarded as the greatest authority on horticulture and agriculture on Pacific Coast; contributor to horticultural journals and widely known for his often-amusing stories in the agricultural press.

Champagne, David B. 1932–52, born: Waterville; corporal, U.S. Marine Corps, Company A, 1st Battalion, 7th Marines, 1st Marine Division, recipient: Medal of Honor (posthumous), Korea, 28 May 1952, "for conspicuous gallantry and intrepidity at the risk of his life above and beyond the call of duty while serving as a fire team leader of Company A, in action against enemy aggressor forces. Advancing with his platoon in the initial assault of the company against a strongly fortified and heavily defended hill position, CPL Champagne skillfully led his fire team through a veritable hail of intense enemy machine gun, small arms, and grenade fire, overrunning trenches and a series of almost impregnable bunker positions before reaching the crest of the hill and placing his men in defensive positions. Suffering a painful leg wound while assisting in repelling the ensuing hostile counterattack, which was launched under cover of a murderous hail of mortar and artillery fire, he steadfastly refused evacuation and fearlessly continued to control his fire team. When the enemy counterattack increased in intensity and a hostile grenade landed in the midst of the fire team, CPL Champagne unhesitatingly seized the deadly missile and hurled it in the direction of the approaching enemy. As the grenade left his hand, it exploded, blowing off his hand and throwing him out of the trench. Mortally wounded by enemy mortar fire while in this exposed position, CPL Champagne, by his valiant leadership, fortitude and gallant spirit of self-sacrifice in the face of almost certain death, undoubtedly saved the lives of several of his fellow marines. His heroic actions served to inspire all who observed him and reflect the highest credit upon himself and the U.S. Naval Service. He gallantly gave his life for his country."

Champlin, James Tift 1811–82, born: Colchester, Connecticut; A.B. *cum laude* Brown University 1834; studied theology, accepted a call from the First Baptist Church, Portland 1838; professor of ancient languages: Waterville College 1841–57, seventh president 1857–67, during the Civil War, the fortunes of Waterville College drained away as most eligible students joined the Union forces, approached Gardner Colby, a native of Bowdoinham, a devout Baptist and a wealthy merchant in Boston, whose original bequest of $50,000 was followed by the erection of Coburn Hall and a bequest, at the time of his death, of $120,000; in response to this act of generosity, the trustees re-named Waterville College, Colby College 1867, Colby's gift was matched by others, new and commodious buildings were built to replace older structures,

Champlin Hall was named in his honor; after his resignation in 1873, removed to Portland where he pursued literary projects; author: *Demosthenes on the Crown* 1843, *Demosthenes Select Orations* 1848, *Aeschines on the Crown* 1850, *Text-Book of Intellectual Philosophy* 1860, *Constitution of the United States, with Brief Comments* 1880.

Chandler, John 1762–1841, born: Epping, New Hampshire; son of a farmer and officer in the French and Indian and Revolutionary Wars, who died in 1776; served in the Continental Army from 1777, participated in the battle of Saratoga; removed to Monmouth, with the assistance of General Henry Dearborn, purchased a tract of land and cleared it for a farm; member: Massachusetts General Court; member: U.S. House of Representatives 1805–09; Kennebec County sheriff 1809–12; commanding brigadier general, USA, during War of 1812, captured by the British, subsequent to the battle of Lundy's Lane in Ontario; a leader in the separation movement, delegate: Maine Constitutional Convention 1819, member, first president: Maine Senate 1820, resigned to become member: U.S. Senate 1820–26, obtained the funding for the arsenal in Augusta and the building of the military road from Bangor to Houlton; director: U.S. Branch Bank, Portland 1829–30; trustee: Bowdoin College 1831–38; collector of U.S. customs, Portland 1829–37; buried in Mt. Pleasant Cemetery, Augusta.

Chandler, Peleg Whitman 1816–89, born: New Gloucester; son of an attorney; A.B. Bowdoin College 1834, L.L.D. 1870, student: Dane Law School, Harvard University; member: Massachusetts bar 1837, practiced in Boston; founder, editor: *Law Reporter* (Boston) 1838–40, the first successful law magazine in the United States; U.S. commissioner of Bankruptcy 1842; member: Boston Common Council 1843–45, president 1844, 1845; Boston city solicitor 1846–53, revised Boston city ordinances from 1850; member: Massachusetts Executive Council 1850; foremost advocate of the Back Bay Improvement, drew up the act of 1859, which established the Boston Public Garden, defeated proposals to divide it into house lots; Republican presidential elector 1860; author: *Bankruptcy Laws of the United States with Rules and Forms in Massachusetts* 1842, *American Criminal Trials* (2 volumes) 1848, *Observations on the Authority of the Gospels, by a Lay Man* 1867, *Memoir of Governor Andrew, with Personal Reminiscences* 1880; son-in-law of Parker Cleaveland.

Chandler, Samuel 1713–75, born: Andover, Massachusetts; son of a farmer; A.B. Harvard College 1735, A.M. 1738, as an undergraduate, survived several serious breaches of the rules, but was awarded the Hopkins Prize for academic excellence; studied theology with Samuel Phillips, began preaching at Chelmsford and in neighboring towns; accepted a call from the Second Congregational Church of York 1741, to succeed Joseph Handkerchief Moody, whose madness had become too florid for him to continue as pastor; a follower of Jonathan Edwards and a supporter of the Great Awakening, joined in the rebuke of ministers that would not allow George

Whitefield to preach from their respective pulpits; after witnessing the results of some very overheated preaching on one congregation, the high pitch of religiosity began to drain from his ministry; grew his own pipe tobacco, excelled as carpenter, joiner, mason, and glazer, kept every clock in his parish in repair, drew legal documents; vehement in his denouncement of the popish elements of the Episcopal church, led prayer for the deliverance of the nation from its Popish Pretender, looked with distaste upon Christmas celebrations; finding the Scotland parish unreceptive, he resigned his pulpit 1749; calls from Thomas Smith to share his parish were refused, preferring to continue keeping school, as he had done for most his ministry, later opened a private school for the teaching of astronomy and navigation, hired by the town of York to keep its public school; starting with three scholars, he soon built it up to number eighty three; continuing his tinkering, he was a regular guest at the home of Sir William Pepperrell, whose clocks and mechanical spit he kept in order; preaching in Gloucester, Massachusetts, at the invitation Rev. John White (father-in-law of Joseph Moody), he was met with such enthusiasm that he was later called to that pulpit as colleague pastor 1751; submitted to rigorous questioning of his faith and principles, wherein the parish found its match in obstinacy; often, the church would take up a collection to have those sermons of his, that especially pleased them, published; Colonial Plaisted came to Gloucester to secure Chandler's service as chaplain for the expedition against Crown Point 1755, where he did well ministering to the ills and sadness of a cold, wet camp in winter; his congregation refused him permission to return to Crown Point for another season; at this point, his wife, who had been mildly psychotic for some time, became violent and had to be kept under close confinement in the parsonage; joined in the blacklisting of Rev. John Cleaveland and his New Lights congregation; publicly bemoaned the rise of Universalism; author: *Address to the People in his Charge, with Regard to Mr. Murry* 1775, *An Attempt to Nip in the Bud, the Unscriptural Doctrine of Universal Salvation* 1776, *Ezekiel's Parable of the Boiling Pot* 1755.

Chaplin, Daniel 1820–64, born: Naples; at age twenty-one, removed to Bangor, where he worked as a clerk in the ship chandlery of Thurston & Metcalf; member of a local militia unit; in the Civil War: was one of the first to enlist as a private in the Second Maine Volunteers 1861; quickly rose in rank to major, USV; appointed colonel of the 18th Maine Volunteers 1862, which later became the 1st Maine Heavy Artillery, led his regiment in the charge at Petersburg, wherein this unit lost more men killed and wounded than any other federal unit; mortally wounded at Deep Bottom; buried in Mount Hope Cemetery, Bangor; father of Winfield Scott Chaplin.

Chaplin, Jeremiah 1776–1841, born: Rowley (later Georgetown), Massachusetts; son of a farmer; A.B. Brown University 1799, first in his class; tutor: Brown University 1799–1800; studied theology with Rev. Thomas Brown, D.D.; pastor of the Second Baptist Church, Boston, pastor: Baptist Church, Danvers, Massachusetts, 1802–

18, principal and professor of theology: Maine Literary and Theology Institute, Waterville 1818, first president: Waterville College (later Colby College) 1821–33; established Waterville Classical Institute (later Coburn Classical Institute); after his resignation, returned to pastoral duties in Rowley, Massachusetts, Wilmington, Connecticut, and Hamilton, New York; author: *The Greatness of Redemption* 1808, *The Evening of Life* 1859, *The Memorial Hour* 1864; son-in-law of John OBrien.

Chaplin, Winfield Scott 1847–1918, born: Glenburn; son of Daniel Chaplin, colonel, USV, commanding officer: 1st Maine Heavy Artillery, killed in action at the battle of Cold Harbor, Virginia, 1864; graduate: U.S. Military Academy 1870, (Hon. A.M. Union College 1885, L.L.D. Harvard University 1893, D. Technology Imperial University of Japan 1915); first lieutenant, U.S. 5th Artillery, USA, 1872–73; professor of mechanical engineering: Maine State College 1873–76, professor of engineering: Imperial University of Japan 1877–82, professor of mathematics: Union College 1883–86, professor of engineering and dean: Lawrence Scientific School (Harvard University) 1886–91, chancellor: University of Washington 1891–97; decorated: Order of the Rising Sun (Japan); fellow: American Academy of Arts and Sciences.

Chase, Charles Henry 1910–81, born: Portland; B.S. U.S. Military Academy 1933, M.S. George Washington University 1969, graduate: Armed Forces Staff College 1947, Army War College 1951, Naval War College 1953; commissioned second lieutenant, USA, 1933, advanced through the ranks to major general 1961; served with 101st Airborne Division, European Theatre, World War II; assistant division commanding officer 1956–57; chief of staff: XVIII Airborne Division 1957–59; chief: military assistance advance group, Cambodia 1959–61; command officer 2nd Infantry Division 1961–62; chief of staff: U.S. Strike Command 1962–64; deputy chief of staff: Allied Forces Central Europe 1964–66; chief of staff: USA, Europe 1967–68, retired 1968; lecturer on management science: Florida Institute of Technology, Melbourne; decorated: Distinguished Service Medal, Silver Star, Legion of Merit with oak leaf cluster, Bronze Star with two oak leaf clusters, decorated by France, Belgium, Holland, Republic of Korea; retired to Satellite Beach, Florida.

Chase, Ethan Allen 1832–1921, born: Turner; student: Hebron Academy, taught school in Georgia 1852–53, began nursery business 1856, removed to Rochester, New York, 1868, organized Chase Brothers, New England Nurseries, branch houses in Augusta, Montréal, Toronto, Saint Louis, Chicago, New York, and Richmond, Virginia; established Alabama Nursery Co., Huntsville 1888, removed to Riverside, California, 1891, organized Chase Nursery Co.; president: National Orange Co., one of the largest orange growing and packing concerns in its day; worked out many problems of irrigation, cultivation and packing; organized the Chase Rose Co.; delegate-at-large: Republican National Convention 1908; father of Lewis Nathaniel Chase, cousin of Solon Chase.

Chase, George 1849–1924, born: Portland; A.B. *summa cum laude* Yale College (valedictorian) ΦBK 1870, L.L.B. Columbia University Law School 1873; member: New York bar 1873; instructor and assistant professor of municipal law: Columbia University Law School 1873–78, professor of criminal law, torts, and procedure 1878–91, dean: Columbia University Law School from 1891; author: *Chase's Edition, Blackstone's Commentaries for American Students, Stephen's Digest of the Law of Evidence, Chase's Cases on Torts,* editor: *New York Law Journal.*

Chase, George Colby 1844–1919, born: Unity; son of a farmer, cousin of Salmon Portland Chase and Elijah Lovejoy; graduate: Maine State Seminary, Lewiston, A.B. Bates College 1868, first in his class, A.M. 1871, D.D. 1893, L.L.D. University of Colorado 1893, Bowdoin College 1905; instructor in Greek and Latin: New Hampton Literary Institution 1868–70, tutor in Greek: Bates College 1870–71, graduate student at Harvard University 1871–72, professor of rhetoric and English literature: Bates College 1872–94, second president and professor of psychology and logic from 1894; father of George Millet Chase.

Chase, George Millet 1873–1938, born: Lewiston; son of George Colby Chase; A.B. Bates College ΦBK 1893, A.M. Yale University 1903; principal: Alfred High School 1893–94, professor of Greek and Latin: Fairmount College, Wichita, Kansas, 1895–99; dean, professor of Greek: American International College, Springfield, Massachusetts, 1901–06; professor of Greek: Bates College 1906–38; secretary of the faculty for twenty-nine years, knew all the Greek inhabitants of Lewiston, personally, spoke modern Greek and delivered talks in their churches and society meetings throughout New England; author: *Questions and Topics in Greek and Roman Statesmanship* 1912, *George C. Chase—A Biography* 1924, coauthor: *Classical Civilization* 1938; member: American Philological Society, New England Classical Association; after his death, his former students placed his portrait in the Bates College library.

Chase, John F. 1843–1914, born: Chelsea; private, 5th Battery, Maine Light Artillery, Chancellorsville, recipient: Medal of Honor, "nearly all the officers and men of the battery having been killed or wounded, this soldier with a comrade continued to fire his gun after the other guns had ceased. This piece was then dragged off by the two, the horses having been shot, and its capture by the enemy was prevented, received forty-eight wounds at Gettysburg." On staff: commander in chief: Grand Army of the Republic; lecturer, general manager: Cyclorama of the Battle of Gettysburg, St. Petersburg, Florida; land developer, holder of some forty-eight patents including one for the bustle hoop skirt, which he sold before it reaped a large sum, and an airplane; buried in St. Bartholomew's Cemetery, St. Petersburg, Florida.

Chase, Joseph Cummings 1878–1965, born: Kents Hill, Readfield; student: Pratt Institute, Pennsylvania Academy, Académie Julian, Paris; exhibited at Paris salon, won 1st and 2nd prize, Grunwaldt poster competition, Paris 1904; painted portraits of six American presidents, many stage notables; as American Expeditionary Forces artist, painted 142 portraits of military leaders and gallant soldiers, 50 of which are in the permanent collection of National Gallery of Art, remainder in Smithsonian; head of art department: Hunter College, served as a judge in the 1923 Miss America pageant; author: *My Friends Look Better Than Ever* 1952, *Face Value* 1962.

Chase, Josiah 1713–78, born: Newbury, Massachusetts; son of a weaver and carpenter; A.B. Harvard College 1738, A.M. 1741, as an undergraduate, enjoyed a Flynt Scholarship; itinerant preacher, distinctly Old Lights in his theology; preached for extended periods in Sutton and Brentwood, New Hampshire; after his marriage to the daughter of Rev. John Tufts, the couple resided in Newbury, Massachusetts, although he preached in Keenborough, New Hampshire, 1746–47; called to new pulpit in Spruce Creek, a village on the road from Kittery Point and what is now Eliot 1749; this new church was within the Middle Parish of Kittery, the pulpit of which was occupied by the New-Lights preacher John Rogers, who was loath to see his parish divided and the settlement of an Old-Light; after his ordination in 1750, the only thing that distinguished his ministry was his extraordinary consumption of rum, usually a quart a day; it comes as no surprise that he met his death in a snowstorm on his way back from a wedding, when he lost his way and drowned in a small creek near his home, some distance from where his hat and wig were eventually found.

Chase, Lewis Nathaniel 1873–1937, born: Sidney; son of Ethan Allan Chase; A.B. Columbia University 1895, A.M. 1898, Ph.D. 1903, student at Harvard University, University of Grenoble; actor with Creston Clarke Co. in Shakespearean and other legitimate roles 1895–96; assistant and tutor of comparative literature: Columbia University 1899–1902; lecturer on literary subjects 1902–03; instructor and assistant professor of English: Indiana University 1903–07; professor of English literature: University of Louisville 1907–08; lecturer: University of Bordeaux 1909–10; instructor and lecturer on contemporary poetry: University of Wisconsin 1916–17; acting assistant professor: University of Rochester 1917–19; professor of English studies: Aligarh (India) Muslim University 1919–22; with Yenching, Peking National, and Peking normal universities 1921–25; visiting professor: California Institute of Technology 1926, Union College 1927–29, Duke University 1929–31, Brown University 1931–33; author: *The English Heroic Play* 1907, *Introduction to Emerson's Compensation* 1906, *Bernard Shaw in France* 1910, *Poe and His Poetry* 1913; editor: *Western Classics for Eastern Students*; director: Brown University project for publication of life and works of Thomas Holley Chivers, in four volumes; achieved wide fame for his poetry reading; gave early, important encouragement to several young poets who later achieved fame, in their own right; with his brother, Martin Aquila Chase, tennis champion of southern California for two years.

Chase, Mary Ellen 1887–1973, born: Blue Hill; A.B. University of Maine 1909, A.M. University of Minnesota 1918, Ph.D. 1922; assistant professor of English Literature: Smith College 1926–29, professor 1929–55; author, her works include: *Jonathan Fisher: Maine Parson, The White Gate, Donald McKay and the Clipper Ships, The Psalms for the Common Reader, The Prophets for the Common Reader.*

Chase, Solon 1822–1909, born: Chases Mill, Turner; graduate: Gorham Academy; farmer, leading and active Greenback campaigner 1876–84; cousin of Ethan Allen Chase and Royal Bird Bradford; his portrait in the Maine statehouse collection.

Chase, Willard Linwood 1897–1983, born: Island Falls; A.B. University of Maine φΒΚ 1920, L.L.D. 1955, A.M. Columbia University Teachers College 1927, Ph.D. 1935; teacher: Orono 1916–17, Old Town 1917–18, Waltham, Massachusetts, 1920–22, superintendent of schools: Canton 1922–24, Boothbay Harbor 1924–25, teacher: Horace Mann School, Columbia University Teachers College 1925–28, assistant professor of education: Boston University 1928–35, headmaster: Country Day School for Boys, Newton, Massachusetts, 1935–40, professor of education: Boston University 1940–53, 1957–61, dean, school of education 1953–57; president: National Council for Social Studies; president: Town Meeting League 1946–47; coauthor: *America in the World* with Marion Lansing and Allan Nevins 1949, *Leaders in Other Lands* with Jeanette Eaton and Allan Nevins 1950, *Pioneer Children of America* with Caroline Emerson and Allan Nevins 1950, *Makers of America* with Marion Lansing and Allan Nevins 1951.

Chase, William Thomas 1839– ?, born: Hallowell; son of a farmer, orphaned at an early age, saw to the education of his sister as well as his own, working on farms in the summer, attending school in the winter, entered Waterville College 1860, left to become the chaplain of a colored regiment at Port Hudson, Louisiana, prevailed upon the commanding officer to allow him to construct a school for the colored troops and educateg them, returning to Waterville College, A.B. 1865, S.T.D. Newton Theological Institution 1869, D.D. University of Chicago 1884; ordained Baptist minister, pastor in Dover, New Hampshire, 1869–74, Lewiston 1874–79, Cambridge, Massachusetts, 1879–84, Minneapolis 1884–89, Ruggles Street Church, Boston 1889–91, Fifth Baptist Church, Philadelphia, from 1891, in Cambridge and Minneapolis oversaw the erection of architecturally significant churches; member, executive committee and board of managers: American Baptist Missionary Union; member, board of managers: American Baptist Publication Society; trustee: Newton Theological Institution; president: Baptist Education Society of Maine.

Chauncey, Charles 1729–1809, born: Boston, Massachusetts; son of the Rev. Charles Chauncey, a Congregational minister, great grandson of President Chauncey of Harvard College; A.B. Harvard College 1748, A.M. 1751; originally intended to enter the ministry but took a job in the counting house of his uncle, Sir William Pepperrell, in Kittery 1748; learned the trade well, became an independent merchant and prospered mightily; purchased the Campernowne estate, near the mouth of what is now known as Chauncey's Creek, at the junction with Deering's Guzzle; married Mary, daughter of Richard Cutts 1756, who died in childbirth two years later, her tombstone served as the inspiration of one of Celia Thaxter's better poems ("In Kittery Churchyard"); appointed notary public of the port of Kittery 1754, appointed justice of the peace 1761; given his intelligence, he could have easily assumed a position of power amongst the Whigs but generally confined himself to letters to newspapers; served on the committee that urged Kittery to stand firm with the city of Boston 1773; chairman of the Kittery Committee of Safety; elected to the First Provincial Congress 1775; carried to the Second Provincial Congress the report that Kittery was daily subjected to British threats and occasional cannon fire 1775; elected by the Massachusetts General Court councillor for the territory formerly known the Province of Maine 1775, as such, he was a part of the executive body of the revolutionary government, declined reelection 1776, and essentially retired from public participation; risked his brig *Hope* on a voyage to Tortuga for a badly needed load of salt; his personal life was sad, his only son went quite mad at the age of sixteen and had to be kept chained in an outhouse; died within a week of recovering his reason in 1789; removed to Portsmouth 1791, even though he continued to serve as justice of the peace and quorum to 1799; being an anti-Federalist, became involved in a riot protesting the Jay Treaty 1795.

Cheever, George Barrell

Cheever, George Barrell 1807–90, born: Hallowell; son of Nathaniel Cheever, M.D., who removed from Salem, Massachusetts, to Hallowell and established the *American Advocate*, brother of Henry Theodore Cheever, grandson of Nathaniel Cheever, first American to shed his blood in the American Revolution; A.B. Bowdoin College 1825, classmate and lifelong friend of Nathaniel Hawthorne, graduate: Andover Theological Seminary 1830; compiled *American Commonplace Book of Prose*, regarded as the best published in the United States, to that time; contributor of poetry and prose to the *North American Review* and others; ordained Congregational minister 1830, pastor: Howard Street Congregational Church, Salem, Massachusetts, 1832–36, took an active part in the controversies surrounding Unitarianism, particularly zealous in support of temperance, published an imaginary dream in the *Salem Landmark*, entitled "Inquire at Amos Giles Distillery," the real Amos Giles was a deacon in Cheever's church, he and his friends were outraged at this gratuitous assault on his character, the offices of the *Landmark* were attacked, by night, and Cheever assaulted, by day, in the streets of Salem, arrested and imprisoned for one month for libel, resigning his pastorate, spent two years in Europe, meanwhile writing letters to the *New York Observer*; pastor: Allen Street Presbyterian Church, New York 1839–44; chief editor: *New York Evangelist* 1845; founding pastor: Church of the Pilgrims, New

York 1846–70; public lecturer, contributor of poems, religious works, and fulminations against slavery; after the repeal of the Missouri compromise, passage of the Kansas-Nebraska and fugitive-slave bills, the Dred Scott decision, Cheever thundered his opposition to the state of things, which echoed and reechoed across the country, his sermons were reprinted in various newspapers, but at least one religious publication intimated that Cheever had gone quite mad, many of his parishioners objected to his tone and the hospitality he extended to the Church Anti-Slavery Society, which advocated nonfellowship with slave holders, commissioned by his church to go to England to explain its position on emancipation 1860; preached on several occasions in the U.S. Senate chamber on "The Rights of the Colored Race to Citizenship and Representation," calling at the White House, immediately before the signing of the Emancipation Proclamation, President Lincoln greeted him as the prime minister of the almighty; resigned his pulpit 1870, donated his house to the American Missionary Association and the American Board of Commissioners for Foreign Missions, retired to his retreat on the Palisades, near Englewood, New Jersey; contributor to the *Biblotheca Sacra*, author: *Commonplace Book of Prose* 1828, *Studies in Poetry* 1830, *Select Works of Archbishop Leighton* 1832, *Commonplace Book of Poetry* 1839, *God's Hand in America* 1841, *Characteristics of the Christian Philosopher: A Discourse on the Virtues and Attainments of Rev. James Marsh* 1843, *Lectures on Hierarchical Despotism* 1844, *Lectures on Pilgrim's Progress* 1844, *Defense of Capital Punishment* 1846, *Wanderings of a Pilgrim in Switzerland* 1845, *Christian Melodies: A Selection of Hymns and Tunes* 1847, *Poets of America* 1847, *The Hill of Difficulty* 1847, *Journal of the Pilgrims, Plymouth, New England, 1620* 1848, *Punishment by Death, Its Authority and Expediency* 1849, *Windings of the River of the Water of Life* 1849, *The Voices of Nature to Her Foster Child, the Soul of Man* 1852, *Powers of the World to Come* 1853, *Thoughts for the Afflicted* 1854, *The Right of the Bible in our Public Schools* 1854, *Lectures on the Life, Genius, and Insanity of Cowper* 1856, *God Against Slavery and the Freedom and Duty of the Pulpit to Rebuke It* 1857, *Guilt of Slavery and Crime of Slaveholding* 1860, *Faith, Doubt, and Evidence* 1881.

Cheever, Henry Theodore 1814–97, born: Hallowell, brother of George Barrell Cheever; A.B. Bowdoin College 1834, correspondent for the *New York Evangelist* in Spain, France, and Louisiana 1835–36, graduate: Bangor Theological Seminary 1839; missionary in Hawaii 1841; editor: *New York Evangelist* 1849–52; secretary and agent: Church Anti-Slavery Society 1859–64; author: *The Whale and His Captors, or The Whale-mans Adventures and the Whale's Biography, Gathered on the Homeward Cruise of the Commodore Preble* 1849, *A Reel in a Bottle for Jack in the Doldrums* 1851, *The Island World of the Pacific* 1852, *Memoirs of Nathaniel Cheever, M.D.* 1853, *Life and Religion in the Sandwich Islands* 1854, *Autobiography and Memorials of Capt. Obidiah Congat* 1855, *The Sea and the Sailor*, derived from the literary remains of Walter Colton 1855, *Short Yarns for Long Voyages* 1855, *Life and Remains of Rev. Walter Colton, U.S.N.* 1856, *The Pulpit and the Pew-Trials and Triumphs of a Year in the Old*

Parsonage, from Leaves of a Pastor's Journal 1858, Wayward Marks in the Moral War with Slavery between the Opening of 1859 and the Close of 1861 1862, Autobiography and Memorials of Ichabod Washburn 1878, Correspondencies of Faith—and Views of Madame Guyon 1885, The Bible Eschatology.

Chenery, William Elisha 1864–1949, born: Wiscasset; graduate: Boston Latin School 1887, A.B. Boston University ΦBK 1887, M.D. Harvard University Medical School 1890, D.Sc. (Hon.) Boston University 1938, D.H.L. Tufts University 1945, postgraduate study at the universities of Freiburg, Vienna, and Berlin, interned with Halle at the *Allgemeine Krankenhaus* in Vienna, practiced in Boston, specializing in laryngology, retiring in 1938; professor of laryngology: Tufts University Medical School 1900–29; chief of staff of the nose, throat, and ear department: New England Deaconess, St. Elizabeth's, New England Baptist, Booth and Roxbury hospitals, established the nose, throat, and ear department at the Forsyth Dental Infirmary; trustee: Boston University 1919–49; in World War I: member, volunteer Medical Corps, prepared 500 young physicians to do plastic surgery; established a fund of $100,000 for Boston University, gave it a library and his own home as a residence for the president, established the William E. and Marion L. Chenery professorship and the Marion Luse Chenery Scholarships in music: Wesleyan College, Macon, Georgia; established the William E. and Marion L. Chenery Library, Tufts University Medical School; gave Emerson College a home for its president; supported, for many years, a missionary in India and the Mission School in Delhi, built the Chenery Memorial Church at Narela, funded the Chenery Memorial Bible Fund of the American Bible Society, the Chenery Memorial Fund of the Massachusetts Bible Society; member: Ancient and Honorable Artillery Company of Massachusetts; cofounder, president: Friends of China (later Sino-American Society); in a tribute to his long and distinguished career, the Boston Symphony Orchestra, in a concert he attended on his eightieth birthday, rose with the audience and played *Happy Birthday to You*.

Cheney, Oren Burbank 1816–94, born: Holderness, New Hampshire; son of the owner of a paper mill; graduate: New Hampton Academical Institute, A.B. Dartmouth College 1839; principal: Farmington Academy, Greenland (New Hampshire) Academy, Stratford (New Hampshire) Academy, Parsonsfield Seminary, pastor: West Lebanon, Maine, 1846, pastor: First Free Will Baptist Church, Augusta 1852; fire having destroyed the Parsonsfield Seminary, Cheney conceived of what became Bates College 1854, secured charter for the Maine State Seminary 1855, became a college 1863, renamed Bates College 1869, first college in New England to graduate women, president to 1894; member: Maine House of Representatives (Whig) 1851; founder: West Lebanon Academy 1851.

Cheverus, Jean Louis Lefebvre, de 1768–1836, born: Mayenne, France; served as assistant, later pastor of Notre Dame de Mayenne; fled the revolution in

France 1792, settled in London, where he founded the Tottenham Chapel; removed to Boston 1796, where he first assisted at Holy Cross church, then took charge of Indian mission churches in Maine; displayed great courage and resourcefulness during a fearsome yellow fever epidemic 1798; his eloquent preaching attracted many Protestants and eased their fears of Roman Catholic perfidity; created bishop of Boston 1808, employed Charles Bulfinch to design the first Catholic church in Boston; returned to France, at the insistence of King Louis XVIII 1823, made bishop of Montauban, later archbishop of Bordeaux and, as peer of France, served in the French Senate 1826–30; founded a retirement system for the clergy of Bordeaux; consecrated cardinal shortly before his death; author: *Statuts du Diocèse de Bordeaux.*

Childs, Harwood Lawrence 1898–1972, born: Gray; A.B. Dartmouth College ΦBK 1919, A.M. 1921, Ph.D. University of Chicago 1928; instructor in public speaking: Dartmouth College 1919–20, instructor in economics 1920–21, assistant professor of economics: Syracuse University 1922–24; associate professor of government: College of William and Mary 1925–27; associate professor of government and head of department of political science: Bucknell University 1928–31; associate professor of politics: Princeton University 1932–46, professor from 1946; regional specialist, Office of War Information, Washington, D.C., 1943–45; Social Science Research Council fellow for study in Germany 1931–32; Guggenheim fellow for study in Germany 1937; founder and first editor: *Public Opinion Quarterly*; member: Enemy Alien Hearing Board, district of New Jersey 1942–43; author: *Public Opinion—Nature, Formation, Role* 1965, numerous papers for scholarly journals.

Childs, John Lewis 1856–1921, born: North Jay; son of a farmer; evinced an interest in flowers and gardening at an early age, at age seventeen, removed to West Hinsdale, New York, where he was employed by a florist 1873, a year later, he leased a few acres and rented a room over a store, announced himself as a seedman and florist, and issued his first catalogue, by 1892, this had grown into several hundred acres and a catalogue, *Childs Seed Catalogue* of 160 pages with a circulation of over a million; constructed the city of Floral Park, Long Island, New York, with banks, stores, residences, &c.; founded *Mayflower* magazine, which grew to a circulation of 300,000; a farm of 800 acres was purchased in Suffolk County, New York, and named Flowerland, which was devoted to wholesale florist business, particularly famous for his new species of gladioli, cannas, and dahlias; member: New York Senate 1894, where he introduced the bill establishing a state normal school in Jamaica, New York, of whose board he became a member and a constant visitor; twice Republican nominee for U.S. House of Representatives; established in Pasadena: California Floral Park 1905; ornithologist and mineralogist of note, close friend of John Burroughs.

Chisholm, Hugh 1847–1912, born: Niagara-on-the-Lake, Ontario, Canada; as a child worked as a train newsboy on the Grand Trunk Railroad (often with his lifelong friend Thomas Edison), established a railway news business in partnership with his brother under the name of Chisholm Brothers; by 1867, had practical control of the newspaper service in trains from Halifax and Chicago and on steamboats on the lines of travel in New England, New York, and Canada; originator of the travel information publishing business, publishers of railway and tourist guides and souvenirs of travel, sold his business to his brothers, removed to Portland 1872, became interested in wood pulp and the manufacture of paper, organized the Umbagog Mill in Livermore Falls 1887, mills in Fairfield; began to develop waterpower at Rumford Falls 1890, organized the Oxford Paper Co., built municipal buildings, hotels, business blocks, worker and management housing; conceived of and had constructed the first floating power plant, which he used at his mill in Bucksport; chief organizer: International Paper Co. 1898, with plants in Maine, New York, New Hampshire, and Vermont, president 1898–1908; buried in Evergreen Cemetery, Portland.

Churchill, Frank Edwin 1901–42, born: Ridlonville (Mexico); studied medicine at University of California at Los Angeles 1921–23; atmosphere pianist for silent films 1923; pianist on radio station KNX (Los Angeles) 1924–29; composer for Walt Disney; among his compositions are: *Who's Afraid of the Big, Bad Wolf, Three Little Pigs*, scores for numerous Silly Symphonies, scores for animated motion pictures: *Snow White* (*Whistle While You Work, Heigh Ho, Someday My Prince Will Come*, &c.), *Bambi* and *Dumbo* (*Watch Out for Mister Stork, Baby Mine, Casey Junior, Tea Time at Four OClock, The Song of the Roustabouts*), for which he received an Academy Award, contributed to the score of *Peter Pan, The Reluctant Dragon*; certain musicologists claim that Churchill had considerable influence on other composers as diverse as Spike Jones, George Antheil, and Bela Bartok; buried in Forest Lawn Cemetery, Glendale, California.

Cilley, Greenleaf 1829–99, born: Thomaston; son of Jonathan Cilley; attended Bath High School; appointed midshipman, USN, 1841; served in the Mediterranean Squadron 1843–45, ordered to U.S. Naval Academy 1846, one month later ordered to the seat of the war with Mexico in the Gulf, served aboard USS *Ohio*, took part in the battle of Vera Cruz, assisted the army in crossing the Medelin River on its march to Alvarado, in the Tuspan Expedition, wounded while storming a shore battery; graduate: U.S. Naval Academy 1849; joined the USS *Raritan*, served in the Gulf squadron to 1850; promoted to master and lieutenant 1855; in the Civil War: promoted to lieutenant commander 1862, commanding officer: USS *Unadilla* at Port Royal, commanding officer: monitor USS *Catskill* at the blockade of Charleston and the bombardment of Fort Sumter, commanding officer: USS *Fort Jackson* at the blockade of Wilmington, North Carolina, placed on the retired list 1865, promoted to commander on the retired list 1867; removed, with his family, to Buenos Aires, Argentina, later to San Isidro; in the war with Paraguay, commanded the steamer *Augustinia*; ascended the Parana and Paraguay Rivers to Corumba, Brazil, where he engaged and equipped a

Eminent Mainers

party of five men, with whom he made the first descent of the River Negra and explored the wilds of Bahia Negra; employed in making plans and estimates and seeking from the Bolivian congress, a railroad concession from Bahia Negra to Santa Cruz de la Sierra; returned to the United States 1876, remained for eight years; returned to Buenos Aires and then settled on his immense sheep ranch in Argentina.

Cilley, Jonathan 1802–38, born: Nottingham, New Hampshire, brother of Joseph Cilley, the first abolitionist to serve in the U.S. Senate, cousin of General Benjamin F. Butler; attended Atkinson Academy, A.B. Bowdoin College ΦBK 1825, read law in the office of John Ruggles, Thomaston; member: Maine bar 1829, practiced in Thomaston; editor: *Thomaston Register* 1829–31; member: Maine House of Representatives 1831-36, speaker 1835–36; member from the 3rd District: U.S. House of Representatives 1836–38 (Jacksonian Democrat), killed in a duel by Representative Graves, of Kentucky; this, along with the murder of Elijah Lovejoy, a few months previous, raised the level of national discourse on slavery to a murderous tone; general abhorrence thus stirred led to stringent laws against dueling; a sketch of his life was written by his Bowdoin classmate, Nathaniel Hawthorne; father of Jonathan Prince and Greenleaf Cilley; buried in Cilley Cemetery, Thomaston, cenotaph in Congressional Cemetery, Washington.

Cilley, Jonathan Prince 1835–1903, born: Thomaston; son of Jonathan Cilley, brother of Greenleaf Cilley; A.B. Bowdoin College 1858; member: Maine bar 1860; in the Civil War: captain, USV, commanding officer: Co. B, 1st Maine Cavalry 1861, while in command, severely wounded and taken prisoner at the battle of Middletown, during the retreat of General Banks from the Shenandoah Valley, 24 May 1862; after being exchanged, promoted to major, USV, served as judge-advocate and examining officer at the central guard house in Washington, took the field with his regiment and ˅ promoted to lieutenant colonel, USV, 1864, he and his regiment played a prominent role in the battles of Farmville, Dinwiddie Court House, Boydon Plank Road, and Appomattox for which he was brevetted brigadier general, USV, for gallant and meritorious service during the war; member: Maine House of Representatives 1867; deputy collector of U.S. Customs at Rockland 1867–76; member: Rockland City Council 1873–75; commissioner of the U.S. District Court 1867–80; adjutant general of Maine 1876–78; editor: *Maine Bugle*.

Clapp, Asa 1762–1848, born: Mansfield, Massachusetts; son of a farmer and local magistrate; during American Revolution: served as a noncommissioned officer in the [James] Sullivan Expedition 1778, after his discharge, walked to Boston, where he served as an officer aboard privateer *Charming Sally*; in one encounter, during a calm, rowed with a party of men over to a British transport and captured it; after the Revolution, involved in merchant trade with the West Indies, while in command of a vessel, lying off Port au Prince, Haiti, successfully evacuated numerous fleeing whites, during the revolution there; in Portland from 1796; a firm supporter of the embargo and President Jefferson 1807, despite the financial ruin it brought him; member: Massachusetts Executive Council 1811; subscribed half his fortune to war effort 1812, the largest subscriber in Maine of stock in the Bank of the United States; delegate: Maine Constitutional Convention 1819; member: Maine House of Representatives 1820–23; considered to be wealthiest man in Maine; great grandfather of Alexander Wadsworth Longfellow, Jr..

Clark, Charles Amory 1841–1916, born: Sangerville; lieutenant and adjutant, 6th Maine Infantry, recipient: Medal of Honor, Brooks Ford, Virginia, 4 May 1863 "having voluntarily taken command of his regiment in the absence of its commander, at great personal risk and remarkable presence of mind and fertility of resource led the command down an exceedingly precipitous embankment to the Rappahannock River and, by his gallantry, coolness and good judgment in the face of the enemy, saved the command from capture or destruction." Buried in Oak Hill Cemetery, Cedar Rapids, Iowa.

Clark, Davis Wasgate 1812–1871, born: Mount Desert; graduate: Maine Wesleyan Seminary, Kents Hill 1833, A.B. Wesleyan University 1836, D.D. 1851; principal and teacher of mathematics and moral philosophy: Amenia (New York) Seminary 1836–43; member: New York Methodist Episcopal Conference 1843–53; editor: *Ladies' Repository*, Cincinnati 1853–64; appointed bishop, Methodist Episcopal Church 1864, first posted to California and Oregon then, in 1866, given the difficult job of presiding in Tennessee, Alabama, and Georgia, became immensely popular, did much to heal the rift left by the Civil War; author: *Elements of Algebra, Mental Discipline, Life and Times of Bishop Hedding, Man All Immortal.*

Clark, Walter Van Tilburg 1909–71, born: East Orland; A.B. University of Nevada 1931, A.M. 1932, A.M. University of Vermont 1934, Litt.D. Colgate University 1958, University of Nevada 1969; graduate instructor in English: University of Nevada 1931–32; fellowship at University of Vermont 1932–34; teacher of English and sports: Cazenovia (New York) public schools 1935–45; took a year's leave to write at Indian Springs Ranch, north of Las Vegas, Nevada, 1941–42; chairman of the English department: Rye (New York) High School 1945, forced to resign due to ill health, spent part of 1946 recovering at Lujan Ranch, Taos, New Mexico, spent 1946–49 writing on the Lewers Ranch in the Washoe Valley, Nevada, resided in Virginia City, Nevada, 1949–54, employed 1950–51 as English teacher and coach at Storey County High School; visiting lecturer in fiction at the Writers' Workshop at the University of Iowa 1951–52, lecturer in English and creative writing: University of Nevada 1952–53, assistant professor of English and chairman of the creative writing program: Montana State University, Missoula 1953–56, professor of creative writing: San Francisco State College 1956, director of the creative writing program 1960–62, with one year's leave in 1960–61 spent as a fellow at the Center for Advanced Studies, Wesleyan University; writer in residence: University of Nevada 1962–71; winner: O. Henry Short Story Award 1945; contributor: *The Atlantic Monthly*, *The New Yorker*, *The Nation*, *Yale Review*, *Saturday Evening Post*, *Holiday*, &c.; author: *The Ox-Bow Incident* 1940, made into a well-regarded motion picture 1943, *The City of Trembling Leaves* 1945, *The Track of the Cat* 1949, made into a motion picture 1954, *The Watchful Gods* 1950; editor: *The Journal of Alfred Doten* (TWO volumes) 1972; gave numerous readings and lectures at colleges and professional organizations, often served as judge for many poetry and fiction awards; member: American Civil Liberties Union; a deeply committed environmentalist, was an early member of the Sierra Club.

Clark, Warren Dearborn 1850–1930, born: East Pittston; descendant of Henry Dearborn; removed to New York 1868, entered the employ of his uncle David B. Dearborn, steamship agent; removed to San Francisco 1877, employee of the shipping and commission house of Williams, Blanchard & Co., later: Williams, Dimond & Co. 1880; partner 1890, senior partner 1914, director; a founder, vice president, stockholder, and general agent for the American-Hawaiian Steamship Co.; general agent for the Brussgaard shipping interests of Norway, for the Mexican States line, for the Osaka Shosen Kaisha line of Japan, for the North German Lloyd and Union Steamship lines; acquired an interest in the Forest Transportation Co., which became the Pacific-Atlantic Steamship Co. (Quaker Line); director: California and Hawaiian Sugar Refining Corp., California Cotton Mills Co., Union Ice Co., Bank of California.

Clarke, Benjamin Franklin 1831–1908, born: Newport; son of a farmer; A.B. Brown University 1863, A.M. 1866, Sc.D. 1897; instructor in mathematics: Brown University 1863–68, professor of mathematics 1868–93, professor of mechanical engineering from 1893, acting president: Brown University 1896–97, 1898–99; member: Providence School Committee.

Clarke, Charles Henry 1864–1946, born: Richmond; son of a clothing manufacturer; attended public schools in Richmond, A.B. Williams College 1887; removed to California, teacher: Hopkins Academy, Oakland, removed to Seattle, traveling salesman for Oliphant & Co., commercial merchandising brokers and manufacturers' agents, later bookkeeper, in partnership with Frank Spencer, bought the Seattle and Tacoma business of the Oliphant Co. 1891, purchased the remainder 1894, formed Spencer, Clarke & Co., Clarke managing the business in Seattle and Tacoma, president 1897, in 1901, Phillip Kelley joined the company, which became Kelley-Clarke Co. (later Kimberly-Clarke Co.), initially handled the sale of canned salmon, the brokerage business was enlarged to include the entire country, exclusive agents for a full range of grocery items, handled product from Proctor & Gamble, California Packing Co., Ghirardelli Chocolate Co., and others, maintained offices in Seattle, Tacoma, Spokane, Portland, Oregon, San Francisco, Los Angeles, Boise, New York, with annual gross sales of over $30 million; president: Kelley Investment Co.; director: Boston National Bank of Seattle, Seattle National Bank, Union Savings & Trust Co., Seattle, Federal Reserve Bank of San Francisco, chairman of the board 1931–35; trustee: Kelley Timber Co.; director: First National Insurance Company of America, General Casualty Company of America, General America Insurance Company of America; member: Seattle board of commissioners 1904–06; member: Bohemian Club of San Francisco.

Clarke, Charles Lorenzo 1853–1941, born: Portland; before entering college, worked as an assistant engineer with the Boston & Maine Railroad Co. on surveying, typographical work, and civil engineering on what became the western division between Boston and Portland; B.S. Bowdoin College φBK 1875, M.S. 1879, C.E. 1880; draftsman for Alexander Holley on Bessemer converters and Siemans furnaces 1876; assistant at the Edison laboratory, Menlo Park, New Jersey, 1880; chief engineer: Edison Electrical Lighting Co., New York 1881–84, designed the dynamos, installed the first Edison electrical lighting central station system, New York 1882; engineer: Telemeter Co., New York 1884–87, Gibson Electric Co. (storage batteries) 1887-89, consulting engineer 1889–1901, consulting engineer: boards of patents, General Electric Co. and Westinghouse 1911–31; author: *Diagonal Functions and their Operation* 1937, various papers, including: "Edison's Electric Railway" 1880, "Electric Motor Diagrams" 1889, "High Frequency Oscillatory and Pulsatory Discharges" 1904, "Loyalty in Business Life" 1913, "Patents" 1914, "The Infinite Duration of Transients" 1915, "Dynamic Balance of Machines" 1916, "Edison and the Incandescent Lamp" 1919, "Step-by-Step Integration of Curve Areas of Phase Significance" 1920; president: Society of Edison Pioneers 1925–26, charter member: American Institute of Electrical Engineers, member of numerous honorary organizations.

Clarke, McDonald 1798–1842, born: Bath; the "Mad Poet of Broadway," a conspicuous figure in New York, with his striking profile and military long coat, a regular attendant of Grace Church, constantly fell in love with one beauty or another, his love poetry was, at first, received happily, later his attentions became irksome, collections of his poetry include: *A Review of the Eve of Eternity, and Other Poems* 1820, *The Elixir of Moonshine, by the Mad Poet* 1822, *The Gossip* 1825, *Poetic Sketches* 1826, *Death in Disguise* 1833, *Poems of McDonald Clarke* 1836, *A Cross and Coronet* 1841, *Afara, a Poem*; his most famous couplet was, "Now twilight lets her curtain down, And pins it with a star"; shortly before his death, he penned a fragment of autobiography that reads, "Begotten among the orange-groves of Jamaica, West Indies. Born in Bath, on the Kennebec River, State of Maine, 18th June, 1798. 1st Love, Mary H. Of New London; last love, Mary T. Of New York; intermediate sweethearts without number. No great compliment to the greatest poet in America-should like the change tho; had to pawn my Diamond Ring (the gift of a lady), and go tick at Delmonico's for Dinner. So much for the greatest poet in America. The greatest poet of the Country ought to have the freedom of the City, the girls of the gentry *gratis*, grab all along the shore the magnificent Mary, and snucks with all the sweet Sisters of Song." Drowned in water running from an open faucet, while confined at Blackwell's Island, New York.

Clarke, Rebecca Sophia 1833–1906, born: Norridgewock; aside for ten years spent in the Midwest, spent her entire life in the house where she was born; under the pen name Sophie May author: *Little Prudy Stories* (six volumes) 1863–65, *Dotty Dimple Stories* (six volumes) 1867–69, *Little Prudy's Flyaway Stories* (6 vol.) 1870–73, *Quinebasset Series* (six volumes) 1871–91, *Flaxie Frizzle Stories* (six volumes) 1876–84, *Little Prudy's Children Series* (six volumes) 1894–1901; known as the Dickens of the nursery.

Clason, Charles Russell 1890–1985, born: Gardiner; A.B. Bates College 1911, L.L.D. 1914, L.L.B. Georgetown University Law School 1914, A.B. Oxford University 1917; instructor in law: Northeastern University 1920–37; member: commission for relief of Belgium, decorated: *Medaille du Roi Albert* (Belgium); member: Massachusetts bar 1917; in World War I: sergeant major, Coast Artillery, USA; assistant district attorney for Western District of Massachusetts 1922–26, district attorney 1927–30; member: U.S. House of Representatives 1937–49 (Republican), unsuccessful candidate for reelection 1948; delegate: Republican National Convention 1952, 1956, 1960; dean: Western New England College School of Law 1952–70; buried in Longmeadow Cemetery, Springfield, Massachusetts.

Clauson, Clinton Ames 1895–1959, born: Mitchell, Iowa; son of a farmer, attended public schools in Otranto Station, Iowa, Lyle, Michigan; in World War I: served as an enlisted man in the USA; graduate: Palmer School of Chiropractic, Davenport, Iowa, 1919; practicing chiropractor in Waterville 1919–38; Waterville city treasurer 1930–31; appointed collector of internal revenue, district of Maine 1934–53; state administrator: Maine War Bond Program 1941–43; wholesaler, retailer in oil, Fairfield 1953–59; mayor of Waterville 1956–57; elected governor of Maine 1959, died in office.

Cleaveland, Parker 1780–1858, born: Byfield, Massachusetts; son of a surgeon in the Revolutionary army and member of the Massachusetts legislature; A.B. Harvard College 1799, M.D. Harvard University Medical School 1823, L.L.D. 1824; school teacher in York 1799–1802, tutor in mathematics and natural philosophy: Harvard College 1803–05, first professor of mathematics and natural philosophy: Bowdoin College 1805–58; librarian, dean of faculty, professor of *materia medica*: Medical School of Maine 1820–58; chair of chemistry, mineralogy, and natural philosophy 1828–58; the mineral *Cleavelandite* named in his honor; author: *Elementary Treatise on Mineralogy and Geology* 1816, first American work on the subject; declined the professorship of mineralogy at Harvard College and the presidency of Bowdoin College

1838; his effectiveness was impaired by his refusal to travel by either steamboat or steam train.

Cleaves, Henry Bradstreet 1840–1912, born: Bridgton; son of a farmer, attended local public school, Bridgton Academy; in the Civil War: enlisted as a private in Company B, 23rd Maine Volunteers 1862, advanced to orderly sergeant, when the regiment was mustered out, he immediately reenlisted, commissioned first lieutenant, USV, his regiment served in the Red River Expedition, later at Cane River Crossing, Pleasant Hill, and Mansefield, after the close of the campaign in Louisiana, served with General Sheridan in the Shenandoah Valley, after the war, was offered, but declined, a commission in the regular army; worked for two years in a blind and sash factory of two years in Bridgton; read law, member: Maine bar 1868, practiced in Bath for one year, removed to Portland; member: Maine House of Representatives 1876–77; Portland city solicitor 1877–79; Maine attorney general 1880–85, achieved prominence through his prosecution of Maine railroad and telegraph companies who had refused to pay a new state tax; elected thirty-seventh governor of Maine (Republican) 1893–97.

Clerque, Francis Hector 1856–1939, born: Bangor; A.B. University of Maine; member: Maine bar 1877, member: U.S. Supreme Court bar; engaged in manufacturing and hydraulic engineering 1880; president: Lake Superior Power Co., Algoma Steel Co., Algoma Central Railroad; began development of the hydraulic power of the Falls of St. Mary's at Sault Ste. Marie, Michigan, and Ontario and the construction and operation of various factories and transportation lines, comprising of blast furnaces, steel rolling mills, iron mines, pulp mills, steamship lines, the Algoma Central Railroad, and Algoma Eastern Railroad; buried in Mt. Hope Cemetery, Bangor.

Clifford, Henry 1904–74, born: Newcastle, son of a merchant; attended Dummer Academy, South Byfield, Massachusetts, Harrow (England) School, School of Political Science, Paris, D.F.A. Villanova University 1953; associated with Guaranty Trust Co., New York 1923–28; assistant curator: Philadelphia (Pennsylvania) Museum of Art 1930–42, curator of paintings and sculpture 1942–64, director 1964–74; research fellow in Aztec art and history: University of Pennsylvania Museum 1964–74, brought many important exhibits to Philadelphia, including Mexican Art Today 1943, Henri Matisse Retrospective Exhibition of Paintings, Drawings, and Sculpture 1948, Vincent Van Gogh 1953, Toulouse-Lautrec 1955, Picasso 1958, Gustave Coubet 1959, Thomas Eakins 1962, A World of Flowers 1963, A Franklin Watkins Retrospective 1964, while organizing the Henri Matisse exhibit, worked closely with Matisse himself, the resulting exhibit was considered the outstanding achievement of his career; instrumental in acquiring the Albert Gallatin collection of postimpressionistic art for the museum; author of the article on Matisse for *Encyclopedia Britannica*, forewords to many art catalogues; artistic director on productions of the Ballet Russe de Monte

Eminent Mainers

Carlo 1936–40; director: Ballet Theatre, New York, Philadelphia Orchestra; founder and first president: Mexican Society of Philadelphia; founder: American-Italy Society of Philadelphia, president 1967–71.

Clifford, Nathan 1803–81, born: Rumney, New Hampshire; student: Haverhill Academy, graduate: Hampton (New Hampshire) Academy, settled in Newfield; member: Maine bar 1827; member: Maine House of Representatives (Democrat) 1830–34, speaker 1832–34; Maine attorney general 1834–38; member: U.S. House of Representatives 1838–1842; U.S. attorney general 1846–48, resigned to serve as peace commissioner in Mexico City at considerable personal risk, recalled by President Taylor; appointed associate justice of the U.S. Supreme Court by President Buchanan, served 1858–81; a New Englander with strong Southern sympathies, presided over the Electoral Commission 1877, although he signed the order certifying Hayes to be president, Clifford refused to recognize Hayes as president, nor would he enter the White House; author: *United States Circuit Court Reports* (two volumes) 1869; buried in Evergreen Cemetery, Portland.

Clough, Herbert Thorndike 1866–1945, born: Rockport; son of a farmer; attended public schools in Rockport; M.D. Dartmouth College Medical School 1895, interned at the Maine Eye and Ear Infirmary, Portland, assistant to Dr. E. E. Holt, removed to Bangor 1899, specialized in diseases of the eye; member: surgical staff, Eastern Maine General Hospital, Bangor; consulting physician: Central Maine General Hospital, Lewiston, Maine, Eye and Ear Infirmary, Portland; consulting ophthalmologist: Bangor & Aroostook Railroad Co.; there being no eyeglass manufacturer in Maine, he constructed his own lens-grinding machines, brought one of the first x-ray machines into Maine and used it at the Maine Eye and Ear Infirmary; interested in radium, from its discovery, studied its uses in Pittsburgh and purchased several needles, used radium in his own work in cases of cancer of the throat and lip and skin cancers of the face, instructed many other physicians in its use; invented several surgical instruments, including a cataract scissor-knife, and, favoring his left hand, adapted several right-hand instruments, particularly cutting instruments, to left-hand application, editor: *Journal of the Maine Medical Association*; devoted much time to the problem of bisecting the arc, prepared several books on the problem, which remained unpublished at his death.

Clute, Howard Merrill 1890–1946, born: North Berwick; son of a lawyer; A.B. Dartmouth College 1911, M.D. 1914, Sc.D. 1941; interned at Mary Hitchcock Hospital, Hanover, New Hampshire; associated with Frank H. Lahey, Boston surgeon, at the Lahey Clinic 1916–35; surgeon in chief: Massachusetts Memorial Hospital 1936–45; professor of surgery: Boston University 1936–45; directing surgeon: Burbank Hospital, Fitchburg, Massachusetts, 1939–46; in World War I: served with the British army in France, later served in the U.S. Army Medical Corps with the rank of colonel, stationed in Boulogne with the Harvey Cushing medical unit; as a surgeon was especially noted for his thyroid operations, devised the special surgical clamp that bears his name; author of over a hundred article, dealing with hyperthyroidism, cancer of the thyroid, colon, and biliary tract, gastric surgery; a founder: American College of Surgeons.

Coatsworth, Elizabeth 1893–1986, born; Buffalo, New York; wife of Henry Beston; graduate: Buffalo Seminary, A.B. Vassar College 1915, A.M. Columbia University 1916, Litt.D. University of Maine 1955, L.H.D. New England College 1958; settled in Nobleboro; recipient: Newberry Award in 1931 for her children's book *The Cat Who Went to Heaven*; author of over ninety books, best known for her children's stories but also wrote fiction, poetry, and memoirs.

Cobb, Calvin Hayes 1889–1961, born: Kittery; grandson of Mark Fernald Wentworth; B.S. U.S. Naval Academy 1911, served aboard USS *Minnesota* during a civilian uprising in Guantanamo, Cuba 1912 and Veracruz, Mexico, 1913, commanding officer: USS *Duncan* during World War I 1916–19, commanded destroyers USS *Monaghan*, USS *Drayton*, USS *Walker* 1919, USS *Percival* 1922–25, commanding officer: USS *Billingsley* and later USS *J. Fred Talbott* 1927–30; assistant U.S. naval attaché in Paris, Madrid, and Lisbon 1930–33, commanding officer: USS *Nitro* 1939–40, on duty at Annapolis 1940–42, commanding officer: USS *Mississippi* 1942, promoted to rear admiral, USN, 1942, commanding officer: Service Squadron South Pacific 1942–44, president of the Naval Examining and Retirement Board 1944–45, commander of naval forces Ryukyus 1945, commandant: U.S. Naval Base, Philadelphia 1945–46, retired as vice admiral, USN, 1946; decorations include Navy Cross and Legion of Merit.

Cobb, David 1748–1830, born: Attleboro, Massachusetts; A.B. Harvard College 1766; studied medicine, practiced in Taunton; member: Provincial Congress 1775; lieutenant colonel Jackson's regiment 1774–76, aide-de-camp General Washington, charged with entertaining French officers and negotiating the evacuation of New York by Sir Guy Carleton's forces; major general of militia 1786; judge of Bristol County Court of Common Pleas 1784–86, during Shays' Rebellion, stated that he would sit as a judge or die as a general, on several occasions, personally defended his court from insurgents; member: Massachusetts House of Representatives 1789–93, speaker; member: U.S. House of Representatives 1793–95; removed to Gouldsboro, Maine, 1796, land agent, farmer, member, president: Massachusetts Senate; member: executive council 1808, lieutenant governor 1809; member, Board of Military Defense 1812; chief justice: Hancock County Court of Common Pleas; buried in Plains Cemetery, Taunton, Massachusetts.

Cobb, Enos 1794–1849, born: Camden; carpenter, joiner, clerk: Navigation Company store; studied medicine and law; in War of 1812: second sergeant, 1st Co, 3rd Regular Massachusetts Minute Guards; traveling agent: Plymouth Beach Lottery Co.; lectured on "Beauties of Education," "Grammar and Rhetoric," "Transportation of Poetry;" author: *The Grammatical Expositor, Elements of the English Language Containing Illustrations of Etymology and Syntax: Being a Fair Delineation of a New System of Teaching English Grammar* 1820; founder and editor: *The Boston Expositor and Philanthropist*; advocate of a city form of government, may very well have been the originator of such a system for the city of Boston 1822; published first American edition of Voltaire's *Candide* 1826; removed to Vermont 1832, special deputy and subpoena officer: Caledonia County; author of a medical text of some 500 pages, which failed to find publication; self-styled poet laureate of the University of Vermont; physiogamist; author: *An Exposition of Dr. Cobb's Art of Discovering The Faculties of the Human Mind and Bodily Infirmaties; To Which Is Added An Autobiographical Sketch Of The Author and a Poetic Description of Several Cities, Towns and Villages Which He Has Visited; to Which Is Also Added, A Guide for Teaching His Art to Others.*

Cobb, Jedediah 1800–60, born: Gray; A.B. Bowdoin College 1820, private medical student of Dr. George Shattuck, Boston, M.D. Medical School of Maine; practiced briefly in Portland before removing to Cincinnati, Ohio, where he was professor of theory and practice of medicine at the Medical College of Ohio; so primitive was transportation along the Ohio River that he and some other men, also bound downriver, constructed a flatboat, which they rowed to Cincinnati; after the first term of 1824–25, he transferred to the chair of anatomy, which he held until 1837, when he transferred to the University of Louisville, resigning in 1852, he reentered the Medical College of Ohio, teaching anatomy there until 1854, when he retired to a farm in Manchester, Massachusetts; served as dean at both institutions, made a journey to Europe in 1830 to purchase artifacts and books for the Medical College of Ohio, in 1832, he taught two courses at the Medical School of Maine.

Cobb, Josephine 1907–1986, born: Portland; graduate: South Portland High School, A.B. Simmons College 1931, A.M. Boston University 1935, postgraduate work in archival sciences at American University; began her career in the rare book division of the Boston Public Library, later served as assistant archivist at the Massachusetts State Archives, where she gained renown as the only person who could decipher the hitherto-undecipherable handwriting of Governor John Winthrop; in 1936 she became the first female to be employed by the newly created National Archives in Washington; began as a cataloguer, later served as expert of photographic records, finally as specialist in iconography 1960–72; worked with Carl Sandburg, Bell Wiley, Marshall Davidson, Lloyd Ostendorf, and other scholars in the field of the Civil War and Abraham Lincoln; long associated with Frederick Hill Meserve and his outstanding collection of early photographs; came to national attention when she picked out the blurred image of Lincoln at Gettysburg; later she was depicted on the first-day cover *cachet* honoring the National Archives; between 1969 and 1971, trained five librarians who would later head the Kennedy, Nixon, Roosevelt, and other presidential libraries; often called upon as consultant and served on many boards, including the advisory board of the Civil War Centennial Commission, the Abraham Lincoln Sesquicentennial Committee, the committee of selection for the Photography Hall of Fame of the American Museum of Photography, advisory committee of the National Capital Landmarks Commission, &c.; president: Columbia Historical Society 1970–71; retired in 1972 to Cape Elizabeth.

Cobb, William Titcomb 1857–1937, born: Rockland; son of a farmer, attended public schools in Rockland, A.B. Bowdoin College 1877, post-graduate student: University of Leipzig, University of Berlin, Harvard University Law School; L.L.D. (Hon.) Bowdoin College 1905, University of Maine 1905; member: Maine bar 1880; president: Cobb-Wight Co., a lime-manufacturing concern, Bath Iron Works; governor of Maine (Republican) 1905–09, a member of the progressive wing of the Republican party, Cobb favored the Hepburn Act of 1906, which brought railroad management to heel, pure food and drug laws, meat inspection laws, and currency reform; a strict prohibitionist (despite the fact that he was known to take a drink, now and again), he enforced the Sturgis law, which allowed him to appoint deputy commissions to rigorously enforce the Maine law.

Coburn, Abner 1803–85, born: Canaan, in that part that is now Skowhegan; son of a lumberman and member of both houses on the Maine legislature, his maternal grandfather died serving as a scout on the Arnold Expedition; attended Bloomfield Academy, became a surveyor 1825, with his father and brother, Philander, formed E. Coburn & Sons 1830, whose business consisted of surveying and buying land and cutting timber; with the death of his father, the concern became A. & P. Coburn, amassed a fortune in lumber, by 1870, was the largest landowner in the state; member: Maine House of Representatives (Whig) 1838, 1840, 1844; presidential elector 1852, 1860; a founder of the Republican party in Maine; elected twenty-fourth governor of Maine 1863–64; chairman: Republican presidential electors 1884; president: Maine Central Railroad; lived most of his life in the same house as his brother and two sisters, none of whom ever married; president of the board of managers of the College of Agriculture and Mechanical Arts, vice president of the board of trustees of Colby College; bequests after his death totaled over $1 million.

Coffin, Charles Albert 1844–1926, born: Skowhegan; L.L.D. (Hon.) Union College 1914, Bowdoin College 1922, Princeton University 1926, Yale University 1919; began his business career with his uncle Charles in Lynn, Massachusetts, spent twenty years manufacturing shoes; formed a syndicate which purchased a large interest in the Thomson-Houston Electric Co., later, general manager, president, purchased control of the Excelsior Electric Co., the Schuyler Electric Company, the Van Depoele Electric Railroad Co., the Brush Electric Co.; organized the Thomson-Houston International Electric Co., brought together Thomson-Houston Electric Co. and the Edison General Electric Co. to form General Electric Co. 1892; president, chairman of the board 1913–22, as the guiding genius of this vast organization, did more than any other man, or group of men to stabilize and stimulate the electrical industry; an organizer of the War Relief Clearing House, later consolidated with the Red Cross; hired Steinmetz; honored by several European nations for humanitarian efforts during World War I; presented to Bowdoin College his collection of paintings and etchings.

Coffin, John Huntington Crane 1815–90, born: Wiscasset; A.B. Bowdoin College 1834, L.L.D. (Hon.) 1884; professor of mathematics on board USS *Vandalia*, USS *Constitution*, at the Norfolk Navy Yard and on the Florida surveys 1836–43, commanding officer: U.S. Naval Observatory, Washington, D.C., 1843–53, chairman of department, professor of mathematics, astronomy, and navigation: U.S. Naval Academy 1853–66; chief editor: *American Ephemeris and Nautical Almanac* 1866–77; member: American Academy of Arts and Sciences, American Philosophical Society; author: "Observations with the Mural Circle at the U.S. Naval Observatory, with Explanations, Formulas, Tables, and Discussions," 1845–49, *The Compass* 1863, *Navigation and Nautical Astronomy* 1868, both prepared for use at the Naval Academy as texts, "Personal Errors in Observations of the Declination of Stars" in *Gould's Astronomical Journal* 1850, *Observations of the Total Eclipse of the Sun, August 1869* 1884.

Coffin, Nathaniel 1710–66, born: Newburyport, Massachusetts; studied medicine under Dr. Tappan, removed to Maine to practice 1738, his practice extended from Kennebunk to the Kennebec, sometimes called upon to treat those that survived scalping; because of his kind treatment of Indians and their sundry injuries due to warfare and hunting, he was always accorded safe passage through their territories; thoroughly debriefed by newly arrived physicians as to new knowledge and techniques from Europe, in turn he would introduce them to medical problems unique to the frontier; father of Nathaniel Coffin.

Coffin, Nathaniel 1744–1826, born: Falmouth (later Portland); son of Dr. Nathaniel Coffin, studied medicine in Portland and in London with surgeon John Hunter 1764–66; known as the most skillful surgeon east of Boston; particularly skilled at trephining and amputations; went aboard HMS *Canso* to try to dissuade Mowatt from burning Portland 1775, after that event, traveled inland with the refugees to minister to their numerous ills during that hard winter, treated many wounded brought into Falmouth by privateers, during the remainder of the Revolution; with John Merrill, founded Marine Hospital; first president: Maine Medical Society.

Coffin, Robert Peter Tristram 1892–1955, born: Brunswick; son of a farmer; A.B. *summa cum laude* Bowdoin College ΦBK 1915, A.M. Princeton University 1916, Rhodes scholar, A.B. Trinity College, Oxon, 1920, B.Litt. 1921, Litt.D. University of Maine 1937; professor of English: Wells College 1921-34; professor of English: Bowdoin College from 1934; during World War I, enlisted man: 72nd Artillery, American Expeditionary Forces 1918–19; fellow: American Academy of Arts and Sciences; author: *Christchurch* 1924, *Book of Crowns and Cottages* 1925, *Dew and Bronze* 1927, *Golden Falcon* 1929, *An Attic Room* 1929, *Laud, Storm Center of Stuart England* 1930, *The Dukes of Buckingham* 1931, *Portrait of An American* 1931, *The Yoke of Thunder* 1932, *Ballads of the Square-Toed Americans* 1933, *Lost Paradise* 1934, *Strange Holiness* 1935 (accorded the Pulitzer Prize for Poetry 1936), *Red Sky in the Morning* 1935, *John Dawn* 1936, *Saltwater Farm* 1937, *Kennebec, Cradle of Americans* 1937, *New Poetry of New England* 1937, *Maine Ballads* 1938, *Collected Poems* 1939, *Captain Abby and Captain John* 1939, *Thomas-Thomas-Ancil-Thomas* 1941, *There Will Be Bread And Love* 1942, *The Substance That Is Poetry* 1942, *Book of Uncles* 1942, *Primer for Americans* 1942, *Mainstays of Maine* 1944, *Poems for a Son with Wings* 1945, *People Behave Like Ballads* 1946, *Yankee Coast* 1947, *The Third Hunger and the Poem Aloud* 1949, *Coast Calender* 1949, *One Horse Farm* 1949, *Maine Doings* 1950, *Apples by the Ocean* 1950, *Sir Isaac Coffin, Admiral and Profit* 1951, *New England, Life in America* 1951.

Colby, Gardner 1810–79, born: Bowdoinham; son of a merchant who was ruined in the War of 1812 and who died soon after; removed with his widowed mother to Charlestown, Massachusetts; after attending grade school, clerked in a grocery store, opened his own dry-goods store at age twenty, became associated with textile mills; during the Civil War, was one of the largest suppliers of woolen cloth for uniforms for the Union Army, engaged extensively in the China trade, became associated with the building of railroads, one of the prime backers of the building of the Union Pacific Railroad, president: Wisconsin Central Railroad; a devout Baptist, tithed from his earliest days, gave heavily to Brown University, of which he was a trustee 1855–79, Newton Theological Institution, of which he was treasurer for many years; in 1864, the trustees of Waterville College, which was in desperate straits, approached Colby for financial assistance, after a visit to the campus, pledged $50,000, with the result that the college was re-named in his honor 1867.

Colcord, Joanna Carver 1882–1960, born aboard ship off New Caledonia of Maine parents, sister of Lincoln Colcord; graduate: Searsport High School, B.S. *cum laude* University of Maine ΦBK 1906, M.S. 1909; certificate: New York School of Social Work 1911; chemist: Agricultural Experimental Station, Orono 1906, assistant district secretary: New York Charity Organization Society 1911, superintendent of district work 1914–25, field representative: American Red Cross to the Virgin Islands 1920–21, general secretary: Minneapolis Family Welfare Association, lecturer: University of Minnesota 1925–29, director, charity organization department: Russell Sage

Eminent Mainers

Foundation, New York 1929–45, member: advisory council, government of the Virgin Islands, U.S. Department of the Interior; a leader in public assistance and social welfare, had an enormous effect on the Roosevelt administration, close personal friend of Eleanor Roosevelt; author: *Broken Home* 1919, *Emergency Work Relief* 1932, *Songs of American Sailormen* 1938, *Your Community* 1939, *Sea Language Comes Ashore* 1945.

Colcord, Lincoln 1883–1947, born at sea off Cape Horn, brother of Joanna Colcord, his father a sea captain, lived aboard ship until he was fourteen, made several voyages to China; graduate: Searsport High School 1900; student at University of Maine 1900–06, A.M. 1922, ΦBK 1924, while in college, wrote the words for *The Maine Stein Song*, later popularized by Rudy Vallée; civil engineer with the Bangor & Aroostook Railroad, while so employed began to write, his first story was published by *Redbook Magazine* 1907, contributor to *American Magazine*, *Collier's*, *Everybody's*, *Cosmopolitan*; staff correspondent: Washington bureau, *Philadelphia Public Ledger* 1916–18; press adviser to Colonel Edward House; associate editor: *The Nation* 1919–20; contributor of poetry and articles on political and nautical matters to the *New York Herald-Tribune*, *New York Evening Post*, *The Freeman*, *The Nation*, *North American Review*, *Harper's Magazine*, *The American Mercury*, *Century Magazine*; contributed a daily article to the *New York Evening Post* covering the hearings on the sinking of the steamship *Vestris* 1928, in an article in the same newspaper exposed as a hoax *The Cradle of the Deep*, the reputed autobiography of Joan Lowell 1929; regular writer of critical pieces on the literature of the sea for *Books* and the *New York Herald-Tribune* literary supplement; staff member: *Today* 1933–34; a founder, editor: *The American Neptune* from 1941; author: *The Drifting Diamond* 1912, *The Game of Life and Death* 1914, *An Instrument of the Gods* 1922, which was compared favorably by critics to the works of Joseph Conrad, published a book-length poem *A Vision of War* 1915, coauthor: *Sailing Days on the Penobscot* 1932, translator: *Giants in the Earth* by Ole Rolvagg 1927; before World War I, he was an advocate of strict neutrality, subsequent to the war, he was a director of the Truth About Russia Committee, formed to combat propaganda that supposedly misrepresented the situation in Russia and advocated recognition of the Soviet government by the United States; an original member of the National Committee to Uphold Constitutional Government; a founder, secretary, director: Penobscot Marine Museum, edited all of its publications; member: Cruising Club of America.

Colcord, Roswell Keyes 1839–1939, born North Searsport; attended public school in Searsport, where he completed a program in mechanical engineering; learned the trade of a shipwright; lured by tales of the gold rush, removed to California 1856, engaged in placer mining in Tuolumne and Calaveras counties, removed to Nevada 1860; superintendent, manager, and owner of mines and mills, close friend of Samuel Clemens; an advocate of the free coinage of silver, a high protective tariff, a high liquor license, restrictions on immigration and naturalization; elected sixth governor of Nevada (Republican) 1891–95, during a period of deep economic depression; as governor, immediately closed down the Nevada statehouse bar, a place, where, like the Augusta House bar, an inordinate amount of state business was conducted between legislators and lobbyists, in an atmosphere of drunken revelry, cut state spending, created the first state board of health, initiated the department of mechanical engineering at the University of Nevada, introduced the secret ballot, advocated female suffrage, declined renomination; appointed by President McKinley superintendent: U.S. Mint, Carson City 1898–1914; on his one-hundredth birthday, received the greetings of Congress and President Franklin D. Roosevelt; uncle of Lincoln and Joanna Colcord.

Cole, Joseph Foxcroft 1837–92, born: Jay; apprenticed with Winslow Homer at Bufford Lithograph Co., Boston; removed to Paris 1860, studied with Emile Charles Lambinet for three years, opened a studio in Boston, where he gained a national reputation as a landscape painter; exhibited at the Paris Salon 1866, 1873, 1874, 1875; divided his life between Boston and Europe, usually spending his summers in Normandy and Belgium, frequent exhibitor at the Royal Academy, London; at the Centennial Exposition, Philadelphia, exhibited three of his best canvases: *Cows Ruminating, Coast Scene in Normandy, Twilight, Melrose Highlands,* for which he received a diploma and a medal 1876.

Cole, Samuel Valentine 1851–1925, born: Machiasport; brother of William Isaac Cole; A.B. Bowdoin College ΦBK 1874, A.M. 1877, graduate: Andover Theological Seminary 1877, D.D. 1898, L.L.D. (Hon.) Bowdoin College 1912; tutor in rhetoric and Latin: Bowdoin College; ordained Congregational minister, pastor: Taunton, Massachusetts, 1889–97; president: Wheaton Female Seminary, Norton, Massachusetts, 1897–1912, began an extensive building campaign that resulted in the construction of twenty-five structures, by the time of his death; president: Wheaton College from 1912; author: *Fidelissima* 1905, *In Scipios Gardens and Other Poems* 1905, *The Great Grey King and Other Poems* 1914, *Goals Afar* 1924.

Collins, Charles 1813–75, born: North Yarmouth; A.B. Wesleyan College 1837; teacher in Augusta High School 1837–38; founding president: Emory and Henry College, Emory, Virginia, 1838–52; elected tenth president: Dickinson College 1852–60; proprietor and president: Tennessee State Female College, Memphis 1860–75; author: *Methodism and Calvinism Compared* 1849.

Colman, Samuel 1832–1920, born: Portland; son of a successful publisher; studied art with Asher Durand in New York; began exhibiting at Academy of Design, New York, at age eighteen; studied in Spain, Italy, France, and England; cofounder: American Water Color Society 1860, first president 1866–67; member: National Academy of Design 1862; member of the Hudson River School, maintained a studio in New York and Newport, Rhode Island; his works hang in the Metropolitan Museum of Art, New York, New York Public Library, Union League Club, Chicago Art Institute, &c.

Colson, Everett Andrews 1885–1937, born: Warren; orphaned at an early age, raised by his grandmother; largely self-taught, studied stenography, typewriting, and other commercial subjects; passed civil service examinations and while still in his teens, received an appointment in the Philippine civil service, later, U.S. marshal in Canton, China; in World War I: served an auditor in the American Expeditionary Forces in France; assistant financial adviser of the government of Haiti from 1920; at the request of Emperor Haile Salassie, Colson was sent by the State Department to act as his financial adviser 1930, oversaw the introduction of a modern infrastructure, such as electricity, radio, and greatly improved educational facilities, oversaw the construction of the first sewer in Ethiopia, the destruction of the last vestiges of slavery; soon assumed the role of chief adviser, deeply involved in the war of words and diplomatic maneuvering, subsequent to the Italian invasion, eventually dispatched to the League of Nations in Geneva, where he acted as representative of Ethiopia, where he did daily battle with the forces of appeasement, led by Anthony Eden; returned to the United States, where he died in a Washington hospital; Salassie sent a representative to the funeral and wrote to Mrs. Colson; broken by the Italian conquest of Ethiopia, he continued to serve the cause of right and justice until his strength was exhausted and his life was sacrificed.

Comstock, Solomon Gilman 1842–33, born: Argyle; removed to Passadumkeag, with his parents 1845; attended East Corinth Academy, Maine Wesleyan Seminary, Kents Hill, Hampden Academy; law student: University of Michigan 1868–69; member: Minnesota bar 1869, in practice in Moorhead, Minnesota, from 1870; Clay County attorney 1872–78, member: Minnesota House of Representatives 1875–84, member: Minnesota Senate 1882–88, member: U.S. House of Representatives (Republican) 1889–91, unsuccessful candidate for reelection 1890; delegate: Republican National Convention 1892; regent: University of Minnesota 1897–1905; manufacturer of agricultural implements; buried in Prairie Home Cemetery, Moorhead.

Conant, Samuel Stillman 1831–85, born: Waterville; son of Thomas Jefferson Conant, biblical scholar and teacher of Greek, Latin, and German at Waterville College; student: Madison University, Hamilton, New York, Berlin, Heidelberg, and Munich; associated with various journals, managing editor: *Harper's Weekly* from 1869 to 1885, when he mysteriously disappeared; translator of Lermontoff's *Circassian Boy* from the Russian 1875.

Condon, Clarence Milville 1875–1916, born: South Brooksville; sergeant, Battery G, 3rd U.S. Artillery, recipient: Medal of Honor, Calalut, Luzon, Philippine

Islands, 5 November 1899, while in command of a detachment of four men, charged and routed forty entrenched insurgents, inflicting on them heavy loss. Buried in Arlington National Cemetery.

Conkling, Mabel Viola Harris 1871–1966, born: Boothbay, daughter of a ship's captain; graduate: Boothbay Harbor High School 1889; studied drawing, painting, and sculpture in Paris at the Julien, Vitti, Whistler, and Colarossi academies, while studying painting with James McNeil Whistler and modeling with Frederick MacMonnies, she decided that sculpture had a stronger appeal, studied with Augustus Saint-Gaudens, Paul Bartlett, and Jean Injalbert, a piece was accepted at the Paris Salon 1900, maintained a studio in New York 1916–40; executed a number of fountain groups and figures for private estates, many bronze figures, particularly of dancers and of noted persons in opera and music, subjects of her portrait figures included Mrs. John Sargent and Queen Marie of Romania, her bas-relief of MacMonnies was donated to Bowdoin College 1964, her *Triumphant Wings* was inspired by the flight of Charles Lindbergh 1927, her work is in the permanent collection of Colby College, the Art Institute of Chicago, the Gardiner Public Library, the Boothbay Harbor Memorial Library, the Cleveland Museum of Art, &c.; a composer of music, she composed *To Maine We Sing*; president: Association of Women Painters and Sculptors 1926–28.

Connor, Seldon *(on the right)* 1839–1917, born: Fairfield; A.B. Tufts University  1859, L.L.D. 1876; studied law in Woodstock, Vermont; in the Civil War: enlisted in the 1st Vermont Volunteers 1861, saw service at Big Bethel, commissioned lieutenant colonel, USV, assigned to the 7th Maine Volunteers 1861, served in the Peninsula campaign, Sharpsburg, Fredericksburg and Gettysburg, sometimes in regimental command, colonel, USV, commanding officer: 19th Maine Volunteers, commanding officer: 1st Division, 2nd Brigade, III Corps December 1863 to March 1864, badly wounded at the wilderness, after gallant service 6 May 1864, promoted to brigadier general, USV, June 1864, mustered out 1866; appointed assessor of internal revenue of the third district of Maine 1868; appointed collector of internal revenue 1874; elected twenty-ninth governor of Maine (Republican) 1876–79; appointed by President Arthur as U.S. pension agent for Maine 1882-86; president: Northern Banking Co., Portland 1887–92; president: Society of the Army of the Potomac 1890; declined election as president of the Maine State College 1892; appointed adjutant general, Maine militia, by Governor Cleaves 1893; buried in Forest Grove Cemetery, Augusta.

Conway, William 1802–65, born: Camden; joined the U.S. Navy in his youth;  while serving as quartermaster at the Warrington Navy Yard in Pensacola, Florida, refused to haul down the national colors when the navy yard was surrendered to Confederate forces 12 January 1861, with the result that he was clapped into irons; later exchanged; a U.S. Army general order was issued commending Conway for the love and reverence thus impulsively exhibited for his country's flag, he was also presented with a gold medal by Maine residents of California; served as signal quartermaster aboard USS *Mississippi*, during which period he complained to then-Lieutenant George Dewey (later admiral of the navy and son-in-law of Ichabod Goodwin), that with the end of the grog ration, "It's a mighty dry birthday for old George Washington," Mr. Dewey; Conway has been honored by the U.S. Navy with the designation of two destroyers as USS *Conway*, DD-70 and DD-507, the latter saw service in World War II (thirteen battle stars), Korea (two battle stars) and Vietnam (Meritorious Unit Citation).

Cony, Daniel 1752–1842, born: Stoughton (that part that is now Sharon), Massachusetts; prepared for medicine, successful practitioner for many years; removed to Fort Western Settlement (later Augusta) 1778; representative and senator: Massachusetts General Court and member: Massachusetts Executive Council; presidential elector 1793, Kennebec County judge of the court of common pleas, judge of probate; delegate: Maine Constitutional Convention 1819; founded and endowed Cony Female Academy (later Cony High School) 1815; grandfather of Samuel Cony, father-in-law of Nathan Weston, great grandfather of Melville Weston Fuller; buried in Cony Cemetery, Augusta.

Cony, Joseph Saville 1834–67, born: Eastport; appointed acting ensign, USN, 1862, commanded several small-boat expeditions along the Carolina coast while serving in USS *Western World*, appointed executive officer in USS *Shokokon*, promoted to acting master, USN, 1863, discharged 1865; lost at sea when his command, *City of Bath*, burned and sank. The U.S. Navy launched a destroyer, USS *Cony* (DD-508), named in his honor, at Bath Iron Works 1943. She was accorded eleven battle stars for World War II and two for Korea.

Cony, Samuel 1811–70, born: Augusta; son of Samuel Cony, Maine adjutant general, grandson of Daniel Cony, cousin of Joseph Hartwell Williams, Melville Weston Fuller; attended China Academy, A.B. Brown University 1829; studied law with Hiram Belcher in Farmington and Reuel Williams in Augusta, member: Maine bar 1832, settled in Old Town, member: Maine House of Representatives (Democrat)

1835–36, member: executive council 1839, Penobscot County judge of probate 1840–46, Maine state land agent 1847–50, Maine state treasurer 1850–55, resettled in Augusta, abolitionist, joined Republican party 1862, member: Maine House of Representatives: 1862–63, elected twenty-fifth governor of Maine 1864–67; buried in Cony Cemetery, Augusta.

Coombs, Delbert Dana 1850–1938, born: Lisbon Falls; attended public school in New Gloucester, received his first instruction in painting from Scott Leighton, noted animal painter, later had lessons from Harry Brown, marine painter of Portland, apprenticed at age twenty to a Portland photographer, became a sign painter in Auburn, caricaturist for James G. Blaine, who employed Coombs in a political campaign; in charge of illustration for the *Lewiston Journal*, exhibited his work at the Poland Spring gallery, the Boston Art Club, the Cobb art gallery in Boston; produced portraits of Chief Justice John A. Peters of the Maine Supreme Judicial Court, governors William King, Alonzo Garcelon, Nelson Dingley, Admiral Royal Bird Bradford, Senator William Frye, all of which hung in the statehouse in Augusta; achieved greatest renown as a painter of landscapes and cattle, which sold widely across the country.

Coombs, Ernest Arthur, yclept Mr. Dressup 1927–2001, born: Lewiston; graduate: North Yarmouth Academy 1945, diploma: Vesper George School of Art 1949; studied commercial art, but developed an interest in the theatre through scenery painting; served as scenery designer for numerous small theatres throughout the United States; became associated with Fred Rogers while employed by the Pittsburgh Miniature Theatre and WQED-TV, removed to Canada to work as his puppeteer on the Canadian Broadcasting System 1963; from 1967 to 1996, appeared as host Mr. Dressup (for his near-limitless supply of costumes) of *Butternut Square*, an immensely popular children's program on the CBC; recipient of the Academy of Canadian Television's Earle Grey Award 1994; spokesman for Canadian Save the Children; member: Order of Canada 1996; author: *Mr. Dressup's Things to Make and Do, Mr. Dressup's 50 More Things to Make and Do, Mr. Dressup's Birthday Book*; summered in Bristol.

Cooney, Barbara 1917–2000, born: Brooklyn, New York; daughter of a stockbroker and an artist, both of Maine descent; A.B. Smith College 1938, studied etching and lithography at the Art Students League 1940, Ph.D. (Hon.) Fitchburg State College 1989, L.L.D. University of Maine at Machias 1994, Westbrook College 1995, Bowdoin College 1996; in World War II: served as second lieutenant, USAWC 1942–43; freelance artist from 1938; daughter-in-law of Guy Murchie 1944–47; settled in Damariscotta; author and illustrator: *The Wreck of Kelly Island* 1941, *The Kellyhorns* 1942, *Captain Pottle's House* 1943, *Chanticleer and the Fox* (adapted from Chaucer, awarded the Caldecott Medal from the American Library Association 1959) 1958, *The Little Juggler: Adapted from an Old French Legend* 1961, *The Courtship, Merry Mar-*

riage, and Feast of Cock Robin and Jenny Wren: To Which Is Added the Doleful Death of Cock Robin 1965, *Snow White and Rose Red* (adapted from Jacob and Wilhelm Grimm) 1966, *Christmas* 1967, *A Garland of Games and Other Diversions: An Alphabet Book* 1969, *Miss Rumphius* (named Best Book of the Year by the *New York Times*) 1982, *Island Boy* 1988, *Hattie and the Wild Waves* 1990, *Eleanor* 1996; illustrator of over one hundred works by other authors; received numerous awards, including another Caldecott Medal for her illustrations for *The Ox-Cart Man* 1980; proclaimed an official state treasure of the state of Maine 1996.

Copeland, Charles 1858–1945, born: Thomaston; orphaned at an early age, supported himself as an apprentice carpenter, clerking in a store and as a bank messenger; associated with the law firm of Gould & Moore, removed to Boston 1876, student: Lowell Institute, associated with Abner Crossman, a designer who also did ornamental sign painting and interior design, while associated with Crossman, Copeland decorated a church in Springfield and a theatre in New York, his first independent assignment was to sketch the old Paine Furniture Building in Boston for an advertisement, later, engaged in similar work, using engraving, copying, and gold leaf application, opened a studio in Boston 1880; illustrator and painter in watercolors; gained a national reputation as an illustrator, singularly successful as an illustrator of textbooks, did much work for Ginn & Co., among which were Colloidi's *Adventures of Pinnochio*, the *Montgomery Histories*, the *Jones Readers*, William J. Long's books on nature, including *Northern Trails*, *Secrets of the Woods*, *Beasts of the Field*, *Fowls of the Air*, *Following the Deer*, Trent's edition of *Robinson Crusoe*, contributed much art work to *Youth's Companion*, including its first cover, did the sketches for Whittier's *Snowbound*, as an artist, best known for his landscapes and marines in watercolor, exhibited at the Society of American Artists, Pennsylvania Academy of Fine Arts, Art Institute of Chicago, Buffalo Academy of Fine Arts, &c., his works are on permanent display at the Pennsylvania Academy, Boston Museum of Fine Arts, &c.

Copeland, Charles Townsend 1860–1952, born: Calais; son of a lumber merchant; graduate: Calais High School, A.B. *cum laude* Harvard College ΦBK 1882, Litt.D. (Hon.) Bowdoin College 1920; English teacher at Englewood (New Jersey) School, student at Harvard University law school; book reviewer and theatrical critic for the Boston *Advertiser*, later for the Boston *Post*; lecturer on English literature: Harvard University 1893–1910, assistant professor of English 1910–1917, associate professor 1917–25, Boylston professor of rhetoric and oratory 1925–28; highly esteemed and influential teacher, his students included: John Reed, Van Wyck Brooks, Walter Lippmann, Waldo Peirce, Robert Benchley, John Dos Passos, Bernard DeVoto, Robert Sherwood, Helen Keller (who was given her first encouragement to write by Copeland), Heywood Broun, Maxwell Perkins, Conrad Aikten, T. S. Eliot, among others; his former students created the Charles Copeland Alumni Association and met annually, on his birthday, in New York from 1906 to 1937, honorary members included E. B. White and Henry Beston; author: *Life of Edwin Booth* 1901, *Freshmen English and Theme Correcting in Harvard College* 1901, editor: *Letters of Thomas Carlyle to His Youngest Sister* 1899, *Tennyson's The Princess, Representative Biography* 1909, *Selections from Wordsworth, Byron, Shelly and Keats* 1909, *The Copeland Reader* 1926, translator: *The Copeland Translations* 1936; commemorated on the cover of *Time* magazine, 27 January 1927; buried in Calais Cemetery.

Copeland, Joseph Tarr 1813–93, born: Newcastle; A.B. Harvard College 1833, studied law in the office of Daniel Webster; removed to St. Clair, Michigan, judge of the county court 1846–49, elected circuit court judge 1851–59, simultaneously served as justice of the Michigan Supreme Court; built the first sawmill in what was to become the great lumbering town of Bay City; retired to his estate near Pontiac; in the Civil War: commissioned lieutenant colonel of the 1st Michigan Cavalry, served under Banks in the Shenandoah Valley, commissioned colonel of the 5th Michigan Cavalry and brigadier general, USV, 1862, assigned to duty in Washington; on the eve of the Gettysburg campaign, with the overhaul of the Cavalry Corps command, his regiments were reassigned to George Custer, detailed to the command of the depot for enlisted men in Annapolis, later to the draft rendezvous in Pittsburgh and the command of the military prison in Alton, Illinois, resigned November 1865; returned to his estate in Michigan, which he operated as a hotel, later removed to Orange Park, Florida, 1878; buried in Magnolia Cemetery, Orange Park; uncle of U.S. Senator Royal Copeland of New York.

Corson, Dighton 1827–1915, born: Somerset County; attended public schools in Waterville, studied law in Waterville and Bangor; member: Maine bar 1853, practiced in Milwaukee, Wisconsin 1853–61, Nevada 1861–76, Deadwood, South Dakota, 1877–89; member: Wisconsin House of Representatives 1857–58; Milwaukee County district attorney 1858–60; district attorney: Storey County, Nevada 1861–65; delegate: South Dakota Constitutional Convention 1885, 1889; judge: Supreme Court of Sourth Dakota 1889–1913; Corson County, South Dakota, named in his honor.

Cox, Oscar Sidney 1905–66, born: Portland; B.S. *summa cum laude* Massachusetts Institute of Technology ΦBK 1924, Ph.B. Yale College 1927, L.L.B. Yale University Law School 1929; member: New York bar, associated with Cadwallader, Wickersham & Taft 1929–34; member: U.S. Supreme Court bar, District of Columbia bar; assistant counsel in charge of taxes: City of New York 1934–38; assistant to general counsel: U.S. Treasury Department 1938–41, discovered the obscure nineteenth-century law making possible the concept of Lend-Lease; general counsel: Lend-Lease Administration 1941–43, Office of Emergency Management 1943–45; assistant U.S. solicitor general 1942–43; general counsel: Foreign Economic Administration 1943–45; member: Cox, Langford & Brown, Washington; director: American Machine & Foundry Co., Nashua Corp., Italian Economic Corp., Belgian American

Development Corp.; chairman: Committee for International Rules of Judicial Procedure from 1961; decorated: officier de la Légion d'Honneur, France, Cross of Commander, Order of Leopold, Belgium, Order of Star of Solidarity, Italy; father of *Maine Times* publisher Peter Cox.

Crafts, Wilbur Fisk 1850–1922, born: Fryeburg; son of a clergyman, temperance worker and outspoken opponent of slavery; A.B. Wesleyan College 1869, A.M. 1871, B.D. Boston University 1871, Ph.D. Marietta College 1896; Methodist minister 1867–79, Congregational minister 1880-83, Presbyterian minister from 1883; founded American Sabbath Union 1889; founder and superintendent: International Reform Bureau; editor in chief: *Christian Statesman* 1901–03, *20th Century Quarterly* from 1896; author of numerous books, including: *Wagons for Eye Gate* 1874, *Trophies of Song* 1874, *The Ideal Sunday School* 1876, *Song Victories* 1877, *Rescue of the Child-Soul* 1880, *Teacher's Edition of the Revised Testament* 1883, *Must the Old Testament Go?* 1883, *The Sabbath for Man* 1884, *Rhetoric Made Racy* 1884, *Successful Men of Today* 1885, *The Temperance Century* 1885, *Reading the Bible with Relish* 1887, *The Civil Sabbath* 1890, *Practical Christian Sociology* 1895, *Protection of Native Races Against Intoxicants and Opium* 1900, *World Book of Temperance* 1908, *History of National Prohibition* 1920; chairman: International Congress on Alcoholism 1915, 1916, member: Union National Committee to Frame Amendment for Constitutional Prohibition.

Cram, Franklin Webster 1846– ?, born: Bangor; began as a newsboy at the Maine Central Railroad terminal in Bangor, later freight porter, station agent: European & North American Railroad 1870, general freight agent, assistant superintendent, general eastern freight agent: Maine Central Railroad 1882-85, traffic manager, treasurer: Acadia Steamship Co., manager of two branch railroads 1882–85, general manager: New Brunswick Railroad 1885–90, Aroostook Construction Co. 1891–94, and from 1892: general manager 1891–94, vice president to 1900, president from 1900, Bangor & Aroostook Railroad, president and director: Northern Maine Seaport Railroad Co., Northern Telegraph Co., Bangor Investment Co., Schoodic Stream Railroad Co.; a prime mover in the establishment of Millinocket and its mills.

Craven, Charles Henderson 1843–98, born: Portland; son of Thomas Tingey Craven, nephew of Tunis A. McD. Craven; received an appointment to the U.S. Naval Academy from Maine 1860, graduated 1863, commissioned ensign, USN, 1863, lieutenant, USN, 1866, lieutenant commander, USN, 1868; during the Civil War: assigned to the South Atlantic blockading squadron 1863–65, took part in the occupation of Morris Island, July 1863, commanded a division at the assault on Fort Sumter by Commodore Stevens, in various attacks on Confederate batteries on the Stone River in 1864, participated in the joint expedition of naval and military forces to cut the Charleston & Savannah Railroad 1864, attached to the USS *Housatonic*, until she was sunk in the first successful submarine attack against a surface warship, served in the attacks against Forts Gregg and Wagner and at the evacuation of Morris Island, captured three boats with eighty men and officers; after the war, attached to the steam frigate USS *Colorado* in European waters 1865–67, lieutenant commander, USN, aboard USS *Wampanoag* (a warship of revolutionary design, regarded as the fastest warship in the world) 1868, served aboard USS *Powhatan*, in the Pacific squadron 1868–69, aboard the storeship USS *Onward*, South Pacific squadron 1869, aboard USS *Nyack*, Pacific fleet 1870–71, USS *Independence* 1872, USS *Kearsarge*, Asiatic station 1872–75, stationed at the Mare Island Navy Yard, California, 1876–78, placed on the retired list, due to poor health 1881; buried in Arlington National Cemetery.

Craven, Thomas Tingey 1808–87, born: Washington, D.C.; son and grandson of naval officers, brother of Tunis A. M. Craven; appointed midshipman from Maine 1822, attached to the Pacific squadron to 1828, promoted to passed midshipman 1828, lieutenant, USN, 1830, commander, USN, 1852, participated in Wilkes's Antarctic Expedition 1840, on duty at the Naval Academy 1851–55, commanded the Potomac squadron after the death of James Ward, commissioned captain, USN, June 1861, assigned to the command of the USS *Brooklyn*, participated in the passage of Forts Jackson and St. Philip, on the lower Mississippi River, below New Orleans 1862, coming upon the flagship, USS *Hartford*, with Admiral Farragut aboard, hard aground and exposed to terrific fire from both Fort Jackson and Fort St. Philip, stopped the engines of the USS *Brooklyn* and deliberately kept her alongside the flagship to divert the fire of the enemy until Farragut could be extracted from his perilous position, became entangled in a chain barricade, from which, with some difficulty, she was extricated, while experiencing terrific fire from Fort St. Philip, butted and fired upon, by the ram CSS *Manassas*, attacked by a rebel steamer, which he silenced, finally, USS *Brooklyn* was subjected to terrific raking fire from Fort Jackson, which she silenced; participated in further operations along the Mississippi, including Vicksburg, commissioned commodore, USN, July 1862, stationed aboard the USS *Niagara* on special service in European waters, commissioned rear admiral, USN, 1866, commandant: Mare Island Navy Yard, California 1867–68, commanded the North Pacific Squadron 1869, port admiral of San Francisco 1870, retired to Kittery Point; buried in Arlington National Cemetery.

Craven, Tunis Augustus McDonough 1813–64, born: Kittery; son and grandson of naval officers, brother of Thomas Tingey Craven; entered the navy as a midshipman in 1829, cruised with various squadrons to 1837, attached to the coastal survey, promoted to lieutenant, USN, 1841; as an officer of the USS *Dale*, took part in the conquest of California 1846–49; after another period with the coastal survey, commanded the USS *Atrato* surveying party of a canal route across the Isthmus of Darien in Columbia (later Panama) 1857; as commander of the USS *Mohawk*, engaged in suppression of the slave trade off Cuba; received a gold medal and diploma from Queen Isabella II of Spain for the rescue of the crew of a Spanish merchant vessel 1860; in the Civil War: promoted to commander, USN, commanding officer: USS *Tuscarora*, which with the USS *Ino* and USS *Kearsarge*, blockaded the CSS *Sumter*, in Gibraltar harbor, until she was abandoned by Captain Raphael Semmes and her crew; transferred his command to the monitor USS *Tecumseh*, served in her in the James River flotilla, held the point of honor as first ship in the line entering Mobile Bay, 5 August 1864; desiring to engage the formidable Confederate ram CSS *Tennessee*, commanded by his former superior, Admiral Franklin Buchanan, CSN, joined the pilot in the pilothouse, and made for the *Tennessee*, struck a torpedo (as mines were then called) and sank rapidly, taking 93 out of 114 officers and men with her; when Craven and the pilot met, simultaneously, at the base of the ladder to the turret and safety, Craven gestured to the him and said, "You first," pilot scrambled to safety, but Craven was lost with his ship; the sudden loss of the USS *Tecumseh* to a torpedo is what caused his friend and neighbor, Captain James Alden, commanding officer: USS *Brooklyn* the second warship in line, to back down and throw the line into confusion, prompting Admiral Farragut's famous command "Damn the torpedoes, four bells, Jouett go ahead"; there have been three naval vessels named in his honor, the first USS *Craven* (torpedo boat destroyer No. 10) was launched at Bath Iron Works 1899, the second USS *Craven* (DD-70) was launched 1918, later served as HMS *Lewes* in World War II, the third USS *Craven* (DD-382) was launched 1937, earned nine battle stars in World War II.

Crocker, Augustus Luther 1850–1925, born: Paris; A.B. Bowdoin College 1873; studied engineering, constructed steel mills in Springfield, Ohio, and Saint Louis; removed to Minneapolis; organizer and first president: Minneapolis Board of Trade; devoted himself to development of river navigation, building dams and reservoirs; Minneapolis navigation director from 1924; organized Upper Mississippi Barge Line Corp.; built many locks and canals; organizer and first president: Minnesota Reclamation League; member, executive committee: National Municipal Reform League; trained first crew at University of Minnesota.

Cronkhite, Bernice Veazie Brown 1893–1983, born: Calais; A.B. Radcliffe College 1916; bibliographer: Harvard University Bureau of Municipal Research; first female teaching assistant at Harvard University; A.M. Yale University 1918, Ph.D. 1920; director: School of Public Service, established Boston Women's Municipal League; appointed dean: Radcliffe College 1923, the youngest in the history of Radcliffe and the United States, to that time, dean: Radcliffe College Graduate School from 1934, the Cronkite Center at Radcliffe was named in her honor; author: *Graduate Education for Women, The Radcliffe Ph.D.* 1956, *The Times of My Life* 1982.

Crosby, Cornelia Thurza "Flyrod" 1854–1942, born: Phillips; daughter of a

starch manufacturer; spent two years at St. Catherine's School, an Episcopal girls' school in Augusta; worked as a bank clerk in Phillips; turned to the outdoors as a remedy for her tuberculosis, began writing for the *Phillips Phonograph* as well as working as a telegrapher 1878; after catching a trout on a dry fly on Rangely Lake, then an unique feat, she was encouraged by Senator William Frye to write about it; correspondent for the *Franklin Journal, Lewiston Journal, Farmington Chronicle, Maine Sportsman*; began writing for the national magazine *Shooting and Fishing*, in charge of the Maine department for *Field and Stream*; publicist for the Maine Central Railroad Co.; an organizer and participant of the first Sportmen's Exposition, Madison Square Garden, New York, received considerable national newspaper notice 1895; in recognition of her activities, made first licensed Maine Guide 1897; among the first to speak for the wearing of distinctive colors by hunters, a policy of catch and release, bag limits, licensing of hunters and fishermen, &c.

Crosby, John 1867–1962, born: Hampden; son of John Crosby, cofounder, with Cadwallader Washburn, of Washburn, Crosby & Co., Minneapolis, nephew of William Drew Washburn; graduate: Phillips Academy, Andover, A.B. Yale College 1890 (member: Skull and Bones), A.M. Harvard University 1893; member: Minnesota bar 1895, practiced in Minneapolis 1895–1910, counsel to Washburn & Crosby from 1899, partner: Kingman, Crosby & Wallace 1902–10, treasurer, president, chairman of the board: Washburn, Crosby Co., which had become the largest flour-milling concern in the world 1910–28, director: after reorganization of Washburn, Crosby and its many subsidiary companies into General Mills, Inc. 1928–51; director: Northwestern National Bank & Trust Co., Northwestern Bancorp; trustee: Farmers and Mechanics Savings Bank, Minneapolis; chosen by the Federal Reserve Bank of Minneapolis to serve as its representative on the Federal Advisory Council of the Federal Reserve System 1936–40; Minneapolis alderman 1897–1901; trustee: Minneapolis Society of Fine Arts, Minneapolis Institute of Arts, Minneapolis Foundation; founder: Northrop Collegiate School for Girls.

Crosby, William George 1805–81, born: Belfast; son of a lawyer and judge; graduate: Belfast Academy, A.B. Bowdoin College 1823, L.L.D. (Hon.) 1870; studied law with his father, Judge William Crosby, practiced for two years in Boston, removed to Portland; delegate: Whig National Convention 1844, supporter of Henry Clay; secretary: Maine State Board of Education 1850; unsuccessful Whig candidate for governor 1852, elected seventeenth governor of Maine by the legislature, no candidate having received a majority, the popular vote being divided between Whig, Democrat, and Free Soil parties 1853, reelected 1854; unsuccessful Democrat candidate for the U.S. House of Representatives; a poet from his college days, author: *Poetical Illustrations of the Athenaeum Gallery*; buried in Grove Cemetery, Belfast.

Cross, Burton Melvin 1902–98, born: Augusta; son of a farmer and Kennebec County deputy sheriff; after graduating from Cony High School 1920, became a florist; member: Augusta Common Council 1933–37, president; member: Augusta board of alderman 1937–41, president; member: Maine House of Representatives 1941–45, Maine Senate 1945–52, majority floor leader 1947, president 1949–52; became acting governor with the resignation of Governor Frederick Payne 24 December 1952, served as governor, in his own right (Republican) 1953–55; unsuccessful candidate for reelection 1954; engaged in the insurance and stock brokerage business to 1971; buried in Forest Grove Cemetery, Augusta.

Croswell, James Greenleaf 1852–1915, born: Brunswick; grandson of Simon Greenleaf, cousin of Alexander Wadsworth Longfellow, Jr.; graduate: Cambridge (Massachusetts) Latin School, A.B. *summa cum laude* Harvard College ΦBK 1873; tutor at St. Marks School, Southboro, Massachusetts, and Harvard College 1877–78; went to Germany as a Parker Fellow and was a student for three years at the universities of Bonn and Leipzig; assistant professor of Greek and Latin: Harvard College 1883–87; headmaster: Brearley School, New York 1887–1915; president: School Masters' Association of New York, Headmasters' Association; member: College Entrance Examination Board, Society of the Cincinnati.

Croswell, Micah S. 1833–1913, born: Farmington Falls; son of a farmer and storekeeper; delicate health allowed for only occasional attendance at Maine Wesleyan Seminary, Kents Hill, studied at Waterville College for two years, made a fishing voyage to Newfoundland that improved his health sufficiently to attend Farnum University, Greenville, North Carolina, for one term, A.B. Amherst College 1856; principal of a seminary in Geneseo, Illinois; went with his brother, recently returned from Hawaii, to Montecello, Minnesota, where they prospered as merchants; while a student at Chicago Theological Seminary, the Civil War broke out; returning to Montecello, joined the local regiment of volunteers, rising in rank to captain and commissary, detached to join Pope's Expedition to quell the Sioux uprising in Minnesota; served as commissary of training camps in Milwaukee; with the rank of major, USV, sent to St. Louis as chief of commissary of the district of the frontier, later department of Arkansas, Fort Smith; mustered out with the brevet rank of lieutenant colonel, USV, 1866; completing the course at Chicago Theological Seminary, ordained at Emporia, Kansas, served in various churches in California, Illinois, Iowa, and Arkansas to 1890; removed to California 1893, managed his oil wells, an orange grove, and a ranch at Croswell Springs; died in Altadena.

Crow, Herbert Carl 1883–1945, born: Highland; student at Carlton College 1900–01, University of Missouri 1906–07; printers assistant 1898; member: editorial staff: *Fort Worth Star-Telegram* 1906–11; associate city editor: *Shanghai China Press* 1911–13; business manager: *Tokyo Japan Advertiser* 1913–14; far eastern representative: Commission on Public Information 1916–18; proprietor: advertising agency, Shanghai 1919–37; special assistant to director: Office of War Information 1941–43; author: *Handbook for China* 1912, *America and the Philippines* 1913, *Japan and America* 1915, *400 Million Customers* (published in English, French, German, Swedish, Danish, Spanish, Dutch, and Polish) 1937, *Master Kung* (published in German and Swedish) 1938, *I Speak for the Chinese* (published in English and Burmese) 1938, *He Opened the Door of Japan* (published in London as *Harris of Japan*) 1939, *The Chinese Are Like That* (published in London as *My Friends the Chinese*) 1939, *Foreign Devils in the Flowery Kingdom* 1940, *America in Stamps* 1940, *Meet the South Americans* 1941, *Japan's Dream of World Empire* 1942, *The Great American Customer* 1943, *China Takes Her Place* 1944, *The City of Flint Grows Up* 1945, numerous articles for periodicals; member: Players Club, New York.

Crowell, Merle 1888–1956, born: North Newport; graduate: Coburn Classical Institute 1906, student at Colby College 1906–07, Litt.D. (Hon.); reporter: *New York Evening Sun* 1911–15; associate editor and staff writer: *American Magazine* 1915–23, editor in chief 1923–29; magazine writer and publicist from 1929; director of public relations: Rockefeller Center 1931–44, originated the erection of an annual Christmas tree and attendant festivities in the Rockefeller Center plaza; senior editor: *Reader's Digest* from 1944.

Crowley, William Robert 1884–1968, born: Bangor, son of a building contractor; attended public schools in Bangor, special student in chemistry at Bowdoin College 1904–09, A.M. 1928; research chemist with E.I. du Pont de Nemours Co., Wilmington, Delaware, 1909–10, associated with the publishing firm of Longmans, Green & Co., New York 1910–39, representative of the introduction of their publications into the New York City school system, involved in all matters connected to their educational department, general manager of the educational and publication department from 1932; an organizer, president: Savannah (Georgia) Shipyards, Inc. 1940–45, the company was involved in producing Liberty and Victory ships during World War II; after obtaining a high rating from the Priorities Committee of the Army and Navy Munitions Board, U.S. Office of Production Management, the company received a $12 million contract from the U.S. Maritime Commission for nine 2,800-ton Coaster-type cargo vessels, which were built and delivered to Great Britain under provisions of the Lend-Lease Act; produced an additional thirty 10,000-ton cargo vessels for the war effort; vice president: Seaboard Marine Service Corp. 1945–48, a ship-maintenance bureau in New York; in addition to his business activities, Crowley maintained a lifelong interest in athletics, captain of his high school football team, played left end on the varsity football team while at Bowdoin College, captain 1907, the year that it won the state championship, subsequently, over a period of over forty years, was a nationally known football referee, officiating at hundreds of games, including a record nineteen Army-Navy games and many Harvard-Yale and Army-Notre Dame contests, as well as several Rose Bowls; after leaving college, served as recreation director at Sing Sing prison where he helped organize a football program and officiated at many prison games; president: New York Public School Athletic League; member: Collegiate Football Rules Committee; president: Eastern Association of Intercollegiate Football Officials 1935–38; contributor of over a hundred articles on sports for various publications, including the *Saturday Evening Post*; author: *Qualitative and Quantitative Analysis* 1910; member: Bowdoin College board of overseers 1942–68, trustee: Brooklyn (New York) Public Library from 1938, member: New York City Board of Education 1939.

Cummings, Joseph 1817–1890, born: Falmouth; A.B. *summa cum laude* Wesleyan University 1840, S.T.D. 1850, Harvard University 1861, L.L.D. (Hon.) Northwestern University 1866; principal: Amenia (New York) Seminary 1843–46, ordained Methodist ministry 1846, filled pastorates in Malden, Chelsea, and Boston, Massachusetts, 1846–53; professor of theology: Methodist General Biblical Institute, Concord, New Hampshire, 1853–54; president: Genesee College, Lima, New York, 1854–57; fifth president: Wesleyan University 1857–75, during his administration, Wesleyan became a co-educational institution 1871; professor of mental philosophy and political economy, Wesleyan University 1875–77; held pastorates in Malden and Cambridge, Massachusetts, 1877–81; John Evans professor of moral and intellectual philosophy, president: Northwestern University 1881–90; author: *Life of the Late Daniel Sillman Newcomb* 1855, *An Elective Presiding Eldership in the Methodist Episcopal Church* 1877; editor: Butler's *Analogy of Religion* 1875.

Curran, Edward Matthew 1903–88, born: Bangor; A.B. University of Maine 1928, L.L.B. Catholic University of America, Washington, 1927, L.L.D. (Hon.) 1967, L.L.D. University of Maine 1970, Georgetown University 1971; member: District of Columbia bar 1929, associate of Milton W. King, Washington 1929–34, assistant corporation counsel: District of Columbia 1934–36, judge: District of Columbia Police Court 1936–40, U.S. attorney, District of Columbia 1940–46, U.S. district judge 194?, chief judge: U.S. District Court, District of Columbia 1966–71, senior U.S. district judge 1971–88, instructor: Catholic University School of Law 1930–35, professor of law: Georgetown University Law School 1943–46; member: Friendly Sons of St. Patrick.

Curtis, Charles Albert 1835–1907, born: Hallowell; student: Maine State Seminary, Yarmouth Academy, A.B. Bowdoin College 1861, A.M.; in the Civil War: Maine state drillmaster 1861, instructor of field officers: 6th Maine Volunteers, assistant adjutant general: staff of General Winfield Scott Hancock, secondd lieutenant, 7th Infantry, USA, for extraordinary merit 1862, 5th Infantry, Fort Craig, New Mexico, brevetted captain 1865 for meritorious service, fought against Texas forces on the Rio Grande 1862, against the Indians of the Southwest 1862–69, retired, because of wounds; as captain 1870, professor of military science and tactics: Norwich University, Norwich, Vermont, 1870–75, 1876–80, St. Augustine's College, Benecia, California, 1875–76; president: Norwich University 1876–80, compiled the first book of regulations published by Norwich University; professor of military science: Shattuck School, Faribault, Minnesota, 1880–85, East Florida Seminary, Gainesville, Florida, 1885–89, Kenyon Military Academy, Sweet Springs, Missouri, 1890–92, Howe School, Lima, Ohio, 1892–93, professor of military science and tactics: University of Wisconsin, Madison from 1895; commanded the largest student corps in the United States; colonel: Minnesota National Guard 1880–85, lieutenant colonel: Florida National Guard 1885–89, Wisconsin National Guard 1901–07; author: *Captured by the Navahoes* 1898, articles for *St. Nicholas*, *Wide Awake*, *Youth's Companion*, *Harper's Young People*, &c.

Curtis, Charles Densmore 1875–1925, born: Augusta; A.B. Pomona College ΦΒΚ 1900, A.M. University of California 1901; member: American Expedition for the Excavation of Cyrene, Tripoli, 1910–11; fellow: American Academy in Rome 1912–15; associate professor of archaeology: American Academy; author: *Roman Monumental Arches* 1908, *Ancient Granulated Jewelry of the Seventh Century, B.C. and Earlier* 1917, *The Bernadini Tomb* 1919; corresponding member: Pontifical Archaeological Society, Rome.

Curtis, Cyrus Herman Kotzschmar 1850–1933, born: Portland; attended public schools in Portland, A.M. (Hon.) Bowdoin College 1913, L.L.D. Ursinus College 1913, University of Pennsylvania 1924, Bowdoin College 1927; at age twelve started his first newspaper *Young America*, which he sold to the boys of Portland, saved his press from being destroyed in the Great Fire of 1866 by placing it in a wagon and dragging it to safety, later started *People's Ledger*, removed to Boston, where he established the *Boston Independent* 1870, removed to Philadelphia 1876, established the *Tribune and Farmer*, which contained a women's column, written by Curtis, himself, when this was criticized by Mrs. Curtis, he turned it over to her, in time it grew a full page, then to an eight-page supplement, finally in 1884, brought out *Ladies' Journal and Practical Housekeeper* as a separate magazine, when Mrs. Curtis retired as editor in 1889, Curtis hired Edward Bok (who later became his son-in-law) as editor; engaged well-known authors, such as Louisa May Alcott to write for *Ladies' Home Journal*; revived *Saturday Evening Post*, the oldest newspaper in the United States 1897, acquired *Country Gentleman* 1912, the *Philadelphia Public Ledger* 1913, the *Philadelphia Telegraph* 1918, the *Philadelphia Press* 1920, the *Philadelphia North American* 1925, the *New York Evening Post* 1923, the *Philadelphia Inquirer* 1930; Curtis Publishing Co.

Eminent Mainers

became the largest in the world, in its day; made many significant benefactions, including the Kotzschmer memorial organ, Portland, then the largest municipal organ in the world, rebuilt Montpelier, Henry Knox's home in Thomaston, made large bequests to Bowdoin College, the Maine General Hospital, the Franklin Institute, the Franklin Memorial, and the University of Pennsylvania, Philadelphia, North Yarmouth Academy, Knox County General Hospital; his daughter, Mary Louise Curtis Bok Zimbalist, endowed the Curtis Institute, Philadelphia, in his memory; an avid sailor, spent much time on the coast on his yacht *Lyndonia*.

Curtis, John 1800–69, born: Bradford; originally a logger, boiled a quantity of spruce gum, sugar, and maple sap in his wife's kettle, spreading it out to cool, chopped the mass into one-inch squares, which he dusted with corn starch and wrapped in tissue paper, selling them as State of Maine Pure Spruce Gum, the first commercial chewing gum, meeting with success, founded Curtis & Son, Inc., erected a factory on Middle Street, Portland, buried in Evergreen Cemetery, Portland; father of John Bacon Curtis.

Curtis, John Bacon 1827–97, born: Hampden; son of John Curtis; took over Curtis & Son, after his father's death, invented several machines for the manufacture of chewing gum, built twelve ships, engaged in dredging, owned the Forest City line of steamboats, pioneer rancher in Nebraska where he owned a 50,000-acre ranch, donated the Curtis Free Public Library to the town of Bradford; buried in Evergreen Cemetery, Portland.

Curtis, Kenneth M. 1931– , born: Curtis Corner, Leeds; graduate: Cony High

School, Augusta 1949, B.S. Maine Maritime Academy, Castine 1952, after serving aboard sundry merchant ships, received his L.L.B. degree from Portland University Law School 1959; served as assistant to Congressman James Oliver 1959–61, employed by the Legislative Research Service of the Library of Congress 1961–62, appointed by President John Kennedy: Maine state coordinator for the area redevelopment administration 1963–64; elected by the Maine legislature: Maine secretary of state 1965–66; won the Democratic nomination for governor, later defeated Governor John Reed, served as governor 1967–75; when elected, he was the youngest governor in the nation; saw many of the points in his Maine Action Plan enacted: reduced the number of state agencies from over two hundred to ten, streamlined financing of schools, created the University of Maine System, bringing the University of Maine and the various state colleges under one board of trustees, secured passage of various environmental laws; won reelection very narrowly in 1970; chaired the New England Governors' Conference, cochaired the New England Regional Commission; chairman: Democratic National Committee 1977; U.S. ambassador to Canada.

Curtis, Oakley Chester 1865–1925, born: Portland; son of a shipbuilder; began his career as a clerk for the Grand Trunk Railway Co., later, became an employee of Randall & McAllister, wholesale dealers in coal, Portland; became manager 1894, president, upon incorporation, became the largest such dealer in Maine; president: Casco Mercantile Bank Co., Union Safe Deposit & Trust Co.; director: United States Trust Co., Merchants Trust Co.; alderman: Portland 1901; member: Maine House of Representatives 1903–04, member: Maine Senate 1905–08, mayor of Portland 1911–14, governor of Maine (Democrat) 1915–17, during his administration, labor for women and boys was restricted to fifty-four hours per week, the school year was lengthened; unsuccessful candidate for reelection 1916.

Curtis, Winterton Conway 1875–1946, born: Richmond; A.B.Williams College φΒΚ 1897, A.M. 1898, Sc.D. 1934, Ph.D. Johns Hopkins University 1901; instructor: Marine Biology Laboratory, Woods Hole 1899–1903, in charge of invertebrate course 1908–11; instructor in zoology: University of Missouri 1901–04, associate professor 1904–08, professor from 1908, acting dean: College of Arts and Science 1939, dean 1940–45; scientific assistant: U.S. Bureau of Fisheries 1907–10; visiting professor: Keio University, Tokyo 1932–33; expert witness: Scopes trial, Dayton, Tennessee 1925; chairman: National Research Council, Division of Biology and Agriculture 1930–31, member: executive board 1935–38; fellow: American Academy of Arts and Sciences; president: American Society of Zoologists 1932; investigator in embryology, morphology, parasitism in platoda and mollusca, and in effects of radiation upon animals, humanistic aspects of biology; author: *Science and Human Affairs* 1922, *Laboratory Directions in General Zoology* 1938, *Textbook of General Zoology* 1948; associate editor: *Journal of Morphology and Physiology* 1927–29.

Cushing, Charles 1734–1810, born: Scituate, Massachusetts; son and grandson of judges of the Massachusetts Superior Court, brother of William Cushing; A.B. Harvard College 1755, A.M. 1758, classmate of John Adams, also of Jacob Bailey, David Sewall, Jonathan Bowman; originally destined for the ministry, but like his friend, John Adams, ultimately chose the law; kept school in Newbury, Massachusetts, 1757, and in Plymouth, Massachusetts, 1758; deputy superintendent of construction at Fort Pownal on the Penobscot River; appointed the first high sheriff of Lincoln County (where his brother William was serving as judge) 1760; colonel of the Lincoln County militia, a matter of considerable burden, given the fact that the French and Indian War was still raging 1759; appointed deputy surveyor of the King's Woods 1761; member: Massachusetts House of Representatives 1775–76; appointed clerk of the Superior

Court of Judicature 1776; commissioned brigadier general of Lincoln County militia 1777; as clerk of the west precinct of Pownalborough, opposed attempts by Episcopalians to obtain relief from provincial taxes for the support of the ministry, which led to a prolonged, vituperative conflict with his neighbor and classmate Jacob Bailey, rector of St. Luke's Parish, religion becoming mixed up with politics, Congregationalists tending toward rebellion, Episcopalians toward Toryism; served as colonel in the disastrous Penobscot Expedition; after his return to Pownalborough, he was seized by one Black John Jones and a party of Tories and carried off to Castine, from which he was subsequently paroled so that he might go to Boston to seek the release of a British major, in exchange 1780; upon his return to Pownalborough, he found his wife still quite unhinged by their ordeal, so he removed with her and his family to Boston; appointed by his brother William to a clerkship of the Massachusetts Supreme Judicial Court 1781; refused reappointment as Lincoln County sheriff; represented Suffolk County for one year in the Massachusetts Senate 1795; justice of the peace and quorum 1798–1805; involved himself in the affairs of the Massachusetts Humane Society.

Cushing, William 1732–1810, born: Scituate, Massachusetts, son and grandson of judges of the Massachusetts Superior Court and members of the Massachusetts Executive Council; A.B. Harvard College 1751, A.M. 1753, A.M. Yale College 1753, as an undergraduate, formed an attachment with his cousin Hannah Phillips, with whom he conceived a child, several years later, while visiting her and her husband, she taunted him about his continuing single status, in response, Cushing pointed to Hannah's latest infant (another Hannah) and stated, "I shall wait for this young lady to grow up, and make her my wife," which he subsequently did; taught school in Roxbury for a year, studied law with Jeremiah Gridley, member: Massachusetts bar 1755; removed to Pownalborough (that part that is now Dresden), in the company of his brother Charles 1755, practiced law; first Lincoln County judge of probate 1760–71; succeeded his father as judge: Massachusetts Superior Court 1772–77; the only Royal judge to side with the revolutionaries; chief justice: Massachusetts Supreme Court 1777–89, his ability to keep Massachusetts courts open and dispensing justice during the Revolution was greatly admired, his most important decision was that the first article of the Massachusetts Commonwealth Constitution stating that all men are born free and equal, slavery was, therefore, abolished, within the commonwealth; declined nominations for governor 1785, 1794; vice president: Massachusetts Constitutional Convention 1788; presidential elector 1788; associate justice: U.S. Supreme Court 1789–1810; upon the rejection of the nomination of Rutledge as chief justice, Cushing was appointed chief justice by Washington, unanimously confirmed by the Senate, but resigned in one week; last survivor of original appointees.

Cushman, Frank Holmes 1891–1946, born: Presque Isle, son of a dentist; removed with his family to Claremont, New Hampshire; graduate: Stevens High School, B.S. Dartmouth College 1913, D.M.D. Harvard University School of Dentistry 1915; practiced in Boston; instructor: Harvard University School of Dentistry 1915, assistant professor 1926, professor of operative dentistry 1929–41; established the first formal instruction in diagnosis in dentistry at Harvard University Medical School 1925; reorganized the teaching of operative dentistry there to conform to sound principles of pedagogy; author of numerous papers on various aspects of school administration and on oral hygiene, dental surgery, diagnosis, and related matters; member: editorial board: *Journal of Dental Education*; served 1915–16 as first lieutenant, Harvard Unit, Royal Army Medical Corps, British Expeditionary Force, first lieutenant, USA Dental Reserve Corps, stationed at the School of Oral and Plastic Surgery, University of Pennsylvania, captain, USA Dental Corps, American Expeditionary Forces, chief of dental service: Base Hospital No. 7, France 1918–19, major, Dental Reserve Corps 1920–25; president: American Academy of Dental Science 1929.

Cushman, Joshua 1761–1834, born: Halifax, Massachusetts; served in Revolutionary army 1777–80; A.B. Harvard College 1787, studied theology, ordained Congregational ministry, pastor in Winslow for twenty years; member: Massachusetts Senate 1810; member: Massachusetts House of Representatives 1811, 1812; member at-large: U.S. House of Representatives 1821–25; member: Maine House of Representatives 1834; buried on Maine statehouse grounds.

Cutler, Elliott Carr 1888–1947, born: Bangor; son of a merchant and logger, grandson of John Lysander Cutler; A.B. Harvard College 1909, M.D. Harvard University Medical School 1913; surgical house officer: Peter Bent Brigham Hospital, Boston, 1913–15, resident surgeon: Harvard unit, American Hospital, Paris, 1915, resident surgeon: Massachusetts General Hospital 1915–16, assistant in surgery: Harvard University Medical School 1915–16; in World War I: went to France with the Harvard University Medical Unit, under Harvey Cushing, served with the American Ambulance Hospital, Paris, organized and directed a Red Cross hospital to assist the French *Service de Santé*; when the United States entered the war, joined another Harvard unit, organized Base Hospital No. 5, attached to the British Army, served at several advanced casualty clearing stations, assigned to an evacuation hospital at Toul, during the battles of Belleau Woods and Château-Thierry attached to Mobile Hospital No. 1 at Coulommiers, chief of surgical services of Evacuation Hospital No. 3 in the St. Mihiel, Argonne, and Aisne offensives; achieved the rank of major, USA Medical Corps; after the armistice, sent to Trier, Germany, with the American Army of Occupation, discharged 1919, promoted to lieutenant colonel Medical Reserve Corps 1924; resident surgeon: Peter Bent Brigham Hospital 1919–21, associate in surgery: Harvard University Medical School 1921–24, instructor in surgery 1921–24; professor of surgery: Western Reserve University (Cleveland) 1924–32; consulting surgeon: New England Peabody Home for Crippled Children from 1932; Moseley professor of surgery: Harvard University Medical School from 1932, surgeon in chief: Peter

Bent Brigham Hospital from 1932; chief medical consultant, with rank of brigadier general, USA, to the secretary of war 1942–45; awarded Distinguished Service Medal with battle clusters for Champagne-Marne, Aise-Marne, St. Mihiel, croix de guerre with palm, Order of the British Empire, member of numerous honorary organizations, recipient of numerous awards; Harvard University overseer, trustee: Noble & Greenough School, Dexter School; coauthor: *Atlas of Surgical Operations* 1939, editor: MacMillan Surgical Monograph Series, member, editorial boards of the *American Journal of Surgery* and *British Journal of Surgery*; Cutler was regarded as one of the foremost surgeons in the country, specialized in heart and brain surgery, first American surgeon to operate on cases of mitral stenosis.

Cutler, Lysander 1807–66, born: Massachusetts; removed to Dexter 1828, merchant, Maine Militia lieutenant colonel during the Aroostook War; after being financially ruined in the panic of 1857, removed to Wisconsin; in the Civil War: commissioned colonel, USV, commanding officer: 6th Wisconsin Infantry 1861–62, promoted to brigadier general, USV, 1862, commanding officer: 2nd Brigade, 1st Division, 1st Corps, heavily engaged in the fierce fighting during the first day at Gettysburg, commanding officer: 1st Brigade, 4th Division, 5th Corps, after the death of General Wadsworth in the Wilderness campaign, assumed command of the 4th Division 1864, commanded his division at Spotsylvania, Cold Harbor, Petersburg, Weldon Railroad, wounded twice in action; brevetted major general, USV, 1864.

Cutler, Nathan 1775–1861, born: Lexington, Massachusetts; son of a farmer; graduate: Leicester Academy, A.B. Dartmouth College 1798; principal: Middlebury Academy (later Middlebury College) 1798–1803; member: Massachusetts bar 1801, removed to Farmington 1803; member: Massachusetts General Court 1809–11, 1819, delegate: Maine Constitutional Convention 1819, member: Maine Senate 1828–29, president 1829; succeeded Governor Lincoln as governor, served 1829–30, because the Maine Senate, of which he was president, had dissolved, a controversy arose as to whether he ought to remain governor, the Maine Supreme Judicial Court, ruled that Joshua Hall, speaker of the Maine House of Representatives, should become governor, until governor-elect Jonathan Hunton assumed office in February 1830; presidential elector at-large 1832; Franklin County treasurer 1838, 1842; a founder of Farmington Academy; member: Maine House of Representatives 1844.

Cutter, Ammi Ruhamah 1705–46, born: Cambridge, Massachusetts; son of a prosperous miller; A.B. Harvard College 1725, A.M. 1728, paid his fees in ground Indian meal, wooden planks, as well as taking care of the college clock; after graduation, remained as laboratory assistant to Professor Greenwood, Hopkins Scholar, and, for one term, taught grammar school; began to preach in North Yarmouth 1729, ordained 1730, his parish included the modern towns of Yarmouth, North Yarmouth, Cumberland, Pownal, Freeport, and Harpswell; warned by his congregation to avoid extreme forms of Arminianism 1733, dismissed by that congregation for failing to accede to its strictures, setting into motion a legal wrangle over title to the parsonage lot that continued until well after his own death; employed by Harvard College to survey its lands on Merriconeag Neck, employed by the town of North Yarmouth to rectify certain errors in the original survey of the town's borders; as physician and surgeon, had a high reputation, paid by the province to tend to the sick at Fort George; served for a long period as clerk to the proprietors, however, served as the town's representative in a legal challenge to those same proprietors; criticized when he failed to alert the Waldo proprietors that certain English settlers were plotting with certain Indians to burn one of the Waldo settlements, information he had gained from the Norridgewock Jesuit, Siresme, whom he entertained at his garrison in North Yarmouth; appointed by the province to supervise the Indian truckhouse at Fort Mary, near Hollis 1742, while there, compiled a lexicon of the Pigwacket dialect; with the coming of war, attempted to save the Pigwackets from Huron atrocities, first grouping them around the truckhouse and finally removing them to Boston 1744; recruited a company for the Louisbourg Expedition, received a commission as captain in Jeremiah Moulton's Third Massachusetts Regiment, detailed to seize and hold the island of Canso, which he did with sufficient zeal that he was rewarded by being appointed chief surgeon to the Louisbourg garrison; succumbing to dysentery, his body was returned to North Yarmouth and buried next to the meetinghouse; father of Ammi Ruhamah Cutter.

Cutter, Ammi Ruhamah 1735–1820, born: North Yarmouth; son of Ammi Ruhamah Cutter; A.B. Harvard College 1752, A.M. 1755, M.D. (Hon.) 1792; joined Crown Point Expedition as surgeon, after three years at Fort Edward, joined the Ranger unit, led by Robert Rogers, at the siege of Louisbourg; received large grants of land in New Hampshire for his service; surveyed the road from Conway to the Connecticut River; founded a smallpox hospital in Portsmouth; justice of the peace 1773; appointed by Continental Congress as physician general of the Hospital in the East; member: New Hampshire Constitutional Convention 1781, longtime president of the New Hampshire Medical Society.

Cutts, James Madison 1805–63, born: Cutts Island, Saco; son of Richard Cutts; law student of William Wirt until the War of 1812 swept away his father's wealth; appointed chief clerk in the second comptroller's office, U.S. Treasury; during the Buchanan and Lincoln administrations was second comptroller 1856–63; his daughter Ada was the wife of Senator Stephen A. Douglas, his wife's sister was the Confederate spy Rose Greenhow.

Cutts, Richard 1771–1845, born: Cutts (later Factory) Island, Saco; descendant of John Cutt, colonial governor of New Hampshire, cousin of Charles Cutts, member: U.S. Senate from New Hampshire; A.B. Harvard College 1790; studied law, had an extensive business in shipping and manufacturing; member: Massachusetts House of Representatives 1799, 1800; member: U.S. House of Representatives (Republican) 1801–13; superintendent general of military supplies 1813–17, appointed first comptroller of the U.S. Treasury 1817–29; brother-in-law of Dolley Madison, father of James Madison Cutts and Richard Dominicus Cutts, one of the great topographers of the nineteenth century; his home on Lafayette Square was a center of culture in Washington; originally buried in St. John's Graveyard, Washington, reinterred in Oak Hill Cemetery, Washington, 1857.

Cutts, Samuel 1726–1801, born: Kittery; apprenticed with Nathaniel Sparhawk, married the daughter of Edward Holyoke, president of Harvard 1762; early and conspicuous member of the Sons of Liberty; principal owner: brig *Resolution*, seized by British authorities at Portsmouth 1769; delegate: New Hampshire Provincial Assembly 1774, 1775; member: Committee of Correspondence; delegate: Fourth and Fifth Provincial Congress 1775, 1776; first justice of the court of common pleas for Rockingham County; chairman: committee that drafted the New Hampshire declaration of independence, June 1776; chairman: Portsmouth Committee of Ways and Means, the local ad hoc Revolutionary Governing Committee, led a mob of some 400 men and boys that took Fort William and Mary, bloodlessly.

d'Abbadie, Bernard-Anselm, Baron de St. Castin 1689–1720, born: Castine; fourth Baron of St. Castin, son of Jean Vincent de St. Castin and Pidiwamika, daughter of Modokawando, chief of the Abenakis; student: Petite Séminaire, Québec; from age fifteen, promoted Abenaki raids on New England; played a leading role in defense of Port Royal 1707, wounded several times, defeated a force significantly greater than his own; assumed title with death of his father 1707; given command of all Indians in Acadia; very successful privateer; appointed to overall command in Acadia 1711; after treaty of Utrecht, attempted to convince the Abenakis to migrate to Cape Breton; removed to France 1714.

d'Abbadie, Jean-Vincent, Baron de St. Castin 1652–1707; born: Bearn, France; colonel of the king's bodyguard, colonel of the Carrigan regiment, which he took to Canada 1665; reestablished French control over southwestern Acadia with his seat at what came to be called Castine, where he established a trading house 1677; married Pidiwamika (Moon Witch), daughter of a local sachem; led a force of 200 Penobscots in the capture of Pemaquid 1696; assisted in the defense of Port Royal, Nova Scotia, 1706, 1707, when he was badly wounded; returned to France 1707, leaving his son in control.

Daggett, Aaron Simon 1837–1938, born: Greene Corner, Greene; a descendant of Henry Dearborn; student: Monmouth Academy, Maine Wesleyan Seminary, Kents Hill, A.B. Bates College 1861; in the Civil War: enlisted in Company E, 5th Maine

Infantry, appointed first lieutenant, USV, participated in the battles of: first Bull Run, West Point, Gaines's Mills, Savage Station, White Oak Swamp, Malvern Hill, Crampton's Gap, Antietam, Fredericksburg, Maryes Heights, Salem Church, Gettysburg, Mine Run, the Wilderness, Spotsylvania, where he particularly distinguished himself at the Angle, North Anna, Cold Harbor, Petersburg, twice wounded, promoted to major, USV, 1863, lieutenant colonel, USV, 1865, brevetted colonel, USV, and brigadier general, USV, for gallant and meritorious service; appointed captain in the regular army by General Grant 1866, major, USA, 1892, lieutenant colonel, USA, 1895, brigadier general, USA, 1901; in the Spanish-American War: led the 10th regiment in the Santiago campaign, El Caney (San Juan Hill) 1898; Philippine Insurrection, where he commanded the south line extending from Bacoor to Manila 1899, commanding officer: U.S. infantry during Boxer Rebellion 1900: Yangtsun, Peking, Imperial City; personally scaled the outer walls of Peking and unfurled the flag, second allied general officer to enter besieged legations; author: *America in the Chinese Relief Expedition* 1903; on his one-hundredth birthday, belatedly received a Purple Heart for his wounds in the Civil War and a Silver Star for gallantry in action against the Boxers, greeted by the president of the United States and a joint resolution of Congress.

Daggett, Windsor Pratt 1884–1958, born: Auburn; graduate: Edward Little High School, Auburn, Ph.B. Brown University 1902; studied expression under Leland Powers and Dr. S. S. Curry, Boston, studied phonetics under William Tilly, Columbia University; professor of public speaking: University of Maine 1907–18; editor: Spoken Word department, *Billboard* 1921–26; lecturer on phonetics: University of Wisconsin, summers 1925–27; lecturer on dramatic diction: American Laboratory Theatre, New York 1925–27; teacher of phonetics and public speaking: Jewish Institute of Religion, New York from 1926; managing director: Naples (Maine) Repertory Theatre, summer 1933; head of drama and speech department: New York School of Vocal Art, Carnegie Hall, New York from 1933; director: Shakespeare Association of America; author and publisher of *The Spoken Word* course with phonographic records and phonetic script 1924.

Dahlgren, Edward C. 1916– , born: Perham; sergeant, U.S. Army, Company E, 142nd Infantry, 36th Infantry Division, recipient: Medal of Honor, Oberhoffen, France, 11 February 1945, "He led the 3rd Platoon to the rescue of a similar unit which had been surrounded in an enemy counter attack at Oberhoffen, France. As he advanced along a street, he observed several Germans crossing a field about one hundred yards away. Running into a barn, he took up a position in a window and swept the hostile troops with submachinegun fire, killing six, wounding others, and completely disorganizing the group. His platoon then moved forward through intermittent sniper fire and made contact with the besieged Americans. When the two platoons had been reorganized, SGT Dahlgren continued to advance along the street until he drew fire from an enemy-held house. In the face of machine pistol and rifle fire, he ran toward the building, hurled a grenade through the door and blasted his way inside with his gun. This aggressive attack so rattled the Germans that all eight men who held the strong point immediately surrendered. As SGT Dahlgren started toward the next house, hostile machinegun fire drove him to cover. He secured rifle grenades, stepped to an exposed position and calmly launched his missiles from a difficult angle until he had destroyed the machinegun and killed its two operators. He moved to the rear of the house and suddenly came under the fire of a machinegun in a barn. Throwing a grenade into the structure, he rushed the position, firing his weapon as he ran; within, he overwhelmed five Germans. After reorganizing his unit, he advanced to clear hostile riflemen from the building where he had destroyed the machinegun. He entered the house by a window and trapped the Germans in the cellar, heard German voices in the house. An attack with rifle grenades drove the hostile troops to the cellar. SGT Dahlgren entered the building, kicked open the cellar door, and, firing several bursts down the stairway, called for the trapped enemy to surrender. Sixteen soldiers filed out with their hands in the air. The bold leadership and magnificent courage displayed by SGT Dahlgren in his heroic attacks were in a large measure responsible for repulsing an enemy counterattack and saving an American platoon from great danger."

Dana, John Wincester 1808–67, born: Fryeburg; son of Judah Dana, great grandson of Israel Putnam and Eleazer Wheelock; graduate: Fryeburg Academy; practiced law, member: Maine House of Representatives 1841–42, Maine Senate 1843–44, president 1844, as president, became acting governor upon the resignation of acting governor David Dunn, 3 January 1844, succeeded the same day by newly elected Governor Hugh J. Anderson; elected fifteenth governor of Maine (Democrat) 1847, 1848, 1849; appointed by President Pierce *chargé d'affaires*, resident minister to Bolivia 1853–59; unsuccessful candidate for governor 1861; sold up and removed to a sheep farm in Rosario, Argentina, died of cholera contracted while nursing the sick.

Dana, Napoleon Jackson Tecumseh 1822–1905, born: Fort Sullivan, Eastport; son of Nathaniel Giddings Dana, captain, USA, after the death of his father, removed with his family to Portsmouth, New Hampshire, 1832; graduate: Phillips Academy, Exeter, graduate: U.S. Military Academy 1842, commissioned second lieutenant, USA, assigned to the 7th Infantry, then stationed at several forts on the Gulf of Mexico, from Pensacola to New Orleans; in Mexican War: with his regiment at the bombardment of Fort Brown, the series of battles that resulted in the capitulation of Monterey, the siege and capitulation of Vera Cruz, the desperate battle of Cerro Gordo, where he was so severely wounded that he was left for dead, thirty-six hours later the burial party discovered the mistake; brevetted captain, USA, for gallant and meritorious conduct at the battle of Cerro Gordo; after the war, served against the Sioux and Chippewas, resigned his commission 1855; at the outbreak of the Civil

War, he was living in St. Paul, Minnesota, engaged in banking and serving as brigadier general of Minnesota militia; commissioned colonel, USV, commanding officer: 1st Minnesota Volunteer Infantry 1861, saw service at the debacle of Ball's Bluff, promoted to brigadier general, USV, February 1862, commanded a brigade in John Sedgwick's II Division, major general, USV, November 1862, served in every major battle of the Army of the Potomac, from Bull Run to Antietam, where he was severely wounded, placed in command of the XIII Corps and the department of the Mississippi, resigned at the close of the war; general agent for the Russian-American Commercial Co., then the largest business concern in Alaska to 1872; superintendent: Great Northern Railroad Co. 1872–88, Chicago, Burlington and Quincy Railroad Co. 1888–95; first deputy commissioner of pensions, Washington from 1895–97; retired to Portsmouth, New Hampshire, where he died and is buried.

Dana, Samuel Trask 1883–1978, born: Portland; A.B. *summa cum laude* Bowdoin College φBK 1904, Sc.D. (Hon.) 1930, M.F. *summa cum laude* Yale University 1907, Sc.D. 1953, Syracuse University 1928, L.L.D. University of Michigan 1953; successively: forest assistant, assistant chief: Offices of Silvics and Forest Investigations, forest economist, assistant chief of the bureau of research: U.S. Forest Service 1907–21, director: Northeastern University Forest Experimental Station 1923–27; Maine forest commissioner 1921–23; professor of forestry, dean: School of Forestry and Conservation, University of Michigan 1927–50, dean: school of natural resources 1950–51, Filibert Roth university professor of forestry 1951–53; member: Hoover Commission on Re-organization of the Executive Branch of Government 1948–49; forest research advisory commission, U.S. Department of Agriculture 1953–58; co-chairman, section on utilization and development of land resources, Mid-Century Conference on Resources for the Future 1953; program commissioner: World Forestry Congress 1959–60; representative of the U.S. Department of Agriculture: General Assembly of the International Institute of Agriculture, Rome 1926; recipient of the first Distinguished Service Award of the American Forest Products Industries 1961; medal for outstanding service in international forestry: 6th World Forestry Congress, Madrid 1966; president: Society of American Foresters 1925–26; author: *Forest and Range Policy—Its Development in the United States* 1956, *California Lands—Ownership, Use, and Management of Forest and Related Lands* 1961, numerous bulletins and articles for professional journals, editor: *History of Activities in the Field of Natural Resources*, University of Michigan 1953, contributor to the *Encyclopedia Britannica*.

Dana, Woodbury Kidder 1840– ?, born: Portland, son of a ship chandler and wholesale grocer; attended public school in Portland, graduate: Lewiston Falls Academy; after school, went to work in mills in Lewiston; in the Civil War: enlisted as a private in Co. K, 29th Regiment, Maine Volunteer Infantry, which became the 2nd Brigade, 1st Division, 19th Corps 1863, participated in the Red River Expedition, the battles of Sabine Cross Roads, Mansfield, Pleasant Hill, Cane River Crossing, Alexandria, and Mansura Chalk Plains; subsequently, the regiment removed to Virginia, where it was involved in the Shenandoah campaign, the battles of Winchester, Fisher's Hill, and Cedar Creek; for gallant conduct in the Red River campaign, promoted to corporal and hospital steward, discharged August 1865; in partnership with Thomas McEwan, established a mill at Westbrook for the manufacture of cotton warps, later the firm became W. K. Dana & Co., incorporated as Dana Warp Mills, came to have 60,000 spindles; inventor of the famous Dana cotton picker, based on the vacuum twisting nozzle method, built like a farm tractor, with two double suction blowers, attached to each are two nozzles, which are, in turn, operated by the picker, the suction blowers are rapidly revolved by the same motive power as the tractor, and create such vacuum as is necessary to rotate the picking end of the nozzles at high speed, the boll is twisted and rapidly drawn into the nozzle and hose into the body of the blower and is opened, fluffed up and passes into a collection bag, making it possible to gin the cotton much more easily than hand-picked cotton; he also provided Westbrook with its first electricity, from his own generating plant, built modern school buildings and a sewer; member: Westbrook Board of Alderman; department commander: Grand Army of the Republic.

Dane, Joseph 1778–1858, born: Beverly, Massachusetts; graduate: Phillips Academy, Andover, A.B. Harvard College 1799; studied law, member: Massachusetts bar 1802, practiced in Kennebunk; delegate: Massachusetts Constitutional Convention 1816, 1819; member: Massachusetts Executive Council 1817; elected to U.S. House of Representatives (Democrat) to fill vacancy caused by the resignation of John Holmes, served 1820–23; first U.S. Representative from Maine; member: Maine House of Representatives 1824, 1825, 1832, 1833, 1839, 1840; member: Maine Senate 1829; buried in Hope Cemetery.

Danforth, Richard Stevens 1885–1962, born: Gardiner; son of a consulting railroad engineer, cousin of John Frank Stevens; B.S. Dartmouth College 1908, C. E. Thayer School of Civil Engineering, Dartmouth College 1909, student: Massachusetts Institute of Technology; engineering and construction work: Portland, Oregon, 1909–13; general manager: Hydro Electric Co., Hood River, Oregon, 1913–14; Pacific Coast sales manager: Kinney Manufacturing Co., San Francisco, 1915–33; district sales manager: Alco Products division, American Locomotive Co. 1933–39; perfected and patented the Danforth anchor, established Danforth Anchor Co., Berkeley, California, 1939; the Danforth anchor possesses unique holding ability and was quickly adopted by the U.S. Navy and became ubiquitous throughout the world, manufactured in sizes running from 2.5 pounds to 10 tons; author: *Oil Flow in Pipe Lines* 1921, *Oil Flow Viscosity and Heat Transfer* 1923.

Darling, John Augustus 1835– ?, born: Bucksport; graduate: Pennsylvania Military Academy 1859; in the Civil War: commissioned second lieutenant, USA, 1861, attached to the 2nd Artillery, after duty at Fort McHenry, Baltimore, ordered to Sedalia, Missouri, commanding officer: battery F, 2nd Artillery, USA, promoted to first lieutenant, USA, aide-de-camp to major general John Dix 1862, active in the Peninsula campaign, conducted the first exchange of prisoners during the war, appointed major, USV, commanding officer: 3rd Pennsylvania Heavy Artillery, USV, which he organized and disciplined, ordered to Fortress Monroe, Virginia, detailed as acting inspector general for the eastern district of Virginia, returned to Fortress Monroe, where he was in command while Jefferson Davis was held prisoner there, brevetted captain and major, USV, for gallant and meritorious service, mustered out of the volunteer service 1865, rejoined the regular army, assigned to the 2nd Artillery, USA, commanding officer: Alcatraz Island 1865–67, took military control of Yerba Buena Island, in command of Fort Mason, San Francisco, in command at Fort Stevens, Oregon, a reduction in army personel required that he be mustered out 1871, reappointed, by special act of Congress, captain, USA, assigned to the 1st Artillery, USA, on duty at the artillery school, Fortress Monroe 1878–79, Fort Trumbull, New London, Connecticut, to 1881, in command of Fort Mason, San Francisco, with duty at Alcatraz Island and the Presidio of San Francisco to 1890, reassigned to Governor's Island, New York, promoted to major, USA, assigned to the 5th Artillery, USA, commanded, at the Presidio, the light and heavy artillery, transferred to the 3rd Artillery, USA, 1896, retired as lieutenant colonel, USA, 1897; under the pen name of August Mignon composed and published many well-known vocal and instrumental pieces in the United States and Europe, including: *Études Melodiques*, *Echoes d'une Casemati*, *Village Deminiscamces*, *Song Without Words*, *Gavotte Militaire*, *Recompense*, *Adrift Together*, *In an Old Church Tower*, *Blessed Dream*, &c.

Davis, Augustus Plummer 1835–99, born: Gardiner; attended public schools in Gardiner, shipped out to California 1849, spent a year mining, joined the navy, discharged at Philadelphia 1855, enlisted as an officer in the French navy and served in the Crimean War; worked for a time, for his father, in Gardiner; with the outbreak of the Civil War, obtained a commission as captain, USV, attached to the 13th Maine Volunteer Infantry, later with the 11th Maine Volunteer Infantry, detached for court martial duty 1861–62; embarked, with his regiment, and participated in the Peninsula campaign, wounded twice at Fair Oaks, subsequently served as division provost marshal to April 1863, commissioned captain, USA, cavalry, stationed at Augusta, brevetted major, USA, March 1865; engaged in business in Gardiner to 1872, removed to Pittsburgh, Pennsylvania, where he started an insurance business and organized the Order of the Sons of Veterans 1881, which, by the turn of the century, had over 2,000 posts in twenty-seven states with membership of over 100,000; buried in Allegheny Cemetery.

Davis, Daniel Franklin Diarrhea 1843–97, born Freedom; son of a minister; attended public school in Stetson, entered Corinna Academy 1863, left school and enlisted as a private in a company raised in Freedom, served to the end of the Civil War, during which he acquired his sobriquet; reentered Corinna Academy, later attended Maine Wesleyan Seminary, Kents Hill; taught school; read law with Lewis Barker, Stetson; member: Maine bar 1868; practiced in East Corinth; member: Maine House of Representatives (Republican) 1871–75, member: Maine Senate 1875–79; as Republican nominee for governor 1879, received 68,967 votes, a plurality of 49.6 percent, incumbent governor Alonzo Garcelon received 21,851 votes, the Greenback candidate received 48,280 votes; no candidate having received a majority, it fell to the legislature to decide the outcome of the election, however, Governor Garcelon, hoping that a legislature with a Democratic majority would reelect him, refuse to certify newly elected Republican legislators, after a period of considerable tumult, the Maine Supreme Judicial Court decided against Garcelon, the Republican majority legislature was seated, and Davis was chosen as thirty-fifth governor of Maine; this was the last gubernatorial election that required a majority of popular votes for election; unsuccessful candidate for reelection 1880; practiced law in Old Town, collector of customs: port of Bangor 1882–86.

Davis, Harlow Morrell 1885–1938, born: Augusta; A.B. Bates College 1907, L.L.B. Harvard University Law School 1910; entered the patent department of the United Shoe Machinery Corp., Boston 1910, remained to his death, assistant manager: patent department 1917, manager 1935; member: U.S. Patent Office Advisory Committee 1934, chairman; father of the actress Bette Davis.

Davis, Henry Gassett 1807–96, born: Trenton; M.D. Yale University Medical School 1839; pioneer orthopedic surgeon, founder of the traction school, first to employ weights and pulleys in treatment; operated a private hospital in New York City for the treatment of club feet, congenital dislocations of the hip, chronic diseases of the joints, and deformities resulting from polio myelitis; author: *Conservative Surgery as Exhibited in Remedying Some of the Mechanical Causes that Operate Injuriously in Health and Disease* 1867.

Davis, Owen Gould 1874–1956, born: Portland; attended public schools in Bangor, student: University of Tennessee 1888–89, Harvard University and Lawrence Scientific School 1891–93; took a job as a geologist and mining engineer at a coal mine in West Virginia 1893–94; hired as a bit actor in the repertory company of Francesca Janauschek, New York, played as many as twenty parts a week; actor, stage manager, press agent, company manager, advance agent, stage director in various theatres; became a playwright, his plays include: *Through the Breakers* 1897, which ran three seasons, wrote over one hundred melodramas, over the next ten years, signed a five-year contract with Sullivan, Harris & Woods 1902, *Confessions of a Wife* 1905, *Nellie, the Beautiful Cloak Model* 1906, which consisted of twenty-one scenes, *Edna, the Pretty Typewriter* 1907, *The Family Cupboard* 1913, *Sinners* 1915, *Forever After*

1918, *The Detour* 1921, *Icebound* which won critical acclaim and for which he received a Pulitzer Prize 1923, this play established Edna May Oliver as an actress, *The Haunted House* 1924, *Easy Come, Easy Go* 1925, signed a contract with Paramount Pictures 1927, *The Nervous Wreck*, produced first as a musical comedy by Florenz Ziegfield, then remade as *Whoopee*, a musical film with Eddie Cantor; numerous film scripts, including *They Had to See Paris* and *So This Is London*, both for Will Rogers, *Jezebel* 1933, adapted *Mr. and Mrs. North* 1931, *No Way Out* 1944, his last play; wrote over two hundred plays, reputed to be America's most prolific and most produced playwright; wrote two autobiographies: *I'd Like to Do It Again* 1931, *My First Fifty Years in the Theatre* 1950.

Davis, Raymond Earl 1885–1970, born: Gorham; B.S. in civil engineering: University of Maine 1911, C.E. 1914, M.S. University of Illinois 1916, D.Eng. University of Maine 1936; started as a topographer 1906, professor of civil engineering, director of engineering materials laboratory: University of California (Berkeley) 1926–52; consulting engineer on numerous public and private projects, including the Tennessee River Authority, Corps of Engineers, USA, U.S. Bureau of Reclamation, Royal Irrigation Department, Thailand, Atomic Energy Commission, U.S. Navy; in World War I: first lieutenant, U.S. Engineering Corps, in World War II: directed or served on advisory committees of several war research projects; twice awarded Wason Medal by American Concrete Institute for most meritorious paper 1931, 1934; Construction Practice Award for notable contribution to art of concrete construction 1948; Turner Gold Medal 1952, Frank E. Richart Award: American Society of Testing Materials 1960, Award of Merit 1964; fellow: American Academy of Arts and Sciences, American Society of Civil Engineers; president: American Concrete Institute; member: Bohemian Club, Commonwealth Club; author of numerous textbooks and technical articles.

Davis, Samuel W. 1845– ?, born: Brewer; ordinary seaman, USN, recipient: Medal of Honor, on board the USS *Brooklyn* during successful attacks against Fort Morgan, rebel gunboats and the ram CSS *Tennessee* in Mobile Bay, on 5 August 1864; despite severe damage to his ship and the loss of several men on board as enemy fire raked her decks from stem to stern, Davis exercised extreme courage and vigilance while acting as a lookout for torpedoes and other obstructions throughout the furious battle that resulted in the surrender of the prize ram CSS *Tennessee* and in the damaging and destruction of batteries at Fort Morgan.

Davis, William Hammett 1879–1964, born: Bangor; L.L.B. George Washington University Law School 1901; examiner: U.S. Patent Office 1902–03; joined preeminent patent legal firm of Betts, Betts, Sheffield, and Betts 1903–06, later formed Pennie, Davis, Marvin, and Edmonds, remained thirty-nine years, eventually as senior partner; head of contracts division of purchase, storage, and traffic: U.S. War Department 1917, legal adviser: secretary of war 1918–19; grew to know and esteem Sidney Hillman and Francis Perkins; deputy administrator: National Recovery Administration, wrote codes for shipbuilding and retail coal; compliance director: N.R.A. 1933–34, chairman: New York State Mediation Board 1937–40, chairman: Twentieth-Century Fund Labor Committee, backed the Wagner Act; member: National Defense Mediation Board, as chairman, defused strikes in automobile plants that would have greatly hindered the war effort; chairman: National War Labor Board, had difficult task of balancing union demands with war effort, grew to have warm relations with George Meany; set standards for collective bargaining; chairman: Office of Economic Stabilization; founded legal firm of Davis, Hoxie, Faithfull, and Hapgood 1945; commissioner: New York City Board of Transportation 1945–47; member: patent advisory board, Atomic Energy Commission 1847–57; chairman: Presidential Commission on Labor Relations in Atomic Installations; chairman, board of trustees: New School for Social Research 1950–57.

Day, Albert 1812–94, born: Wells; joined the Washingtonians, an early temperance group; member: Massachusetts House of Representatives 1856; secured charter for the first inebriate asylum in the country, Boston 1857; first superintendent to 1867; M.D. Harvard University Medical School 1866; managed the Washingtonian asylum effectively, reformed thousands of habitual drunkards; superintendent: New York Inebriate Asylum, Binghamton 1867–72; founder and superintendent: Greenwood Institute, Boston 1870–73; superintendent: Washingtonian Asylum 1875–93; founding member: American Association for the Cure of Inebriates 1870.

Day, Holman Francis 1865–1935, born: Vassalboro; A.B. Colby College 1887, Litt.D (Hon.) 1907; managing editor: Union Publishing Co., Bangor, 1889–90, editor and proprietor: *Dexter Gazette*, special writer for the *Lewiston Journal, Boston Herald*; managing editor: *Lewiston Daily Sun*; major and military secretary to Gov. John F. Hill 1901–04; author: *Up in Maine* 1900, *Pine Tree Ballads* 1902, *Kim o'Ktaadn* 1904, *Squire Phin* 1905, later dramatized as *The Circus Man; Along Came Ruth* 1924, *Blow the Man Down* 1916, *King Spruce: A Novel, The Rider of the King Log* 1919, *When Egypt Went Broke* 1920, *All Wool Morrison* 1921, *The Loving Are the Daring* 1923, *Leadbetter's Luck* 1923, *Clothes Make the Pirate* 1925, *John Lang* 1926, *When the Fight Begins* 1926, *Starwagons* 1928, *Ships of Joy* 1932; maker of numerous silent movies; retired to Monterey, California.

Deane, Charles 1813–89, born: Biddeford; graduate: Thornton Academy; financial reverses forced him into trade, eventually became a partner in Waterston, Pray and Co., Boston, retired with ample fortune 1864; devoted himself to historical research; member: Massachusetts Historical Society 1849, American Antiquarian Society 1851; A.M., ΦΒΚ (Hon.) Harvard University 1856; edited eleven volumes of Massachusetts Historical Society's *Proceedings*, found a copy of the long-lost *History of* the *Plymouth Plantation* by Governor Bradford; author: *Some Notices of Samuel Gorton* 1850, *First Plymouth Patent* 1854, *Bibliography of Gov. Hutchinson's Publications* 1857, *Wingfield's Discourse on Virginia* 1860, *Letters of Phillis Wheatley* 1864, *Smith's True Relation* 1866, *Remarks on Sebastian Cabot's Mappe Monde* 1867, *Memoir of George Livermore* 1869, *The Forms in Issuing Letters—Patent by the Crown of England* 1870; editor: Bradford's *Dialogue, or Third Conference Between Old Men and Young Men* 1870; regarded as peerless in his unbiased, judicious, and tireless pursuit of minute historical research.

Dearborn, Henry 1751–1829, born: North Hampton, New Hampshire; studied and practiced medicine in Portsmouth; when the news of the battles of Lexington and Concord arrived, organized a troop of sixty volunteers and marched with them to Cambridge; appointed captain in Colonel Starks's regiment, participated in the battle of Bunker Hill after marching across Charlestown Neck under galling fire 1775; accompanied the Arnold Expedition to Québec, where he was captured and taken to Halifax, Nova Scotia, and exchanged 1777; appointed major, participated in the taking of Fort Ticonderoga; as lLieutenant colonel, led a charge to cover the retreat at the battle of Monmouth, for which he received the thanks of general Washington; accompanied General John Sullivans Expedition to upstate New York to punish the Iroquois Nation; appointed major general New Hampshire militia, served on Washington's staff; present at the surrender of Cornwallis at Yorktown; settled in Pittston (that part which is now Gardiner), served as U.S. marshal, District of Maine 1790; Bowdoin College overseer 1794–98; member: U.S. House of Representatives 1793–97; appointed secretary of war 1801–09; appointed collector of customs, port of Boston 1809–12; in the War of 1812, commissioned major general, USA, captured York (later Toronto) and Fort George, after the war, commanded the military district of New York City; appointed minister plenipotentiary to Portugal 1822–24; retired to Roxbury, Massachusetts, paying annual visits to his farm in Pittston; Fort Dearborn (Chicago) named in his honor; originally buried in Mount Auburn Cemetery, later reinterred in Forest Hills Cemetery, Boston.

Dearing, John Lincoln 1858–1916, born: Webster; A.B. Colby College 1884; graduate: Newton Theological Institution 1889; ordained Baptist minister 1888, missionary to Yokohama, Japan; president: Yokohama Baptist Theology Seminary 1894–1908, professor of theology and ethics; wrote, in Japanese: *Outline of Theology* 1895, superintendent: American Baptist Union for Japan, China, and the Philippines 1908–11; editor: *The Christian Movement in the Japanese Empire*.

Deering, Charles 1852–1927, born: South Paris; son of William Deering, brother of James Deering; graduate: Maine Wesleyan Seminary, Kents Hill, U.S. Naval Academy 1873, commissioned ensign, USN, advanced to master, USN; while serving aboard the flagship of the Asiatic squadron served as personal escort, at the request of

148   Eminent Mainers

ex-President U. S. Grant and Mrs. Grant, in their tour of China and Japan 1879, resigned 1881; secretary: Deering Harvester Co. to 1902; with merger with McCormick and formation of International Harvester, served as chairman of the board: International Harvester Co. 1904–16; showed genuine talent for painting, began its study in the 1870s, returned to Paris and occupied the studio of Anders Zorn 1893, encouraged by his lifelong friend, John Singer Sargent, to sever his business connections and devote himself to portrait painting, for which he had a decided talent, family responsibilities required him to abandon art as a vocation, but he continued to paint and to encourage young artists; was, for many years, trustee: Art Institute of Chicago; after his retirement from business, purchased a group of homes in Sitges, near Barcelona, Spain, which he planned to make into an art center and school, later, he purchased and restored a castle near Tarragona, Spain, he also developed an extensive property south of Miami, Florida, lent generous support to the U.S. Department of Agriculture experimental station and the New York Botanical Garden nearby; endowed a professorship in botany at Northwestern University, where, after his death, his heirs built the Charles Deering Library; edited and published *Life of William Henry Schuetze* 1903, *William Deering* 1913; decorated: the order of Alfonso XII and Isabella the Catholic of Spain, the Mérite Agricole and Palmes Académiques of France, the Nichan Iftikhar of Tunisia, Double Dragon of China.

Deering, James 1859–1925, born: South Paris; son of William Deering, brother of Charles Deering; student: Northwestern University and Massachusetts Institute of Technology; entered Deering Harvester 1880; vice president of International Harvester after merger with McCormick 1901–19, director 1919–25; chevalier: Legion of Honor (France), officer of the crown (Germany); philanthropist; builder of Vizcaya, a most opulent mansion in Miami; died at sea, returning from France.

Deering, Nathaniel 1791-1881, born: Portland; graduate: Phillips Academy, Exeter, A.B. Harvard College 1810; entered the counting house of Asa Clapp in Portland; member: Maine bar 1815, practiced in Canaan, later in Skowhegan 1815–36, while in Canaan, Lydia Maria Child wrote the once-famous epigram upon his name:
> Whoever weds the young lawyer at C.
> Will surely have prospects most cheering
> For what must his person and intellect be,
> When even his name is N. Deering?

removed to Portland 1836; editor: *Independent Statesman*, a Whig newspaper; author: *Carabassset or the Last of the Norridgewocks*, a play 1830, *The Clairvoyant*, a comedy, *Buzzaris*, a tragedy of the Greek revolution 1851, several short stories, including: *The Donation Visit, Timotheus Tuttle, Tableaux Vivants, Mrs. Sykes*, a body of church music.

Deering, Nathaniel Cobb 1827–87, born: Norway; graduated from North Bridgton Academy; member: Maine House of Representatives 1855–57, removed to

Osage, Iowa, in lumber business; clerk: U.S. Senate to 1865; special agent for the Post Office Department for the district of Nebraska, Minnesota, and Iowa 1865–69; national bank examiner for Iowa 1872–77; member: U.S. House of Representatives (Republican) 1877–83, chairman: Committee on Expenditures in the Department of State; unsuccessful candidate for renomination 1882; president of a large cattle company in Montana; buried in Osage (Iowa) Cemetery.

Deering, William 1826–1913, born: South Paris; attended public school in South Paris, Maine Wesleyan Seminary, Kents Hill, employed by the South Paris Woolen Manufacturing Co., manager from 1849; removed to Portland 1861, manufacturer of cloth and uniforms for the Union Army; cofounded, Deering, Milliken & Co. 1865, owners of sundry woolen and cotton mills, with branch offices in Boston and New York, sold his interest to Seth Milliken 1870; removed to Plano, Illinois, where, with the Rev. E. H. Gammon, founded Gammon & Deering Co., sole proprietor from 1878; manufactured the Marsh harvester, which superseded the reaper, and which was working a revolution in grain harvesting, after much experimentation, added the Appleby twine self-binder 1880; perfected the ball-bearing 1892; produced in 1896, the first self-propelled farm machine, for which he won a gold medal at the Paris Exhibition of 1900 and made officer of the French Legion of Honor; Deering Harvester Co. merged in 1902 with the McCormick Co. to form International Harvester Co.; president, board of trustees: Northwestern University, Garrett Biblical Institute; father of Charles and James Deering.

Delabarre, Edmund Burke 1863–1945, born: Dover; student at Brown University 1882–83, A.M. Amherst College 1886, A.M. Harvard University 1889, Ph.D. University of Freiburg 1901; associate professor of psychology: Brown University 1891–96, professor 1896–32; director: Harvard University Psychology Laboratory 1896–97; fellow: American Academy of Arts and Sciences; author: *Über Bewegungsemfindugen* 1891, *Report of the Brown-Harvard Expedition to Nauchuck, Labrador* 1900, *Dighton Rock History* 1916, *Inscribed Rocks of Narragansett Bay* 1913–23, *Rocks of New England* 1928; officer of the Military Order of Saint James of the Sword (Portugal).

Dennett, Carl Pullen 1874–1955, born: Bangor; student: University of Maine Law School 1895–96; brokers clerk, New York 1893, bank clerk 1894, partner: Pearl and Dennett, brokers 1895–1910; financial vice president, director and member, executive committee: Griffin Wheel Co. 1910–14, trustee representing controlling interest 1914–19; trustee of various estates from 1919; president: General Capital Co. 1929–43; president and director: Capital Managers, Inc.; director: New York Central Railroad System, Florence Stove Co., John Hancock Mutual Life Insurance Co., First National Bank of Boston, Capital Managers, Inc., United-Car Fastener Corp.; vice-chairman: American Red Cross Commission to Switzerland 1918–19; vice chairman:

Industrial Advisory Committee of First Federal Reserve District; member: Bohemian Club, San Francisco, Bath and Tennis, Everglades Club, Palm Beach; author: *Prisoners of the Great War* 1919, *That Reminds Me* 1948.

Dennison, Aaron Lufkin 1812–95, born: Freeport; son of a shoemaker; at age eighteen, apprenticed to a watchmaker in Brunswick, where he learned the prevailing method of manual watchmaking, removed to Boston 1833, where he set himself up as a watchmaker; studied mass-production techniques employed at the Springfield Armory; surmounting the difficulties of manufacturing tiny parts; founded, in Roxbury, the Waltham Watch Co. (originally the American Horologue Co.) 1850, where he manufactured the first inexpensive factory-made watches in the United States; his brother Eliphelet, applying the same techniques of mass-production to the manufacture of paper boxes founded the Dennison Manufacturing Co., originally in Brunswick, later in Framingham, Massachusetts.

Dennison, Winfred Thaxter 1873–1919, born: Portland; graduate: Phillips Academy, Exeter 1892, A.B. Harvard College 1896, L.L.B. Harvard University Law School 1900; member: New York bar 1900, practiced in New York; assistant U.S. district attorney, Southern District of New York 1906–09, special assistant to U.S. attorney general in sugar and other customs fraud prosecutions 1909–10, assistant U.S. attorney general 1910–14; member: Philippine Commission and secretary of the interior, Philippine Islands 1914–16.

Derry, George Herman 1878–1949, born: Portland; son of a coal dealer; attended parochial schools in Portland, served as secretary to the bishop of the diocese of Maine, student: Holy Cross University 1895–96, St. Johns Juniorate, S.J., Frederick, Maryland 1896–99, graduate *summa cum laude*: Schools of Social Science and Philosophy, Stonyhurst College, England 1902, postgraduate study: Johns Hopkins University 1902–04, Ph.D. Holy Cross University 1908, S.T.D. Catholic University, Paris 1910, L.L.D. Marquette University 1927, Litt.D. Xavier University 1940; professor of Latin, Greek and comparative literature: Saint Francis Xavier University 1904–06, Holy Cross University 1906-08, principal: Jordan High School, Lewiston 1908–09, Milford (Massachusetts) High School 1910–14, junior master: English High School, Boston 1915–16, assistant professor of political science: University of Kansas 1917–19, acting head of department of economics: Bryn Mawr College 1919–20, head of economics department: Union College 1920–25, professor and head of department of sociology: Marquette University 1925–27, president: Marygrove College, Detroit 1927–37, during his administration, Marygrove went from an enrollment of one hundred students to being the second largest Catholic college for women in the United States, introduced an educational program derived from that of the Jesuits, emphasizing the classics for women, after his resignation: national director of social education, Knights of Columbus; gave more than five hundred lectures in the United States,

Canada, and Mexico on the evils of communism; president: St. Joseph's College, Standish 1941–47; director, social education, Supreme Council, Knights of Columbus from 1947; associate editor: *Knights of Columbus Historical Series*; contributor to the *Catholic Encyclopedia*; author: *Handbook for Discussion Groups* 1947, *How the Reds Get That Way* 1948; decorated: Knight Commander, St. Gregory the Great by Pope Pius XI 1932.

Des Jardins, Arthur Ulderic 1884–1964, born: Waterville; student: Montréal (Québec) College 1898–99, St. Joseph's College, Trois-Rivières, Québec 1900-01, M.D. University of Pennsylvania 1912, special course in radiological physics: Cambridge University, England, 1920, M.S. in radiology: University of Minnesota 1924; in charge of Fairfield Tuberculosis Sanitarium 1913–14; assistant surgeon: American ambulance, American Hospital, Paris, 1914–15; assistant to Dr. Joseph Blake, Hospital Militaire 76, Ris Orangis, France, 1915–16; surgery fellow: Mayo Foundation, Rochester, Minnesota, 1917, roentgenology fellow 1920, pathologic surgery fellow 1917, head: therapeutic radiology department: Mayo Clinic 1920, professor of radiology: Mayo Foundation from 1936; honorary staff member and trustee: Miles Memorial Hospital, Damariscotta; instructor: military surgery: Fort Riley, Kansas, 1917–18; pathologist: Central Medical department laboratory, Dijon, France, 1918, evacuation hospital, number 2, Baccarat, France, 1918, pathologist and commanding officer: 3rd Army Laboratory, Coblenz, Germany, 1919, promoted from captain to lieutenant colonel, Medical Corps, USA, 1917–24; retired to Walpole, buried in Old Harrington Cemetery, Bristol.

Dickinson, Roscoe Gilkey 1894–1945, born: Brewer; B.S. Massachusetts Institute of Technology 1915, Ph.D. California Institute of Technology 1920; assistant in theoretical chemistry: Massachusetts Institute of Technology 1915–16, research assistant in chemistry: California Institute of Technology 1917–26, national research fellow 1920–23, assistant professor of physical chemistry: California Institute of Technology 1926–28, associate professor 1928–38, professor from 1938, acting dean of graduate school 1942–45; engaged in war research: Office of Science Research and Development from 1941.

Dillingham, Pitt 1852–1926, born: Norridgewock, son of a Universalist clergyman; attended public school in Waterville, A.B. Dartmouth College 1873, B.D. Harvard University Divinity School 1876; ordained Unitarian minister 1876, appointed to the Harvard Church, Charlestown, Massachusetts, to 1888, selected to represent the American Unitarian Association at the International Conference of Unitarian Churches, Liverpool 1882, accepted the pastorate of the First Unitarian Church, Buffalo 1888, failing health required him to resign, resumed preaching at churches in Uxbridge, Massachusetts, 1892–93, Brockton, Massachusetts, 1894–95; associated with the Calhoun Colored School and Settlement, founded by his sister, Mabel

Dillingham 1892 in Lowndes County, Alabama, as co-principal and chaplain 1895–1909; wrote and lectured widely and devoted himself to the increase of self-respect and prosperity of blacks; contributor: Land Tenure Among the Negroes (*Yale Review* 1892), described credit and crop mortgaging systems that operated to limit black enterprise and success, other articles included: "Settlement Work in the Cotton Belt" (*The Outlook*), "Black Belt Settlement Work" (*Southern Workman*); organized the Calhoun Land Company to oppose abuses on the part of people willing to profit from the difficulties confronting blacks and was instrumental in increasing black prosperity and independence; under his guidance, the school acquired large tracts of land that were sold in small farm lots to encourage permanent settlements and develop community spirit; after his resignation in 1909, associated with the Robert Gould Shaw Settlement House and Associated Charities, Boston; member, advisory board: Massachusetts Child Labor Committee; secretary, treasurer, president: Street Manual Training School, Minter, Alabama.

Dingley, Edward Nelson 1862–1930, born: Auburn; son of Nelson Dingley, Jr.; attended public schools in Lewiston, Bates College 1879–80, A.B. Yale College 1883, L.L.B. Columbian (later Georgetown University) College Law School 1885; member of the staff of *Boston Advertizer* and *Boston Record* 1886–87; part-owner and editor: *Leavenworth* (Kansas) *Times* 1887–88, editor and publisher: *Kalamazoo Telegraph* and *Press* 1888–1909; member: Michigan House of Representatives 1899–1903, floor leader, chairman: Ways and Means Committee; delegate: Republican National Convention 1900; unsuccessful Progressive party candidate for the U.S. House of Representatives 1912, 1914; associate editor, tariff and fiscal specialist: *New York Herald* 1919–20; publicist for the Republican National Committee; member of speakers bureau and editorial writer; founded the Dingley Syndicate, which directed his and the writings of others to newspapers across the nation; clerk: U.S. House of Representatives Ways and Means Committee 1921–24, framed revenue legislation, in particular, the Fordney-McCumber tariff bill, guided members of both houses in financial intricacies; served for six years as fiscal expert for the Republican majority on the U.S. Senate Finance Committee; author: *Life and Times of Nelson Dingley, Jr.* 1901, *Unto the Hills* (a statement of the more important politico-economic questions affecting America, from a purely American perspective) 1922.

Dingley, Nelson, Jr. 1832–99, born: Durham; brother of Frank Lambert Dingley; attended common schools in Unity, Waterville Seminary, Waterville College; A.B. Dartmouth College 1855, L.L.D. (Hon.) 1895, Bates College 1874; member: Maine bar 1856, purchased the *Lewiston Weekly Journal* 1856, added the *Evening Journal* 1865, co-editor with his brother Frank; member: Maine House of Representatives (Republican) 1862–65, 1868, 1873, speaker 1863–64; elected twenty-eighth governor of Maine 1874–76; delegate: Republican National Convention 1876, 1880; member: U.S. House of Representatives 1881–99, chairman: Committee on Ways and Means;

author of the infamous Dingley tariff 1897; declined appointment as secretary of the treasury; appointed by President McKinley to an international commission to settle a dispute with Canada over the Alaskan boundary and Alaskan seal fisheries 1898; president: Congressional Temperance Society; Bowdoin College overseer 1873–74; father of Henry McKenney Dingley; died in Washington, D.C., buried in Oak Hill Cemetery, Auburn.

Dinsmore, Samuel P. 1822–82, born: Bristol; A.B. Bowdoin College 1844; member: Maine bar, practiced in Bangor; editor: *Bangor Mercury*; took an active part in the presidential canvass for John C. Frémont 1856; removed to New York to practice law 1857; appointed by President Lincoln to a position in the War Department, subsequently became financial editor of the *New York Evening Post*, frequent contributor to the *North American Review*.

Dix, Dorothea Lynde 1802–87, born: Hampden; daughter of a physician, owner of the largest drug store in Boston, granddaughter of the proprietor of Dixmont; kept a girls' school in Boston 1821–35, where character development was primary; tutor to the children of William Ellery Channing; agreeing to teach Sunday school in East Cambridge (Massachusetts) House of Correction exposed her to the horrific conditions prevailing in such settings in those days 1841, she made a thorough investigation of conditions extant in jails, pest houses, and places for the confinement of the insane 1841–43, published her findings and submitted a petition to the Massachusetts legislature, in behalf of the insane persons confined within the commonwealth in cages, closets, cellars, stalls, pens; chained, naked, beaten with rods, and lashed into obedience 1843, began her campaign for amelioration, responsible for the founding or rebuilding of mental hospitals in Massachusetts, Maine, New Jersey, Alabama, South Carolina, North Carolina, Maryland 1845–52, traveled in Europe, where she attacked the inhumane lunacy laws of Scotland, visited hospitals and asylums in Norway, Holland, Italy, Russia, and Greece 1854–57, convinced Queen Victoria to institute a royal commission to investigate conditions prevailing in the British Empire; during the Civil War, appointed by President Lincoln to be superintendent of nurses 1861–65; after the war, retired to the New Jersey State Insane Hospital, where she lived until her death; author: *The Garland of Flora* 1829, *Conversations about Common Things*, *Alice and Ruth*, *Evening Hours*, other books for children, *Prisons and Prison Discipline* 1845; buried in Mount Auburn Cemetery, Cambridge, Massachusetts; in 1942, the U.S. Navy launched USS *Dorothea L. Dix* (AP-67), which received five battle stars in World War II.

Dobbin, Carroll Edward 1892–1967, born: Jonesport; son of a sailor; attended public schools in Jonesport, A.B. Colby College 1916, D.Sc. 1941, Ph.D. Johns Hopkins University 1924, D.Eng. Colorado School of Mines 1952; geology laboratory assistant in his junior and senior years at Colby College; assistant geologist in oil section: U.S. Geological Survey 1918, assigned to fieldwork in Oklahoma, chief of field work in the ranger division of Texas 1919, coal section 1920, employed in the fuel section (coal and oil) 1924–27, regional geologist in the conservation division, stationed in Denver 1928–59; Dobbin conducted extensive field research in the geology of petroleum, gas, and coal in the western United States, particularly in Montana and Wyoming; the data compiled was reproduced extensively; recipient: U.S. Interior Department Honor Award 1959; president: American Association of Petroleum Geologists 1958–67; president: Rocky Mountain Geologists 1947–48, Colorado Society of Engineers 1951; member: American Academy of Arts and Sciences, American Institute of Mining Metallurgists and Petroleum Engineers; author of numerous bulletins and papers for the U.S. Geological Survey and professional journals.

Dole, Charles Fletcher 1845–1927, born: Brewer; A.B. Harvard College 1868, A.M. 1870, graduate: Andover Theological Seminary 1873; minister: Plymouth Church, Portland 1874–76, First Congregational Church (Unitarian), Jamaica Plain, Massachusetts, 1876–1910; author: *The Citizen and the Neighbor* 1889, *Early Hebrew Stories* 1896, *The Problems of Duty* 1900, *Noble Womanhood* 1900, *The Spirit of Democracy* 1906, *The Hope of Immortality* (originally an Ingersoll lecture at Harvard University) 1906, *The Burden of Poverty* 1912, *The New American Citizen* 1918, *A Religion for the New Day* 1920; president: Association to Abolish War; trustee: Tuskegee Institute 1897–1916; father of James Dole, Hawaiian pineapple magnate.

Dole, Daniel 1808–78, born: Skowhegan; A.B. Bowdoin College, graduate Bangor Theological Seminary; missionary to Hawaiian Islands; president: Oahu College; father of Sanford Dole: president of the Hawaiian Republic and first governor of Hawaii.

Donnell, Harold Eugene 1887–1966, born: Mount Desert; student: Coburn Classical Institute, Colby College, Harvard College, law student: University of Baltimore 1924–25; principal and superintendent of schools: various Maine schools 1909–15; lecturer on criminal subjects 1920–66; superintendent: Maine Reformatory for Men 1920–24, Maryland Training School for Boys 1924–30, superintendent of Maryland prisons and administrator, department of corrections 1930–58; member: Maryland probation and parole board 1936–53; in World War I: lieutenant, USN, administrator and educational officer: U.S. Naval Prison, Kittery 1918–20; new prison named in his honor 1964; author of numerous articles on crime and prisons.

Dorman, Edmund Lawrence 1911–62, born: Portland; B.S. Harvard College 1933, L.L.B. Harvard University Law School 1936; founded Film Foundation of America (for dissemination of legal education through motion pictures in collaboration with Felix Frankfurter and Harvard University Law School faculty) 1937; president: American Institute of Motion Pictures, New York, 1939–46; created: Nobel Science Series, Literature Series, Presidential Series (with leading candidates for president of the United States), Documentary Series (with Albert Einstein, Thomas Mann, and others), feature motion pictures, confidential government films to further war effort, and documentary films for the Department of State and as coordinator of Inter-American Affairs (closely associated with Nelson Rockefeller), documentary features for the Protestant Film Commission and the International Committee of the Young Men's Christian Association; in collaboration with the U.S. Military Academy 1946–49; vice president in charge of production: United World Film (wholly owned subsidiary of Universal-International, J. Arthur Rank Organization, London); formed Dorman Electronics for worldwide distribution of television products 1949, president; merged interests with Remington-Rand International, division of Sperry-Rand Corp. 1956; president: Bradd Realty Corp., Houston, Texas, Edmund L. Dorman & Co., New York from 1959.

Dorr, Temple Emery 1840–1913, born: Bradley; attended public school in Bradley, employed in summers rafting logs on the Penobscot River, removed to California 1862, engaged in prospecting and mining, settled in Saginaw, Michigan, 1866, employed by Eddy, Avery & Co., rafting logs on the Cass River, agent for the firm, secured an interest in the firm and with C. K. Eddy in numerous large lumbering operations; on the death of Newell Avery, formed a partnership with Simon Murphy, styled Murphy and Dorr Co. 1879, bought and operated a large sawmill in Bay City; president: Tittabawasee Boom Co., which handled more logs than any such concern in the world; with the decline of lumbering in Michigan, became interested in redwood timber in California, along with his brother-in-law Selwyn Eddy and Simon Murphy, secured control of the Pacific Lumber Co., which became the largest producer of redwood lumber in the world, also had extensive iron ore holding in Minnesota; presented Saginaw, Michigan, with a magnificent auditorium.

Douglas, Alice May 1865–1943, born: Bath; state superintendent for peace and arbitration, Women's Christian Temperance Union; secretary: Young People's Work of Women's Home Missionary Society, Methodist church, Maine conference; executive: Maine Branch, American School Peace League; Maine correspondent, Lake Mohonk Conference on International Arbitration; general investigator for Eugenics Section, Carnegie Institution; director: Maine Conference Deaconess Home, Portland; editor: *Pacific Banner* and *The Acorn*; founder: Peace Maker's Band; author: *Phlox, May Flowers, Gems Without Polish* 1889, *The Pine and the Palm, Olive Leaves, Peace Bells, Quaker John in the Civil War, Self-Exiled from Russia, How the Little Cousins Formed a Museum, The Peace Makers, A Friend Indeed, Jewel Gatherers.*

Douglas, Paul Howard 1892–1976, born: Salem, Massachusetts, of Maine parents; raised by his stepmother in the remote Piscataquis County settlement of Onawa (Elliottsville), attended high school in Newport, A.B. φBK Bowdoin College 1913, A.M. Columbia University 1915, attended Harvard University 1915–16, Ph.D. University of Chicago 1920; taught economics at the University of Illinois 1916–17, Reed College 1917–18; engaged in industrial relations with the Emergency Fleet Corporation 1918–19; returned to the teaching of economics at the University of Washington 1919–20, professor of industrial relations at University of Chicago 1919–49; served on numerous state and national commissions and committees; alderman: city of Chicago 1939–42; unsuccessful candidate for the Democratic nomination for U.S. Senate 1942; during World War II, despite his membership in the Society of Friends, joined the U.S. Marine Corps as a private, rising in rank to lieutenant colonel, accorded the Bronze Star for bravery; elected as a Democrat to the U.S. Senate 1949, served until 1967, having been defeated for reelection in 1966; chairman: Committee on Economic Report (Eighty-fourth Congress), Joint Economic Committee (Eighty-sixth and Eighty-eighth Congresses); chairman of the President's Committee on Urban Affairs 1967–68, chairman: Committee on Tax Reform 1969; after his death in Washington, D.C., he was cremated and his ashes scattered in Jackson Park, Chicago; his second wife Emily Taft Douglas (daughter of the sculptor Loredo Taft) severed in the U.S. House of Representatives 1945–47.

Dow, Lorenzo 1825–99, born: Sumner; A.B. Wesleyan College 1849; taught school in Vermont for a year, went around Cape Horn to California 1850–53, removed to New York, where he studied law, removed to Topeka, Kansas, 1854; elected judge, Kansas Supreme Court 1855; mayor of Topeka 1859; editor: *Kansas Tribune*; with coming of the Civil War, devoted himself to improvements in ordinance, invented the waterproof cartridge adopted by U.S. government, manufactured by Remington Arms Co. with which he became associated; in 1866, took up engineering, cleared away the old Spanish dike on the Magdalena River, Columbia, and established a steamboat line; removed to Colorado 1873, engaged in mining, in 1896; organized Dow Composing Machine Co. to develop and market the typesetting machine invented by his son Alexander, which came to dominate the market.

Dow, Neal 1804–97, born: Portland; son of Quakers; sent to the Friends Academy in New Bedford, Massachusetts; merchant and manufacturer; chief of the Portland fire department 1839; subsequent to the report made to the Maine legislature by James Appleton, organized the Maine Temperance Union 1838; mayor of Portland 1851–58, in his first term as mayor drafted a bill for the prohibition of the manufacture and sale of intoxicating liquors throughout the state, entitled A Bill for the Suppression of Drinking-Houses and Tippling Shops, provided for search of suspected places, for seizure, condemnation, and confiscation of such liquor found and the punishment by fine and imprisonment of those trafficking in it; ignoring his friends, who were appalled at the radical nature of the bill, secured a hearing before the legislature and through persuasive rhetoric and moral suasion, secured approval of what came to be known as the Maine Law 1851; president: World Temperance Convention in New York City 1853; member: Maine House of Representatives 1858–59; in the Civil War:

appointed colonel of the 13th Regiment, Maine Volunteers, accompanied General Butler's expedition to New Orleans, commissioned brigadier general, USV, 1862, assigned the command of the forts below New Orleans, subsequently in command of the district of Florida; at the battle of Port Hudson, twice wounded and taken prisoner, sent to Libby Prison, where he was held for a year, eventually exchanged for Confederate General W. F. H. Lee; broken in health, resigned his commission 1864; Prohibition party candidate for president of the United States 1880; buried in Evergreen Cemetery; father of Frederick Neal Dow.

Doyen, Dorcas 1813–36, born: Temple; daughter of neer-do-wells, she became a servant at the age of thirteen in the household of Nathan Weston, chief justice of the Maine Supreme Judicial Court; a remarkably intelligent woman, proficient in several languages and extremely well-read, she left the Weston household in Augusta at age seventeen and, eventually, made her way to New York City, where, under the *nom d'amour* of Helen Jewett, she became a very expensive and sought-after prostitute; she was hacked to death and set on fire by a patron who was eventually found to be not guilty of this heinous and extremely renown case; novelists as diverse as Joseph Holt Ingraham (*Frank Rivers: or, the Dangers of the Town*) and Gore Vidal (*Burr*) have made fictive use of the murder, and Doyen has been the subject of nonfiction works, such as *Their Sister's Keepers: Prostitution in New York City 1830–70* by Marilyn Wood Hill and *The Murder of Helen Jewett, The Life and Death of A Prostitute in Nineteenth-Century New York.*

Dresser, Horatio Willis 1866–1954, born: Yarmouth; son of Julius A. Dresser, an itinerant newspaper editor, his mother was a student of Phineas P. Quimby; removed to Webster, Massachusetts, Dansville, New York, Denver, Colorado, and Oakland, California, where he received the bulk of his early education; leaving school at age thirteen, became a telegraph operator and railroad agent in California 1879–82; stenographer and bookkeeper in Boston 1885–88; A.B. Harvard College 1895, A.M. 1904, Ph.D. 1907; founder, editor, and publisher *The Journal of Practical Metaphysics* 1895-98; associate editor: *The Arena* 1898–99; founder, editor, publisher: *The Higher Law* 1899–1902; assistant in philosophy: Harvard College 1903–11, professor of philosophy, Ursinus College, Collegeville, Pennsylvania, 1912–13, instructor in church history: New Church Theological School, Cambridge, 1913–14, lecturer on practical philosophy 1893–1912; author: *The Power of Silence; An Interpretation of Life in its Relation to Health and Happiness* 1895, *The Perfect Whole: The Heart of It* 1896, *In Search of a Soul* 1897, *Voice of Hope* 1898, *Methods and Problems in Spiritual Healing* 1897, *Voices of Freedom* 1900, *Education and the Philosophical Ideal* 1900, *The Christian Ideal* 1901, *A Book of Secrets* 1902, *Man and the Divine Order* 1903, *Health and the Inner Life* 1906, *The Greatest Truth* 1907, *The Philosophy of the Spirit, A Study of the Spiritual Nature of Man and the Presence of God, A Physician to the Soul* 1908, *A Message to the Soul* 1910, *Human Efficiency: A Psychological Study of Modern Problems* 1912,

In *Modern Life* 1914, *Handbook of the New Thought* 1907, *The Victorious Faith: Moral Ideals in War Time* 1917, *On the Threshold of the Spiritual World: A History of the New Thought Movement* 1919, *The Open Vision* 1920, *Spiritual Health and Healing* 1922, *Psychology in Theory and Application* 1925, *History of Ancient and Medieval Philosophy* 1926, *Outlines of the Psychology of Religion* 1929, *Knowing and Helping People* 1933; editor: *The Spirit of the New Thought* 1917, *The Quimby Manuscripts: Showing the Discovery of Spiritual Healing and the Origin of Christian Science* 1921.

Dresser, Julius A. 1838–93, born: Maine; an itinerant newspaper editor, he visited Phineas Quimby for relief of a nervous disorder 1860, quickly convinced of the efficacy of Quimby's methods, he was given access to Quimby's yet-unpublished manuscripts; edited newspapers in Yarmouth, Maine, Webster, Massachusetts, Dansville, New York, Denver, Colorado, and Oakland, California; removing to Boston, in 1882, with his wife, founded the monthly *Mental Healing*; gradually modified Quimby's system until it was a new theory of disease and healing, which came to be known as New Thought, which differed markedly from Christian Science, another Quimby-derived religion; while not denying the existence of the real world, held that the Omnipresent Wisdom controlled all nature and only by right thinking could health and prosperity be obtained; author: *The True History of Mental Science* 1899; father of Horatio Willis Dresser.

Drummond, Thomas 1809–90, born: Bristol; graduate: Lincoln Academy, A.B. Bowdoin College 1830; read law in Philadelphia; member: Pennsylvania bar 1833; removed to Galena, Illinois, 1835; appointed by President Taylor: judge of the U.S. District Court for Illinois 1850, served to 1869, when he was appointed, by President Grant (a personal friend from Galena): judge of the seventh U.S. Circuit Court, holding jurisdiction over Illinois, Wisconsin, and Indiana; made many notable decisions, particularly on the applicability of admiralty law on shipping on the Great Lakes, protecting it from divergent and conflicting laws of the several states, a question long undecided in American courts; English admiralty law held that such laws were only applicable to tidewater, Drummond, however, held that the law applied to all navigable waters within the territory of the United States, upheld by the U.S. Supreme Court and incorporated into American and English law texts as elementary law; during the Civil War, when General Burnside, commanding officer of the department, suppressed the publication of articles in a Chicago newspaper he thought seditious and disloyal, Drummond publicly denounced this order as an act of military usurpation, asserting that freedom of speech is protected by the United States Constitution; so great was the tumult, that President Lincoln revoked the order, later, the U.S. Supreme Court approved of the reasoning of Judge Drummond; he undertook to enforce the law impartially in the prosecution of extensive whisky frauds; the receivers that he appointed to run various railroads, subsequent to their default following the Panic of 1873, performed their tasks with unique success, later, his work was commended by various railroad experts and upheld by the U.S. Supreme Court; tributes to his ability and sagacity were paid, at his death, by many, including Lord Coleridge, lord chief justice of Great Britain, and William Howard Taft; Judge Kennesaw Mountain Landis had his portrait hung in the chambers of the U.S. District Court in Chicago.

Dryden, John Fairfield 1839–1911, born: Temple; attended public schools in Temple and Worcester, Massachusetts, attended Yale College, forced to withdraw, due to illness, shortly before graduation; took an interest in the Friendly Societies of England, where wage-earners could purchase life insurance for a small weekly or monthly premium, approached several businessmen of Newark, New Jersey, with his plan 1873, together, they obtained a charter from the New Jersey legislature, establishing the first American Friendly Society, which wrote policies for two years; founder, secretary: Prudential Insurance Co. of America 1875, this was the real birth of industrial insurance on this continent, elected president 1881; in a period of twenty-five years the numbers of Americans with life insurance went from less than 2 percent to 17 percent, with a total value of policies of more than $1 trillion; also involved in the organization of various street railways, banks, and other financial establishments in New Jersey, New York, and Pennsylvania; member: U.S. Senate from New Jersey (Republican) 1902–08, chairman: Committee on Relations with Canada, Committee on Enrolled Bills; candidate for reelection but withdrew due to a deadlock in the legislature; vice president: Fidelity Trust Co., Newark, New Jersey, director: Merchants National Bank, Newark, United States Casualty Co., New York; buried in Mount Pleasant Cemetery, Newark, New Jersey.

Dunham, Alanson Mellen Mellie 1853–1931; born: Norway; snowshoe maker for Peary, among others; fiddler, taken up by Henry Ford; on the Keith Circuit; credited by many for resurgence of interest in square dancing.

Dunham, George Lura 1859–1927, born: North Paris; graduate: Hebron Academy, A.B. Colby College ΦBK 1882, A.M. 1883; taught classics at Portland High School 1882–85, removed to Brattleboro, Vermont, engaged in shoe manufacture with brothers Charles and Lyndon; president and treasurer: Dunham Brothers, which came to be the largest shoe manufacturer in Vermont, gained a national reputation 1910–27; organized and president: Brattelboro Memorial Hospital; member: Vermont House of Representatives 1917–19, member: Vermont Senate 1920–21.

Dunlap, Robert Pinckney 1794–1859, born: Brunswick; son of John Dunlap, a soldier in the French and Indian War, merchant in Brunswick, member: Massachusetts general court and a founding overseer of Bowdoin College; brother of David Dunlap; A.B. Bowdoin College 1815, studied law with Benjamin Orr, Topsham, member: Massachusetts bar 1818, practiced in Brunswick; member: Maine House of Representatives 1821–22, Maine Senate 1824–28, 1831–34, president 1827–28, 1831; member: executive council 1829–31; eighth governor of Maine 1838–43, reelected, annually, three times; in his terms as governor, strove well to overcome the difficulties engendered by the Panic of 1837; member from Second District: U.S. House of Representatives (Democrat) 1843–47; collector of customs, Portland 1848–49; postmaster of Brunswick 1853–57; Bowdoin College overseer 1821–59, president, board of overseers 1843–59; as general grand high priest of the General Grand Royal Arch Chapter of the United States, served as national head of the Freemasons in America for eight years; buried in Pine Grove Cemetery, Brunswick.

Dunn, David 1811–94, born: Cornish; member: Maine bar 1833; practiced in Poland Corner; member: Maine House of Representatives 1840–44, speaker 1843–44, as speaker, became acting governor with the resignation of acting governor Edward Kavanagh 1 January 1844, resigned as speaker and, thus, acting governor 3 January 1844, succeeded by John Winchester Dana, president of the Maine Senate, who was succeeded the same day by newly elected Governor Hugh J. Anderson; member: Maine Senate 1845–46, president 1846; clerk in the Washington, D.C., post office 1857–61.

Dunn, Esther Cloudman 1891–1977, born: Portland; A.B. Cornell University 1913, Ph.D. University of London 1922, Litt.D. (Hon.) Smith College 1956; English instructor: Bryn Mawr College 1913–17, instructor and director of English composition: Smith College from 1922, assistant professor to 1924, associate professor 1924–26, professor from 1927, chairman, department of English, Mary Augusta Jordan chair of English from 1944; after her death, the Esther Cloudman Dunn chair of Comparative Literature was established at Smith College; author: *Ben Johnson's Art—Elizabethan Life and Literature as Reflected Therein* 1925, *The Literature of Shakespeare's England* 1936, *Shakespeare in America* 1939, *Pursuit of Understanding; Autobiography of an Education* 1945, coauthor: *Trollope Reader* 1947.

Dunn, Henry Wesley 1877–1958, born: Waterville; son of a merchant and manufacturer; graduate: Coburn Classical Institute, A.B. Colby College ΦBK 1896, L.L.D. (Hon.) 1936, L.L.B. Harvard University Law School 1902, A.M. Yale University 1917; principal: Monson Academy 1896-97, submaster: Worcester Classical High School 1897–98, Hotchkiss School 1898–99; member: Massachusetts bar 1902, practiced law in Boston, associated with the firm of Powers, Hall & Jones, 1902–12; dean: College of Law, State University of Iowa 1912–14, where he established the case study of law; associated with Fisk, Richardson, Herrick & Neave 1914–16; chairman: Massachusetts Committee to Consolidate the Laws 1916–17; professor of law: Yale University Law School 1917–18; member: Herrick, Smith, Donald & Farley, Boston 1919–31; professor of finance: Harvard University Graduate School of Business Administration 1931–44, where he developed a course in investment management.

Dunn, William 1834–1902, born: Lisbon; quartermaster, USN, recipient: Medal of Honor, "on board the USS *Monadnock* in action during several attacks on Fort Fisher, 24 and 25 December 1864; and 13, 14, and 15 January 1865. With his ship anchored well inshore to insure perfect range against severe fire of rebel guns, Dunn continued his duties when the vessel was at anchor, as her propellers were kept in motion to make her turrets bear, and the shooting away of her chain might cause her to ground; disdainful of shelter despite severe weather conditions, he inspired his shipmates and contributed to the success of his vessel in reducing the enemy guns to silence." Buried in West Bowdoin Cemetery.

Dunnell, Mark Hill 1823–1914, born: Buxton; A.B. Waterville College 1843, A.M. 1852, L.L.D. (Hon.) Shurtliff College 1868; principal: Norway and Hebron Academies 1849–54; member: Maine House of Representatives 1854, Maine Senate 1855; Maine state superintendent of schools 1855–59; delegate: Republican National Convention 1856; practiced law in Portland from 1860; in the Civil War: colonel, USV, commanding officer: 5th Maine Infantry 1861–62; consul at Vera Cruz, Mexico 1862–63; removed to Minnesota 1865; member: Minnesota House of Representatives 1867; Minnesota state superintendent of public education 1867–70; member: U.S. House of Representatives (Republican) 1871–83, 1889–91, unsuccessful candidate for speaker; unsuccessful candidate for U.S. Senate 1883; delegate: Republican National Convention 1892; a founder and regent of Pillsbury Academy; father of Mark Boothby Dunnell; buried in Forest Hill Cemetery, Owatonna, Minnesota.

Dunster, Edward Swift 1834–88, born: Springvale; a descendant of Henry Dunster, first president of Harvard College; A.B. Harvard College 1856, M.D. New York College of Physicians and Surgeons 1859; practiced in New York; in the Civil War: assistant surgeon, USV, served in West Virginia and in the Peninsula Campaign, acting as medical inspector and director of hospitals; after serving in Philadelphia, Washington, and West Point, resigned 1866; returned to practice in New York, specializing in obstetrics and the diseases of women and children; editor: *New York Medical Journal* 1866–72; resident physician at the hospitals on Randall's Island 1869-73; professor of obstetrics and the diseases of women and children: University of Vermont 1868-71, Dartmouth College medical department 1871-73, University of Michigan Medical School from 1873; some of his articles for professional journals include: "Relations of the Medical Profession to Modern Education," "Logic of Modern Medicine," "Notes on Double Monsters," "History of Anæsthesia," "The Comparative Mortality in Armies from Wounds and Disease," "History of Spontaneous Generation."

Dunton, William Herbert 1878–1961, born: Augusta; student: Cowles Art School, Boston; Art Students League, New York; student of Leon Gaspard; murals in Missouri state capitol, Jefferson City; Peoria Society of Applied Arts, Witte Memorial

Museum, San Antonio, Texas, Museum of New Mexico, Santa Fe, *Fall in the Fort Hills* at the White House, Washington, D.C., portrait of Frank Riley at the Arizona Pioneers Historical Society, Tucson.

Dyer, George Leland 1849–1914, born: Calais; son of George Washington Dyer, prominent lawyer and patent attorney in Washington, D.C., brother of Philip Sidney Dyer; graduate, *cum laude*: U.S. Naval Academy 1870; promoted to ensign, USN, 1871, service aboard USS *Plymouth*, on the European, West Indies, and Africa stations 1870–73, service aboard USS *Minnesota* and USS *Frolic*, North Atlantic station 1873–74, promoted to master, USN, 1873, aboard USS *Frolic*, South Atlantic station 1875–77, instructor in mathematics: U.S. Naval Academy 1877–80, promoted to lieutenant, USN, 1879, service aboard USS *Constitution* 1880–81, USS *Despatch*, hydrographic duties in the Gulf of Samana, Dominican Republic, and West Indies station 1881–82, assistant to hydrographer, U.S. Hydrographic Office, Washington 1883–88, promoted to hydrographer, U.S. Hydrographic Office 1888–89, flag lieutenant, USS *Charleston*, Pacific station, present during the first Hawaiian revolution 1890–93, head of department of languages and director of ships: U.S. Naval Academy 1893–95, executive officer: USS *Vevuvius*, service in the Atlantic preventing filibuster activity against Cuba 1896–97, naval attaché, American Embassy, Madrid, Spain, at the outbreak of the Spanish-American War 1897–98, in that war: commanding officer: USS *Stranger*, blockade duty off Havana 1898, commanding officer: USS *Yankton*, patrol duty on the Cuban coast 1898–1901, commanding officer: USS *Rainbow*, Asiatic station 1902–03, commanding officer: USS *Albany*, Asiatic station 1903–04, governor of Guam 1904–05, promoted to captain, USN, 1905, commandant: Charleston (South Carolina) Navy Yard, Port Royal (South Carolina) Navy Station, and 6th Naval District 1906–08, promoted to commodore, USN, 1908; retired to the orange grove and home, styled The Anchorage, he had maintained from 1882 in Winter Park, Florida.

Eames, Emma Hayden 1865–1952, born: Shanghai, China; sister of Hayden Eames, daughter of a clipper captain, first cousin of General Thomas Worcester Hyde; returned to America with her parents and raised by her grandmother in Bath, where she attended public school; removed to Boston to study voice with Clara Munger, also trained in the Delsarte system under Annie Payson Call 1882; made her first professional appearance as Marguerite in *Faust* 1885; on the advice of William Gericke, conductor of the Boston Symphony Orchestra, studied in Paris with Mathilde Marchesi 1886–88; attracted the attention of Charles Gounod, who recommended her for the part of Juliette in his opera *Romeo et Juliette*, Paris Opera 1889; remained at Paris Opera for two years, sang the title role in de la Nux's *Zaira* and Columbe in Saint-Saens's *Ascario*, reprised her role of Marguerite at Covent Garden, London, 1891, became quite popular with the English royal family, performed often at Buckingham Palace; made debut at Metropolitan Opera House, New York, 1881, appeared regularly until 1909 in such roles as Tosca, appeared in nineteen operas, some of which were: *The Magic Flute, Aida, Cavalleria Rusticana, Die Walküre, The Marriage of Figaro*; sang with Madame Schumann-Heink, Geraldine Farrar, Enrico Caruso, Nellie Melba, and Emma Calvé; first truly great American female singer, was appearing with Caruso at San Francisco when the great earthquake occurred 1906; decorated by Queen Victoria with Jubilee Medal 1897, designated officer: French Academy of Music; author: *Some Memories and Reflections* 1927; her voice was noted for its ease and flexibility and her command of the technique of florid singing, also noted for her beauty and stage presence.

Eames, Hayden 1863–1938, born: Shanghai, China, brother of Emma Eames, raised in Bath; graduate: U.S. Naval Academy 1882, served in U.S. Navy 1882-94; general manager: Pope Tube Co. 1893–1900, manager: carriage department, Pope Motor Co. 1895–1900; with Westinghouse Electric Co. 1900–03; proprietor: American Distributing Co., distributors of automobile parts; manager: Studebaker Automobile Co. 1907–10; in World War I: lieutenant colonel in charge of many small ordnance producers.

Eastman, Seth 1808–75, born: Brunswick; cousin of Eastman Johnson; graduate: U.S. Military Academy 1829, classmate and lifelong friend of General Robert E. Lee; commissioned second lieutenant, USA, detailed to the topographical corps, drawing master: U.S. Military Academy 1833–41, as captain, USA, served in the Seminole War 1840–41, Fort Snelling, Minnesota, 1841–48, while there, produced a large body of paintings and drawings detailing the life of the Sioux, exhibited at the annual show of the National Academy of Design, New York, member from 1838; detailed to the bureau of the commissioner of Indian affairs, where he prepared the illustrations for Henry Schoolcrafts *History and Statistical Information Respecting the...Indian Tribes of the United States*, in six volumes 1856; after service on the frontier, military governor of Cincinnati, Ohio, retired 1863; kept on active duty at Elmira, New York, and at Fort Mifflin, Pennsylvania, served on the board of examination of credentials for promotions within the army to 1867, brevetted colonel and brigadier general, USA, 1869; retained, at full pay, by special act of Congress, painted Indian scenes in the Indian Affairs room and views of West Point and western forts in the Military Affairs room, United States Capitol 1867–70; author: *Treatise on Topographical Drawing* 1837, which became a standard text at West Point for years.

Eckstorm, Fannie Hardy 1865–1946, born: Brewer; daughter of a fur buyer, landowner and naturalist; graduate: Abbot Academy, Andover, Massachusetts, A.B.

Smith College 1888; Brewer superintendent of schools 1889–91, employed by D. C. Heath & Company, Boston, publishers; author: *The Woodpeckers* 1901, *The Bird Book* 1901, *David Libbey: Penobscot Woodman and River-Driver* 1907, *The Indian Legends of Mount Katahdin* 1924, *The Penobscot Man* 1924, *The Katahdin Legends* 1924, *Minstrelsy of Maine: Folksongs and Ballads of the Woods and the Coast* 1927, *The Attack on Norridgewock* 1924, *The Handicrafts of the Modern Indians of Maine* 1932, *Maine Maps of Historical Interest* 1939, *Who Was Paugus?* 1939, *Jeremiah Pearson Hardy: A Maine Portrait Painter* 1939, *Indian Place-Names of the Penobscot Valley and the Maine Coast* 1941, *Old John Neptune and Other Indian Shamens* 1945; one of the first two women elected to the American Ornithologists Union; co-founder: Folk-Song Society of the Northeast.

Edes, Robert Thaxter 1838–1923, born: Eastport; son of a Congregational minister; A.B. Harvard College 1858, M.D. Harvard University Medical School 1861; in the Civil War: commissioned assistant surgeon, USN, 1861, passed assistant surgeon, USN, 1862-65, surgeon of the second division of the mortar flotilla at the capture of the forts below New Orleans, later at Vicksburg and Port Hudson, assigned to the USS *Blackhawk*, flagship of the Mississippi squadron, later attached to the USS *Colorado*; assistant professor of *materia medica*: Harvard University Medical School 1870–75, professor 1875–84, Jackson professor of clinical medicine 1884–86; removed to Washington, professor: Georgetown and Columbia University medical schools; resident physician: Adams Nervine Asylum, Jamaica Plain, Massachusetts, 1891–97; author: *Therapeutic Hand-Book of U.S. Pharmacoplia* 1883.

Edwards, Llewellyn Nathaniel 1873–1952, born: Otisfield; son of an apple grower, brother of Dayton James Edwards; B.C.E. University of Maine 1898, C.E. 1901, D.Eng. (Hon.) 1927; draftsman: Boston Bridge Works, bridge designer: Boston & Maine Railroad Co. 1903–06, Chicago & Northwestern Railroad Co. 1906–07, structural engineer: Grand Trunk Railroad Co. 1907–12, in charge of the reconstruction of five bridges on the Lewiston branch in Maine; engineer in charge of design and construction of Coteau Bridge over the St. Lawrence River near Valleyfield, Québec, which had an overall length of seven-eighths of a mile, two swing spans, and seventeen fixed truss spans that were floated into position upon substructure piers; engaged in the exploration and estimation of costs of structures on a proposed railway line in Canada 1912–13; supervising engineer of bridges: Toronto Department of Works 1913–19, prepared estimates, plans, and specifications for and controlled and inspected construction of new street railway and highway bridges, retaining walls and other projects within the city, designed and constructed the Olympia Bridge, a reinforced concrete arch pedestrian bridge at Toronto Island; employed by the U.S. Bureau of Roads as senior highway bridge engineer 1919–21; assigned to District No. 6, comprised of Texas, Oklahoma, Arkansas, and Louisiana, formulated the plans for several bridges in Oklahoma; bridge engineer: Maine State Highway Commission

1921–28, designed the so-called cobwork bridge between Orrs and Bailey's Islands, a then-unique solution to tide flow, extreme weather conditions, and expense; his largest bridge was the Hancock-Sullivan span across the Taunton River; designed concrete arch-bowstring bridges: Norridgewock, the International Bridge across the St. John River, between Madawaska and Edmundston, New Brunswick, which aided greatly the development of the paper industry in that region, Chisholm Park Bridge across the Androscoggin River at Rumford, the largest open spandrel concrete arch bridge in Maine; returned to the U.S. Bureau of Roads 1928, continued to retirement in 1943; did considerable research in Great Britain on Roman roads and construction methods; author: *The Evolution of Early American Bridges* 1934, *Glossary of Terms and Compendium of Information Relating to Bridge Materials and Construction* 1937; took a considerable part in the preparation of *Specifications for Highway Bridges* for the American Association of State Highway Officials, which was accepted as standard by most state agencies.

Elliott, Maxine pseudonym of Jessie Carolyn Dermot 1868–1940; born: Rockland, daughter of a sea captain, sister of Gertrude Elliott; attended Notre Dame Academy, Roxbury, Massachusetts; completed several journeys with her father to South America and Spain; having determined to have a career on the stage, she removed to New York, at age sixteen, where she studied with Dion Boucicault, made her first appearance 1890, opposite the English actor, E. S. Willard, after several minor roles, she appeared as Beatrice Selwyn in *The Professor's Love Story*, in 1893, she played Violet Woodman in *The Prodigal's Daughter*, engaged by Rose Coghlan as leading lady and in her repetoire as Dora in *Diplomacy*, Alice Verney in *Forget Me Not*, Grace Harkaway in *London Assurance*, in 1895; became a member of Augustin Daly's company, where she matured into one of the foremost actresses of the American stage; while with Daly, played Sylvia in *A Midsummer's Dream*, Olivia in *Twelfth Night*, repeated her performances in London; removed to San Francisco 1897, leading lady in the Frawley stock company, toured Australia, created the part of Alice Adams in *Nathan Hale*, played the heroine in *An American Citizen*, *The Cowboy and the Lady*, *When We were Twenty-One*, played the lead in *Her Own Way* 1903, where she received great acclaim, when she repeated the role in London 1905; she received the personal plaudits of King Edward VII, spent two years in the lead in *The Great Match*; mistress of J. P. Morgan, Sr.; first woman since Laura Keene to own and manage her own theatre, Maxine Elliott's Theatre, built in New York 1908, attended to every detail of her productions, which were generally well-received; decorated by Belgium for war work: Order of the Crown; lived in retirement in Cannes, France, where she entertained the likes of the Duke and Duchess of Windsor and Winston Churchill, who returned often to her villa overlooking the Mediterranean to paint; buried in the Protestant Cemetery, Cannes, France.

Ellis, Charles Alton 1876–1949, born: Parkman; A.B. Wesleyan College 1900, C.E. University of Illinois 1922; draftsman, checker, squad foreman: American Bridge Co. 1902–08; assistant professor of engineering: University of Michigan 1908–12; designing engineer: Dominion Bridge Co. 1912–14; assistant professor of engineering: University of Illinois 1914–15, professor of structural engineering 1915–21; vice president: Strauss Engineering Corp. 1921–32, while at Strauss, did most of the design work and calculations for the Golden Gate Bridge, for which he has never received proper credit, construction engineer 1932–34; professor and head of division: Purdue University 1934–46; lecturer in civil engineering: Northwestern Technical Institute from 1946; designer: Montréal Harbor Bridge.

Elwell, Frank A. 1857–1902, born: Portland; son of Edward H. Elwell; after attending public school in Portland, apprenticed as a printer with the *Portland Transcript*, later serving as foreman of the printing room, made frequent contributions on athletic topics; one of the first in Portland to master the bicycle; organizer, president of the Portland Wheel Club; a founder of the L.A.W. and served as chief consul for the Maine division; organized the Blue Nose tour of Canada, led several parties that traversed portions of Canada and brought attention to the need for modern, macadamized roads; after the death of his father, resigned his position at the *Transcript*, and devoted his time to the organization and leading of bicycle tours in Europe, the first of their kind and the beginning of that form of tourism in several European countries; built one of the first motorcycles, and on it, and subsequent improved models, made the first traverse of North Africa as well as tours of Asia, the Holy Lands, and the Balkans; intending to begin commercial production of a motorcycle of his design in Waltham, Massachusetts, he died subsequent to an accident on Long Island, New York, while demonstrating the virtues of his design to prospective investors; his wife was the daughter of J. H. Lamson, a prominent photographer, and niece of Charles Henry Lamson, inventor of numerous bicycle improvements as well as kites of international renown.

Elwell, James William 1820– ?, born: Bath; son of a ship's chandler, in Bath and later in New York; attended Bath Academy; at age twelve, entered the employ of James R. Gibson, ship's chandler; at age fifteen, was in charge, removed to New York, where he became his father's partner in John Elwell & Co. 1838, established shipping lines between New York and the principal ports of the South, as well as South America and the West Indies; after his father's death, the company became James W. Elwell & Co. 1852; served five consecutive terms on the arbitration committee of the Merchants Exchange, a court of equity with powers of the New York state supreme court; an original incorporator of the Shipowners Association, Marine National Bank; trustee: Union Mutual Life Insurance Co., Niagara Fire Insurance Co., Great Western Insurance Co., Chicago & Northwestern Railroad Co., Galena & Chicago Railroad Co., Great Eastern Railroad Co., Columbus, Chicago & Indiana Central Railroad

Co., Atlantic & Pacific Railroad Co., Chicago, Danville & Vincennes Railroad Co., American Congregational Union, Seaman's Friend Society of New York; organized the Brooklyn Helping Hand Society 1871; president: Fresh Air Fund; president: Mariners' Family Asylum (Sailors' Snug Harbor), Staten Island; by 1896, was the oldest merchant doing business on South Street.

Emerson, Ellen Russell 1837–1907, born: New Sharon; daughter of a physician; attended public school in New Sharon, Mount Vernon Seminary, Boston; pioneer ethnologist/anthropologist; contact, as a girl, with H. W. Longfellow sparked her interest in American Indian customs, received encouragement and assistance from John Wesley Powell; author: *Poems* 1865, *Indian Myths: or Legends, Traditions and Symbols of the Aborigines of America Compared with those of Other Countries, Including Hindostan, Egypt, Persia, Assyria and China* 1884, *Masks, Heads and Faces, with some Considerations Respecting the Rise and Development of Art* 1891, *Nature and Human Nature* 1901, *British Ballads from Maine, Indian Place-Names of the Penobscot and the Maine Coast*.

Emerson, George Barrell 1797–1881, born: Wells; son of a physician; A.B. Harvard College 1817, L.L.D. (Hon.) 1859, principal: Leominster (Massachusetts) Academy 1817–19, mathematics tutor at Harvard College 1819–21, principal: English High School, Boston 1821–23, opened and ran a private school for young ladies in Boston 1823–56; an organizer of the Boston Mechanics' Institution; a founder and president: Boston Society of Natural History 1837–43; instrumental in persuading the legislature to fund the geological survey of Massachusetts, took charge of the botanical department of that survey; president: American Institute of Instruction, instrumental in establishing the Massachusetts Board of Education; member: American Academy of Arts and Sciences; author: *Observations on a Pamphlet, Entitled Remarks on the Seventh Annual Report of the Hon. Horace Mann, Secretary of the Massachusetts Board of Education* 1844, *Report on the Trees and Shrubs Growing Naturally in the Forests of Massachusetts* 1846, *History and Design of the American Institute of Instruction* 1849, *Education in Massachusetts: Early Legislation and History* 1869, *A Report on the Trees and Shrubs Growing Naturally in the Forests of Massachusetts: Originally Published Agreeably to an Order of the Legislature by the Commissioners on the Zoological and Botanical Survey of the State* 1875, *Reminiscences of an Old Teacher* 1878, *Manual of Agriculture* 1881.

Emerson, James Ezekiel 1823–1900, born: Norridgewock; attended public school in Bangor 1829–39, while working as a carpenter, farmer, sawmill worker, removed to Lewiston 1850, established a factory for making woodworking machinery, invented a machine for boring, turning, and cutting the heads on bobbins, used in cotton mills; removed to California 1852, superintendent of several sawmills; inventor of circular and band saws with removable teeth; removed to Trenton, New Jersey, 1859; manufacturer of edged tools and, during the Civil War, swords and sabres; when the American Saw Co. was organized to manufacture his saws with moveable teeth, he was made superintendent and under his administration, became one of the largest in the country; also invented a swage for spreading sawteeth to a uniform width and shape and cutting the edge in a single operation, a combined anvil, shears, and punching machine, and many other useful devices; president: Emerson, Smith, and Co., saw works in Beaver Falls, Pennsylvania.

Emerson, John Brown 1805–70, born: Edgecomb; shipmaster, commanding officer: brigs *Lexington* and *Henry Kneeland*; noting the inefficiency of steam-driven paddle wheels aboard ocean going ships, invented a spiral propeller, consisting of an open barrel, the heads of which were connected by spirals of angled iron, thus, containing elements of the screw propeller, he tested the model on a small vessel in the Sheepscot River, obtained a patent 1834, later constructed a vessel in New Orleans that utilized this form of propulsion; brought several actions against patent infringement by John Ericsson, some reaching the U.S. Supreme Court; after his death, the U.S. Congress voted a sum of $25,610 for the relief of John B. Emerson, a royalty of $10 per ton, of five vessels constructed using the Ericsson propeller, most importantly, the USS *Princeton*, generally considered to be the first screw man-of-war, the Senate report also went on, "Your committee believes that the infringement of his patent by the United States gave encouragement to other ship-builders to do the same thing, and that Mr. Emerson, in consequence, suffered damages greatly in excess of the sum above stated"; at the beginning of the Civil War, he was imprisoned in Louisiana for his Unionist predilections; after his release, he retired to Newcastle, where he died.

Emerson, Luther Orlando 1820–1915, born: Parsonsfield; cousin of Usher Parsons; graduate: Parsonsfield Seminary, D.Mus.(Hon.) Findlay College; received a musical education from I. B. Woodbury, began as a choral director, church organist and composer in Salem, Massachusetts, later removed to Boston; church organist and musical director: Bulfinch Street Church; associated with the publishing firm of Oliver Ditson & Co. from 1857; his compilation of hymns *Golden Wreath* sold 40,000 copies in the first year; called to take charge of the music in the Second Congregationalist Church, Greenfield, Massachusetts, and of the musical department of Powers Institute, Bernardson; published his second hymnal *Sabbath Harmony*, which was followed by his third *The Harp of Judah* 1863, was immensely popular, selling 30,000 copies in three months; declined an invitation from Lowell Mason to become his associate; directed over 300 musical festivals, composed some 80 songs, quartets, and piano pieces, 3 masses and many church anthems, wrote the music for very popular Civil War song *We Are Coming, Father Abraham* (words by William Cullen Bryant).

Emerson, William Ralph 1833–1917, born Alton, Illinois; son of Dr. William R. Emerson, a native of Kennebunk and brother of George Barrell Emerson, who had removed to Alton at the behest of Elijah P. Lovejoy; subsequent to the murder of

Lovejoy and the death of Dr. Emerson, both in 1837, W. R. Emerson and mother removed back to Kennebunk; attended Boston public schools while boarding with George Barrell Emerson; began his architectural career in partnership with Jonathan Preston 1854–61, practiced under his own name until he partnered with Carl Fehmer 1864, the firm of Emerson & Fehmer designed several townhouses in Back Bay, Boston, and at least one cottage in Newport, Rhode Island, charter member: Boston Society of Architects 1867; oversaw the restoration of the Old Ship Church in Hingham; in his subsequent career, he designed in high Gothic Victorian, as in the Massachusetts Homeopathic Hospital, or in the popular stick style, as in the Forbes residence and the William Ellery Channing Eustis residence, both in Milton, Massachusetts; designed numerous cottages in Maine for people such as Frederick Law Olmstead, Thomas Blake (son of George Fordyce Blake), J. Montgomery Sears, among others; several churches.

Emery, Charles Henry 1862–1950, born: Portland; graduate: Westbrook Seminary, Shaw's Business College, Portland; while in school, worked for his father's wholesale beef business, removed to Chicago 1881, employed by Libby, McNeil & Libby, a food-canning business, superintendent of the can-making department 1890; patented a machine to solder the square cans which the company had adopted for its packed meat, thus eliminating the need for hand soldering, left Libby, McNeil & Libby 1890; general manager: Sea Coast Canning Co., Eastport, which was operating some forty sardine-packing houses along the coast, applied the automatic can-making and soldering and sealing machines, thus revolutionizing this aspect of the sardine business, entered the sardine business as an independent under the name of Independent Canning Co. 1908–12; recalled by Libby, McNeil & Libby in 1914, sent to Alaska to improve the canning of salmon 1914, sent to Camden, New Jersey, to operate the tomato-packing operation of the company 1916; subsequent to his retirement in 1924, operated citrus groves in Anaheim, California, and in Howey-in-the-Hills, Florida; while at Libby, initiated the use of corned beef hash and veal loaf, both from recipes of his wife.

Emery, Henry Crosby 1872–1924, born: Ellsworth; son of Lucilius Alonzo Emery, grandson of John Crosby; A.B. Bowdoin College 1892; A.M. Harvard University 1893, Ph.D. Columbia University 1896, L.L.D. (Hon.) Bowdoin College 1913; instructor in political economy: Bowdoin College 1896–1900, professor: Yale University 1900–15, the youngest full professor at Yale, to that date; appointed chairman: U.S. Tariff Board by President Taft, completely revamped the tariff schedule, investigated the industrial effects of the tariff, gathered statistics on various dutiable articles, output, information regarding costs of production, general conditions of competition, here and abroad, served 1909–13; resigned from Yale University and was associated with Guaranty Trust Co. from 1915; sent by Morgan Guaranty to Saint Petersburg to study industrial and financial conditions in Russia 1916, escaped Russian Revolution on foot, captured by German forces, released from prison in Berlin with lapse of German monarchy and assisted the Weimar Republic; manager: Pekin branch of the Asia Banking Corp. of New York 1921–24, died returning from China, buried at sea; Bowdoin College overseer 1910–24; author: *Speculation on the Stock and Produce Exchanges of the United States* 1896 (his doctoral dissertation at Columbia) remains an authoritative analysis of the economics of exchange, *Politician, Party and People* 1913.

Emery, Lucilius Alonzo 1840–1920, born: Carmel; graduate: Hampden Academy, A.B. Bowdoin College 1861, A.M. 1864, L.L.D. (Hon.) 1898; member: Maine bar 1863, practiced in Ellsworth; Hancock County Attorney 1867–71; member: Maine Senate 1874, 1875, 1881; Maine attorney general 1876–79; associate justice: Maine Supreme Judicial Court 1883–1911, chief justice 1906–1911; professor of medical jurisprudence: Medical School of Maine 1889–1912; lecturer on Roman law: University of Maine from 1896; author: *Concerning Justice* 1914; Bowdoin College overseer 1874–1907, trustee 1907–20; son-in-law of John Crosby, father of Henry Crosby Emery.

Emery, Stephen Albert 1841–1891, born: Paris; attended Colby College 1859–60; music student: University of Leipzig, University of Dresden 1862–63; professor of harmony and piano: New England Conservatory 1864–81, professor of composition and theory: Boston University 1881–91; assistant editor: *Musical Herald*; author: *Elements of Harmony* 1879, *Foundation Studies in Pianoforte Playing* 1882, published over 150 compositions, including string quartets, piano sonatas, songs, &c.

Emmons, Chansonetta Stanley 1858–1937, born: Kingfield; sister of F. E. and

F. O. Stanley; school teacher, student: Western Maine Normal School, Farmington; received encouragement from her brothers, who had become portrait photographers, removed to Boston, taught art in public schools and studied painting, settled in Dorchester; with a borrowed camera, immediately demonstrated great skill in capturing unromantic, truthful photographic studies, after the death of her husband, spent winter of 1896–97 in Kingfield; began a career of professional photography; prize winner: *Youth's Companion* Sixth Annual Photography Show 1901; demonstrated great skill as a printer; master member: Society of Arts and Crafts, Guild of Photographers.

Estes, Dana 1840–1909, born: Gorham; after Civil War service, became bookseller, formed with Charles Lauriat: Estes and Lauriat in Boston, first company to combine publishing with wholesale/retail; publisher of Guizot's *History of France*, also the publisher of Scott, Dickens, Thackery, Hugo, Dumas, Laura Richards, and others, prominent in the establishment of the International Trademark Convention; donated land in Gorham for state normal school, (now University of Southern Maine).

Evans, Clinton Buswell 1848–1923, born: Fryeburg; A.B. Dartmouth College 1873; reporter and night editor: *Springfield Republican* 1873–83, financial editor: *Chicago Tribune* 1883–88, founder: *The Economist* 1888, president: Economist Publishing Company.

Evans, George 1797–1867, born: Hallowell; attended Hallowell and Monmouth academies, A.B. Bowdoin College 1815, L.L.D. (Hon.) 1847, overseer 1827–45, trustee 1845–67; married Ann Dearborn, daughter of Henry Dearborn; member: Maine bar 1818, practiced in Gardiner, later removed to Hallowell; member: Maine House of Representatives 1825–29, speaker 1829; member: U.S. House of Representatives (Whig) 1829–41; member: U.S. Senate 1841–45, chairman: Committee on Finance; in Washington, he was highly regarded as fiscal expert and parliamentarian; among those considered for the vice presidency under Zachary Taylor 1848, appointed by President Taylor, chairman of the Mexican claims commission; Maine attorney general 1853–56; first president: Portland & Kennebec Railroad, president: Maine Historical Society; buried in Oak Grove Cemetery, Gardiner.

Everett, Charles Carroll 1829–1900, born: Brunswick; son of Ebenezer Everett, an attorney, Bowdoin College trustee and cousin of Edward Everett; A.B. Bowdoin College 1850 (Hon. A.M., D.D., L.L.D.), student at Medical College of Maine, student at University of Berlin (his primary teacher was Hegel's successor, Georg Andreas Gabler), S.T.D. Harvard University Divinity School 1859; instructor, professor of languages, and college librarian: Bowdoin College 1853–57 (his tenure was vetoed by the board of overseers because he was a Unitarian); pastor: Unitarian Church, Bangor 1859–69; Bussey professor of theology: Harvard University Divinity School from 1869, dean: Harvard University Divinity School from 1878, taught the first courses in comparative religions in the United States; author: *The Science of Thought* 1869, *Fichte's Science of Knowledge: A Critical Exposition* 1884, *Essays on Poetry, Comedy and Duty* 1888, *Religion Before Christianity, Ethics for Young People* 1892, *The Gospel of Paul* 1893, *Essays: Theological and Literary* 1901; chairman, editorial board: *The New World*, an undenominational theological quarterly.

Fahey, Myrna 1933–1973, born: Carmel; graduate: Pemetic High School, Southwest Harbor, where she was a cheerleader; a part in a school play decided her in favor of the life of an actress; runner-up in the Miss Maine contest 1952, runner-up in the Miss Rheingold contest 1956; removed to California where she apprenticed at the Pasadena Playhouse for a year; began doing commercials for television, appeared on *Wagon Train, Bonanza, Perry Mason, Thriller, Marcus Welby, M.D., Batman*, co-starred, with Tony Franciosa, in the movie *The Story on Page One* 1959, appeared as Vincent Price's character's sister in *The Fall of the House of Usher* 1960, returned to television where she starred in a sitcom *Father of the Bride* 1961, at this time, she appeared on the cover of *TV Guide*, where her good looks were compared to those of Elizabeth Taylor; succumbed to cancer, buried in Mt. Pleasant Cemetery, Bangor

Fairfield, Arthur Philip 1877–1946, born: Saco; attended Bowdoin College 1895–97, served aboard USS *Columbia* during the Spanish-American War, B.S. U.S. Naval Academy 1901, instructor at Annapolis 1906–09, commanding officer: USS *McDougal* and USS *Gregory*, in World War I: member of the general staff of Admiral Sims, London and Queenstown, Ireland; commanding officer: USS *Argonne* 1922, USS *Chester* 1930–32, graduate: U.S. Naval War College 1933, assistant chief of the Bureau of Navigation 1933–35, promoted to rear admiral, USN, 1934, commanding officer: Cruiser Division Seven 1935–36, member of the General Board 1937–38, assistant chief of Naval Operations 1938–39, commanding officer: Battery Division 2, USS *Idaho* flagship 1939–41, retired as vice admiral, USN, 1941; decorated: Navy Cross, Order of the Crown (Belgium), Commander, Order of the British Empire, Order of St. Olaf of Norway.

Fairfield, John 1737–1819, born: Boston, Massachusetts; son of a prosperous merchant; A.B. Harvard College 1757, A.M. 1760; after graduation, kept school in Roxbury and Manchester, Massachusetts, and Arrowsick Island, Maine; chosen as the moderator (as well as selectman) of the first town meeting in Pownalborough, held in the garrison house in Wiscasset 1760; called by the newly divided parish of Pepperrellborough (now Saco) 1762; his ordination occasioned one of the great feasts in Maine history; even though the congregation had only ten members, a meal of sixtyfour pounds of beef, forty-three pounds of pork, numerous fowls, a barrel of beer, two gallons of rum, and two quarts of brandy was consumed; married the daughter of Ichabod Goodwin, who was also the widow of Foxwell Cutts]; though he was a Whig and, therefore, suffered no political problems with his congregation, the parish refused to increase his salary to compensate for the great inflation occasioned by the Revolution; this, his growing blindness, and bickering over theology caused the congregation to dwindle; Fairfield resigned 1798, only to be immediately unsuccessfully run by the Democrats to oppose George Thacher for the U.S. House of Representatives.

Fairfield, John 1797–1847, born: Saco; graduate: Limerick Academy, made several trips to the South as a manufacturer's representative; studied law with Ether Shepley; member: Maine bar 1826; reporter of decisions: Maine Supreme Judicial Court 1832–35; member (Third District 1835-37, Fourth District 1837-38): U.S. House of Representatives (Democrat) 1835–38; during his term, the Graves-Cilley duel took place, at considerable personal risk, introduced legislation that resulted in Graves being expelled from the House; resigned to serve as tenth governor of Maine

1838–39, unsuccessful candidate for reelection 1840, elected twelfth governor of Maine 1841–43, during his term, the so-called Aroostook War took place, during which he became a national hero for his willingness to challenge Great Britain; resigned to serve in U.S. Senate 1843–47; nominated for vice president on Democratic ticket 1844; died an agonizing death, as the result of allowing a quack to introduce acid into his knee to alleviate a chronic knee malady; buried in Laurel Hill Cemetery, Saco, cenotaph in Congressional Cemetery, Washington.

Farley, William 1835– ?, born: Whitefield; boatswain's mate, USN, recipient: Medal of Honor, "served aboard USS *Marblehead* off Legareville, Stono River, 25 December 1863, during an engagement with the enemy on John's Island. Behaving in a gallant manner, Farley animated his men and kept up a rapid and effective fire on the enemy throughout the engagement, which resulted in the enemy's abandonment of its positions, leaving a caisson and one gun behind."

Farmer, Hannah Tobey Shapleigh 1823–91, born: Berwick; daughter of a school teacher, surveyor, justice of the peace, deputy sheriff, representative to the Massachusetts General Court; after the deaths of her father, brother, and two sisters from tuberculosis, removed to Eliot with her mother, in near-destitute conditions; helped by becoming an itinerant mantua-maker; met and married Moses Gerrish Farmer, preceptor of Eliot Academy; immediately joined in his chronic inventing, patenting her head protector 1883; became involved in charitable and philanthropic activities; during the Civil War, raised large sums for the public benefit of wounded soldiers; in memory of her son, constructed a large dwelling in Eliot, Rosemary Cottage, for the purpose of sheltering and feeding weary and needy women and children 1888; writing under the pseudonym Mabelle, wrote prose and poetry; buried in Eliot.

Farmer, Moses Gerrish 1820–93, born: Boscawen, New Hampshire; son of a farmer and lumberman; attended local school and studied piano while assisting his father, after whose death in 1837, Farmer enrolled in Phillips Academy, Andover, attended Dartmouth College before a bout with typhoid fever obliged him to withdraw; worked part of 1842 in a civil engineer's office in Portsmouth, later taught school in Portsmouth; preceptor: Eliot Academy 1843–44, where he met and married Hannah Tobey Shapleigh, principal: Belknap School for Girls, Dover, New Hampshire, 1844–45; aside from his interest in mathematics, he tuned pianos, played church organ; devised a machine to print window shades on paper, rather than linen, as was then the fashion and which proved very successful; began to study electricity, constructed what must have been the first electric railroad, powered by batteries, which he exhibited in various places in Maine and New Hampshire 1845; offered the position of wire examiner on the new telegraph line from Boston to Worcester, assumed control of the line from Boston to Newburyport, removed his family to Salem 1848–51; invented an electric-striking apparatus for fire alarm purposes, with the

Eminent Mainers

assistance of William Channing, induced the city of Boston to install, what was to become, the first electrical fire alarm system in the world, Farmer acting as superintendent 1851–53; discovered the means of duplex and quadruplex telegraphy 1855; invented aluminum electroplating 1856; while serving as superintendent of a tobacco-extracting factory in Somerville, invented an incandescent light bulb, lighted his parlor in Salem 1859; finding that well-cell batteries were impractical for this purpose, devised and patented a self-exciting dynamo 1868; selected as electrician at the U.S. Torpedo Station at Newport, Rhode Island, 1872–81, closely associated with Admiral Royal Bird Bradford; consulting electrician to the United States Electric Light Co.; retired to Eliot, where he is buried.

Farnham, Ralph 1756–1861, born: Lebanon; last survivor of the battle of Bunker Hill; settled in Acton 1779; invited, in 1860, to a benefit concert, held in his honor, at Tremont Temple in Boston.

Farnham, Thomas Jefferson 1804–48, born: Maine; lawyer in Peoria, Illinois, prior to 1837; removed to New York, where his wife was matron of the women's section of the prison at Sing Sing; organized a party of immigrants, which adopted the motto "Oregon or the Grave" 1839, eventually reached Fort Vancouver, engaged by Marcus Whitman to draft a petition requesting United States government protection of Oregon, which he carried to Washington, made voyage to Sandwich Islands (Hawaii) and Monterey, California; author: *Travels in the Californias* 1844; instrumental in securing release of English and American prisoners held by Mexican authorities for insurrectionary activities; author: *Travels in the Great Western Prairies, the Anahuac and Rocky Mountains, and in the Oregon Territory* 1841; settled in San Francisco 1847; his published writings had an enormous impact, particularly during the gold rush; buried in the mission cemetery in Santa Barbara, California.

Farrington, Edward Holyoke 1860–1934, born: Brewer; brother of Wallace and Oliver Farrington; B.S., M.S. University of Maine, M.S. Sheffield Scientific School, Yale University 1882; chemist: Connecticut Agriculture Experimental Station, New Haven, 1887–89, Experimental Station, U.S. Department of Agriculture, Washington, D.C. 1887–89; chemist: Illinois Agriculture Experiment Station, Champaign 1890–94; professor of dairy husbanding: University of Wisconsin 1894–1927; chemist: World's Fair dairy test 1893; author: *Testing Milk and Its Products* 1896, *Dairy Products* 1927; originated the alkaline test for acidity in dairy products, high-pressure oven test for water in dairy products, milk sediment test, butterfat percentage test, considered by many to be the father of the modern dairy industry.

Farrington, Oliver Cummings 1864–1933, born: Brewer; brother of Edward Holyoke and Wallace Farrington; B.S. University of Maine 1881, M.S. 1888, Ph.D. Yale University 1891; laboratory assistant: Yale University 1890–91; assistant: American Museum of Natural History 1893; curator of geology: Field Museum, Chicago, from 1894; president: American Association of Museums 1915–16; fellow: Geological Society of America; member: Field Museum expedition to Brazil 1922–23; author: *Gems and Gem Minerals* 1903, *Meteorites* 1915.

Farrington, Wallace Rider 1871–1933, born: Orono; brother of Edward Holyoke and Oliver Cummings Farrington; B.S. University of Maine 1891; began career as newspaperman as a reporter for the *Bangor Daily News, Kennebec Journal*, editor and founder: *Rockland Daily Star*; editor: *Pacific Commercial Advertiser*, Honolulu; created through merger: *Honolulu Star-Bulletin*; a founder and chairman of the board of regents of the University of Hawaii; territorial governor of Hawaii 1921–29.

Fassett, Francis Henry 1823–1908, born: Bath; apprenticed to Isaac Cole, carpenter; later studied architecture in Boston and New York; after the Great Fire of 1866, commissioned to build a large number of structures in Portland, including the original building of the Maine Medical Center, Sacred Heart Church, the Baxter Library, Portland High School, the Keith Theatre, the pedestal for the Longfellow memorial; other commissions include the Sagadahoc County Courthouse, Bath, several structures for the Maine Insane Hospital, Augusta; one of his more accomplished students (and later partner) was John Calvin Stevens.

Felch, Alpheus 1804–96, born: Limerick; son of a merchant; graduate: Phillips Academy, Exeter, A.B. Bowdoin College 1827; studied law, member: Maine bar, practiced in Houlton 1830–33; advised by a physician to go West for his health, got as far as Monroe, Michigan, where he contracted cholera, remained, served as Monroe village attorney, removed to Marshall, Michigan, 1833; member: Michigan House of Representatives 1835–37; Michigan state bank examiner 1838–39; Michigan state auditor general 1842; a founder and first regent: University of Michigan 1842–47; associate justice: Michigan Supreme Court 1842–45; governor of Michigan 1846–47, resigned in order to serve in the U.S. Senate (Democrat) 1847–53, chairman: Committee on Audit and Control, Committee on Public Land; president of the commission to settle Spanish and Mexican war claims 1853–56; Tappan professor of law: University of Michigan 1879–84; as governor, responsible for the building of the St. Mary's Falls Canal at Sault Sainte Marie, an essential component in the industrial development of the Great Lakes, oversaw the movement of the capital from Detroit to Lansing; father-in-law of Claudius Buchanan Grant; buried in Forest Hill Cemetery, Ann Arbor.

Ferrero, Willy 1906–1954, born: Portland; son of Italian immigrants, returned with his family to Italy as a child; at the age of six, conducted a performance of the Teatro Costanzi in Rome, at age eight, conducted symphonic concerts in various European capitals, met with great acclaim and extravagant praise from other musicians; continued to conduct through World War I; graduated from the Vienna Academy of Music 1924; his compositions include a symphonic poem *Il Mistero dell aurora*, several pieces for chamber orchestra, several film scores.

Fernald, Albert E. 1838–1908, born: Winterport; first lieutenant, Company F, 20th Maine Infantry, USV, recipient: Medal of Honor, "at Five Forks, Virginia, 1 April 1865, during a rush at the enemy, Lieutenant. Fernald seized, during a scuffle, the flag of the 9th Virginia Infantry, CSA." Buried in Oak Hill Cemetery, Winterport.

Fernald, Bert Manfred 1858–1926, born: West Poland; son of a farmer,

 attended public school in Poland and Hebron Academy; while attending a business school in Boston, the death of his father required him to return home to manage the family farm; the cash crop was sweet corn, which was sold to a local cannery; along with his brothers-in-law, organized Fernald, Keene & True Co. with Fernald as manager, later president; came to own six corn canneries, marketed under the Poland and Alice Rose labels; member: Maine House of Representatives 1897–99, Maine Senate 1900–1901; unsuccessful Republican candidate for governor 1903, elected governor of Maine 1909–1911; as a proponent of tourism, opposed exploitation of waterpower, particularly in the Rangely Lakes region; proposed several forest, water, and wildlife protection measures; established Maine forestry district; oversaw the construction of the new Maine Statehouse; the Fernald Law of 1909 prevented export of Maine-generated electricity; in warm alliance with Percival Baxter; appointed to fill unexpired term of Edwin C. Burleigh in U.S. Senate 1916 (Republican), chairman: Committee on Public Buildings and Grounds, elected in own right 1918, reelected 1924, died in office; a warmly regarded figure in the Senate, known for his humor, opposed United States membership in League of Nations and World Court; president: Poland Telephone Co.; director: Fidelity Trust Co.; president: National Canners Association; denounced measures for government regulation of meat packers as stifling; buried in Highland Cemetery, West Poland.

Fernald, Charles Henry 1838–1921, born: Mount Desert; son of a farmer; at age sixteen, found employment on a local shipping line, worked summers, attended local public school in the winter; graduate: Maine Wesleyan Seminary, Kents Hill, A.M. Bowdoin College 1871, Ph.D. Maine State Agricultural College 1885; during the Civil War: seaman, master's mate, acting ensign, USN, 1862, saw service aboard: USS *Housatonic*, USS *Stettin*, USS *Carnation*, USS *Patapsco*, USS *George W. Rogers*; student of Agassiz at Penekese; principal: Litchfield Academy 1865, Houlton Academy 1866–71, professor of natural history: Maine State Agriculture College (later University of Maine) 1871–86, professor of zoology, chairman of department: Massachusetts Agriculture College and director of the graduate school 1886–1910, amassed the largest collection of *microlepidoptera* in the world; author: *Catalogue of the Tortricidæ of North America* 1882, *Butterflies of Maine* 1884, *Grasses of Maine* 1885, *Sphingidae of New England* 1886; father of Henry Torsey Fernald.

Fernald, Frank Lysander 1835–1919, born: Kittery; served several years as shipbuilder; entered USN, 1854; chief draftsman: Boston Navy Yard 1868; assistant naval constructor 1871; in England, France, and Germany studying marine design 1875–79; member: naval advisory board, design and construction of USS *Atlanta*, USS *Boston*, USS *Chicago*, USS *Dolphin* 1887–91; commanding officer: construction of USS *Charleston*, USS *San Francisco*, USS *Monterey*, Union Iron Works, San Francisco 1891-95; commanding officer: naval construction, Navy Yard, New York, commanding officer: construction of USS *Maine* (BB-10, the second battleship of that name), USS *Cincinnati*; special duty in England, China, Burma, Baltimore, Wilmington (Delaware), and New York Navy Yard, new construction.

Fernald, Guy Goodwin 1865–1939, born: Wilton; son of a merchant and undertaker; student: Wilton Academy, Farmington State Normal School, St. Johnsbury (Vermont) Academy, A.B. Dartmouth College 1893, A.M. 1893, M.D. Dartmouth College Medical School 1899; interned at Mary Hitchcock Memorial Hospital, Hanover, New Hampshire; member of staff: McLean Hospital, Waverly, Massachusetts; assistant to Dr. C. August Hoch for five years, had charge of male patients and their nurses for four years; resident physician and psychiatrist: Massachusetts State Reformatory, West Concord, 1908–35; principal: boys' division, Perkins School for the Blind 1893–94; disciplinarian: Friends School, Providence, Rhode Island, 1895–96; during a year's leave of absence 1917–18, made a survey of feeble-mindedness in Maine for the National Committee for Mental Hygiene; director of survey and secretary of the Maine Commission on Provision for Study of Feeblemindedness; author: *The Defective Delinquent Class: Differentiating Tests* 1912, *Report on the Maine Commission for the Study of Feeblemindedness* 1919, numerous articles, including appropriate literature for reformatory inmates, his paper "Character: An Integral Mentality Function" 1918, was the basis of his psychiatric teaching that in clinical personality studies investigation of character and its deviations as expressed in behavior should supplement the grading of intelligence; developed the first penal institution psychopathic laboratory for classification on basis of mentality; member: American Association for the Study of the Feebleminded, American Association for Clinical Criminology, American Prison Association, Massachusetts Society for Mental Hygiene.

Fernald, Merritt Caldwell 1838–1916, born: South Levant; left fatherless at age five; began teaching, while still a boy, A.B. Bowdoin College 1861, A.M. 1864, Ph.D. 1881, L.L.D. (Hon.) 1902; principal: Goulds Academy, Bethel 1863, post-graduate student at Harvard University, where he studied analytical chemistry and mineralogy 1864; principal: Houlton Academy 1865–66, principal: Foxcroft Academy 1866–68; professor of mathematics, acting president: Maine State College of Agriculture and Mechanic Arts, later University of Maine 1868–79, president 1879–1893, professor of philosophy 1898–1908; contributor of numerous papers on meteorology, mathematical tables, records of barometrical, geodesic, and astronomical works; father of Merritt Lyndon and Robert Heywood Fernald.

Fernald, Merritt Lyndon 1873–1950, born: Orono; son of Merritt Caldwell Fernald, brother of Robert Heywood Fernald; attended the University of Maine for one year, asked by Sereno Watson, curator of the Gray Herbarium, Harvard University, to be his assistant; B.S. Harvard College 1897, D.C.L. (Hon.) Acadia University, Nova Scotia 1933, D.Sc. University of Montréal 1938; assistant in Gray's Herbarium, Harvard University 1891–92, curator 1935–36, director from 1937; instructor in botany: Harvard University 1902–05, assistant professor 1905–15, Fisher professor of natural history 1915–49; assistant editor: *Rhodera* (organ of New England Botany Club) 1899–1928, editor in chief from 1924; author of some 900 papers and monographs on botany, much of his research involved persistence of ancient species in temperate North America of ancient types of plants which survived geological upheaval and glacial invasions from the Cretaceous age; in 1910, made a study of botanical evidence given in Norse sagas relating to the discovery of North America, he published in *Rhodora* a paper called "Notes on Plants of Wineland the Good," in which he demonstrated that the southern limit of Leif Ericson's voyage must have been in southern Labrador or northern Newfoundland, a theory now widely accepted by historians; at the request of the president of the legislative council of Newfoundland, wrote *The Botanical Evidence of Marine Conditions in Hamilton Inlet, Labrador* 1926, wherein he showed that by investigation of the flora and fauna of the inlet determined by different conditions of salinity or freshness of water, the original boundary between Newfoundland and the Dominion of Canada could be determined, this paper was essential in the considerations of the Privy Council in London, which awarded 110,000 square miles of Atlantic watershed to Newfoundland; editor: *Gray's Manual of Botany* seventh edition, *Gray's Manual of Botany* ninth edition; author: *Edible Wild Plants of Eastern North America* (with Alfred Kinsey); fellow: American Academy of Arts and Sciences; recipient: gold medal, Massachusetts Horticultural Society 1940.

Fernald, Walter Elmore 1859–1927, born: Kittery; M.D. Medical School of Maine 1881; assistant physician: State Insane Hospital, Mendota, Wisconsin, 1882–87, superintendent: Massachusetts School for the Feeble-Minded from 1887; professor of mental disease: Tufts University Medical School from 1887, lecturer on mental diseases of children: Harvard University Medical School; author: *Report of the Commission to Investigate the Question of the Increase of Criminals, Mental Defectives, Epilectics and Degenerates* 1911; considered to the foremost expert on retardation in the United States.

Fessenden, Francis 1839–1906, born: Portland; son of William Pitt Fessenden; A.B. Bowdoin College 1858, overseer 1879–86; studied law with his grandfather and at Harvard University Law School; removed to New York to study for the New York bar 1860; in the Civil War: rose from captain, USV, to major general, USV, assigned to the 19th U.S. Infantry, stationed in Indianapolis, Indiana, recruiting; joined General Buell's army in Tennessee, severely wounded at Shiloh; appointed colonel, 30th Maine Volunteers, ordered to Louisiana 1864, participated in the Red River campaign, led his regiment at the battles of Sabine Cross Roads, Pleasant Hill; commanding officer: 3rd Brigade, Emory's Division, XIX Corps, Monett's Bluff, where he was credited with directing the charge that saved the retreating army, but losing his right leg as a result of exposing himself to enemy fire; promoted to brigadier general, USV, 1864, major general, USV, 1865, commanding officer: 1st Division, USA, West Virginia Department 1865, commanding officer: 1st Brigade, Hancock's Division; commanding officer: Maryland and Shenandoah district of refugees, freedmen, and abandoned lands 1866; member of the military commission that tried and condemned William Wirtz, commandant of Andersonville Prison; after declining a commission in the regular army, mustered out 1866; member: Maine bar; mayor of Portland 1876; Bowdoin College overseer, compiled his father's letters and papers; by appointment of Congress: member, Board of Managers, National Home for Disabled Veterans (Togus); buried in Evergreen Cemetery, Portland.

Fessenden, James Deering 1833–82, born: Westbrook; son of William Pitt Fessenden; A.B. Bowdoin College 1852, student: Harvard University Law School; member: Maine bar 1856, practiced with his father in Portland; in the Civil War: recruited a company for the 2nd U.S. sharpshooters (Berdan's sharpshooters); mustered into service as captain, USV, 1861; assigned to the staff of General David Hunter, engaged in operations on the Carolina coast, recruited, organized, and disciplined the first regiment of Negro troops in U.S. Army 1862, brought the regiment to such proficiency in drill and discipline as to convince officers opposed to such a plan that blacks could make good soldiers; after the regiment was disbanded, served as aide-de-camp, with rank of colonel, USV, in Admiral Dupont's attack on Charleston 1863; served under General Hooker at Lookout Mountain; operations in support of General McPherson at Resaca, Kennesaw Mountain, and the battle of Peach Tree Creek; ordered to report to General Sheridan, where he participated in Sheridan's famous ride to Cedar Creek; commanded the post at Winchester; commanded a district in South Carolina, later Maryland; brevetted major general, USV, commanding officer: U.S. Volunteers 1866; after being mustered out resumed the practice of law in

Eminent Mainers

Portland, appointed register of bankruptcy; mayor of Portland 1876; member: Maine House of Representatives 1872–74; buried in Evergreen Cemetery, Portland.

Fessenden, Samuel 1784–1869, born: Fryeburg; son of a Congregational minister; graduate: Fryeburg Academy, A.B. Dartmouth College ΦBK 1806, L.L.D. (Hon.) Bowdoin College 1846; studied law with Daniel Webster and Judah Dana, Fryeburg; member: Massachusetts bar 1809, practiced in New Gloucester; closely associated with Simon Greenleaf; member: Massachusetts House of Representatives (Federalist) 1814–16, Massachusetts Senate 1818–19; elected major general of militia; his strong advocacy of Federalism and his strong antislavery stance made higher elective office, once Maine separated from Massachusetts, difficult; member: Maine House of Representatives 1825, 1826; Liberty party candidate for governor 1847; widely known as a leader of abolitionists in Maine; vice president of the first meeting of the New England Anti-Slavery Society, president 1836; visited black families, took them to church, made major efforts to see to their education, proposed a black man for admission to U.S. District Court as an attorney 1844; removed to Portland 1824; associated with Thomas Deblois; president: Cumberland County Bar Association; Bowdoin College overseer 1822–29; declined election to the presidency of Dartmouth College; natural father of William Pitt Fessenden.

Fessenden, William Pitt 1806–69, born: Boscawen, New Hampshire; natural son of Samuel Fessenden (or, some say, Daniel Webster), half-brother of T. A. D. Fessenden, son-in-law of James Deering; removed from his mother's care (whom he never saw again) and taken to Fryeburg, by his father, at the age of a few days; attended Fryeburg Academy, A.B. Bowdoin College 1823, L.L.D. (Hon.) 1858, Harvard University 1864; member: Maine bar 1827, practiced in Fryeburg 1827–29, removed to Portland 1829; formed a partnership with his father; declined nomination for U.S. House of Representatives 1831, 1838; member: Maine House of Representatives 1831, 1839, 1845–46, 1853–54; delegate: Whig National Convention 1832, 1840, 1848, 1852; accompanied Daniel Webster on tour of Western states 1837; formed a partnership with William Willis 1835; member: U.S. House of Representatives 1840–42; an organizer of the Republican party in Maine; member: U.S. Senate 1854–64, 1865–69 (Republican), chairman: Committee on Finance, chairman: Committee on Public Buildings and Grounds, chairman: Committee on Appropriations; member, Board of Regents: Smithsonian Institution; his first speech in the Senate opposing the Kansas-Nebraska bill was widely noted and established his reputation as an orator of note and firm opponent of slavery; secretary of the treasury: 1864–65, assumed office at a point when the finances of the country were in dire straits, through skillful manipulation of bond sales, was able to stave off national bankruptcy; opposed strict reconstruction and the impeachment of Andrew Johnson, Fessenden's vote saving Johnson from conviction was his last political act; Bowdoin College overseer 1843–60, trustee 1860–69; father of James Deering, Francis and Samuel Fessenden; buried in Evergreen Cemetery, Portland; a U.S. Revenue Cutter, USRC *Fessenden*, was launched in 1865.

Field, Elias 1882–1949, born: Phillips; son of a lawyer; graduate: Boston Latin School, A.B. Harvard College 1903, L.L.B. Harvard University Law School 1906; member: Massachusetts bar 1906, formed a partnership with two classmates: Brown, Field & Murray, later Brown, Field & McCarthy; primarily a trial lawyer, also attracted corporate clients, including numerous insurance companies; special assistant to the U.S. attorney general 1920–23; counsel for the government in the *United States Shoe Machinery Company* v. *United States*, in which the company was charged with violation of the Clayton Anti-Trust Act, the decision in favor of the government claim invalidated tying clauses imposed by the company in leasing shoe machinery; counsel for the U.S. Alien Property Custodian in a case that involved principles applicable in liquidating partnerships between Americans and enemy aliens; selected by the American Legion to defend an impoverished veteran accused of murder, prevailed against seemingly insurmountable odds; assisted Arthur D. Hill in his defense of Sacco and Vanzetti 1927; lecturer: Northeastern University School of Law 1914–45; legislative counsel for the city of Boston 1920–21; regional counsel for the U.S. Railroad Administration; in World War I: commissioned captain, 101st Engineers, USA, transferred to 1st Army Headquarters, promoted to major, judge advocate general's department, stationed in Bordeaux 1918-19; decorated by the French government: Order of the Silver Palms, officer of the National Academy.

Field, Richard Hinckley 1903–78, born: Phillips; nephew of Elias Field; graduate: Phillips Academy, Exeter 1922, A.B. Harvard College 1926, L.L.B. *magna cum laude* Harvard University Law School 1929; member: Massachusetts bar 1929, Maine bar 1973; member: Brown, Field & McCarthy, Boston 1930–42; assistant counsel, special commission on control and conduct of public utilities in Massachusetts 1929–30; regional attorney: Massachusetts Office of Public Affairs, Boston 1942–43; chief legal adviser and acting general counsel, Washington, 1943–44, general counsel 1944–46; visiting professor of law: Harvard University Law School 1946–47, professor 1947–68, Story professor of law 1968–73; counsel: Murray, Plumb & Murray, Portland 1973–78; visiting American professor: University of London, Institute of Advanced Studies 1970–71; consultant: Economic Stabilization Administration 1950–51; Maine Advisory Commission on Rules of Evidence 1973–78; member: board of selectman, town of Weston, Massachusetts, 1956–58, town moderator 1962–68; fellow: American Bar Foundation; chief reporter, division of jurisdiction between state and federal courts: American Law Institute 1960–68; president, board of trustees: Cambridge School 1949–55; permanent secretary: Harvard College, class of 1926, 1926–51; as a classmate and friend of Alger Hiss, raised money for his defense; coauthor: *Materials for a Basic Course in Civil Procedure* 1953, revised editions 1968, 1973, *Maine Civil Practice* 1959, revised edition 1970, *Maine Evidence* 1976.

Fillebrown, Charles Bowdoin 1842–1917, born: Winthrop; son of a dentist, brother of Thomas Fillebrown; student: Maine Wesleyan Seminary, Kents Hill 1858–61, Phillips Academy, Exeter 1862, student at Massachusetts Institute of Technology 1866–67; in Union Army 1862–66, 24th Maine Infantry, 29th Maine Infantry, three years as aide-de-camp, 1st Brigade, 1st Division, 19th Corps; Brigade staff: Banks's Red River Expedition, division staff: Shenandoah Valley campaign; associated with Jordan, Marsh & Co., wholesale dry-goods jobbers 1868–69; salesman for Sargent Brothers & Co. 1869–72; Boston agent for Great Falls Bleachery 1872–74, partner 1874–77; established C. D. Fillebrown & Co. 1877; president and general manager: Glenark Knitting Co., Woonsocket, Rhode Island, 1881–1903; founder and treasurer: Massachusetts Single Tax League 1892, president 1899–1909, single tax propagandist from 1896; author: *The Single Tax, Its Breadth and Catholicity* 1898, *After Dinner Mongraphs* 1899, *Boston Object Lessons* 1899, *The Catholic Church and the Single Tax* 1900, *Cornhill and the Single Tax* 1901, *Washington Street and the Single Tax* 1901, *The College Professors and the Single Tax* 1902, *Ground Rent and the Professional Economists* 1902, *Boston Land Lords and the Single Tax* 1903.

Fillebrown, Thomas 1836–1908, born: Winthrop; son of a dentist, brother of Charles Fillebrown; student: Towle Academy, Maine Wesleyan Seminary, Kents Hill, M.D. Medical School of Maine 1883, D.M.D. Harvard University Dental School 1869; practiced dentistry in Winthrop, lectured on dental subjects at the Portland School of Medical Instruction 1878–83; chairman, Department of Operative Dentistry andOral Surgery: Harvard University Dental School 1883–1904; president: American Dental Association 1898.

Fisher, Clark 1837–1903, born: Levant; C. E. Rensselaer Polytechical Institute 1858; during the Civil War: joined U.S. Navy, in engagements at White House landing, Pocotaligo, bombardment of Fort Sumter, taken prisoner at Magnolia Springs, South Carolina, but escaped; after the war, chief engineer, USN; experimented with petroleum oil as a fuel for the navy; with the death of his father, Mark Fisher, who had originally started the Eagle Anvil Works in Newport, Maine, took over the management of the Eagle Anvil Works (the largest such concern in the country), now in Trenton, New Jersey; between 1874 and 1891, was issued numerous patents: an improved railroad spike, cast iron anvil, rail joints, a combination anvil and vise, a spring motor, a lifting jack, &c.; after his death, which was the result of a railroad derailment, his widow, Harriet White Fisher, made national news by assuming the presidency of the Eagle Anvil Works, later, compounded that attention by setting off, in her Locomobile (with chauffeur and a ton of supplies), for a round-the-world journey, which she completed three years later, thus, becoming the first woman to have done so.

Fisher, Ebenezer 1815–79, born: Plantation Number Three (later Charlotte); student at Maine Wesleyan Seminary, Kents Hill, D.D. Lombard University 1862; at age sixteen, removed to Sharon, Massachusetts, where he worked for his brother-in-law in a furniture manufactory; taught school in Charlotte 1834–38; founded the Universalist Society of Milltown 1839; member: Maine House of Representatives (Whig) 1840; member: Maine Universalist convention 1840; pastor: Universalist Church, Addison Point 1841-47, Salem, Massachusetts 1847–53, South Dedham 1853–58; founding president: Saint Lawrence University, Canton, New York 1858–79.

Fisher, Jonathan 1768–1847, born: New Braintree, Massachusetts; son of a soldier killed in the Revolution; A.B. *cum laude* Harvard College 1792; studied theology in Cambridge, demonstrated a remarkable knowledge of Hebrew; Congregational minister: Blue Hill 1796–1837; wood engraver, portrait and landscape painter; devised a phonetic alphabet and a system of stenography, which he used in preparation of his sermons; compiled a Hebrew lexicon; wrote and illustrated a volume entitled *Scripture Animals: or, Natural History of the Living Creatures Named in the Bible* 1834, published another volume entitled *Miscellaneous Poems: Including a Sketch of the Scriptures to the Book of Ruth; Satan's Great Devise, or Lines on Intemperance; I and Conscience, or A Dialogue on Universalism; and a Few Others on Various Subjects* 1827.

Fitch, Aubrey Wray 1883–1978, born: St. Ignace, Michigan, of Maine parents; B.S. U.S. Naval Academy 1906, served aboard USS *Wyoming*, attached to the Grand Fleet, in World War I; qualified as naval aviator 1930, graduate: Naval War College 1938, commanding officer: Pensacola Naval Air Station 1938-40, promoted to rear admiral, USN, 1940; commanding officer: Patrol Wing Two, later, commanding officer: Carrier Division One (flagship USS *Saratoga*), as such fought the battle of Coral Sea, 7–8 May 1942; commanding officer: all aircraft in South Pacific Fleet 1942, commanding officer: all naval air forces of the United States 1943; promoted to vice admiral, USN, 1943, deputy chief of naval operations for air 1944, superintendent: U.S. Naval Academy 1945–47, retired as Admiral, USN, to Newcastle 1947.

Flagg, Edmund 1815–90, born: Wiscasset; son of an attorney, cousin of Daniel Webster; A.B. Bowdoin College 1835; teacher at a classical school in Louisville, reporter for the *Louisville Daily Journal* 1836–61; author: *The Far West* 1838; member: Missouri bar 1837; editor: *St. Louis Daily Commercial Bulletin* 1838, publisher: *Louisville Literary Newsletter*; law partner of Seargent Prentiss, while editor of the *Vicksburg* (Mississippi) *Whig*, fought a duel with the editor of the *Vicksburg Sentinel* 1842, in which he was severely wounded; removed to Marietta, Ohio, editor: *Weekly Gazette Mutual Insurance* 1842–44; returned to St. Louis, where he edited the *Evening Gazette* and served as court reporter in St. Louis County 1844–48; went to Germany as secretary to Edward Hannegan, American minister to Berlin 1848; later appointed consul in Venice and acted as correspondent to several American newspapers; wrote several plays: *DeMolai* 1838, *Ruy Blas* 1845, *Mary Tudor* 1847, *Catherine Howard* 1847, author of several books: *Carrero, or the Prime Minister* 1848, *Francis of Valois* 1848, *The Howard Queen* 1848, *Edmund Dantes* (a sequel to *The Count of Monte Cristo)*1849, *Blanche of Artois* 1850; editor: *Saint Louis Democratic Times* 1851; author: *Venice, the City of the Sea, From the Invasion of Napoleon in 1797 to the Capitulation to Radetzky, in 1849* (two volumes) 1853; contributed articles for *United States Illustrated* 1853–54; appointed statistician for the U.S. Department of State, Washington, prepared: *Relations of the United States with All Foreign Nations* (four volumes) 1856–57, which was highly commended, here and abroad; later he was employed in the Department of the Interior, in charge of copyrights 1861–70; practiced law in Fairfax County, Virginia, from 1870.

Flavin, James 1906–76, born: Portland; B.S. U.S. Military Academy; after serving in the army, turned actor, made numerous appearances on television productions, such as *Man With A Camera, The Roaring Twenties, The Addams Family, &c.*; often playing tough cops or crack Marine sergeants, appeared on Broadway in *The Front Page*, his movies include: *King Kong* 1933, *Baby, Take a Bow* 1934, *The Littlest Rebel, Man on the Flying Trapeze* 1935, *Sweethearts* 1938, *Rose of Washington Square* 1939, *Broadway Melody of 1940* 1940, *Buck Privates* 1941, *Yankee Doodle Dandy, Iceland, My Man Godfrey, The Grapes of Wrath, Fingers at My Window, Kid Glove Killer* 1942, *Thank Your Lucky Stars, Murder on the Waterfront, Footlight Glamour* 1943, *Hollywood Canteen, Four Jills in a Jeep, Here Come the WAVES, Laura* 1944, *Operation Pacific, Anchors Aweigh, God is My Co-Pilot, Mildred Pierce, Conflict, Murder, He Says, The Shanghai Cobra* 1945, *Easy to Wed, Angel on my Shoulder, The Strange Loves of Martha Ivers, Nobody Lives Forever* 1946, *Nightmare Alley, The Fabulous Dorseys, Desert Fury* 1947, *One Touch of Venus* 1948, *My Dream is Yours, Mighty Joe Young, Abbott and Costello Meet the Killer* 1949, *Million Dollar Mermaid* 1952, *Abbott and Costello Go to Mars* 1953, *Francis in the Haunted House* 1956, *Mister Roberts, Good Times, In Cold Blood* 1967; buried in Holy Cross Cemetery, Culver City, California.

Fletcher, Loren 1833–1919, born: Mount Vernon; graduate: Maine Wesleyan Seminary, Kents Hill; removed to Bangor 1853, stonecutter, clerk; removed to Minneapolis 1856; engaged in lumber and flour business; a founder and director of the First National Bank, Minneapolis, from 1864; member: Minnesota House of Representatives 1872–86, speaker 1880–86; member: U.S. House of Representatives 1893–1903, 1905–07 (Republican), chairman: Committee on Expenditures on Public Buildings; buried in Lakeview Cemetery, Minneapolis.

Flint, Charles Rundlett 1850–1934, born: Thomaston; his father, Benjamin Flint and an uncle, Isaac Flint Chapman, established the firm of Flint & Chapman 1837, which built ships in Thomaston and Bath and owned and managed the second largest fleet of merchant ships under the American flag (the largest being the Sewall fleet of Bath); removed with his parents to Brooklyn, New York, 1858, attended public schools in Thomaston, Brooklyn, New York, the Warren Johnson School, Topsham, and Polytechnic Institute of Brooklyn, from which he graduated in 1868; dock clerk in New York, receiving and delivering cargoes; clerk: William R. Grace & Co. 1869; New York partner of Bryce, Grace & Co. of Peru; organized Gilchrist, Flint and Co. 1871, ship chandlers; acquired a quarter interest in W. R. Grace & Co. 1872, during the next four years, visited all the countries of South America, partner: Grace Brothers & Co. 1876; Chilean consul in New York, resigned 1879, when Chile declared war on Peru, his firm being the financial agents for the Peruvian government; during that war, rendered great assistance to Peru through the purchase and delivery of munitions; organizer, president: United States Electric Light Co., first to illuminate rooms with incandescent light in New York; visited Brazil in 1884, arranged for the export of large quantities of rubber to the United States; entered his father's firm, Flint & Co. 1886; consul of Nicaragua, consul general of Costa Rica; U.S. delegate: first International Conference of American States, Washington 1889; proposed the establishment of a Bureau of American Republics, which was unanimously adopted, the concept was adopted by U.S. Secretary of State James G. Blaine; construction of the Pan-American Building was funded by Andrew Carnegie; acted as U.S. agent in negotiating a treaty of reciprocity with Brazil; acted for President Piexoto in the purchase of munitions and war vessels in the da Gama revolution in Brazil 1893, within twenty-five days, he purchased, converted, armed, and equipped six high-speed vessels of 10,000 tons displacement, known as the Dynamite Fleet, which enabled the Brazilian government to prevent the restoration of the monarchy; in the Sino-Japanese War 1894–95, Flint purchased the cruiser *Esmeralda* from Chile and delivered it to Japan; during the Spanish-American War, assisted the U.S. Navy in procurement of munitions and ships abroad; as a result of messages from his agents, he was able to convey to John D. Long, U.S. secretary of the navy, the first news of the departure of the Spanish fleet from Cape Verde and later the direction it was sailing, he was also able to inform the government of the sailing of colliers to rendezvous with the Spanish fleet off Venezuela; during the Russo-Japanese War, he was given de Rothchild credits for account of the Russian government in excess of 150,000,000 francs and purchased for Russia eight submarine boats and ten torpedo boats in the United States; under Russian diplomatic passport, visited the Czar and Grand Duke Alexis in St. Petersburg and advised high government officials on war activities; later, he accompanied Admiral Brousiloff on a secret mission to Turkey and Greece; the czar later presented him with a charka of rock crystal bordered with gold and set with rubies and diamonds, bearing the imperial seal; organized Flint, Dearborn & Co. 1889, a consolidation of competing lines of sailing vessels to California; earned his sobriquet Father of the Trusts, through his organization of sundry combinations; brought about the formation of United States Rubber Co. 1891, of which he was treasurer, and on whose behalf he went to Brussels 1906 and negotiated with King Leopold for the entire rubber output of the Belgian Congo; he also organized the American Woolen

Co., the American Chicle Co., Clarksburg Fuel Co., Computing Scale Co. of America, Computing-Tabulating-Recording Co. (the predecessor of International Business Machines, Inc.), the new president of which, Thomas J. Watson, Flint hired away from the National Cash Register Co., Fairmount Coal Co., International Time Recording Co., Mechanical Rubber Co., National Starch Co., Rubber Goods Manufacturing Co., Sen Sen Chicklet Co., Sloss-Sheffield Steel and Iron Co., Somerset Coal Co., United States Bobbin and Shuttle Co.; founder, chairman: American Committee for the Encouragement of Democratic Government in Russia 1917; noted big game hunter; owned and raced the famous sloop *Gracie*, an owner of the successful America's Cup defender *Vigilant*; author: *Memories of an Active Life* 1923.

Fogler, Raymond Henry 1892–1996, born: South Hope; B.S. University of Maine 1915, L.L.D. 1939, M.S. Princeton University 1917, L.L.D. (Hon.) Colby College 1958, D.Sc. Nasson College 1962; executive secretary: agricultural extension service, University of Maine 1917–19; with W. T. Grant Co. 1919–32; director of personnel and real estate: Montgomery Ward & Co., Chicago 1932–40, retail operations manager, vice president, general operating manager, director 1932–38, president 1938–40; president, general manager: W. T. Grant Co. 1940–50, president 1950–52; assistant secretary of the U.S. Navy 1953–57; director: Centennial Insurance Co., Grand Union Co.; trustee: Atlantic Mutual Insurance Co., the Grant Foundation; endowed the Fogler Library, University of Maine.

Follansbee, Elizabeth A. 1837–1919, born: Pittston; attended school in New York and France, student at University of California Medical School, University of Michigan Medical School, M.D. Women's Medical College of Pennsylvania 1877; intern: New England Hospital for Women and Children, Boston; practiced in San Francisco for six years (as such, was the first female physician to practice in California), removed to Los Angeles 1882; an original member of the faculty of University of Southern California Medical School, served for twenty-five years as professor; member: Daughters of the American Revolution, Colonial Dames.

Folsom, George 1802–69, born: Kennebunk; graduate: Phillips Academy, Exeter, A.B. Harvard College 1822; studied law with Judge Ether Shepley in Saco; member: Maine bar 1824; practiced law in Framingham and Worcester, Massachusetts; chairman, Publications Committee of the American Antiquarian Society, published the society's second volume of transactions; removed to New York 1837; secretary, librarian: New York Historical Society 1841, editor: *Collections*; author: *History of Saco and Biddeford, With Notices of Other Early Settlements, and of the Proprietary Governments in Maine, Including the Provinces of New Somersetshire and Lygonia* 1830, *A Catalogue of Original Documents in the English Archives, Relating to the Early History of the State of Maine* 1858, *Expedition of Captain Samuel Argall: Afterwards Governor of Virginia, Knight et cetera to the French Settlements in Acadia and to Manhattan Island, A.D. 1613*

1841, *A Few Particulars Concerning the Directors General or Governors of New Netherlands* 1841, *Historical Sketch of the New York Historical Society* 1841, *Dispatches of Hernando Cortes: The Conqueror of Mexico, Addressed to the Emperor Charles V, Written During the Conquest, and Containing a Narrative of its Events* 1843, *Mexico in 1842…to which is added an account of Texas and Yucatan and the Santa Fe Expedition, Memoirs of Hon. Thomas Lindall Winthrop, L.L.D.: Second President of the American Antiquarian Society* 1857; member: New York Senate (American or Know Nothing party) 1844; chargé d'affaires in the Netherlands 1850–55; editor: *Historical Magazine* 1858–59; president: American Ethnological Society 1859–69; member: American Geographical and Statistical Society, Deaf and Dumb Society, Union League Club; a founder of the Century Association; died in Rome.

Ford, Francis 1882–1953, born: Portland; older brother of John Ford; actor on Broadway and stock, began movie career with Thomas Edison 1907, later with Vitagraph and Universal; director of shorts and action serials; appeared in many of his brother John Ford's films, including: *Stagecoach, Drums Along the Mohawk, Tobacco Road, My Darling Clementine, The Quiet Man,* &c.

Ford, John (born: Sean Aloysius Feeney) 1895–1973, born: Cape Eliza-

beth; son of a saloon keeper, younger brother of Francis Ford; raised on Munjoy Hill in Portland, graduated from Portland High School; after a short stint at University of Maine removed to Hollywood, where he worked for his brother Francis and appeared as an extra in several films, including *The Birth of A Nation*; his important silent films include: *The Iron Horse* and *Four Sons*; regarded by many as the greatest American film director, he was a folk artist, a master storyteller, and a poet of the moving image, he raised the musical score to a level of importance often superior to that of the dialogue; recipient of six Oscars for *The Informer, The Grapes of Wrath, How Green Was My Valley, The Quiet Man, The Battle of Midway, December 7th.*; during World War II, was chief of the photographic branch of the OSS and rear admiral USNR; buried in Holy Cross Cemetery, Culver City, California.

Ford, Sewell 1868–1946, born: South Levant; son a merchant, Civil War soldier in the 1st Maine Cavalry, later, a sailor aboard the USS *Brooklyn*; graduate: Haverhill (Massachusetts) High School 1887; reporter: *Haverhill Daily Laborer and Gazette, Baltimore Globe, Baltimore World, New York Dispatch*, editor: American Press Association 1893–1903; began writing short stories, essays, and novelettes for magazines in 1900; author: *Horses Nine* 1903, *Truegate of Mogador* 1906, *Shorty McCabe* 1906, *Side-Step-*

ping with Shorty 1908, *Cherub Devine* 1909, *Just Horses* 1910, *Torchy* 1911, *Odd Numbers* 1912, *Trying Out Torchy* 1913, *On With Torchy* 1914, *Shorty McCabe on the Job* 1915, *Torchy, Private Secretary* 1916, *Wilt Thou, Shorty?* 1917, *Torchy and Vee* 1918, *Shorty McCabe Looks 'Em Over* 1918, *Shorty McCabe Gets the Hall* 1919, *Meet 'Em with Shorty McCabe* 1921, *Inez and Trilby May* 1921, *Trilby May Crashes In* 1922; his character Shorty McCabe, a genial professor of physical culture and homely philosopher and wit, achieved great popularity, Torchy was perhaps the best-known office boy in America, regarded, by many as one of the most droll and attractive figures in modern humorous fiction; both Torchy and Shorty McCabe were the subjects of motion pictures, Shorty's marriage was the subject of an editorial in the *New York Tribune* 1917.

Foss, Herbert Louis 1871–1937, born: Belfast; seaman, USN, recipient: Medal of Honor, "on board the USS *Marblehead* during the operation of cutting the cable from Cienfuegos, Cuba, 11 May 1898, when, facing the heavy fire of the enemy, Foss set an example of extraordinary bravery and coolness throughout this action." Buried in Forest Hill Cemetery, Hingham, Massachusetts.

Foster, Ben 1852–1926, born: North Anson; son of John Burt Foster, brother of John McGaw Foster; student at the Art Students League and of Abbott Thayer, New York; removed to Paris 1885; student of Luc Olivier Merson and Aimé Morot; exhibited in the Paris Salon; returned to New York 1887; received medals for four oil paintings exhibited at the World's Columbian Exhibition, Chicago, 1893; primarily a painter of landscapes and sheep, night effects and woodland scenes, his *Lulled by a Murmuring Stream* was exhibited at the Paris Exhibition of 1900 and purchased by the French government for inclusion into the Luxembourg gallery collection, the only other American painter, so honored, to that date, was Winslow Homer; recipient: Carnegie Prize, National Academy of Design, New York, 1906, recipient: Inness Gold Medal, National Academy of Design 1909; member: Society of American Artists 1897; associate: National Academy 1901; member: National Institute of Arts and Letters; some of his works include: *A Dreary Road, Fontainebleau Forest, A Maine Hillside, Now Day Is Over, First Days of Spring, All in a Misty Moonshine, A Windy Day, The Evening Star, The Shephard, The Swineherd, The Laggard*.

Foster, Stephen Clark 1799–1872, born: Machias; blacksmith, shipwright; member: Maine House of Representatives 1834–37, 1847; member, president: Maine Senate 1840; member from the Sixth District: U.S. House of Representatives 1857–61 (Republican); delegate: peace convention 1861; buried in Forest Hill Cemetery, Pembroke.

Fox, Jabez 1705–1755, born: Woburn, Massachusetts; son of a Congregational minister, his mother was a member of the Indian-fighting Tyng family of Falmouth;

A.B. Harvard College 1727, A.M. 1730; kept school in Woburn for a year, gave consideration to becoming a physician, trained for the ministry, but his voice failed him; removed to Falmouth, when appointed by the Massachusetts House of Representatives to be the notary for the port of Falmouth 1741; married a widow with children and a fine mansion; in a town meeting, long renown for its particular disorderliness, Fox was chosen to represent Falmouth in the Massachusetts House of Representatives 1745, reelected 1746, 1747, and 1750–52; promptly upon becoming a member of the general court was appointed to farm the excise for York County, which meant that he collected taxes due on such things as tea, coffee, arrack, coaches, and chariots; during the war years of 1748–49, served as subcommissary on the eastern frontiers, in which he was responsible for storage of provisions, ammunition, snowshoes, taking care of sundry whaleboats, and delivering clothing, &c.; signed the treaty of Falmouth 1749; engaged by the Plymouth Company to lay out a town on the Kennebec; had a financial interest in the towns of Wiscasset and Gorham, and lobbied on their behalf in the general court; came into conflict with Enoch Freeman, when he opposed Freeman's appointment as administrator of Thomas Westbrook's estate; appointed justice of the peace for York County 1748, failed to prevent the rescue, by a Falmouth mob, of two prisoners being taken to the York County jail for the murder of several Indians 1748; raised from the House of Representatives to Provincial Council 1752, when the council met in Falmouth in 1754, Governor Shirley resided in Fox's mansion; died soon thereafter of consumption, his funeral was preached by Thomas Smith; buried in the Eastern Cemetery, Portland.

Fournier, William G. 1913–43, born: Norwich, Connecticut; sergeant, U.S. Army, Company M, 35th Infantry Division, entered service at Winterport, recipient: Medal of Honor (posthumous), "for gallantry and intrepidity above and beyond the call of duty: as a leader of a machine-gun section charged with the protection of other battalion units, his group was attacked by a superior number of Japanese, his gunner killed, his assistant gunner wounded, an adjoining gun crew put out of action; ordered to withdraw from this hazardous position, SGT Fournier refused to retire but rushed forward to the idle gun and, with the aid of another soldier who joined him, held up the machine-gun by the tripod to increase his field action, opened fire, and inflicted heavy casualties upon the enemy, but while so engaged both these gallant soldiers were killed, but their sturdy defense factored in the following success of the attacking battalion." Buried in National Cemetery of the Pacific, Honolulu, Hawaii.

Fowler, Joseph William 1894– ?, born: Monmouth; graduate: Monmouth Academy 1911, B.S. U.S. Naval Academy 1918, M.S. Massachusetts Institute of Technology 1921, graduate: U.S. Naval War College 1929; commissioned ensign, USN, 1917, advanced through the ranks to rear admiral, USN, 1946; production officer: Navy Yard, Mare Island, California, 1940–42, assistant industrial manager (naval work in private yards): San Francisco 1942–45, commanding officer: San Francisco

Naval Shipyard 1945, director: industrial survey, Office of the Secretary of the Navy 1946–48, director: Defense Supply Management Agency 1952; vice president: Disneyland, Anaheim, California, Walt Disney Productions, Burbank, California; decorated: World War I Victory Medal and Clasp, Yangtze Service Medal, World War II: Legion of Merit, Victory Medal, pre-Pearl Harbor Medal, Order of Merit, Chile; member: Society of Naval Engineers, member: Bohemian Club, San Francisco.

Frank, Melvin Porter 1841– ?, born: Gray; son of a farmer; attended Lewiston High School, Maine State Seminary, Lewiston, Lewiston Falls Academy, A.B. Tufts University 1865; studied law in the firm of Shepley & Strout, Portland; member: Maine bar 1868; practiced in Portland; member: Maine House of Representatives 1876, 1879, drafted the legislation that abolished capital punishment, the first in the nation; chosen speaker 1879; unsuccessful Democratic candidate for U.S. House of Representatives 1880, unsuccessful Democratic candidate for governor 1896.

Freeman, Enoch 1706–88, born: Eastham, Massachusetts; son of Captain Samuel Freeman, member: Massachusetts House of Representatives; A.B. Harvard College 1729, A.M. 1732; although he kept school in Barnstable and Eastham during vacations, he determined to go into trade subsequent to graduation; enrolled as a student at Samuel Grainger's business school and apprenticed to Hugh Hall, merchant; after his apprenticeship was up, became a contract salesman for Hall, who was a Barbadian and one of the few merchants in Boston who imported black slaves; business frequently took him to Falmouth, to which he removed to permanently 1742, originally working for Samuel Waldo, getting out forest products; because of his mathematical abilities, found himself designing and overseeing the construction of fortifications; dispatched to Boston 1774 to plead for military reinforcements from the general court; appointed captain of militia 1744, appointed major of the 2nd Regiment 1746, commanding officer of the Canada Soldiers on the Eastern frontiers 1748, appointed commander of the battery in Falmouth and commander over the forces in his majesty's service in the County of York 1750; appointed register of deeds, judge of the court of common pleas, as judge, known to fine people for not having attended church, fined loggers 4s for swearing a single oath and women 6s for fornication; served as agent for absentee landlords, paying their taxes and minding their boundaries; proprietor of Pearsontown and Topsham; quite orthodox in his religion, it was thought to be good thing that Freeman happened to be out of town when George Whitefield brought his revival to Falmouth, opposed New Light preachers, who often became his political enemies; disliked Episcopalians, so much so that he appealed to the Society for the Propagation of the Gospel not to support the mission of John Wiswall; elected register of deeds 1761, appointed judge of probate for Cumberland County 1770; disliked recent acts of parliament as much as he disliked mobs, joined in a boycott of several ships in harbor 1769, refused to administer an oath to a man who wanted to testify against the mob that assaulted the comptroller of customs, when overruled in this by

Governor Hutchinson, Freeman blandly responded that the men named in the warrants all had good alibis; he and son Samuel joined the Falmouth Committee of Correspondence 1774, soon after, Freeman was elected to the Massachusetts House of Representatives, which elevated him to the council, but Governor Gage refused to accept him; called the county congress, which chose him as president; delegate to the first Provincial Congress; with the purge of loyal military officers, appointed to the 1st Cumberland Regiment; collected supplies for the relief of Boston; as chairman of the Committee of Safety, attempted to keep mobs under control; declined election to the Provincial Committee of Safety by the Provincial Congress; attempted to control the mob led by Samuel Thompson that had come to town to attack HMS *Canceaux*; when Thompson seized Captain Mowatt, Freeman, and General Jedidiah Preble went surety for Mowatt, who promptly broke parole and regained his ship, the mob jailed Freeman and Preble, who regained their freedom by purchasing 4s worth of liquor for their captors; subsequent to the burning of Falmouth by Mowatt, Freeman busied himself in caring for the survivors and preparing for another British invasion, which came in 1779, in the form of two schooners and eight sloops, bearing several hundred men; mustering all the available militiamen in the entrenchments he had constructed years before, Freeman and his small force repelled several attempted landings and eventually fired on the fleet, itself, at which point, the fleet withdrew; at this point, Freeman began a gradual decline that only ended at his death in 1788.

Freeman, John Ripley 1855–1932, born: West Bridgton; son of a farmer; B.S. Massachusetts Institute of Technology 1876, Sc.D. (Hon.) Brown University 1904, Tufts University 1905, University of Pennsylvania 1927, Yale University 1931; principal assistant engineer: Essex Co., Lawrence, Massachusetts, 1876–85, assistant to Hiram F. Mills, regarded by many as the foremost waterpower engineer in the United States, brought him into contact with the foremost experts in waterpower and hydraulics; engineer and special inspector: Associated Factory Mutual Fire Insurance Companies of Boston 1876–86, chief of its corps of inspectors, reorganized the corps along scientific lines, conducted experiments for the improvement and standardization of fire prevention apparatus, conducted scientific investigations into the causes of fires, simultaneously maintained a private consulting practice in waterpower, municipal water supplies, and factory construction, did an outstanding job, became president and treasurer of a combination of similar companies in Providence, Rhode Island (State, Enterprise and American Fire Insurance companies), from 1903, consolidated as Manufacturers Mutual Fire Insurances Co., raised their risk from $65 million to $3 billion; by 1932, had over 10,000 industrial clients; author: *Report on New York's Water Supply* 1900, *Report of the Commissioner on Additional Water Supply for the City of New York* 1903, this report laid the groundwork for the Catskill Mountain water supply, with which he was associated until his death; chief engineer for the damming of the Charles River, twice offered and declined professorship of civil engineering, Massachusetts Institute of Technology, also refused the presidency; member of the commission which located the supply and designed the works for a water supply from the Owens River to the city of Los Angeles 1906; consultant to numerous cities for the increase of their water supplies; member of the Isthmus Canal Commission 1905–08, 1915, advised the secretary of war on such problems as the choice between a sea-level canal, in Panama, as opposed to a system of dams, locks, and lake, favored by Chief Engineer John F. Stevens; employed by the Chinese government 1917–20 as consultant in the rebuilding of 400 miles of the Grand Canal and control of floods along the Yellow River; after 10 years of work, persuaded the U.S. government to set up an hydraulics laboratory, which was completed 1932, on the grounds of the Bureau of Standards, Washington; author: *Regulation of Elevation and Discharge of the Great Lakes* 1923, *Hydraulic Laboratory Practice* 1929, his *Earthquake Damage and Earthquake Insurance* 1932 was the culmination of years of research concerning earthquakes and his efforts to convinced geophysicists and seismologists of the true nature of earthquakes; his papers include: *Experiments Relating to Hydraulics of Fire Streams* 1890, *The Nozzle as an Accurate Water Meter* 1891, both accorded the Norman Gold Medal of the American Society of Civil Engineers, *The Safeguarding of Life in Theatres* 1905, *The Fire Protection of Cities* 1915, *Flood Control of the River Po in Italy* 1930, awarded the Cross Medal of the American Society of Civil Engineering, *General Review of Current Practice in Water Power Production in America* 1924, read before the first world power conference in London, *The Need for a National Hydraulic Laboratory for the Solution of River Problems* 1924; granted a number of patents on useful appliances, including: automatic fire extinguishers 1889, typewriter cabinets 1895, hose nozzles 1896, valve controlling mechanisms for sprinkler systems 1896, flume screens 1901, molded strainer screens for well and filters 1922, apparatus for forming cellular concrete walls, and apparatus and methods for constructing and sinking caissons; president: American Society of Mechanical Engineers 1904–05, American Society of Civil Engineers 1923–24.

Freeman, Samuel 1743–1831, born: Falmouth (that portion that became Portland); son of Enoch Freeman; attended Harvard College, originally a surveyor, school teacher, later became an active patriot during the Revolution; secretary of the Cumberland County Convention 1774, delegate: Massachusetts Provincial Congress 1775; member: Massachusetts General Court 1776, 1778; clerk of the Cumberland County courts 1775–1820; register of probate to 1804, judge of probate 1804–20; postmaster of Portland 1776–1805; a founder of Bowdoin College, overseer 1794–96, 1799–1819, vice president of the board 1813–15, president 1815–19, treasurer and trustee 1796–99; author: *The Massachusetts Justice* 1803, *Probate Directory* 1803, editor: *Journal of Rev. Thomas Smith* 1821.

Freese, John Henry 1876–1930, born: Bangor; A.B. Harvard College 1902, student at Harvard University Law School; assistant clerk: Maine Supreme Court 1897–99; as observer at Harvard University Observatory, made first photograph of the spectrum of starlight, giving vast new data on the composition of the universe, described in "Making of the Universe," *Century Magazine* December 1902, contributor to magazines and professional journals, translator of Aristotle's *The Art of Rhetoric*, *The Coming Conquest of England* by August Niemann, *The Bibliotheca of Myriobiblion* by Plotinus, others.

French, Edward Sanborn 1883–1968, born: Portland; son of a ticket agent of the Boston & Maine Railroad; graduate: Somerville (Massachusetts) Latin School, A.B. Dartmouth College 1906, A.M. 1935, L.L.D. (Hon.) Middlebury College 1947; while in college, worked in various capacities for the Boston & Maine Railroad, after graduation, continued on to 1908, general manager: White River Railroad Co. in Vermont 1908–20, president 1920–27; when the railroad was abandoned after a disastrous flood, appointed receiver of the Springfield (Vermont) Electric Railway 1920, which was reorganized as the Springfield Terminal Railway, president to 1930; vice president, director: John T. Slack Corp., Springfield, a manufacturer of wool 1922–30; vice president, general manager: St. Johnsbury & Lake Champlain Railroad Co. 1925–30; president: Montpelier & Wells River Railroad Co., Barre & Chelsea Railroad Co. 1926–30, Mystic Terminal Co., comprised of Boston waterfront terminals serving the Boston & Maine Railroad Co. 1927–30; vice president, director: Woodbury Granite Co., Burlington, Vermont, 1927–30; director: Rock of Ages Granite Corp. 1927–30; director of national banks in Barre and Brattleboro; owned a hardware business, a farm machine company, a group of mines and mills manufacturing talc; president: Boston & Maine Railroad 1930–52, chairman of the board 1952–55; president: Maine Central Railroad 1932–52; placed the first streamlined passenger train in the East 1935, inaugurated the first railroad-owned airline in the country, the Boston & Maine-Central Vermont Airways 1933; took over both railroads in the midst of the Great Depression, managed to gain the confidence of institutional and individual investors, reorganized the debts and left them in far better financial shape than when he began; director: Jones and Lamson Machine Co., Springfield from 1942, president 1955–64, when the company was sold to Textron, Inc.; director: National Life Insurance Co., Montpelier, Union Mutual Life Insurance Co., Portland, New England Public Service Co., Oxford Paper Co., American Enka Co., Saco-Lowell Shops, H. P. Hood & Sons, the Federal Reserve Bank, Boston; trustee: Dartmouth College 1935, life trustee from 1941.

French, John Edward 1900–41, born: Skowhegan; B.S. U.S. Naval Academy 1921; promoted through the ranks to lieutenant commander, USN; while serving as navigator aboard USS *Arizona*, was killed in the Japanese attack on Pearl Harbor.

Friend, Victor Alonzo 1870–1952, born: Brooklin; son of a storekeeper and owner of coastal trading vessels; attended public schools in Fitchburg, Massachusetts, Bates College, graduate: Portland Business College 1892; engaged in food manufacturing and packing 1892–1952; in association with his brother, Leslie Friend, organized the firm of Friend Brothers, Inc., bakers and canners, of which he was president 1921–52; trustee: Boston University, Tufts University, Dean Academy, Franklin, Massachusetts; president: Melrose Orchestral Association 1921–52; a prominent Universalist layman, attended various state and national conventions, for many years, was the president of the Universalist General Convention; chairman: Massachusetts Committee of Catholics, Protestants and Jews; member: Massachusetts Executive Council 1944–48; collected guns as a hobby and presented Tufts University with his large collection 1941.

Frisbee, John B. 1825–1903, born: Phippsburg; gunner's mate, USN, recipient: Medal of Honor, "served on board the U.S. Steam Gunboat *Pinola* during the action against Forts Jackson and St. Philip, and during the taking of New Orleans, 24 April 1862, while engaged in the bombardment of Fort St. Philip, Frisbee, acting courageously and without personal regard, closed the powder magazine which had been set afire by enemy shelling and shut off his avenue of escape, thereby setting a high example of bravery." Buried in Fairview Cemetery, Winnegance, Phippsburg.

Frost, Charles 1710–56, born: New Castle, New Hampshire; son of John Frost, a British naval officer, who had settled in New Castle and acquired considerable property and civil honors, as well as marrying the sister of Sir William Pepperrell; A.B. Harvard College 1730, A.M. 1733, his undergraduate career included several serious infractions, including the theft of a goose, for which he was fined 7s; the year that he received his masters degree was also the year that he came into his inheritance, which included lands in East New Jersey, Berwick, Kittery, and the wilder parts of Maine; chosen as notary for Kittery in 1732–33; removed permanently to Falmouth in 1738, where he served as clerk to Thomas Westbrook's commercial interests; lived in what came to be known as Frost's Garrison, in Stroudwater, married his cousin Joanna Pepperrell Jackson; appointed justice of the peace 1739, settled down to a life of business, law, and farming; Frost was regarded as a great nuisance by Rev. Thomas Smith, by whom he had been criticized for foreclosing a certain mortgage in a sermon, also, the Great Awakening in Falmouth had begun at Frost's Garrison and Frost remained its fervent supporter, even though most of his peers came to dislike its excesses; farmed on a larger scale than most, sent barrels of peas to Governor Belcher, who found them to be wonderful; complained to his uncle, General Pepperrell, that enlistments for the Louisbourg Expedition had drained the countryside of workers, however, after the victory, Frost supplied Pepperrell's table lavishly; as judge, was criticized for his heavy-handed enforcement of laws proscribing certain activities on the Sabbath; being opposed to the Excise Act, he stood for and won a seat in the Massachusetts House of Representatives 1755; after his death, his widow operated the garrison as a tavern, which remained a local landmark for over a century.

Frost, Charles Sumner 1856–1931, born: Lewiston; son of a lumber merchant and mill owner; graduate Lewiston High School, B.S. Massachusetts Institute of Technology 1876; employed by the architectural firm of Peabody and Stearns (Boston); removed to Chicago 1881, associated with Henry Ives Cobb in the firm of Cobb & Frost 1882–89, practiced alone to 1898, then was associated with Alfred Granger in the firm of Frost & Granger; in the course of his career, designed several important railway stations and offices in the Central and Northwestern states, including the Chicago & Northwestern Railway Company's general office building and terminal, the terminal buildings for the Lake Shore & Michigan Southern Railway Co., Union Station in St. Paul, Minnesota, the Great Northern Railway station in Minneapolis, the Hill Office and Bank Building, St. Paul, the eighteen-story Borland Building and municipal pier in Chicago, numerous residences and clubhouses, including the Union Club and the Calumet Club in Chicago, the Newberry Library, his commissions in Maine include: Charles Frost cottage, Dr. Richard C. Cabot cottage, Clifford Barnes cottage, all in Northeast Harbor; often called upon to arbitrate conflicting claims and as inspector of buildings to pass on their safety and structure.

Frost, John 1738–1810, born: Kittery; grandson of Major Charles Frost, who was killed by the Indians 1697, son of Major, Deacon, Register of Probate, and Judge Charles Frost, brother of Simon Frost; entered the British army, at an early age, made captain, served in the Louisbourg Expedition, under General Amherst 1758; served in the Ticonderoga and Crown Point Expedition 1759; assisted in the capture of Montréal 1760; returned to Kittery until the outbreak of the Revolution; at the siege of Boston, served as a lieutenant in the Maine regiment, promoted to colonel, served with Washington in the campaigns in New York and New Jersey, commanded his regiment at Saratoga, later at Stillwater and Bemis Heights; after being promoted to brigadier general, served in the middle and Southern states; after the war, retired to his estate in Kittery; served as a justice of the York County Court of Sessions; member: Massachusetts Governor's Council.

Frost, John 1800–59, born: Kennebunk; student at Bowdoin College, A.B. Harvard College 1822, L.L.D. (Hon.) Marietta College 1843; principal: Mayhew School, Boston 1823–27, conducted a school for young ladies in Philadelphia 1827–38; professor of English language at the Philadelphia Central High School 1838–45; devoted himself to the compilation of histories and biographies, utilizing a corps of assistants, published over 300 works, including *History of the World* (three volumes) 1844, *Pictorial History of the United States* (two volumes) 1844, *Beauties of English History*, *Wild Scenes of a Hunter's Life*, *Illustrious Mechanics*, *Book of Heroes*, *Book of the Army*, *Book of the Navy*.

Frost, Simon 1705–66, born: Kittery (that portion that is now Eliot); grandson of Major Charles Frost, who was killed by the Indians 1697, son of Major, Deacon, Register of Probate, and Judge Charles Frost, brother of John Frost; A.B. Harvard College 1729, A.M. 1732; kept school in Kittery, returned to Boston to be sworn as deputy secretary of the province 1735; known as a serious and pious man, not one to frequent the fleshpots of the capital; returned to Kittery 1740, where he got caught up in the religious revival of the day; in spite of this, he still quite capable of advertising the sale of a parcel of black slaves, recently arrived in Kittery aboard ship; appointed register of probate for York County 1744, appointed justice of the peace 1745, elected to the Massachusetts House of Representatives 1747–49; appointed first justice of the court of common pleas 1749, sat for one session as special justice on the superior court; father-in-law of Alpheus Spring.

Frye, Alexis Everett 1859–1936, born: North Haven; son of a ship captain and orange grower; L.L.B. Harvard University Law School 1890, A.M. 1897, L.L.D. (Hon.) University of Redlands 1923; engaged in the making of relief maps of Hyde Park, Massachusetts, 1880–83; teacher of methods and practices: Chicago Normal School 1883–86; delivered some 1,500 lectures on educational topics 1886–90; member: Massachusetts bar 1890; superintendent of schools: San Bernandino, California, 1891–93; traveled extensively in Africa, Asia, and Europe 1893–98; superintendent of public schools, Republic of Cuba 1899–1901, organized and equipped public schools in Cuba, awarded the Medal of Legion of Honor (Cuba) 1900; captain Comoany E, 7th California National Guard 1893, helped organize Harvard University Battery, captain: Harvard Graduates Company 1898, lieutenant Company K, 1st Massachusetts Artillery 1898–99; life fellow: American Geographical Society; author: *Child and Nature* 1888, *Brooks and Brook Basins* 1891, *Mind Charts* 1891, *Primary Geography* (considered to the first geography text written for grammar schools in the United States) 1895, *Complete Geography* 1895, *Elements of Geography* 1898, *Home and School Atlas* 1898, *Geografic Elemental* (Cuba), *Manual para Maestros* 1899, *School Law of Cuba* 1899, *Grammar School Geography* 1901, *First Steps in Geography* 1903, *Home Geography* 1911, *New Geography, Book One* 1917, *The Brooklet's Story* 1927.

Frye, Jonathan c.1704–25, born: Andover, Massachusetts; cousin of Joseph Frye; A.B. Harvard College 1723, distinguished himself, as an undergraduate, by leading the student riot of 1722; having fallen in love with the thirteen-year-old daughter of Reverend John Rogers, who, understandably, opposed the match, Frye enlisted as a common soldier in Captain Lovewell's company 1725; while serving as chaplain, spied a lone Indian, a member of the Sokokis tribe, at a distance, to whom they gave chase; after scalping this Indian, his party was set upon by a much superior force; after a fierce, prolonged battle, the Indians withdrew, possibly because of the death of the chief, Paugus; Frye and two others of the wounded lapsed, eventually, Frye convinced the others to leave him, as he was unafraid of death, his body was not recovered; Cotton Mather publicly mourned his loss, the Pigwacket fight, also known as Lovewell's fight, became the topic of much verse, including the first published work by Henry

Wadsworth Longfellow; Fannie Eckstorm posited that rather than heroic, Frye had actually joined the militia in order to get scalp money, so he could wed, that he stirred up Lovewell's force, in spite of better judgment, to give chase, and that the date of the fight was changed so that it would not be seen that Frye had gone scalping on the Sabbath.

Frye, Joseph 1711–1794, born: Andover, Massachusetts; student at Harvard College for two years; justice of the peace and member of the Massachusetts general court; ensign in Hale's regiment at the capture of Louisbourg 1745, as colonel, in command of a regiment, captured at Fort William Henry by Montcalm, made good his escape by killing the Indian who had charge of him 1757; appointed major general of Massachusetts militia by the Massachusetts Provincial Congress 1775, appointed brigadier general by the Continental Congress, but resigned soon after because of debility 1776; retired to Fryeburg; the town of Fryeburg consists, largely, of land granted to him in recognition of his service at Louisbourg and Fort William Henry 1762.

Frye, William Pierce 1831–1911, born: Lewiston; grandson of Joseph Frye; A.B. Bowdoin College 1850, L.L.D. (Hon.) 1889, Bates College 1881; read law in office of W.P. Fessenden; practiced law in Rockland and later in Lewiston; member: Maine House of Representatives 1861, 1862, 1867; Republican presidential elector 1864; mayor of Lewiston 1866; Maine attorney general 1867–69; member: Republican National Committee 1872–84; member: U.S. House of Representatives 1871–81 (Republican), member: Judiciary and Ways and Means Committees; member: U.S. Senate 1881–1911, president *pro tempore* 1895–1911, longer than any other man, twice second in line of succession to the U.S. presidency; member: committees on Foreign Affairs, Privileges, and Elections; strong advocate of United States intervention in Cuba; U.S. peace commissioner, subsequent to the Spanish-American War 1898; influenced, in part, by Admiral Royal Bird Bradford, advocated retaining control of Cuba, Guam, the Philippines, and Puerto Rico; instrumental in achieving a solution to the Samoan crisis, fishing rights with Canada, disposition of the *Alabama* claims award; Bowdoin College overseer 1872–81, trustee 1881–11; for many years, held the record for largest trout caught (ten pounds); cousin of Edward Parsons Tobie, brother-in-law to Alonzo Garcelon; buried in Riverside Cemetery, Lewiston.

Fuller, Melville Weston 1833–1910, born: Augusta; son of an attorney, brother of Henry Weld Fuller, grandson of Nathan Weston and Henry Weld Fuller I; A.B. Bowdoin College ΦBK 1853, L.L.D. (Hon.) 1888, Northwestern University 1888, Harvard University 1891, Yale University 1901; read law in the office of his uncle, George Melville Weston, Bangor; student: Harvard University Law School 1854–55; member: Maine bar 1855; editor: *Augusta Age* 1855, a prominent Democratic weekly; Augusta city solicitor; member: Augusta City Council; removed to Chicago 1856, clerk in the law office of S. K. Dow, formerly of Maine, later, became his partner to 1860; member: Fuller & Ham 1862–64, Fuller, Ham & Shepard 1864–66, Fuller & Shepard 1866–68, Fuller & Smith 1869–77; early won recognition for his meticulous preparation and keen intelligence, facility of speech, skill in procedure, and his commanding grasp of fundamental principles of jurisprudence; he rejected many attractive offers from railroads, corporations, and banks, preferring to retain his independence to take cases that interested him; one case that commanded much public attention was that of Rev. Charles Edward Cheney, rector of the Christ Protestant Episcopal Church, Chicago, who had been deposed by an ecclesiastical court for expressing his belief in doctrines contrary to established principles of his denomination, Fuller appeared as counsel for the rector, before the church tribunal and astonished both the church and the legal profession by the scope of his knowledge of canon law and patristic literature; in another case, Fuller represented the city of Chicago in its long and bitter contest with the Illinois Central Railroad over control of the Lake Michigan shore, Fuller prevailed against a stunning array of forensic horsepower with his tenacious, resourceful argumentation; a close friend and admirer of Stephen A. Douglas; delegate: Democratic National Convention 1864, 1872, 1876, 1880; member: Illinois House of Representatives 1863–64; delegate: Illinois Constitutional Convention 1862; chief justice of the United States (the first chief justice so designated, his predecessors having been commissioned as chief justice of the U.S. Supreme Court) 1888–1910, wrote 800 decisions and 29 dissents, including the majority opinion in *Pollock* v. *Farmers Loan and Trust Company* 1895, wherein he declared the federal income tax unconstitutional; began the tradition of the judicial handshake, where, before each session, each justice shakes the hand of all the other justices, indicting unity of purpose, if not opinion; at his urging, Congress created the U.S. Circuit Court of Appeals; member: International Court of Arbitration 1900–10; he was one of Venezuela's two members on a five-man tribunal that met in Paris to settle the boundary dispute with British Guiana 1897; regent and chancellor: Smithsonian Institution; Bowdoin College overseer 1875–79, trustee 1894–1910; died at his summer home in Sorrento, buried in Graceland Cemetery, Chicago.

Fuller, Weston Earle 1879–1935, born: Phillips; son of a wholesale hardware merchant, cousin of Melville Weston Fuller; C. E. Cornell University 1900; instructor in hydraulics and mechanics: Cornell University 1900–02; assistant engineer: Ithaca Water Co. 1902–03; associated with the engineering firm of Hazen & Whipple, New York, from 1903; supervisor of the construction of water filtration plants in Watertown, New York, construction of the New York State Hospital for the Insane, Poughkeepsie; chief draftsman, junior partner 1907, partner 1915, when the firm became Hazen, Whipple & Fuller, traveled across the country and Canada, studying water and sewerage problems and supervising the design or improvement of water and sewerage systems and filtration plants, including those of Toronto, Canada, Peekskill, New York, Springfield, Massachusetts, Portland, Maine, Pittsburgh, Pennsylvania, West

Palm Beach, and Miami, Florida, where he was responsible for a unique method of disposing of sewerage by pumping it into the rapidly flowing outgoing current of the sea channel at ebb tide; devised the general design of the Passaic River Valley sewer, New Jersey, resigned from Hazen, Whipple & Fuller 1922; became professor of civil engineering: Swarthmore College, chairman of department 1924, resigned 1929; formed firm of Fuller & Everett, New York 1931, represented the Commonwealth of Massachusetts in the Connecticut River controversy with Connecticut 1928–30, represented the waterpower interests of New York state in the tri-state case on the Delaware River; known throughout the profession for his analysis of flood data and the prediction of occurrence and severity, these formulae were presented in his "Flood Flows," which he read before the American Society of Civil Engineers 1913, and for which he received the Fuertes Graduate Medal at Cornell University 1914.

Furbish, Catherine (Kate) 1834–1931, born: Exeter, New Hampshire; removed to Brunswick at early age; taxonomist, artist, founder: Josselyn Botanical Society; her folios of watercolor paintings of all of Maine's flowering plants and trees are held in Special Collections at the Bowdoin College Library.

Furlong, Atherton Bernard 1849–1919, born: Greenwood; cousin of Addison Verrill, student: Norway Academy, studied music and painting in Boston and Europe; tenor soloist, Boston 1873; director: Park Street Church choir, solo tenor: Holy Trinity Church choir, Brooklyn, New York 1872–77; associated with Dudley Buck 1877–80; sent to England as the representative American oratorio and ballad tenor 1880, sang in St. James Hall, London, and with leading oratorio societies of England, Paris, and Berlin, sang in state concert: Buckingham Palace, with Adelina Patti 1887; director and proprietor: College of Vocal Art, Toronto, from 1888; animal and landscape painter, exhibited at American Academy of Design, &c.; member: Company D, 74th Regiment, New York National Guard, took part in quelling the Fenian raid into Canada 1866–67; author: *Echoes of Memory* 1887, *People of the Blue* 1918, composer of numerous songs; father of Charles Wellington Furlong.

Furlong, Charles Wellington 1874–1967, born: Portland; son of Atherton Bernard Furlong; graduate: Massachusetts Normal Art School 1895, student: Cornell University, Harvard University, *École des Beaux Arts*, *Académie Julian*, Paris; member of faculty: Cornell University 1896–1904, 1906–10, Clark University, Boston University; paintings in leading American art exhibits, life drawings of now extinct Ona and Yahgan Indians in permanent collection of Smithsonian Institution; lecturer at educational institutions and before learned societies in the United States and England; leader of expeditions and explorations in Africa, Near East, South America, Central America, Tierra del Fuego, and Patagonia; discovered the sunken wreck of USS *Philadelphia* near Tripoli 1904; in World War I: rose from private. to major, general staff, commissioned 1929, expert consultant: military intelligence 1943; member:

American Peace delegation, Paris 1918, special military aide to President Woodrow Wilson; military observer and intelligence officer in the Balkans and Near and Middle East 1919; received Distinguished Service Medal twice, recipient: croix de guerre (Greece), Medal for Bravery (Montenegro) and others, including palms of French Academy; fellow: Royal Geographic Society; author: *The Gateway to the Sahara* 1909, *Tripoli in Barbary* 1911, *Leter Buck* 1921, contributor to ethnological collections of various museums and educational institutions, records of explorations to Tierra del Fuego and Patagonia (including the only song, speech, and hand and footprint records extant of the Ona and Yahgan Fuegian tribes) acquired by Stefanson collections, Dartmouth College 1960.

Galland, Joseph Stanislaus 1883–1947, born: Biddeford; A.B. University of Maine 1906, B.S. 1907, A.M. University of Wisconsin 1913, Ph.D. 1914; teacher of romantic languages at Kemper Military Academy, University of Wisconsin, Syracuse University, University of Michigan, and Indiana University to 1925; head of department of romantic languages, Northwestern University from 1925; in World War I: cryptographer with French army at Arras and Amiens fronts, with American Expeditionary Forces at St. Mihiel, Argonne, and Moselle army of occupation; chevalier Legion d'Honneur; author: *French Composition* 1922, *Spanish Grammar Review* 1923, *Spanish Composition* 1924, *Elementary Spanish Reader* 1925, *Progressive French Reader* 1929, *Nineteenth-Century French Prose* 1930, *Nineteenth-Century French Verse* 1932, *Progressive French Grammar* 1932, *An Historical and Analytical Bibliography of the Literature of Cryptography* 1945, *A Study of the Structural Elements of the French Language* 1941; editor: Balzac's *Le Chabert* 1929, *Ten Favorite French Stories* 1935.

Gamage, Harvey Farrin 1898–1976, born: Bristol, son of a carpenter; graduate: Lincoln Academy; joined his father as a house carpenter in Bristol 1917, began working in boatyards in East Boothbay 1918, established his own boatyard in South Bristol 1924; built over 100 oak and cedar-hulled draggers, 60 to 100 feet in length, also turned out oceanographic research vessels, minesweepers, schooners, and replicas of noted sailing vessels, including *Shenandoah* 1964, an 108-foot replica of an 1849 revenue cutter; *Clearwater*, a reproduction of a Hudson River sloop; his *Albatross* was selected by the Smithsonian Institution for inclusion in its watercraft collection; during World War II: built minesweepers and PT boats for the U.S. Navy.

Gammon, Elijah Hedding 1819–91, born: Gilmore Pond Plantation (later Lexington); son of a farmer; admitted to Maine conference of Methodist Episcopal Church 1843; pastor: Wilton 1843–51, Saint Charles, Illinois, 1853, Jefferson Street Church (Chicago) 1854–58, presiding elder: Charles district, Rock River conference 1855–58; partner: Newton & Co., Batavia, Illinois, manufacturers of farm equipment 1858–61, partner in manufacturing harvesting equipment with J. D. Easton 1861–68, with William Prindle 1868–70, with William Jones 1868–70; partner: Gammon and

(James) Deering 1870–79, manufactured the Marsh harvester; founder and vice president: Plano (Illinois) Manufacturing Co. 1880–91, manufactured twine-binding harvesters; endowed Maine Wesleyan Seminary and Garrett Bible Institute, founded: Gammon Theological Seminary (Atlanta) for educating black Methodist clergy.

Gannett, Guy Patterson 1881–1954, born: Augusta; son of William Howard Gannett, cousin of Henry Gannett; graduate: Phillips Academy, Andover, student: Yale College 1901–02, L.L.D. (Hon.) Portland University 1951; joined the W. H. Gannett Co. as treasurer 1902–21, organizer, president: Guy Gannett Publishing Co. 1921–54, purchased the *Portland Press* and *Portland Herald, Portland Evening Express, Portland Sunday Press, Waterville Sentinel, Maine Farmer*, Augusta, all in 1921; merged the *Press* and *Herald*, discontinued the *Maine Farmer* 1924, acquired the *Portland Evening Express* 1925, thus acquiring all the newspapers published in Portland; purchased the *Kennebec Journal* 1929; organized Guy Gannett Broadcasting Services: operated WGAN, began radio broadcasting 1938, began television broadcasting 1954, operated WGUY 1947–52; vice president: Fidelity Trust Co. 1928–30, president 1930–33; an organizer: Financial Institutions, Inc., a Maine holding company that controlled twelve banks; director: Central Maine Power Co. 1910–25, vice president 1916–25; president: Salina (Kansas) Light, Power & Gas Co.; vice president, treasurer: United Water, Gas & Electric Co., Hutchinson, Kansas; vice president, director: Augusta Trust Co.; director: Federal Light & Traction Co., New York, Springfield (Missouri) Railway & Light Co., Union Mutual Life Insurance Co.; member: Augusta Common Council 1907–11, harbor master 1910–27; trustee: Bates College 1929–54, Portland University Law School 1950–54; member: Maine House of Representatives (Republican) 1917, Maine Senate 1919; member: Republican National Committee 1920–28; member: Maine Turnpike Authority 1941–42; in World War I: captain with the American Red Cross, assigned to the hospital in Neufchâteau for training, later attached to the base hospital of the 6th Division, participated in the Argonne campaign; an early and enthusiastic advocate of civil aviation, appointed by the governor of Maine to a committee 1917, chaired by Admiral Robert E. Peary, to study the possibilities of a naval air station on Casco Bay, which ultimately became Brunswick Naval Air Station; member: Maine Citizens Coordinating Committee for Defense 1940; chairman: Maine Aeronautics Commission 1941–43; member, Special Committee of the Office of Civil Defense, established to study the enrollment of private airplanes and pilots for emergency service, approved 1941 by Fiorello H. La Guardia, national defense commissioner, this later became the Civil Air Patrol, of which Gannett was made wing commander for Maine with rank of lieutenant colonel, later, colonel, adviser to the national commander.

Gannett, Henry 1846–1914, born: Bath; grandson of Barzillai Gannett, cousin of William Henry Gannett; S. B. Lawrence Scientific School, Harvard University 1869, M. E. Hooper Mining School, Harvard University 1870, L.L.D. (Hon.) Bowdoin College 1890; assistant: Harvard University Observatory, accompanied Professor Pickering to Spain to observe an eclipse of the sun 1870–71; topographer: Hayden survey 1872–79; chief geographer: U.S. Geological Survey from 1882; geographer: U.S. census 1890, 1900, 1910, assistant director of census of Puerto Rico 1902, Cuba 1907–08; pioneer in the use of lantern slides for educational purposes; co-organizer: U.S. Board of Geographic Names, chairman 1894–1914; geographer: Conservation Commission 1908–09; associate editor: *National Geographic Magazine*, chairman: U.S. Geographic Board; a founder and president: National Geographic Society 1910–14; a founder of Geological Society of America, Association of American Geographers; chairman: commission to judge the claims of Robert E. Peary; referred to as the father of American mapmaking; author: *Manual of Topographic Surveying, Statistical Atlases: 10th., 11th., 12th Censuses, Commercial Geography, Dictionary of Altitudes, Standard Compendium of Geography, Census of Puerto Rico, Census of Cuba, Census of the Philippines, The Contour Map of the U.S., Magnetic Declination in the U.S., Statistics of the Negro of the United States* 1894; Mount Gannett in the Wind River range, the highest point in Wyoming, was named in his honor 1906; among the first to scale Mount Whitney.

Gannett, William Howard 1854–1948, born: Augusta; son of a baker, grandson of Barzillai Gannett, cousin of Henry Gannett; student: Augusta public schools to the age of eight, conducted a blind cousin from house to house, where he tuned pianos, and to a store where he conducted a stationery and music business; clerked in stationery store until 1872; worked for a short time in Boston; clerk for Joseph Piper & Co., Augusta, operators of a small variety store; later worked in a similar store owned by Joseph Clapp 1876, later purchased this store in partnership with Wallace Morse under the name of Gannett & Morse; engaged in the lumber business in Skowhegan 1887, returned to Augusta 1888, began to promote through advertising in monthly magazines a medicinal lozenge called Oxien; Augusta had by this time become a center for the publication of rural periodicals; recognizing that the profit lay with the magazine publisher, established *Comfort* magazine 1888, which very quickly grew to a monthly run of one-half million copies; built a five-story plant and commissioned Hoe & Co. of New York to design a web-perfector press, the first perfector press in the United States 1892; monthly subscription rates grew to over one million by 1900, the first American magazine to do so, established a London office for the distribution of a European edition; assembled a newspaper combination, including the *Portland Press Herald*, originally to silence criticism, which he passed on to his son Guy 1922; member: Maine House of Representatives 1903–05; devoted himself to the restoration of Fort Western, which he presented to the city of Augusta; sponsored annual winter sports carnivals on his estate Ganeston Park; author: *My Voyage of Life* 1936; an enthusiastic flyer, in his later years, devoted much of his time to flights throughout the Americas, including a flight to Alaska and across the Andes; Maine governor: National Aeronautic Association.

Garcelon, Alonzo 1813–1906, born: Lewiston; son of a farmer and colonel in the

militia; attended Monmouth, Waterville, and Lincoln academies; A.B. Bowdoin College 1836; taught for three terms at Alfred Academy; student: Dartmouth College Medical School, studying under the famous Dr. Muzzey, who removed to the Medical College of Ohio (Cincinnati) 1838; accompanying Dr. Muzzey, he received his M.D. 1839; practiced in Lewiston for sixty-seven years, first physician in Maine to operate for mastoid disease and goiter; maintained a farm, built the first cotton mill in Lewiston, president of the Androscoggin Railroad; originally a Whig, but his admiration of Jackson's stand against nullification caused him to become a Democrat, later, because of his dislike of slavery, he became a Free Soiler, later became a Republican, rejoined Democrats in response to impeachment of Andrew Johnson; established the *Lewiston Journal* 1847, Lewiston's first newspaper; influential in the establishment of Androscoggin County and the choice of Auburn as county seat; member: Maine House of Representatives 1853, 1857, Maine Senate 1855; during the Civil War: served as Maine surgeon general, saw service at the first battle of Bull Run, the Peninsula campaign, and Antietam, invalided home for malaria, after his recovery, returned to the army and served until Appomattox; unsuccessful Democratic candidate for the U.S. House of Representatives 1868; mayor of Lewiston 1871, the first Democrat to hold that office; as Democratic candidate for governor 1878, ran third behind the incumbent governor Republican Seldon Connor and the Greenback-Labor candidate John Smith, no candidate having achieved a majority, the legislature chose Garcelon as thirtieth governor of Maine, served 1879–80, unsuccessful candidate for reelection 1879, when he came in third behind the Republican candidate, Daniel Davis, who had not received a majority of the popular votes cast, and the Greenback candidate; Garcelon refused to certify newly elected Republican legislators, hoping that, once again, a Democratically controlled legislature would return him to office; a period of great tumult resulted, eventually the Maine Supreme Judicial Court ruled against Garcelon and Davis was elected by the legislature; returned to the practice of medicine, trustee: American Medical Association 1882–1901, vice president 1901; at the age of ninety, presented with a loving cup and a gold-headed cane by the American Medical Association; brother-in-law to William Pierce Frye; died from accidental asphyxiation by illuminating gas, buried in Garcelon Cemetery, Lewiston.

Gardiner, Robert Hallowell I (born Hallowell) 1782–1864, born: Bristol, England; son of Loyalist refugees, grandson of Silvester Gardiner; returned with his family to Boston 1792, attended Boston Latin School and Phillips Academy, Andover, Derby Academy, A.B. Harvard College φBK 1801, A.M. 1804; inherited

204   Eminent Mainers

estate on Kennebec from maternal grandmother, added Gardiner to name, spent two years in England and France observing scientific farming methods; introduced superior breeds of animals, improved farm machinery and new varieties of fruit and grains; founded the Gardiner Lyceum 1821, the forerunner of American agricultural and technical schools, which gave instruction in mathematics, mechanics, navigation, and those branches of natural philosophy and chemistry that are calculated to make scientific farmers and mechanics, first institution of its kind to receive public monies from a state legislature; member: Maine House of Representatives 1822; Bowdoin College overseer 1811–41, vice president of the board 1819–29, president 1829–41, trustee 1841–60; president of the Maine Historical Society 1846–55.

Gardiner, Silvester 1717–86, born: South Kingston, Rhode Island; son of a cordwainer; studied medicine in Boston, England, France 1727–35; practiced in Boston; unhappy about the haphazard distribution of medicinal drugs, set up his own apothecary at the Sign of the Unicorn and Mortar, met with such great success that he set up others in Meriden and Hartford, Connecticut; achieved considerable fame with his successful removal of a large kidney stone 1741; proposed the establishment of a hospital for smallpox victims 1761; became the chief promoter and largest owner of the Kennebec Company 1753; as a proprietor, established the towns of Gardiner and Pittston, devoted much of his time and fortune in the development of the lower Kennebec; as a Tory, forced to flee to Halifax, Nova Scotia and eventually to London, during the Revolution; proscribed and banished, his property was seized and sold, later, because of provision (largely the work of Benjamin Vaughan) in the Treaty of Paris 1783, his heirs were able to recover much of it; returned to Newport, Rhode Island, 1785, only to die suddenly the next year; buried at Trinity Church, Newport; grandfather of Robert Hallowell Gardiner.

Gardiner, William Tudor 1892–1953, born: Newton, Massachusetts; son of Robert Hallowell Gardiner II; graduate: Groton Academy 1910; A.B. Harvard College 1914, played on the varsity football team, won the national intermediate sculling championship and double sculling championship with Sullivan Sargent 1913, student: Harvard University Law School 1914–17, L.L.D. (Hon.) Bates College 1929, University of Maine 1932, Bowdoin College 1945; during World War I: enlisted in the USA as a private, 1st Maine Heavy Artillery, reorganized as the 56th Pioneer Infantry, passed through the ranks to first lieutenant, participated in the Meuse-Argonne campaign, after the armistice, served in the army of occupation; member: Maine bar 1919, joined the firm of Andrews & Nelson, Augusta, partner 1921, at which time the firm became Andrews, Nelson & Gardiner; member: Maine House of Representatives 1921–25, speaker: 1925; governor of Maine 1929–33 (Republican); chairman of the board, director: Incorporated Investors, Boston 1933; chairman, vice chairman of the board: Pacific Coast Co., San Francisco 1932; chairman of the board: National Dock & Storage Warehouse Co., Boston 1945; director: United States Smelting, Refining

& Mining Co., Northwest Airlines, Inc., Rayonier, Inc.; vice president, assistant treasurer, director: Parker Corp.; trustee: National Dock Trust; corporator: Gardiner Savings Institution; trustee: Bates College; member, Aviation Committee: New England
Council; in World War II: commissioned major, USAAF, promoted through the ranks
to colonel, went overseas 1942, served as liaison between the service of supply and
the air force; intelligence officer: Provisional Troop Carrier Command, joined the
planning staff for the North African invasion and landed with the Air Service Command on 8 November 1942; chairman: Joint Rearmament Committee in rearming
the French 1942–43; intelligence officer: 51st Troop Carrier Wing, participated in the
airborne invasion of Sicily as observer and navigator on a C-47 airplane; as representative of Troop Carrier Command, accompanied General Maxwell Taylor on a clandestine mission to Rome, then well behind German lines, to confer with the Italian
high command about the possibility of an Italian armistice and a subsequent allied airborne occupation, given the pessimism of the Italian chief of staff, General Carboni,
it seemed wise to cancel the invasion, some elements being already in the air; chairman: Joint Air Commission, which equipped the French air force in North Africa,
Sardinia, and Corsica; served with G-5 Civil Affairs at Supreme Headquarters, Allied
Expeditionary Force in England; director of intelligence: 8th Air Force 1944–45;
awarded the Silver Star 1942, the Air Medal, Legion of Merit 1943, chevalier of the
French Legion of Honor, croix de guerre with palm, commander of the Order of Ouis-
sam Alaouite Cherifien of Morocco 1944; member: Cruising Club of America; killed
in an airplane crash in Schnecksville, Pennsylvania; buried in Christ Church Cemetery, Gardiner.

Garland, Mary J. 1834–1901, born: Machias; taught school in Maine for a year,
removed to Montréal where she taught for nine years in a boarding school for girls;
student at Vassar College 1870, student with Mme. Mathilde Kriege in kindergarten
training, Boston 1871; opened a private kindergarten in Boston, first in United States;
what became Garland Junior College was melded into Simmons College 1976.

Garland, William May 1866–1948, born: Westport; son of a Methodist clergyman, cousin of James Jewett; attended public schools in Waterville, L.L.D. (Hon.)
University of Heidelberg 1936; clerk in the dry goods firm of R. H. White & Co.,
Boston 1882; removed to Daytona Beach, Florida where he drove a stagecoach in
Volusia County 1884–86; associated with the Illinois Trust and Savings Bank to 1890;
after contracting tuberculosis, removed to Los Angeles; auditor: Pacific Cable Co.
1890–94; president: W. M. Garland & Co. 1894–1948, dealers in real estate; founder,
vice president: Western Air Express 1926–30; president: California Real Estate Association, president: National Association of Realtors 1917–18, president: California
State Chamber of Commerce 1929–30; as chairman of the Merriam for Governor
Committee, associated with Charles C. Teague in the campaign to defeat Upton Sinclair's bid for the governorship of California 1936; president: Los Angeles Realty

Board, board of Los Angeles Public Library, president: California Safety Council 1935–37; established the William May Garland Trophy 1938, to be awarded every year to the California city with the best safety record; a leader in the development of the Port of Los Angeles; president: International Aviation Meet 1913, held at Dominguez field, near Los Angeles; served on the staff of Governor James Gillette 1906-10; delegate: Republican National Convention 1900, 1924, 1928, 1936, 1940; member: International Olympic Committee 1922; member: U.S. Olympic Committee, secured Olympics for Los Angeles 1932, president: Organizing Committee for 1932 Olympics; grand marshal: Tournament of Roses, Pasadena, California, 1932; president: Community Development Association 1922–32; played a prominent part in the construction of the Los Angeles coliseum, scene of the Tenth Olympics Games, and the swimming stadium adjoining the coliseum, in Exposition Park; decorated: Knight of the Belgian Order of Leopold, Order of the White Lion (Czechoslovakia), Légion d'Honneur (France), Red Cross of Honor (Germany), Commander of the Order of Orange-Nassau (Netherlands), Commanders Cross of the Order of Polonia Restituta (Poland); given to population prognostician, was among the first to predict that Los Angeles would become the third largest city in the country; for years, he had billboards erected in the Los Angeles region on which were posted his predictions on a variety of matters; to advertise his Hollywoodland subdivision, had erected the now-famous Hollywood sign.

Garman, Charles Edward 1850–1907, born: Limington; graduate: Lebanon Academy, A.B. Amherst College ΦΒΚ 1872, A.M. 1880, D.D. 1896; principal: Ware (Massachusetts) High School 1872, in World War II: commissioned major, USAAF, promoted through the ranks to colonel; went overseas 1872–75; B.D. Yale University Divinity School 1879, recipient: Hooker fellowship; Walker instructor in mathematics: Amherst College 1880, associate professor 1882, professor of mental and moral philosophy from 1892; the number of his students who later occupied chairs of philosophy and psychology was large and distinguished; upon his retirement, in 1906, a number of his former students compiled a volume, *Studies in Philosophy and Psychology*, dedicated to him and containing the essences of his influence over many diverse minds; for many years a trustee of Mount Holyoke College; after his death, a posthumous volume, *Letters, Lectures and Addresses of Charles Edward Garman* was published 1909.

Gatley, George Grant 1868–1931, born: Portland, son of immigrants from Wales; graduate: U.S. Military Academy 1890, promoted through the ranks to brigadier general 1917; organized 17th Battery, service in Philippine Islands 1903–05, participated in various operations against the Moros, in Cuba: Second Intervention 1906–09, organized and instructed Cuban field artillery 1909–13, on Mexican border 1913–15, commanding officer: 55th field artillery brigade, commanding officer: 42nd Division (Rainbow Division, so named by Douglas MacArthur, because it was formed of National Guard units from across the nation), the first American division to arrive in Europe: Champagne Marne, Aisne Marne, San Mihiel, Meuse Argonne, occupation of Germany.

George, Gladys (pseudonym of Gladys Anna Clare) 1900–54, born: Patten; child actress in vaudeville, stock, Broadway, silent films, leading lady during 1930s and 1940s; her films include: *Red Hot Dollars* 1919, *The Women in the Suitcase, Homespun Folks, Below the Surface* 1920, *The Easy Road, The House Jazz Built, Chickens* 1921, *Straight Is the Way* 1934, *Valiant Is the Word for Carrie* (for which she was accorded an Oscar nomination) 1936, *They Gave Him a Gun, Madame X* 1937, *Love Is a Headache, Marie Antoinette* 1938, *Here I Am a Stranger, Roaring Twenties, I'm from Missouri* 1939, *A Child Is Born, The House Across the Bay, The Way of All Flesh* 1940, *The Lady From Cheyenne, Hit the Road, The Maltese Falcon* 1941, *The Hard Way* 1942, *The Crystal Ball, Nobody's Darling* 1943, *Minstrel Man, Christmas Holiday* 1944, *Steppin' in Society* 1945, *The Best Years of Our Lives* 1946, *Millie's Daughter* 1947, *Alias a Gentleman* 1948, *Flamingo Road* 1949, *Undercover Girl, Bright Leaf* 1950, *He Ran All the Way, Silver City, Lullaby of Broadway, Detective Story* 1951, *It Happens Every Thursday* 1953; buried in Valhalla Memorial Park, North Hollywood, California.

Gestefeld, Ursula Newell 1845–1921, born: Augusta; founder of a system of thought, known as Science of Being; instructor for Exodus Club, Chicago 1897; became Church of the New Thought and College of Science of Being, first pastor of this church and head of college; author: *The Metaphysics of Balzac* 1898, *The Builder and the Plan* 1898, *Reincarnation or Immortality* 1899, *The Science of the Larger Life* 1905, *The Master of the Man* 1907; buried in Graceland Cemetery, Chicago.

Gibson, Paris 1830–1920, born: Brownfield; son of a farmer and logger, brother of Augustus Abel Gibson; attended public school in Brownfield; graduate: Fryeburg Academy, A.B. Bowdoin College 1851; member: Maine House of Representatives 1851; farmed in Brownfield, removed to Minneapolis 1858, built the Cataract flour mill, the first flour mill at the falls of Saint Anthony; operated the North Star woolen mill; financially ruined in the Panic of 1873; removed to Fort Benton, Montana, 1879, first to raise merino sheep, on a large scale, in northern Montana; led by the journal of the Lewis and Clark Expedition to the great falls of the Missouri, where he founded the city of the same name, now the largest city in Montana 1884; with the cooperation of James J. Hill, built the St. Paul, Minneapolis & Manitoba Railroad; organized the Great Falls Water Power Co., Town Site Co.; bestowed upon Great Falls its public park system, the first in the Northwest; developed the gold, silver, coal, and iron deposits in the vicinity; delegate: Montana Constitutional Convention 1889; member: Montana Senate 1889, advocated the establishment of the University of Montana; member: U.S. Senate 1901–04 (Democrat); strong supporter of Theodore Roosevelt and the Progressive movement; buried in Highland Cemetery, Great Falls.

Gignoux, Edward Thaxter 1916–88, born: Portland; A.B. *cum laude* Harvard College 1937, L.L.B. *magna cum laude* Harvard University Law School 1940, L.L.D. (Hon.) Bowdoin College 1962, University of Maine 1966, Colby College 1974, Nasson College 1974, Bates College 1977, Husson College 1983, St. Joseph's College 1984; member: District of Columbia bar 1941, Maine bar 1946; associate: Slee, O'Brien, Hellings & Ulsh, Buffalo 1940–41, Covington, Burling, Rublee, Acheson & Shorb, Washington 1941–42, partner: Verrill, Dana, Walker, Philbrick & White-house, Portland 1946–57; U.S. district judge, Portland from 1957, judge: United States Temporary Emergency Court of Appeals 1980–87; member of council and chairman, visiting committee: Harvard University Law School; member, advisory panel: U.S. Department of State; assistant Portland city counsel 1947–48; member: Portland City Council 1949–55, chairman 1952; member: U.S. Judiciary Conference, chairman, Subcommittee on Supporting Personnel 1968–70, chairman, Standing Committee on Rules of Practice and Procedure 1980–87; editor: *Harvard Law Review* 1939–40; trustee: Maine Medical Center, Maine Eye and Ear Infirmary, Portland Symphony Orchestra; member, board of overseers: Harvard University; in World War II: major, USA, 1942–46, decorated: Bronze Star, Legion of Merit; recipient: Learned Hand Medal 1984, Edward J. Devitt Distinguished Service to Justice Award 1986; the federal court house in Portland is named in his honor.

Gilbreth, Frank Bunker 1868–1925, born: Fairfield at Fairground Farm; graduate: English High School, Boston 1885, L.L.D. (Hon.) University of Maine 1920; passed entrance examinations for entrance into Massachusetts Institute of Technology but decided to continue his technical education in night school and entered the employ of a firm of Boston construction engineers; starting as a bricklayer's apprentice, he advanced steadily in the firm's service until he became general superintendent; mastering many trades in the course of this progress, began business for himself as a general contractor in Boston 1895, erecting mills, factories, power plants, dams, canals, and industrial establishments of all kinds in many sections of the country and in Europe, establishing branch offices in New York, San Francisco, and London; invented an improved scaffold for bricklayers, the yankee hod carrier, a method of waterproofing cellars, concrete mixers, conveyors, an accurate measurer and feeder and other labor-saving devices, he also formulated the cost-plus-fixed sum contract, the first of its kind, and began his pioneering work to promote efficiency and eliminate fatigue and waste, he developed his system of progress reports and photographing progress pictures to keep accurately informed of the status of each project, the results of this pioneer application of management principles and practice in the field of construction led to improvements in selection and training of workers as well as to betterment and invention of machines and devices, this led to field and laboratory studies, in collaboration with his wife, Lillian, to determine the best equipment and surroundings for efficient performance of work; devised the micromotion and the eyelegraph processes of determining fundamental units of work and methods of industrial education, he also installed a number of motion-study laboratories and formulated a plan for standardizing progress of personnel; the results of these studies were published as *Field System, Concrete System* 1908, *Bricklaying System* 1909, *Motion Study, Primer of Scientific Management* 1911, *Time Study, Fatigue Study* 1916, *Applied Motion Study* 1917, *Motion Study for the Handicapped* 1919, wrote many articles on education, management, personnel problems, and the re-education of crippled soldiers, delivered numerous addresses and read papers before scientific and engineering societies; founder: the Society for the Promotion of the Science of Management, later renamed the Taylor Society 1912; established a fatigue museum in Providence, Rhode Island, 1913; leading engineering societies and technical colleges all over the world adopted motion studies and other of his principles of management; his life was immortalized in the book *Cheaper by the Dozen*, written by two of his daughters; his wife, Lillian, was the inventor of the modern sanitary napkin, among other things.

Gill, Laura Drake 1860–1926, born: Chesterville; sister of Adam Gill; prepared at Classical School for Girls, Northampton, Massachusetts, where her aunt was head; A.B. Smith College 1881, A.M. 1885, D.C.L. (Hon.) University of the South 1907; studied mathematics at the universities of Leipzig 1890–92, Geneva 1892, Sorbonne 1892–93; had charge of the first party of Red Cross nurses dispatched to Cuba, subsequently detailed to select and place nurses at the Leiter General Hospital, Chickamauga, Tennessee, and Montauk Point, New York; reorganized Cuban school system after the Spanish-American War with support of General Leonard Wood; dean: Barnard College 1901–08, while at Barnard, established a bachelor's degree in science, secured three city blocks, planned the first dormitory, Brooks Hall, begun in 1907; organized and directed the first vocational bureau for college women for the Women's Educational and Industrial Union of Boston 1909–11; engaged in additional organization work at the University of the South and at Trinity College 1914–15; during World War I: special agent in field organization for the employment service of the U.S. Department of Labor; after the war, spent three years as an educational worker in the Pine Mountain settlement in Kentucky; joined the staff of Berea College.

Gillars, Mildred Elizabeth Sisk, yclept Axis Sally 1900–88, born: Portland; graduate: Conneaut (Ohio) High School, attended Ohio Wesleyan University, hoping to become an actress, she majored in dramatic arts; after dropping out of Ohio Wesleyan University, she was variously employed as a sales clerk, waitress, cashier, &c.; she later lived in Greenwich Village, where she worked in stock companies, musical comedies, and vaudeville, in Paris, she worked as a sales clerk and governess, spent a period in North Africa; in 1935, she removed to Berlin, where she was an English instructor at the Berlitz School of Languages; became involved with Dr. Max Otto Koischwitz, Nazi propagandist and former professor at Hunter College, and, after his return to Germany, an official of Radio Berlin; she was hired to broadcast music and act in radio plays that were little but thinly disguised Nazi propaganda; called herself Midge at the mike, but was commonly known as Axis Sally; her broadcasts were heard all over Europe, North Africa, and in the United States, she showed an uncanny, intimate knowledge of individual soldiers and their movements; she often acquired such knowledge impersonating Red Cross workers at prisoner-of-war camps; after the war, she blended in to the horde of displaced persons in Germany, eventually, she was arrested 1946, returned to the United States and indicted on eight counts of treason; in a trial that lasted for six weeks, she was found not guilty on seven counts but convicted for the part she played in the broadcast of *Vision of Invasion*, a harrowing radio play that described the bloody defeat awaiting the allies on D-day 1949; spent twelve years in Alderson Federal Prison for Women, paroled 1961; taught music at a Catholic convent near Columbus, Ohio, and finally finished her degree at Ohio Wesleyan 1973.

Gilman, Jeremiah Howard 1831–1909, born: Thomaston; student: Bowdoin College, graduate: U.S. Military Academy 1856, commissioned second lieutenant, USA, assigned to the 1st U.S. artillery; served at Fort Brown, Texas, 1856–57, Fort Adams, Rhode Island, 1857–58, and Fort Barrancas, Pensacola, Florida, 1858–61; before the outbreak of Civil War, while in command of a company at Fort Barrancas, when confronted by state militia, who had come to demand the surrender of the fort, fired on them, driving them, precipitately, away, this is considered by many to be the first shot of the Civil War, two days later, Gilman spiked the guns of Fort Barrancas and removed as much ammunition and supplies as he could and withdrew to Fort Pickens, where he held out stubbornly until reinforced by the U.S. Navy; Fort Pickens was the only federal fort in the Southern states (aside from Fortress Monroe) to remain in federal hands; received a bronze medal from the New York Chamber of Commerce; promoted to first lieutenant, USA, and captain, USA, two months later; made chief of artillery of General McCook's division in Kentucky, later, made inspector and acting chief of artillery of the Army of the Ohio, serving in Tennessee, Alabama, and Mississippi; after Shiloh, brevetted major, USA, for gallant and meritorious services at the battle of Shiloh, Tennessee, 1862, advance on and siege of Corinth, operations in North Alabama, chief of artillery and ordnance officer: battle of Perryville, named inspector of artillery in the Army of the Cumberland, in Rosecrans, Tennessee, campaign, brevetted lieutenant, USA, for gallant and meritorious services at the battle of Stones River, Tennessee, 1862, served as inspector: subsistence department of the Army of the Cumberland 1863, chief of commissariat of the Department of the Susquehanna 1863–64, purchasing commissary of subsistence at Baltimore 1864–65; after the war, acted as chief of commissary in various departments, eventually becoming assistant commissary general, retired 1895, promoted colonel, USA, on the retired list 1904; known to history as the hero of Fort Pickens, his high sense of integrity earned him the sobriquet of "Honest Gilman"; had a talent for painting, did creditable work in oils and watercolors; contributor: "With Slemmer in Pensacola Harbor," *Battles and Leaders of the Civil War* 1885.

Gilman, Luthene Claremont 1857–1942, born: Levant; graduate: Maine Central Institute, Pittsfield, L.L.B. Columbia University Law School 1883; member: Washington bar, practiced in Seattle, member: Lewis and Gilman 1884–92, Stratton, Lewis, and Gilman 1892–97, Preston, Carr, and Gilman 1897–1903; Seattle city attorney 1887–88; delegate: Washington constitution convention 1889; member: Washington House of Representatives 1893 (Democrat); general counsel for the Great Northern Railroad from 1903; removed to St. Paul, Minnesota, 1909, assistant to James J. Hill, president, Great Northern Railroad 1909–14; after the retirement of Hill, removed to Portland, Oregon, 1914; president: Spokane, Portland & Seattle Railroad and affiliated lines 1914–18, vice president: Great Northern Railroad 1920–37.

Gilmore, Albert Field 1871–1943, born: Turner; son of a farmer; A.B. Bates College ΦBK 1892, A.M. 1895, Litt.D. (Hon.) 1924, C.S.B. 1922; principal: Kennebunk High School, superintendent of schools: Turner, principal: Litchfield Academy; with American Book Co. 1897–1917; first reader: First Church of Christ, Scientist, Brooklyn, New York 1914–17; chairman: Christian Science Committee on Publications, New York, 1917–22; president: the Mother Church, Boston, 1922–23; editor: *Christian Science Weekly* and monthly magazine 1922–29; trustee: Christian Science Publication Society from 1932; member: Maine House of Representatives 1941–42; author: *Birds Through the Year* 1909, *Birds of Field, Forest and Park* 1918, *East and West of Jordan* 1929, *Fellowship—The Story of a Man and a Business* 1929, *Yes, 'Tis Round: The Log of a Far Journey* 1933, *The Bible: Beacon Light of History* 1935, *Links in Christianity's Chain* 1938, *Who Was this Nazarene?: A Challenging and Definitive Biography of the Master* 1941, *The Christ at the Peace Table* 1943 .

Ginn, Edward 1838–1914, born: Orland; took charge of his father's farm at age nine, worked as a cook in a logging camp, shipped out on a fishing schooner to the Grand Banks, taught school in the winters; A.B. Tufts University 1862, A.M. 1865; associated with the publishing firms of D. Appleton & Co. and Crosby, Ainsworth & Co., Boston; undertook, on his own, the publication of Craik's *English of Shakespeare*, this was followed by his publication of other school texts; founder, with Daniel Collamore Heath: Ginn & Heath Co., later D. C. Heath & Co., in its day, the largest publisher of school texts in the world; founder: World Peace Foundation.

Goddard, Anson Morrill 1859–1932, born: Auburn; son of Charles William Goddard I, brother of Charles William Goddard II, grandson of Anson Peaselee Morrill; A.B. Bowdoin College 1882, student: Harvard University Law School; member: Maine bar 1885, practiced in Augusta; Augusta city solicitor 1887–92; retained by a New York firm to prepare the evidence for the case of *Charles W. Hotchkiss v. Bon Air Coal & Iron Company* and conducted the case, won the largest damage award to date by a Maine jury 1908; induced by William Howard Gannett to withdraw from the practice of law and become editor and manager of *Comfort* magazine, a monthly with a circulation of one million 1909; spent twenty-two years selecting all material published and writing an editorial for each issue, gaining for himself a national reputation for trenchant wit and depth of scholarly thinking on issues of national importance.

Goddard, Charles William I 1825–1889, born: Portland; A.B. Bowdoin College 1844, student at Harvard University Law School 1844–46; member: Maine bar 1846, removed to Lewiston; Androscoggin County attorney 1854–57, 1857–61; member: Maine Senate 1857–61, president 1858, chairman: Judiciary Committee; appointed by President Lincoln: consul general, Constantinople, 1861–64, while consul, formulated a code for the regulation of the U.S. consular courts operating in Islamic countries; appointed by Governor Chamberlain: chairman, Maine commission for the equalization of municipal war debt; first justice of the Superior Court of Cumberland County; postmaster of Portland 1871–84; sole commissioner to revise Maine law 1881–83; professor of medical jurisprudence: Medical School of Maine 1872–89; son-in-law of Anson Peaslee Morrill, father of Anson Morrill Goddard and Charles William Goddard II.

Goddard, Charles William II 1879–1951, born: Portland; graduate: St. Paul's School, Garden City, New York, A.B. Dartmouth College 1902; reporter: *Boston Post* 1903; member, editorial staff: *New York Sunday American* 1904–18; devoted himself to writing motion picture scenari 1918–23; feature writer: *American Weekly*, where his brother Morrill was editor; playwright: *The Ghost Breaker, The Misleading Library*, &c.; author of numerous photoplays, including: *The Perils of Pauline, The Exploits of Myra, The Seven Pearls*, &c.

Goddard, Henry Herbert 1866–1957, born: Vassalboro; a descendant of Edward Winslow, cousin of Pliny Earle Goddard; his father was a farmer, who died subsequent to an accident, his mother was a Quaker preacher who left Herbert in the care of neighbors so that she might visit every Quaker meeting in the United States; attended Oak Grove Seminary (where his roommate was Rufus Jones; they would room together through Moses Brown and Haverford), graduate: Moses Brown School, Providence, Rhode Island, A.B. Haverford College ΦBK 1889, Ph.D. Clark University 1899, the topic of his dissertation was the mind cure of Phineas Quimby; football coach and instructor in Latin, mathematics, and botany: University of Southern California 1887–88, teacher and principal: Oak Grove Seminary 1891–96; professor of psychology and pedagogy: Pennsylvania State Normal School, West Chester, Pennsylvania, 1899–1906; psychologist and director of research: Training School for Feeble-Minded Boys and Girls, Vineland, New Jersey, 1906–18; professor of abnormal and clinical psychology: Ohio State University 1922–38; author: *The Kallikak Family* 1912, *Feeble Mindedness: Its Causes and Consequences* 1914, *School Training of Defective Children* 1914, *The Criminal Imbecile* 1915, *Juvenile Delinquency* 1921, *Two Souls, One Body*

1927, *The Training of the Gifted Child* 1927, several other works; coined the word "moron" and the phrases "juvenile delinquent" and "gifted child"; created the first test for intelligence in the United States at the behest of United States armed forces during World War I; president: American Association for the Study of the Feeble-minded 1914–15.

Goddard, Morrill 1866–1937, born: Portland; son of Charles William Goddard I, brother of Charles William Goddard II; A.B. Dartmouth College 1885; editor, foreign and war correspondent from 1885; editor: *American Weekly Magazine*, city editor: *New York World* 1888, as editor of the *Sunday World* 1898–1923, dealt effectively with strong religious opposition to the issuance of Sunday papers, issued the first colored comic section; editor: *Morning Journal* (later *American*), editor: *American Magazine* 1898, which had a circulation of over six million, the largest in the world; as supervisor of the first Hearst motion pictures, supervised the making of the first newsreel 1913; member: The Society for Psychical Research, the Corinthian Yacht Club; author: *What Interests People and Why* 1935; died in Brooklin, Maine.

Goddard, Pliny Earle 1869–1928, born: Lewiston; son of a Quaker minister, cousin of Henry Herbert Goddard; graduate: Oak Grove Seminary, A.B. Earlham College 1892, A.M. 1896; lay missionary to Hupa Indians of California; Ph.D. University of California 1906; assistant professor 1906–09, assistant curator of anthropology: American Museum of Natural History, New York, curator from 1914; lecturer on anthropology: Columbia University 1916–17; author: *Life and Culture of the Hupa* 1903, *The Morphology of the Hupa Language* 1904, *Hupa Texts* 1904, *The Phonology of the Hupa Language* 1907, *Kato Texts* 1909, *Chipewyan Texts* 1912, *Analysis of a Lake Dialect, Chipewyan* 1912, *Indians of the Southwest* 1913, *Indians of the Northwest Coast* 1913, *Dancing Societies of the Sarsi Indians* 1914, *Chilula Texts* 1914, *Sarsi Texts* 1915, *The Beaver Indians* 1916; editor: *The American Anthropologist* 1915–20; founder and co-editor with Franz Boas: *International Journal of American Linguistics*; president: American Folk-Lore Society 1914–16.

Godfrey, Ard 1813– ?, born: Orono; removed to Saint Anthony's Falls (later Minneapolis), Minnesota Territory 1847, and constructed the first dam and mill at that site, he later served as the first postmaster of Minneapolis; his home is the oldest frame structure extant in Minneapolis and is on the National Register; later removed to Minnehaha Falls, on the Elk River, where he constructed another dam and mill, founded the village of Orono.

Golden, Richard 1854–1909, born: Bangor; began career as actor in comedy *Fashion* 1867; coauthor, producer, and star in *Old Jed Prouty* 1889, gave thousands of performances, with which he became closely identified.

Goodale, George Lincoln 1839–1923, born: Saco; son of Stephen Lincoln Goodale; apprenticed to an apothecary, A.B. Amherst College φBK 1860, A.M., L.L.D. (Hon.); assistant in chemistry and botany 1860–61, student: Medical School of Maine, M.D. Harvard University Medical School 1863, M.D. Medical School of Maine 1863; practiced in Portland 1863–65; Portland city physician; lecturer on anatomy, surgery, and *materia medica*: Medical School of Maine; failing health required him to take leave; journeyed to California via Panama; inspecting, on commission, certain mining properties and ascending Mount Shasta; professor of applied chemistry: Bowdoin College, and professor of *materia medica*, Medical School of Maine 1868–72; founded, with C. F. Brackett: *Bowdoin Scientific Review*; his first botanical paper attracted the attention of Asa Gray, who invited him to become instructor in botany: Harvard University 1872, assistant professor 1873, professor 1878, after Gray's death, succeeded him as Fisher professor of natural history; curator: Botanical Museum and Botanical Garden, Harvard University, 1879; initiated the famous glass flower collection 1886, journeyed to Dresden, Germany, to induce Leopold and Rudolf Blaschka, renowned makers of glass marine models, to work exclusively for Harvard; author of the first physiologic botany in United States; associate editor: *American Journal of Science*; president: American Association for the Advancement of Science 1890; retired from Harvard in 1909.

Goodale, Stephen Lincoln 1815–97, born: South Berwick; clerked in his father's apothecary, removed to Saco 1838, began cultivating and studying trees and shrubs; secretary: Maine Board of Agriculture 1856–73, collected and disseminated data on methods of cultivation, treatment, and propagation; published an annual compendium; founder and trustee: Maine State College of Agriculture and Mechanical Arts (predecessor of University of Maine); associated with Gail Borden in establishing a condensed milk factory in Farmington Falls 1863; inaugurated the manufacture of beef extract with the Liebig process; president: Saco and Biddeford Savings Institution; president and chemist: Cumberland Bone Co.; author: *The Principles of Breeding or Glimpses at Physiological Laws Involved in the Reproduction and Improvement of Domestic Animals* 1861; father of George Lincoln Goodale, grandfather of Joseph Lincoln Goodale.

Goodall, Louis Bertrand 1851–1935, born: Winchester, New Hampshire; woolen manufacturer; settled in Sanford, founder: Mousam River Mills; founder, president, and chairman of the board: Goodall Worsted Co., which had a near-monopoly on the production of automobile upholstery; member from the First District: U.S. House of Representatives 1917–21 (Republican); philanthropist; buried in Oakdale Cemetery, Sanford.

Goodblood, Clair 1929–1951, born: Fort Kent; corporal, USA, Company D, 7th Infantry Division, recipient: Medal of Honor (posthumous), near Popsu-don, Korea,

24 and 25 April 1951, "CPL Goodblood. a member of Company D, distinguished himself by conspicuous gallantry and intrepidity, at the risk of his life above and beyond the call of duty in action against an armed enemy of the United Nations. CPL Goodblood, a machine gunner, was attached to Company B in defensive positions on thickly wooded key terrain under the attack of a ruthless foe; in bitter fighting which ensued, the numerically superior enemy infiltrated the perimeter, rendering the friendly position untenable; upon order to move back, CPL Goodblood voluntarily remained to cover the withdrawal and, constantly vulnerable to heavy fire, inflicting withering destruction on the assaulting force; seeing a grenade lobbed at his position, he shoved his assistant to the ground and flinging himself upon the soldier attempted to shield him; despite his valorous act both men were wounded; rejecting aid for himself, he ordered the ammunition bearer to evacuate the injured man for medical treatment. He fearlessly maintained his one-man defense, sweeping the onrushing assailants with fire until an enemy banzai charge carried the hill and silenced his gun. When friendly elements regained the commanding ground, CPL Goodblood's body was found lying beside his gun and approximately one hundred hostile dead lay in the wake of his field of fire. Through his unflinching courage and willing self-sacrifice the onslaught was retarded, enabling his unit to withdraw, regroup, and resecure the strongpoint. CPL Goodblood's inspirational conduct and devotion to duty reflect lasting glory on himself and are in keeping with the noble traditions of the military service." Buried in Chandler Cemetery, Burnham.

Goodenow, John Holmes 1832–1906, born: Alfred; son of Daniel Goodenow, grandson of John Holmes, cousin of Noah Brooks; A.B. Bowdoin College 1852, overseer 1879-1906; practiced law in Alfred with Nathan Dane Appleton; member: Maine House of Representatives 1858, Maine Senate, president 1861–62; appointed by President Lincoln: consul general in Constantinople (subsequent to Charles William Goddard) 1864–73, at the ceremony in the White House coincident to his appointment, Lincoln quoted from memory a lengthy speech made by John Holmes in the U.S. Senate; secretary of legation 1873–75.

Goodrich, Leland Matthew 1899–1990, born: Lewiston; A.B. Bowdoin College ϕBK 1920, Sc.D. (Hon.) 1952, A.M. Harvard University 1921, Ph.D. 1925; instructor in political science: Brown University 1922–23, assistant professor 1926–31, associate professor 1931–46, professor 1945–46; professor of international organization and administration: Columbia University 1950–67, acting department chairman: public law and government 1965–66, James T. Shotwell professor of international relations 1967–68; visiting lecturer in government: Harvard University 1949–50; professor of international organization and administration: Fletcher School of Law and Diplomacy from 1944; director: World Peace Foundation 1942–46; member: secretary general's commission to review organization and activities, United Nations Secretariat 1961; author: *Korea—A Study of United States Policy in the United Nations*

1956, *The United Nations* 1959, *The United Nations in a Changing World* 1974, coauthor: *Charter of the United Nations: Commentary and Documents* 1949, revised 1969, *The United Nations and the Maintenance of International Peace and Security* 1955, coeditor: *Documents on American Foreign Relations, Vol. IV* 1942; member: International Secretariat, United Nations Conference on International Organization 1945; chairman of board of editors: *International Organization* 1947–54; trustee: World Peace Foundation; trustee, overseer: Bowdoin College; member: Foreign Policy Association, Council on Foreign Relations; director: Academy of Political Science from 1973.

Goodwin, Daniel Raynes 1811–90, born: North Berwick, A.B. *summa cum laude* Bowdoin College 1832, D.D. 1855, L.L.D. (Hon.) Episcopal Divinity School, Philadelphia 1868; master: Hallowell Academy, graduate: Andover Theological Seminary; succeeded H. W. Longfellow as professor of modern languages, Bowdoin College 1835–53, librarian 1838–53; deacon: Episcopal church 1847, ordained priest 1848; president: Trinity College (Hartford) 1853–60; elected ninth provost: University of Pennsylvania 1860–68; dean: Episcopal Divinity School, Philadelphia 1868–83, professor of systematic divinity 1876–90; member: American Philosophical Society, American Academy of Arts and Sciences, American Oriental Society; founding president: Society of Biblical Literature and Exegesis; author of some ninety-six pamphlets, tracts, reviews, speeches, and treatises on ethics, theology, ecclesiastical controversy, and philology, including *Southern Slavery in its Present Aspects* 1864, *The New Realistic Divinity neither the Religion of the Bible and Prayer-Book nor of the Holy Catholic Church* 1879, *Memorial Discourse on Henry W. Longfellow* 1882, *Notes on the Revision of the New Testament Revision* 1883, *Christian Eschatology* 1885; most influential leader of evangelical branch of the Episcopal church in America; son-in-law of Samuel Vaughan Merrick.

Goodwin, Ichabod 1794–1882, born North Berwick; graduate: Berwick Academy; entered the counting house of Samuel Lord, in Portsmouth, New Hampshire; began, at age twenty, as a supercargo, made numerous voyages, became a ship's master and owner; member: New Hampshire House of Representatives 1838, 1843, 1844, 1850, 1854, 1856; delegate: New Hampshire Constitutional Convention 1850; delegate: Whig National Convention 1832, 1848, 1852, vice president 1832, 1848; nominated several times for governor and member of the U.S. House of Representatives by the Whig party; an early and enthusiastic organizer of the Republican party in New Hampshire; elected twenty-ninth governor of New Hampshire 1859, 1860–61; with the outbreak of the Civil War, rather than delay by calling a special session of the New Hampshire legislature, appealed directly to the public for funds to put volunteer regiments in the field, which enabled him to raise and equip ten regiments, and which the New Hampshire legislature later legalized by enacting retroactive enabling legislation; president, director: Eastern Railroad Co., later part of Boston & Maine Railroad Co.; director: Portland, Saco & Portsmouth Railroad Co., president

1847–71; president, director: Piscataqua Exchange Bank (later First National Bank); director: Portsmouth Savings Bank; his home in Portsmouth is extant, is on the National Register of Historic Places, and is in the Strawberry Banke restoration area; father-in-law of Admiral George Dewey, USN.

Goodwin, John Noble 1824–87, born: South Berwick; A.B. Dartmouth College 1844; studied law with John Hubbard; member: Maine bar 1848, practiced in South Berwick; member Maine Senate 1854, member: Committee to Revise Code of Statutes; member from the 1st District: U.S. House of Representatives 1861–63 (Republican), member: committees on the interior and on pensions; appointed, by President Lincoln, first chief justice and first governor of the Arizona Territory 1863–65, organized territory and established Prescott, named for W. H. Prescott, Goodwin's favorite author, as capital; Arizona territorial delegate: U.S. House of Representatives 1865–67; subsequently practiced law in New York; buried in Forest Grove Cemetery, Augusta.

Gordon, Gary Ivan 1960–93, born: Lincoln; master sergeant, USA, recipient: Medal of Honor (posthumous), "Master Sergeant Gordon distinguished himself by actions above and beyond the call of duty on 3 October 1993, while serving as sniper team leader, U.S. Army Special Operations Command with Task Force Ranger in Mogadishu, Somalia. Master Sergeant Gordon's sniper team provided precision fire from the lead helicopter during an assault and at two helicopter crash sites when subjected to intense automatic weapons and rocket propelled grenade fire. When Master Sergeant Gordon learned that ground forces were not immediately available to secure the second crash site, he and another sniper unhesitatingly volunteered to be inserted to protect four critically wounded personnel, despite being well aware of the growing number of enemy personnel closing on the site. After his third request to be inserted, Master Sergeant Gordon received permission to perform his volunteer mission. When debris and enemy ground fire at his site caused them to abort the first attempt, Master Sergeant Gordon was inserted one hundred meters south of the crash site. Equipped with only his sniper rifle and a pistol, Master Sergeant Gordon and his fellow sniper, while under intense small arms fire from the enemy, fought their way through a dense maze of shanties and shacks to reach the critically injured crew members. Master Sergeant Gordon immediately pulled the pilot and the other crew members from the aircraft, establishing a perimeter which placed him and his fellow sniper in the most vulnerable position. Master Sergeant Gordon used his long-range rifle and sidearm to kill an undetermined number of attackers until he depleted his ammunition. Despite the fact that he was critically low on ammunition, he provided some of it to the dazed pilot and then radioed for help. Master Sergeant Gordon continued to travel the perimeter, protecting the downed crew. After his team member was fatally wounded and his own ammunition exhausted, Master Sergeant Gordon returned to the wreckage, recovering a rifle with the last five rounds of ammunition and gave it to the pilot with the words, 'Good luck.' Then armed only with his pistol, Master Sergeant Gordon continued to fight until he was fatally wounded. His actions saved the pilot's life. Master Sergeant Gordon's extraordinary heroism and devotion to duty were in keeping with the highest standards of military service and reflect great credit upon his unit and the United States Army." Buried in Lincoln Cemetery, Lincoln.

Gordon, Nathaniel 1826–62 born: Portland; member of a well-established seafaring family; Gordon, master of the ship *Erie*, was apprehended off the Congo with a load of some 800 slaves, bound for Cuba; brought to New York, tried, and convicted of the capital crime of piracy; despite the reception of a monster petition bearing some 5,000 signatures delivered by former Senator Evans, requesting clemency, Lincoln refused to commute the sentence and Gordon was hanged, the only man ever executed by the United States for slaving.

Gordon, Robert Winslow 1888–1961, born: Bangor; graduate: Phillips Academy, Exeter 1906, A.B. Harvard College 1910; assistant in English: Harvard University 1912–18, assistant professor of English: University of California (Berkeley) 1918–25; Seldon fellow: Harvard College 1925–26; special consultant in music: Library of Congress, Washington from 1927; in charge of Archive of American Folk-Song, Library of Congress from 1929; member: American Folk-Lore Society, Kentucky Folk-Lore Society, American Folk Dance Society, Folk-Song Society of the Northeast, Society for the Preservation of Spirituals, American Dialect Society, Modern Language Association of America, International Commission of Popular Arts; author of numerous works on folk-song.

Gore, George 1855–1933, born: Hartland; raised in Westbrook; catcher for S.D. Warren Co. baseball team, played professionally for various teams in the New England League to 1878; member: Chicago White Stockings 1879–87, National League Championship 1880, 1881, 1882, 1885, 1886; led the league in batting and hitting 1880, scored the most runs (5) in a single game 1880, stole 7 bases in one game, led the league in runs scored (86) 1881, led the league in runs (99) and walks (29) 1882, led in walks (61) 1884, led in walks (102) 1886, most extra base-hits in one game (three doubles and two triples) 1885; member: the predecessor of the New York Giants 1887–89; member: Players League 1890; rejoined the Giants 1891–92, retired 1894; businessman in Nutley, New Jersey.

Gorges, Sir Fernando 1565–1647, born: Ashton Phillips, Somerset, England; related to both Sir Walter Raleigh and Sir John Popham; commander of a small body of troops fighting for Henri IV of France, 1589, knighted 1591; led a colorful military career, thereafter, served in Spain, &c.; appointed by King James, governor of Plymouth (England), met George Weymouth 1605, upon his return from Maine, and took into his household, for a period of three years, the three Indians Weymouth had kidnaped, instructed them in English and gleaned from them much information about their native place; with Sir John Popham, obtained from King James I, grants of incorporation of two companies for settlement of the New World, styled the First and Second Colonies, to be administered by the Council of Virginia 1606, the second became the Plymouth Colony; dispatched three ships with one hundred potential settlers and two of the Indians as interpreters, to the mouth of the Kennebec 1607; dispatched John Smith and two ships 1615, an expedition that came to naught, dispatched Richard Vines 1616–17, who encamped at Saco for the winter; received a grant, with John Mason from the Royal English Council for a grant of land between the Merrimac, Kennebec, and St. Lawrence Rivers, styled Laconia 1622; established Saco and Agamenticus, later York; as president of the council, gave his approbation to a grant to John Endicott and his associates, of Massachusetts, "so far as it should not be prejudicial to my son, Robert Gorges's, interests" 1628; received from King Charles I a charter establishing him to be lord proprietor of the Province of Maine 1639, with extraordinary powers of legislation and government, transmissible to his heirs and assigns, bounded by the Piscataqua and Kennebec Rivers; he had patronage of churches, could establish laws in commerce with representatives of the freeholders, with penalties extending to liberty, property and life, he could erect courts, with dire ecclesiastical and admiralty jurisdiction, make war, raise, organize, and command troops, regulate markets and tolls, designate ports of entry, exact duties on merchandise; he appointed his son, Thomas Gorges, deputy governor, who removed to Agamenticus; his concept that colonies should be a royal endeavor and kept under royal control was a threat to the Puritans of Massachusetts Bay; the English civil war and Gorges's age prevented true fulfillment of his plan; eventually, the freeholders formed a body politic and submitted themselves to the jurisdiction of Massachusetts Bay.

Gould, Arthur Robinson 1857–1946, born: East Corinth; removed to Presque Isle 1887; lumberman, operated mills in Fort Fairfield and Presque Isle; builder of the Maine and New Brunswick Power Co., built and operated an electric railroad from Presque Isle to Caribou, linking with the Canadian Pacific Railroad; president: Aroostook Valley Railroad Co. 1902–46; member: Maine Senate 1921, 1927; member: U.S. Senate 1926–31 (Republican), chairman: Committee on Immigration; buried in Mt. Hope Cemetery, Bangor.

Gould, George Milbury 1848–1922, born: Auburn; enlisted as a drummer boy in the Union Army at age thirteen, 63rd Ohio Volunteers, discharged for ill health, reenlisted, discharged for ill health 1864; A.B. Ohio Wesleyan University 1873, S.T.B. Harvard University Divinity School 1874, studied at universities of Paris, Leipzig, and Berlin, M.D. Jefferson Medical College 1888; author: *A Compend of the Diseases of the Eye* 1886, invented cemented bifocal glasses; ophthamologist: Philadelphia Hospital 1892–94; a temperamental man, given to passionate disagreement with those that opposed his then-radical but now accepted theories of eye strain and human health; president: American Academy of Medicine 1895; began to correspond with the writer Lafcadio Hearn, who eventually became a longtime resident in Gould's home, wrote a response to a critical biography of Hearn: *Considering Lafcadio Hearn* 1908; author: *The Students Medical Dictionary* (eleven editions), *A Pocket Medical Dictionary* 1892, *A New Medical Dictionary* 1894, went through numerous editions, *An Illustrated Dictionary of Medical Biology and Allied Subjects*, *A Dictionary of New Medical Terms* 1894, *Medicine and Surgery* 1896–1905, *A Cyclopedia of Practical Medicine and Surgery* 1900; founded and edited: *Medical News* 1891-95, *Philadelphia Medical Journal* 1898–1900; author: *Suggestions for Medical Writers* 1900; founded and edited: *American Medicine* 1901–06; author: *An Autumn Singer* 1892, *The Meaning of Life and the Method of Life* 1893, *The Infinite Presence* 1910, *Biographic Clinics* (six volumes) 1903-09, *The Jefferson Medical College of Philadelphia* (two volumes) 1904; editor: *Life and Letters of Edmund Clarence Stedman* (two volumes) 1910.

Gower, Frederick Allen 1851–84, born: Sedgwick; son of a Baptist minister, after his father's death, his mother became the principal of the Ladies Collegiate Institute, Worcester, Massachusetts, 1859; graduate: Abbot School, Farmington, student at Brown University 1869–70, withdrew to assist his uncle, George Gower, a lumber merchant in New Haven, Connecticut, intending to matriculate at Yale College, financial concerns required him to return to Providence 1873; reporter, later editor: *Providence Evening Press*; as member of the lecture committee of the Franklin Lyceum, engaged Alexander Graham Bell for a lecture and demonstration of the recently invented telephone, joined with Bell to familiarize the public with the telephone; invented the telephone harp, a device for producing loud effects on the lecture platform; went to Great Britain to look after Bell's interests 1878; engaged by Cornelius Roosevelt of New York to go to France to introduce the Bell instrument; invented a competing, and some say, superior instrument to the Bell telephone; after rigorous tests conducted by the British army and navy and prominent scientific men and government officials, established a monopoly in England and France for the production and installation of the Gower telephone; member: Royal Institute of Great Britain; married his cousin, Lillian Norton (aka ÒNordicaÓ) 1883; lost his life trying to cross the English Channel in a balloon.

Grant, Albert Weston 1856–1930, born: East Benton, cousin of George Bernard Grant; removed with his parents to Stevens Point, Wisconsin; graduate: U.S. Naval Academy 1877, rose through the ranks to vice admiral, USN, 1918; service aboard USS *Pensacola*, USS *Lackawanna*, USS *Aliance*, USS *Passaic*, USS *Iroquois*; detailed to the Norfolk Navy Yard, where he received torpedo training; served at the Naval War College, service aboard USS *Trenton*, USS *Richmond*, USS *Saratoga*, USS *Yorktown*; detailed to Norfolk Navy Yard, where he supervised pioneer electrical work aboard USS *Pensacola*; service aboard USS *Concord*; promoted to lieutenant, USN, 1893; service aboard USS *San Francisco*; service at U.S. Naval Academy as instructor

1894–97; aboard USS *Helena*, during the Spanish-American War, aboard USS *Massachusetts*, battle of Santiago, service aboard USS *Machias*, promoted to lieutenant commander, USN, 1900; instructor at U.S. Naval Academy 1900–02; executive officer: USS *Oregon* 1902–03, commanding officer 1903–05, promoted to commander, USN; in charge of the department of seamanship, U.S. Naval Academy; author: *The School of the Ship*, which was a standard text at the academy for many years; duty at the U.S. Naval War College; commanding officer: USS *Arethusa* 1907–08; aboard USS *Connecticut* as chief of staff: Atlantic Fleet (the Great White Fleet) during its around-the-world cruise 1908–09; promoted to captain, USN, 1909, commanding officer: Fourth Naval District, commanding officer: Philadelphia Navy Yard 1910–13, commanding officer: construction of USS *Texas* 1913–14, commanding officer (first commander or plankholder): USS *Texas* 1914–15, commanding officer: Submarine Force, Atlantic Fleet 1915–17, commanding officer: Battleship Force One, Atlantic Fleet 1917, vice admiral, USN, commanding officer: Western Atlantic 1918–1919, commanding officer: Washington, D.C. Navy Yard; superintendent: Naval Gun Factory 1919–20; a destroyer, USS *Albert W. Grant* (DD-649), named in honor, was launched 1942, received seven battle stars in World War II.

Grant, Claudius Buchanan 1835–1921, born: Lebanon; A.B. University of Michigan 1859, A.M. 1862, L.L.D. (Hon.) 1891; teacher and principal of Ann Arbor (Michigan) High School 1859–62; during the Civil War, rose from captain to colonel, 20th Michigan Volunteers 1862–65, participated in the battles of Fredericksburg, Vicksburg, from the Wilderness to Appomottax; studied law at University of Michigan 1865–66, member: Michigan bar 1866, member: Felch (Alpheus) & Grant; recorder and postmaster: Ann Arbor; member: Michigan House of Representatives 1870–74, chairman: Committee on Education, speaker *pro tempore*; regent: University of Michigan 1870–80; practiced law at Houghton 1873–82; judge: circuit court 1881–89, associate justice, Michigan Supreme Court 1883–1909, chief justice 1888, 1899–1908; member: Grand Army of the Republic, Military Order of the Loyal Legion; son-in-law of Alpheus Felch; buried in Forest Hill Cemetery, Ann Arbor.

Grant, George Bernard 1849–1917, born: Farmingdale; son of a shipwright, cousin of Albert Weston Grant; graduate: Bridgton Academy, student: Chandler Scientific School, Dartmouth College, B.S. Lawrence Scientific School, Harvard University 1873; while in college, conceived of the mechanical calculating machine (unaware, at that time, of the previous, unfulfilled attempts at a similar concept by Babbage), obtained his first patents in 1872 and 1873; with the financial aid of Professor Wolcott Gibbs of Harvard University and Fairman Rogers of Philadelphia, constructed the first mechanical calculating machine, Grant's Difference Engine, exhibited at the Philadelphia Exposition 1876, stood 5 feet high, 8 feet long, weighed nearly one ton and had 15,000 parts, cost $10,000, sold remarkably well (the original model is preserved at the University of Pennsylvania), awarded a gold medal by the

Eminent Mainers

Franklin Institute 1877; never ceased in making further improvements, several of his later models are preserved at the Smithsonian Institution in Washington; because of his need for much more precise gears than were then available became a founder of the American gear cutting business, founded Grant's Gear Works, Inc. Boston, Philadelphia, and Cleveland; author: *Chart and Tables, for Bevel Gears* 1885, *A Handbook on the Teeth of Gears, Their Curves, Properties and Practical Construction, With Orthographs* 1885, *Chart and Tables for Bevel Gears* 1885, *Odentics; or, the Theory and Practice of the Teeth of Gear Wheels* 1891, *Grants Gear Book of 1892* 1892, *A Treatise on Gear Wheels* 1897; an enthusiastic botanist, accumulated one of the largest private herbaria in the United States; Charles Babbage is generally credited with the invention of the first mechanical calculator, however, he was thwarted in its construction by that problem which Grant overcame, that is, the manufacture and use of precision gears, in which Grant became the acknowledged world leader.

Grant, Lemuel Pratt 1817–93, born: Frankfort; son of a farmer; at an early age, became a rod man on a railway surveying crew, working on the Philadelphia & Reading line; assistant engineer under Edgar Thompson; chief engineer of the Georgia Central Railroad 1840; recognized that the small village of Marthaville, which would later be renamed Atlanta, would become the nexus of railroad and, subsequently, manufacturing and mercantile activity in northern Georgia, hence, his title as Father of Atlanta; superintendent of every railroad to converge on Atlanta, assistant to L. O. Reynolds on the Central Railroad of Georgia 1841, returned to the Georgia Central Railroad, grading the bed to Marthaville 1843, chief engineer and superintendent: Montgomery & West Point Railroad 1845, oversaw construction from Chehaw to Opelika, resident engineer: Georgia Railroad Co. 1848–51, chief engineer: Atlanta & West Point Railroad 1851–53; engaged in the construction of railroads in Louisiana, Mississippi, and Texas 1853–58; president: Southern Pacific Railroad Co. 1858; chief engineer of the Georgia Western Railroad and other proposed lines in Alabama 1859; in the Civil War: captain of Engineers, CSA, planned and oversaw construction of the defenses of Atlanta; after the war, devoted himself to rebuilding southern railroads and the city of Atlanta; superintendent: Atlanta & West Point Railroad 1866–81, president: Georgia Pacific Railroad, president: Western Railroad; grew rich on wise investments in real estate, was the largest landowner within the city of Atlanta, donated Grant Park to the city of Atlanta.

Gray, Oliver Crosby 1837–1905, born: Jefferson; son of a prominent physician and graduate of Harvard University Medical School; A.B. Waterville College 1855, A.M. 1868, L.L.D. (Hon.) 1885; removed to Minnesota, superintendent of schools: Minneapolis 1855–57, principal: Monticello (Minnesota) Seminary 1857–59, principal: Female Seminary, Princeton, Arkansas 1859–61; in the Civil War: member: 3rd Arkansas Cavalry, CSA, 1861–65; president: Saint John's College, Little Rock, Arkansas, 1871–74; professor of mathematics: University of Arkansas 1874–85; mayor of Fayette, Arkansas, and superintendent of schools 1886–87; professor of mathematics: University of Arkansas 1886–95; principal: Arkansas School for the Blind from 1895.

Greeley, Jonathan Clark 1833– ?, born: Palermo; attended local public school and Lincoln Academy; removed to Palatka, Florida, on the St. John's River, engaged in mercantile trade, served as alderman; member: Florida House of Representatives, the only unionist in that body to 1864; to avoid conscription into the Confederate Army, ran the blockade to Key West, made his way back to Maine; after the war, returned to Jacksonville, where he was a merchant; appointed deputy collector of internal revenue, assistant assessor 1866–73; appointed Duval County treasurer 1868–75; mayor of Jacksonville 1873–75; chairman of the Committee on Public Works; alderman; unsuccessful candidate for lieutenant governor 1882; member: Florida Senate 1883; unsuccessful candidate for U.S. House of Representatives 1884; delegate: Florida Constitutional Convention 1885; closely associated with Frank Hawthorne; a founder, principal stockholder, and depositor: Florida Savings Bank, ruined in the yellow fever epidemic of 1888; agent of the Land Mortgage Bank of Florida, Ltd., London; loaned some $2 million on real estate, purchased 75,000 acres of phosphate lands, and erected a processing plant.

Green, Joseph Foster 1811–97, born: Bath; appointed midshipman USN, 1827, assigned to the USS *Vandalia* in the Brazilian squadron; studied at the naval school in Norfolk 1833; promoted to passed midshipman; cruised the Mediterranean aboard the USS *Potomac*; commissioned lieutenant, USN, 1838; stationed in the West Indian and Brazilian squadrons; in the war with Mexico, served aboard the USS *Ohio* and took part in all the important naval engagements on the Pacific Coast; promoted to commander, USN, 1855; stationed at the Charlestown Navy Yard and at Annapolis 1850–58; when the Civil War broke out, Green was on ordnance duty; commissioned captain, USN, 1862; commanded the steam sloop USS *Canandaigua* to 1864, taking part in the bombardment of Fort Wagner 1863; after the war, on ordnance duty at the Charlestown Navy Yard 1866–68; promoted to commodore, USN, 1867, rear admiral, USN, 1870; served on board: USS *Dolphin*, USS *Vandalia*, USS *Grampus*, USS *Columbia*; commanding officer: USS *America*, commanding officer: USS *Canandaigua*; served in Pacific Squadron, Brazil Squadron, Mediterranean Squadron, South Atlantic Blockading Squadron; commanding officer: Southern Squadron, Atlantic Fleet, flagship USS *Congress*; commanding officer: North Atlantic Squadron, flagship USS *Worcester*; retired 1872.

Greene, Charles Lyman 1862–1929, born: Gray; son of William Warren Greene, a physician, who was a professor of surgery at the Medical School of Maine and the University of Michigan, famed for having revived a patient who had been declared dead and already placed in a coffin, through the ingenious use of an injection of phosphoric acid, the patient outlived the doctor by thirty years, also performed the first successful removal of a goiter; student: University of Michigan Medical School, M.D. University of Minnesota 1890, postgraduate work: Harvard University Medical School, Johns Hopkins University Medical School, London, Paris, Heidelberg; professor of medicine and chief of the department of medicine: University of Minnesota 1892–1915; author: *The Medical Examination for Life Insurance and Its Associate Clinical Methods* 1900, *Extreme Dilation of the Heart Due to Valvular Disease, with Special Reference to Treatment by the School Method, Medical Diagnosis* 1907, six editions, several chapters for the medical works of Sir William Osler, in World War I: lieutenant colonel, USA Medical Corps.

Greene, Gladys Georgiana, yclept Jean Arthur 1905–91, born: New

York City; daughter of a photographer who removed to Portland to take over the photographic studio of J. W. and Charles Henry Lamson; attended grammar school and Portland High School before removing to New York, at age fifteen, to work as a model; because of her father's relationship with John Ford, was able to obtain a bit part in his *Cameo Kirby* 1923, after which she obtained roles in numerous westerns, with the coming of talkies, her voice became an asset, quit Hollywood briefly to play Broadway 1932, with John Ford's *The Whole Town's Talking* 1935, she became a star of light comedy, working with Frank Capra and George Stevens; was accorded critical acclaim for her appearance on Broadway in *Peter Pan* 1950; starred in the short-lived *The Jean Arthur Story* on television 1956; taught drama at Vassar College; her films include: *Cameo Kirby, The Temple of Venus* 1923, *Biff Bang Buddy, Fast and Fearless, Bringin Home the Bacon, Travelin Fast, Thundering Romance* 1924, *Seven Chances, Drug Store Cowboy, The Fighting Smile, A Man of Nerve, Tearin Loose, Hurricane Horseman, Thundering Through* 1925, *Under Fire, Born to Battle, The Fighting Cheat, Double Daring, Lightning Bill, The Cowboy Cop, Twisted Triggers, The College Boob, The Block Signal* 1929, *The Masked Menace* (serial), *Husband Hunters, The Broken Gate, Horse Shoes, The Poor Nut, Flying Luck* 1927, *Wallflowers, Warming Up, Brotherly Love, Sins of the Fathers* 1928, *The Canary Murder Case, Stairs of Sand, The Greene Murder Case, The Mysterious Dr. Fu Manchu, The Saturday Night Kid, Half-Way to Heaven* 1929, *Street of Chance, Young Eagles, Paramount on Parade, The Return of Dr. Fu Manchu, Danger Lights, The Silver Horde* 1930, *The Gang Buster, Virtuous Husband, The Lawyer's Secret, Ex-Bad Boy* 1931, *Get That Venus, The Past of Mary Holmes* 1933, *Whirlpool, The Defense Rests, The Most Precious Thing in Life* 1934, *The Whole Town's Talking, Public Hero No. 1, Party Wire, Diamond Jim, The Public Menace, If You Could Only Cook* 1935, *Mr. Deeds Goes to Town, The Ex-Mrs. Bradford, Adventures in Manhattan, More Than a Secretary* 1936, *The Plainsman* (as Calamity Jane), *History Is Made at Night, Easy Living* 1937, *You Can't Take It With You* 1938, *Only Angels Have Wings, Mr. Smith Goes to Washington* 1939, *Too Many Husbands, Arizona* 1940, *The Devil and Miss Jones* 1941, *The Talk of the Town* 1942, *The More the Merrier, A Lady Takes a Chance* 1943, *The Impatient Years* 1944, *A Foreign Affair* 1948, *Shane* 1953.

Greene, William Lyman 1828–1914, born: Kennebunkport; raised on his grandfather's farm, learned the printing trade, employed by the University Press and the Riverside Press, Cambridge, Massachusetts; entered the office of *The Congregationalist* 1855, junior partner 1856, as head of the publishing department, saw the newspaper grew into one of the leading religious periodicals in the country, the firm was reorganized as W. L. Greene & Co. 1867, continued to publish *The Congregationalist* to 1901, when it was sold to the Congregational Sunday School and Publishing Society, his firm also published *The Student and Schoolmate* from 1862, with William Adams (Oliver Optic) as editor; spent his retirement touring the Holy Lands.

Greenleaf, Moses 1777–1834, born: Newburyport, Massachusetts; son of Moses Greenleaf; kept a general store in New Gloucester and Bangor 1799–1818; in real estate business, helped settle Williamsburg; spent life furthering settlement of central Maine; surveyed roads, located stone and mineral deposits, secured charter for Piscatiquis Canal and Railroad Co. 1833, provided valuable information to miners, land developers, and legislators through his publications and maps; author: *Map of the District of Maine from the Latest and Best Authorities* 1815, *A Survey of the State of Maine in Reference to its Geographical Features, Statistics and Political Economy* 1829; uncle of John A. Poor, who is said to have derived his consuming interest in railroad development from Greenleaf.

Greenleaf, Simon 1783–1853, born: Newburyport, Massachusetts, son of Moses Greenleaf; raised in New Gloucester; A.M. (Hon.) Bowdoin College 1817, L.L.D. Harvard University 1834, Amherst College 1845, University of Alabama 1852; studied law with Ezekiel Whitman, later chief justice: Maine Supreme Judicial Court; member: Cumberland County bar 1806, practiced in Standish for one year, removed to Gray 1807, removed to Portland 1818, where he had an extensive practice in maritime and equity law; member: Maine House of Representatives 1820; reporter: Maine Supreme Judicial Court 1820–32, during this time, he traveled the circuit with the judges, being retained in countless cases; appointed Royall professor of law: Harvard University Law School 1833–48; generally regarded as foremost expert on common law, in his day; author: *A Brief Report of Cases Argued and Determined by the Supreme Court* (nine volumes) 1820-32, *Full Collection of Cases, Overruled, Denied, Doubted or Limited in their Application* 1821, *A Brief Inquiry into the Origins and Principles of Free Masonry* 1820, *A Treatise of the Law of Evidence* vol. 1 1842, vol. 2 1846, vol. 3 1853, *Life of Joseph Story* 1845, *Examination of the Testimony of the Four Evangelists, by the Rules of Evidence Administered in Courts of Justice, with an Account of the Trial of Jesus* 1846, *Cruise's Digest of the Law of Real Property, Revised and Abridged for the use of American Students* (seven volumes) 1848-50; author of the constitution of Liberia; father of Patrick Henry Greenleaf.

Greenough, James Bradstreet 1833–1901, born: Portland; graduate: Boston Latin School, A.B. Harvard College φΒΚ 1856, student: Harvard University Law School; removed to Marshall, Michigan; studied law privately, member: Michigan bar, practiced in Calhoun County for eight years; tutor in Latin: Harvard University 1865, assistant professor 1873, professor 1883–1901; author: *Analysis of the Latin Subjunctive* 1870; his study of Sanskrit led to his offering regular courses, and, with the establishment of a department, was made head 1880; primarily responsible for *Harvard Studies in Classical Philology* 1890, obtaining from his own class of 1856 the endowment needed for its publication; coauthor: *Allen and Greenough Latin Grammar* 1872, which served as a standard text for more than a half century, this was followed by a long series of Allen and Greenough Latin texts; adapted for the stage Thackery's *The Rose and the Ring* 1880, author of two original comedies: *The Queen of Hearts* 1875, *The Blackbirds* 1877, author of the book and lyrics of the comic opera *Old King Cole* 1889, and the Latin words for the Harvard hymn *Hymn for Commencement*; an early advocate of the higher education for women, took an active part in promoting the Society for the Collegiate Instruction of Women, which evolved into Radcliffe College, chairman: Radcliffe's administrative board; author: *Words and Their Ways in English Speech* 1901.

Greenwood, Chester 1858–1937, born: Farmington; student: Wilton Academy; at age fifteen, invented the Greenwood Ear Protector (earmuffs), at age sixteen began manufacture, at age nineteen, secured patent, by 1883, was producing 30,000 pairs annually, by 1936, the number had increased to 400,000; he conducted a bicycle business and sold electrical supplies in the 1890s, later, he sold and installed steam heating systems of his own design; built and operated a steamboat on Clearwater Lake, near Farmington; co-founder, president, manager: Franklin Telephone & Telegraph Co. 1893; designed and manufactured special machinery for other manufacturers, in particular: machines for making rolling pins, wood handles, spools, also invented doughnut hooks, portable camps, the spring steel rake, steel bows for archery, a washing machine, a cotton picker, an umbrella holder, &c.; built a profitable business block in Farmington, developed Greenwood Avenue as part of an extensive residential area; treasurer: Highland Park Realty & Construction Co.; ardent prohibitionist, chairman: Prohibition party local committee, Prohibition party candidate for Maine State Senate 1894; president: Center Meeting House Society 1925–37; buried in Fairview Cemetery, Farmington.

Gregory, Hansen Crockett 1832–1921, born: Clam Cove (now Glen Cove), Rockport; ship captain, reportedly in 1847 stuck a fried cake on the spoke of his wheel, thus creating the doughnut, another story has it that, being dissatisfied by the uncooked center of fried cakes, cut out the center and, in this way, created the doughnut; died at Sailors' Snug Harbor, Staten Island, New York; on the one-hundredth anniversary of this invention, Gregory's birthplace was marked by a bronze plaque and celebrations were held across the country; plans for the erection of a 300-foot-high statue of Gregory by Victor Kahill on the summit of Mount Battie in Camden came to naught.

Griffen, Eugene 1855–1907, born: Ellsworth; graduate: U.S. Military Academy 1875; commissioned second lieutenant, USA, assigned to the corps of engineers; on duty at the Engineer School of Application, Willetts Point, New York, to 1878; in charge of surveying parties in Colorado, New Mexico, Arizona, and Texas; quarter-master, later adjutant: battalion of engineers, Willetts Point; commissioned first lieu-tenant, USA, 1879; assistant professor of civil and military engineering and the art of war: U.S. Military Academy 1883–85; aide-de-camp to General Winfield Scott Han-cock (as well as son-in-law) 1885–86; chief engineer: Division of the Atlantic and the Department of the East 1885–86; commissioned captain, USA, 1887; assistant engi-neer, commissioner, District of Columbia 1886–88, resigned 1889; first vice president: General Electric Co. 1892, president: British-Thomson-Houston Co. from 1893; in the Spanish-American War: in volunteer service, organized 1st Volunteer Engineers, colonel, USV, commanding officer: 1st U.S. Volunteer Engineers 1898, served in Puerto Rico 1898–99, brigadier general, USV, 1899.

Griffin, Walter 1861–1935, born: Portland; son of a ship figurehead carver, stu-dent: Boston Museum of Fine Art, Art Students League, New York and Paris, pupil of R. Collin and Jean Paul Laurens; lived principally in France 1883–1915; art instructor and director: School of Art Society of Hartford 1898–1907; recipient: medal of honor, San Francisco Exposition 1915, gold medal: Pennsylvania Academy of Art; works hang in: Memorial Art Gallery, Rochester, New York, Albright-Knox Art Gallery, Buffalo, Brooklyn Museum of Art, Imperial Art Museum, Tokyo, Luxembourg Gallery, Paris; member: National Academy of Art.

Griswold, William McCrillis 1853–99, born: Bangor; son of Rufus Griswold, patron, publisher, and literary executor of Edgar Allan Poe; graduate: Phillips Acad-emy, Exeter, A.B. Harvard College 1875; as a child began his lifelong study of periodi-cal literature; spent several years in Europe, subsequent to his graduation from college; employed by the Library of Congress 1882–88; under the pseudonym of G. P. Index published a general index to *The Nation*, volumes 1–30, much to the astonishment of the editors of *The Nation* 1880; published: *G. P. Index Annual* 1882–85, *Annual* (index to periodicals annually from 1887), *A Directory of Writers for the Literary Press in the United States* 1884, *Descriptive List of Novels and Tales* (ten volumes) 1891–92, *The Novels of 1897*, *Passages from the Correspondence and Other Papers of Rufus W. Griswold* 1898; contributed book reviews and political editorials to *The Nation*.

Grover, Cuvier 1828–85, born: Bethel; son of a physician and delegate: Maine Constitutional Convention 1819, brother of Lafayette Grover; graduate: U.S. Military

Academy 1850 (4/44); assigned to the 1st Artillery; served on railroad explorations, crossed the Rockies with the Isaac Stevens expedition 1853; promoted to first lieutenant, USA, 1855, captain, USA, 1858; on the Utah Expedition against Mormons 1858–59; commanding officer: Fort Union (New Mexico) 1861, when a force of Confederates demanded his surrender, he burned his supplies and, making a forced march, got his command over the Missouri River; commissioned brigadier general, USV, commanding officer: 1st, brigade, 2nd Division of III Corps, Army of the Potomac: Yorktown, Fair Oaks, Savages Station, Glendale, Malvern Hill, Harrison's Landing, Bristoe Station, Second Bull Run; in the Gulf: commanding officer: 4th Division, XIX Corps: Vermillion Bend, Port Hudson; commanding officer: 2nd Division, XIX Corps: Opequon, Winchester, Fisher's Hill, Cedar Creek where he was wounded; commanding officer: XIX Corps, brevetted major general, USV; commanding officer: district of Savannah; after the war: appointed lieutenant colonel, USA, of the 38th Cavalry, a black unit, later colonel, USA, commanding officer: 1st Cavalry, died on active duty, buried at West Point.

Grover, Lafayette 1823–1911, born: Bethel; son of a physician and member of the Maine Constitutional Convention 1819, brother of Cuvier Grover; graduate: Goulds Academy, student: Bowdoin College for two years, studied law in the office of Asa Fish, Philadelphia; member: Pennsylvania bar 1850; sailed around the Horn to San Francisco 1851, removed to Salem, Oregon; clerk: U.S. District Court; prosecuting attorney: second judicial district 1852; served as first lieutenant in the company of volunteers he helped recruit to fight in the Rogue River Indian War 1853–54; member: Oregon House of Representatives 1853–56, speaker: 1856; president: U.S. board of commissioners appointed to assess spoliation of property destroyed in the Indian wars; member: Oregon Constitutional Convention 1857; first member from Oregon: U.S. House of Representatives (Democrat) 1857–59; organizer, manager: Willamette Woolen Manufacturing Co.; established the Salem Flouring-mills Co., the first mill in Oregon to ship flour to foreign countries; chairman: Democratic State Committee 1866–70; elected fourth governor of Oregon 1870–77, while governor, introduced tugboat service at the mouth of the Columbia River, built locks at Willamette Falls, opening the Willamette River to waterborne traffic, constructed the Oregon Statehouse, the penitentiary, the state university, the agricultural college, and an asylum for the deaf and blind; as governor, refused to issue a certificate of election to presidential elector Dr. J. W. Watts, a Republican 1876, gave the certificate to the Democratic elector, with next highest vote, later overruled by the electoral commission; member: U.S. Senate 1877–83 (Democrat), chairman: Committee on Manufactures, member: committees on military affairs, public lands, tailroads, yerritories; played a prominent part in the exclusion of Chinese immigrants; buried in Riverview Cemetery, Portland, Oregon.

Gunnison, Almon 1844–1917, born: Hallowell; son of a Congregational minister; student: Dalhousie College, Green Mountain Institute, Tufts College, B.D. Saint Lawrence University 1868, D.D. 1880; ordained Universalist minister, pastor: Bath 1868–71, All Souls Church, Brooklyn, New York, 1871–1891, First Church (the largest Universalist congregation in the United States), Worcester, Massachusetts, 1891–98; sixth president: Saint Lawrence University, Canton, New York, 1898–1914; editorial contributor: *Christian Leader*; author: *Rambles Overland* 1886, *Wayside and Fireside Rambles* 1893.

Guptill, Arthur Leighton 1891–1956, born: Gorham; B.S. Pratt Institute, Brooklyn, New York, 1912, student at Massachusetts Institute of Technology 1914–16; registered architect 1916, partner: Bearse and Guptill, architects, designers, and illustrators, New York 1919–25; freelance advertising artist, teacher in professional art schools 1916–37; art director: Reinhold Publishing Corp. 1930–37; contributor: "Guptill's Corner" in architectural magazine *Pencil Point* 1934–37; executive vice president: Watson-Guptill Publications, 1937–51, president from 1951; editor and publisher: *American Artist* magazine; fellow: Royal Society of Arts, London, member: American Architecture Association; founding president: American Amateur Artists Association; editor, designer, and publisher: *Type Specimens* 1940, *Lumiprinting* 1942, *Studio Secrets* 1943, *Oil Painting for the Beginner* 1944, *Masks* 1945, *Animal Drawing and Painting* 1946, *Pastel Painting* 1947, *Painters' Question and Answer Book* 1948, *Scratchbook Drawing* 1949, *How to Draw the Dog* 1950, *Type and Lettering* 1950, *Watercolor Painting for the Beginner* 1951, *Figure Indication* 1952, *Art and Hand-Lettering* 1952, *How to Make a Living as a Painter* 1954, *Is That Me?* 1947, *Brush and Ink* 1949, *Scripts* 1950, *Casein Painting* 1950, author: *Sketching and Rendering in Pencil* 1922, *Free-Hand Drawing Self-Taught* 1933, *Pen Drawing* 1947, *Watercolor Painting, Step by Step* 1955.

Gurney, Edward John 1914–96, born: Portland; attended public schools in Skowhegan and Waterville, B.S. Colby College 1935, L.L.B. Harvard University Law School 1938, L.L.M. Duke University Law School 1948; member: New York bar 1939, Florida bar 1949; practiced law in New York 1938–41, Winter Park, Florida, 1948–96; member: U.S. House of Representatives (Republican) 1963–69, member: U.S. Senate 1969–75; Winter Park city commissioner 1952–58, mayor 1961–62; in World War II: rose from private to lieutenant colonel, USA, 1941–46, served in Europe, decorated: Silver Star, Purple Heart.

Hacker, Jeremiah 1801–95, born: Brunswick; after a common school education, became an itinerant teacher of penmanship; converted to Quakerism, with his wife, Submit Tobey, settled in Portland, began the publication of the weekly newspaper *The Portland Pleasure Boat*, "J. Hacker, Owner, Master, and Crew," the paper's sections were divided into cabins, the motto was "Truth Against Error—Victory or Death" 1845; this quickly became a forum for dissenters and liberals; Hacker supported abolition of slavery, the repeal of the fugitive slave law, the underground railway, the establishment of reform schools for the segregation of juvenile offenders; persuaded the governor and legislature that selling large tracts of Maine land to land agents was wrong and that quarter sections ought to be sold, at low cost, to the landless, provided that they settle upon it and begin improvements; a fire destroyed his press in 1864, shortly thereafter, he began the publication of *Chariot of Wisdom and Love*; removed to Berlin, New Jersey, 1866, and began publishing a newspaper; his later years, in Vineland, New Jersey, were spent writing tracts and vituperative doggerel, as in his *The Last Song of Jeremiah Hacker*; buried in Siloam Cemetery, Vineland.

Hackett, Arthur 1884–1969, born: Portland; graduate: Worcester (Massachusetts) High School; studied violin with Michael Reidel, voice with Arthur J. Hubbard and Vincent V. Hubbard, Boston, studied acting with Arthur Weinschenk, Paris; tenor, made many concert tours in the United States, five tours with Geraldine Farrar, soloist in churches in New York; made operatic debut in *Rigoletto*, Grand Opera, Paris, 1924, in Europe 1924–27; singing under the name of Granville, sang with Nellie Melba on her farewell tour of the British Isles 1926; soloist with New York Philharmonic, Boston Symphony Orchestra, &c.; sang at many music festivals; sang leading role on tour with *The King's Henchman*; professor of voice, chairman: Vocal Department, University of Michigan 1930–53.

Hale, Eugene 1836–1918, born: Turner; brother of Clarence Hale; graduate: Hebron Academy, A.M. (Hon.) Bowdoin College 1869, L.L.D. Bates College 1882, Colby College 1886, Bowdoin College 1896; member: Maine bar 1857, associated with Howland & Strout of Portland, removed to Orland, later to Ellsworth; partner: Robinson & Hale, later: senior partner: Hale & Emery, Hale & Hamlin; prosecuting attorney for Hancock County 1858–66; in the Civil War: served as lieutenant in the Maine militia, aide-de-camp to Governor Washburn, when drafted in 1863, hired a substitute in lieu of active service; member: Maine House of Representatives 1867–68, 1879–80; member from the Fifth District: U.S. House of Representatives 1869–1879 (Republican), unsuccessful candidate for reelection 1878; declined appointments to the cabinets of Presidents Grant and Hayes as postmaster general and secretary of the navy; member: U.S. Senate 1881–1911, chairman: Committee on Census, Committee on Private Land Claims, Committee on Printing, longtime chairman of the Senate Naval Affairs Committee; a key figure in the development of the modern U.S. Navy, an opponent of the Spanish-American War and the retention of the Philippines; excoriated by Theodore Roosevelt for his reluctance to allow the U.S. Navy to send the Great White Fleet on its around-the-world cruise; member: National Monetary Commission which framed the Aldrich central bank plan of 1910; son-in-law of Senator and Secretary of the Interior Zachariah Chandler of Michigan, father of Frederick Hale; buried in Woodbine Cemetery, Ellsworth; the U.S. Navy launched USS *Hale* (DD-133), named in his honor, at Bath Iron Works 1918, a second USS *Hale* (DD-

642) was launched, also at Bath Iron Works, in 1943, she earned six battle stars in World War II.

Hale, Frederick 1874–1963, born: Detroit, Michigan; son of Eugene Hale, grandson of Senator and Secretary of the Interior Zachariah Chandler of Michigan, cousin of Robert Hale; student: Lawrenceville School, graduate: Groton Academy, A.B. Harvard College 1896, student at Columbia University Law School 1896–97; member: Maine bar, practiced in Portland from 1899; member: Maine House of Representatives 1905–06; member: Republican National Committee 1912–18; member: U.S. Senate 1916–40 (Republican), chairman: Committee on Canadian Relations, Naval Affairs Committee, Appropriations Committee; buried in Woodbine Cemetery, Ellsworth.

Haley, Ora 1845–1919, born: East Corinth; brother of George Haley; graduate: East Corinth Academy; largest livestock grower and dealer in Wyoming from 1871.

Hall, Edwin Herbert 1855–1938, born: North Gorham; son of a farmer and logger; student: Gorham Academy, A.B. Bowdoin College 1875; principal: Goulds Academy, Brunswick High School 1875–77, A.M. 1878, Ph.D. Johns Hopkins University 1880, L.L.D. (Hon.) Bowdoin College 1905; while at Johns Hopkins 1879, noted a peculiar effect of magnetic action, usually described as a difference of potential transverse to the lines of current flow, which appears when a magnetic field is applied perpendicular to the current, which came to be known as the Hall effect; after graduation from Johns Hopkins, remained for one year as assistant in physics, awarded a Tyndall scholarship, which entitled him to foreign travel for one year, visited Helmholtz's laboratory in Berlin and addressed the physics section of the British Association for the Advancement of Science on the Hall effect; instructor in physics: Harvard University 1881–88, assistant professor 1888–95, professor 1895–1914, Rumford professor of physics 1914–1927; author: *Descriptive List of Elementary Exercises in Physics for Admission to Harvard College* 1886, written at the behest of President Eliot, *A Textbook of Physics* 1891, *Lessons in Physics* 1904, *College Laboratory Manual of Physics* 1904, *Elements of Physics* 1912, coauthor: *The Teaching of Chemistry and Physics* 1902; with his promotion to assistant professor, he gave courses in heat engines and dynamics, which, subsequently, became the basis for professorships at Harvard; his main research dealt with thermal and thermoelectrical effects, was the first to call attention to the role of positive ions in electrical conductivity, later incorporated into the wave theory of metallic conduction; his last book: *A Dual Theory of Conduction in Metals* 1938, pertained to this research; served as a special police officer during the Boston police strike of 1919; president: Charles William Eliot Memorial Association; first honorary member: American Association of Physics Teachers.

Hall, John Hancock 1781–1841, born: Falmouth (that portion that later became Portland); son of Stephen Hall; inventor of the first metal- planing machine and, sequentially, became the first producer of breech-loading firearms made with interchangeable parts, something usually (and quite erroneously) credited to Eli Whitney, whose rifles did not, in fact, have truly interchangeable parts, and even at that, Whitney could not have produced his rifles without borrowing Hall's planing machine; applied for first patent 1811; had his shop on the Royal River in North Yarmouth, demonstrated for President James Monroe on his visit to Portland 1817, which resulted in the first large order from United States government; removed to Harper's Ferry to oversee construction of machinery and jigs 1819, remained until his death in 1841; Hall's rifle became the United States government general issue rifle, used in the Seminole wars, the Mexican war, and persisting into the Civil War, when it finally was rendered obsolete; two of his sons became congressmen from Missouri, one of whom also became governor of Missouri.

Hall, Robert Browne 1858–1907, born: Bowdoinham; began the study of the cornet in childhood, after playing in bands in Maine and Boston, made director of the Bangor Band 1882, later served as director of the Waterville Band from 1890; his numerous march compositions led to his being referred to as the New England March King; buried in Evergreen Cemetery, Richmond.

Hall, William Augustus 1815–88, born: Portland; son of John Hall, grandson of Stephen Hall; attended Yale College, removed to Randolph County, Missouri 1840; member: Missouri bar 1841; in Mexican war: captain USA; judge: circuit court 1847–61; delegate: Missouri Constitutional Convention 1861; member: U.S. House of Representatives 1862–65 (Democrat); delegate: Democratic National Convention 1864; buried in Hall Cemetery, Darkville, Missouri; brother of Willard Preble Hall, member of Congress and governor of Missouri, father of Uriel Sebrae Hall, member of Congress and William Preble Hall 1848–1927, graduate: U.S. Military Academy 1868; assigned primarily to the western frontier until the Spanish-American War, was in the fight with the Apaches at Whitestone Mountain, Arizona, 1873, Big Horn and Yellowstone Expeditions 1876, attacked by hostile Indians while in command of a reconnoitering party on the White River, Colorado, 1879, during that fight, went to the rescue of a fellow officer who was surrounded by about thirty-five warriors, for which he was awarded the Medal of Honor; served as adjutant general of Puerto Rico 1899–1900; member of the distinguished army marksmanship teams 1879–92, buried in Arlington National Cemetery.

Hamblen, Archelaus Lewis 1894–1971, born: Surry; B.S. University of Maine 1916; commissioned in the USA Infantry 1916, served in the 15th Machine Gun Battalion in France, during World War I; graduate: Infantry Staff School, USA, advanced course 1928, assistant professor, later professor of military science and tactics: University of Arkansas 1928–32, graduate: Command and General Staff School 1934, Army War College 1937; duty with War Department general staff 1941-42, promoted to brigadier general, USA, 1942; assistant chief of staff for supply at Allied Headquarters, London 1942–43, assistant chief of staff for supply, later assistant to the plans officer, Allied Headquarters, North Africa 1943–44, assistant chief of staff for supply: U.S. component, Allied armies in Italy 1944–45, assistant chief of staff for plans in the Mediterranean theatre of operations 1945–46, retired 1954; decorations include: two Distinguished Service Medals, Legion of Merit, Bronze Star, Commendation Ribbon.

Hamilton, Frederick William 1860–1940, born: Portland; attended public schools in Portland, A.B. Tufts University φBK 1880; filled various capacities for the Portland & Ogdensburg Railroad Co. 1880–89; after a course at Tufts University Divinity School, ordained Universalist minister, held parishes at Pawtucket, Rhode Island, and Roxbury, Massachusetts; director of Boston associated charities 1896–1907; active member of the Boston Public School Association, whose main goal was to keep politics out of the Boston school system; member: Massachusetts School Board 1909–20; author: *The Church and the Secular Life* 1904, three prize essays, one of which, "Restriction of Immigration," was prepared for the Public Opinion Co., another on the Venezuelan boundary dispute was for the American Humane Society, another was on restricting individual wealth, for the Dartmouth College Foundation; trustee, acting president: Tufts University 1905–06, fourth president 1905–12; after his resignation, served briefly as the pastor of the North Cambridge Universalist Church; business manager of a Boston forestry company.

Hamlen, James Clarence 1852–1936, born: Portland; joined his father in the lumber and cooperage business, established in 1846, president: J. H. Hamlen and Co. from 1903, exporter of sundry goods to Martinique and other islands in the Caribbean, first and for many years the only American company to trade with Senegal, shipping ice, fruit, and lumber; holder of timberlands in Maine, Arkansas, Kentucky, and Nova Scotia; operated cooperage plants in Nova Scotia and found it necessary to build and man its own ships, which were built at Liverpool, Nova Scotia, and at its own yard in Portland, where it also built vessels for the U.S. Navy during World War I; director: Casco National Bank, Fidelity Trust Co.; Democratic candidate for U.S. Senate, U.S. House of Representatives, mayor of Portland; federal fuel administrator for Maine during World War I; an avid yachtsman, an intimate friend of Sir Thomas Lipton; after the eruption of Mount Peleé, which destroyed St. Pierre on Martinique (including the Hamlen home and offices), he personally mounted his own relief expedition and secured a congressional appropriation to the same end 1902.

Hamlet, Harry Gabriel 1874–1954, born: Eastport; son of a U.S. Revenue Service officer; attended public schools in Dorchester, Massachusetts, student: Massachusetts Institute of Technology 1892–93, B.S. U.S. Coast Guard Academy 1896; promoted through the ranks to rear admiral 1932, retired as vice admiral 1934; his first assignment was aboard the cutter USRC (later USCGC) *Bear*, on that vessel when it made a relief expedition to the Arctic 1897–98 to rescue the crews of four whaling vessels; assigned to the Naval War College 1900, one of the first coast guard officers so assigned; after his graduation reassigned to the *Bear* 1901, served aboard vessels of the service on both coasts and in Alaskan and arctic waters; assigned to the 3rd Naval District 1917; organized the various activities and the training of personnel at Naval Section Bases 6 and 9, Bensonhurst, New York; joined U.S. Naval Forces at Brest, France, 1918, assumed command of the USS *Marietta*; while in command, he rescued the crew and officers of the USS *James* that was sinking in a gale; personnel officer and in charge of ship operations: Coast Guard Headquarters, Washington, 1919–22; commanding officer: cutter USCGC *Mojave*, Honolulu, 1922, cruised the Orient and Philippine Islands; assigned to the Philadelphia Navy Yard 1924, superintendent of reconditioning, outfitting, and commissioning of twenty destroyers turned over to the coast guard by the navy; he also trained the crews when the vessels were placed into commission; he organized the Coast Guard Destroyer Force and was placed in command; superintendent: U.S. Coast Guard Academy, New London, Connecticut, 1928–32; commandant: U.S. Coast Guard 1932–36, during his term, the service completed a vast ice map that coast guard oceanographers had worked on for twenty years and which aided the U.S. Weather Bureau in forecasting the probability of icebergs; shortly before his retirement, he was appointed to the newly organized Federal Maritime Commission and proceeded to the West Coast to conduct hearings on a maritime strike that was seriously affecting the nation's shipping industry as sympathy walkouts spread to the East Coast; chairman: Personnel Advisory Committee for the U.S. Senate Committee on Commerce, which was dealing with maritime problems and legislation designed to improve the U.S. Merchant Marine 1934–36; awarded the Congressional Gold Life Saving Medal for his service aboard the USS *Marietta* 1920, Silver Star, commander: Order of the Crown of Italy; president: Retired Officers Association 1946–54.

Hamlin, Alfred Dwight Foster 1855–1926, born: Constantinople; son of Cyrus Hamlin; A.B. Amherst College 1875, student of architecture: Massachusetts Institute of Technology 1876–77; taught drawing for two years at Miss Porter's School, Farmington, Connecticut; student: *École des Beaux Arts*, Paris 1878–81, on return, entered firm of McKim, Mead, and White, New York; instructor in architecture: Columbia University 1887, assistant professor 1889, adjunct professor 1891, professor of history of architecture 1904, director of department from 1911; associated with Professor Charles Ware in the designing of the American School for Classical Studies, Athens 1884–86; architect of many public buildings, including the library buildings in Newark, Jersey City, Paterson, Cleveland, and Providence; author: *A Textbook of the History of Architecture* 1896, *European and Japanese Gardens* 1902, *In Memoriam, Rev. Cyrus Hamlin* 1903, *A History of Ornament, Ancient and Medieval* 1916, *A History of Ornament, Renaissance and Modern* 1923; regularly contributed to *Architectural Record* 1915–1926; awarded the Cross of George I, Greece 1920; chairman: Arts Committee for the completion of the Cathedral of St. John the Divine, New York; father of Talbot Faulkner Hamlin, eminent architectural historian.

Hamlin, Augustus Choate 1829–1905, born: Columbia Falls; nephew of Hannibal Hamlin; A.B. Bowdoin College 1851, M.D. Harvard University Medical School 1855; in the Civil War: assistant surgeon, 2nd Maine Infantry, brigade surgeon, medical director: XI Corps 1862–63, lieutenant colonel and medical inspector: Army of the Potomac, Army of the South, siege of Fort Wagner; staff of General Thomas; recipient: Chevalier, Order of St. Anne, Russia, 1878; Maine surgeon general 1882–86; mayor of Bangor; owned an orange grove in DeLand, Florida, and while there, the Hamlin variety of orange was named for him; purchased the Mount Mica farm and pursued the mining of tourmaline, author *The Tourmaline* 1873, *The History of Mount Mica* 1895; purchased the old jail on Paris Hill and presented it to the village as a library; buried in Mount Hope Cemetery, Bangor.

Hamlin, Charles 1837–1911, born: Hampden; son of Hannibal Hamlin; student: Bridgton and Bethel Academies, A.B. Bowdoin College 1857; practiced law in Orland 1858–61; in the Civil War: commissioned major, USV; helped organize the 1st Maine Heavy Artillery (which sustained the second heaviest losses of any regiment during the war) 1862, assistant adjutant general 2nd Division, III Corps, under Major General Hiram Berry, USV, commended for valor at Little Round Top, Gettysburg, 2 July 1863, at engagements at Kelly's Ford, Locust Grove, and Mine Run, assisted General A. P. Howe, inspector of artillery, at Harpers Ferry, relieved General Sigel during Early's raid on Washington; at Ford's Theatre the night of Lincoln's assassination, called out troops to put down possible insurrection, commanded the streets of the capital; resigning as brevet brigadier general, USV; Bangor city solicitor 1867–68, register of bankruptcy 1867–78, reporter: Maine Supreme Court 1868–1900; member: Maine House of Representatives 1883, 1885, speaker 1885; president: Eastern Maine General Hospital; organized Bangor Building and Loan Association 1885; owned woolen mills in Pittsfield and Old Town; lecturer: University of Maine law school 1899–1911; chairman, Executive Committee: Maine Gettysburg Commission, which erected sixteen monuments on the battlefield; author: *The Life and Times of Hannibal Hamlin* 1899, *Insolvent Laws of Maine*.

Hamlin, Cyrus 1811–1900, born: Waterford; son of a farmer, cousin of Hannibal Hamlin, Ralph Waldo Emerson; after his father's death, worked for his brother-in-law, Charles Farley, in his jewelry store in Portland 1827; came under the influence of Rev. Edward Payson; entered Bridgton Academy 1829, A.B. Bowdoin College 1834, D.D., L.L.D. (Hon.), Harvard University, University of the City of New York, graduate: Bangor Theological Seminary 1837; missionary to Turkey, under the auspices of the American Board of Commissioners for Foreign Missions 1838; established a seminary for the training of teachers and translators, Bebek 1840; due to persecution of the Armenian Protestants of Turkey, Hamlin, as a protected foreigner, set up a variety of industries left wanting by the absence of the Armenians, including a steam-powered gristmill and large bakery; with the coming of the Crimean War, found himself supplying the needs of the British Royal Navy and Army, some ten tons of bread, per diem, the profits from which were devoted to the construction of a church and school buildings, as well as the work of the American Board of Commissioners for Foreign Missions; at odds with the board over a scheme of vernacular education, resigned and became the organizer and founding president of Robert College, Constantinople 1860–77, the establishment of the school met with the determined opposition of Jesuit missionaries, who had been unable to obtain a similar concession from the Turkish sultan, as well as the French and Russian embassies; professor of theology: Bangor Theological Seminary 1877–80; president: Middlebury College 1880–85; author: *Cholera and Its Treatment* 1865, *Among the Turks* 1877, *My Life and Times*, translator of numerous works into Armenian; a vocal opponent of free trade, contributor of numerous papers and articles on free trade and international relations; father of Alfred Dwight Foster Hamlin.

Hamlin, Hannibal 1809–91, born: Paris Hill; son of a farmer, cousin of Cyrus

Hamlin; attended district school, Hebron Academy; with Horatio King, purchased the *Oxford Jeffersonian*, a weekly political paper, published in Paris 1829; studied law in the firm of Fessenden & Deblois, Portland, member: Maine bar 1833, practiced in Hampden, later Bangor; member: Maine House of Representatives 1836–40, 1847, speaker 1837, 1839–40; unsuccessful candidate for U.S. House of Representatives 1840; member: U.S. House of Representatives 1843–47 (Democrat), chairman: Committee on Commerce; identified with the antislavery wing of his party, on one occasion, he was intentionally detained by President Polk at the White House, Hamlin managed to slip away and arrived in the House at the last moment for a critical vote; presented the Wilmot proviso and secured its passage; member: U.S. Senate 1848–57 (Democrat), 1857–61 (Republican), chairman: Committee on District of Columbia, member: Committee on Manufactures, Committee on Mines and Mining, Committee on Post Offices and Post Roads, Committee on Foreign Affairs; resigned from the Senate when elected twentieth governor of Maine (Republican) 1857, resigned six weeks later so as to return to the U.S. Senate; resigned to become vice president of the United States 1861–65, pressured Lincoln to issue the Emancipation Proclamation, from an early date, and was allowed to view and amend it before its issuance; member, board of regents: Smithsonian Institution 1861–65, 1870–82; appointed collector of the Port of Boston

1865–66; resigned to become member: U.S. Senate (Republican) 1869–81; appointed U.S. minister to Spain 1881–82; while vice president, the Senate on recess, enlisted in the Maine Coast Guard and served as cook at Fort McClary in Kittery; first politician, of national stature to recognize the importance of Decoration (later Memorial) Day, campaigned to see it accorded the status of a national holiday; buried in Mount Hope Cemetery, Bangor.

Hanley, Charles Clark 1851–1934, born: Warren; son of a lighthouse superintendent; schooled in Bristol, Maine, Charlestown, and Winchester, Massachusetts; learned piano-case making with the Chickering Co., Boston; established himself as a boat builder in Sandwich, Massachusetts, 1875, later moved to Bourne, then finally to Quincy, retiring in 1925; one of the best known of the rule-of-thumb yacht designers at a time where there were few university-trained marine architects; the most famous of his designs is the Cape Cod catboat, vessels varying in length between 20 and 28 feet, in their class unbeatable; these boats were sometimes referred to as Hanley's Orphans, because most racing associations forbade them from racing against any of their own vessels; his *Harbinger* once beat the entire fleet of varied racing yachts at Marblehead, his *Genesee*, built 1899, won the Canada Cup in the international races on the Great Lakes 1899, 1900, his *Kit*, built 1896, won the Long Island Sound championship 1901; models of some of his designs are on permanent display at the Massachusetts Institute of Technology; Professor George Owen, of that institution, said that Hanley had a genius for proportion which makes him worthy to rank among the world's best yacht builders; he invented many appliances for construction but never took out patents on them.

Hanna, Marcus Aurelius 1842–1921, born: Bristol; son of the keeper of the Pemaquid Point lighthouse; sergeant, Company B, 50th Massachusetts Infantry, recipient: Medal of Honor, Port Hudson, Louisiana, 4 July 1863, voluntarily exposed himself to a heavy fire to get water for comrades in rifle pits; after the war, became the keeper of the Pemaquid Point Lighthouse 1869–73, as keeper of the Cape Elizabeth light, received much attention, as well as the gold medal from the United States Life Saving Service for his daring rescue of two crewmen from the *Australia* 1885; buried in Mt. Pleasant Cemetery, Portland; the U.S. Coast Guard commissioned a cutter, USCGC *Marcus Hanna*, named in his honor, in 1998.

Hanscom, Elizabeth Deering 1865–1960, born: Saco; A.B. Boston University ΦBK 1887, A.M. 1893, Ph.D. Yale University 1894; teacher, later, professor of English: Smith College from 1894; author: *Lamb's Essays—A Biographical Study* 1891, *The Friendly Craft* 1908, *Sophia Smith and the Beginnings of Smith College* 1925, *The Heart of the Puritan* 1917.

Hanscom, John Forsyth 1842–1912, born: Eliot; nephew of Isaiah and William L. Hanscom; in the Civil War: USV, 1862–63, appointed naval constructor, on duty: navy yards League Island, Pennsylvania, Boston; Bureau of Construction advisory board: Chester, Pennsylvania, 1883–84, New York 1887–88; member: board of inspection and survey 1889–91, 1895–1903; superintendent of construction for battleships USS *Maine* and USS *Alabama* 1898–1903; senior member, board member for ships building on the Atlantic coast; retired as rear admiral, USN, 1904.

Harding, Carroll Rede 1888–1963, born: Hallowell; C.E. Cornell University 1910, L.L.D. (Hon.) Hobart College 1954; with Alaska-Canada Boundary Survey 1909, American Bridge Co. 1910–11, International Waterways Commission 1912, Costa Rica-Panama Boundary Survey 1912–13; draftsman: Southern Pacific Railroad, chief draftsman, assistant construction engineer, construction engineer, assistant to president 1913–47; director or officer of various subsidiaries; designed and built Suisun Bay Bridge 1926–30; director and president: Pullman Co. 1947–58.

Hardison, Wallace Libby 1850–1909, born: Caribou; removed, at age nineteen, to Humboldt County, California, a year later, removed to Bradford, Pennsylvania, where his brothers were in the oil-drilling business, in which he prospered; member: Pennsylvania House of Representatives for one term; located a source of oil in Santa Paula, California, established the Union Oil Company of California; became involved in gold mining in Peru, established the Inca Mining Company of Peru; owner, publisher *Los Angeles Herald* 1900–04; killed by a Southern Pacific railroad locomotive while crossing the tracks in Roscoe on his way to visit his orange grove in Monte Vista; father of Allen Crosby Hardison, uncle of Charles Collins Teague, Chester W. Brown.

Hardy, Benjamin Franklin 1808–86, born: Kennebunk; left as an orphan at age four; A.B. Haverford College, M.D. University of Pennsylvania Medical School 1840, practiced in New Bedford, Massachusetts, for a few years before being appointed Royal Hawaiian court physician and physician in charge of the marine hospital of the Hawaiian Islands 1856–62; removed to San Francisco, established the San Francisco Lying-In Hospital and Foundlings Asylum, where he acted as manager, physician, and surgeon until his death.

Hardy, Sylvia 1823–88, born: Wilton; grew to well over seven feet tall and weighed over four hundred pounds, after working as a practical nurse became a giantess for P. T. Barnum for many years; she became particularly close to General and Mrs. Tom Thumb, who visited her often in Wilton after her retirement.

Harper, Joseph Morrill 1787–1865, born: Limerick; graduate: Freyburg Academy, studied medicine, practiced in Canterbury, New Hampshire; assistant surgeon:

4th Infantry, USA, during War of 1812; member: New Hampshire House of Representatives 1826–27, New Hampshire Senate 1829–30, president: New Hampshire Senate 1830, ex officio governor of New Hampshire 1831; member: U.S. House of Representatives 1831–35 (Jacksonian); justice of the peace and quorum 1835–65; president: Mechanics Bank of Concord 1847–56; his son, Charles Augustus Harper, was colonel in chief of the Texas Rangers during the war with Mexico; buried in Village Cemetery, Canterbury.

Harris, George 1844–1922, born: East Machias; son of a logger and mill owner, brother of Samuel Harris; graduate: Washington Academy, East Machias, A.B. Amherst College 1866, D.D. (Hon.) 1883, graduate: Andover Theological Seminary 1869, D.D. Harvard University 1899, L.L.D. Dartmouth College 1899, L.L.D. Wesleyan University; ordained Congregational ministry 1869, minister: High Street Congregational Church, Auburn, 1869–72, Center Church, Providence, Rhode Island, 1872–83; Abbot professor of Christian theology: Andover Theological Seminary 1883–99, president of the faculty 1896–99; an editor: *Andover Review* 1884–94; placed on trial 1886, with Egbert Smyth, for heterodoxy, acquitted by the Massachusetts Supreme Court, in 1892, after several years of litigation; president: Amherst College 1899–1912; editor: *Hymns of Faith* 1887, author: *Moral Evolution* 1896, *Inequality and Progress* 1897, *A Century of Change in Religion* 1914.

Harris, Samuel 1814–99, born: East Machias; brother of George Harris; A.B. Bowdoin College ΦBK 1833, L.L.D. (Hon.) 1871, D.D. Williams College 1855, student at Andover Theological Seminary 1835-38; principal: Limerick Academy 1833–34, ordained Congregational minister 1841, pastor: Congregational Church, Conway, Massachusetts, 1841–51, pastor: South Congregational Church, Pittsfield, Massachusetts, 1851–55; professor of systematic theology: Bangor Theological Seminary 1851–55; fifth president and professor of mental and moral philosophy, trustee and overseer ex-officio: Bowdoin College 1867–71; Dwight professor of systematic theology: Yale University Divinity School 1871–95; author: *Zaccheus: The Scriptural Plans of Beneficence* 1844, *Kingdom of Christ on Earth* 1874, *The Philosophical Basis of Theism* 1883, *The Self Revelation of God* 1886, *God the Creator and Lord of All* 1896, contributor to *Bibliotheca Sacra*.

Hartford, George Huntington 1833–1917, born: Augusta; removed to St. Louis, where he was hired by George F. Gilman, the son of a wealthy tanner and ship owner, to go to New York and purchase and resell clipper ship cargoes at cargo prices; by eliminating middlemen, the price of tea, in particular, was drastically lowered to the consumer; first sold tea by mail, offering money-back guarantees, developed a buyer's club, opened their first store in New York city 1859, employed promotional techniques: large, illuminated signs, elaborate interior decorations, brass bands, national advertising in magazines; added coffee and other groceries to the line; incorporated the Great Atlantic and Pacific Tea Co., the first national chain 1869, which by the twentieth century, was the largest retailer in the United States; used the new transcontinental railroad to provision stores; established a system of peddlers and distinctively painted wagons to serve rural areas; after the retirement of Gilman in 1878, Hartford, who had been general manager, and his sons, assumed control of the company; donated the Hartford Fire Station to the city of Augusta, built on the site of his birth; buried in the Rosedale Cemetery, Orange, New Jersey.

Hartley, Edmund Marsden 1877–1943, born: Lewiston; student: Cleveland School of Art, student of Nina Waldbeck, Kenyon Cox; member: Blue Rider Group, Munich; exhibited at Autumn Salon, Berlin, Armory Show, New York 1913, Dresden, Berlin, Provincetown 1916, Ogunquit 1917, Bermuda 1918, New Mexico 1919–20, lived in Provence 1926–28, New Hampshire 1930, Cape Cod 1931, Mexico and Berlin 1932–33, Maine 1934–35, Nova Scotia 1936, and settled in Maine 1937; his works hang in: the Museum of Modern Art and the Metropolitan Museum of Art, New York, Columbus Museum of Art, the Phillips collection, Hirshhorn Museum, and National Gallery of Art, Washington, Walker Art Museum, Minneapolis, Art Institute of Chicago, Cleveland Museum of Art, Philadelphia Museum of Art, Olin Arts Center, Bates College, Ogunquit Museum of American Art among others; author: *Twenty Five Poems* 1923, *Adventures in Art* 1921, *Androscoggin* 1940, *Sea Burial* 1941, *Autobiography*.

Harvey, Harold Brown 1884–1949, born: Parkman; B.S. Massachusetts Institute of Technology 1905; lecturer: Northwestern University School of Commerce; electrical engineer with Becker Brothers, Chicago, and chief engineer: American Maintenance Co. 1906; factory manager: Henry Newgard and Co., electric construction and manufacturing 1910–15; founder and president: Marquette Electric Switchboard Co.; president: Harvey Electric Co., brass forgings 1919–21; founder and president: Harvey Metal Corp. from 1923, aluminum, brass, and copper forgings for automotive, aircraft, railroad, and general industries; president: Burr Oak Coal Co.; inventor: magnetic metal separator and early high-voltage equipment, pioneer in aluminum and brass forging industry, originator of drop forgings of brass and various processes in the forging of nonferrous metals; president: Rotary Club of Chicago which originated and sponsored first Boys' Week in Chicago 1919–20; trustee: Massachusetts Institute of Technology; author: *Rotary's Message to Garcia, Renaissance of the Bronze Age*.

Haskell, Clement Caldwell 1847– ?, born: East Livermore; son of a merchant; attended public schools in Livermore, graduate: Livermore Academy 1871, M.D. Medical School of Maine 1875; practiced in Boston 1875–76, removed to Maitland, Florida, where he practiced medicine and maintained an orange grove; with three others, organized a company to build a railroad from Sanford to Tampa 1879, which attracted much attention, in that it was the, then, southernmost railroad in the United States, and the first spade full of earth was turned by President Grant 1880; after building forty miles of track, the Plant Investment Co., became involved and completed the road to Tampa 1885; Haskell served as director and treasurer to 1892; treasurer: Plant Steamship Co., which connected Tampa to Havana, Mobile, and South America; director: Associated Railway Land Department of Florida; resigned to devote his time to a wholesale butter, cheese, and grocery business in Sanford; founder, president: Sanford Loan & Trust Co.; trustee: Orange Belt Investment Co.; brother of Edwin Bradbury Haskell.

Haskell, Edwin Bradbury 1837–1907, born: Livermore; graduate: Maine Wesleyan Seminary, Kents Hill; entered the *Portland Advertiser* 1854, reporter for the *Boston Journal* 1857, *Boston Herald* 1860; purchased an interest in the *Herald* 1865, served as editor to 1887; purchased an interest in the *Minneapolis Journal*, partner of Alden Blethen; brother of Clement Caldwell Haskell.

Haskell, Henry Leland 1840–1908, born: Clinton; brother of Frank W. Haskell; in Civil War: enlisted as private: Company A, promoted to sergeant major 125th New York Infantry, rose to captain, USV, discharged for wounds 1864, reenlisted 1867, entered as second lieutenant, USA, assigned to the 12th U.S. Infantry; promoted through ranks to brigadier general, USA, 1904; served in campaigns against the Apaches in Arizona and the Nez Perce in Idaho; received the surrender of Geronimo at Fort Bowie, New Mexico, 1879, also present at the capture of Sitting Bull; in the Spanish-American War: led his battalion at El Caney, after which he was mentioned in the dispatches as heroic, later led his unit in the Philippines during the insurrection; placed in command of Fort Thomas, Kentucky; retired to San Francisco; buried in San Francisco National Cemetery; member: Sons of the American Revolution.

Haskell, Llewellyn Solomon 1815–72, born: New Gloucester; educated at the Gardiner Lyceum, became a druggist in Philadelphia 1834, formed a partnership with Thomas B. Merrick, removed to New York, where he became a noted entrepreneur, espoused a progressive philosophy of the interrelationship of man, nature, and community 1841; resided on the summit of Orange Mountain, New Jersey, 500 acres of which he subdivided into Llewellyn Park, the earliest planned community, with the assistance of the architect Alexander Jackson Davis, who also designed Haskell's villa "Eyrie" and numerous other large dwellings for the community; devoted the rest of his life to the landscaping of Llewellyn Park and construction of villas.

Haskin, William Lawrence 1841–1936, born: Houlton; son of an army officer; graduate: Mexico Academy, Oswego, New York 1852-57, C.E. Rensselaer Polytechnical Institute 1861; in the Civil War: promoted through the ranks from second lieutenant, USA, to brigadier general, USA, brevetted for Port Hudson for good conduct and gallant service throughout the war; after the war, served in New York, South Carolina, Maine, California, Oregon, and Connecticut; commanding officer: of a regiment in Cuba, commanding officer: all regular troops in Cuba 1902.

Hatch, Edward 1832–89, born: Bangor; sailor, graduate: Norwich (Vermont) Military Academy 1852; removed to Iowa, where he was a lumberman; in the Civil War: one of the first volunteers to arrive in Washington, put on duty at the White House, April 1861, ordered to take charge of a camp of instruction at Davenport, Iowa, commissioned captain, USV, 2nd Iowa Cavalry, USV, which he helped raise 12 August 1861, promoted to major, USV, 5 September 1861, lieutenant, USV, 11 September 1861, engaged at New Madrid and Island Number Ten; colonel, USA, commanding officer: 1st Brigade: engaged at the battles of Iuka, Corinth, Coffeville; on Grierson's Raid through central Mississippi, commanding officer: 5th Cavalry Division, Army of the Tennessee, severely wounded at Wyatt, in west Tennessee, succeeded in delaying Hood's invasion; brevetted major general, USV, and major general, USA, for the battles of Franklin and Nashville, where he and his division played a particularly distinguished role, mustered out 1866, commissioned colonel, USA, commanding officer: 9th Cavalry USA, a command that he held for twenty-three years, brevetted brigadier general and major general, USA, 1867; commanding officer: Department of Arizona and New Mexico 1876–80, president of the Ute investigating committee, which made a treaty with that tribe 1880, returned to New Mexico, where he took the field against the Apache chief, Victorio, whom he defeated; died on active duty at Fort Robinson, Nebraska, buried at the National Cemetery, Fort Leavenworth, Kansas.

Hatch, Rufus 1832–93, born: Wells; removed to Wisconsin 1851; laid first rails in Wisconsin; original member of Chicago Board of Trade; made unsuccessful attempt to take over the Chicago & Northwestern Railroad; removed to New York, managed the highly successful Northwestern Pool; in a series of *Rufus Hatch's Circular* attacked the Vanderbilt interests in general and stock watering in particular; organized the Open Board of Brokers, which posed such a threat to the stock exchange that it was subsumed by the stock exchange and Hatch was offered its presidency, which he refused; president: Pacific Mail Steamship Line, Iron Steamboat Co.; attempted to purchase Yellowstone National Park from the United States government; referred to as Uncle Rufus; affected clerical garb; expert organist; coined the terms "bears," "bulls," and "lambs" of Wall Street.

Hawes, Jesse 1843–1901, born: Corinna; attended public schools in Corinna and Belvidere, Illinois; in the Civil War: private, 9th Illinois Cavalry, USV, served 1861–65, engaged in the campaigns in Missouri, Arkansas, and Mississippi, wounded at Jacksonport, Arkansas, 1862, later captured at Pontotoc, Mississippi, taken to various Confederate prisons and finally to Cahaba Prison, Selma, Alabama, where he was incarcerated for nine months before being exchanged, later wrote a book *Cahaba*

1888, where he detailed his life as a prisoner of war; M.D. University of Michigan Medical School 1868, M.D. Long Island College Hospital, Brooklyn, New York, 1871; studied physical diagnosis at Bellevue Hospital, New York, postgraduate work in antiseptic surgery with Joseph Lister in London, diseases of women at Mount Sinai Hospital, New York, 1880, studied at the New York Post-Graduate Medical School and Hospital 1890; established a private practice of general medicine and surgery in Greeley, Colorado, 1872; professor of obstetrics: University of Denver Medical School 1890–92; surgeon for the Colorado & Southern Railway Co., Union Pacific Railroad Co.; credited with the invention of several surgical instruments and appliances; president: Union Bank, Greeley 1877–1901; author of numerous articles for medical journals, including: "A New Compressor Testis" 1884, "Ovarian Hernia" 1886, "Typhoid Fever" 1890, "A New Splint for Nasal Fractures and Deformities" 1887, "The Local Use of Guaia in the Treatment of Frequent, Painful Urination" 1900; a trustee and regent: Colorado State Normal School (later University of Northern Colorado); vice president: American Medical Association 1893, president: Colorado Medical Association 1884–85, president: Colorado State Board of Medical Examiners 1889–90.

Hawkins, Dexter Arnold 1825–86, born: Canton; son of a Universalist minister, his maternal grandfather was in the crew of the *Bonhomme Richard* in its fight with HMS *Serapis* 1779; early showed a marked ability in mathematics, appointed, at age sixteen, as a civil engineer, by Oxford County, to lay out a new road, taught mathematics at Bethel Academy, Bridgton Academy, A.B. Bowdoin College 1848; lecturer on public instruction at the Maine State Normal School 1848–52; principal: Topsham Academy 1849; read law in the office of William Pitt Fessenden; student: *L'École des Drôits* in Paris, Harvard University Law School; commissioned by the governor of Maine to study the schools, systems, and methods of instruction in Germany, France, and Austria; practiced law in New York City from 1854; during the Civil War, assisted in the raising of two regiments, active in the care of returning wounded and sick soldiers; active in establishing U.S. Department of Education 1867; advocated a system of independently controlled public schools; drew up Act to Secure to Children the Benefits of Elementary Education, passed by New York State 1874; instrumental in driving the Tweed Ring from power and correcting other political irregularities in New York City; author: *Sectarian Appropriations of Public Moneys and Properties*, wherein he demonstrated severe antagonism to the success of the Roman Catholic church in obtaining such appropriations, *Extravagances of the Tammany Ring* 1871, *Traditions of Overlook Mountain* 1873, *The Roman Catholic Church in New York City and the Public Lands and Public Money* 1880, *Free Trade and Protection* 1883, *The Redemption of the Trade Dollar* 1886; published many papers and articles on the subjects of bimetallism, silver and other financial matters; delivered an address before the Committee on Coinage of the U.S. House of Representatives, entitled *The Silver Problem* 1886; delivered an address before Syracuse University, entitled *The Anglo-Saxon Race, Its History, Character and Destiny* 1875.

Hawthorne, Frank Warren 1852– ?, born: Bath; attended public school in Bath, A.B. Bowdoin College 1874; managed father's business for eleven years, occasional contributor to newspapers and journals, composed and read a poem at the Bath Centennial Celebration 1881; an earnest Democrat, appointed to Governor Plaisted's military staff as lieutenant 1881–85; removed to Florida, where he founded the *Jacksonville* (Florida) *Morning News* 1885, secretary and treasurer: News Publishing Co., editor: *News-Herald* 1888, organized the Florida Publishing Co., editor: *Times-Union* from 1888, remained at his post during great yellow fever epidemic, surviving while most of his coworkers died; Hawthorne, Florida, named in his honor.

Hayden, Cyrus 1843– ?, born: York; carpenter, USN, recipient: Medal of Honor, "on board the USS *Colorado* during the attack and capture of the Korean forts, 11 June 1871. Serving as a color bearer of the battalion, Hayden planted his flag on the ramparts of the citadel and protected it under heavy fire from the enemy."

Hayes, John Lord 1812–87, born: South Berwick; son of an attorney, nephew of Nathan Lord; graduate: Berwick Academy, A.B. Dartmouth College 1831, L.L.D. 1860, student at Harvard University Law School 1833–34; member: New Hampshire bar 1835, practiced in Portsmouth; clerk: U.S. Circuit Court of New Hampshire; author: *The Probable Influence of Icebergs Upon Drift* 1844; member: Boston Society of Natural History 1845; organized the Katahdin Ironworks 1846, employed by the Canadian government as consul in Washington for the advocacy of the reciprocity treaty, appointed to represent New England iron manufacturers in Congress to receive tariff and protection 1846; removed to Washington 1851, organized and was secretary of the Mexican, Rio Grande and Pacific Railway Co., obtained a charter from the Mexican government for a railroad to cross Mexico to the Pacific 1854; appointed by President Lincoln as chief clerk, U.S. Patent Office 1861–65; secretary: National Association of Wool Manufactures, lobbied to raise wool tariff 1867, first business interest to be so organized; editor: *Bulletin of the National Association of Wool Manufacturers*; chairman: U.S. Tariff Commission from 1882; his recommendations incorporated in tariff of 1883; a gifted taxidermist, studied geology, his paper on glaciation, presented before the American Association of Geologists in 1843, was regarded as the most advanced in its day; author of some sixty works, including: *The Iron Mines of Nova Scotia, Jackson's Vindication as the Inventor of Anaesthetics, The Hudson Bay Question, The Protective Question Abroad and at Home, Sheep Industry in the South, Reminiscences of the Free-Soil Movement in New Hampshire* 1843, many papers and pamphlets on wool growing and manufacture; buried in Mt. Auburn Cemetery, Cambridge, Massachusetts.

Hayes, Joseph 1835–1912, born: South Berwick; graduate: Phillips Academy, Andover, A.B. Harvard College 1855; removed to Wisconsin, where he engaged in banking, later in Iowa, he practiced civil engineering, returning to Boston, where he was a real estate broker; in the Civil War: major 18th Massachusetts Regiment, USV, 1861, promoted through the ranks to brigadier general, USV, 1864, commanding officer: 1st Division, V Corps, distinguished himself at Sharpsburg, Fredericksburg (where his regiment charged Maryes Heights three times), Chancellorsville, and Gettysburg; at the battle of the Wilderness, he was severely wounded by a bullet that left a deep furrow in his skull, recommended by both Generals Warren and Meade for promotion to brigadier general, USA; taken prisoner during General Warren's attempt to seize the Weldon Railroad in the siege of Petersburg, confined at Libby Prison for several months, after his exchange, made U.S. commissioner of supplies in seceded states 1865, commanding officer: 1st Brigade of Ayress 2nd Division, V Corps, present at the surrender at Appomattox; brevetted major general, USA, declined a commission in the regular army, mustered out 1865; mining engineer in Colorado, introduced hydraulic mining to Columbia, became the president of a coal mining company; suffering from his head wound, became a recluse in a small Pennsylvania town, died in Bloomingdale's sanitarium, New York, buried in South Berwick.

Hayes, Thomas Sumner 1902–59, born: Bath; Ph.B. Georgetown University 1924; teacher in Ponce and San Juan (Puerto Rico) high schools 1924–27, principal: Humaçao High School, Arecibo 1927–32, instructor in English: University of Puerto Rico 1931–41, assistant professor 1941–42, professor of English literature and university librarian from 1942; secretary to the governor of Puerto Rico 1942–43; columnist: *El Mundo de San Juan* 1949–51.

Healey, James Augustine 1830–1900, born near Macon, Georgia; son of an Irish immigrant plantation owner and a former black slave; student at Quaker schools in Flushing, Long Island, and Burlington, New Jersey; first graduate of Holy Cross, Worcester, Massachusetts, 1849; studied in Montréal and Paris 1849–54; secretary to Bishop John Fitzpatrick, Boston 1854–57; an interesting aspect of his life was that with his father's death in 1855, Healey and his siblings, all of whom were members of Catholic orders, inherited numerous slaves and land, rather than manumit the slaves, they were sold, along with the plantations, making Healey and his siblings comfortable for the rest of their lives; rector of the Cathedral of the Holy Cross, Boston 1857–66, St. James Church, Boston 1866–75; second bishop of Portland 1875–1900, originally, his see included New Hampshire, as well as Maine; in 1884 New Hampshire became a separate diocese; first black Roman Catholic bishop in the United States.

Healy, James Augustine 1890–1975, born: Portland; born in the same room as was Henry Wadsworth Longfellow and named for Bishop Healy; son of a steward and purser on various passenger vessels; attended the North School until removing with his parents to New York city 1903; became a page on the floor of the New York Stock

Exchange 1904, gained a reputation for being the youngest telephone clerk on the floor, eventually engaged by the firm of Shearson, Hammill & Co.; during World War I, served as secretary to Herbert Hoover, director of the Commission for Relief in Belgium (later American Relief Administration), awarded by Belgium the Order of the Crown; served as secretary of the American Committee for Relief in Ireland 1920–22; purchased a seat on the New York Stock Exchange 1924, partner: Kinkead, Florentino & Co., set a record for most shares sold in one hour (160,000); maintained a summer home on Chebeague Island; began making large bequests to Mercy Hospital 1947, which named a portion of itself the John and Catherine Healy Memorial Wing; made bequests of modern art by Reginald Marsh, Arthur Davies, George Luks, George Bellows, Eugene Higgins, and Edward Steichen to the Portland Museum of Art (then the L. D. M. Swett Museum); donated to Colby College what came to be known as the James Augustine Healy collection of nineteenth- and twentieth-century literature, which contains one of the finest collections of Irish literature and printing anywhere; awarded a doctorate in humane letters by 1955 Colby College; spoke out publicly against plans for an oil refinery in Casco Bay.

Heath, Daniel Collamore 1843–1908, born: Salem; attended public schools in

Salem and Farmington, Nichols Latin School, Lewiston, A.B. Amherst College 1868, A.M. 1871; principal: Southboro (Massachusetts) High School 1868–70, student at Bangor Theological Seminary 1870–72, Farmington superintendent of schools 1873–74; representative for the book publishing firm of Ginn Brothers, Rochester, 1874, opened a branch in New York 1875, became a member of the firm, whose name was changed to Ginn & Heath Co. 1876, after re-organization 1886; president: D. C. Heath and Co., the largest producer of textbooks in the world; selected by the University of Chicago to take charge of the publications of University of Chicago Press and publications of the various departments and schools of the university.

Henry, Frank Forrest 1870–1961, born aboard the clipper ship *Apersham* in the

Indian Ocean, raised in Thomaston, where he attended public schools, removed to Buffalo, New York, 1887; employed by the Lehigh Valley Transportation Co. 1887; the company operated a fleet of lake steamers; Henry acquired a familiarity with the Buffalo waterfront and the shipment of flour, made assistant general manager 1892, left the company 1893; associated with Washburn, Crosby Co. (John Crosby, Cadwallader Washburn), a milling concern of Minneapolis, Minnesota; placed in charge of the Buffalo project, where Washburn, Crosby built mills and the immense grain silos that still grace the Buffalo waterfront, with the result that Buffalo became the largest flour-milling and exporting center in the world; director: Washburn, Crosby 1910, vice president 1924, executive vice president 1925, with the reorganization of Crosby, Washburn into General Mills 1928, Washburn, Crosby became its Buffalo subsidiary, president 1928–31, chairman of the board 1931–37, an original director of General Mills 1928–49, chairman of General Mills operating board 1928–36, which had overall charge of the company's operating policy; director: Great Northern Railroad Co., Buffalo, Rochester & Pittsburgh Railway Co., Keystone Warehouse, Manufacturers & Traders Trust Co.; trustee: Erie County Savings Bank, trustee, president: Forest Lawn Cemetery 1938–52, trustee: Buffalo Orphan Asylum.

Herrick, Anson 1812–68, born: Lewiston; son of Ebenezer Herrick; printer, founder, and editor: *Citizen,* Wiscasset, 1833, *New York Atlas,* New York, 1838; member: New York City Board of Alderman 1854–56; naval storekeeper, New York 1857–61; member: U.S. House of Representatives (Democrat) 1863–65; delegate: Union National Convention, Philadelphia 1866; buried in Green-Wood Cemetery, Brooklyn.

Hersey, Ira Greenlief 1858–1943, born: Hodgdon; graduate: Ricker Classical Institute; member: Maine bar 1880, practiced in Houlton; unsuccessful Prohibitionist candidate for governor 1886; member: Maine House of Representatives 1909–12, member: Maine Senate 1913–16, president 1915–16; member: U.S. House of Representatives, Fourth District 1917–29 (Republican), chairman: Committee on Expenditures for Public Buildings; judge of probate: Aroostook County 1934–42; buried in Evergreen Cemetery, Houlton.

Hersey, Mark Leslie 1863–1934, born: Stetson; A.B. Bates College 1884, graduate: U.S. Military Academy 1887, A.M. Bates College 1902, L.L.D. (Hon.) 1919, University of Maine 1921; commissioned second lieutenant, 19th Infantry 1887, served with the 9th Infantry in Arizona to 1891, professor of military science and tactics: University of Maine 1891–95, served in Cuba during the Spanish-American War, served with the 9th Infantry in the Philippine Insurrection and in the Boxer Rebellion in China, promoted through ranks to major general, USA, 1919; with Philippine Constabulary 1909–14, chief: Mindinao Constabulary 1909–14, in World War I: commanding officer: 155th Infantry 1917, participated in the St. Mihiel and Meuse Argonne offensives, commanding officer: 4th Division: march to Rhein, Army of Occupation; represented the American Expeditionary Forces at the Versailles Peace Conference; awarded the D.S.M., Légion d'Honneur, croix de guerre with palm, retired 1924; the U.S. Navy launched a transport, USS *General M. L. Hersey* (AP-116), named in his honor, in 1944; she was accorded one battle star for World War II and two for Korea.

Hersey, Samuel Freeman 1812–75, born: Sumner; son of a farmer; graduate: Hebron Academy 1831, removed to Bangor; in lumber business in Lincoln, Milford, and Stillwater; came to own 75,000 acres of timberland in Wisconsin and Minnesota; founded Stillwater, Minnesota, where he built extensive sawmills; member: Maine House of Representatives 1842, 1857, 1865, 1867, 1869; member: executive council 1852-54; delegate: Republican National Convention 1860, 1864; member: Republican National Committee 1864–68; member: Maine Senate 1868–69; member from the Fourth District: U.S. House of Representatives 1873–75, died in office; buried in Mount Hope Cemetery, Bangor; in his will, left large bequests to the Bangor Public Library and Westbrook Seminary, established a summer retreat on the Penobscot for the Universalist Sunday School of Bangor.

Hesseltine, Francis Snow 1833–1916, born: Bangor; A.B. Waterville College 1863 (as of 1866); in the Civil War: commissioned captain, USV, rose in rank to lieutenant colonel, USV, commanding officer: 13th Maine Infantry, recipient: Medal of Honor, at Matagorda Bay, Texas, 29–30 December 1863, "In command of a detachment of one hundred men, conducted a reconnaissance for two days, baffling and beating back an attacking force of more than a thousand Confederate cavalry, and regained his transport without loss." Later held public office in Georgia; buried in Wyoming Cemetery, Melrose, Massachusetts.

Heywood, Charles 1839–1915, born: Waterville; commissioned second lieutenant, USMC 1858, stationed at the Brooklyn Navy Yard; sent to Staten Island to quell quarantine riots; stationed aboard the USS *Niagara*, involved in repatriating Africans taken from slavers; then at Greytown, Nicaragua, guarding the captured filibusterer, William Walker; during the Civil War, commanding officer: marine detachment on board USS *Cumberland*, took his detachment into Norfolk to fire the navy yard, personally fired the last gun as she sank in her battle with CSS *Virginia* (ex-USS *Merrimac*), brevetted major, USMC for this action; at Hatteras Inlet and at the capture of Forts Clark and Hatteras; commanding officer: marine detachment on board the USS *Hartford* at Mobile Bay, where he was brevetted lieutenant colonel, USMC, for distinguished gallantry, took part in the capture of Forts Morgan, Gaines, and Powell, and the ram CSS *Tennessee*; after the war, fleet marine officer, European station, aboard USS *Franklin* 1867, fleet marine officer, North Atlantic station, commanding officer: a force of 1,000 marines, based at Key West, in anticipation of war with Spain and deployment to Cuba 1876, commanding officer: marine barracks, Washington, during labor riots was sent to Baltimore, Reading, and Philadelphia, commanding officer: marine barracks, Mare Island, California, 1880–83, Brooklyn Navy Yard 1883–85, commanding officer: two battalions of marines and a battery of naval artillery sent to Panama during a revolution there 1885, so hazardous was his duty there that he received the thanks of the commander in chief of the North Atlantic station and of the secretary of the navy; appointed colonel commandant of the Marine Corps 1891, raised to brigadier general, USMC, 1899, becoming the first Marine Corps general officer 1899; major general, USMC, 1902, retired 1903; during his tenure as commandant repeatedly fought off Congressional attempts to disband the corps, of which he tripled the size; buried in Arlington National Cemetery; in 1940, the U.S. Navy commissioned USS *Heywood*, which received twelve battle stars during World War II.

Higgins, Milton Prince 1842–1912, born: Standish; son of a farmer and mechanic; student: Standish and Gorham academies; apprenticed in the machine shops of the Amoskeag Manufacturing Co., Manchester, New Hampshire; B.S. Dartmouth College 1868; draftsman and engineer: Washburn and Moen Manufacturing Co., Worcester, 1868; superintendent: Washburn shops at the Worcester Free Institute (later Worcester Polytechnical Institute) 1869–96; a pioneer in industrial training, many of his methods were adopted throughout the country; his address "The Education of Machinists, Foreman, and Mechanical Engineers," delivered before the American Society of Mechanical Engineers 1899, was enthusiastically received, reprinted, and disseminated throughout the country; founder and president: Norton Emery Wheel Co. (later, the Norton Co.) from 1885, Norton came to be the preeminent manufacturer of grinding wheels and abrasives in the world, with manufacturing facilities in Worcester, Germany, France, Great Britain, and Canada; founder and president: Plunger Elevator Co. 1896–1904, when it was sold to the Otis Elevator Co.; founder and president: Worcester Pressed Steel Co. from 1904.

Hilborn, Samuel Greeley 1834–99, born: Minot; student: Hebron Academy, Goulds Academy; A.B. Tufts University 1859; member: Maine bar 1861, removed to California, practiced law in Vallejo; member: California Senate 1875–79, delegate: California Constitutional Convention 1879; removed to San Francisco; U.S. district attorney for the district of California 1883–86, removed to Oakland 1887; member: U.S. House of Representatives 1892–94, 1895–99 (Republican); unsuccessful candidate for reelection 1898; lived in retirement in Washington, D.C.; buried in Rock Creek Cemetery, Washington.

Hildreth, Horace Augustus 1902–88, born: Gardiner; son of an attorney; A.B. Bowdoin College 1925, L.L.B. Harvard University Law School 1928; joined the law firm of Ropes, Gray, Best, Coolidge & Rugg, Boston, later settled in Portland; member: Maine House of Representatives 1940–42; Maine Senate 1942–1944, president 1943–44; governor of Maine (Republican) 1945–49, chairman: New England Governors' Conference 1947, National Governors' Conference 1947–48; unsuccessful candidate for the Republican nomination for U.S. Senate 1948; president: Bucknell University 1949–67; U.S. ambassador to Pakistan 1953–57.

Hill, Frank Alpine 1841–1903, born: Biddeford; A.B. Bowdoin College ΦBK 1861, Litt.D. (Hon.) 1894; principal: Limington Academy, principal: high schools in Biddeford, Milford, Massachusetts, and Chelsea, Massachusetts, 1861–86; headmaster: English High School, Cambridge, Massachusetts, 1886–93; secretary: Massachusetts Board of Education 1893–1903, successor to Horace Mann, strove mightily to improve Massachusetts public schools, introduced teacher certification, improved teacher training, &c.; active in promotion of the interests of the adult blind; trustee: Boston Museum of Fine Arts, Massachusetts Institute of Technology, Massachusetts

Agricultural College; editor: *Holmes' Fourth Reader* 1888 *Holmes' Fifth Reader* 1889; coauthor: *Civil Government of the United States* 1890, *History of the United States for Schools* 1894; author: *Seven Lamps for the Teacher's Way.*

Hill, James 1734–1811, born: Kittery; shipbuilder; at age twenty, enlisted for the Crown Point Expedition 1755, built boats for the Hudson River and Lake George; kept a diary which remains the major source of information about William Johnson and Rogers Rangers; shipwright: HMS *Achilles* to Jamaica, England, and America; settled in Newmarket, New Hampshire, 1761; shipbuilder, landowner, held numerous public offices, signed Association Pact of 1776, petition to Committee of Safety to deal with Tories; captain, Pierce's Island defense; part of General Sullivan's defense of Portsmouth; lieutenant New Hampshire militia in company against Burgoyne at Saratoga; colonel 1784, brigadier general 1788; member: New Hampshire Provisional Congress 1775; first member of first legislature 1784; member: New Hampshire Constitutional Convention 1792.

Hill, John Fremont 1855–1912, born: Eliot; son of a farmer, attended public school in Eliot, M.D. Medical School of Maine 1877, did his training at Long Island College Hospital, Brooklyn, New York; practiced in Boothbay Harbor for a year, removed to Augusta 1879; associated with his father-in-law, Peleg O. Vickery in publishing periodicals; president: Vickery & Hill Publishing Co., with branch offices in Boston, New York, and Chicago; member: Maine House of Representatives 1889–92, chairman of the Committee on Railroads; member: Maine Senate 1893–97, chairman of the Committee on Railroads; Republican presidential elector 1896; member: executive council 1899–1900; governor of Maine (Republican) 1901–05; a leading promoter of the Augusta, Hallowell & Gardiner Electric Railroad, the Rockland, Thomaston & Camden Street Railway, also associated with the Quincy (Illinois) Gas & Electric Co., the Decatur (Illinois) Gas & Electric Co., the Peoria (Illinois) Gas & Electric Co., large electric railway and lighting properties in Indiana, the Rockland-Rockport Lime Co.; president: Augusta National Bank; trustee: Augusta Savings Bank, Kennebec Savings Bank; his first wife, Lizzie Vickery, was the daughter of P. O. Vickery, his second wife, Laura Colman Ligget, was the daughter of Norman Colman, U.S. secretary of agriculture under Grover Cleveland; buried in Forest Grove Cemetery, Augusta.

Hill, Lysander 1834–1914, born: Union; A.B. Bowdoin College 1858, A.M. 1861; member: Maine bar 1860, practiced in Thomaston, taking Jonathan Prince Cilley as partner; in the Civil War: captain Company I, 20th Maine VOL 1862–63, invalided home because of typhoid fever; practiced patent law in Alexandria, Virginia, and Washington, D.C.; register of bankruptcy: Eighth Judicial District, Virginia 1867–68; judge: circuit court 1869–70; chairman: Virginia Republican State Committee 1867–69; delegate: Republican National Convention 1868; removed to Chicago

1881; devoted himself to patent law to 1904; gained a national reputation, when he appeared before the U.S. Supreme Court in the celebrated Bell Telephone case and for his successful defense of George Westinghouse and his patent on the air brake; author: *The Two Great Questions — The Existence of God and The Immortality of the Soul* 1909.

Hill, William G. 1881–1958, born: Chebeague Island; after attending grammar school on Chebeague, became nationally known as a crack rifle shot, after besting Annie Oakley in a competition at Rangely Lakes, where he hit 99 out of 100 clay pigeons, Oakley hit 88; recommended by Oakley to the Remington Arms Co., he was hired by them and served for 40 years as their New England sales representative; monopolized for 25 years New England and Canadian shooting titles; as a demonstrator, astounded watchers by his ability to split a playing card, held sidewise, in two; on at least one occasion hit 500 thrown glass balls, without a miss; during World War I, founded the Hill Tackle Co., in World War II: served as a rifle instructor to an estimated 2.5 million Army enlisted men.

Hillard, George Stillman 1808–79, born: Machias; A.B. Harvard College 1828, A.M. 1831, L.L.B. Harvard University Law School 1832, L.L.D. (Hon.) Trinity (Hartford) College 1857; member: Massachusetts bar 1833; editor: *The Jurist, The Christian Register*, purchased an interest in the *Boston Courier* and served as assistant editor 1856–61; member: Massachusetts House of Representatives 1835; president: Boston Common Council 1846–47; delivered a series of twelve lectures before the Lowell Institute 1847; member: Massachusetts Senate 1850; delegate: Massachusetts Constitutional Convention 1853; Boston city solicitor 1854–55; U.S. attorney for Massachusetts 1866–71; member, board of overseers: Harvard University 1871–75; author: *Memorial of Daniel Webster* 1853, *Six Months in Italy* 1863, *Political Duties of the Educated Classes* 1866, *Life and Campaigns of George B. McClellan* 1864, *Life of George Ticknor* 1873; editor: *The Poetical Works of Edmund Spencer* (five volumes) 1835; translator: Guizot's *Essay on Character and the Influence of George Washington* 1840.

Hinckley, George Walter 1853–1950; born: Guilford, Connecticut; student: Guilford Institute, Connecticut State Normal School, A.M. (Hon.) Colby College 1912, L.L.D. 1939, D.D. Bowdoin College 1927; ordained Baptist minister 1880, pastor: West Hartford, Connecticut, 1880–82, Windsor, Connecticut, 1882–84, missionary in Maine for three years; founder and editor: *Good Will Record*, founder: Goodwill Home and School, Fairfield; author: *Story of Good Will Farm* 1892, *Good Will Short Talks* 1901, *Some Boys I Know* 1902, *Something Happened* 1903, *Story of Dan McDonald* 1904, *In Camp with Boys* 1908, *Some Good Will Boys* 1910, *Roughing It with Boys* 1912, *Letters From Applehurst* 1923, *A Long Trip at Home* 1926, *Camping In* 1927, *Ten Nights in a Bungalow* 1928, *The Weekadays Feast* 1929, *My Friends the Trees* 1930, *A Month of Forestry* 1931, *In Sunset Park* 1932, *At Good Will East* 1933, *Reinsophy* 1934, *As I Re-*

member It 1935, *Fifty Years with the Good Will Record* 1937, *The Man of Whom I Write*.

Hincks, Edward Winslow 1830–94, born: Bucksport; removed to Bangor 1845, became a printer for the *Whig & Courier*, removed to Boston 1849, member: Massachusetts House of Representatives 1855, in the Civil War: on 18 December 1860, wrote to Major Robert Anderson, commanding officer of Forts Sumter and Moultrie, and offered to him a volunteer force, appointed second lieutenant, USA, 1861, lieutenant and colonel of the 8th Massachusetts Volunteer Infantry (a ninety-day regiment of Massachusetts militia), which on the march to Washington, saved the frigate USS *Constitution* from destruction by a secessionist mob in Annapolis and repaired the railway and bridge at Annapolis Junction; colonel of the 19th Massachusetts Infantry, one of the regiments involved in the disaster at Balls Bluff; during the Peninsular campaign, wounded at Glendale, warmly commended by generals Burns and Sedgwick; wounded twice at Sharpsburg, brigadier general, USV, 1862, while convalescing, served on recruiting and court martial duty, commanding officer: prison camp at Camp Lookout, Maryland, 1864, commanding officer: a Negro division of the XVIII Corps in the Petersburg campaign, on recruitment and draft duty until his resignation 1865, commissioned lieutenant colonel, USA, 1866, assigned to the 40th Infantry, USA, later to the 25th Infantry, USA, retired with the rank of colonel, USA, brevetted brigadier general, USA, and major general, USA; governor of the National Home for Disabled Volunteers at Hampton, Virginia, to 1873, transferred to a similar post at Milwaukee, Wisconsin, to 1880; retired to Cambridge, Massachusetts, buried in Mt. Auburn Cemetery.

Hincks, Edward Young 1844–1927, born: Bucksport; brother of William B. Hincks; A.B. Yale College 1866 (member: Skull and Bones), A.M. 1883, student at Union Theological Seminary 1866–67, B.D. Andover Theological Seminary 1870, D.D. Yale University 1885; ordained Congregational minister 1870, pastor: State Street Church, Portland 1870–81, professor of biblical theology: Andover Theological Seminary 1908–1919, professor of biblical literature: Harvard University from 1919; author: *Progressive Orthodoxy* 1886, *The Divinity of Christ* 1893.

Hincks, William Bliss 1841–1903, born: Bucksport; brother of Edward Young Hincks; sergeant major (highest rank: major) 14th Connecticut Infantry, recipient: Medal of Honor, "During the highwater mark of Picketts charge on 3 July 1863, the colors of the 14th Tennessee C.S.A. were planted fifty yards in front of the center of SGT Major Hincks's regiment. There were no Confederates standing near it but several were lying down around it. Upon a call for volunteers by Major Ellis, commanding, to capture this flag, this soldier and two others leaped the wall. One companion was instantly shot. SGT Major Hincks outran his remaining companion, running straight and swift for the colors amid a storm of shot. Swinging his saber over the prostrate Confederates and uttering a terrific yell, he seized the flag and hastily returned to his lines. The 14th Tennessee carried twelve battle honors on its flag. The devotion to duty shown by SGT Major Hincks gave encouragement to many of his comrades at a crucial moment of the battle." Buried in Grove Cemetery, Bridgeport, Connecticut.

Hinds, Asher Crosby 1863–1919, born: Benton; graduate: Coburn Classical Institute, Waterville, A.B. Colby College 1883, L.L.D. (Hon.) 1906; member: editorial staff, *Portland Daily Advertiser* 1884–85, *Portland Press* 1885–1902; speakers clerk: U.S. House of Representatives 1889–91, parliamentary clerk: U.S. House of Representatives 1895–1911; member from the 1st District: U.S. House of Representatives 1911–17 (Republican); editor: *Rules, Manual, and Digest of the House of Representatives, Parliamentary Precedents of the House of Representatives* 1899, *Hinds's Precedents of the House of Representatives* 1908; Hinds's immense work, consisting of eight volumes of 1,000 pages each, with 40,000 footnotes, had an immense influence on the work of the Congress; parliamentarian: Republican National Convention 1900, 1904, 1908; trustee: Colby College; buried in Evergreen Cemetery, Portland.

Hinkley, Holmes 1793–1866, born: Hallowell; apprenticed at age fourteen to a carpenter; removed to Boston 1815, maker of patterns for machinery 1823, established a machine shop on Boston Neck 1826, built the first steam locomotive made in New England; began to construct, in 1840, the Hinkley-style locomotive, utilizing a new and ingenious design and his fuel-efficient boiler; established the Hinkley Locomotive Works, in Boston 1848, which became, in the 1850s, one of the major locomotive concerns in the country; retired 1857; during the Civil War: made shot and shell for the federal government; established the Hinkley and Williams Works in 1864; his locomotive *Lion*, originally constructed for the Whitneyville and Machias Railroad in 1846, is on display in the Maine State Museum in Augusta and is considered to be the oldest locomotive, extant, in New England and ninth in the country.

Hiscock, Ira Vaughn 1892–1986, born: Farmington; A.B. Wesleyan University 1914, A.M. 1916, Sc.D. (Hon.) 1939, M.P.H. Yale University 1921, A.M. 1931, M.D. Connecticut Medical Society 1933; bacteriologist: Connecticut Department of Health 1914–17; in World War I: first lieutenant, USA, 1918–19, in World War II: colonel, USA, 1942, chief of public health, civil affairs division, U.S. War Department 1943–45; member of faculty: Yale University 1920–60, professor of public health *emeritus* 1960–86; author: *Health and Welfare in Honolulu, Hawaii* 1929, *Public Health in Hawaii* 1935, *Ways to Community Health Education* 1939, *District Health Administration* 1936, *Practitioner's Library of Preventive Medicine*; contributor of health surveys, articles to scientific magazines; member: New Haven Board of Health from 1928, president 1942; president: Connecticut State Public Health League 1951–52; vice chairman: Health Committee, National Boy Scouts of America; member: Connecticut State Public Health Council from 1952; president: National Health Council 1938–40; vice president: National Social Welfare Assembly; sometime officer in several national health affiliated agencies; president: Accredited School of Public Health 1957, National Society for the Prevention of Blindness 1958; member, Health Administration Commission: World Health Organization 1951–66; decorated: Legion of Merit, recipient: Sedgwick Medal, American Public Health Association; president: American Public Health Association 1955–56.

Hitchcock, Roswell Dwight 1817–87, born: East Machias; graduate: Washington Academy, A.B. Amherst College 1836, D.D. Bowdoin College 1855, University of Edinburgh 1885, L.L.D. Williams College 1873, Harvard University 1886, student at Andover Theological Seminary 1836–39, tutor at Amherst College 1839–42; ordained Congregational minister 1845, pastor: First Congregational Church, Exeter, New Hampshire, 1845–52; Collins professor of natural and revealed religion: Bowdoin College 1852–55; Washburn professor of church history: Union Theological Seminary 1855–87, president 1880–87; an editor: *American Theological Review* 1863–70, president: Palestine Exploration Society, trustee: Amherst College; author: *Life of Edward Robinson* 1862, *Complete Analysis of the Holy Bible* 1869, *Hymns and Songs of Praise* 1874, *Socialism* 1879, *Eternal Atonement* 1888.

Hobbs, John Edward 1829–1919, born: North Berwick; brother of Ichabod Goodwin Hobbs; farmer from boyhood, manufacturer of attachable steel sleigh runners (his invention) from 1885, manufacturer of his patented double-ender spring sleigh; vice president: American Forestry Association; author of the Maine forest law (which became the model for other states); chairman of the forestry commission which pressured President Benjamin Harrison to withdraw 100 million acres of federal land from sale and create a U.S. forest reserve.

Holden, Carl Frederick 1895–1953, born: Bangor; B.S. U.S. Naval Academy 1917, M.S. Harvard University 1924; commissioned ensign, USN, 1917, promoted through the ranks to rear admiral, USN, 1945, vice admiral, USN, 1952; duty in destroyers, Queenstown, Ireland, and Brest, France, 1917–19; executive officer, navigator, engineering officer 1919–22; on staff of commanding officer: destroyer scouting force, Atlantic 1924–27; member: U.S. Naval Mission to Brazil, Rio de Janeiro 1927–30; communications officer: USS *Arizona* 1931–32; commanding officer: USS *Tarbell* 1932–34; district communications officer, 14th Naval District, Honolulu 1934–36; navigator: USS *Idaho*; commanding officer: USS *Ramapo* 1936–38; in charge of radio shore activities, office of director of naval communications, Department of the Navy, Washington 1938–40; executive officer: USS *Pennsylvania* 1940–42 (present at Pearl Harbor attack, 7 December 1941); communication officer: U.S. Fleet 1942, director of naval communications 1942–43; commanding officer: USS *New Jersey* (first commander or plankholder), task force 38 and 58, Pacific 1943–45; commanding officer: cruiser division 18, Pacific; commanding officer: training command,

Atlantic Fleet 1946–52; commanding officer: U.S. Naval Base, New York 1948–52; president: Federal Telecommunication Laboratory from 1952; awarded Legion of Merit with gold star in lieu of 2nd V for combat, Bronze Star with gold star in lieu of second V for combat, Asian Pacific Medal with eleven stars, Philippine Liberation Medal with two stars.

Holden, Joseph W. 1816–1900, born: Otisfield, sawmill and gristmill operator; gained national fame as a proponent of the theory that the earth is flat; lectured widely, including the Maine State Fair, Lewiston, 1892, the Columbian Exposition, Chicago 1893, Bowdoin College 1896; conducted several experiments that proved the validity, to his satisfaction, of his theory; his tombstone reads "Prof. Joseph W. Holden—Born Otisfield Aug. 24, 1816: March 30, 1900—Discovered that the Earth—is flat and stationary and—that the sun and moon do move"; endowed an ice cream social that continues to this day, on the last Sunday in August, at the Raysville Free Baptist Church.

Holden, Liberty Emery 1833–1913, born: Raymond; son of a farmer; attended public school in Sweden, Goulds Academy, Bethel, student at Waterville College 1854–56, A.B. University of Michigan 1858, A.M. 1861; professor of rhetoric and English literature: Kalamazoo (Michigan) College 1858–61; superintendent of schools: Tiffin, Ohio, 1861–62; member: Ohio bar 1862; engaged in the real estate business in Cleveland, Ohio; became interested in iron mines in the Lake Superior region; manager: Pittsburgh and Lake Angeline mine 1862–72; removed to Utah, acquired an interest in silver-lead mines 1872; founder and president: Salt Lake Academy 1872–85; owner, editor: *Cleveland Plain Dealer* from 1885, president: Plain Dealer Publishing Co.; built the first large apartment house in Cleveland; a founder and first chairman: National Bimetallic League 1884, at his direction, data were collected and published which created a national interest in the free coinage of silver; trustee: Western Reserve University, Adelbert College, Cleveland School of Art, president: Western Reserve Historical Society; delegate: Democratic National Convention 1888, 1896; Ohio commissioner: World's Columbian Exposition 1893.

Holmes, Ernest Shurtliff 1887–1960, born: Lincoln; brother of Fenwicke Lindsay Holmes; Ph.D. (Hon.) and fellow: Andhra Research University, India; founder 1927 and dean: Institute of Religious Science and Philosophy (later Church of Religious Science), Los Angeles; founder: *Science of Mind* magazine, a national publication; honorary member of cultural, scientific, and literary institutions in the United States, Mexico, Argentina, Brazil, Portugal, Italy, and India; author of numerous books of new psychology and spiritual philosophy.

Holmes, Fenwicke Lindsay 1883– ?, born: Lincoln; brother of Ernest Shurtliff Holmes; A.B. Colby College ΦΒΚ 1905, student: Hartford Theological Seminary

1908–10; Latin teacher: Attleboro (Massachusetts) High School 1907–08; minister: Rincon (California) Congregational Church 1911–12, Congregational Church, Venice, California, 1912–17; a founder: Metaphysical Institute, Long Beach, California, 1917, Southern California Metaphysical Institute, Los Angeles 1917; lecturer on psychology and metaphysics 1917–26; pastor: First Church of Divine Science, New York, from 1926; author: *The Law of Mind in Action* 1919, *How to Develop Faith That Heals* 1919, *Being and Becoming* 1920, *Practical Healing* 1921, *What Is Mental Science?* 1921, *Songs of the Silence* 1921, *The Science of Mind-Psychology and Metaphysics* 1924, *The Twenty Secrets of Success* 1926, *Visualization and Concentration—How to Choose a Career* 1926, numerous articles for newspapers and magazines.

Holmes, John 1773–1843, born: Kingston, Massachusetts; A.B. Brown University 1796, A.M. 1799; member: Massachusetts bar, practiced in Alfred; member: Massachusetts General Court 1802–03, 1812; member: Massachusetts Senate 1813–14; a commissioner to divide the islands in Passamaquoddy Bay between the United States and Great Britain according to the Treaty of Ghent 1816; member from the First District: U.S. House of Representatives 1817–20, chairman: Committee on Expenditures of the Department of State; delegate: Maine Constitutional Convention 1819; member: U.S. Senate 1820–27, 1829–33, chairman: Committee on Finance, Committee on Pensions; member: Maine House of Representatives 1836–37; U.S. attorney for Maine 1841–43; Bowdoin College trustee 1821–43; grandfather of Noah Brooks, John Homes Goodenow; buried in Eastern Cemetery, Portland.

Homans, Amy Morris 1848–1933, born: East Vassalboro; student: Vassalboro Academy, Oak Grove Seminary; A.M. Bates College 1909, D.Ped. Russell Sage College 1930; preceptress: Oak Grove Seminary 1867–69; principal: Hemenway School, Boston; removed to Wilmington, North Carolina, to act as an instructor, and later principal, in the school started by her aunt, Amy Morris Bradley, for the benefit of poor whites; instructor: Tileston Normal School; principal: McRae and Chapbourn School, Wilmington, North Carolina, 1869–77; in charge of educational work founded by Mary Hemenway 1877–1909; organized and directed: Boston Normal School of Household Arts 1886–98, Boston Normal School of Gymnastics 1888–1909; professor of hygiene and director of department: Wellesley College 1908–18; fellow: American Physical Education Association from 1931.

Homer, Winslow 1836–1910, born: Boston, Massachusetts, of Maine parents; removed, with his family to Cambridge 1842, apprenticed to a Boston lithographer 1854, upon completion of his apprenticeship, took a room at Ballous *Pictorial* building and began an independent career; removed to New York 1859, opened a studio in Nassau Street, attended night school at the Academy of Design and took lessons from Frederick Rondel; commissioned by *Harper's Weekly* to make sketches of the scene of President Lincoln's first inaugural 1861, subsequently crossed the Potomac with the first volunteers, stayed with the Army of the Potomac throughout the Civil War, making numerous works, reproduced in *Harper's Weekly*; exhibited oils and watercolors at the Academy of Design, New York, including his *The First Goose at Yorktown, Home, Sweet Home*, and *Prisoners at the Front*; exhibited at the Paris salon of 1867; associated with John LaFarge in Paris, returned to New York, 1868; made home on Prout's Neck from 1882; his *Snap the Whip* and *The American Type* were exhibited at the Centennial Exhibition, Philadelphia, 1876; exhibited at the Paris Exhibition of 1877, where his work and their American flavor was much noted; his later works include: *A Voice from the Cliffs, Tynemouth, Life Line, Eight Bells, Fog on the Banks, Undertow, High Seas*, &c.; buried in Mount Auburn Cemetery, Cambridge, Massachusetts.

Hooper, Lucien Obed 1896– ?, born: Biddeford; student: Boston University, Harvard University 1918; associate editor: *Boston Commercial* 1919–23; investment analyst: E. A. Pierce & Co. 1923–27; head, research department: Frazier Jelke & Co. 1927–38; market letter writer: Shearson, Hammill & Co. 1928–41; director of research: W. E. Hutton & Co. 1941–63, senior analyst from 1963; contributor of articles to financial and economic journals, signed column in *Forbes* magazine; mayor: Westwood, New Jersey, 1934–37; trustee: Cushing Academy; member: New York Social Security Analysts.

Hopkins, Neville Monroe 1873–1945, born: Portland; B.S. Columbian University 1899, M.S. 1900, Ph.D. 1902, graduate student: Harvard University 1901; instructor in chemistry: Columbian University 1899–1902, assistant professor: George Washington University 1902–23; professional engineering lecturer: College of Engineering, New York University, from 1934; member of faculty: Institute for Industrial Progress; member: Munroe, Hall, and Hopkins, consulting engineers; electrician: General Electric Co.; editorial representative: *Electorial World and Engineer*; trustee and in charge of electrical division: Institute of Industrial Research; vice president and electrical engineer: Electric Tachometer Co.; electrical engineer, in charge of power plant design and construction at all U.S. Navy yards and stations 1905–08; expert engineer: U.S. Office of Public Roads from 1909; inventor of electrical and mechanical devices, including the electric tachometer, electromechanical flashlights and focusing devices, electrical rectifiers, burglar and firm alarms, a pneumatic system for preventing the lapse of water pipes, double, collapsible tubes as chemical containers, fire-retardant materials, tobacco-processing machinery, torpedo belts for ship protection, a chronograph method of control for deflecting torpedoes; his instrument for measuring high temperatures was awarded the John Scott Medal: Franklin Institute 1900; temporary assistant: U.S. Embassy, Paris; at outbreak of World War I, volunteer: French Red Cross and with the French army in its retreat from Mons to Paris; chairman: Belgian Scholarship Commission; U.S. technical adviser, design of gun division, USA, from 1917; major USA, consulting engineer: Aircraft Fireproofing Corp., Union Carbide and Carbon Co., in charge of research division: Union Carbide Laboratories; president: New-Mix Products, International Tube Co.; inventor and developer: Televotes, Radiovotes, inventor of Synchronous Electric Registration and Voting System, making possible mass voting by radio and newspaper announcement, automatic radio-electric survey system showing the number of radio receiving sets tuned into any particular broadcasting station wavelength, inventor: submersible battle cruiser, long-range naval and anti-aircraft guns, high-explosive anti-aircraft shells and battleship-wrecking bombs, blast meter and system for the U.S. Army for measuring the force of high explosives in the field, electric chronograph for ballistic measurements, inactivator for destroying criminal time bombs and infernal machines, designer of torpedo and magnetic bomb-protection equipment, super rocket guns and rocket missiles; author: *Model Engines and Boats* 1898, *Twentieth-Century Magic* 1904, *Experimental Electro-Chemistry* 1905, *The Strange Case of Mason Brant* 1916, *The Raccoon Lake Mystery* 1917, *Over the Threshold of War* 1918, *The Outlook for Research and Invention* 1919, *The Inventor and His Workshop*, *The Horrors of the Grew Mystery*, also some one hundred articles in scientific and engineering journals; charter member and founder: American Electrochemical Society, fellow: American Association for the Advancement of Science, American Institute of Electrical Engineers, Society of American Military Engineers, American Chemical Society.

Hopkins, Pauline Elizabeth 1859–1930, born: Portland; at age fifteen, won a prize of ten dollars, in gold, for her essay "The Evils of Intemperance and Their Remedies"; organized and sang in Hopkins Colored Troubadours, which presented concerts and recitals; editor: *Colored American* 1900–04, first magazine for blacks published in the United States in the twentieth century, founded the publishing house of P. E. Hopkins & Co. 1905; author and composer: *Slaves' Escape: or the Underground Railroad* (also known as *Peculiar Sam*) 1879; author of a series of biographical sketches: *Famous Women of the Negro Race*, *Famous Men of the Negro Race*; author: *Away From Accommodation: Radical Editors and Protest Journalism* 1900–1910; coined the term "Negro Renaissance"; contributed twenty-one biographies to *Dictionary of American Negro Biography*; author: *Contending Forces: A Romance Illustrative of Negro Life North and South* 1900, *Of One Blood: Hagar's Daughters, A Story of Southern Caste Prejudice* 1902, *Winona: A Tale of Negro Life in the South and Southwest* 1902, *A Primer of Facts Pertaining to the Early Greatness of the Possibility of Restoration by Its Descendants, with Epilogue* 1905; contributor: *Voice of the Negro, New Era Magazine*; died in obscurity and poverty in the Cambridge (Massachusetts) Relief Hospital, subsequent to severe burns, suffered when her nightgown caught fire; buried in the Garden Cemetery, Chelsea, Massachusetts.

Hopkins, Timothy 1859–1936, born: Hallowell; born: Timothy Nolan, the son of an immigrant from Ireland, who departed from Maine to seek his fortune in the gold fields of California, sent for his family, but was drowned the day they departed from New York; his mother found employment in the household of Mark Hopkins in San Francisco; her son was made a member of the family, which formally adopted him in 1878; prepared to enter Harvard College, but ill health prevented this, entered the service of the Central Pacific Railroad 1880, which had been built by his adoptive father and Collis P. Huntington, Charles Crocker, and Leland Stanford; treasurer 1883–92, when the Central Pacific Railroad Co. was organized in 1885, he served as its first treasurer and as a director, resigned 1892, when his adoptive mother married Edward Searles from Methuen, Massachusetts, an interior decorator, many years her junior; when Hopkins protested this, he was disinherited; in bringing suit, he was unsuccessful, the defense being led by General Thomas Hubbard, Searles expressed his appreciation by presenting Searles Hall to Bowdoin College, as well as underwriting much of the cost of Hubbard Hall, named for General Hubbard, who was at that time, president of the board of trustees of Bowdoin College; president: Southern Pacific Milling Co.; director: Wells, Fargo Bank & Union Trust Co., Pacific Telephone & Telegraph Co., Union Ice Co.; grew violets and chrysanthemums on his large estate in Menlo Park for the San Francisco trade; an original trustee: Stanford University; founded the Hopkins Marine Station at Pacific Grove, which he gave to Stanford University; trustee: public school system of San Mateo County; author: *The Kelloggs in the Old World and the New* (three volumes) 1903, *John Hopkins and Some of His Descendants* 1932.

Hornberger, H. Richard 1924–97, born: Trenton, New Jersey; M.D. Cornell University College of Medicine; combat surgeon: 8055th Mobile Army Surgical Hospital (MASH) in Korea 1952–53; settled in Bremen, practiced in Waterville; author (under the pen name Richard Hooker): *M*A*S*H* 1968, *M*A*S*H Goes to Maine* 1971, *M*A*S*H Goes to Paris* 1974, *M*A*S*H Goes to London* 1975, *M*A*S*H Goes to New Orleans* 1975, *M*A*S*H Goes to Hollywood* 1976, *M*A*S*H Goes to Morocco* 1976, *M*A*S*H Goes to Vienna* 1976, *M*A*S*H Goes to Montreal* 1977, *M*A*S*H Goes to Moscow* 1977.

Horne, Nellie Mathes 1870– ?, born: Eliot; graduate: Commercial College, Boston; studied art with U. D. Tenney and others; collaborator in studies with Ulysses Dow Tenney on notable portraits, painted Edward Everett Hale, William Dean Howells, Hon. Frank Jones, Navy Secretary John D. Long, ten living ex-mayors of Portsmouth, and others; her portrait of Belva Lockwood is in the National Portrait Gallery in Washington.

Howard, Oliver Otis 1830–1909, born: Leeds; graduate: North Yarmouth Academy, A.B. Bowdoin College ΦBK 1850, overseer 1866–70, trustee 1892–1909; worked his way through Bowdoin by teaching at various grammar schools, graduate: U.S. Military Academy 1854, received his appointment from his uncle, Representative John Otis; served in the Seminole War, assistant professor of mathematics and first lieutenant of ordnance: U.S. Military Academy; in the Civil War: colonel, 3rd Maine, USV, at first Manassas, commanded a brigade composed of three Maine regiments and one Vermont regiment in Heintzelman's division, brigadier general USV, commanding officer: a brigade of the II Corps, participated in the battles of Yorktown, Fair Oaks; recipient: Medal of Honor, led the 61st New York Infantry in a charge in which he was twice severely wounded in the right arm, necessitating amputation; major general USV: commanding officer: II Corps, commanding officer: XI Corps: Chancellorsville, Gettysburg (in tactical command of the army of the Potomac from the death of General Reynolds to the arrival of General Meade), Lookout Mountain, Missionary Ridge; commanding officer: IV Corps: Atlanta campaign, commanding officer: Army of the Tennessee: march to the sea, Bentonville; known as the praying general; after the war, headed the Bureau of Refugees, Freedmen, and Abandoned Lands (commonly known as the Freedmen's Bureau) 1865–72; founder and third president: Howard University 1869–74; peace commissioner to the Apaches, boldly rode into Cochise's camp and brought an end to the decade-long Cochise war 1872; superintendent: U.S. Military Academy 1881-82; major general, USA, commanding officer: departments of the Platte, Pacific, and Atlantic 1882–88, his conduct of the war against and subsequent pursuit of the Nez Perce is still a matter of intense controversy, caught, as he was, between his admiration and respect for Chief Joseph, on the one hand, and the rapaciousness of white settlers and the bland acceptance of inconsistency in the enforcement of treaty provisions by the federal government, on the other hand; became closely associated with Albert Smiley and the Lake Mohonk Conference of the Friends of the Indian; founder: Lincoln Memorial University 1895; author: "Report of Brigadier general O. O. Howard," in *Report of the Secretary of War, 1877*, 1877, "The True Story of the Wallowa Campaign," in *North American Review* July, 1879, *Nez Perce Joseph: An Account of His Ancestors, His Lands, His Confederates, His Enemies, His Murders, His War, His Pursuit, and Capture* 1881, *Autobiography* (two volumes) 1907, *My Life and Experiences Among Our Hostile Indians* 1907, *Famous Indian Chiefs I Have Known* 1908; retired to Burlington, Vermont, where he is buried in Lake View Cemetery.

Howard, Volney Erskine 1809–89, born: Norridgewock; student: Bloomfield Academy, A.B. Waterville College; member: Mississippi bar 1837; member: Mississippi House of Representatives 1836; reporter: Mississippi High Court Errors and Appeals; co-editor: *The Mississippian* 1836; author: *The Statutes of Mississippi* (seven volumes) 1840; unsuccessful candidate for U.S. House of Representatives 1840; removed to San Antonio, Texas 1844, delegate: Texas Constitutional Convention 1845; member: U.S. House of Representatives 1849–53 (Democrat), unsuccessful candidate for reelection 1852; appointed major general of California militia to put down vigilante activities, San Francisco 1856; district attorney, Los Angeles 1861–70; member: California Constitutional Convention 1878–79; judge: Los Angeles Superior Court 1880–84; buried in Fort Hill Cemetery, Los Angeles.

Howard, William A. 1807–71, born: Maine; distinguished himself, as a child, for leading an expedition to rescue an American vessel captured by the British for infringing on the fishery laws; entered the U.S. Navy 1824, resigned his commission to accept a captaincy in the Revenue Marine 1828; so successful was he in rescuing vessels in distress on the New England coast that he was presented a silver service by the merchants of Boston; appointed by the German Confederation second in command of the Weser fleet, constructed a navy yard and dry dock 1848–61; in the Civil War: raised a regiment of marine artillery which was attached to the Burnside Expedition; began organizing, in New York, a regiment of heavy artillery for service with the Army of the James; commanded the defenses around Portsmouth and Norfolk, Virginia; at the close of the war, returned to the Revenue Service as captain; first to hoist the American flag over Alaska, after its transference from Russia; superintended the building of steam launches for the Revenue Marine.

Howe, Albion Parris 1818–97, born: Standish; graduate: U.S. Military Academy 1841, commissioned second lieutenant, USA, assigned to the 4th Artillery; on garrison duty and service on the frontier; professor of mathematics: U.S. Military Academy; in the Mexican War: adjutant: 4th Artillery 1846–55, brevetted captain, USA, 1847, for gallant and meritorious conduct at the battles of Contreras and Cherubusco; instructor at the Artillery School, Fortress Monroe, Virginia; in the Civil War: served at Harper's Ferry 1861, appointed chief of artillery of the Army of the Potomac 1862, brevetted major, USV, for bravery at Malvern Hill, 1862, brevetted lieutenant colonel, USV, for gallant action at Salem Heights, Virginia, 1863, brevetted colonel, USV, for daring and meritorious work at the battle of Rappahannock Station, Virginia, 1863, brevetted brigadier general, USV, 1865, brevetted major general, USV, for faithful and meritorious service during the war 1865, participated in the battles of Yorktown, Williamsburg, Seven Days, Second Bull Run, South Mountain, Antietam, Fredericksburg, Gettysburg, Mine Run; as a member of President Lincoln's honor guard, accompanied Lincoln's body from Washington to Springfield, Illinois; member: military commission that tried the Lincoln assassination conspirators; mustered out 1866; rejoined the regular army, with rank of major, USA; served on the Pacific Coast, retired with the rank of colonel, USA, 1882; buried in Mt. Auburn Cemetery, Cambridge, Massachusetts.

Howe, Lucien 1848–1928, born: Standish; A.B. Bowdoin College 1870, A.M. 1873, M.D. Long Island College Hospital (Brooklyn) 1871, M.D. Bellevue Hospital Medical College 1872; founder and surgeon-in-charge: Buffalo Eye and Ear Infirmary 1876, ophthamalic surgeon: Buffalo General Hospital from 1885; founder, director: Howe Laboratory of Ophthamalogy, Harvard University Medical School 1926; devised the test for trachoma, devised a prophylactic wash that virtually rid mankind of the scourge; secured legislation in New York, known as the Howe Law, which requires newbornes to be treated, now ubiquitous; author: *The Muscles of the Eye* (two volumes), *Universal Military Education* 1916, *The Hereditary Eye Defects* 1927, numerous papers on ophthalmological subjects; in his day, Howe was the most renown eye surgeon in the country; awarded the Leslie Dana gold medal of the National Committee for the Prevention of Blindness 1927; president: American Ophthalmological Society 1918–19, Eugenics Research Society.

Howe, Timothy Otis 1816–83, born: Livermore; graduate: Maine Wesleyan Seminary, Kents Hill; member: Maine bar 1839; practiced in Readfield; member: Maine House of Representatives 1845; removed to Green Bay, Wisconsin; judge of the circuit court, justice: Wisconsin Supreme Court 1850–53; unsuccessful candidate for U.S. Senate 1856; member: U.S. Senate 1861–79 (Republican), chairman: Committee on Enrolled Bills, Committee on Revolutionary Claims, Committee on the Library, Committee on Foreign Relations; spoke strongly for the Negro suffrage bill 1861, urged the right of the federal government to establish territorial governments over the seceded states, spoke against the policies of President Johnson and voted for his impeachment; opposed the Chinese-exclusion bill; unsuccessful candidate for reelection 1878; commissioner for the purchase of the Black Hills from the Indians; appointed postmaster general by President Arthur 1882–83; delegate: International Monetary Congress, Paris, 1881; declined appointments as chief justice, U.S. Supreme Court and Ambassador to Great Britain; buried in Woodlawn Cemetery, Green Bay, Wisconsin.

Hubbard, John 1794–1869, born: Readfield; son and grandson of physicians; A.B. Dartmouth College 1816; principal: Hallowell Academy 1816–18, principal: Dinwiddie (Virginia) Academy 1818–20; M.D. University of Pennsylvania Medical School 1822, L.L.D. (Hon.) Waterville College 1851; practiced in Dinwiddie County, Virginia, 1822–29, after a year of graduate work at the University of Pennsylvania, returned to Maine and practiced in Hallowell 1830; member: Maine Senate 1842–43; elected sixteenth governor of Maine (Democrat) 1850–53, while governor, signed the Maine Law, the nation's first Prohibition law; obtained a reform school for juvenile delinquents, a state agricultural school (later the University of Maine); unsuccessful candidate for re'lection 1852; after his terms as governor, resumed the practice of medicine but was appointed by the U.S. Treasury Department as special agent to inspect Maine customhouses 1856, his territory was extended to include all of New England 1858; appointed by President Buchanan to the commission created by the reciprocity treaty with Canada to settle disputes between Canada and the United States over fisheries along the Northern coast 1859; father of Thomas Hamlin Hubbard and John Barrett Hubbard.

Hubbard, John 1849–1932, born: South Berwick; graduate: U.S. Naval Academy 1870, while at Annapolis, served as stroke for the academy's rowing team; commissioned ensign, USN, 1871, master 1873, lieutenant, USN, 1878, lieutenant commander, USN, 1898, commander, USN, 1901, commanding officer: USS *Nashville* and naval forces on the Isthmus of Panama, played an important role in the Revolution of 1903, which resulted in the establishment of the Republic of Panama, captain, USN, 1905, first commanding officer (or plankholder): USS *Minnesota* (BB-22), as such participated in the circumnavigation of the globe by the Great White Fleet 1907–09, rear admiral, USN, 1909, commander in chief: Asiatic fleet 1910, member: General Board; retired 1911; Hubbard Hall (aka the Boathouse), at the U.S. Naval Academy was named in his honor, in 1930, the first structure there named for a living person.

Hubbard, Thomas Hamlin 1838–1915, born: Hallowell; son of Dr. John Hubbard, brother of John Barrett Hubbard; A.B. Bowdoin College 1857, A.M. 1860, L.L.D. (Hon.) 1894, L.L.B. Albany Law School 1861; member: Maine bar 1860, New York bar 1861, Supreme Court of the United States bar 1870; in the Civil War: commissioned first lieutenant, USV; adjutant, 25th Maine Infantry 1862, lieutenant colonel, USV, helped raise the 30th Maine Infantry 1863, USV 1864, brevetted brigadier general, USV, for meritorious services; played a large role in the construction of the dams that saved the Red River Expedition, also assisted in the construction of a pontoon bridge, utilizing the decks of some twenty-eight steamboats, across the Atchafalaya River, for the passage of General Banks's army, for which he received the commendation of Admiral Porter; mustered into the regular army, transferred to the Army of the Potomac; took part in the Shenandoah Valley campaign of 1864–65, resigned 1865; member: law firm of Barney, Butler & Parsons, later, Butler, Stillman, and Hubbard, New York, 1875–96; became associated with Collis P. Huntington; vice president and director: Southern Pacific Railroad Co. 1896–1900, president: Mexican International Railroad Co. 1897–1901, Houston & Texas Central Railroad Co. 1894–1901, president: Guatemala Central Railroad Co. 1901–12, International Bank from 1905, president and chairman of the board: International Banking Corp. from 1904, president: Pacific Improvement Co. from 1903, director: National Bank of Commerce, director and chairman, executive committee: Toledo, St. Louis & Western Railroad Co., director: American Light & Traction Co., Wabash Railroad Co., Western Union Telegraph Co., director and member, Finance Committee: Metropolitan Life Insurance Co.; trustee: Bowdoin College, Albany Law School; president Peary Arctic Club; Cape Thomas Hubbard the most northerly point of Axel Heiburg Land named in his honor; contributed the Hubbard Library to Bowdoin College; in response to a large donation, the Hallowell Social Library was renamed Hubbard Free Library, in his honor 1893; Bowdoin College overseer 1874–89, trustee 1889–1915; commander in chief: Loyal Legion of the United States.

Hughes, Charles Frederick 1866–1934, born: Bath; son of a ship carpenter; graduate: U.S. Naval Academy 1888; commissioned ensign, USN, 1890; on USS *Monterey* at Battle of Manila Bay 1898; served in the hydrographic office, Philadelphia, 1899–1900; gunnery officer: USS *Massachusetts* 1900-04; navigator, later, executive officer: USS *Washington* 1906–08; commanding officer: USS *Birmingham* 1911–12, commanding officer: USS *Des Moines* 1912–13, at Vera Cruz during Diaz revolution 1912; chief of staff, Atlantic Fleet 1913–14; commanding officer: USS *New York* 1916–18, flagship of American squadron, served with British Grand Fleet in the North Sea 1917–18; commanding officer: Philadelphia Naval Yard 1918–20, commanding officer: 2nd Battleship Division 1920–23; president: Naval War College, Newport, Rhode Island, 1923–24; admiral, commander in chief, U.S. Fleet (CINCUS) 1924–27, chief of naval operations 1927–30; succeeded by Admiral W. V. Pratt; decorated: Distinguished Service Medal, Order of Leopold (Belgium), Venezuelan Order of the Liberator; greatly beloved by the fleet for his shiphandling and rugged manners; while he was chief of naval operations, his father was laboring as a carpenter on board USS *Constitution*; in the 1940, the U.S. Navy launched USS *Charles F. Hughes* (DD-428), she received four battle stars in World War II, an armored personnel carrier, USS *Admiral C .F. Hughes* (AP-124), named in his honor, was commissioned 1944; buried at Arlington National Cemetery

Hume, Frank Merton 1867–1939, born: Bridgewater; son of a lumberman,  attended public school in Bridgewater, the Abbott Family School, Little Blue, Farmington, graduate: Riverview Military Academy, Poughkeepsie, New York, failed the physical for entrance to U.S. Military Academy (bad eyesight), attended Cornell University until the death of his father required his return to Bridgewater, engaged in the hardware business in Houlton, postmaster of Houlton 1897–1914; joined the National Guard in 1894, captain, Company L, 2nd Maine Infantry; in the Spanish-American War, served as captain, Battery B, 1st Maine Volunteer Artillery, also served on the Mexican border in 1916; in World War I: colonel, 2nd Maine Infantry, later 103rd U.S. Infantry; recipient: DSO for Meuse-Argonne, croix de guerre for gallantry at Toul; appointed by President Coolidge: collector of U.S. Customs, Section 1 (Maine and New Hampshire) 1927; buried in Greenwood Cemetery, Houlton; his portrait is in the Maine Statehouse collection.

Hume, William 1803–1902, born: Waterville, removed to Califonia 1852, returned to Maine to fetch his two brothers, established Hapgood, Hume, and Co. 1864, first cannery on Columbia River and on the Pacific Coast, first salmon cannery; at death owned more than half of all canneries in the Northwest.

Hussey, Obed 1792–1860, born: Paris; of Nantucket Quaker stock; invented a machine for the manufacture of hooks and eyes, a mill for crushing cane, an artificial-ice machine, a steam plow, a grinding machine for corn, an ice-making machine, and near-myriad other useful devices, most important of which was a mowing and reaping machine, which he patented 1833; located his manufactory in Baltimore; when he demonstrated his machine in Great Britain in 1851, Prince Albert purchased two for use on the royal estates; sued by Cyrus McCormick for infringement, the patent office found for Hussey 1848; killed in 1860, when, having exited a standing railroad train, bound for Portland from Boston, to secure a drink of water for a squally child, he was thrown under the train by a sudden jolt.

Hustus, Walter L. 1921–99, born: Fairfield; graduate: South Portland High School; entered the U.S. Air Force October 1942, served as a tail gunner aboard a B-17, assisted in twenty successful missions until shot down in 1943, near Orenburg, C   , 1943, after hiding for three days, taken prisoner and held in the now-famous *Stalag 17*; upon liberation, resumed service in the air corps, participating in the Berlin airlift and the rescue of eleven downed airmen in Greenland, earning, in the process, the Distinguished Flying Cross, six air medals, a Purple Heart, and numerous other awards; subsequent to his retirement in 1951, served as a Maine forest ranger at Bradbury Mountain State Park in Pownal until his retirement in 1971.

Hutchings, William 1764–1866, born: York, son of a soldier who had partici-pated in the siege of Louisbourg; removed, with his family, to Penobscot 1768; in the American Revolution: served in the siege of Castine, taken prisoner by the British, released, enlisted in McCobb's regiment of Massachusetts militia, entered service at Newcastle, stationed at Cox's Head, on the Kennebec River; father of fifteen chil-dren; last surviving veteran of the American Revolution in Maine, last but three in the United States.

Hutchison, John Irwin 1867–1935, born: Bangor; A.B. Bates College ΦBK 1889, graduate student: Clark University 1890–92, Ph.D. *magna cum laude* University of Chicago 1896; instructor in mathematics: Cornell University 1894–1903, assistant professor 1903–10, professor from 1910; author: *Differential and Integral Calculus* 1902, *Elementary Treatise on the Calculus* 1912; recognized, internationally, as a leading research mathematician, made many contributions to mathematical journals on such subjects as: theta and automorphic functions, birational transformations, quartic and cubic surfaces, zeta function and Dirichlet series; an accomplished pianist and enthu-siastic singer, he was also a plant hybridizer of note, producing several new varieties of narcissi.

Hyde, Thomas Worcester 1841–99, born: Florence, Italy; son of Zina Hyde, a brigade-major in the War of 1812, raised in Bath; A.B. Bowdoin College 1861; in the Civil War: commissioned major, USV; assigned to the 7th Maine Infantry, served with that regiment in the Peninsula campaign, second Bull Run; recipient: Medal of

Honor, at Antietam, Maryland, "led his regiment in an assault on a strong body of the enemy's infantry and kept up the fight until the greater part of his men had been killed or wounded, bringing the remainder safely out of the fight"; made inspector general of the left grand division 1863, provost-marshal of the VI Corps, aide-de-camp to General John Sedgwick, lieutenant colonel, USV, 1 December 1863, colonel, USV, 22 October 1864, brevetted brigadier general, USV, 2 April 1865, commanding officer: 3rd Brigade, 2nd Division, VI Corps: Shenandoah and Richmond campaigns; member: Maine Senate 1874–76, president 1875–76; mayor of Bath 1876–78; member, board of managers: National Soldiers Home, Togus; member: board of visitors: U.S. Military Academy 1877; founder, president, general manager: Bath Iron Works from 1891; author: *Following the Greek Cross; or, Memories of the 6th Army Corps* 1894; buried in Hyde Mausoleum, Oak Grove Cemetery, Bath; father of John Sedgwick Hyde, Edward Warden Hyde.

Ingalls, Melville Ezra 1842–1914, born: Harrison; graduate: Bridgton Academy, student: Bowdoin College, LL.B. Harvard University Law School 1863; president: Boston City Council; member: Massachusetts Senate 1867; president: Cincinnati, Indianapolis & Lafayette Railroad 1870–1905, chairman of the board 1905–12; under his management what had been known as the old Big Four, viz., the Cincinnati, Indianapolis, St. Louis & Chicago Railroad Co. (the successor to the Cincinnati, Indianapolis & Lafayette Railroad Co.) was consolidated with the Cleveland, Cincinnati, Chicago & Indianapolis Railroad Co., that company, in turn, acquired the Cincinnati, Wabash & Michigan Railroad Co., the Cairo, Vincennes & Columbus Railroad Co., the Peoria & Eastern Railroad Co., all of which became the Cleveland, Cincinnati, Chicago & St. Louis Railroad Co., commonly known as the Big Four; between 1889 and 1891, this system grew from 400 miles to 2,200 miles; succeeded Collis P. Huntington as president and director of the Chesapeake & Ohio Railroad 1888–1900; an originator of the Central Freight Association, which had charge of freight rates and traffic regulations west of the Alleghenies and east of the Mississippi; originated the Joint Traffic Association, which had as its object the elimination of rebates and the regulation of rates, later declared unconstitutional by the U.S. Supreme Court; a founder and president: Cincinnati Art Museum; the developer of Virginia Hot Springs.

Ingalls, Rufus 1820–93, born: Denmark; graduate: U.S. Military Academy 1843, assigned to Dragoons/quartermaster; served on frontier duty at Fort Jesup, Louisiana, and Fort Leavenworth, Kansas, 1843–46; commissioned second lieutenant, USA, 1845; in the war with Mexico, took part in engagements at Embudo and Pueblo de Taos, promoted to first lieutenant, USA, 1847; appointed assistant quartermaster with rank of captain, USA; ordered to California, served at Monterey, Los Angeles, and Fort Yuma; accompanied Steptoe's expedition across the continent 1854–55; on duty in Vancouver, Washington, 1855–56, while stationed there, along with his classmate and lifelong friend, U. S. Grant, being impressed with the high prices being paid for ice in San Francisco, arranged for the cutting of ice and its shipment to San Francisco, contrary headwinds prevented the vessel from reaching port before the cargo melted away; on the commission to examine the war debt of Oregon and Washington Territory 1856–60; at the outbreak of the Civil War: served in the defense of Fort Pickens, Florida, to July 1861, as major, USA, aide-de-camp to General McClellan 1861; chief quartermaster of the Army of the Potomac 1862, performed his duties with great skill and dispatch to 1865; participated in the battles of South Mountain, Antietam, Fredericksburg, Chancellorsville, Gettysburg, and Mine Run; promoted to brigadier general, USV, 1863, brevetted lieutenant colonel, and brigadier general, in the regular army for meritorious and distinguished services 1864; chief quartermaster of the armies against Richmond: participated in the battles of the Wilderness, Spotsylvania, Cold Harbor, Petersburg, Appomattox; present, along with General Seth Williams, at General Lee's surrender, in Wilmer McLean's parlor; brevetted major general, USV, 1865; assistant quartermaster general 1866, chief quartermaster of the Department of the Atlantic 1867–75, Pacific 1876–78, Missouri 1878–81, quartermaster general of the army 1882 with rank of brigadier general, USA, retired 1883; resided in Oregon for eight years, died in New York, buried in Arlington National Cemetery.

Ingraham, Joseph Holt 1809–60, born: Portland; son of Joseph Holt Ingraham, merchant, and Ann Tate Ingraham, niece of Admiral George Tate and principle beneficiary of his will; at age seventeen, shipped out on a trading vessel trading in South America; A.B. Bowdoin College 1833; professor of languages: Jefferson College, Natchez, Mississippi; published his *Southwest by a Yankee* 1836, *The American Lounger* 1836, *Lafitte* 1836, *Frank Rivers: or, the Dangers of the Town* 1840, a fictional account of the murder of Dorcas Doyen, *Rafael; or Twice Condemned* 1845, *The Prince of the House of David; or, Three Years in the Holy City* 1855, *The Pillar of Fire; or, Israel in Bondage* 1859 (which later served as the basis of Cecil B. DeMille's film *The Ten Commandments*), *The Throne of David, from the Consecration of the Shepard of Bethlehem to the Rebellion of Prince Absalom* 1860, *The Sunny South* 1860; ordained priest: Protestant Episcopal Church 1855, priest: Jackson, Mississippi, 1852, missionary: Aberdeen, Mississippi, 1853–54, rector: Saint John's Church, Mobile, Alabama, 1855–58, Christ Church, Holly Springs, Mississippi, 1859–60, killed by the accidental discharge of a pistol; father of Prentiss Ingraham, famous soldier of fortune and author.

Jackson, George Pullen 1874–1953, born: Monson; son of George Frederick Jackson; student: Royal Conservatory of Music, Dresden, Germany 1897–98, Vanderbilt University 1900–01, Ph.B. University of Chicago ΦBK 1904, Ph.D. 1911; with Huston Biscuit Co., Birmingham, Alabama, 1895–97; teacher of German: Kansas State Agriculture College, Manhattan 1905–06, Case School of Applied Science, Cleveland 1906–07, special instructor in German: University of Chicago 1908–10, instructor in German: Oberlin College 1910–12, Northwestern University 1912–13, assistant professor of German: University of North Dakota 1913–18, associate professor: Vanderbilt University 1918–26, professor 1926–43; president: University Philharmonic Society, Grand Forks, North Dakota, 1913–18; founder: Nashville Symphony Orchestra 1920, founder: Tennessee Music Teachers Association; organizer, manager: Old Harp Singers of Nashville, organizer: Tennessee State Harp Singing Association 1933; member: American Musicology Society; president: Southeastern Folklore Society 1946; editor: *Southeastern Folklore Quarterly*; chairman: folklore division, Southern Atlantic Modern Language Association, president 1948; president: Tennessee Folklore Society 1942, International Folk Music Council; author: *The Rhythmic Form of the German Folk Songs* 1916, *White Spirituals in the Southern Uplands: The Story of the Fasola Folk, Their Songs, Singing, and Buckwheat Notes* 1933, *Spiritual Folk-Songs of Early America: Two Hundred and Fifty Tunes and Texts* 1937, *Down-East Spirituals* 1943, *White and Negro Spirituals* 1943, *Story of the Sacred Harp* 1944, *Another Sheaf of White Spirituals* 1952; editor: *American Folk Music for High School and other Choral Groups* 1947, *Sing, Brothers, Sing* 1948; author of articles in: *Modern Language Notes, Modern Philology, American Mercury, Virginia Quarterly Review, World Today, Journal of American Folklore, Southern Folklore Quarterly, Georgia Review, Groves Dictionary of Music and Musicians*.

Jackson, Sumner Waldron 1885–1945, born: Spruce Head, South Thomaston, son of a quarryman; A.B. Bowdoin College 1909, M.D. Jefferson Medical College, interned at Massachusetts General Hospital, went with the Harvard Unit to France to tend to allied wounded in World War I, first commissioned in the French army and later in the U.S. Army Medical Corps; subsequent to the end of the war, returned to the United States, along with his wife, a French national and their infant son; his wife, finding the United States uncongenial, convinced Jackson to return to France 1919; there being then no reciprocity, Jackson was required to retake all of his exams to qualify as a physician; hired by the American Hospital in Neuilly, a suburb of Paris, quickly rose to the level of director of urology; in the course of his work treated Ernest Hemingway, Gertrude Stein, Zelda and F. Scott Fitzgerald, and many other members of the American ex-patriot community; with the outbreak of World War II, elected to remain at his post, treating wounded resistance fighters and helping downed airmen escape capture; his thirteen-year-old son, Philip, was dispatched to St. Nazaire, where he took photographs of German naval installations; betrayed shortly before the Normandy invasion, he and his family were eventually sent to German concentration camps, his wife and son survived but Jackson was killed when the British attacked and sank the prison ship on which he was being held in Lubeck Bay; accorded the U.S. Medal of Freedom and various levels of the French Legion of Honor, cited by Field Marshal Montgomery and General Dwight D. Eisenhower for his work with the resistance.

Jenks, Francis Haynes 1812–88, born: Bath; son of William Jenks; graduate: Boston Latin School, awarded a silver medal, presented by the Marquis de Lafayette; began his business career in Boston, removed to Baltimore; noting, on a trip to England, that banks were encumbered with valuables and silver plate left for safekeeping without remuneration, conceived of the safety deposit business, wherein, for a fee, people could rent individual boxes in a fireproof, secure vault; obtained the charter for the first such business from the New York legislature 1861, president: Safe Deposit Co. of New York 1865–85; operated numerous, similar businesses in London, Paris, Chicago, Boston, &c.; father of Francis Mankin Jenks, developer of Riverside Drive, West End Avenue, and the Upper West Side of New York, generally; presented to the Medical School of Johns Hopkins University (of which he was a trustee) the most valuable collection of human monstrosities and deformities in existence.

Jewett, Albert Gallatin 1802–85, born: Pittston, brother of Daniel Tarbox Jewett; A.B. Waterville College 1826; member: Maine bar 1829, practiced in Bangor; Penobscot County attorney for five years; appointed by President Polk as chargé d'affaires in Peru 1845–48; resided in France, returned to the United States; settled in Georgia; operated a steamboat line on the Chagres River in Panama, with his brother D. T. Jewett 1850–53; removed to Belfast 1854, mayor of Belfast 1863–64, 1867.

Jewett, Charles Coffin 1816–68, born: Lebanon; brother of John Punchard and George Baker Jewett; A.B. Brown University 1835, taught for two years at Uxbridge (Massachusetts) Academy, graduate: Andover Theological Seminary 1840, while at Andover, made a special study of Oriental languages and history, intending to become a missionary; principal: Wrentham (Massachusetts) Academy for one year; librarian and professor of modern languages: Brown University 1841–43; visited libraries and purchased books for Brown University in Europe 1843–45; again taught at Brown University 1845–48; assistant secretary and librarian: Smithsonian Institution 1848–58, introduced new and original methods of card cataloguing; first superintendent: Boston Public Library 1858–68; author: *Facts and Considerations Relative to Duties on Books* 1846, *A Plan for Stereotyping Catalogues by Separate Title* 1851, *On the Constructing of Catalogues of Libraries with Rules and Examples* 1852, *Notices of Public Libraries in the United States* 1854.

Jewett, Daniel Tarbox 1807–1906, born: Pittston; son of a farmer, brother of Albert Gallatin Jewett; attended local schools, entered Waterville College 1826, transferred to Columbia College 1828, A.B. 1830; taught Latin, Greek, and algebra at a private school in Virginia for a year, had charge of another school in Boston while a student at Harvard University Law School; member: Maine bar 1834, practiced in Bangor; city solicitor 1834–37; operated a steamboat line on the Chagres River in Panama with his brother Albert 1850–53; removed to California, gold miner for two years; returned to Bangor, removed to Saint Louis, Missouri, 1857; enjoyed a large practice and was known, locally, as the Nestor of the St. Louis bar; member: Missouri House of Representatives 1867–68; delegate: Republican state convention 1870; appointed member, to fill an unexpired term: U.S. Senate 1870–71 (Republican); buried in Bellefontaine Cemetery, St. Louis.

Jewett, James Richard 1862–1943, born: Westport; cousin of William May Garland, as a child spent several years at sea with his parents, his father being master of a sailing ship, made voyage to China via Cape Horn 1869–71; A.B. *summa cum laude* Harvard College ΦBK 1884, Harvard University fellowship 1884–87, Ph.D. University of Strasbourg 1891; instructor of Semitic languages: Harvard University 1887–88, Brown University 1890–91; associate professor: Semitic languages and Oriental history: Brown University 1891–95, professor: University of Minnesota 1895–1902; professor of Arabic language and literature: University of Chicago 1902–11; professor of Arabic: Harvard University 1911–33; fellow: American Academy of Arts and Sciences; editor: *Harvard Semitic Series*, co-operating editor: *American Journal of Semitic Languages*, co-editor: *Journal of the American Oriental Society*; endowed the Margaret Weyerhauser Jewett professorship of Arabic at the American University in Beirut to honor his wife 1929, endowed the James Richard Jewett chair of Arabic at Harvard University 1936.

Jewett, John Punchard 1814–84, born: Lebanon; brother of Charles Coffin and George Baker Jewett; worked in a Salem, Massachusetts, book bindery, sold books in Salem, removed to Boston 1847, opened a bookstore/publishing house, first to publish *Uncle Tom's Cabin or Life Amongst the Lowly* in book form 1852, obtained the endorsements from the leaders of the Abolition movement, brought the book to the attention of political leaders, had it translated into German; published tracts on abolition, feminism, temperance, and religion including Margaret Fuller's *Women of the Nineteenth Century*; became interested in the manufacture of safety matches, opened a factory in Roxbury, Massachusetts; close personal friend of Charles Sumner, Wendell Philips, John A. Andrew, and John A. Whittier; removed to New York city 1867, died in Orange, New Jersey.

Jewett, Sarah Orne 1849–1909, born: South Berwick; daughter of Theodore

 Herman Jewett; graduate: Berwick Academy, lived her entire life in the house in which she was born; author: *Deephaven* 1877, *Old Friends and New* 1880, *Country By-ways* 1881, *The Mate of Daylight* 1883, *A Country Doctor* 1884, *A Marsh Island* 1885, *A White Heron and Other Stories* 1886, *Betsey Leicester* 1887, *The Story of the Normans* 1887, *Tales of New England* 1888, *The King of Folly Island and Other Stories* 1889, *Strangers and Wayfarers* 1890, *The Country of the Pointed Firs* 1896, *The Tory Lover* 1901; buried in the Portland Street Cemetery, South Berwick.

Johnson, Charles Fitz Abner 1826–1902, born: Sullivan; removed to California during the gold rush, returned penniless; located in Presque Isle, formed C. F. A. Johnson & Phair Co., dealers in lumber, manufacturers of starch; having become interested in ostrich raising, dispatched his son Edward to South Africa, who, after remaining a year, returned with twenty-three birds; located their enterprise in Fallbrook, California, later in Coronado; this was the first ostrich farm in the United States; his two most fractious male birds, Jim Blaine and Tom Reed, became the progenitors of many of the ostriches in the country; a resident of Long Beach, associated with Jotham Bixby, served as the first mayor of Long Beach and three terms in the California House of Representatives.

Johnson, Franklin Winslow 1870–1956, born: Jay; graduate: Wilton Academy, A.B. Colby College φBK 1891, A.M. 1894, L.H.D. (Hon.) 1916, L.L.D. University of Maine, Brown University 1933, D.C.L. Acadia University 1938; principal: Calais High School 1891–94, Coburn Classical Institute, Waterville, 1894–1905, Morgan Park (Illinois) Academy 1905–07, assistant principal: University of Chicago High School 1907-09, principal 1909–19, professor of education: Columbia University Teachers College 1919–29; fifteenth president: Colby College 1929–42, during his administration, Colby College procured a new site on Mayflower Hill, raised a $7,000,000 building fund (during the depths of the Great Depression), and began the process of construction on the new campus; author: *Problems of Boyhood* 1914, *Administration and Supervision of the High School* 1925, numerous papers and articles for professional journals.

Johnson, Jonathan Eastman 1824–1906, born: Lovell; son of Philip C. J. Johnson, Maine attorney general for many years, brother of Philip Carrigan Johnson, cousin of Seth Eastman; student: public schools in Augusta, where he began to work in pastels and do portraits in black and white; removed to Washington, D.C., with his parents 1845, began to do portraits of distinguished men; spent two years at the Royal Academy at Düsseldorf, later studied at the Hague; painted his first important paintings: *The Savoyard* and *The Card Players*, established himself in Paris, returned to the United States 1856, painted amongst the Indian tribes, north of Lake Superior 1856–57, settled in Washington long enough to paint *My Old Kentucky Home*, established a studio in New York 1858; member: National Academy of Design from 1860; his genre paintings include: *The Husking Bee, The Kentucky Home, The Stagecoach*; his portraits include those of presidents John Quincy Adams, Chester Arthur, Grover Cleveland, and Benjamin Harrison; Commodore Vanderbilt, Daniel Webster, John D. Rockefeller, Dolley Madison, H. W. Longfellow, Nathaniel Hawthorne, and others; his works hang in the Metropolitan Museum of Art, New York, the White House, the Corcoran Gallery, the U.S. Treasury Department, in Washington, the capitol in Albany, in the Century, Knickerbocker, and Union League clubs in New York.

Johnson, Philip Carrigan, Jr. 1828–87, born: Lovell; son of Philip C. J. Johnson, brother of Eastman Johnson; entered the U.S. Navy as midshipman 1846, present at the bombardment of Vera Cruz and Tuspan during the war with Mexico, served aboard USS *Ohio* in the Pacific squadron 1847–48, spent the next four years at the Naval Academy and attached to the Brazil squadron, attached to the coastal survey 1854–59, promoted to lieutenant, USN, 1855, attached to USS *San Jacinto* cruising the African coast 1859–61; in the Civil War: commanding officer: USS *Tennessee* in the Western Gulf squadron, present at the bombardment and passage of Forts Jackson and St. Philip, promoted to lieutenant commander, USN, 1862, attached to USS *Katahdin* in the Western Gulf squadron 1864–65, stationed at the Naval Academy 1865–66, attached to the USS *Sacramento* 1866–68, promoted to commander, USN, 1867, served as fleet captain of the South Pacific squadron 1868–70, promoted to captain, USN, 1874, commanding officer: USS *Omaha* and USS *Richmond* in the South Pacific squadron 1874-76, attached to the Mare Island Navy Yard, commanding officer: training ship USS *New Hampshire* 1877-81, promoted to commodore, USN, commanding officer: Portsmouth Navy Yard 1884-87, promoted to rear admiral, USN, shortly before his death in Kittery.

Johnston, Alnah James 1896–1987, born: Portland; A.B. Wellesley College 1918, graduate study at Harvard; began her teaching career at Bennett Junior College, Millbrook, New York; acted briefly on Broadway before taking a teaching position with Yenching College for Women, Peking, China; headmistress: Dana Hall School 1938–62, the Johnston dormitories there are named in her honor; president: National Association of Principals of Schools for Girls; at age eighty-one, wrote: *The Footprints of the Pheasant in the Snow*, based upon her journal and travels in China.

Jones, Augustine 1838–1925, born: South China; orphaned at early age; graduate: North Yarmouth Academy, A.B. Bowdoin College 1860, A.M. 1863, L.L.B. Harvard University Law School 1867; principal: Oak Grove Seminary, Vassalboro 1860–63; law student of Governor John Andrew, later administered his estate; member: Massachusetts bar 1867, practiced law in Boston 1867–79; selected by John Greenleaf Whittier to represent the Society of Friends in a series of discourses on the Universal Church, in Boston 1874; member: Massachusetts House of Representatives 1878; principal: Friends School, Providence, Rhode Island, 1879–1904; author: *Life of Joseph Dudley, Second Governor of Massachusetts* 1899; his pamphlet *Peace and Arbitration* was printed in three editions of over 100,000 copies; delegate of the Peace Society of Boston and from the Society of Friends to the Universal Peace Congress, London 1890.

Jones, Charles 1804–59, born: Stroudwater; early entered the employ of a relative, Hezekiah Winslow, proprietor of a shipping commission firm in Portland, later a partner in Winslow & Jones; organized, president: the Portland Co., for the manufacturing of all equipments of a railroad and of all other articles of wood and metal, this company was established in connection with various railroads then organized in Portland, especially the Atlantic & St. Lawrence Railroad Co.; organized, president: Portland Gas Light Co., the first in the state; a dominant factor in Portland real estate; an amateur architect, designed several notable buildings, also designed locomotives built by the Portland Co.; director: Widows' Wood Society, Portland Benevolent Society; father of Elizabeth Jones Pullen.

Jones, Chester Morse 1891–1972, born: Portland; A.B. Williams College 1913, D.Sc. (Hon.) 1942, M.D. Harvard University Medical School 1919; intern: Massachusetts General Hospital 1918–19, on staff 1919–54, board of consultants 1957–64; member of faculty: Harvard University Medical School 1921–72, clinical professor of medicine 1940–57, traveling fellow to Strasbourg, France, 1924–25, Henry Pickering Walcott fellow in clinical medicine 1925–28; acting associate professor of medicine: Vanderbilt University Medical School 1940–41; member: missions to Austria, Greece, and Italy 1947–48; consulting physician: Office of U.S. Surgeon General 1944–46; Shattuck lecturer: Massachusetts Medical Society 1958; chairman: American Board of Internal Medicine 1955–57; president: Harvard University Medical School Alumni Association, American Gastroenterological Society 1936, American Clinical and Climatological Society 1951; author: *Digestive Tract Pain* 1938; member, editorial board: *New England Journal of Medicine*, *Gastroenterology*, *Annals of Internal Medicine*; author of numerous articles and papers on digestive tract physiology and disease for professional journals.

Jones, Eli 1807–90, born: China; attended local district school, enabled to attend the Friends School, Providence, Rhode Island, through its charitable fund 1827;

began to speak publicly at the Friends meeting in China at the age of fourteen; organized a temperance society well in advance of the Washington movement and exerted
considerable influence in Maine and the subsequent passage of the Maine Law; married Sybil Jones 1833 and shared her missionary travels thereafter.

Jones, Rufus 1863–1948, born: South China, son of a farmer, nephew of Sybil
Jones; graduate: Oak Grove Seminary, A.B. Haverford College φΒΚ 1885, A.M. 1886,
L.L.D. (Hon.) 1922, studied at University of Heidelburg 1897, University of Pennsyl-
vania 1893–95, A.M. Harvard University 1901, Litt.D. Whittier College 1948, S.T.D.
Harvard University 1920, Columbia University 1933, Colby College 1937, L.L.D.
Swarthmore College 1922, Earlham College 1929, Williams College 1936, D.Th.
Marburg University 1925, D.D. Yale University 1935, L.H.D. Colgate University
1942; teacher: Moses Brown School, Providence, Rhode Island, 1887–89, principal:
Oak Grove Seminary 1889–93, ordained minister of the Society of Friends from 1890;
instructor in philosophy and ethics: Haverford College 1893–1901, assistant professor
1901–04, professor 1904–34; editor: *The Friends Review* 1893, *The American Friends
Review* 1894–1912; trustee: Bryn Mawr College from 1896, president of board of
trustees: Bryn Mawr College 1916–36, trustee: Brown University, University of
Yenching; founder and president: American Friends Service Committee 1917–27,
1933–44, which was accorded the Nobel Prize for peace 1947; during the First World
War, the committee helped rebuild French villages and took care of tens of thousands
of French war orphans, following the armistice, Jones and his coworkers undertook
the care of German children, at one time feeding as many as 1,200,000 a day, helped
restore Polish refugees to their home, fought typhus in Poland, famine in Russia, and,
subsequently, plagues throughout the world, during the Spanish Civil War, cared for
children of both sides, in 1938, Jones led a committee which visited Germany to
arrange for relief of the Jews, joined with other religious leader in 1948 to plead for
peace between the Jews and Moslems of Palestine, who were asked to establish a
Truce of God, establishing a holy area of peace in Jerusalem; named among the ten
foremost religious leaders in America by Rabbi Stephen Wise; author: *Life of Eli and
Sybil Jones* 1889, *Practical Christianity* 1899, *A Dynamic Faith* 1901, *A Boy's Religion
From Memory* 1902, *Autobiography of George Fox* 1903, *Social Law in the Spiritual World*
1904, *The Double Search* 1905, *The Abundant Life* 1908, *Quakerism, A Religion of Life*
1908, *Studies in Mystical Religion* 1909, *The Children of the Light* 1909, *Selections from
Clement of Alexandria* 1910, *The Quakers in the American Colonies* 1911, *Stories of
Hebrew Heroes* 1911, *Spiritual Reformers in the Sixteenth and Seventeenth Centuries* 1914,
The Inner Life 1916, *St. Paul, the Hero* 1917, *The World Within* 1918, *The Story of
George Fox* 1919, *The Remnant* 1920, *Nature and Authority of Conscience* 1920, *A Ser-
vice of Love in Wartime* 1920, *Later Periods of Quakerism* 1921, *The Boy Jesus and His
Companions* 1922, *Spiritual Energies in Daily Life* 1922, *Religious Foundations* 1923, *Fun-
damental Ends of Life* 1924, *The Life and the Message of George Fox* 1924, *The Church's
Debt to Heretics* 1925, *Finding the Trail of Life* 1926, *The Faith and Practices of Quakers*

1927, *The New Quest* 1928, *The Trail of Life in College* 1929, *Some Exponents of Mystical Religion* 1930, *George Fox: Seeker and Friend* 1930, *Pathways to the Reality of God* 1931, *A Preface to Christian Faith in a New Age* 1932, *Mysticism and Democracy in the English Commonwealth* 1932, *Haverford College—A History and an Interpretation* 1933, *Re-Thinking Religious Liberalism* 1935, *Testimony of the Soul* 1936, *Some Problems of Life* 1937, *The Eternal Gospel* 1938, *Flowering of Mysticism* 1939, *Small Town Boy* 1941, *Spirit of Man* 1941, *New Eyes for Invisibles* 1943, *The Radiant Life* 1944, *The Luminous Trail* 1947, *A Call to What is Vital* 1948; healed the rift between orthodox and Hicksite Friends.

Jones, Stephen Alfred 1848–1915, born: China; student: Friends School, Providence, Rhode Island, Coburn Classical Institute, A.B. Dartmouth College 1872, A.M. 1875, Ph.D. 1885; instructor in Greek and Latin: Spiceland (Indiana) Academy 1872–74, professor of Greek and Latin: Pennsylvania College 1874–82, student: University of Münster (Germany) 1882–83, University of Bonn 1883–85, investigating Greek and Latin texts 1885–87, principal: Colorado Springs High School 1887–89; president: Nevada State University 1889–94, director: Nevada Agricultural Station 1889–94, professor of pedagogy: State Normal School, San Jose, California, 1895–1915.

Jones, Sybil Jones 1808–73, born: Brunswick; grew up in Augusta, student: Friends School, Providence, Rhode Island, 1824–25, teacher for eight years, married Eli Jones 1833, settled in South China, later Dirigo; recognized by the Friends meeting as a gospel minister and missionary; preached in Nova Scotia, New Brunswick, Liberia, England—where she was the first in that country to call for total abstinence—on the Continent, Syria, Palestine, founded the Friends School in Ramallah 1870; at some risk, explained the Quaker concept of the equality of the sexes to Muslim women; mother of Richard Mott Jones, aunt of Rufus Jones.

Jordan, Eben Dyer 1822–95, born: Danville Junction; orphaned at age four and left to his own devices; at age fourteen, removed to Boston, at age sixteen, became a messenger boy for William P. Tenney & Co., drygoods merchant on Salem Street, at age nineteen, opened his own small store at the corner of Mechanic and Hanover Streets, annual sales went from $8,000 to $100,000, per annum, in four years; sold his interest in the business 1848; established Jordan, Marsh & Co. on Milk Street 1851; went to Europe to arrange for direct purchase of various drygoods 1853, weathered the Great Panic of 1857, built a retail store on Washington Street with eleven acres of floor space and 3,000 employees; by the turn of the century, Jordan, Marsh & Co. was the largest retail establishment in the United States; established a free night school for his operatives; funded the construction of Jordan Hall and underwrote a grand opera company for several years; principal owner: *Boston Globe*.

Jordan, Edwin Oakes 1866–1936, born: Thomaston; son of a ship captain; B.S. Massachusetts Institute of Technology 1888, Ph.D. Clark University 1892, Sc.D. (Hon.) University of Cincinnati 1920, student: Pasteur Institute, Paris 1896; chief assistant bacteriologist: Massachusetts Board of Health 1888–90; lecturer on biology: Massachusetts Institute of Technology 1889–90; fellow in morphology: Clark University 1890–92; associate in anatomy: University of Chicago 1892–95, instructor 1893–95, assistant professor of bacteriology: University of Chicago 1895–1900, associate professor 1900–1907, professor 1907–33; chairman: Department of Hygiene and Bacteriology, University of Chicago 1914–33; chief of serum division and trustee: McCormick Memorial Institute for Infectious Diseases; editor: *Journal of Preventative Medicine* 1926–36, co-editor: *Journal of Infectious Diseases* 1904–36; director: International Health Division, Rockefeller Foundation; author: *General Bacteriology* 1908, standard texts, in many editions and translations, *Food Poisoning* 1917, coauthor: *A Pioneer in Public Health—W. T. Sedgwick* 1924, *Epidemic Influenza* 1927, *The Newer Knowledge of Bacteriology and Immunology* 1928; president: Society of American Bacteriologists 1905.

Jordan, Samuel 1729–1802, born: Biddeford; son of Captain Samuel Jordan, mill and land owner, step-son of Rev. Thomas Smith; celebrated his fifteenth birthday (and his mother's remarriage) by joining a snowshoe company sent into the wilderness to search out hostile Indians; A.B. Harvard College 1750, A.M. 1753, being a son of the frontier and having already served as a soldier, the vagaries of college discipline were almost too much for him to bear, managed to graduate after having been degraded for riotous behavior; settled on Jordan land in Biddeford, took his father's place as selectman, representative to the Massachusetts General Court 1756–65, justice of the peace 1761; removed to Jordan's Island, Gouldsborough, 1769, wintered on the Union River; appointed justice of the peace for Lincoln County 1773; appointed to the committee appointed to pass on prizes seized by the committees of safety for violations of association regulations; reported to the general court, from the Union River, that many of the inhabitants of that region were on the verge of capitulation to the British army 1777; he remained faithful to the Revolutionary government; resigned his position as justice of the peace and returned to Saco 1788, where he lived quietly until carried off by smallpox.

Jordan, Wayne C. 1885–1924, born: Lewiston; son of Lyman Jordan, grandson of Ebenezer Knowlton, cousin of Carl Milliken; A.B. Bates College ΦBK 1906, A.B. Oxford University (second to become a Rhodes scholar in Maine) 1909; New Hampshire county secretary: Young Men's Christian Association 1910–13, sent by the association to China, where he was put in charge of the cities of Wuchang, Hunan, and Hankow, an area of intense religious turmoil 1913–21, transferred to the interior province of Shensi 1921, where the vicissitudes of the Chinese civil war made his work difficult; died of typhus.

Josselyn, John *c.* 1610–75, born: Kent, England; brother of Henry Josselyn, deputy governor of the province; settled in Black Point, author: *New Englands Rarities Discovered in Birds, Beasts, Fishes, Serpents, and Plants of that Country; Together with the Physical and Chyrurigical Remedies wherein the Natives Constantly Use to Cure their Distempers, Wounds and Sores—Also a Perfect Description of an Indian Squaw, in all her Bravery; with a Poem Not Improperly Conferred upon Her* 1672, an uneven work, combining accurate observation with wild fantasy, for example, that certain Indians were capable of conversing extempore in perfect hexameter verse or that barley frequently degenerates into oats, characterized early New Englanders as inexplicably "covetous and proud...all like Ethiopians, white in the teeth only, full of ludification, injurious dealings, and cruelty"; author: *A Chronological Table of the Most Remarkable Passages from the First Discovery of the Continent of America to 1673* 1673, *An Account of Two Voyages to New England; Wherein You Have the Setting Out of a Ship with the Charges, and a Description of the Country* 1676, all three books were reprinted in Boston 1865;

Jostberg, Richard Edwin 1923–93, born: Portland; B.S. U.S. Naval Academy 1944, M.S. George Washington University 1971; commissioned ensign, USN, 1944, advanced through the ranks to captain, USN, 1965; commanding officer: nuclear attack submarine USS *Tulabee* 1959–63, Polaris missile submarine USS *Henry L. Stimson* 1965–67; project manager, deep submergence, Washington, 1969–73, retired 1973; chief engineer: Clinch River Breeder Reactor, Project Management Corp. 1973–76; general manager: Commonwealth Research Corp., Chicago 1976–81; director, nuclear safety: Commonwealth Edison Co., Chicago 1981–84, assistant vice president 1984–85; consultant, nuclear industry 1986–93; president: Canterbury Improvement Association 1982–83; decorated: Bronze Star, Legion of Merit, with cluster, Purple Heart; member: American Nuclear Society.

Judd, Sylvester 1813–53, born: Westhampton, Massachusetts; son of Sylvester Judd, noted antiquarian; A.B. Yale College 1836, declined a professorship at Miami University, graduate: Harvard University Divinity School 1840; ordained pastor of the Unitarian Church, Augusta 1840–53; author: *A Young Man's Account of His Conversion from Calvinism* 1839, *Margaret, a Tale of the Real and Ideal, including Sketches of a Place not before described* 1845, a didactic poem in defense of Unitarian doctrine entitled *Philo, an Evangeliad* 1850, *Richard Edney and the Governor's Family* 1850, *The Church, in a series of Discourses* 1854, another volume, a loosely constructed tale of old New England, interspersed with descriptions of nature, illustrated by Felix Darley, was intended to promote the cause of liberal Christianity and the principles of world peace and temperance 1856; frequently in demand as a lecturer on social questions, especially opposition to war and slavery and support for temperance; in his later years, advocated the idea of birthright in the church, that is, that children ought to have the same rights within the church as adults, an idea that spread from his own church to many others; son-in-law of Reuel Williams.

Kaler, James Otis 1848–1912, born: Winterport; great nephew of Benjamin Thompson, Count Rumford; at age seventeen, began work at the *Boston Journal*, removed to New York 1870, associated with Frank Leslie and Norman Monro as an editor for the *New York Sun* and *Evening Telegram* to 1877, special correspondent to the *Boston Globe*; superintendent of schools: South Portland from 1898; under the pen name of James Otis, wrote very popular juvenile fiction, his works include: *Toby Tyler or, Ten Weeks With A Circus* (made into a movie by Walt Disney), *Raising the Pearl, Tim and Tip, Jenny Wren's Boarding House, Teddy and Carrots, Two Merchants of Newspaper Row* 1896, *Across the Delaware, Hunting in Africa: Adventures in Big Game Country* 1884, *A Runaway Brig; or An Accidental Cruise* 1888, *The Castaways, or, On the Florida Reefs* 1888, *The Grazango Diamond, When Israel Putnam Served The King, Little Joe, The Wreck of the Circus, Jack the Hunchback: A Story of Adventure on the Coast of Maine* 1892, *The Search for the Silver City: A Tale of Adventure in the Yucatan* 1893, *Josiah in New York, or, A Coupon From the Fresh Air Fund* 1893, *Chasing A Yacht, or, the Theft of the Gem* 1894, *The Boys' Revolt: A Story of the Street Arabs of New York* 1894, *The Boys of 1745 at the Capture of Louisbourg* 1895, *How Tommy Saved the Barn* 1895, *An Island Refuge: Casco Bay in 1676* 1895, *Wrecked on Spider Island; or, How Ned Rogers Found the Treasure* 1896, *The Capture of The Laughing Mary: A Story of Three New York Boys in 1776* 1898, *Joel Harford* 1898, *The Charming Sally, Privateer Schooner of New York* 1898, *The Cruise of the Comet: The Story of a Privateer of 1812* 1898, *Morgan: The Jersey Spy* 1898, *Captain Tom:The Privateersman of the Armed Brig Chasseur* 1899, *Down the Slope* 1899, *At the Siege of Quebec* 1899, *The Life Savers: A Story of the United States Life-Saving Service* 1899, *The Life of John Paul Jones* 1900, *Amos Dunkel, Oarsman: A Story of the Whale Boat Navy of 1776* 1901, *When We Destroyed the Gaspee: A Story of Narragansett Bay in 1772* 1901, *The Story of Old Falmouth* 1901, *With Porter in the Essex* 1901, *With The Regulators: A Story of North Carolina in 1768* 1901, *The Cruise of the Enterprise; being a story of the struggle and defeat of the French Privateering Expedition Against the United States in 1779* 1902, *How the Twins Captured a Hessian* 1902, *The Story of Pemaquid* 1902, *Minute Boys of the Mohawk Valley* 1905, *The Lightkeepers: A Story of the United States Lighthouse Service* 1900, *Aboard the Hylow on Sable Island Bank* 1907, *Commodore Barney's Young Spies: A Boy's Story of the Burning of the City of Washington* 1907, *Minute Boys of South Carolina* 1907, *The Wreck of the Ocean Queen* 1907, *Afloat in Freedom's Cause* 1908, *Cruise of the Phoebe* 1908, *Minute Boys of Long Island* 1908, *The Stowaways Aboard the Ellen Marie* 1908, *The Minute Boys of New York* 1909, *The Sarah Jane, Dickey Dalton, Captain: A Story of Tugboating in Portland Harbor* 1909, *The Wireless Station at Silver Fox Farm* 1910, *Mary of Plymouth: A Story of the Pilgrim Settlement* 1910, *The Minute Boys of Boston* 1910, *Stephen of Philadelphia: A Story of Penn's Colony* 1910, *Mr. Stubbs's Brother: A Sequel to Toby Tyler* 1910, *Geography of Maine* 1910, *Boy Scouts in the Maine Woods* 1911, *Adventures in Mexico* 1911, *Hannah of Kentucky* 1912, *Seth of Colorado; A Story of the Settlement of Denver* 1912, *Benjamin of Ohio: The Story of the Settlement of Marietta* 1912, *The Club at Crows' Corner* 1915.

Kalloch, Isaac Smith 1831–87, born: East Thomaston (Rockland); expelled from Colby College 1848; ordained Baptist minister 1850; called to lead the Tremont Temple, Boston, largest church in United States; thought by many to be the greatest preacher in United States, obliged to resign under cloud of adultery 1857; removed to Kansas, founded town of Ottawa; a founder of Bluemont Central College (later Kansas State University); owner and editor *Western Home Journal*, founder: Leavenworth, Lawrence & Galveston Railroad (predecessor of the Atchison, Topeka & Santa Fe Railroad); removed to San Francisco 1875, built the Metropolitan Temple, largest Baptist church in United States; became leader of the populist Workingman's movement, candidate for mayor, shot and severely wounded by Charles De Young, editor of the *San Francisco Chronicle*, who was, in turn, shot and killed by Kalloch's son Milton, who was acquitted 1879; elected mayor, served two-year term; removed to Whatcome, Washington (later Bellingham); died following a stroke.

Kavanagh, Edward 1795–1844, born: Damariscotta Mills, Newcastle; son of an Irish immigrant owner of extensive mills and a shipyard; attended Jesuit colleges in Montréal and Georgetown, D.C., graduate: St. Mary's College, Baltimore, 1813; member: Maine bar, practiced in Damariscotta Mills; member, board of selectman of Newcastle 1824–27; member: Maine House of Representatives 1826; secretary: Maine Senate 1830; member from the Third District: U.S. House of Representatives 1831–35 (Jacksonian), unsuccessful candidate for reelection 1834; chargé d'affairs to Portugal 1835–41; member: Maine Boundary Commission 1842; member: Maine Senate 1842, 1843, president 1843; following John Fairfield's resignation to become a U.S. senator, Kavanagh became the thirteenth governor of Maine (Democrat) 1843–44; Kavanagh was the first Roman Catholic governor of Maine; while governor, engaged in a spirited debate with the federal government for failing to protect Maine's interests in the Webster-Ashburton treaty; buried in St. Patrick's Catholic Cemetery, Newcastle.

Keegan, George Joseph 1921–91, born: Houlton; graduate: Van Buren Boys High School, valedictorian 1938; member: Civilian Conservation Corps 1939; student at Harvard College 1940–43; enlisted in the Army Air Corps Reserve; bomber pilot, flew fifty-six combat missions from New Guinea to Okinawa; A.B. Harvard College 1947; graduate student at Columbia University; recalled to duty, special mission in China; at Pentagon: expert on Soviet science, technology, and education, had much to do with the revival of interest in science in American schools; aide to President Eisenhower 1954; colonel, USAF, B-47 bomber pilot, Strategic Air Command; commanding officer: three bomber squadrons, director of operations for all Strategic Air and Reconnaissance Operations in Alaska; senior planner: U-2 operations over Cuba during the missile crisis 1962; worked with Lockheed in the development of the SR-71 supersonic photo plane; A.M. George Washington University 1965; chief of Air Force Intelligence in South Viet Nam 1967–69, gave the first warning of the Tet

Offensive, possibly saving Saigon from falling to the enemy; recipient: Distinguished Flying Cross; major general, USAF, chief of intelligence for all U.S. forces in the Pacific, reported on Soviet preparations for a nuclear strike against mainland China, deputy chief of staff for Operations and Plans, U.S. Air Force Logistics Command 1970; deeply troubled that the Congress and the American people were not being informed of Soviet preparations for war, resigned his position and began a worldwide speaking tour; vice president: U.S. Strategic Institute; military editor: *Strategic Review* 1977; co-chairman: Coalition for Peace Through Strength; president: Institute of Strategic Affairs; recipient: Distinguished Service Medal with oak leaf cluster, Legion of Merit with three oak leaf clusters; founder: *Soviet Military Thought* series.

Keith, Adelphus Bartlett 1855–1958, born: Appleton; son of a farmer, who removed, with his family, to Iowa 1865; left the farm in 1871 to learn the printing trade, devoted himself to various aspects of the newspaper business, edited and published the *Dennison* (Iowa) *Bulletin*, issued a German edition of the newspaper, associated with several other Iowa publications; editor: *Des Moines Leader*; delegate to the Democratic National Convention 1884, 1888; removed to Montana 1889; editor: *Montana Farming and Stock Journal*; managing editor: *Helena Daily Journal*; private secretary to Governor Richards 1893–97; official custodian of the state armory and state supplies; editor: *Montana Western Mining World*; editor: *Butte Inter-Mountain* 1897–1900; editor: *Helena Daily Herald* 1900–01; president: Montana State Press Association 1897–98; managing editor and political writer for the daily *Butte Miner* 1901; edited the *Pacific Woodman* for four years and the *Montana Workman* for one year; past head consul in woodcraft and past supreme steward in the Fraternal Union of America; president: Montana Auxiliary Fraternal Congress 1903; student of metaphysics, anatomy, and physiology; graduate: American Institute of Phrenology, New York, 1877; his life work was the development of a new system of metaphysics, involving practical and self-applicable methods of thought control, by which mental fatigue was eliminated.

Kellogg, Elijah 1813–1901, born: Portland; son of Elijah Kellogg; A.B. Bowdoin College 1840, graduate: Andover Theological Seminary 1843; pastor: Harpswell Congregational Church 1844–55, 1885–1901; chaplain: Seamans Friend Society, Boston 1855–65; author of numerous works for boys, including: *Good Old Times* 1867, *Charlie Bell, the Waif of Elm Island* 1868, *The Ark of Elm Island* 1869, *Lion Ben* 1869, *Arthur Brown, the Young Captain* 1870, *The Boy Farmer of Elm Island* 1870, *Hard-Scrabble of Elm Island* 1870, *Norman Cline* 1870, *The Young Shipbuilders of Elm Island* 1870, *The Sophomore of Radcliffe* 1872, *Stout Heart, or, the Student from Across the Sea* 1873, *Brought to the Front, or, The Young Defenders* 1876, *The Mission of Black Rifle* 1876, *Forest Glen, or, The Mohawk's Friendship* 1877, *Merry Xmas*, a farce in two acts, written for a college performance and published in 1910, his *Spartacus to the Gladiators* was, for many years, a standard recitation piece; despite wealth from his writing (and which he dispersed in acts of charity), he remained at the Harpswell church, until his death, where he is buried in the churchyard.

Kendall, Bion Freeman 1827–63, born: Bethel; A.B. Dartmouth College 1852; obtained the position of clerk in a federal department in Washington, served as astronomer in the Isaac Stevens's railroad survey expedition to the Northwest; became a lawyer in Olympia, Washington Territory, secretary of the territorial legislature; active in the timber trade; at the beginning of the Civil War: made a clandestine journey through the southern states and made a report to General Winfield Scott on the condition, resources, and war material in the several seceding states 1861; appointed superintendent of Indian affairs for the Washington Territory; editor of a newspaper; assassinated by a man who believed that his father had been libeled by that journal.

Kendell, Charles West 1828–1914, born: Searsmont; graduate: Phillips Academy, Andover, student at Yale College; removed to California; miner; proprietor and editor: *San Jose Tribune* 1855–59; member: California bar 1859, practiced law in Sacramento; member: California Assembly 1861, 1862; removed to Hamilton, Nevada, 1862; member: U.S. House of Representatives 1871–75 (Democrat); removed to Denver, practiced law; assistant librarian: Interstate Commerce Commission, Washington, D.C., 1892–1914; buried in the Congressional Cemetery, Washington.

Kent, Edward I 1802–77, born: Concord, New Hampshire; nephew of Prentiss

Mellen; A.B. Harvard College 1821, classmate and close friend of Ralph Waldo Emerson, Josiah Quincey, and Robert Barnwell, L.L.D. (Hon.) Waterville College 1855; removed to Topsham to study law with Benjamin Orr, practiced in Bangor from 1825; chief justice: Court of Sessions 1827; member: Maine House of Representatives 1829–38; mayor of Bangor 1836–38; unsuccessful candidate for governor 1836; elected ninth governor of Maine (Whig) 1837–38, so close were the results that the Supreme Judicial Court was called upon to decide the validity of some returns; unsuccessful candidate for governor 1838, 1839, elected eleventh governor of Maine 1840–41, it was this election that gave rise to the once-famous political song: *Have You Heard the News from Maine?*; unsuccessful candidate for governor 1841; appointed commissioner to determine the northern boundary with Canada, under provisions of the Webster-Ashburton Treaty 1843; delegate: Whig National Convention 1848; U.S. consul at Rio de Janeiro 1849–53; associate justice: Maine Supreme Judicial Court 1859–73; chairman: Maine constitutional commission 1875; buried in Mt. Auburn Cemetery, Cambridge, Massachusetts.

Kent, Edward Austin 1853–1912, born: Bangor; graduate: École des Beaux Arts, Paris; began the practice of architecture in Syracuse with J. L. Sillsbee, removed to Chicago with Sillsbee for two years 1882–84, began to practice independently in Buffalo; among his designs were: Temple Beth Zion, the W. O. Chapin building, the First Unitarian Church (which continues to receive favorable comment by architectural historians), numerous residences, other commissions included the Kent House, a hotel on the grounds of the Chautauqua Institution; lost his life with the sinking of RMS *Titanic*; his body was recovered, along with the miniature, entrusted to him by Mrs. Helen Candee, for safekeeping, and was subsequently buried in Buffalo's Forest Lawn Cemetery, the inscription on his tombstone reads "Greater love hath no man than this, that a man lay down his life for his friends."

Kent, Rockwell 1882–1971, born: Tarrytown Heights, New York; son of a mining engineer and lawyer; student: Episcopal Academy of Connecticut, Horace Mann School, New York, student: Columbia University; studied art with William Merritt Chase, Robert Henri, Hayes Miller, Abbott Thayer; settled on Monhegan Island 1904, where he built his own house and supported himself as a lobsterman; first exhibited his paintings at the National Academy of Design, New York 1905; landscape and figure painter, wood engraver, lithographer; represented at Metropolitan Museum of Art, New York, Art Institute of Chicago, Brooklyn Museum of Art, other American museums, Pushkin Museum, Moscow, Hermitage, St. Petersburg; exhibited in the United States, South America, and Europe; chairman: National Council for American-Soviet Friendship; recipient: Lenin Prize for strengthening peace among the nations 1967; member: National Academy, National Institute of Arts and Letters; author: *Wilderness* 1927, *Voyaging* 1924, *North by East* 1930, *Rockwellkentiana* 1933, *Salaminia* 1935, *This Is My Own* 1940, *Its Me, O Lord* 1955, *Of Men and Mountains* 1959, *Greenland Journal* 1963, *After Long Years* 1968.

Keyes, Erasmus 1810–95, born: Brimfield, Massachusetts; removed at an early age to Augusta, son of a prominent physician; secured an appointment to U.S. Military Academy at West Point, graduated 1832; commissioned second lieutenant, 3rd Artillery 1833; aide-de-camp to General Scott (whose favorite Keyes became) 1837–41; captain 3rd Artillery 1841, served at New Orleans and Fort Moultrie, Carolina 1842–44; member: board of visitors, U.S. Military Academy, instructor in field artillery and cavalry: U.S. Military Academy 1844–48; served on Pacific coast 1851-60; military aide to General Scott, lieutenant colonel, USA, 1861; commanded a brigade at first Manassas, colonel, USA, and brigadier general, USA, 1861; commanding officer: 1st Volunteer Cavalry, commanding officer: IV Corps in the Peninsula campaign; major general, USA, resigned 1864, after a dispute with his commanding officer, General John Adams Dix; removed to San Francisco, president: Maxwell Gold Mining Co. 1867–69, vice president: California Vine Culture Society for Napa County; author: *Fifty Years Observations of Man and Events* 1884; Camp

Keyes, Augusta, was named in his honor; died in Nice, France, ultimately buried at West Point.

Kidder, Wellington Parker 1853–1924, born: Norridgewock; at age fifteen, patented an improvement in rotary steam engines; invented the web adjustable press 1874, later conceived the idea of a press printing from a continuous roll of paper, this was the first self-feeding, moving bed, and stationary platen press ever constructed; constructed the first cylinder web perfected press 1884, made it possible to print four times as fast as presses then in use, it could be adjusted to cut any desired length of paper, very rapidly adopted worldwide for fast printing jobs; invented an attachment that made it possible to print in two colors, simultaneously; invented a complete system of electroplating machinery; invented a consecutive numbering machine, which made it possible to print tickets, banknotes, &c. at a rate of 700,000 per day per machine; invented the Franklin typewriter, the first visible writing typewriter constructed 1887, produced the Wellington typewriter which was manufactured in Canada and distributed throughout the British empire, under the name Empire, this machine was also manufactured in Belgium and in Germany, where it was known as the Adler typewriter; invented the first noiseless typewriter 1895; organized the Parker Typewriter Co., Buffalo 1895, for its manufacture and distribution; designed and manufactured a steam car 1902.

Kimball, Francis Hatch 1845–1919, born: Kennebunk; attended public school in Kennebunk to age fourteen, entered the employ of a relative in Haverhill, Massachusetts, where he gained his first practical experience in architecture, helping erect structures; in the Civil War: enlisted in the U.S. Navy; entered the architectural office of Louis P. Rogers, Boston 1867, who soon formed a partnership with Gridley Bryant; sent to Hartford, Connecticut, to prepare working drawings for the Charter Oak Life Insurance Company's building and a business block for the Connecticut Mutual Life Insurance Co.; supervising architect: Trinity College, Hartford 1873–78, sent by the architect, William Burgess, to London to familiarize himself with the drawings; removed to New York, where he opened an office in association with Thomas Wisedell, his first work was the remodeling of the old Madison Square Garden; his Casino Theatre, in the Moorish style, at the corner of Broadway and 39th Street, where he demonstrated his mastery of applied terra cotta detail; called upon by the city of New York to prepare construction code for the construction of theatres, in particular, means to suppress fire; designed the Fifth Avenue Theatre and the Garrick Theatre; devised the pneumatic caisson approach to the construction of foundations, an advance quickly adopted by the building industry and particularly important in the construction of skyscrapers; consulting architect: Metropolitan Life Building, whose foundation was built with his method, the tallest building in country, in its day; he also designed churches, homes, warehouses, and railroad stations as well as numerous office buildings, including the Standard Oil Company building.

Kimball, Sumner Increase 1834–1923, born: Lebanon; son of a lawyer; A.B. Bowdoin College 1855, Ph.D. 1891; member: Maine bar 1858, practiced in North Berwick; member: Maine House of Representatives 1859; clerk and chief clerk, Second Auditors Office, U.S. Treasury Department 1862–71; chief: Revenue Marine Service and Life Saving Service 1871–75; general superintendent: United States Life Saving Service and chief officer of the bureau 1878-1916; rid the service of political appointments, oversaw the construction of numerous life-saving stations on all coasts, oversaw the design and construction of superior watercraft, dramatically increased the success rate of marine rescues; U.S. delegate to the International Marine Conference, Washington, 1889, chairman of the Committee on Life-saving and Apparatus; organized, by act of Congress, the U.S. Coast Guard by combining the Life Saving Service and the Revenue Cutter Service 1915; founder: U.S. Coast Guard Academy, retired at age eighty-one at three-quarters pay, a unique distinction; president: Board of Life Saving Appliances; acting chief clerk, acting comptroller, acting solicitor: U.S. Treasury; author: *Organization and Methods, at the U.S. Life Saving Service* 1889, *Joshua James, Lifesaver* 1909

Kimball, William Wallace 1828–1904, born: South Paris; attended public school in South Paris, after clerking in a store and teaching in district schools, removed to Boston 1848; traveling salesman; located in Chicago 1857, opened a piano and organ warehouse, moved his showrooms to the Crosby Opera House; his business destroyed in the Great Fire of 1871, began selling out of his house, using the billiard room as an office and the stable as shipping department; incorporated W. W. Kimball Co. 1882; came to be largest manufacturer of pianos and organs in world.

Kimball, William Wirt 1848–1930, born: South Paris; son of William King Kimball; graduate: U.S. Naval Academy 1869; commissioned ensign 1870, promoted through the ranks to rear admiral 1908; served on North and South Atlantic, European, Asiatic stations; in first class of officers at Torpedo Station, Newport, 1870; assisted in the capture of American steamers on the Orinoco 1872; torpedo officer on first two torpedo craft in U.S. Navy 1874; engaged in the development of magazine and machine guns in the 1880s; designed, constructed, and operated the first armed cars used by U.S. forces; assisted in occupation of Panama 1885, reported to Congress on the progress of the Panama canal 1886; executive officer: USS *Detroit* in the Enchadas affair in Rio Harbor 1884; engaged in development of submarine boats in early 1880s, (John P. Holland, inventor of the Holland boats, wrote of him, "submarining owes more to him than any other living man"), organized first torpedo boat flotilla in the USN; commanding officer: Atlantic Torpedo Boat Flotilla, in the war with Spain; commanding officer: USS *Caesar*, USS *Abarenda*, USS *Glacier*, USS *Supply*, USS *Vixen*, USS *Concord*, USS *Wheeling*, USS *Alert*, first commanding officer or plankholder USS *New Jersey*; member: Board of Construction, Examination and Retirement 1907–09; commanding officer: Nicaragua Expeditionary Squadron 1909;

recalled to active duty during World War I, president of officers and officer in charge, history section: Office of Operations; senior officer present: second action at Matanzas Bar.

King, Cyrus 1772–1817, born: Scarborough; brother of William King, half-brother of Rufus King, son of a lumber dealer; graduate: Phillips Academy, A.B. Columbia College 1794; member: Saco bar 1797; major general: Massachusetts Militia; a founder of Thornton Academy; member (at-large 1813-15, Fourteenth District 1815–17): U.S. House of Representatives 1813–17 (Federalist); buried in Laurel Hill Cemetery, Saco.

King, Horatio 1811–97, born: Paris; son of a farmer; at age seventeen, went to work for the *Paris Jeffersonian*, purchased the paper with Hannibal Hamlin 1830, later became sole owner; sold out to the *Eastern Argus* 1838; removed to Washington, D.C.; secured a clerkship in the U.S. Post Office 1839, head of foreign mail division 1850, where he drastically improved mail service to Europe; appointed first assistant postmaster general 1854, served under presidents Pierce and Buchanan; appointed postmaster general 1861; although a Democrat, took an uncompromising stand against abuses of the franking privilege by Southern congressmen, thus becoming the first federal official to deny the legality of secession; practiced law in the District of Columbia, member of the board of commissioners to carry out the Emancipation Proclamation in the District of Columbia; author: *Sketches of Travel, or, Twelve Months in Europe* 1878, *Turning on the Light* 1895, a defense of the Buchanan Administration; secretary: Washington Monument Society; father of Horatio Collins King; buried in Congressional Cemetery, Washington.

King, Horatio Collins 1837–1918, born: Portland; son of Horatio King; A.B. Dickinson College ΦΒΚ 1858, studied law with Edward Masters Stanton, later U.S. secretary of war; member: New York bar 1861; in the Civil War: commissioned captain, USV; served on the staffs of Generals Casey, Heintzelman, Augur, Wesley Merritt, and Thomas Devin, as major and quartermaster, USV; recipient: Medal of Honor, Dinwiddie Courthouse, Virginia, 31 March 1865, "While serving as a volunteer aide, carried orders to the reserve brigade and participated with it in the charge which repulsed the enemy." Later brevetted colonel, USV; returned to the practice of law in New York to 1870; associate editor: *New York Star* 1870–72; associated with Henry Ward Beecher as business manager of the *Christian Union*; publisher *Christian at Work*; appointed judge advocate general on the staff of President Cleveland 1884–88; Democratic nominee for New York secretary of state 1895; author: *The Plymouth Silver Wedding* 1873, *The Brooklyn Congregational Council* 1876, *King's Guide to Regimental Courts-Martial* 1882, editor: *Proceedings of the Army of the Potomac* 1879–87; buried in Green-Wood Cemetery, Brooklyn, New York.

King, Rufus 1755–1827, born: Scarborough; son of Richard King, a lumber dealer, half brother of William and Cyrus King; graduate: Dummer Academy, Byfield, Massachusetts, A.B. Harvard College 1777; studied law with Theophilus Parsons in Newburyport; aide to General John Sullivan, in the unsuccessful Rhode Island Expedition 1778; delegate: Continental Congress 1784–89, proposed that slavery be prohibited in the states created out of the Northwest Territory 1785, although this proposal was never voted on, it became part of the Northwest Ordinance 1787; appointed commissioner of the Commonwealth of Massachusetts to determine its boundaries with New York and to convey to the United States lands claimed west of the Alleghenies 1787; delegate: U.S. Constitutional Convention 1788, a drafter and signer of United States Constitution; became a citizen of New York 1788; member: U.S. Senate 1789–96, 1813–25; a warm advocate of John Jay's mission to Great Britain and the subsequent treaty, wrote a number of articles under the pseudonym of Camillus advocating its adoption; minister plenipotentiary to Great Britain 1796–1803, 1825–26; unsuccessful candidate for vice president of the United States 1804, 1808, unsuccessful candidate for governor 1816, unsuccessful candidate for president of the United States 1816, last Federalist to be nominated for president; director: First National Bank of the United States; an opponent of the so-called Missouri Compromise, in his last act as senator, proposed buying the freedom of slaves through sales of U.S. public lands, had his wise counsel been heeded, the Civil War might have been averted; father of James Gore King, banker, a founder of the New York Stock Exchange, and a prime mover in the creation of the Erie and other canals, the Erie and other railroads, and John Alsop King, reformer and governor of New York; his home in Queens is extant and is on the National Register of Historic Places; buried in Grace Church graveyard, Queens, New York.

King, William 1768–1852, born: Scarborough; brother of Cyrus King, half-brother of Rufus King, son of a lumber dealer; as a youth, worked lumber mill in Saco, later in Topsham, later owned a mill in Topsham, opened a general store; representative to Massachusetts General Court from Topsham 1795–99, removed to Bath 1800; in time, became one of the largest ship owners in the United States; founder and president of the first bank in Bath, owned much real estate in Maine (Kingfield was named in his honor); one of the incorporators and principal owners of the first cotton mill in Maine, erected in Brunswick 1809; member Massachusetts House of Representatives from Bath (Democrat) 1804–06, member for Lincoln County: Massachusetts Senate 1807–11, 1818–19; proposed the Betterment Act, which compelled original proprietors of wild lands or speculators therein to sell at first value lands cleared and improved by squatters or else pay them for the improvements, also proposed the Toleration Act, which ended the requirement that towns were compelled to support a minister; leader in separation movement, delegate, president: Maine Constitutional Convention 1819; first governor of Maine 1820–21, while governor, in order to encourage industrial growth, advocated tax rebates for manufacturers who built factories; resigned to become U.S. commissioner for the adjustment of Spanish claims in Florida 1821–24; commissioner of public buildings in Maine, obtained the services of architect Bulfinch and saw to the erection of the Maine Statehouse in Augusta; collector of customs in Bath 1831–34; unsuccessful Whig candidate for governor 1835; major general of Massachusetts militia, colonel, USA, recruiting officer of U.S. Volunteers in the War of 1812, recruited a regiment in Bath; trustee: Maine Literary and Theological Institution, later Colby College 1821–48, Bowdoin College overseer 1797–1821, trustee 1821–49, vice president of the board 1836–49; buried in Oak Grove Cemetery, Bath.

Kinnison, David 1736–1851, born: Wells; owned a farm in Lebanon, formed a political club and held secret meetings in a tavern, participated in the Boston Tea Party, served as minuteman at Lexington and Concord, served with the Continental Army to 1781, returned to Wells; in the War of 1812: although well into his sixties, enlisted and fought at the battle of Sacketts Harbor and was badly wounded at the battle of Williamsburgh; learned to read at age 62, married and buried 4 wives, sired 22 children, at age 110 walked to Chicago, could and did make 20 miles a day, addressed an antislavery meeting with considerable effect 1848; last survivor of the Boston Tea Party.

Klain, Zora 1884–1952, born: Norway; A.B. Clark University 1912, A.M. Pennsylvania State College 1917, Ph.D. University of Pennsylvania 1924; instructor: MacDonough (Maryland) Academy 1912–15, assistant professor of German: Pennsylvania State College 1915–22, assistant professor of psychology and education: University of Rochester 1924–25, chairman of department and professor of education: Rutgers University from 1925; author: *Quaker Contributions to Education in North Carolina* 1925, *Educational Activities of New England Quakers* 1928, contributor of numerous articles for educational journals.

Klingelsmith, Margaret Center 1859–1931, born: Portland; L.L.B. University of Pennsylvania Law School 1898, L.L.D. (Hon.) 1916; the first female graduate of University of Pennsylvania law school, the first female to obtain an L.L.D. from the University of Pennsylvania; her essay *The Tendency of Commercial Law in Crimes and Torts* won Meredith Prize; librarian: Biddle Law Library, University of Pennsylvania, 1899–1931, increased its holdings from 8,000 volumes to 80,000, was acknowledged as the leading law library in United States; author: *University of Pennsylvania: The Proceedings at the Dedication of the New Building of the Department of Law* (two volumes) 1915, *Stetham's Abridgment of the Law* (two volumes) 1915; vice president: University of Pennsylvania 1916; author of numerous essays and biographies including those of James Wilson and Jeremiah Sullivan, contributed to magazines and did much work for Lewis and Pepper's *Digest of Decisions and Encyclopedia of Pennsylvania Law 1754–1898* (twenty-three volumes) 1898-1906.

Knight, Margaret 1838–1914, born: York; made her first invention at age twelve: a device to prevent weaving shuttles from flying; worked in upholstery, learned daguerreotype, ambrotype, and photography; worked at Columbia Bag Co., Springfield, Massachusetts, invented the machinery necessary to make a square-bottomed bag, forced to defend her patent against infringement, produced 1,867 drawings in her successful legal action; later invented a window frame and sash, several household implements; her sleeve valve engine was incorporated into the Willys-Knight motorcar; held a total of twenty-seven patents; buried in Newton (Massachusetts) Cemetery.

Knox, George William 1829–92, born: Belgrade; removed to Washington, D.C., and began Knox's Express Co. 1864, which came to be the largest private express company in the country; for twenty years was U.S. mail contractor; delivered materials for the Washington Monument, the State, War and Navy Building, the Library of Congress, and a variety of other important structures.

Knox, Henry 1750–1806, born: Boston, Massachusetts; son of a ship captain and owner of a wharf; employed by Wharton & Barnes, booksellers; a large, robust man, often engaged in wrestling matches between the North and South snds of Boston; joined a military company at age eighteen, later second in command of the Boston grenadier corps; derived his knowledge of military matters from conversing with British officers who frequented his bookstore and from reading texts on such matters as artillery, fortifications, &c.; through the explosion of his fowling piece, lost two fingers on his left hand, which he kept wrapped in a colorful scarf; married Lucy Flucker, daughter of the secretary of the colony and granddaughter of Samuel Waldo; associated with the Sons of Liberty; while serving with the Revolutionary Army during the siege of Boston, his bookstore was robbed and pillaged; engaged in recruitment of soldiers, later, appointed to artillery and given the chore of dragging fifty-five cannon from Fort Ticonderoga to Boston, essential in driving the British from that city; served on the court martial of Major André, the British spy; superintended the crossing of the Delaware River, his stentorian voice was heard above the noise of the storm that covered that maneuver; at the battle of Trenton, Knox's artillery was the decisive factor in victory, participated in the battle of Princeton; after the army went into winter quarters, Knox was detailed to go to Springfield, Massachusetts, to oversee the casting of cannon; associated with General Greene in the planning of the defenses of the Hudson River; covered the American retreat at Monmouth, with his artillery; directed the placement and firing of artillery at Yorktown; promoted to major general 1782; chairman of the committee of officers that drafted a petition to Congress for redress of back pay and other grievances, failure of Congress to address these grievances led to the Newburg addresses, Knox personally quelled the rebellious attitude of those disaffected officers; founded the Society of the Cincinnati 1783; after the war and Washington's retirement, served as commanding officer of the army; served as secretary of war under the Confederation 1785–89, and later under President Washington 1789–94; founded the U.S. Military Academy, pressed for the creation of a navy; removed to his wife's vast estate in Maine, where he conducted many improvements; died as a result of getting a chicken bone stuck in his throat; buried in Elm Grove Cemetery, Thomaston; grandfather of Henry Knox Thatcher.

Kotzschmar, Herman 1829–1909, born: Finsterwalde, Brandenburg; at age nineteen, organized the Saxonia Band and took it to the United States; after the tour, lingered and was approached to take over the Jibbenainosay Band, based at the Portland Museum on Union Street 1849. Subsequently became a teacher and the pianist for the Sacred Music Society; organist at First Parish 1851–98; helped to organize Haydn Association in 1853, conductor 1869–98; composer of sacred music, vocal quartets, song, piano pieces, &c.; teacher of Cyrus Curtis and John Knowles Paine.

Kyes, Preston 1875–1949, North Jay; graduate: Wilton Academy, A.B. Bowdoin College 1896, A.M. 1900, Sc.D. (Hon.) 1921, graduate student: Harvard University 1898-1900, M.D. Johns Hopkins University Medical School 1900; associate: Royal Prussian Institute of Experimental Therapy, Frankfort-am-Main 1900–02, 1904–06; fellow: Rockefeller Institute for Medical Research, New York 1902–05; associate: Memorial Institute for Infectious Diseases, Chicago 1904–09, associate in anatomy: University of Chicago Medical School 1901–02, instructor 1902–04, assistant professor 1904–06, assistant professor of experimental pathology 1906–12, assistant professor of preventive medicine 1912–16, associate professor 1916–18, professor 1918–40; an internationally known authority in pathology and anatomy, did much research primarily relating to bacterial disease, toxins and antitoxins, venoms and the human spleen, venom hemolysis, fixed tissue phagocytes, serum therapy in pneumonia; editor: *American Journal of Immunology, The University of Chicago Science Series*; trustee: Farmington Memorial Hospital, North Jay Library.

Ladd, Edwin Fremont 1859–1925, born: Starks; B.S. University of Maine 1884; assistant chemist: New York Experimental Station, Geneva, New York, 1884–90, professor of chemistry and pharmacy, North Dakota Agricultural College 1890–1912, dean 1912–16, president 1916–21; pressed on the North Dakota state legislature some of the earliest pure food laws in the nation as North Dakota state chemist, state food commissioner from 1902, state inspector of weights, grades, and measures 1918–21; for the purpose of testing wheat and determining actual food value, constructed an experimental flour mill and bakery, where he subjected cereal products to the most searching tests known to science, introduced a new system of grading, based on laboratory tests and milling value rather than weight or appearance; having the authority to revoke the license of any miller who failed to observe the new regulations, he revolutionized the existing milling methods of North Dakota, bringing him into intense conflict with milling interests; secured legislation to require hotel and restaurant inspections; conducted the most advanced tests on paint and varnish; advocated state-owned grain elevators; co-founder of the Farmers' Non-Partisan League, which, by 1916, controlled every major state office; denied a passport to attended the Peace Convention, he was characterized by the U.S. attorney general as a radical, a red, a dangerous person; a leader in the fight for the Pure Food and Drug Act; member: U.S. Senate 1921–25 (Republican), chairman: Committee on Public Roads and Surveys, opposed the entry of the United States into the League of Nations, contending that it was not a league of peoples but that of governments, opposed the World Court, contending that it was a court of exploitation; opposed the Four Powers Pact, contending that it was based on oppression; opposed the Federal Reserve System, contending that it gave too much power to unelected individuals; contended that the U.S. Supreme Court did not have the right to overturn acts of Congress; succeeded Senator Lenroot as the chairman of the Senate investigative committee that bared the oil scandals, generally known as Tea Pot Dome; supported the presidential candidacy of Robert La Follette, rather than Coolidge 1924, outraged Republicans stripped him and other so-called radicals of their committee chairmanships; editor: *North Dakota Farmer* 1899–1906, author: *Manual of Analysis* 1898, *Mixed Paints* 1908; buried in Glenwood Cemetery, Washington, D.C.

Ladd, Horatio Oliver 1839–1932, born: Hallowell; son of General Samuel Greenleaf Ladd, second adjutant general of the Maine militia and the owner of a hardware business; A.B. Bowdoin College 1859; principal: Farmington (Maine) Academy 1859–61; graduate: Yale University Divinity School 1863; served as an army chaplain in the Civil War; pastor of the Olivet (Michigan) Congregational Church and professor of rhetoric and oratory at Olivet College 1868–69, Congregational minister at Romeo, Michigan, 1869–73, principal: New Hampshire State Normal School, Plymouth 1873–76; founder and president: University of New Mexico 1881–89; founder: Ramona and U.S. Indian Schools, Santa Fé; supervisor of the U.S. census in New Mexico 1890; pastor: Hopkinton (Massachusetts) Congregrational Church 1890–91; took orders in the Protestant Episcopal Church; rector: Trinity Church, Fishkill, New York, 1891–96, later served as rector of Grace Church, Jamaica, Long Island, New York; author: *The Memorial of John S. C. Abbott* 1878, *The War with Mexico* 1881, *Ramona Days* 1889, *The Founding of the Episcopal Church in Dutchess County, New.York* 1895, numerous articles for periodicals; son-in-law of John S. C. Abbott.

Ladd, William 1788–1841, born: Exeter, New Hampshire; son of a wealthy ship captain; A.B. Harvard College ΦBK 1798; at age twenty, commanding officer of a merchant brig, out of Portland, spent a few years in Florida, operating a free-labor experiment to point the way to a peaceful abolition of slavery, turned to scientific farming in Minot 1812; founded the American Peace Society 1828, author: *A Brief Illustration of the Principles of War and Peace, by Philanthropos* 1831, *An Essay on a Congress of Nations* 1840, tirelessly propagandized state legislatures, the Congress, and the White

House with delegations, petitions, and political pressure for his plan for a Congress of Nations that would provide for the general welfare and a Court of Nations that would settle international disputes judicially or diplomatically; first to recognize that any international court would have to be independent of the executive body, recognized that the realization of peace required the securing of justice; taking a page from Rufus King, advocated the sale of public lands to purchase the freedom of slaves; licensed Congregational ministry 1837; first to point out the relationship between pacifism and feminism in his *On the Duty of Females to Promote the Causes of Peace* 1836; feeling that the principle of nonresistance was the only solid and substantial foundation, persuaded the American Peace Society to condemn all war, defensive as well as offensive; after his death, the American Peace Society became international, sponsoring Peace Conventions in Brussels, Paris, London, and elsewhere; eventually the International Court of Arbitration and League of Nations were founded, incorporating many of the first principles laid down by Ladd; Bowdoin College overseer 1825–40.

Lamson, Charles Henry 1847–1930, born: Augusta; engaged as a watchmaker and optician; inventor of luggage carrier for bicycles and novel types of kites and aeroplanes for use in meterological observations; pioneer in the construction of flying machines; was the first to obtain patent for a method of tilting or warping the wings of kites and aeroplanes for the purpose of balancing or turning in flight; the Wright brothers experimented with a Lamson kite before building their own.

Lane, Gertrude Battles 1874–1941, born: Saco; graduate: Thornton Academy 1892, a year's course at Burdett College of Business and Shorthand; assistant editor: Cyclopedia Publishing Co. 1896–1902; contributor of essays, poems, and book reviews to the *Boston Transcript, Boston Beacon*; household editor: *Women's Home Companion* 1903, managing editor 1909, editor in chief from 1912; raised subscription rate from 700,000 to 3.5 million, fought against child labor, unsanitary grocery stores, devoted space to the education of women for the vote, health care for infants and mothers, regularly published articles by the presidents of the United States, Eleanor Roosevelt had a regular column, published Kathleen Norris, Edna Ferber, Sinclair Lewis, Willa Cather, Booth Tarkington, Pearl Buck, Sherwood Anderson,and others; during World War I, served with Herbert Hoover in the U.S. Food Administration, orchestrated and disseminated information about food, energy, and clothing; member: White House Conference on Child Health and Protection 1930–31; vice president: Crowell Publishing Co. from 1923; managing editor: *American Magazine* 1933; author: *A Peculiar Treasure* 1939.

Lane, Horace M. 1837–1912, born: Readfield; at age nineteen removed to Brazil, mastered the language, reorganized education in Brazil, returned to United States, studied medicine and settled in Missouri 1863; called to Brazil by Presbyterian Board of Foreign Missions; despite the loss to his wife, eight children, and a large medical practice, departed for S‹o Paulo, established Ecola Americana, had some 18,000 students, made an enormous impact on Brazil; organizer and president: Mackenzie College, the most influential educational institution in Brazil.

Langdon, Timothy 1746–08, born: Boston, Massachusetts; A.B. Harvard College 1765, A.M. 1767; removed to Wiscasset 1769, where he was the only resident lawyer for many years, built a fine house, which was a landmark on Fort Hill to 1891; appointed crown lawyer (prosecuting attorney for the province); member: Wiscasset Committee of Correspondence; elected by the town to the Third Provincial Congress 1775, upon his return, found that his friend, Abiel Wood, had been declared a public enemy, by the Provincial Congress, in response to unflattering statements made about John Hancock and Samuel Adams, as well as trading voyages to Nova Scotia, succeeded, with the aid of Thomas Rice, of having the charges quashed at town meeting; appointed Lincoln County register of probate, Jonathan Bowman protested this appointment to the council, which suspended the appointment and appointed Roland Cushing in his place; appointed justice of the peace and quorum 1776, where he mainly engaged in apprehending deserters from the Continental Army and resident Tories, his conduct in this disagreeable chore was often marked by humanity and kindness, sufficiently so that he was upbraided by Benedict Arnold; his last appointive position, before alcoholism rendered him incompetent, was an admiralty judge for the Province of Maine 1778–85; dropped from the list of justices of the peace 1790; from that time, he sold his mansion and wandered about, from Pownalborough to Vassalborough, Norridgewock, Farmington, Orono, and the upper reaches of the Kennebec, writing an occasional writ in return for drink; dropped from the list of attorneys licensed to practice 1800; eventually found dead, sitting on his chair, at Hinkley's Plain, Hallowell.

Langlais, Bernard 1921–77, born: Old Town; student: Corcoran School of Art, Washington, D.C., 1948–50, Brooklyn Museum School 1949–51, Skowhegan School of Painting and Sculpture 1949–50, Grande Chaumier, Paris, France, 1952–53, Art Academy of Oslo, Norway, 1954–56, D.F.A. University of Maine 1973; one-man show: Leo Castelli Gallery, New York, Governor Dummer Academy, Allan Stone Gallery, Grippi & Waddell Gallery, Lee A. Ault & Company, Inc., Alpha Gallery, Phillips Academy, Exeter, Seton Hall University, Brooklyn Museum, University of Maine, others; exhibited in group shows: Museum of Modern Art, New York, Carnegie International, Whitney Museum, Colby College, Art in Embassies, XX Siècle Gallerie, Hobe Sound Gallery, Dallas Museum of Contemporary Art, San Francisco Museum of Art Assemblage, Art Institute of Chicago, Barone Gallery, Brooklyn Museum, Kornblee Gallery, Martha Jackson Gallery, Camino Gallery, others; represented in permanent collections: Philadelphia Museum of Art, Philadelphia Zoological Gardens, Art Institute of Chicago, Olsen Foundation, Whitney Museum, Singer Sewing Machine collections, Chrysler Museum, others; numerous private collections;

visiting artist: Pennsylvania State University 1971; member: Maine Arts and Humanities Commission 1972–77; recipient: Maine Arts and Humanities Award 1971, Ford Foundation Purchase Award 1963, Skowhegan School of Painting and Sculpture, Maine Artist Award 1975, Fulbright scholar 1954–55, Guggenheim fellow 1972–73, National Endowment for Arts Award 1977–78, established Bernard Langlais Scholarship: Skowhegan School of Painting and Sculpture endowed 1979; buried in Cushing.

Lansil, Walter Franklin 1846–1925, born: Bangor; after attending public schools in Bangor, studied art in Paris at the Julien Academy and with J. P. Hardy in Bangor; settled in Boston; known, in particular, for his rendering of luminous effects, such as sunrises and sunsets; some of his noted paintings are *Crossing the Georges, Sunset, Boston Harbor, View of Charlestown, with Shipping.*

Larrabee, William Clark 1802–59, born: Cape Elizabeth; A.B. Bowdoin College 1828; ordained Methodist minister 1828, principal: Alfred Academy 1828–30, tutor: Wesleyan College 1830, principal: Oneida Conference Seminary (the first Methodist school of higher education in New York State), Cazenovia, New York, 1831–32, principal: Maine Wesleyan Seminary, Kents Hill, 1836–41; assisted in first geological survey of Maine, professor of mathematics and natural science: Indiana Asbury University (now DePauw), Greencastle, 1841–50, president: 1849–50; editor: *Ladies' Repository*, Cincinnati, 1852; first superintendent of education, State of Indiana, 1852–54, 1856–59; member: board of visitors, U.S. Military Academy, Bowdoin College overseer 1839–43; author: *Evidences of Natural and Revealed Religion* 1850, *Wesley and his Coadjutors* (two volumes) 1851, *Asbury and his Coadjutors* (two volumes) 1851, *Rosebower* 1854.

Laughlin, Gail 1868–1952, born: Robbinston; A.B. Wellesley College 1894, L.L.B. Cornell University Law School 1898; founder: *The Agora*, winner: Cornell University debate prize and leader of Cornell University Collegiate debate team 1898; editorial writer: *New York Commercial* 1898–99; practiced law in New York 1899–1902; lecturer: National Woman Suffrage Association 1902–06; practiced in Denver 1908–14, San Francisco 1914–24, Portland from 1924; member: U.S. Supreme Court bar; member: Maine House of Representatives 1927–31, 1933–35; member: Maine Senate 1937–41; reporter of court decisions 1941; member: Colorado Board of Pardons 1911–14; secretary: state executive committee: Progressive Party of Colorado 1913–14; vice chairman: National Woman's Party, member: Republican State Central Committee of California 1920–22; a founder and director: National League for Woman's Service; president: Woman's Literary Union of Portland 1927–29; a founder and first president: National Federation of Business and Professional Women's Clubs 1919–20; president: California Civic League 1918–20; writer on tariff and other economic questions; author of law making women eligible for jury duty in California and successfully defended its constitutionality.

Lawrence, George Warren 1875–1939, born: South Gardiner; E.E. University of Maine 1898; after service in Cuba, during the Spanish-American War as a corporal in the 8th Company, U.S. Signal Corps, joined the testing department: General Electric Co., Schenectady 1901; electrical engineer: American Smelting and Refining Co., Monterey, Mexico, 1903; installation engineer and construction foreman: General Electric Co., Boston, 1904; manager, treasurer: Greenfield (Massachusetts) Electric Light and Power Co. 1905, vice president 1920, president from 1926; president: Turners Falls (Massachusetts) Power & Electric Co. from 1919; combined several utility companies to form the Western Massachusetts Companies, president from 1927.

Leach, Herbert Wood 1858–1934, born: Penobscot; son of a farmer; shipped out as a common seaman 1872, made several voyages to sundry parts of the world, returned to New York *via* Australia 1879; against his better judgment, signed on to an Arctic expedition to be lead by Lieutenant Commander George DeLong, USN, aboard the *Jeanette*, whose purpose was to determine whether Wrangel Island was in fact a part of a huge continent including Greenland, joining ship at San Francisco, Leach found himself aboard *Jeanette*, which journeyed north into the Bering Sea, where it became trapped in the ice, north of Siberia, eventually being crushed by the ice; the men of the expedition evacuated ship, dragging supplies, and three boats across the ice to Bennett Island over a period of six weeks, where they encountered open ocean, embarking in the three boats, they set out for the mouth of the Lena River, one boat was lost in a gale, another, bearing DeLong and twelve of the crew, made land, only to starve, the third boat, with Leach frozen at the tiller, made landfall, where help was finally received by Russian authorities, eventually making their way to Yakutsk by sled, a distance of 1,200 miles; after returning to the United States, Leach was discharged from the navy, made a lecture tour, and found employment in a shoe factory in Brockton, Massachusetts, where he worked for forty years; awarded a Medal of Honor by the U.S. Congress 1890, awarded a $25-per-month pension by Congress 1898; as the last survivor of the DeLong Expedition, present at the unveiling of a memorial to DeLong at Woodlawn Cemetery, New York, 1928; after Leach died, he was buried in Penobscot.

Leadbetter, Danville 1811–66, born: Leeds; graduate: U.S. Military Academy 1836; assigned to the engineers, served in all parts of the country in the construction of fortifications; constructed harbors, lighthouses, primarily around Mobile Bay; resigned his commission and was appointed chief engineer of the state of Alabama 1857, during the Civil War: commissioned brigadier general, CSA, 1862, saw to the defenses of Mobile, constructed the line on Missionary Ridge, accompanied General Longstreet on the Knoxville campaign, chief engineer on the staff of General Joseph E. Johnson; after defeat of the South, escaped to Mexico and later Canada, where he died in Clifton, subsequently buried in Magnolia Cemetery, Mobile.

Leadbetter, Guy Whitman 1893–1945, born: Bangor; son of the manager of the MacGregor Spool Mill, Lincoln; A.B. Bowdoin College 1916, in his senior year, was captain of the football team and set the intercollegiate record for the hammer throw, which stood for many years; M.D. Johns Hopkins University Medical School 1920, after a year of postgraduate work in orthopedics at Johns Hopkins and Baltimore Children's Hospital, surgical resident: Lakeside Hospital, Cleveland 1921–22, orthopedic resident: Johns Hopkins University Hospital 1922–23, practiced in Washington from 1923, specialized in orthopedic surgery, where he achieved international fame; associate orthopedist, Emergency Hospital to 1935, thereafter: orthopedist in chief; associate professor, later clinical professor: George Washington University Medical School; author: *The Problem of the Fractured Hip* 1945, numerous papers, many relating to fractures of the neck of the femur; during World War II: consultant to the secretary of war; secretary to the Orthopedic Committee of the National Research Council; president: American Academy of Orthopedic Surgeons 1945; an accomplished pianist, also had a well-trained baritone voice, was a linguist, and well versed in astronomy, geology, entomology, scientific photography, anthropology, and archeology.

Leighton, Marshall Ora 1874–1958, born: Corinna; B.S. Massachusetts Institute of Technology; resident hydrogeographer: U.S. Geological Survey 1902, chief: division of hydroeconomics 1903–06, chief hydrogeographer 1906–13, consulting engineer from 1913; advisory hydrographer: U.S. Inland Waterways Commission 1907–09, in which capacity he rendered report on flood control by reservoirs, pioneering present flood control program of United States 1907–09; member: Northern New Jersey Flood Commission 1903–04, Passaic River District Flood Commission 1905–06, Florida Everglades Engineering Commission 1913, chairman: National Service Commission, Engineering Council 1915–20, president: National Public Work Department Association 1920–21; organized U.S. hydrographic survey of Hawaii 1909; explored Mexico and the Andes for hydro-electric power sites 1923–24; vice president and chief engineer: East Tennessee Development Co. (predecessor of the Tennessee Valley Authority) 1925–27; chief of public works: Washington Metropolitan District Civilian Defense 1941–43; author of numerous U.S. government reports on water supplies and waterpower.

Leslie, Annie Louise 1870–1948, born: Perry; A.B. Mount Holyoke College 1892; teacher, public schools: White River Junction, Vermont, 1893–95, Rockville, Connecticut, 1895–97, Mt. Clemens, Michigan, 1897–1904; dramatic editor: *Pittsburgh Dispatch* 1917–18; editor of "Experience" column and editorial writer: *Detroit News*, as Nancy Brown from 1918; author: *Experience, Dear Nancy, Column Folks, Nancy's Family, Acres of Friends, Column House, Come Again, Home Edition*; a 98-foot stone carillon tower, dedicated to peace, was erected in her honor by "Experience" column contributors, on Belle Isle, Detroit, 1940; recipient: Distinguished Alumnae Award, Mt. Holyoke College 1942.

Lewis, Charles Hildreth 1837–1906, born: Alton; B.S. Norwich University 1855; government surveyor and civil engineer in Minnesota and Iowa; in the Civil War: commissioned captain, USA, 1861, participated in the battles of Shiloh, Stone River, Murfreesboro, Missionary Ridge, Chickamauga, and Sherman's march to the sea, brevetted lieutenant for distinguished service at the battle of Nashville; after the war, mined in Colorado for two years, removed to New York where he engaged in the brokerage business; member: New York Stock Exchange; owned valuable real estate along the Maine Coast, founded the town of Sorrento 1887; advanced large amounts of money to Norwich University, which was on the verge of closing; in recognition of his generosity, he was elected president of Norwich University 1880 and the name was changed to Lewis College by the Vermont legislature (the old name was restored, at his request in 1884), served until 1892.

Lewis, Robert Benjamin 1798–1859, born: Hallowell; grandson of a black servant to Dr. Silvester Gardiner, who, subsequent to attempting to poison his employer, was pensioned off to a farm on Cobbosseecontee Stream; preacher; inventor of numerous useful devices, including a hemp stalk stripper; author: *Light and Truth; collected from the Bible and Ancient and Modern History, containing the Universal History of the Colored and the Indian Races, from the Creation of the World to the Present Time* 1844, which thoroughly anticipates modern Afrocentric thought.

Libby, George D. 1919–50, born: Bridgton; sergeant, U.S. Army, Company C, 3rd Engineer Combat Battalion, 24th Infantry Division, recipient: Medal of Honor (posthumous), "near Taejon, Korea, 20 July 1950, SGT Libby distinguished himself by conspicuous gallantry and intrepidity above and beyond the call of duty in action. While breaking through an enemy encirclement, the vehicle in which he was riding approached an enemy roadblock and encountered devastating fire which disabled the truck, killing or wounding all the passengers except SGT Libby. Taking cover in a ditch SGT Libby engaged the enemy and despite the heavy fire crossed the road twice to administer aid to his wounded comrades. He then hailed a passing M-5 artillery tractor and helped the wounded aboard. The enemy directed intense small arms fire at the driver and SGT Libby, realizing that no one else could operate the vehicle, placed himself between the driver and the enemy, thereby shielding him while he returned the fire. During this action he received several wounds in the arms and body. Continuing through the town the tractor made frequent stops and SGT Libby helped more wounded aboard. Refusing first aid, he continued to shield the driver and return the fire of the enemy when another roadblock was encountered. SGT Libby received additional wounds but held his position until he lost consciousness. SGT Libbys sustained, heroic actions enabled his comrades to reach friendly lines. His dauntless courage and gallant self-sacrifice bing the highest credit upon himself and uphold the esteemed traditions of the U.S. Army." Buried in Arlington National Cemetery.

Lincoln, Charles Monroe 1866–1950, born: Bath; member of staff: *New York Herald*, editor: Paris edition, assistant of James Gordon Bennett 1895–1906; managing editor: *New York World* 1910–20, managing editor: *New York Herald* 1920–24, member: editorial staff, *New York Times*, specialist in international affairs 1926–44; president: James Gordon Bennett Memorial Corporation; explored for James Gordon Bennett, rival routes of proposed canal between Caribbean and Pacific, reporting in favor of Panama; collaborated with Marconi, in proof of the feasibility of wireless telegraphy 1899, collaborated with Glenn Curtiss in demonstration of the meaning of airplane work in war 1910.

Lincoln, Enoch 1788–1829, born: Worcester, Massachusetts; son of Levi Lincoln, governor of Massachusetts, member: U.S. House of Representatives, U.S. attorney general and acting U.S. secretary of state, brother of Levi Lincoln, Jr., also governor of Massachusetts; student at Harvard College 1806–08, A.M. (Hon.) Bowdoin College 1821, trustee ex-officio 1827–29; studied law in Worcester, with his brother Levi, member: Massachusetts bar 1811, practiced in Salem, removed to Fryeburg 1812, assistant U.S. district attorney 1815; member: U.S. House of Representatives 1818–26 (Republican); governor of Maine 1826–29; largely through his influence, Augusta was chosen as the new seat of government of the state, died subsequent to giving an oration commemorating the laying of the cornerstone of the statehouse; buried at the foot of Capitol Park; author of a poem *The Village*, descriptive of scenery and life in Fryeburg 1816, contributor of articles on Indian languages and French missions in Maine to the first volume of the *Maine Historical Collections*; at the time of his death, had accumulated a large amount of material on Indian tribes and languages but which remained in manuscript.

Little, Charles Coffin 1799–1869, born: Kennebunk; as a boy, removed to Boston and found employment in a shipping house, later in the bookstore of Carter, Hilliard & Co., member of the firm of Hilliard, Gray, Little, and Wilkins until 1837, when he formed a partnership with James Brown, styled Charles Little & Co., later, Little, Brown, and Co.; this company became the largest publishers of law texts in the United States, as well as the largest importer of English works, including the *Encyclopædia Britannica*, sundry English dictionaries, and other standard works; member: Massachusetts House of Representatives 1836–37.

Little, Clarence Cook 1888–1971, born: Brookline, Massachusetts; A.B. Harvard College 1910, D. Sc. (Hon.) Harvard University 1914; researcher in genetics; president: University of Maine 1922–25; president: University of Michigan 1925–29; subsequently head of Roscoe B. Thayer Memorial Laboratory on Mount Desert.

Little, Daniel 1724–1801, born: Haverhill, Massachusetts; son of a tanner, who removed, with his family to the new town of Hampstead, New Hampshire, where he asked to call the first town meeting, later serving as deacon, selectman, moderator, and justice of the peace; loath to send his child to college, he sent young Daniel to study with Stephen Sewall, in Newburyport, where he acquired Latin, Greek, and Hebrew, later he studied theology with Joseph Moody in York; failing to acquire the pulpit of the Second Church of Portsmouth, he kept school in Wells, preaching occasionally in Berwick and York; Joseph Moody attempted to convert him to New-Lights but failed; accepted the unanimous call to the pulpit of the Second, or, East Parish of Wells 1751; although, he called himself a Calvinist, he had no strong feelings on theology and rewrote the church's confession of faith to eliminate all references to the Trinity, the Atonement, and Election, since none had the authority of scripture, after his death, his church became Unitarian; A.M. Harvard College 1766; appointed "Missionary to the Eastward" by the trustees of the Eastern Mission 1769, which, in time, earned him the sobriquet Apostle of the East; finding the Penobscots deficient in English, he compiled a Penobscot grammar, so as to better communicate with them but made no headway in converting them from the Catholicism they learned from Jesuits; as an itinerant preacher, went from barn to meadow, wherever there were sufficient numbers to address; with the coming of revolution, he made his way to Watertown, where he convinced the authorities that he could, indeed, make steel; the Massachusetts General Court voted him funds to erect a building, build a furnace and a blacksmith's forge, and acquire tools; as he later recorded in the *Memoirs* of the American Academy of Arts and Sciences (of which he was a charter member), his attempts were not successful; he also announced a cure for cancer, by means of clay poultices; he studied chemistry and natural science, particularly the migration of fish; published his weather observations, collected minerals and Indian relics, collected early manuscripts for the Massachusetts Historical Society; climbed what is now Mount Washington in 1784; making his way, Down East, to repair the ravages of war, he found more damage done by religious revivalists, whose ignorant ravings he eschewed, than by British forces; sent by the governor of Massachusetts to negotiate a treaty with the Penobscots, he was reproved by their chief and told that ministers ought not to have anything to do with public business; approached Henry Knox, in an attempt to get the Waldo heirs to fund the construction of a school and the maintenance of a permanent missionary; acquired the first sleigh in Wells 1770, acquired the first wheeled conveyance seen in Wells 1792; Bowdoin College trustee 1794–99; father-in-law of Silas Moody.

Littledale, Clara Savage 1891–1956, born: Belfast; A.B. Smith College 1913; first female reporter: *New York Evening Post*, editor: women's page, resigned 1914; press chairman: National Women Suffrage Association 1914; associate editor: *Good Housekeeping* 1915, reported on political developments in Washington, D.C., to Europe to report on war 1918; managing editor: *The Magazine for Parents* 1926; chief editor: *Parents* from 1928; far-reaching influence through 1,675,000 subscribers, frequently appeared on radio, television, and lecture circuit, sought to translate technical studies on nutrition, family health, child training, vocational guidance into practical and understandable articles, supported laws prohibiting child labor, advocate of better schools, health facilities, expanded childcare facilities; coauthor: *Parents Magazine Book of Baby Care* 1952, buried in Vine Lake Cemetery, Medfield, Massachusetts.

Littlefield, Charles Edgar 1851–1915, born: Lebanon, son of a Free Will Baptist preacher, brother of Arthur S. Littlefield; graduate: Foxcroft Academy, apprentice carpenter, pattern-maker: Bodwell Granite Co., Vinalhaven; at age nineteen, had charge of a gang of men doing construction and repair work, as well as the boxing of granite for shipment; removed to Rockland 1874, began the study of law, member: Maine bar 1876; in practice in Rockland in partnership with Jonathan Prince Cilley, later joined by brother Arthur Littlefield; member: Maine House of Representatives 1885–89, speaker 1887–89; Maine attorney general (second youngest to date) 1889–93; member from the Second District: U.S. House of Representatives 1889–1908 (Republican), chairman: Committee on Expenditures in the Agriculture Department, member: Judiciary, Merchant Marine, and Fisheries Committees; a member of the reform wing of the Republican party, he led the fight in the House for stringent laws regulating corporate accountability, his anticanteen bill, his bill against compulsory pilotage, and his attempt to secure legislation against shipping liquor into Prohibition states attracted national attention; delegate: Republican National Convention 1892, chairman, Maine delegation, delegate-at-large 1896; resigned his seat 1908, resumed the practice of law in New York, in partnership with his son, Charles William Littlefield; appointed referee or master in a dispute between Virginia and West Virginia 1909; director: Equitable Life Assurance Society; his abilities as an indefatigable orator made him a favorite at numerous public gatherings; buried in Achorn Cemetery, Rockland.

Littlefield, George H. 1842–1919, born: Skowhegan; corporal, Company G, 1st Maine Veteran Infantry, recipient: Medal of Honor, "at Fort Fisher, North Carolina, 25 March 1865, the color sergeant having been wounded, this soldier picked up the flag and bore it to the front, to the great encouragement of the charging column." Buried in Cotton Cemetery, Richmond.

Locke, John 1792–1856, born: Fryeburg; M.D. Yale University Medical School 1819, geologist on explorations of the Northwest Territories and the state of Ohio; professor of chemistry at the Medical College of Ohio for many years; a pioneer in the sciences of botany, geology, and electricity, made numerous discoveries, particularly in terrestrial magnetism; constructed numerous instruments for use in optics, physics, electricity, and magnetism, including the gravity escapement for regulator clocks, patented 1844, an electrochronograph, subsequently purchased by the U.S. Naval Observatory in Washington, he devised a spirit level, patented 1850, that is still in

Eminent Mainers

use; contributed to the proceedings of various scientific societies and to *American Journal of Science*, author of texts on botany and English grammar.

Lombard, Alvin 1856–1937, born: Springfield; son of a millwright and mechanic; attended local schools, went to work in a shingle mill at age twelve, later employed by his father as a wheelwright, supervised the construction of a number of tanneries and operated a sawmill owned by his father, owned a mill of his own, in Lincoln, cutting timber in the winter and milling it in the summer, during this period, invented a waterwheel governor, removed to Boston 1886 to manufacture it, remained in Boston for seven years, returned to Maine, settling in Waterville, where he designed and patented the Lombard barker and braker attachment, a machine used to strip bark from logs 1898, received a patent on a pulp crusher 1899, established the Waterville Iron Works, received the patent on his caterpillar tractor 1901, the first practical use of the caterpillar tread, organized the Lombard Traction Machine Co., Waterville; because of its great pulling power and its ability to traverse almost any terrain, the Lombard tractor came into wide use in all kinds of heavy work, including operations in the woods, on farms, on construction jobs, and for snow plowing; he later sold the manufacturing rights to the Phoenix Manufacturing Co., Eau Clair, Wisconsin; he built, for his own use, three steam automobiles, with which he traveled about the state; buried in Pine Grove Cemetery, Waterville.

Long, John Davis 1838–1915, born: Buckfield; son of Zadoc Long, a merchant; graduate: Hebron Academy, A.B. Harvard College 1857, L.L.D. (Hon.) Harvard University 1880; principal: Westfield Academy, Massachusetts 1857–59; student: Harvard University Law School 1860–61, studied law in the office of Peleg Chandler, in Boston, member: Maine bar 1861, practiced in Buckfield 1861-63, removed to Boston; member: Massachusetts House of Representatives 1875–78, speaker 1876–78; lieutenant governor of Massachusetts 1879, governor (Republican) 1880–83, reelected twice, annually; as governor, attempted to abolish capital punishment within the commonwealth; member: U.S. House of Representatives 1883–89; U.S. secretary of the navy 1897–1902; president: Board of Overseers, Harvard University; fellow: American Academy of Arts and Sciences; author: *The Republican Party, Its History, Principles and Policies*, 1898, *The New American Navy* (two volumes) 1912, published a translation of Virgils ®nied 1879; Long is credited with much of the success of the navy during the Spanish-American War; during his tenure as secretary of the navy: the campus of the U.S. Naval Academy was largely rebuilt, Bancroft Hall was planned and begun, naval repair facilities greatly expanded, he created the general board, adopted wireless radio communications, merged the Engineer Corps with the line, began the acquisition of submarine boats; buried in Hingham (Massachusetts) Cemetery; the U.S. Navy launched a destroyer, USS *Long* (DD-209), named in his honor, in 1919, she was sunk after a fierce battle in Lingayen Gulf in 1945 and was accorded nine battle stars for World War II.

Longfellow, Alexander Wadsworth II 1854–1934, born: Portland; son of Alexander Wadsworth Longfellow I, cousin of William Pitt Preble Longfellow, nephew of Henry Wadsworth Longfellow, grandson of Stephen Longfellow, great-grandson of Peleg Wadsworth and Asa Clapp; A.B. Harvard College 1876, special student in architecture: Massachusetts Institute of Technology 1876–78, École des Beaux Arts, Paris 1879–81; associated with the architectural firm of Cabot & Chandler, Boston 1878–79, encouraged by his employers to travel in France and study the vernacular architecture 1879–81, associated with the architectural firm of H. H. Richardson 1881–86, supervising architect: Francis Lee Higginson house, Boston 1881–83, Hay-Adams houses, Washington 1884–86; established the architectural firm of Longfellow and Alden 1886–96, Boston and Pittsburgh, designed the Allegheny Carnegie Library, Pittsburgh City Hall, Cambridge City Hall, Edwin Abbot house (now Longy School of Music) Cambridge, several residences in Longfellow and Hubbard Parks, Cambridge, the Duquesne Club, Pittsburgh, &c., dissolved partnership, aligned himself with his brother R. K. Longfellow 1895, designed Phillips Brooks House, Semitic Museum, Arnold Arboretum, Agassiz House, two dormitories at Radcliffe College, Oliver Wendell Holmes and Abraham Lincoln Schools, the original Boston elevated train station, the Maine Historical Society, Portland, Merrill Memorial Library, Yarmouth, the R. Buckminster Fuller house, Bear Island, (which, according to some sources, had an immense impact on the thinking of R. Buckminster Fuller, Jr.), the Herbert Brown residence, Falmouth Foreside, Memorial Chapel, Yarmouth, Nova Scotia; president: Boston Museum of Fine Arts, Boston Athenaeum; fellow: American Institute of Architects.

Longfellow, Henry Wadsworth 1807–82, born: Portland; son of Stephen

Longfellow III, grandson of Peleg Wadsworth; his first published poem was *The Battle of Lovewell's Pond*, which appeared in the *Portland Gazette*; A.B. Bowdoin College 1825, his schoolmates included John S. C. Abbott, James W. Bradbury, Nathaniel Hawthorne, Horatio Bridge, William Pitt Fessenden, Seargeant Prentiss, and Calvin Stowe; while a junior at Bowdoin College, was offered the newly created chair of modern languages, provided that he first study in Europe, spent the better part of a year in Paris, studying French language and literature, removed to Madrid, Spain, where he met Washington Irving, whose *Sketch Book* had a profound influence on him as a youth, later removed to Italy, where he spent a year, later he studied at the University of Göttingen before returning home in 1829; as a professor at Bowdoin College, he excelled as a teacher, wrote and edited textbooks, translated prose and poetry, published his *Outre Mer*, a volume of sketches of his European travels; offered the chair of modern languages at Harvard College 1835, before he assumed his duties, made another trip to Europe for the particular purpose of familiarizing himself with German and Scandinavian literature and language, taught at Harvard College for eighteen years; the most popular American poet of the nineteenth century, honored here and abroad, his bust was placed in Westminster Abbey after his death; buried in Mt. Auburn Cemetery, Cambridge.

Longfellow, Samuel 1819–92, born: Portland; son of Stephen Longfellow III, grandson of Peleg Wadsworth, brother of Henry Wadsworth Longfellow; graduate: Portland Academy, A.B. Harvard College 1839, S.T.B. Harvard University Divinity School 1842, while at divinity school fell under the influence of the transcendentalists; prepared a new hymn book for the Unitarians; known for his kindliness and focus on the children of his congregations; regarded himself as a theist rather than Christian; pastor: Unitarian Church, Fall River, 1848–51, pastor: Second Society, Brooklyn, New York, 1857–60, pastor: Unitarian Society, Germantown, Pennsylvania, 1877–82; author: *A Book of Hymns for Public and Private Devotion* 1846, *Hymns of the Spirit* 1864, *Hymns and Verses* 1894, *Life of Henry Wadsworth Longfellow* 1891, *Memoir and Letters* 1894; compiled jointly, with Henry Lee Higginson: *Thalatta: A Book for the Sea-Side* 1853.

Longfellow, Stephen I 1722–90, born: Byfield Parish, Newbury, Massachusetts; son of Lieutenant Stephen Longfellow, the prototype of *The Village Blacksmith*, nephew of Chief Justice Samuel Sewall, cousin of Sir William Pepperrell; A.B. Harvard College 1742, A.M. 1745, as an undergraduate, held Browne and Hollis scholarships; kept school in York, until approached by Rev. Thomas Smith, on behalf of the Falmouth selectmen, who offered to him £200, per annum, to be schoolmaster in Falmouth; elected parish clerk 1750, town clerk and notary public for the port of Falmouth 1751, acted as clerk of courts until Cumberland County was established 1760, appointed clerk and register of probate, as well as justice of the peace, in 1761, he was elevated to quorum; came to be extremely well-regarded, known for his wit and humor; managed a lottery to build Tukey's Bridge, helped finance a scalping expedition, helped care for Maine's quota of Acadian exiles; with the coming of revolution and his dislike of mobs, joined in the loyalist's address to Governor Hutchinson, joined in the boycott of British goods, and participated in the Cumberland County convention of Committees of Safety 1774; lost his home on Free Street and other properties worth £1,000 in the burning of Falmouth, retired to his farm in Gorham and devoted himself to agriculture for the rest of his life; Longfellow was probably suspected of being a loyalist, his son Samuel Longfellow was indicted by the state as a Tory, but after he was imprisoned by the British (he was later to die in jail), his name was stricken from the list of proscribed persons.

Longfellow, Stephen III 1775–1849, born: Gorham; son of Stephen Longfellow II; A.B. Harvard College ΦBK 1798, L.L.D. Bowdoin College 1828, studied law with Salmon Chase (father of Salmon Portland Chase), Portland; member: Maine bar 1801, practiced in Portland; delegate: Hartford Convention 1814; member: Massachusetts General Court 1814–16; presidential elector 1816; member: U.S. House of Representatives 1823–25 (Federalist); president: Maine Historical Society 1834; compiled sixteen volumes of Massachusetts court cases and twelve volumes of Maine cases; Bowdoin College overseer 1811–17, vice president of the board 1815–17, trustee 1817–36, vice president of the board 1833–36; president: Maine Historical Society; son-in-law of Peleg Wadsworth, father of Henry Wadsworth Longfellow, Samuel Longfellow, and others; buried in Western Cemetery, Portland.

Longfellow, William Pitt Preble 1836–1913, born: Portland; A.B. Harvard College 1855, B.S. Lawrence Scientific School (Harvard University) 1859; studied architecture in the office of Edward C. Cabot, Boston; assistant architect: U.S. Treasury Department 1869–72, practiced in Boston; first editor: *The American Architect and Building News* 1875–80; adjunct professor of architecture: Massachusetts Institute of Technology 1881–82; trustee: Boston Museum of Fine Arts from 1882; a founder, secretary: Boston Society of Architects; chairman: architectural section, board of judges, Columbian Exposition, Chicago 1893; author: *Abstract of Lectures on Perspective* 1889, *The Column and the Arch* 1898, compiled: *Cyclopedia of Architecture in Italy, Greece, and the Levant* 1895; nephew of H. W. Longfellow, great nephew of Edward Preble, grandson of Stephen Longfellow and William Pitt Preble.

Longley, James Bernard 1924–80, born: Lewiston; student: Bowdoin College 1947, L.L.B. University of Maine Law School 1957; general agent: New England Mutual Life Insurance Co., Lewiston 1963; member: Maine bar; president: Longley Associates, dealers in insurance, Lewiston 1948–74; partner: Longley & Buckley, Lewiston 1958–74; governor of Maine 1975–1979 (Independent); director: Casco Bank & Trust Co., treasurer, director: First Federal Savings and Loan Association; lecturer: universities of Wisconsin, Colorado, Arkansas, Connecticut, at the Wharton School, and at Purdue; athletic director: Healey Home for Boys 1958–70; chairman: Maine Management and Cost Survey of State Government 1972–73; trustee: Central Maine General Hospital, president: Maine Underwriters; chairman, board of editors: American Society of Chartered Life Underwriters; buried in Mt. Hope Cemetery, Lewiston.

Lord, Edward Thomas Sumner 1871–1953, born: Limington, son of a headmaster of Limington Academy; A.B. Dartmouth College ΦBK 1891, A.M. 1894, Litt.D. (Hon.) Bates College 1939; instructor in English and mathematics: Worcester (Massachusetts) Academy 1891–92; New England agent: D. C. Heath & Co., publishers 1892–93; manager, educational department: Charles Scribner & Sons 1893–1901; president: Lothrop Publishing Co., Boston 1901–02; vice president, director, manager, educational department: Charles Scribner & Sons 1902–47.

Lord, Everett William 1871–1965, born: Surry; A.B. Boston University ΦBK 1900, A.M. 1906, L.L.D. (Hon.) Mount Union College 1926, Litt. D. Portia College 1938; superintendent of schools: Ellsworth 1893–95, Bellows Falls, Vermont, 1900–02; assistant commissioner of education: Puerto Rico 1902–08; secretary: National Child Labor Committee 1908–10; executive secretary: Boston University; organizer: College of Business Administration, Boston University, dean 1913–41; organized College of Business Administration: University of Puerto Rico 1926, dean 1926–29; organized Portland Junior College 1933, dean 1933–38; author: *Lessons in English* 1905, *Pedagogia Fundamental* 1907, *Children of the Stage* 1910, *The Boy and His Job* 1911, *Commercial Spanish* 1916, *Ethics of Business* 1926, *The Money Value of Education* 1927, *Books for Business Men* 1931, *Plan for Self-Management* 1936, *Student Persistence in American Colleges* 1938, *Business Is Business* (verse), *Legend of the Adman* (verse).

Lord, Frederick Taylor 1875–1941, born: Bangor; A.B. Harvard College 1897, M.D. Harvard University Medical School 1900; house officer: Massachusetts General Hospital 1900–01, visiting physician 1912–35, member: consultation board from 1935; assistant in clinical medicine: Harvard University Medical School 1905–09, instructor 1909–30, clinical professor of medicine 1930–35; member: American Red Cross commission to Serbia 1917; first to investigate the antipneumococcic sera, did much to make serum available to physicians; author: *Diseases of the Bronchi, Lungs and Pleura* 1915, *Pneumonia* 1922, *Lober Pneumonia and Serum Therapy* 1938; prepared the sections on influenza and diseases of the pleura for Osler's *Modern Medicine*.

Lord, Herbert Mayhew 1859–1930, born: Rockland; brother of Jere Williams Lord; A.B. Colby College 1884, A.M. 1889, L.L.D. (Hon.) 1920, Tufts University 1929; reporter, editor, part- owner: *Rockland Courier-Gazette*; newspaper reporter: Cardiff, Tennessee; clerk: Committee of Ways and Means, U.S. House of Representatives 1894–98; in the Spanish-American War: major and paymaster, USA, promoted through the ranks to brigadier general 1919; in World War I: director of finance, supervised the disbursement of $24 billion; awarded Distinguished Service Medal; chief of finance, U.S. Army 1920–22; after retirement: appointed director of the United States budget by President Harding 1923, served to 1929; known for his remarkable memory, able to quote figures in the billions, to the exact cent, without notes; trustee: Colby College.

Lord, John Abel 1872–1946, born: Phippsburg; son of a shipwright; apprenticed under noted shipwrights William Pattee and Frederick Rideout; while serving as a clerk in the Swanton, Jamason Hardware Co., recruited by Thomas W. Hyde to work at the Bath Iron Works, 1894, sent a year in the shipyard and two years in the mold loft; appointed assistant ship's draughtsman by the U.S. Navy 1898, remained at the Iron Works for three years; designed, blueprinted, and prepared the specifications for the training brig USS *Boxer*, launched at the Portsmouth Navy Yard, Kittery, 1903; assigned to the Puget Sound Navy Yard, Bremerton, Washington, 1902, returned to Bath Iron Works 1906, where he served as navy inspector for the construction of the scout cruiser USS *Chester*, later served as chief carpenter on her trials and commissioning; attached to the Brooklyn Navy Yard 1911–15, where he served as construction officer on USS *Arizona* and USS *New York*; in World War I, served aboard the minelayer USS *Baltimore*, before returning to Bath Iron Works as inspector of destroyers and of patrol craft in Boothbay and Camden; in 1922, transferred to Portsmouth Navy Yard as shop superintendent; chosen to superintend the reconstruction of USS *Constitution* at the Boston Navy Yard, recruited many superannuated shipwrights from Bath (including the father of chief of Naval Operations, Admiral Charles Hughes) to accomplish the task; after USS *Constitution* was relaunched in 1931, he was retired with the rank of commander; during World War II, recalled by the Bureau of Ships, serving first as assistant to the supervisor of ships at Bath Iron Works, later transferred to the office of the chairman of the U.S. Maritime Commission for duty with the technical division of the chief of the wood construction section.

Lord, Nathan 1792–1870, born: South Berwick; A.B. Bowdoin College 1809, D.D. 1828; teacher at Phillips Academy, Exeter, graduate: Andover Theological Seminary 1815, L.L.D. (Hon.) Dartmouth College 1864; pastor: Congregational Church, Amherst, New Hampshire, 1816–28; Dartmouth College trustee 1821–28, sixth president of Dartmouth College 1828–63, as president, greatly expanded and improved the physical plant and academic capabilities of Dartmouth College, established the Chandler School of Science and Arts 1851; despite his policy of admitting black students, whom were treated with every courtesy, his outspoken support of slavery as an institution countenanced by the Bible and therefore, by God, caused the board of trustees considerable discomfort, particularly in the middle of the Civil War; the board of trustees passed resolutions of loyalty, without censuring Lord, whom they greatly esteemed, this was interpreted by Lord as censure, so he resigned; author: *Two Letters to Ministers of All Denominations on Slavery* 1855, *A True Picture of Abolitionism* 1863, a compendium of his sermons, letters, and essays was published posthumously.

Lord, Phillips H. 1902–75, born: Hartford; graduate: Phillips Academy, Andover, A.B. Bowdoin College 1925; principal: Plainville (Connecticut) High School 1925–27; creator of radio characters and radio dramas: *Seth Parker, Uncle Abe and David, Country Doctor, the Stebbins Boys, Cruise of the Schooner Seth Parker, G-Men, Gang-Busters, We the People, Mr. District Attorney, Sky Blazers, Counterspy, Policewoman, Treasury Agent, The Black Robe*; starred in the motion picture *Way Back Home*; composer of hymns; author: *Seth Parker's Hymnal, Seth Parker's Album, Sunday at Seth Parker's, Uncle Hosic, Way Back Home, Scrap Book*; settled in Ellsworth

Loring, Charles Joseph 1918–1952, born: Portland; major, U.S. Air Force, 8th Fighter-Bomber Squadron, 8th Fighter-Bomber Wing, recipient: Medal of Honor (posthumous), "near Sniper Ridge, North Korea, 22 November 1952, Major Loring distinguished himself by conspicuous gallantry and intrepidity at the risk of his life above and beyond the call of duty. While leading a flight of four F-80 aircraft on a close support mission, Major Loring was briefed by a controller to dive-bomb enemy gun positions, which were harassing friendly ground troops. After verifying the location of the target, Major Loring rolled into his dive bomb run. Throughout the run, extremely accurate ground fire was directed on his aircraft. Disregarding the accuracy and intensity of the ground fire, Major Loring aggressively continued to press the attack until his aircraft was hit. At approximately four thousand feet, he deliberately altered his course forty five degrees to the left, pulled up in a deliberate, controlled maneuver, and elected to sacrifice his life by diving his aircraft directly into the midst of the enemy emplacements. His selfless and heroic action completely destroyed the enemy gun emplacements and eliminated a dangerous threat to United Nations ground forces. Major Loring's noble spirit, superlative courage, and conscious self-sacrifice in inflicting maximum damage on the enemy exemplified valor of the highest degree and his actions were in keeping with the finest traditions of the U.S. Air Force." Commemorated at the National Memorial of the Pacific (wall of the missing), Honolulu, as well as in Portland, Loring Air Force Base was named in his honor.

Loring, Charles Morgridge 1832–1922, born: Portland; after making several voyages to the West Indies on his father's vessels, determined that the sea was not his metier, he removed to the then-tiny town of Minneapolis where he amassed a small fortune through milling and merchandising, retiring from business he devoted himself to improving Minneapolis through the creation of parks, parkways, and playgrounds; despite some local opposition he prevailed upon the Minnesota legislature to create a parks commission, of which he was president; through his efforts Mount Rubidoux was made into the first bird sanctuary in the United States; Central Park was renamed Loring Park in his honor; founder and president: American Park Association; son-in-law of Frank Mellen Nye.

Loring, Harold Amasa 1879– ?, born: Portland; pioneer in study of American aboriginal music, lived with several tribes; appointed supervisor of Indian music by the commissioner of Indian Affairs at the direction of Theodore Roosevelt.

Loring, Nicholas 1711–63, born: Hull, Massachusetts; son of a farmer and the ruling elder of the church in Hull; orphaned at an early age, sent to live with his uncle, Reverend Israel Loring of Sudbury; A.B. Harvard College 1732, A.M. 1735; began preaching in Hull, Sudbury, and Dedham 1735, called by the church at North Yarmouth, which had just survived the Arminianism of Ammi Ruhamah Cutter 1736; having married a woman of considerable estate from Rhode Island, he and Madame

Loring raised eight children, who came to church in the summer barefoot in order to encourage the shoeless poor to attend, likewise; Loring's brother and sister also emigrated to North Yarmouth; Ammi Ruhamh Cutter, captain of militia, a noted Indian fighter and Loring's predecessor, continued to attend church in North Yarmouth, striding down the aisle, glaring contemptuously at his successor; when the Indian wars resumed, Loring enlisted as a sentry, on the occasion of a man being killed by Indians in the neighborhood, Loring grabbed his musket and joined in the pursuit and was presented with a tomahawk dropped by one of the Indians; received George Whitefield and the Great Awakening with an enthusiasm noted as far away as Boston; when Loring died of consumption, the funeral provided by the town was extremely lavish; buried in the Indian Fighters' Burying Ground, leaving fifty-three grandchildren and ninety-seven great-grandchildren; his female black slave Billinder, who had originally come to North Yarmouth from Rhode Island as part of his wife's dowry, lived on as a familiar figure in Portland well into the nineteenth century; father-in-law of David Mitchel.

Lovejoy, Clarence Earle 1894–1974, born: Waterville; A.B. Columbia University 1917, student: Sorbonne, Paris 1919, A.M. Colby College 1937, L.L.D. (Hon.) Parsons College 1959; reporter: *Pittsfield* (Massachusetts) *Journal* 1910–12, *Berkshire* (Pittsfield) *Evening Eagle* 1912–13, *Meriden* (Connecticut) *Morning Record* 1914, with *New York Times* 1915–20, 1934–62, boating editor; founder: *Bronxville* (New York) *Press* 1925, editor, publisher 1925–27, alumni executive, editor: *Columbia Alumni News* 1927–47, educational consultant, college counselor to students, director: College Admissions Counseling Service 1947–74; in World War I: first lieutenant, 38th Infantry, 3rd Division, USA, 1917–19, with AEF, captain 22nd, 16th, and 26th Infantry, USA, 1920-25, captain, associate professor, military science and tactics: Rutgers University R.O.T.C. 1921–25, in World War II: colonel, military intelligence reserve, active as colonel, USA, 1942–46, director: security and intelligence division: Military District No. 1, New York, overseas: director, public relations division, European Theatre of Operations by appointment of General Eisenhower, continued by General McNarney, decorated: Silver Star, Legion of Merit, Bronze Star; author: *The Story of the Thirty-Eighth* 1919, *The Lovejoy Genealogy* 1930, *So You're Going to College* 1940, *Lovejoy's Complete Guide to American Colleges and Universities* 1948, *Lovejoy's College Guide* 1952, *Lovejoy's Vocational School Guide* 1955, *Lovejoy's Scholarship Guide* 1957, *Lovejoy's Prep School Guide* 1958, editor, publisher: *Lovejoy's Guidance Digest* (monthly), contributor to newspapers, magazines, military educational journals.

Lovejoy, Elijah Parish 1802–37, born: Albion; son of a farmer and Presbyterian minister, brother of Owen Lovejoy, cousin of Nathan Farwell; A.B. Waterville College 1826; removed to St. Louis, Missouri, 1827, established a school, became the editor of a political newspaper supporting Henry Clay for president 1829–33, took a course at the theological seminary in Princeton, New Jersey, 1833, licensed Presbyterian preacher, filled pulpits in New York and Newport, Rhode Island, returned to St. Louis, editor: *Saint Louis Observer* (Presbyterian newspaper) 1833–36, advocated temperance and abolition of slavery; editor: *Alton* (Illinois) *Observer* 1836–37, his press was destroyed three times by pro-slavery mobs, during the fourth assault, Lovejoy was murdered, became a national symbol for the abolitionist movement; for fear of desecration, his grave in the Alton City Cemetery was originally left unmarked, it is now the site of a one hundred-foot-high, granite column; it was at a memorial service for Lovejoy in Hudson, Ohio, that John Brown made his first public pronouncement, vowing to avenge Lovejoy's murder and to wage war against slavery; his *Memoir* was published, posthumously, by his brothers, with an introduction by John Quincy Adams 1838.

Lovejoy, Owen 1811–64, born: Albion; brother of Elijah Lovejoy, cousin of Nathan Farwell; attended Bowdoin College 1830–33; present at his brother's murder; ordained Congregational minister, pastor: Princeton, Illinois, 1839–56; delegate: National Abolitionist Convention, Buffalo, 1847; member: Illinois House of Representatives 1854, regarded as the leading abolitionist in Illinois; member: U.S. House of Representatives 1857–64 (Republican), chairman: Committee on Agriculture, Committee on District of Columbia; author of the bill abolishing slavery in all U.S. territories; buried in Oakland Cemetery, Princeton, Illinois, cenotaph in Congressional Cemetery, Washington.

Low, Frederick Ferdinand 1828–94, born: Frankfort (that part that is now Winterport); apprenticed to the East India trading company of Russell, Sturgis and Co., Boston, 1843, attended lectures at Faneuil Hall and the Lowell Institute; joined in the gold rush to California 1849, mined in Marysville, removed to San Francisco, accomplished the merger of nearly all steamship lines on San Francisco Bay and Sacramento River 1854; an incorporator of the California Steam Navigation Co.; member: U.S. House of Representatives 1861–63 (Republican); collector of customs: San Francisco 1863; elected ninth governor of California as a Union Republican 1863–67, while governor, Low was appointed by President Lincoln to the commission created to investigate the California Railroad 1864; founder: University of California; U.S. minister to China 1869–74, during this period, was empowered to negotiate with Korea for the protection of shipwrecked seamen and for a treaty of commerce and navigation 1871; joint manager: Anglo-California Bank 1874–91, played a large hand in the commercial development of Hawaii; originally buried in Laurel Hill Cemetery, San Francisco, later reinterred in Cypress Lawn Cemetery, Colma, California.

Luce, Robert 1862–1946, born: Auburn; son of a lawyer; attended public schools in Auburn, Lewiston, and Somerville, Massachusetts; A.B. Harvard College 1882, L.L.D. (Hon.) Bates College 1923; member, editorial staff: *Boston Globe* 1884–88, founded Luce's Press Clipping Bureau, Boston and New York, 1888, which was the first of its kind in the United States; member: Massachusetts House of Representatives 1899, 1901–08; member: Massachusetts bar 1908, president: Republican State Convention 1910, lieutenant governor of Massachusetts 1912; delegate Massachusetts Constitutional Convention 1917-19; president: Republican Club of Massachusetts 1918; regent: Smithsonian Institution 1929–31; member: U.S. House of Representatives (Republican) 1919–35, 1937–41, chairman: Committee on Elections, Committee on World War I Veterans, Library Committee; unsuccessful candidate for reelection 1940; author: *Electric Railways* 1885, *Writing for the Press* 1886, *Going Abroad* 1897, *Congress—An Explanation* 1926, *Legislative Procedure* 1922, *Legislative Assemblies* 1924, *Legislative Principles* 1930, *Legislative Problems* 1935, the last four were a four-volume series on the science of legislation and are considered to be among the most exhaustive and authoritative works on the subject; buried in Mount Auburn Cemetery, Cambridge.

Lunt, Orrington 1815–97, born: Bowdoinham; son of a merchant and member of the Maine House of Representatives; clerked in his father's store from the age of fourteen, partner 1837; clerk and treasurer: town of Bowdoinham 1837–42; removed to Chicago 1842, rented half of a storefront on the Chicago River, undertook a general commission business with the delivery of a small cargo of oats from Buffalo; leased a hundred feet on the river and erected a grain house, by 1862, was the leading grain merchant in Chicago, handling over three million bushels of wheat per annum; charter member of the Chicago Board of Trade; member of the committee that went to Washington to urge improvement of Chicago's harbor 1853; elected water commissioner, president, treasurer 1855–61; a founder, director, vice president, auditor: Galena & Chicago Railroad Co., the first railroad to reach Chicago; founder, secretary, and treasurer: Northwestern University, personally chose the site for the erection of the university in what was to become Evansville (named for his brother-in-law, John Evans), donated the Orrington Lunt Library (which was replaced, eventually, as the main university library by the Charles Deering Library); a founder, life member, president: Chicago Bible Society; a founder, acting president: Garrett Biblical Institute.

Lyman, John Goodwin 1886–1967, born: Biddeford; educated in Montréal and at the Hotchkiss School, Lakeville, Connecticut, student at McGill University 1905–07, student at the Royal College of Art, London, student of Jean-Paul Laurens, Paris, 1908–09, Henri Matisse 1909–10, settled in Montréal, established an atelier with Hazen Sise, Georgie Holt, and Andre Bieler; reviewer for *The Montrealer*; professor of fine art: McGill University from 1948, chairman of the department from 1951; founded the Eastern Group of Painters 1939, the Contemporary Art Society for Artists and Laymen; regarded as the first modernist painter in Canada, his works are exhibited in the National Gallery of Canada, Musée du Québec, Montréal Museum of Fine Arts, University of Manitoba, McGill University, Art Gallery of Hamilton,

Beaverbrook Gallery, Fredericton, Musée d'Art, Montréal; died in Barbados.

Lyon, James 1735–94, born: Newark, New Jersey; A.B. College of New Jersey (later Princeton University) 1759, A.M. 1762; licensed to preach by the Presbyterian Synod of New Jersey, preached in Nova Scotia 1765–72, in Machias from 1772; during the Revolution, chairman: Machias Committee and Correspondence, offered to General Washington to lead a raid on Nova Scotia; shares with Francis Hopkinson the honor of first American composer, his tune book *Urania* 1761, containing seventy psalm-tunes, twelve anthems, and fourteen hymns, six of which were of his own composition, was the first book of music published in what became the United States, with tunes composed therein.

MacDonald, George Everett 1857–1944, born: Gardiner; printer's apprentice: *Truth Seeker*, New York 1875, foreman and assistant editor, newspaper work in California and Washington 1887–93, assistant editor *Truth Seeker* 1893–1909, editor 1909–36, president: Truth Seeker Co.; author: *Fifty Years of Free Thought.*

Mace, Aurelia Gay 1835–1910, born: Strong; member: United Society of Believers in Christ's Second Appearing (Shakers) from an early age, signed covenant at age twenty-three, second elderess, Sabbathday Lake 1860–66, 1869–80, trustee from 1896, had financial control of colony, played large part in establishing the Shaker brush industry, introduced Shakers' lemon syrup and balsam pillows to public; achieved national fame in 1890 when she mistook Charles Lewis Tiffany for a tramp, gave him lemonade, brushed his clothes, insisted that he sit down for the noon meal, and sent him off with a box lunch, Tiffany responded by sending her a set of silver engraved "Aurelia," the story appeared in newspapers and a book; regular contributor: *Shaker Manifesto*; maintained wide correspondence, particularly with Leo Tolstoy, a collection of her letters was published as *Aletheia: Spirit of Truth* 1899; is credited with the invention of the wire hanger.

MacMillan, Donald Baxter 1874–1970, born: Provincetown, Massachusetts, son of a ship captain lost at sea 1885; attended public schools in Provincetown and Freeport, A.B. Bowdoin College 1898, A.M. 1910, D.Sc. (Hon.) 1918, Boston University 1937; principal: Levi Hall School, North Gorham, 1898–1900, instructor at Swarthmore (Pennsylvania) preparatory school 1900–03, Worcester (Massachusetts) Academy 1903–08, joined Admiral Robert E. Peary's expedition to the Arctic 1908, made fifteen subsequent voyages to the north, member of the Cabot Labrador party 1910, engaged in an ethnological study of Eskimos and Indians of Northern Labrador 1911–12, head of the Crocker Land Expedition under the auspices of the American Museum of Natural History 1913–17, after his ship was wrecked on the Labrador coast, continued in another ship, establishing his base camp at Etah, Greenland, explored hundreds of miles, discovered two islands and an immense glacier, found the cached records of the Nares Expedition of 1876, collected specimens for the museum and also discovered incontrovertible evidence of coal deposits on Ellesmere Island, which proved that the Arctic once had a temperate climate, after his return, finding the United States at war, became a navigation officer in the aviation section of the navy, with the rank of commander, later rear admiral, USN; after the war, served as anthropology professor at Bowdoin College; led an expedition to Hudson Bay 1920, Baffin Island 1921, North Greenland 1923–24, where he conducted experiments on atmospheric electricity and the northern lights, in 1925, led an expedition that included three navy amphibious airplanes, led the Field Museum Expedition to Greenland 1926, another to Labrador and Baffin Island 1927–28, established a school for Eskimos at Nain, led the Baffin Island Expedition 1929, Iceland and Baffin Island 1930, an aerial exploration of Labrador 1931, the Bowdoin-Button Island Expedition of 1934, Resolution Bay and Baffin Island Expedition of 1937, Baffin Bay-North Greenland 1938; Tallman Foundation professor of anthropology: Bowdoin College 1932–33; author: *Four Years in the White North* 1917, *Etah and Beyond* 1927, *Kah-da* 1929, *How Peary Reached the Pole* 1936, numerous magazine articles; buried in Provincetown Cemetery.

Macurdy, Grace Harriet 1866–1946, born: Robbinston; A.B. Radcliffe College ΦBK 1888; teacher of classics: Cambridge School for Girls 1888–93, instructor in Greek: Vassar College 1893–99, student: University of Berlin 1899–1900, Ph.D. Columbia University 1903; author: *The Chronology of Extant Plays of Euripides* 1905; associate professor: Vassar College 1903, professor 1916, chairman of department 1923–46; author: *Troy and Paeonia* 1925, *Hellenistic Queens* 1932, *Vassal Queens and Some Contemporary Women in the Roman Empire* 1940; member: American Philological Association, American Linguistic Society; awarded: King's Medal for Service in the Cause of Freedom (Great Britain) 1946.

MacVane, John Franklin 1912–84, born: Portland; graduate: Phillips Academy, Exeter, A.B. Williams College 1933, Rhodes Scholar, B.Litt. Exeter College, Oxford 1936; reporter, ship news columnist: *Brooklyn Daily Eagle* 1935–36, reporter: *New York Sun* 1936–38, subeditor: *London Daily Express* 1938–39, *Continental Daily Mail*, Paris, 1939, correspondent: Exchange Telegraph Agency, International News Service covering the fall of France; reporter, war correspondent, assigned to the British army by National Broadcasting Co., London, 1940–42, North African campaign, Morocco-Algeria-Tunisia 1942–43, British and American armies, covered Casablanca Conference 1943, landed with the 16th Infantry, USA, 1st Infantry Division, Normandy on D-day, later with the First Army 1944–45, French Deuxième Division Blinde, Paris, 1944; United Nations correspondent, National Broadcasting Co., covering United Nations Security Council 1946, Berlin airlift 1948, United Nations General Assembly, Paris, 1951–52; producer, moderator: weekly radio, television panel show *United or Not*, American Broadcasting Co., 1950–52; with United

Nations General Assembly, Paris, 1951–52, United Nations correspondent: American Broadcasting Co. 1953–78; Photo Communications Co. 1978–84; writer commentator: documentary television film series *Alaska, The New Frontier* for National Educational Television 1960; author: *Journey into War* 1943, *War and Diplomacy in North Africa* 1944, *Embassy Extraordinary: The United States Mission to the United Nations* 1961, *On the Air in World War II* 1979; decorated: Purple Heart, chevalier and officer: Légion d'Honneur, Médaille de la Libertée, American Association for the United Nations Award 1960; president: Association of Radio-Television Analyists 1948–49, 1955–56; president: United Nations Correspondents Association 1964; governor: Society of Silurians; member: American Society of the French Legion of Honor.

Madockawando *circa* 1630–98, adopted son of Assaminasqua, chief of the Penobscots; became chief of the Penobscots, whose lands were divided between the French and English by the treaty of Breda 1667, brought under French influence by Baron de St. Castine, who married Madockawando's daughter; in King Philip's War, attempted to reach an accord with the English, reaching an unsatisfactory conclusion to negotiations with the English commissioners, declared war on the English, by the close of 1675, held some fifty captives, most of whom reported being treated well; in a treaty reached at Casco 1678, the English were enabled to return to their farms on condition of their paying rent to the Indians; in Queen Ann's War, the sacking of Castine's fort led to the resumption of hostilities 1688; led the raid on York 1691, in which the settlement was leveled, some seventy-five persons, including Shubael Dummer, were killed and eighty-five prisoners taken, failed to take the garrison, with the loss of many warriors; his humane treatment of Thomas Cobbet and Mrs. Shubael Dummer were widely noted; when the English built Fort William Henry at Pemaquid, he hastened to Québec to inform Frontenac; consented to a treaty with the English 1693, but was unable to gain the ascent of various chiefs who had come under the influence of French Jesuit emissaries, forced to recommence hostilities, was probably killed by Captain Pascho Chubb at a conference at Pemaquid; succeeded by the fierce Moxus.

Magoun, George Frederic 1821–96, born: Bath; A.B. Bowdoin College ΦBK 1841, D.D. Amherst College 1867, attended Yale University Divinity School, S.T.B. Andover Theological Seminary 1847; ordained Congregational minister 1848; founded home-mission: Shullsberg, Wisconsin, 1848, pastor: Galena, Illinois, Davenport and Lyon, Iowa; trustee: Iowa College, Davenport, 1846; first president: Grinnell College 1862–84; teacher of moral and mental philosophy, had to deal with disastrous fires and a tornado that leveled the entire campus 1882; wrote many articles and one book: *Asa Turne: A Home Missionary and Patriarch and His Times* 1889; active in the founding of the Republican party in Iowa; delegate to three peace congresses in Europe.

Magoun, Henry Albert 1863–1931, born: Bath; student at Massachusetts Institute of Technology 1883; draftsman: Goss Marine Iron Works, Bath, and its successor, Bath Iron Works; later with Charles Mosher, builder of fast boats, boilers, and engines, New York; Columbian Iron Works and Dry Dock Co., Baltimore; Harlan and Hollingsworth, Wilmington, Delaware; in charge of engine department: Hyde Windlass, Bath, 1907–09, designed steering gear for destroyers USS *Craven* and USS *Dahlgren*; superintendent: marine department, Sparrows Point, Baltimore, designed compound and triple-expansion steam engines; assistant to president: New York Shipbuilding Co. 1907, vice president 1907–26, in charge of all shipbuilding, including battleships, cruisers, mine layers, tugboats, lightships, barges, lighthouse tenders; president: Atlantic Coast Shipbuilders Association 1923–24.

Main, Amos 1707–60, born: York; fitted for college by Joseph Moody; A.B. Harvard College 1729, A.M. 1732; as undergraduate, Main defended himself from being beaten by the sophomores, in part, by carrying a pistol, for which he was degraded and fined; kept school and assisted the Reverend John Brown, of Haverhill, between degrees; kept school in York 1735; removed to the frontier town of Rochester, New Hampshire, 1737, chosen clerk of the first town meeting in that place, later served as the first minister; the town built him a garrisoned parsonage and gave him all of the income from parsonage lands; also served as lawyer, physician, and schoolmaster; because of the near-constant threat of Indian attack, Main was dispatched to Portsmouth to beg for military assistance, he returned with a large and ancient cannon, which, after many years of service, burst during a Fourth of July celebration; very highly regarded by his contemporaries, in 1896, the city of Rochester erected a bronze statue of him on the central square.

Malcolm, Daniel 1725–69, born: Georgetown; ship owner and captain, removed to Boston where he owned two houses; a leader of the Sons of Liberty, associate of Samuel Adams, John Hancock, and Harrison Gray Otis; became a very active antagonist of customs officials, refused entry to comptroller of customs, despite his having a writ of assistance, besieged by king's troops, rescued by a mob; when the attorney general referred the question to England, it was ruled that the courts in America had no right to issue writs of assistance, a major triumph for the Colonial cause 1766; after smuggling in sixty pipes of wine, called and presided over a meeting of the merchants in Boston, which voted not to import any British goods for a year and a half, the first movement of the merchants against the Acts of Parliament 1768; Malcolm raised a mob to prevent the seizure of John Hancock's sloop *Liberty*, the first clash with armed forces of England; his tombstone in Copps Hill cemetery was used by British troops for target practice.

Mann, Edwin Jonathan 1878–1954, born: West Paris, son of Lewis Mann, a manufacturer; student: Goulds Academy, Bethel, high schools in Bryant Pond and

South Paris, B.S. University of Maine 1900; associated with his father's firm, L. M. & W. E. Mann & Son, manufacturers of wooden clothespins, handles, and related wooden objects, became partner 1904, when the firm became L. M. Mann & Son, upon the death of his father, Mann became sole owner and manager, modernized the plant in West Paris, built a new facility in Bryant Pond 1925, by 1954, output had reached 75,000,000 handles annually, with eighty employees; most of the wood needed came from company timberlands in Oxford County; an incorporator: South Paris Savings Bank; director: Norway National Bank; trustee: West Paris Library (the current, highly idiosyncratic building he built as a memorial to his brother, Arthur L. Mann); member: West Paris School Committee.

Manson, Frederic E. 1860–1945, born: Searsport; A.B. Bates College 1883, A.M. 1886; editor: *Augusta Journal* 1888–91, *Lowell* (Massachusetts) *Evening Mail* 1891–92, New England news director: *Boston Journal* 1892–93, managing editor, editor in chief: *Grit*, Williamsport, Pennsylvania, 1895–1945; author: *Pennsylvania Masonry*.

Marble, Albert Prescott 1836–1906, born: Vassalboro; A.B. Colby College φBK 1861; removed to Beaver Dam, Wisconsin, to accept professorship in mathematics at Wayland University 1862; principal: Worcester Academy 1866–68; superintendent of Wisconsin schools 1868–94, raised the quality of education to nationally noted level; put in charge of New York City's first three high schools 1896; founding president: National Educational Association; author: *Sanitary Conditions for School Houses* 1891; trustee: Wellesley College.

Marriner, J. Theodore 1892–1937, born: Maine; A.B. Dartmouth College 1914, A.M. Harvard University 1915, Ph.D. 1918; assistant in English: Harvard University 1916–18; third secretary: legation of Stockholm 1918–21, second secretary: legation at Bucharest, American delegate: coronation of King and Queen of Romania, first secretary: embassy on duty in Western Europe 1923–26, secretary of legation: Berne and secretary American delegation to preparatory commission on reduction and limitation of armament: Geneva 1926–27, chargé d'affairs: Switzerland, head American representative: Disarmament Commission, member: American mission to Paris for signature of general pact renouncing war 1928, advisor: American delegation, London Naval Conference 1931, accompanied Prime Minister Laval on his trip to Washington, D.C.; murdered in Beirut by a deranged Armenian; author: "Transylvania and its Seven Castles," *National Geographic Magazine*, March 1926.

Mason, Luther Whiting 1828–96, born: Turner; son of a farmer and pump maker, after whose death, Mason attended village school in Gardiner and the Gardiner Lyceum, later attended Gorham Academy; studied with Lowell Mason at the Boston Academy of Music; choir supervisor: St. Timothy's Episcopal Church, Baltimore, supervisor of musical education: Louisville, Kentucky, 1853–56, Cincinnati 1856–64, while in Cincinnati, invented the National System of music charts and books, which brought him immediately success and fame; in 1864, served as drum major and fifer in the 138th Ohio Regiment of Volunteers; head: Musical Education System in Boston from 1864; invited to become instructor of musics in the Imperial School of Music in Japan, introduced Western tonality, set up educational facilities (school music in Japan was called Mason-song), made the first transcriptions of traditional *koto* music in Western notation, closely associated with Edward Morse 1880–82, one of his students there was Suzuki Shinichi, the founder of the Suzuki method of violin playing; later, traveled extensively in Europe, collecting songs and studying methodology; closely associated with Edwin Ginn, Ginn & Company published his *National Music Course* in four volumes and numerous other volumes of musical instruction; died in North Buckfield, where he is buried; see *Luther Whiting Mason: International Music Educator*, Sondra Wieland Howe, Harmonie Park Press, Warren, Michigan, 1997.

Mason, Otis Tufton 1838–1913, born: Eastport; A.B. Columbian University (later George Washington University) 1861, A.M. 1862, Ph.D. 1879, L.L.D. (Hon.) 1898; director: Columbian University preparatory school 1861–84; curator of ethnology: National Museum (Smithsonian Institution) from 1884, head curator: Department of Anthropology from 1902; founder: Anthropology Society of Washington; anthropological editor: *American Naturalist*; author: *The Hupa Indian Industries*, *Women's Share in Primitive Cultures* 1894, *Origins of Inventions* 1895, *Primitive Transportation*, *The Land Problem*, *Cradles of the North American Indians*, *The Antiquities of Guadeloupe*, *Aboriginal Basket Making* (two volumes) 1904, contributor to numerous articles and papers published by the Smithsonian Institution.

Mathews, Shailer 1863–1941, born: Portland; A.B. Colby College 1884, A.M. 1887, graduate: Newton Theological Institution 1887, student: University of Berlin 1890–91, D.D. Colby College 1901, Oberlin College 1908, Brown University 1914, Miami University 1922, University of Glasgow 1928, Chicago Theological Seminary 1933, University of Rochester 1926; professor of rhetoric: Colby College 1887–89, professor of history and political economy: Divinity School, University of Chicago, 1889–94, associate professor: New Testament history and interpretation 1894–97, professor 1897–1905, professor of systematic theology 1905–06, professor of history and comparative theology 1906–33, dean 1899–1933; editor: *The World Today* 1903–11, *Biblical World* 1918–20; trustee: Carnegie Foundation for Peace from 1914; author: *Select Medieval Documents* 1891, *The Social Teachings of Jesus* 1887, *A History of New Testament Times in the Life of Christ* 1901, *Principles and Ideals for the Sunday School* 1903, *Hope in the New Testament* 1905, *The Church and the Changing Order* 1907, *The Social Gospel* 1909, *The Gospel and Modern Man* 1909, *Scientific Management in the Churches* 1911, *The Making of Tomorrow* 1913, *The Individual and the Social Gospel*

1914, *The Spiritual Interpretation of History* 1916, *Patriotism with Religion* 1918, *The Validity of American Ideals* 1922, *The Contributions of Science to Religion* 1924, *The Faith of Modernism* 1924, *Outline of Christianity* 1927, *Jesus on Social Institutions* 1928, *The Atonement and the Social Process* 1930, *The Growth of the Idea of God* 1931, *Immortality and the Cosmic Process* 1933, *Christianity and Social Process* 1934, *Creative Christianity* 1935, *New Faith for Old—An Autobiography* 1936, *Is God Emeritus?* 1940; brother of Edward Mathews.

Maxcy, Kenneth Fuller 1889–1966, born: Saco; A.B. George Washington University φBK 1911, M.D. Johns Hopkins University Medical School 1915, D.P.H. 1921; resident house officer: Johns Hopkins University Hospital 1915–16, assistant resident pediatrician 1916–17; assistant in medicine: Henry Ford Hospital, Detroit 1917; fellow: Johns Hopkins University School of Hygiene and Public Health 1919–21; assistant surgeon; surgeon: U.S. Public Health Service 1921–29, professor of bacteriology and preventive medicine: University of Virginia Medical School 1929–36, professor of public health and preventive medicine: University of Minnesota 1936–37, professor of bacteriology: Johns Hopkins University School of Hygiene and Public Health 1937–38, professor of epidemiology 1938–54; consultant: Rockefeller Foundation, health division 1937–40, 1942–45, 1948–52; member: National Advisory Health Council 1942–46; consultant: secretary of war, Army Epidemiology Board 1941–49; trustee: International Polio Congress; chairman: Committee on Research and Ctandards, American Public Health Association 1939-46; recipient: Sedgwick Memorial Medal 1952; editor: *Papers of Wade Hampton Frost* 1941, *Rosenau's Preventive Medicine and Hygiene* 1956; buried in Arlington National Cemetery.

Maxim, Sir Hiram Stevens 1840–1916, born: Sangerville; brother of Hudson Maxim, son of a sometime Millerite farmer, wood turner, blacksmith, trapper, tanner, miller, carpenter, and mason; at a very early age, demonstrated remarkable ability at whittling, bound out to a carriage maker in Abbot, hypothesized an helicopter, a repeating gun mechanism, and built what he claimed was the first tricycle (with the first wheel spokes in tension, rather than compression) and an automatic mousetrap; worked for a time in a threshing factory in upstate New York; removed to Huntington, Canada, where he was a prizefighter and bartender, as well as a painter of decorations; patternmaker at a machine shop in Fitchburg, Massachusetts, learned mechanical drafting; foreman of a philosophical instrument manufactory in Boston, obtained his first patent for an improved curling iron 1866; foreman at the Novelty Iron Works and Ship Building Co., New York; invented various improvements in steam engines and the Maxim automatic gas machine, which became ubiquitous; turned his attention to electricity 1877, produced an incandescent lamp which burned for 1,000 hours; designed a process for flashing electric carbons, whereby each filament was evenly coated, exhibited his self-regulating current machine at the Paris Exposition of 1881, for which he was decorated by the French government: chevalier,

Légion d'Honneur; returned to London as the representative of the United States Electric Light Co. 1883; beginning in 1881–82, developed the first, fully automatic machine gun, capable of shooting ten rounds per second; developed cordite, a cord-like explosive propellant; organized the Maxim-Nordenfelt Gun Co., later Maxim, Nordenfelt, and Vickers Co., later Vickers, Sons, and Maxim Co.; later invented the pom-pom gun or automatic cannon with explosive shells; his elaborate experimentations in powered flight led to his flying a steam-powered airplane ten years before the Wright brothers' first flight, powered by a lightweight steam engine that produced six horsepower for every pound of weight; also patented a twin-rotor helicopter, driven by a gasoline engine; invented the modern aerial bomb, the steam inhaler for asthmatics, and numerous other diverse inventions, including both electric and internal combustion-driven motorcars, built by the Pope Manufacturing Co. from 1899; immigrated to England in protest of what he considered to be unfair treatment by the U.S. government; decorated by the sultan of the Ottoman Empire with the Grand Order of Medjideh, by the Emperor of China with the Order of the Double Dragon, knighted by King Edward VII 1901; refused a seat in Parliament; representative of the Diesel interests in the British empire; author: *Progress in Aerial Navigation* 1890, *Report on Aerial Machines 1842–1893*, *Monte Carlo Facts and Fallacies* 1904, *Artificial and Natural Flight* 1908, *A New System for Preventing Collisions at Sea*, wherein he anticipated the invention of radar 1912, *My Life* 1915, editor: *Li Hung Chang's Scrapbook* 1913; buried in West Norwood Cemetery, London; father of Hiram Percy Maxim, automobile designer, inventor of the silencer for firearms.

Maxim, Hudson (originally named Isaac) 1853–1927, born: Orneville; brother of Hiram Maxim; student: Maine Wesleyan Seminary, Kents Hill, for seven years; his interest in chemistry led to wide reading and experimentation in the subject, he formulated a hypothesis, in 1875, concerning the compound nature of atoms (published "The Principle of Force and Demonstration of the Existence of the Atom" in the *Scientific American Supplement* 1889) not unlike the atomic theory later accepted by scientists; with a classmate from Kents Hill, invented a durable ink, started a publishing house and a mail order business based upon their books, *The Real Penwork Self-Instructor in Penmanship*, *Bible Pearls of Promise*, and *Golden Gems of Penmanship*; while working for his brother, began to experiment with explosives 1888, built a dynamite and powder factory in Maxim, New Jersey, 1890; there, with R. C. Schuppenhaus, developed Maxim-Schuppenhaus smokeless powder, the first made in the United States and the first to be adopted by the U.S. government; later invented a smokeless cannon powder, used in enormous quantities in World War I; sold his factory and powder inventions to E. I. du Pont de Nemours & Co. 1897; remained a consulting engineer, invented maximite, a high explosive bursting powder which, when placed in torpedoes, resists the shock of firing and the greater shock of penetrating armor plate without bursting, later detonated by a delay action fuse, also a Maxim invention; invented stabillite, so-called for its great stability, and motorite a self-combustive substance used to power torpedoes; during World War I: served as chairman of the Committee on Ordnance and Explosives of the Naval Consulting Board; hypothesized the existence of atomic energy and methods for exploiting it, television, and superhighways; buried at Maxim Park, New Jersey; author: *The Maxim Aerial Torpedo: a new system of throwing high explosives from ordnance* 1897, *The Science of Poetry and the Philosophy of Language* 1910, *Defenseless America* 1915, *Dynamite Stories, and some interesting facts about explosives* 1916.

Mayall, Samuel, Jr. 1816–92, born: North Gray; son of Samuel Mayall, an immigrant English weaver, who built one of the first woolen mills, if not the first, in Maine, and who believed that when he died, his soul would transmigrate into a sheep, as a consequence, he built his tomb, still extant, out of split granite in a meadow near his mill; member: Maine House of Representatives 1845, 1847–48; Maine Senate 1847–48; member: U.S. House of Representatives 1853–55 (Democrat); delegate: Republican National Convention 1856; removed to Saint Paul, Minnesota, 1857, held extensive land holdings; in Civil War: captain, USV, wounded twice, captured and escaped several times; buried in Oakland Cemetery, St. Paul.

Mayall, Thomas Jefferson 1826–88, born: North Berwick; first found employment in a paper mill in Roxbury, Massachusetts, soon began inventing; made improvements in papermaking machinery, devised the first rubber drive belt, devised the first cylinder printing machine, from which came the wallpaper and calico printing industry, chores formally done with blocks, his later wallpaper machine was capable of printing one thousand rolls per diem, devised a method of making satin-faced paper, of vulcanizing rubber 1841, an automatic battery, a revolving cannon, which, driven by steam, was capable of loading and firing forty shots per minute and was widely adopted in European armies; bombshells with sharpened edges to bore through the sides of warships, a coffee-hulling machine, self-activating drawbridges for railroads; at the time of his death, Mayall was working on an electric elevated railway, an electric-cable railway, and a pneumatic railway; Mayall held a total of two hundred patents in the United States and seventy in Great Britain.

Mayo, Bernard 1902–79, born: Lewiston; student: University of Maine 1920-22, A.B. George Washington University ΦBK 1924, A.M. 1925, Ph.D. Johns Hopkins University 1931; associate professor of history: National University (merged with George Washington University 1954) 1926–27, professor of American history 1927–37, dean, school of economics 1929–33, lecturer: American University 1928–29, professor of American history: American University graduate school 1936, professor of American history: Georgetown University graduate school 1937–49, professor of American history: University of Virginia 1940–46; visiting professor of American history: Harvard University 1946–47, Lamar memorial lecturer: Mercer

University, Macon, Georgia, 1958, Thomas Jefferson scholar: University of Virginia 1962–63; recipient: Alumni Achievement Award: George Washington University 1943, president: Virginia Social Science Association 1960–61; author: *Henry Clay, Spokesman of the New West* 1937, *Jefferson and the Way of Honor* 1951, editor (for the American Historical Association): *Instructions to the British Ministers to the United States 1791–1812* 1941, *Thomas Jefferson and His Unknown Brother Randolph* 1942, *Jefferson Himself: The Personal Narrative of a Many-Sided American* 1942, *Myths and Men; Patrick Henry, George Washington, Thomas Jefferson* 1959; member: advisory commission for the publication of the papers of Thomas Jefferson 1943–79.

McCulloch, Hugh 1808–95, born: Kennebunkport; student at Bowdoin College

1824–26; studied law in Kennebunk and Boston, member: Massachusetts bar 1832; removed to Indiana 1833, cashier and manager: Fort Wayne branch of the Bank of Indiana 1835; president: State Bank of Indiana 1856–63; comptroller of the U.S. Treasury 1863–65, launched the Greenback or national banking system, began the creation of national banks; as secretary of the treasury 1865–69, recommended retirement of notes and return to gold standard, managed to convert over a billion dollars in short-term debt into a funded debt; partner: Jay Cooke, McCulloch, and Co., re-organized as McCulloch and Co. 1873, agent in London 1870–76; once again called upon to serve as secretary of the treasury 1884–85; author: *Men and Measures of Half a Century: Sketches and Comments* 1888; buried in Rock Creek Cemetery, Washington; a U.S. revenue cutter, USRC *McCulloch*, named in his honor, participated in the battle of Manila Bay 1898.

McCollum, John Hildreth 1843–1915, born: Pittston; son of a Congregational

minister; graduate: Phillips Academy, Andover 1861, student: Dartmouth College 1861–62, S.M. 1910; enlisted in the 30th Massachusetts Infantry, USV, served as a hospital steward to 1865, saw action in the attacks on the forts below New Orleans, the battle of Baton Rouge, the siege of Vicksburg, and in the Shenandoah Valley, at the battles of Winchester and Cedar Creek; after being mustered out April 1865, entered Harvard University Medical School, M.D. 1869; house surgeon: Boston City Hospital 1869–70, assistant superintendent Marine Hospital, Chelsea, Massachusetts, 1870–71, in general practice in Boston, developed an interest in contagious diseases, appointed assistant to the Boston city physician, in charge of vaccination and smallpox patients, vaccinated over 75,000 persons, appointed Boston city physician from 1881, during his administration, contagious disease virtually disappeared; McCollum is credited with the realization that the administration of diphtheria antitoxin in 3,000 to 5,000 units was ineffectual, increased the dose one hundred-fold with dramatic effects; superintendent and director: Boston City Hospital 1908–15; instructor in contagious disease: Harvard University Medical School 1896, assistant professor 1903, professor 1908–13.

McDonald, John Daniel 1863–1952, born: Machias; B.S. U.S. Naval Academy 1884, commissioned ensign 1886, promoted through the ranks to vice admiral 1920; served aboard USS *Monterey*: Spanish-American War 1898, led a mixed landing force of sailors and Marines to destroy a large rifle held by rebel insurgents, Olongapo, Philippine Islands, 1901, at Naval Torpedo Station, Newport, Rhode Island, 1904, navigator: USS *Ohio* 1904–07, commanding officer: First Lighthouse District 1907–08, commanding officer: USS *Castine* 1908–09, USS *Chattanooga* 1909–10, USS *Hancock* 1911, USS *Virginia* 1911–13; at Naval War College 1913–15; chief of staff: Atlantic Fleet 1915–16, commanding officer: USS *Arizona* (first commander or plankholder) 1916–18, commandant: Navy Yard, New York 1918, vice admiral, USN, commandant: 14th Naval District, retired 1924.

McGilvery, Freeman 1823–64; born: Prospect; became a sailor at an early age, master before he had turned twenty-one; while in Rio de Janeiro, heard of the outbreak of the Civil War, hastened back, raised a battalion of artillery, in which he was captain; instrumental at the battle of Cedar Mountain in preserving the left flank of the Union Army 1862; subsequently engaged at Sulphur Springs, second Bull Run, Chantilly, and Antietam; promoted to major, USV, commanding officer: 1st Brigade of the volunteer artillery reserve, Army of the Potomac 1863; commissioned lieutenant colonel, USV; at Gettysburg, repelled two Confederate attacks on Sickles's position, during the third assault, was driven back along with the rest of Sickles's command, managed to form a new line, without infantry assistance, that defended an 800-yard gap in the federal line, later commanded the reserve artillery, which played a significant role in repelling Pickett's charge; promoted to colonel, USV, commanding officer: 1st Maine Mounted Artillery 1863, commanding officer: reserve artillery at Petersburg; appointed chief of artillery of the X Corps, while engaged at Deep Bottom, was wounded in the finger, discounting the severity of the wound, he continued with his duties until gangrene set in, died of the effects of chloroform; one of the forts guarding Petersburg was named in his honor; 1 September was set aside by the Maine legislature and governor as Freeman McGilvery Day; buried in Village Cemetery, Searsport.

McGraw, John Harte 1850–1916, born: Barker Plantation, Penobscot County; son of an Irish immigrant logger who drowned in the Penobscot River; attended public schools in Penobscot and Washington Counties, clerked in a retail store while attending school in Danforth; manager of a grocery store, four years later, entered into a partnership with his brother in a general store in Danforth; removed to San Francisco 1875, drove a horsecar for a few months, removed to Seattle, Washington, 1876; clerk in the Occidental Hotel, subsequently acquired an interest in the American

Hotel, where he was manager until 1878, when the hotel burned to the ground; appointed to the Seattle police force, city marshal 1879, chief of police 1880–82; while a policeman, devoted much of his spare time and much of his salary to the creation of the collection of the Seattle Public Library; member: Washington bar 1886; King County sheriff 1882–84, in his second term, suppressed anti-Chinese rioting and fell into political disfavor, losing reelection to a third term; president: Seattle First National Bank 1890–93; elected third governor of Washington (Republican) 1893–97, during his tenure, a new statehouse was erected in Olympia, successfully uncovered a political intrigue involving fraud between members of the Board of Capitol Commissioners and an architect and syndicate; after his term as governor, his successor, John Rankin Rogers, audited McGraw's accounts as King County sheriff and found that he owed $10,000 to the state; in order to regain his fortune, removed to the Klondike, where he successfully engaged in mining for two years; after his return to Seattle, president: Puget Sound Realty Associates; director: Hanford Irrigation & Power Co.; first president: Associated Chambers of Commerce of the Pacific; vice president: Alaska-Yukon-Pacific Exposition, Seattle 1909; died of typhoid fever, buried in Mount Pleasant Cemetery, Seattle.

McIntyre, Rufus 1784–1866, born: York; A.B. Dartmouth College ΦBK 1809; member: Maine bar 1812, practiced in Parsonsfield; served in War of 1812; member: Maine House of Representatives 1820; prosecuting attorney for York County 1820–43; member: Maine Boundary Commission 1820; member from the First District: U.S. House of Representatives 1827–35 (Jacksonian); Maine state land agent 1839–40, it was McIntyre's arrest, by Canadian authorities, that was the proximate cause of the Aroostook War; U.S. marshal 1853–57; Bowdoin College overseer 1821–60; buried in Middleroad Cemetery, Parsonfield.

McKusick, Victor Almon 1921– , born: Parkman; twin brother of Vincent McKusick; student: Tufts University ΦBK 1940–43, M.D. Johns Hopkins University Medical School 1946, D.Sc. (Hon.) New York Medical College 1974, University of Maine 1978, University of Rochester 1979, Memorial University, Newfoundland, 1979, Aberdeen University 1988, Bates College 1989, Colby College 1991, University of Chicago 1991, M.D. Liverpool University 1976, Edinburgh University 1984, University of Zurich 1990; training in clinical medicine, laboratory research: Johns Hopkins University/U.S. Public Health Service 1946–52; instructor in medicine: Johns Hopkins University Medicine School 1951–54, assistant professor 1954–57, associate professor 1957–60, chief, division of genetics 1957–73, professor of medicine 1960–85, professor of epidemiology and biology 1969–78, William Osler professor of medicine 1978–85, chairman, Department of Medicine 1973–85; physician in chief: Johns Hopkins University Hospital 1973–85, university professor of medical genetics from 1985; founding president: the Human Genome Organization (HUGO), the international co-ordinating body for the human genome initiative; delineated Marfan syndrome and other heritable disorders of connective tissue, established the usefulness of gene mapping and genetics as a part of medical discipline, studied heart sounds and murmurs and adapted a device for sound spectrography; author: *Heritable Disorders of Connective Tissue* 1956, *Cardiovascular Sound in Health and Disease* 1958, *Medical Genetics* 1964, *Human Genetics* 1964, *On the X Chromosome of Man* 1964, *Mendelian Inheritance in Man* 1966, *Medical Genetics of the Amish* 1978, *A Model of Its Kind* 1989, *Osler's Legacy* 1990, *A Century of Biomedical Science at Johns Hopkins* 1993; founding co-editor in chief: *Genomics Journal*.

McKusick, Vincent 1921– , born: Parkman; twin brother of Victor McKusick; A.B. Bates College ΦBK 1943, B.S., M.S. Massachusetts Institute of Technology 1947, L.L.B. *summa cum laude* Harvard University Law School 1950, L.L.D. Colby College 1976, Nasson College 1978, Bates College 1979, Bowdoin College 1979, Suffolk University 1983; law clerk to Chief Judge Learned Hand of the U.S. Court of Appeals, Second District 1950–51, Justice Felix Frankfurter of the U.S. Supreme Court 1951–52; member: Maine bar 1952, practiced in Portland; partner: Pierce, Atwood, Scribner, Allen & McKusick and predecessors 1953–77; chief justice: Maine Supreme Judicial Court 1977–92; president: Conference of Chief Justices of the United States 1990–91, presided at the first meeting of the United States of the Conference of International Appellate Judges.

McLellan, Isaac 1806–99, born: Portland; graduate: Phillips Academy, Andover, classmate and close friend of Nathaniel Willis; A.B. Bowdoin College 1826; practiced law in Boston, renewed his friendship with Willis, who was then editing the *Monthly Magazine*, contributing numerous poems and articles to that publication; associate editor: *Daily Patriot*, constant contributor to the *New England Magazine* and the *Knickerbocker*, removed to New York 1851; a passionate hunter, gave up the practice of law and devoted himself to field sport and poetry; author: *The Year and Other Poems* 1832, *The Fall of the Indian* 1830, *Poems of the Rod and Gun* 1886, *Haunts of Wild Game, War Poems*, &c.

McNear, George Washington 1837–1909, born: Washington; son of a shipowner; showed a proficiency for mathematics and navigation, began shipping out on his father's vessels 1852, after making several voyages abroad and along the Atlantic Coast, landed in New Orleans 1854, took command of a schooner plying the Mississippi River and Lake Pontchartrain, became part-owner and master of a steamboat plying the same waters 1856–60, sold his interest and went to California, formed a partnership with his brother, John A. McNear, in Petaluma: McNear and Brother, commission and grain merchants, opened a branch in San Francisco 1861, sent the company's first shipload of grain to Europe 1867, partnership dissolved 1874, established G. W. McNear, San Francisco, incorporated 1909 as George W. McNear, Inc., with branches in London and Liverpool, became one of the leading shippers on the

Pacific Coast, concentrated his shipping facilities in Port Costa, California, where he built warehouses and wharfs where as many as ten deepwater ships could load simultaneously, acquired the warehouses and flour mills of Starr & Co. in Vallejo and Wheatport 1895, owned some twenty-five warehouses in the interior of the state, providing storage for over eight million bushels of grain; builder, president: Oakland Street Railroad Co.; president: First National Bank, Oakland, Port Costa Water Co., Port Costa Milling Co.; instrumental in merging the old Produce Exchange with the Merchants' Exchange, of which he was president; owned a ranch in Contra Costa County where he raised cattle and fruit and a ranch in Merced County, where he grew cotton and grain.

Merriam, Henry Clay 1837–1912, born: Houlton; brother of Cyrus Knapp Merriam; A.B. Colby College 1864 (as of 1867), L.L.D. (Hon.) 1908; in the Civil War: captain, USV, 20th Maine 1862, brevetted lieutenant for Antietam, captured at the battle of the Wilderness, POW at Andersonville, successful on his third attempt at escape; joined General Ulman's Louisiana Expedition to organize Negro troops, placed in command of the 1st Louisiana Native Guard, the first all-black regiment in the U.S. Army, which he led at Fort Blakely, the last assault of the war; recipient: Medal of Honor, Fort Blakely, Alabama, 9 April 1865, "Volunteered to attack the enemy's works in advance of orders and, upon permission being given, made a most gallant assault," brevetted colonel, USV; mustered out 1865, appointed major, USA, 1866; commanded the 38th Infantry, commanded the infantry reserve in Custer's Indian campaign in Kansas 1867, commanded Fort McIntosh 1876; during the Mexican Revolution, bombarded the Mexican federal troops of Pablo Quintana, redressing outrages against Americans, crossed the Rio Grande and rescued U.S. commercial agent Haines, who had been captured by Mexican revolutionaries; promoted lieutenant colonel, USA 2nd Infantry 1876; assigned to the Department of the Columbia 1876; during the Nez Perce war of 1877, received the highest commendation of his commander, General O. O. Howard, for his service in Idaho and Washington, his successful management of Indian tribes, which resulted in their settlement on reservations and the opening of vast territories to settlers; promoted colonel, USA, 1885; commanded Fort Laramie, Wyoming, 1885–89; during the Sioux War 1890–91, commanded all troops along the Cheyenne River, South Dakota, disarmed 300 of Sitting Bull's followers during their stampede subsequent to Sitting Bull's death; appointed brigadier general, USA, 1897; commanded the Department of the Columbia, which included Alaska, charged with devising and implementing a rescue of starving miners in the Klondike, in midwinter, suppression of striking miners in the Coeur d'Alene region of Idaho; during the Spanish-American War, major general, USV; his command was increased to include Hawaii and the entire Pacific Coast; organized, equipped, instructed, and forwarded troops to the Philippines; assigned to the Department of the Colorado and the Missouri 1899, retired 1901; advanced to major general, USA, on the retired list, by special act of Congress 1903; champion rifle shot:

U.S. Army 1883–85; invented the Merriam pack, for which he received a gold medal from the French Academy of Inventors; buried in Arlington National Cemetery.

Merrick, Samuel Vaughan 1801–70, born: Hallowell; grandson of Samuel Vaughan, son of John Merrick, tutor to the Vaughan family, who subsequently married the sister of Dr. Benjamin Vaughan, and was cashier of the Hallowell Bank and sur-veyor of the Canada Road; attended public school in Hallowell to age fifteen, when he removed to Philadelphia and worked for an uncle, a wine merchant; organized a fire insurance company in Philadelphia 1820, he and his partner, John Agnew, won fame for their construction of an improved type of fire engine; a founder and first president of the Franklin Institute 1842–54; after study in Europe, brought about gas production and street lighting in Philadelphia 1836; established the Southwark foundry 1835, which produced the best marine steam engines in the country, utilized in the most advanced vessels of the day, for example: the first screw-propelled steam frigate: USS *Princeton* 1843, USS *Mississippi*, USS *San Jacinto*, USS *Wabash*; intro-duced the steam hammer to the United States; constructed prefabricated iron frame lighthouses for the Florida Coast (several of which are extant); first president of the Pennsylvania Railroad 1847–49; president: Sunbury & Erie Railroad Co. 1856; direc-tor: Catawissa Railroad Co.; member: American Philosophical Society.

Merrill, Augustus 1843–95, born: Byron; in the Civil War: enlisted as sergeant, later as captain, Company B, 1st Maine Veteran Infantry, recipient: Medal of Honor, at Petersburg, Virginia 2 April 1865, "with six men, captured sixty-nine Confederate prisoners and recaptured several soldiers who had fallen into the enemy's hands." Later brevetted major, USV; buried in Graceland Cemetery, Chicago.

Merrill, Elmer Drew 1876–1956, born: East Auburn; son of a farmer; attended local public schools, B.S. University of Maine ФBK 1898, M.S. 1904, Sc.D. (Hon.) 1925, student: George Washington University Medical School 1900–01, Sc.D. Har-vard University 1936, L.L.D. University of California 1935, Yale University 1951; assistant in natural science: University of Maine 1898–99; assistant agrostologist: U.S. Department of Agriculture, Washington, D.C., 1899–1902; botanist: Bureau of Agri-culture, Manila, Philippine Islands, 1902, Bureau of Agriculture, Bureau of Forestry 1902–03, Bureau of Government Laboratories 1903–05, Bureau of Science from 1906; associate professor of botany and head of department: University of the Philippines 1912–19, professor 1916–19; director: Bureau of Science, Manila 1919–23; in his twenty-one years in the Philippines, Merrill accumulated a remarkable botanical library and an herbarium representative of the many thousands of species of plants extant and described many of them botanically; dean: College of Agriculture and director: Agricultural Experimental Station, University of California 1923–29; profes-sor of botany: Columbia University 1930–35; director: New York Botanical Garden 1930–35; professor of botany: Harvard University, director: Arnold Arboretum, administrator: botanical collections: Harvard University 1935–46, Arnold professor of botany: Harvard University 1946–48; specialist in taxonomy and phytogeography of Philippine, Polynesian, and Indo-Malayan plants; member: American Academy of Arts and Sciences, American Philosophical Society, Deutsche Botanical Gesellschaft, Royal Netherlands Botanical Society, Linnean Society; president: American Botanical Society 1934, Taxonomic Society of America 1946; author of over 500 papers and books on the botany of North America, China, Philippines, Malaya, and Polynesia, including: *Dictionary of Plant Names of the Philippine Islands* 1903, *A Flora of Manila* 1912, *An Interpretation of Rumphius Herbarium Amboinense* 1917, *Species Blancoanae, A Critical Revision of the Philippine Species of Plants Described by Blanco and Llanos* 1918, *Enumeration of Philippine Flowering Plants* (four volumes) 1922–26; in 1937, he completed the compilation of a Polynesian botanical bibliography covering the period from 1773 to 1935; completed 1938, a bibliography of all botanical literature of East Asia; editor: *Philippine Journal of Science*; while on an expedition to China, was captured by bandits and managed to ransom himself and two companions for five gold Mexican dollars and a watch 1917; in World War II: acted as special consultant to the secretary of war, prepared emergency food manuals for U.S. troops serving in the Pacific theatre, in which edible, nonpoisonous plants were described; made a member of the Order of Orange-Nassau by Queen Wilhelmina of the Netherlands 1948; first American botanist to receive the Medal of the Linnean Society of London 1939; Guggenheim fellowship for the study of Indo-Malayasian and Philippine flora 1952.

Merrill, George W. 1837– ?, born: Turner; A.B. Bowdoin College 1859; removed to Evansville, Indiana; studied law, member: Indiana bar 1861; in the Civil War: first lieutenant, USV, Company F, 60th Indiana Volunteers, promoted to captain, USV, captured at Munfordsville, exchanged; removed to Nevada, district attorney 1865–77; member: Nevada House of Representatives 1880–82, speaker 1882; U.S. minister to Hawaii 1885–89 (his successor was John Leavitt Stevens).

Merrill, Moses Emery 1803–47, born: Brunswick; graduate: U.S. Military Academy 1826, commissioned second lieutenant, USA, attached to the 5th Infantry, assigned to frontier duty in Illinois, Missouri, Michigan, Wisconsin to 1845; promoted to lieutenant, USA, 1833, captain, USA, 1837; took part in the military occupation of Texas 1845–46; in the Mexican War, saw action at Palo Alto, Resaca de la Palma, Monterey, the siege of Veracruz and the capture of San Antonio, Cherubusco; killed while leading a column in attack at Molino del Rey.

Merrill, Samuel 1822–99, born: Turner; after receiving a grade school education in Turner, began to teach school at age seventeen, later superintendent of schools; removed to Tamworth, New Hampshire, 1847; engaged in merchandising; elected as an abolitionist to the New Hampshire House of Representatives during the tumultuous period following the repeal of the Missouri Compromise and the election of

John P. Hale and James Bell to the U.S. Senate 1854–56; removed to McGregor, Iowa, 1856, where he was a merchant and banker, member: Iowa General Assembly (House of Representatives) 1859–62, resigned to serve in the Civil War; commissioned colonel, USV, commanding officer: 21st Iowa Volunteer Infantry, served under General Grant in the Western Department, took part in the battles in Missouri, severely wounded at the battle of Hartsville, Missouri; mustered out and granted a pension, which he donated to the hospital in Des Moines, Iowa; merchant and banker to 1868, elected seventh governor of Iowa (Republican) 1868–72, declared against depreciated currency, campaigned to have the word "white" dropped from the Iowa constitution as a qualification of electors, literally broke the ground for the Iowa capitol building with a plough, as chairman of the capitol building commission, combated speculation and jobbery, introduced significant reforms in the public schools of Iowa, required that before he could give a pardon for a capital offense, he had to, personally and privately, interview the plaintiff; after his retirement from office, served as president of the Citizens National Bank, Des Moines; removed to Los Angeles, California, 1889, where he engaged in banking; buried in Woodland Cemetery, Des Moines, Iowa.

Merry, John Fairfield 1840–1916; born: Edgecomb; entered USN, 1862; service in the Civil War and Spanish-American War; commanding officer: Naval Station Honolulu, began construction of Pearl Harbor naval facilities, where Merry Point was named in his honor; retired as rear admiral, USN.

Metcalf, Wilder Stevens 1855– ?, born: Milo; removed, with his parents to Elyria, Ohio, 1856; A.B. Oberlin College 1878; engaged in the butter and cheese business for nine years; removed to Lawrence, Kansas, 1887, associated with a farm mortgage business; L.L.B. University of Kansas Law School 1897, member: Kansas bar 1897; when the Spanish-American War broke out, Metcalf was colonel, 1st Kansas Volunteer Infantry, commissioned major, USV, 20th Kansas Volunteer Infantry, while on service with his regiment, in the Philippines, was shot through the ear at Caloocan and through the foot in the advance on Bocaue; even though the wound was painful, stayed in command of his battalion, was lifted onto his horse, and continued the advance for several miles, ordered to the rear by General MacArthur, who recommended his brevet to brigadier general; upon rejoining his regiment, was still unable to mount a horse, so he commanded from a buggy in several engagements, mustered out 1899; delegate: Republican National Convention 1900; member: Lawrence (Kansas) school board.

Metcalf, William Henry 1896–1968, born: Waite; graduate: Dennysville High School; in Canada, during World War I, joined Sixteenth Scottish Battalion; at Arras led, on foot, a tank division into a German position; awarded the Victoria Cross; taken up by British Royal family, invited to participate in the 1938 coronation of King George VI, but felt that he couldn't leave his garage in Eastport in the care of the hired man; buried with full British military honors in Eastport.

Millay, Edna St. Vincent 1892–1950, born: Rockland; at age fourteen, won the *St. Nicholas Magazine* Gold Badge for Poetry; her poem *Renascence* brought her early acclaim 1912; student: Barnard College, A.B. Vassar College 1917, Litt. D. (Hon.) Tufts University, Russell Sage College 1933, Colby College 1937, L.L.D. University of Wisconsin 1933, L.H.D. New York University 1937; after Vassar, moved in with her sister Kathleen in Greenwich Village, appeared briefly as an unpaid actress in Provincetown Players productions in their theatre on MacDougal Street; her *A Few Figs from Thistles* 1920 caused some critics to hail her as the most outstanding female poet of the age, *Aria da Capo* 1921, an antiwar play, *Second April* 1921, a collection of poems, *The Lamp and the Bell* 1921, a play, *Two Slatterns and a King* 1921, a play, *The Harp-Weaver and Other Poems* won the Pulitzer Prize for poetry 1923, *Justice Denied in Massachusetts* 1927, a poem commemorating the Sacco-Vanzetti trial, she also made a personal appeal to the governor of Massachusetts and was arrested as one of the death watch demonstrators before the statehouse in Boston; her book for the opera *The King's Henchman* 1927, a lyric drama of Saxon England, commissioned by the Metropolitan Opera Co., music by Deems Taylor, proved the most popular American opera, to that point; *The Buck in the Snow* 1928, poems, *Fatal Interview* 1931, a collection of sonnets and one of the few volumes of poetry to appear on bestseller lists, *The Princess Marries a Page* 1932, a play, *Wine from These Grapes* 1934, poems; co-translator of Baudelaire's *Flowers of Evil* 1936, *Conversations at Midnight* 1937, poems, *Huntsman, What Quarry?* poems 1939, *There Are No More Islands Any More* 1940, poem, a plea for American intervention in World War II, *Collected Sonnets* 1941, *The Murder of Lidice* 1942, a much-acclaimed poem inspired by the destruction of a Czech village of that name and the massacre of its inhabitants by the German army, *Collected Lyrics* 1943, *Poem and Prayer for an Invading Army* 1944; Millay stood apart from most of her contemporaries in her frankness, clarity, and naturalness of style, her acceptance and enjoyment of the Bohemian lifestyl,e and the "vicissitudes and transience of love."

Millay, Kathleen Kalloch 1896–1943, born: Rockland; sister of Edna St. Vincent Millay; student at Vassar College 1917–20, author: *Wayfarer* 1926, *Against the Wall* 1929, *The Very Little Giant* 1934, *Whirligiggle and the Kings Beard* 1934, *Plup Plups House Warming* 1935, *The Evergreen Tree* 1927, *The Hermit Thrush* 1929, *The Beggar at the Gate* 1931, *Of All the Animals* 1932, *Persephone* 1932, *Black of the Moon* 1934, *The Man Who Would Become A Bird* 1935, *Hollywood Wife* 1939, *After Tomorrow, Judy Listens In, Harum Scarum, Mad Money, Grafted Fruit, Nobody's Business, Mr. Nightingale, Thaw Country.*

Millett, Lewis Lee Red 1920– ?, born: Mechanic Falls; captain, U.S. Army, Company E, 27th Infantry Regiment, recipient: Medal of Honor, Soam-Ni, Korea, 7 February 1951, "Capt. Millett, Company E, distinguished himself by duty in action. While personally leading his company in an attack against a strongly held position he noted that the 1st Platoon was pinned down by small arms, automatic, and anti tank fire. Capt. Millett ordered the 3rd Platoon forward, placed himself at the head of the two platoons, and, with fixed bayonet, led the assault up the fire-swept hill. In the fierce charge Capt. Millett bayoneted two enemy soldiers and boldly continued on, throwing grenades, clubbing and bayoneting the enemy, while urging his men forward by shouting encouragement. Despite vicious opposing fire, the whirlwind hand-to-hand assault carried to the crest of the hill. His dauntless leadership and personal courage so inspired his men that they stormed into the hostile position and used their bayonets with such lethal force that the enemy fled in wild disorder. During this fierce onslaught Capt. Millett was wounded by grenade fragments but refused evacuation until the objective was taken and firmly secured. The superb leadership, conspicuous courage, and consummate devotion to duty demonstrated by Capt. Millett were directly responsible for the successful accomplishment of a hazardous mission and reflect the highest credit on himself and the heroic traditions of the military service."

Milliken, Carl E. 1877–1961, born: Pittsfield; son of a farmer and logger, grandson of Ebenezer Knowlton, cousin of Wayne Jordan, son-in-law of George Colby Chase; attended public schools in Augusta, A.B. Bates College ΦBK 1897, L.L.D. (Hon.) 1917, A.B. Harvard College 1899, L.L.D. Colby College 1918; associated with his father's lumber business, Mattawamkeag Lumber Co., Island Falls, 1899; treasurer, general manager: Stockholm (Maine) Lumber Co. 1900–19, president: Katahdin Farmers Telephone Co. 1904–25; member: Maine House of Representatives 1909–11, Maine Senate 1912–16, president 1913–14; governor of Maine (Republican) 1917–21, first Maine governor to be elected through a direct primary; member of a group of Maine residents engaged in the production of a series of motion pictures, based on the literature of the outdoors with Maine scenery; secretary: Motion Picture Association of America (the so-called Hays Office) 1926–47, a voluntary self-censorship unit for the movie industry, Milliken was the spokesman in defense of films passed by the association, often in the face of criticism by religious organizations, which contended that the content of sexuality and violence in many films contributed to delinquency in the young, his defense of the film industry brought him into conflict with the National Council of Churches from which he resigned 1931; managing trustee: Teaching Films Custodians, Inc. 1947–58, a nonprofit organization maintained by the film industry for the distribution of historical films to schools; an official delegate representing the United States at the International Conference on Education Cinematography, Rome, 1934; represented the Motion Picture Producers and Distributors of America at a conference held in London 1935, on production code administration for the European motion picture industry; accompanied John D. Rockefeller, Jr., on a tour of the United States in behalf of the Interchurch World Movement 1921; president: Northern Baptist Convention; president: American Baptist Foreign Mission Society; died in a nursing home in Springfield, Massachusetts.

Milliken, Seth Mellen 1836–1920, born Poland; student: Yarmouth Academy, Hebron Academy; became a miller's assistant in Minot, at age seventeen; was soon placed in charge of the mill; at age nineteen, became a grocer in Portland in partnership with his brother-in-law David True 1860; co-founder: Deering, Milliken & Co. 1865, suppliers of dry goods and textiles; when William Deering withdrew, Milliken became president: Milliken & Co. 1869, which became the largest combine of textile mills in United States, through the ownership or control of forty-two textile milling companies; Milliken was among the first to see the possibilities of industrial development in the South, in particular, the development of reliable steam power freed textile mills from the need to be on or near a source of waterpower, hence, the movement of mills to the source of cotton; he was also the director of the National City Bank, New York, the Bowery Savings Bank, the New York Life Insurance Co., Trust Company of New York, Mercantile National Bank; was able to keep his holdings solvent during the Panic of 1907, winning him the admiration and confidence of Theodore Roosevelt and J. P. Morgan; Republican presidential elector 1896; became a familiar sight in New York, driving fast trotting horses; father of Margaret Milliken Hatch, whose foundation continues to promote good works.

Mills, Hiram Francis 1836–1921, born: Bangor; S.B. Rensselaer Polytechnical Institute 1856, A.M. (Hon.) Harvard University 1889; served as apprentice engineer on the Hoosac and Bergen tunnels, with power projects in Cohoes, New York, and Billerica, Massachusetts; opened his own office in Boston 1868, consulting engineer in many parts of United States and Latin America; designed the stone dam in Bangor 1866; principle work in Massachusetts; chief engineer, Essex County, Lawrence locks and canals; at Lowell undertook experiments which led to the perfection of piezometer turbine designs; author: *Flow of Water in Pipes* 1923; consulting engineer: Boston Metropolitan Water and Sewerage Board, designed water supply, drainage, and sewerage systems; chairman: Committee on Water Supply and Sewers, Massachusetts Board of Health 1886–1914; dissatisfied with current thinking on water purification, constructed at Lowell the most advanced laboratory in the world, constructed the first sand filter, reduced the incidence of typhoid in Massachusetts by 90 *percent*; published in: *Proceedings of the American Academy of Arts and Sciences, Journal of the Franklin Institute, Transactions of the American Academy of Civil Engineers, Journal of New England Water Works Association*; endowed Elizabeth Worcester Mills Foundation for Cancer Research, Harvard University; member of the corporation: Massachusetts Institute of Technology, chairman of its Committee on Mechanical Engineering and Applied Engineering.

Mitchel, David 1728–96, born: Pembroke, Massachusetts; removed to North Yarmouth, with his family 1733; A.B. Harvard College 1751, A.M. 1754, as an undergraduate, held a Browne Scholarship; kept school in Falmouth; because of poor eyesight, gave up on becoming a Congregational minister; his poor eyesight did not prevent him from seeing, from shore, a distress signal on Boon Island; married the daughter of Nicholas Loring, on one occasion, while returning home from courting her, he was attacked by an Indian brandishing a tomahawk, fortunately for him, the gate to the Mitchel stockade was open, so he galloped in, unharmed; although he never joined the bar, he practiced law in North Yarmouth; Yarmouth town clerk 1762–96, appointed justice of the peace 1764, as deacon, conducted religious services in the absence of a minister, cared for the poor, helped the illiterate with their letters and led community activities; served on the town committee formed to reply to the Boston Committee of Safety 1774, also served on the standing Committee of Correspondence, attended the Cumberland County Convention and served on the committee detailed to draft its resolutions 1774; delegate to the Provincial Congress at Watertown 1775; appointed to supersede the governor's appointment as in command of the Cumberland Regiment; copied the Declaration of Independence into the Yarmouth town records with a bold hand; appointed special justice of the Cumberland County Court of Pleas 1775, made a permanent justice in that court 1778, became chief justice 1781–86; campaigned for the federal Constitution and was a member of the ratifying body 1788; elected to the Massachusetts House of Representatives 1791, since none of the candidates for the Massachusetts Senate had achieved a majority, he was chosen for the upper house and continued to serve in the senate for several years; in the general court he campaigned for the establishment of a college in the district, particularly in North Yarmouth, but when the choice was Brunswick, he cooperated completely and was chosen first Bowdoin College treasurer, having made a considerable fortune from selling forest lands, he was very successful in the selling of the six townships assigned to the establishment of Bowdoin College, also served as trustee 1794–96; stricken by a stroke while attending the senate in Boston, he was able to return home before his death.

Monteux, Doris Hodgkins 1895–1984, born: Salsbury Cove, Bar Harbor; a professional singer when she met and married Pierre Monteux 1928; co-founded the

Domaine School for Conductors and Orchestral Players, Hancock, 1941; author: *Everyone Is Someone, It's All in the Music* 1965; after Monteux's death, established the Pierre Monteux Memorial Foundation.

Monteux, Pierre 1875–1964, born: Paris, France; student: Paris Conservatory, studied violin with Maurin and Berthelier, solfeggio and harmony with Lavignac, counterpoint and fugue with Leneoveu; recipient of honorary doctorates from University of California, Mills College, University of Maine, Stanford University; viola player, later: conductor of concerts and Ballet Russe, conductor: Metropolitan Opera Company, New York 1917–19, Boston Symphony 1919–24, with William Mengelberg at the Concertgebouw Orchestra, Amsterdam 1920–30, conductor: Paris Symphony Orchestra from 1930, conductor: San Francisco Symphony Orchestra 1934–52, principal conductor: London Symphony Orchestra from 1961, only French conductor to have conducted both the Berlin Philharmonic Orchestra and Vienna Philharmonic Orchestra before 1950, divided 1938 season with Toscanini and Rodzinski at National Broadcasting Company, New York; in World War I: private in French infantry, participated in battles of Verdun, Rheims, Soissons, and Argonne, decorated: French Legion of Honor, Commander of the Crown of Roumania, Commander of Orange-Nassau; married Doris Hodgkins of Hancock 1928, with her, founded the Domaine School for Conductors and Orchestral Players and served as its director; buried in Hancock.

Moody, Grenville 1812–87, born: Portland; descendant of Rev. Samuel Moody, cousin of Ralph Waldo Emerson; removed with his parents to Baltimore, where his father became the principal of the first female seminary in Baltimore; became a clerk in his brothers store in Norwich, Ohio, 1831; licensed as a local preacher by the Methodist Episcopal church 1835, received into the Ohio conference, held various pastorates in the state, appointed to Morris Chapel in Cincinnati 1860; invited to take command of the 74th Ohio Volunteers 1861, consulted with his congregation and accepted commission with their permission; at Stones River he received nickname "Fighting Parson," where he was wounded four times and had his horse shot from under him but would not leave the field, brevetted brigadier general, USV; resigned 1863, due to debility; after the war, returned to his ministry in various pastorates; retired to his farm in Jefferson, Ohio; died as result of an accident on his way to preach a memorial service before a part of the Grand Army of the Republic.

Moody, Joseph (yclept Handkerchief Moody) 1700–53, born: York; son of Samuel Moody (a); as a child, accidently killed Ebenezer Preble, a playmate, with the discharge of a pistol; A.B. Harvard College 1717, A.M. 1721; schoolmaster in York 1717–32, also served as York registrar of deeds, county treasurer, justice of the peace, and judge of the court of common pleas; ordained Congregational ministry 1732, pastor of the new second parish (Scotland or North parish) of York, where he gained fame for his powerful praying as well as the other fine qualities of his ministry;

in 1738, began constantly wearing a handkerchief over his face, acquired a reputation for second sight, when, in the midst of a very long prayer to God, recommending success for the forces of General Pepperrell at Louisbourg, he suddenly cried "It is done. It is delivered into our hands," subsequently, it was seen that his outburst had occurred at the moment of capitulation; model for Hawthorne's *Minister of the Black Veil*; removed from his position by an ecclesiastical council, by reason of insanity 1741; father of Samuel Moody (d), grandfather of Samuel Moody (e).

Moody, Joshua 1697–1749, born: New Castle, New Hampshire; son of Samuel Moody (b.); obtained his early schooling in New Castle under Edward Wigglesworth; A.B. Harvard College 1716, A.M.; expelled twice during his undergraduate career; became the first Falmouth town clerk 1719; at the time of the Falmouth Indian conference of 1721, he was a lieutenant of militia and carried an Indian messenger to Norridgewock in a whaleboat; became involved in the political struggle between Governor Shute and the Massachusetts General Court, his father having been dismissed, Moody insulted a party of politicians who had come to the fort in Falmouth, they subsequently had him lowered in rank from lieutenant to sergeant; by 1724, he was serving as captain under Thomas Westbrook in his campaign on the frontier; subsequent to that Indian war and the death of his father, settled permanently in Falmouth, where he was involved in land speculation with his brother Samuel; appointed justice of the peace 1729, declined elevation to judge of the court of common pleas, preferring to remain justice of the peace until his death; during the next Indian war did not serve in the field but was active in the purchasing of "Whale Boats, Warehouse room, Medicines and Attendance on the sick soldiers and Expresses"; elected to the Massachusetts House of Representatives 1732; when Thomas Smith heard that Moody was dying, he made a hazardous journey on snowshoes in order to be with him when he died.

Moody, Samuel (a) 1676–1747, born: Newbury, Massachusetts; great grandfather of Grenville Moody, Ralph Waldo Emerson, father of Joseph Moody; A.B. Harvard College 1697, A.M. 1700; agreed to be chaplain to the garrison at York 1698, ordained Congregational ministry at York 1700, where he preached to the end of his life; in the beginning, faced, along with the rest of the town, great hardship, given the desolation left by Indian raids; the house built for him by the town was heavily fortified; during his entire tenure, the danger of Indian attack was never entirely absent, his parishioners commonly attended services armed; chaplain on the abortive Port Royal Expedition 1707; was among the signers of the treaty with the Abenakis, signed at Portsmouth 1712; widely known for his serene confidence in God's immanent presence and grace, for many generations, stories of Father Moody's more peculiar beliefs and statements were favored stories to be told; sent by the Massachusetts Congregational convention to Rhode Island as a missionary amongst the Baptists and Quakers, where he met with some success, established the first Congregational body in Providence, which subsequently attempted to lure him back as their regular preacher, but to no avail 1723; initially supported George Whitefield's New Light revival, even allowing him to preach in his pulpit in York, later developments caused him concern and so, he served as a member of the convention of ministers that met in Boston to pass judgment on the religious revivals that followed George Whitefield's preaching 1743; despite his age and infirmities, accompanied the William Pepperrell expedition to Cape Breton, after the capitulation of the citadel, took particular pleasure in destroying crosses and images with his own axe, preached the first Protestant sermon in that place 1745; often preached, by invitation, to the Massachusetts General Court; author: *The Vain Youth*.... 1707, *The Doleful State of the Damned; Especially Such as go to Hell* 1710, *Judas the Traitor Hung up in Chains* 1714, *Smoking Flax Inflamed, or, Weary Sinners Encouraged to go to Christ* 1718, *A Sermon Preached Before His Excellency Samuel Shute*.... 1721, Mr. *Moody's Discourses to the Little Children* 1721, an account of the life and death of Joseph Quasson, an Indian 1726.

Moody, Samuel (b) *c.*1667–1729, born: Portsmouth, New Hampshire; son of a Congregational minister; A.B. Harvard College 1689, A.M.; preached in Hadley, Massachusetts, 1693–94, New Castle, New Hampshire to 1704, preached for several years on the Isle of Shoals to a particularly rough crowd; in 1705 he was in command of forty men at St. John's Fort, Newfoundland; in 1709 he was in command of the fort at Casco Bay; corresponded with Father Sébastien Râle, served as the organ of communications between the British authorities and the Indians; as a result of the Treaty of Peace concluded at Utrecht and the cessation of hostilities, both in Europe and America, Moody was approached by a delegation of Indians, under a flag of truce, with the result of the conclusion of hostilities in Maine, ratified by a treaty signed at Portsmouth 1713; with the demolition of Fort Casco and the surrounding houses, by order of the authorities in Boston, Moody and his family removed to Portland Neck, where there was only one other family, named Ingersoll 1716; allowed, by the council, to erect a fortified house (on the beach at what is now the corner of Fore and Hancock Streets) and arm, at his own expense, other inhabitants of the Neck; his home was, for many years, the most prominent in the village; chosen selectman for seven years, justice of the peace, justice of the court of common pleas of York County, member of the delegation, sent by the council, to demand restitution for Indian raids in 1720; after the destruction of the settlement on Merrymeeting Bay (in what is now the town of Bowdoinham), the destruction of Brunswick, and other raids east of the Kennebec 1722, Moody was second-in-command of military forces on the coast; because of a quarrel between Governor Shute and the house of representatives, Moody was summoned to Boston, interrogated by the house and, in the absence of Governor Shute, dismissed by Lieutenant Governor Dummer, for the reason that Moody had been disposed to obey the orders of the governor, rather than those of the legislature; after his death, buried in the Eastern Cemetery; father of Samuel Moody (c).

Moody, Samuel (c.) 1699–1758, born: New Castle, New Hampshire; son of Major Samuel Moody; removed with his family to Falmouth (that portion that is now Portland), where his father directed the resettlement of that place, subsequent to the devastation wrought by the Indian wars; A.B. Harvard College 1718, A.M. 1721, his undergraduate career was prominent in the size and number of fines incurred; apprenticed with a Dr. Davis; appointed army surgeon 1722, detailed to Falmouth and Saco, commended by Thomas Westbrook; married the sister of Esther Wheelwright; settled in Falmouth, where he practiced medicine and succeeded his father as a chief resident proprietor, fought numerous and protracted suits against squatters and tenants; built boats, cut lumber, smoked salmon, and kept a tavern; served, at different times, as assessor, clerk of the First Parish, town clerk, notary public, and justice of the peace, captain of the town militia, represented Falmouth in the general court 1738, 1740, 1743; served on the committee for erecting blockhouses; attended the army in conflicts with the Indians; after 1730, spent most of his time in Brunswick, served as surgeon on the Kennebec during the war years 1739–42; at the siege of Louisbourg, commanded a company of the second Massachusetts regiment; from 1746 to the time of his death, served at Forts Frederick, Richmond and George, where he combined the jobs of military commander, surgeon, truckmaster, and justice of the peace; died while in command of Fort George at Brunswick, buried in the First Parish cemetery, Brunswick.

Moody, Samuel (d.) 1726–95, born: York; son of Rev. Joseph Moody; A.B. Harvard College 1746, A.M. 1749, A.M. Dartmouth College 1779; his father's derangement becoming complete, while an undergraduate Moody had to struggle to stay in school, held Hollis and Browne Scholarships, waited on tables; in a period where the study of Hebrew had declined, mastered the language sufficiently to give a declamation in that language; also showed considerable interest in science; attempted to follow his father into the ministry, but could not secure a permanent pulpit; although he considered himself to be a Calvinist, he went to the mat with Rev. Joseph Bellamy and his famous *True Religion Delineated*, wherein Bellamy asserted that only Calvinism logically explained how it was that a good God could create sin, in his *An Attempt to Point out the Fatal and Pernicious Consequences of the Rev. Mr. Joseph Bellamy's Doctrines* (1759), Moody suggested that the Calvinistic God is a nauseating creature, far better to assume that sin was a creation of man's free will; Bellamy, in his *The Wisdom of God* replied to Moody and suggested that God had created sin for His glory; giving up his desire to preach, he was appointed justice of the peace for York 1754, busied himself witnessing documents and the treaty with the Penobscots; he also devoted much time in his attempt to secure compensation, from the general court, for the suffering his grandfather, Samuel Moody (a) experienced at Port Royal and Louisbourg; obtained permission from the First Parish of York to erect a schoolhouse on parsonage land; one of his great successes was taking the poor boy Joseph Willard in, preparing him, and sponsoring him at Harvard College and, in time, seeing Willard become one of the better-regarded presidents of that school; Lieutenant Governor William Dummer left an endowment for the establishment of a Free Grammar School, which was established at Byfield, Massachusetts, 1763; Moody was unanimously chosen master by the trustees, his brother Joseph (father of Samuel Moody [e]) kept the academy farm and boarded the students; in time, Moody came to the highest-regarded schoolmaster in the colonies; Dummer graduates constituted 25 percent of the undergraduate body at Harvard College and it was felt that they were the best prepared; Moody believed in cleanliness and physical exercise, on occasion, in warm weather, he would suspend classes so that the school could swim in the tidal creek adjacent; on one occasion, the student Edward Preble, upon being reproved by Moody for hovering too close to the stove and subsequently disarming Moody of the shovel, with which Moody was about to whack the recalcitrant Preble, was proclaimed a hero by the astonished Moody (if Wellington could say that the battle of Waterloo was won on the playing fields of Eton, it could be also said that the grit and determination of Preble in the War with Tripoli was clearly indicated in the schoolroom at Governor Dummer Academy); when Moody hired a French dancing master for the school, the uproar was tremendous; Moody always attended Harvard commencements and felt no compunctions in informing his former student, President Joseph Willard, of deficiencies in food and orations; appointed justice of the peace 1768, elected to the Massachusetts House of Representatives 1775; by 1782, the mental illness that claimed his father was beginning to be evident in Moody's behavior, by 1790, the board of trustees obtained his resignation, after which he returned to York; invited to become master of Berwick Academy, he chose, instead, to make extended trips on horseback to visit former students, staying often with President Joseph Willard at Harvard; eventually he died while one such trip, after over-exertion in a snowstorm at Exeter, New Hampshire; he was buried in the York meetinghouse graveyard.

Moody, Samuel (e) 1765–1832, born: Byfield, Massachusetts; son of Joseph Moody, who kept the farm school at Governor Dummer Academy, nephew of Samuel Moody (d); A.B. Dartmouth College ΦBK 1790, A.M. 1793; teacher at Hallowell Academy, delegate: Maine Constitutional Convention 1819; Bowdoin College overseer 1799–1813.

Moore, Anne Carroll 1871–1961, born: Limerick; after graduation from Bradford Academy, began study of law with her father; subsequent to his death 1891, enrolled in the Pratt Institute Library School, Brooklyn, New York, 1892; after graduation in 1896, became the children's librarian of the Pratt Institute Free Library, where many of her innovations were adopted, worldwide; in particular, her initiation of storytelling and poetry reading to children; through her various publications deeply influenced the first generation of children's librarians; published: *A List of Books for a Children's Library* 1903; influenced Stockholm to adopt the first children's library in Europe 1911; hired by New York Public Library to superintend work with children

1906, built collections, hired and directed children's librarians, insisted there be no restrictions on children as patrons; disliked much children's literature, highly influenced new authors; friend and correspondent with Leo Frank, defended him before he was lynched in Atlanta 1915; doted on her handpuppet Nicholas; author: *Nicholas: A Manhattan Christmas* 1924, *Nicholas and the Christmas Curse* 1932; reviewer for *Bookman, Herald Tribune, Hornbook*.

Moore, Bryant Edward 1894–1951, born: Ellsworth; son of a druggist; attended public schools in Ellsworth, B.S. U.S. Military Academy 1917, commissioned second lieutenant, USA, rose through the rank to major general, USA, 1944; first assigned to the 50th Infantry, transferred to 15th Infantry, Tientsin, China, 1919; stationed at Vancouver Barracks, Washington, 1921; instructor in military science: U.S. Military Academy 1924; student: Infantry School, Fort Benning, Georgia, 1929–30; stationed at Fort Williams, Maine, 1930–32, Schofield Barracks, Hawaii, with the 35th Infantry 1932–35, Fort Jay, New York, 1935–37; professor of military science and tactics: College of the City of New York 1937–38; student: Command and General Staff School, Fort Leavenworth, Kansas 1938–39; instructor in military science and tactics. University of Illinois 1939–42; sent with a task force to Australia, which occupied New Caledonia, subsequently re-organized to constitute the American Division, served as assistant chief of staff for intelligence and operations; commanding officer: 164th Regiment, first regiment in ground combat with the Japanese on Guadalcanal, defended Henderson Field and counter-attacked in October 1942, made a successful offensive near Koli Point, November 1942, defended a major portion of the American position west of the Matanikau River during November and December 1942, rotated home 1943; assistant division commander: 104th Infantry, Camp Adair, Oregon; accompanied this regiment to the European Theatre 1944; assumed command of the 8th Infantry Division, January 1945, under his command, this division played a decisive role in the attack of the VII Corps across the Roer River to the Rhine River, clearing the German army from the Cologne Plain, in the reduction of the Ruhr pocket and in the elimination of the German army east of the Rhine; after V-J day, he moved with his division to Camp Leonard Wood, Missouri; late in 1945, went overseas to command the 88th Division in Venezio Giulia, Italy; commanding general: Trieste U.S. Troops, Free Territory of Trieste; chief of public information, U.S. War Department, Washington, 1948; superintendent: U.S. Military Academy 1949–51; commander, IX Corps, Korea, 1951; died of a heart attack in Korea subsequent to a helicopter crash in the Han River; decorated: Distinguished Service Medal with two oak clusters, Silver Star with cluster, Legion of Merit with cluster.

Moore, Edward Bruce 1851–1915, born: North Anson; born on a farm, son of a civil engineer and architect who designed a number of public buildings in Alabama and Texas, where he had extensive land holdings, railroad and steamship interests, who died in 1853, the mother moved the family to Grand Rapids, Michigan; during the Civil War, two elder brothers serving in the Union Army were wounded, the mother removed to Washington to nurse them; page: U.S. Senate 1866–67, attended National University law school, member: District of Columbia bar 1881; assistant examiner: U.S. Patent Office 1883, law clerk 1898, principal examiner 1899–1901, assistant commissioner 1901–13, commissioner 1907–13; U.S. delegate: International Patent Congress, Stockholm 1908; successfully negotiated treaty with Germany relating to non-working American patents; special diplomatic representative to arrange conventions relating to patents with Denmark, Sweden, Norway, Russia, Austria, Italy, France, Spain, and Belgium 1909; special expert attaché: American delegation, International Congress of American States; prepared convention relating to patents, copyrights and trademarks adopted by U.S. Congress 1911; chairman: American delegation to Convention of International Union for Protection of International Property 1911.

Moore, Ella Maude 1849–1922, born: Warren; as a young girl composed the poem *Rock of Ages*, winner of $500 prize from the *Youth's Companion* magazine; author: *Songs of Sunshine and Shadow* 1880.

Moore, Harrison Bray ?– ?, born: Windham; attended public school in Windham, removed to New York, later Brooklyn, started in the lighterage business 1863, incorporated as New York Lighterage and Transportation Co. 1874, founder and president from 1874; his company was responsible for the delivery of all construction materials, rails, locomotive, &c. for the Southern Pacific Railroad, later for the elevated railroads in New York and Brooklyn; personally designed and oversaw construction of all vessels and barges for the company; designer and builder of *Pampero*, the fastest vessel in the world 1904 (the record for fastest vessel afloat next went to that of Charles Rundlett Flint; vice president: National Bank of Deposit; foreign freight agent of the Philadelphia & Reading Railroad.

Moore, Henry Dyer 1842–1930, born: Steuben; son of a shipwright and ship captain, brother of John Godfrey Moore, Martha Gallison Moore Avery; student: Cherryfield Academy, removed to Rochester, New York, 1860; employed by his uncle, Henry Dundas, a wool merchant; in the Civil War: enlisted in the 2nd Maine Cavalry, served to the end of the war; after the war, bookkeeper: W. E. Garrett & Sons, snuff manufacturers, Philadelphia; bought the business in association with George Wilson 1893, later the firm controlled three other snuff manufacturers: Stewart Ralph Snuff Co., Philadelphia, Ivey Owen Snuff Co., Lynchburg, Virginia, and Weyman & Bruton Co., Nashville, Tennessee, of which he was president; merged his properties with Atlantic Snuff Co., an alliance with James B. Duke, president of the American Tobacco Co.; Atlantic Snuff Co. absorbed the snuff business of American Tobacco, the consolidation known as American Snuff Co., of which Moore was president; under the decision of the U.S. Supreme Court 1911, which dissolved the American

Eminent Mainers

Tobacco Co., as a monopoly in violation of the Sherman Anti-Trust Act, the American Snuff Co. was also forced to disintegrate; Moore remained in control of several of the constituent parts and remained president or board member to his death; organized the Haddonfield (New Jersey) National Bank and First National Bank of Ocean City, New Jersey; vice president: Security Trust Co.; director: Camden Safe Deposit & Trust Co.; constructed the Montana Railroad 1897, a stretch of one hundred sixty miles through the Rocky Mountains connecting with the Northern Pacific Railroad Co. at Lombard, Montana; owner of an 11,000-acre tract of wheat land in central Montana adjoining the Montana Railroad; built and endowed the Steuben community hall.

Moore, Hoyt Augustus 1870–1958, born: Ellsworth; A.B. Bowdoin College ΦBK 1895, L.L.D. (Hon.) 1939, L.L.B. Harvard University Law School 1904; member: New York bar 1904, practiced in New York, in office of predecessor of Cravath, Swaine, and Moore; partner 1913–57; counsel to Cravath, Swaine, and Moore 1958; Bowdoin College overseer 1929–33, trustee 1933–58, vice president of the board 1948–58.

Moore, John Godfrey 1847–99, born: Steuben; son of a shipwright and ship captain, brother of Henry Dyer Moore, Martha Gallison Moore Avery; student: Cherryfield Academy, East Maine Conference Seminary, Bucksport; began as an employee of his uncle, a lumber dealer in New York; established himself as a dealer in lumber and railroad ties; with John Evans, established Evans and Moore, which became the National Dredging Co., Wilmington, Delaware; built government piers and breakwaters in Buffalo, New York, and Cleveland, Ohio; made extensive improvements on the Delaware River between Philadelphia and Wilmington; organized the Mutual Union Telegraph Co. 1880, erected wires between Boston, New York, Philadelphia, and Washington, strung lines wherever the business required, soon had an extensive network, after a particularly bitter and extended competitive war, the Western Union Co. was compelled to come to terms, leasing the Mutual Union lines for ninety-nine years 1882, his able management won the praise of the entire business community, the highest compliment came from the Western Union Telegraph Co., which invited him to become a director, which he was, until his death; established the financial firm of Moore & Schley 1885, purchased a seat on the New York Stock Exchange 1886, acquired a controlling interest in the Chase National Bank, with branches in Philadelphia and Washington; became known as a prime money mover, closely identified with the operations of the Havemeyers, the Rockefellers, J. Pierpont Morgan, James J. Hill, and William C. Whitney; personally negotiated the deals whereby the New York, New Haven & Hartford Railroad Co. acquired the New England Railroad Co., the acquisition of the New York, Susquehanna & Western Railroad Co. by the Erie Railroad Co., and the acquisition of the Seattle, Lake Shore & Western Railroad Co. by the Northern Pacific Railroad Co.; director and corporate officer of numerous companies and corporations; instituted the original suit to test the constitutionality of the first income tax law 1894–95, which the U.S. Supreme Court, in the opinion written by Chief Justice Meville Weston Fuller, declared unconstitutional; built the Washington County railroad from Ellsworth to Calais; developed the village of Grindstone Neck; his daughters gave Schoodic Point to Acadia National Park.

Moran, Edward Carleton 1894–1967, born: Rockland; son of an insurance salesman; attended public schools in Rockland, A.B. Bowdoin College 1917; in World War I: first lieutenant, Battery A 73rd Artillery, Coast Guard Artillery Corps; associated with his father in E. C. Moran Co., Rockland, an insurance business 1919, president from 1928; delegate: Democratic National Committee 1928, 1932; unsuccessful candidate for governor 1928, 1930; member from the Second District: U.S. House of Representatives 1933–37, helped draft the Merchant Maritime Act of 1936, which created the U.S. Maritime Commission; member: U.S. Maritime Commission 1937–40; state director: Office of Price Administration 1942; second assistant secretary of labor 1945; chairman: Rockland City Council 1946-47; buried in Achorn Cemetery, Rockland.

Morgan, James Appleton 1845–1928, born: Portland; grandson of a major of Massachusetts militia who participated in Arnold's march to and subsequent retreat from Québec, son of a physician, fur-trapper, and founder of Saginaw, Michigan; removed, with his family, to Racine, Wisconsin, A.B. Racine College 1867, A.M. 1870, L.L.B. Columbia University Law School 1869; associate counsel for the Erie and Northern Pacific railroads 1875–85; president: New York & Palisade Railroad Co.; president: Shakespeare Press Publishing Co., founder: *Appleton's Journal*, developed a theory that the Shakespeare plays as printed in the 1623 folio are not always strictly monographs but the work of many actors and stage censors improving them constantly from their original mounting by Shakespeare, in support of this theory published the Bankside edition of Shakespeare in twenty volumes 1888–92; founder and president Shakespeare Society of New York 1885–1925; author: *Selections of Macaronic Poetry* 1872, *De Colyar on the Law of Guaranty* 1874, *Addison on Contracts, Principles of Evidence, The Law of Literature: Reviewing the Laws of Literary Property in Manuscripts; Books, Lectures, Dramatic, and Musical Compositions; Works of Art, Newspapers, Periodicals et cetera; Copyright Transfers, and Copyright and Piracy; Libel and Contempt of Court by Literary Matter et cetera: With An Appendix of the American, English, French and German Statutes of Copyright* (three volumes) 1875, *The Shakespeare Myth* 1884, *Shakespeare in Fact and Criticism* 1884, *Shakespeare Pronunciation as Derived from Puns in the Plays* 1884, *Study in the Warwickshire Dialect* 1884, *Shakespearean Commentations* 1885, *Digesta Shakespeareana* 1887, *The People and the Railways; A Popular Discussion of the Railway Problem in the United States by Way of Answer to The Railway and the Republic* 1888, *Society and the Fad* 1890; editor: *Addison on Contracts* 1875, *Best on the*

Principles of Evidence 1876, *Forsyth on Trial by Jury* 1876, *The Bankside Restoration Shakespeare* (five volumes) 1905–08, *Mrs. Shakespeare's Second Marriage and the Transference of 16 Non-Quarto Plays to the First Folio* 1925.

Morgan, Jonathan 1775–1871, born: Brimfield, Massachusetts; student at Brown University, Union College; removed to Alna 1812, lawyer; built the first steamboat in Maine (reportedly driven by a screw propellor, not paddlewheels), christened by him *Alpha*, but generally known as Morgan's Rattler for the racket produced by the machinery, used as a towboat at the mouth of the Kennebec 1816; removed to Portland 1820; librarian: Maine Charitable Mechanics Association; justice of the peace; clerk: Congress Square Unitarian Church; author: *English Grammar* 1814, his own translation from the Greek of the Old Testament 1816, *A Synopsis of Disease* 1860; invented an improved coffee mill, a woodstove, a lifting pump, various farm implements, an oil lamp, manufacturer of glue.

Morrell, Daniel Johnson 1821–85, born: North Berwick; attended public school in North Berwick and Friends School, Philadelphia; removed to Johnstown, Pennsylvania, 1855; general manager and president: Cambria Ironworks to 1884; president: First National Bank of Johnstown 1863–84; president of the Johnstown City Council for many years; member: U.S. House of Representatives 1867–71 (Republican), chairman: Committee on Manufactures; a major figure in the development of Johnstown, he became one of the greatest ironmasters of his day, a strong voice in the Republican party, a man who looked upon Andrew Carnegie as an upstart in the business, first to employ the Bessemer system, Cambria was the largest producer of steel in the United States 1871–76, trained many of the outstanding steelmakers of the early twentieth century; for many years, president: American Iron and Steel Association; progressive in his treatment of operatives: instituted an eight-hour day when the norm was twelve, built a hospital, a library, and established a night school; concerned for the integrity of the so-called Johnstown Dam, offered to repair it at his own expense, the offer was refused with dire consequences a few years later; commissioner to the Paris Exposition 1878; buried in Grandview Cemetery, Johnstown.

Morrill, Anson Peaslee 1803–87, born: Dearborn, that part that is now Bel-grade; son of a millwright, brother of Lot Myrick Morrill; infrequently attended local public school, assisted his father in his carding and gristmill, taught school in Miramichi, New Brunswick; storekeeper, postmaster of Dearborn 1825–41; member: Maine House of Representatives (Democrat) 1834–35; sheriff of Somerset County 1839; purchased a bankrupt woolen mill in Readfield and put it on a paying condition 1844; Maine state land agent 1850–53; left the Democratic party over the question of prohibition 1853; ran third in the number of votes cast as Prohibition and Free Soil parties (Wildcat) candidate for governor 1853; as Republican candidate for governor, having failed to obtain a majority of votes, the election results were decided by the legislature, appointed eighteenth governor of Maine 1855, Morrill was the first Maine governor to be a Republican; unsuccessful candidate for reelection 1855; delegate: Republican National Convention 1856; member from the Third District: U.S. House of Representatives 1861–63 (Republican); president: Maine Central Railroad Co. 1871–87; member: Maine House of Representatives 1881–82; buried in Forest Grove Cemetery, Augusta.

Morrill, Edmund Needham 1834–1909, born: Westbrook; son of a tanner and currier; graduate: Westbrook Seminary 1855; superintendent of Westbrook schools 1856–57; removed to Brown County, Kansas, 1857; erected a sawmill; member: Free State Legislature 1857, elected member of the Kansas House of Representatives, under the Lecompton constitution 1858; in the Civil War: enlisted as a private in Company C, 7th Kansas Cavalry, USV, 1861, promoted to captain, USV, assigned to commissary, brevetted major, USA, mustered out 1865; located in Hiawatha, Kansas; clerk of the Brown County District Court 1866–70, county clerk 1866–73; founded the first bank in Brown County, president 1887–1909; founded the Morrill Free Public Library, Hiawatha, 1882, founded Hiawatha Academy 1889; loaned the money necessary for William Allen White to purchase the *Emporia Gazette*; member: Kansas Senate 1872–74, 1876–80, president *pro tempore* 1877; member: U.S. House of Representatives (Republican) 1883–91, as chairman of the Pensions Committee, framed and secured passage of the Morrill Bill 1890, which did much to relieve the Republican party of charges that it had been faithless to old soldiers, received the thanks of Senator Henry Cabot Lodge, among others; governor of Kansas 1894–96, unsuccessful candidate for reelection; president: First National Bank, Leavenworth, director: National Bank of Kansas City; died in San Antonio, Texas, buried in Mount Hope Cemetery, Hiawatha.

Eminent Mainers

Morrill, Lot Myrick  1812–83, born: Dearborn, that part that is now Belgrade; son of a miller, brother of Anson Morrill; attended local public school, worked in his father's mill, clerked in a general store, attended Waterville College 1830–31; read law in Readfield with Judge Edward Fuller, member: Maine bar 1837; practiced in Readfield, later Augusta; formed a partnership with James Bradbury 1841; member: Maine Senate 1854–56, president 1856; originally a Democrat, but broke with the party over slavery and Prohibition, elected twenty-second governor of Maine (Republican) 1858–60; member: U.S. Senate 1861–69, 1869–76, chairman: Committee on Audit and Control of the Contingent Expense, special committee to investigate the Crédit Moblier and the financing of the Union Pacific Railroad; member: Committee on District of Columbia, Committee on Appropriations, Committee on the Library, while in the Senate, was an ardent supporter of emancipation and suffrage for former slaves, voted for the impeachment of Andrew Johnson; resigned from the Senate to become U.S. secretary of the treasury 1876–77; collector of customs, Portland 1877–83; buried in Forest Grove Cemetery, Augusta; a U.S. Revenue Cutter, USRC *Lot M. Morrill*, was named in his honor.

Morrill, Walter Goodale 1840–1935, born: Williamsburg; captain, Company B, 20th Maine Infantry, recipient: Medal of Honor, at Rappahannock Station, Virginia, 7 November 1863, "Learning that an assault was to be made upon the enemy's works by other troops, this officer voluntarily joined the storming party with about fifty men of his regiment, and by his dash and gallantry, rendered effective service in the assault." Buried in Village Cemetery, Pittsfield.

Morse, Charles Townsend 1842– ?, born: Thomaston; removed to California to search for gold; settled in Santa Clara, purchased from R. W. Wilson a vegetable seed producing company, later restyled C. C. Morse & Co. 1877; in time, Morse became known as the "Vegetable King" and built an opulent mansion that is extant and is on the National Register of Historic Places; in 1930 his son merged the company with the Ferry Seed Company, forming the Ferry-Morse Seed Company, which continues to be one of the largest such concerns in the world.

Morse, Charles Wyman 1856–1933, born: Bath; A.B. Bowdoin College 1877; engaged in shipping business while still in college 1873–77; formed C. W. Morse & Co.: ice and lumber shipping firm, removed to Wall Street 1897; organized Consolidated Ice Co. 1899, merged with other companies to form American Ice Co., manipulated stock through Ice Securities Corp., made over $12 million before irregularities and corruption ended his company's control over ice; formed Consolidated Steamship

Co. 1905, had near-monopoly over East Coast shipping, came to be called "Admiral of the Atlantic Coast"; gained control of twelve banks, including the Knickerbocker Bank and Bank of North America; failed in attempt to corner the copper market, which resulted in the Panic of 1907; investigated and indicted, imprisoned in Atlanta Penitentiary 1910–12, retained Harry Dougherty, later U.S. attorney general under Harding, feigning illness through consumption of chemicals and soapsuds, Morse was pardoned by President Taft, who was convinced that Morse was near death; organized Hudson Navigation Co., sued for unfair competition 1915; contracted by Shipping Board to build thirty-six ships during World War I; borrowed money from Emergency Fleet Corp., indicted for conspiracy to defraud government when an investigation revealed that he had used the money to build shipyards instead of ships; indicted for using the mails to defraud prospective investors; the government was eventually awarded $11.5 million from Morse's Virginia Shipbuilding Corp. 1925; returned to Bath, funded construction of Morse High School.

Morse, Edward Sylvester 1838–1925, born: Portland; brother of George Frederic Morse; student: Bethel Academy, Ph.D (Hon.) Bowdoin College, A.M. Harvard, D.Sc. Yale University, L.H.D. Tufts University; draftsman for the Portland Company, where he designed locomotives; member: Portland Natural History Society; assistant to Louis Agassiz at Museum of Comparative Zoology, Harvard University; a founder, secretary: *The American Naturalist* 1866–78, supplied most of the drawings; the results of his original research on brachoipods, which he found to be worms, rather than mollusks, secured for him recognition from Darwin and other eminent scientists and his early election to the National Academy of Science; lecturer on zoology: Bowdoin College and Maine State College; as lecturer, crisscrossed the nation, an early and articulate proponent of Darwin; interest in shells led him to Japan where he founded the Department of Zoology at the Imperial University; founded the first marine laboratory in the Pacific, at Enoshima; his interest in pottery and ceramics led to the first archaeological explorations in Japan; worked with Professor Ernest Fenellosa of Harvard which led to Morse's appointment as director of the Peabody Museum, Salem; was on the staff of the Boston Museum, keeper of the Japanese pottery, as such, laid down the basis of the collection of Asian art which many consider to be the finest in the world; invented a solar heater, which received wide note; his book: *Japanese Homes and Their Surroundings* had an enormous impact, seminal work in Craftsman period, Frank Lloyd Wright, Greene and Greene, and others; author: *Observations on the Terrestrial Pulmoifera of Maine, Including a Catalogue of All the Species of Terrestrial and Fluviatile Mollusca Known to Inhabit the State* 1864, *The Brachopoda, A Division of Annelida* 1870, *Remarks on the Adaptive Oration of the Mollusca* 1871 (which earned the admiration of Darwin), *On the Tarsus and Carpus of Birds* 1872, *First Book of Zoology* 1875, *Catalogue of the Morse Collection of Japanese Pottery* 1901, *Glimpses of China and Chinese Homes* 1902, *Mars and Its Mystery* 1906 (resulted from his close friendship with astronomer Percival Lowell), *Japan Day by Day* (two volumes) 1917; president:

Eminent Mainers

American Association for the Advancement of Science 1885, Boston Society of Natural History; first American to be decorated by the emperor of Japan: Order of the Sacred Treasure 1922.

Morse, Harold Marston 1892–1977, born: Waterville; graduate: Coburn Classical Institute, A.B. *summa cum laude* Colby College ΦBK 1914, Sc.D. 1934, A.M. Harvard University 1915, Ph.D. 1917, Doctor: University of Paris 1946, University of Vienna 1952, University of Rennes 1953, University of Maryland 1955, Brooklyn Polytechical Institute 1956, Modena 1975, D.Sc. Kenyon College 1948, University of Pisa 1948, LaSalle University 1960, Williams College 1959, Harvard University 1965, University of Maine 1971, L.L.D. Xavier University 1961, Litt.D. Yeshiva University 1962; his doctorial thesis published as *Certain Types of Geodesic Motion on a Surface of Negative Curvature*; in World War I: private, USA, with ambulance corps in France, awarded: croix de guerre, second lieutenant U.S. Coast Artillery Reserve 1919–24; Benjamin Pierce Instructor in mathematics: Harvard University 1919–20, assistant professor: Cornell University 1920–26, Brown University 1926–28, associate professor: Harvard University 1928–29, professor 1929–35; after the publication of his thesis, made an important discovery announced in his *Relations Between the Critical Points of a Real Function of Independent Variables* 1925, this led to a new branch of mathematics commonly known as Morse theory, which represented a bold and unexpected synthesis of analysis and topology (homology theory): *Calculus of Variations in the Large* 1934, lecturer: International Congress of Mathematics, Zurich 1937, Cambridge, England, 1950, professor of mathematics: Institute for Advanced Studies, Princeton, 1935–62; in World War II: consultant: Office of the Chief of Ordnance; chairman: War Preparedness Committee of the American Mathematics Society 1940–42, division of mathematics: National Research Council 1950–52; a founder of the National Science Foundation; author: *Topological Methods in the Theory of Functions of a Complex Variable* 1947, *Critical Point Theory in Global Analysis and Differential Topology* 1969, *Variational Analysis; Critical Extremals and Sturmian Extensions* 1973, *Global Variational Analysis: Weierstrass Integrals on a Riemannian Manifold* 1976.

Morse, Ruggles Sylvester 1815–93, born: Leeds; clerk in the Tremont House, Boston, 1838, clerk in the Astor Hotel, New York, to 1849, caught gold fever and made an unsuccessful foray to California in search of gold, returned to Maine but was soon in New Orleans; after clerking in the Arcade Hotel, became a half-owner of the City Hotel and the proprietor of the St. James and the St. Charles hotels, the latter was considered to be the most sumptuous hotel south of New York and was owned by Enoch Redington Mudge; Morse began the construction of what has come to be called the Victoria Mansion in 1858, employing Henry Austen of New Haven as architect and Gustave Herter of New York as decorator; despite the onset of the Civil War and Morse's apparent adherence to the Southern cause, construction continued and he and his wife began to summer in Portland from 1866.

Mortimer, Frederick Craig 1857–1936, born: Waterville; crippled from childhood; A.B. Colby College 1881, A.M. 1932; joined the staff of the *Rochester* (New York) *Democrat and Chronicle*, became assistant city editor, removed to New York 1886, assistant city editor: *New York Times*, with which he continued to retirement 1926; wrote: "Topics of the Times," a column of informal comments on the news he introduced in 1896, described by the *Providence Journal* as a group of essays "as well written as Addison's, as bright as Steele's and always within the scope of current interest," this column was so popular that it was continued, by other hands, long after his death; also responsible for the selection of poetry on the editorial page of the *Times*, furthered the careers of many poets, including Rudyard Kipling; a student of French literature, studied medicine, followed developments in the field, and engaged in controversies on medical subjects; his comments on scientific matters were so sound that Charles Steinmetz sought him out to congratulate him on them.

Morton, Charles Gould 1861–1933, born: Cumberland; son of Brigadier General Charles Gould, USA, graduate: U.S. Military Academy 1883, promoted through the ranks to major general, USA, 1917; after six years of frontier duty at Fort Douglas, Utah, and Fort Lewis, Colorado, professor of military science and tactics: East Florida Seminary, Gainesville 1889, Florida State Agricultural College, Lakeland 1890; during Spanish-American War: lieutenant 1st Maine Volunteers; after the war, sent to Philippines, engaged actively the insurgents; graduate: Army War College 1905; returned to the Philippines 1905; inspector general: Department of the Colorado 1907–09, Department of the Great Lakes 1910–11, Philippines 1911–12; commanding officer: 10th Division on Mexican border 1916–17; in World War I: commanding officer: 26th Division, was in combat at Belfort, Meuse-Argonne; after the war commanding officer: Department of Hawaii, commanding officer: IX Corps, San Francisco; decorated: Distinguished Service Medal with citation for exceptional meritorious and distinguished service, "He commanded the 29th Division from the date of its organization until the end of hostilities and led his division with skill and ability in the successful operations east and northeast of Verdun which forced the enemy to maintain this front with strong forces, thus preventing an increase in hostile strength between the Argonne and the Meuse," croix de guerre with two palms, commander, Legion of Honor; buried in Arlington National Cemetery; in 1944, the U.S. Navy commissioned the USS *General C.G. Morton* (AP-138), she received three battle stars for Korea.

Morton, Eliza Happy 1852–1916, born: North Deering; graduate: Westbrook Seminary; began teaching at age sixteen, specializing in geography; head of department: Normal Department, Battle Creek College, 1880–83; secretary, treasurer: Maine Seventh-day Adventist Tract Society, Review and Herald Publishing Co., Portland; author: *Lessons on the Continent* 1883, *Potter's Elementary Geography* 1888, *Potter's Advanced Geography* 1901, *Thought—Its Origin and Power* 1905, *Star Flowers, or Songs* *in the Night* 1912; composer of numerous texts for songs and hymns, most famous: *Songs My Mother Sang , My Mission, Longing for Rest;* buried in Evergreen Cemetery, Portland.

Moses, George Higgins
1869–1944, born: Lubec; son of a clergyman; attended public schools in Eastport, graduate: Phillips Academy, Exeter, A.B. Dartmouth College 1890, A.M. 1893, L.L.D. (Hon.) George Washington University 1921, Dartmouth College 1928, Litt.D. Lincoln Memorial University 1929; private secretary to David Goodell, governor of New Hampshire 1889–90; manager: *New Hampshire Republican;* private secretary to the chairman of the New Hampshire Republican State Committee during the political campaign of 1890; reporter, news editor, managing editor, part owner, president: *Monitor* and *Independent Statesman,* Concord 1898–1918; close associate and political confidant of Senator William Chandler, acted as his unofficial representative; private secretary to Governor John McLane during the sessions of the Portsmouth Peace Conference 1905; secretary: New Hampshire Forestry Commission 1893–1906; delegate at large: Republican National Convention 1908, 1916, 1928 (permanent chairman), 1932, 1936, 1940; envoy extraordinary and minister plenipotentiary to Greece and Montenegro 1909–12, a prime mover in the project to form a Balkans federation, the plan for which was drawn with his advice, decorated by the Greek and Montenegrian governments, fiscal agent of the Royal Hellenic government 1913–15; chief of the editorial department of the Republican Publicity Association, Washington 1915–18; elected to fill an unexpired term in U.S. Senate 1918, member until 1933 (Republican), when he was defeated for renomination by Styles Bridges; a strong opponent of the Versailles Peace Treaty and United States entry into the League of Nations; chairman: Committee on Printing, member: Committee on Post Offices and Post Roads, Committee on Rules, Committee on Foreign Relations, president *pro tempore* 1925–33; president: New Hampshire Constitutional Convention 1938; manager of Leonard Wood's campaign to secure the Republican nomination for president 1920; author: *John Stark* 1890, *New Hampshire Men* 1893; buried in Franklin (New Hampshire) Cemetery.

Mosher, Thomas Bird
1852–1923, born: Biddeford; went to sea at an early age with his father, a shipmaster, augmented a meager education with much reading on board ship, traveled to England and Germany, wrecked on the Devonshire coast, became a clerk and bookkeeper in a Portland publishing house, formed a partnership with Ruel T. McLellan in a stationery and publishing house 1882, began publishing choice and limited editions of books of *belle-lettres* 1891; editor and publisher *The Bibelot* from 1895, a reprint of poetry and prose largely from scarce editions and sources not widely known, complete in twenty-one volumes 1915; editor and publisher first American edition of *The Germ* 1898, Swinburne's *Poems and Ballads* 1899, Rosetti's *Poetical Works* 1902, published the first facsimile reprint of Fitzgerald's *Omar Khayyam* 1902, a similar facsimile edition of Whitman's *Leaves of Grass;* Mosher's

books became highly prized for their scholarly editing, tasteful typography, and æsthetic format, rivaling the best work of Kelmscott Press.

Moulton, Jeremiah 1688–1765, born: York; carried into captivity when York was destroyed 1692, later released by Benjamin Church, thereafter, took an avid part in the Indian wars; led, in 1722, an expedition against Norridgewock, which was found deserted, carried off the papers of Father Râle, but left the church and village standing, in 1724, led 200 men in an attack on Norridgewock, most of the inhabitants were killed, along with Father Râle, despite Moulton's orders that he be spared; as colonel of Massachusetts militia, led a regiment at Louisbourg 1745; later served as sheriff of York County, member: executive council, judge of common pleas, and probate judge.

Mudge, Benjamin Franklin 1817–79, born: Orrington; nephew of Enoch Mudge, brother of Thomas Hicks Mudge and Zachariah Mudge; A.B. Wesleyan University 1840, studied law, member: Massachusetts bar, practiced in Lynn 1844–59, mayor of Lynn 1852; removed to Kansas 1862, Kansas state geologist 1864–65, professor of natural sciences and higher mathematics: Kansas State Agricultural College, Lawrence, 1865–73, explored the cretaceous formations of western Kansas, discovered forty-five new species of dinosaurs; president: Kansas State Teachers Association 1867, Kansas Academy of Sciences 1868–79, lecturer on geology: Kansas State University, Lawrence, 1873–79; frequent contributor to the *Transactions* of the Kansas Academy of Sciences, author: *First Annual Report of the Geology of Kansas* 1866.

Mulford, Clarence Edward 1883–1956, born: Streator, Illinois; settled in Fryeburg; author: the *Hopalong Cassidy* series, many other western novels.

Munsey, Frank Andrew 1854–1925, born: Mercer; Litt.D. (Hon.) Bowdoin College 1919, L.L.D. New York University; removed, with his parents to Gardiner, Bowdoin, Litchfield, Livermore Falls, and finally, Lisbon Falls, where he attended grammar school while working as a store clerk; while his father served in the 20th Maine Volunteer Infantry, during the Civil War, he also helped provide for his family; learned telegraphy, worked in Portland, later, manager: Western Union telegraph office in Augusta, where he made the acquaintance of James G. Blaine and William Henry Gannett, who suggested to Munsey the possibilities of publishing; with an accumulation of manuscripts, removed to New York 1882, started his first magazine *Golden Argosy* (the first pulp magazine), later called *Argosy*, did most of the writing and editing himself 1885; established *Munsey's Weekly*, later called *Munsey's Magazine* 1888, which would have the largest paid circulation in the world, subsequently established *Puritan* and *Junior Munsey* 1897, *All-Story Magazine*, *Scrap Book*, *Cavalier*, *Railroad Man's Magazine*, *Woman*, *Live Wire*; purchased many magazines simply to destroy them, *i.e. Godey's Lady Book*, *Peterson's Magazine*, "Let Munsey kill it" became a common phrase; purchased and sold, merged and destroyed a bewildering number of newspapers; created the New York *Herald-Tribune* through merger; introduced the Sunday newspaper, much condemned by ecclesiastics but very popular with the public; a banker and creator of the Mohican chain of groceries; with George Perkins, made it possible for Theodore Roosevelt (who referred to him as "the wild ass of the desert") to bolt the Republican party in 1912 and start the Progressive party; opposed entry into the League of Nations; decorated by France with the Légion d'Honneur for war relief work as well as his generosity to the American Hospital in Neuilly; Munsey left the bulk of his $40 million estate to the New York Metropolitan Museum of Art; author: *A Tragedy of Errors* 1889, *The Story of the Founding and Development of the Munsey Publishing House*; buried in the Hillside Cemetery, Lisbon Falls.

Murphy, Frank Morrill 1854–1940, born: Jefferson; removed to Manitowoc, Wisconsin, with his parents, where he attended school; in the employment of Thomas Windiate, Manitowoc, Wisconsin; worked in lumber camps in Wisconsin; developed a stage line to California 1872–77; removed to Arizona, associated with Diamond Joe Reynolds in developing the Congress mine; secretary and promoter: Santa Fe, Prescott & Phoenix Railroad Co. 1891–92, president from 1904; president: Prescott National Bank from founding to 1910; president: Prescott & Eastern Railroad Co., Bradshaw Mountain Railroad Co., Arizona & California Railroad Co.

Murphy, Nathan Oakes 1849–1908, born: Jefferson; brother of Frank Morrill Murphy; taught school in Wisconsin; engaged in mining and railroad building in Arizona; secretary of Arizona Territory 1889–92; delegate: Republican National Convention 1892; governor of Arizona Territory 1892–93, 1898–1902; territorial delegate to U.S. House of Representatives 1895–97 (Republican); retired to Coronado, California; originally buried in Masonic Cemetery, San Diego, reinterred in Rock Creek Cemetery, Washington.

Murphy, Simon Jones 1815–1905, born: Windsor, son and grandson of loggers; attended public school in Whitefield; at age eighteen, left Whitefield with a clean axe and the clothes on his back, entered the employ of a sawmill in Milford; in partnership with James Thissell, established his own mill 1840, which failed 1843, established another mill 1843; superintendent of the Franklin Adams mill 1845; formed a partnership with Jonathan Eddy and Newell Avery, styled Eddy, Murphy & Co., which operated mills in the Bangor area; became interested in Michigan, to which he removed 1865; with the death of Eddy, the firm became Avery & Murphy; purchased large block of white pine lands on the Muskegon and White Rivers, organized the S. J. Murphy Lumber Co. 1886; erected a mill in Green Bay, Wisconsin; employing bandsaws, milled out in excess of 25 million board feet per annum; acquired control of the Pacific Lumber Co., which owned large tracts of redwood timber in Eureka and Scotia, California, also associated with iron mining in Michigan, copper mining in Arizona, railroads, electric power generation, manufacturing, and oil production;

organized the Murphy Oil Co., Whittier, California; director: American Exchange National Bank, Union Trust Co., Michigan Fire & Marine Insurance Co., Standard Life & Accident Insurance Co., Edison Illuminating Co., all of Detroit; constructed several large office buildings in Detroit, including the Penobscot Building, long the tallest building in Michigan; raised belted Galloway cattle on his extensive ranch in Arizona; pioneered in irrigation systems on his large orange groves in Whittier; father of William Herbert Murphy.

Murphy, William Herbert 1855–1929, born: Bangor; son of Simon Murphy; removed, with his family, to Detroit, Michigan, 1866; graduate: Central High School, student: University of Michigan 1875–77; underwent treatment for impaired hearing and studied music in Boston; worked at a sawmill in Bay City, Michigan, owned by his father; organized Murphy Power Co., which erected the first large power plant in Detroit, which later became Detroit Edison; an employee at the power plant, Henry Ford, talked Murphy into organizing the Detroit Automobile Co. (the first automobile manufacturing company in Detroit) for producing the Ford motor car, after Ford withdrew, reorganized as the Cadillac Motor Car Co. 1902; organized the Lincoln Motor Co.; manufactured the Liberty aviation engine; managed the Penobscot buildings, Detroit, including the Greater Penobscot Building, long the tallest building in Michigan, the Marquette, the Murphy, and the Telegraph buildings; founder and president: Detroit Symphony Orchestra, endowed the music school at University of Michigan; president and director: Pacific Lumber Co. (a corporation originally chartered in Maine), which held a large tract of redwood timber in Humboldt County, California, produced 100 million board feet of lumber, per annum; president and director: Murphy Oil Co. of Los Angeles, developed the oil field at Signal Hill, Long Beach; an enthusiastic lover of music, formed an orchestra while attending high school in Detroit, later established a similar organization in Bay City; a founder 1904, and chief financial supporter of the Detroit Symphony Orchestra, chief builder of Detroit Symphony Hall, to which he presented a very large pipe organ 1924, chief financial backer of the University of Michigan Music School.

Muskie, Edmund Sixtus 1914–96, born: Rumford; son of a Polish immigrant tailor, who shortened the family name from Marciszewski; A.B. *cum laude* Bates College ΦBK 1936, L.L.B. Cornell University Law School 1939, numerous honorary degrees; member: Massachusetts bar 1939, Maine bar 1940, U.S. District Court bar 1941, New York bar 1981, U.S. Supreme Court bar 1981; practiced in Waterville 1940, 1945–55; in World War II: enlisted in the USN, and served in the Atlantic and Asiatic-Pacific theaters 1942–45; member, secretary: Waterville Board of Zoning Adjustment 1948–55, district director of the Maine Office of Price Stabilization 1951–52, Waterville city solicitor 1954; member: Maine House of Representatives 1946, 1948, 1950, Democratic floor leader 1949–51; governor of Maine 1955–59; member: U.S. Senate 1959–80 (Democrat), chairman: Committee on the Budget,

Subcommittee on Environmental Pollution, Public Works, Subcommittee on Arms Control, assistant majority whip; resigned to become U.S. secretary of state 1980–81; unsuccessful Democratic candidate for vice president 1968; unsuccessful candidate for the Democratic nomination for president of the United States 1972; partner: Chadbourne & Parke, Washington, D.C., 1982–96; national executive director: AMVETS 1951; author: *Journeys* 1972, coauthor: *Presidential Promises and Performances* 1980; buried in Arlington National Cemetery.

Neal, John 1793–1876, born: Portland; cousin of Neal Dow; after clerking for a short time in Boston, removed to Baltimore, where he opened a dry goods firm, which promptly failed 1816; turned immediately to literature, published his first novel *Keep Cool* 1817; a vocal advocate of physical fitness and training, thought by many to be the originator of athletic gymnasia in the United States; removed to England 1823, being attracted to the warm reception there of his fiction, lived in household of Jeremy Bentham; known as "Yankee Neal"; contributor to *Blackwood's* and other British periodicals of articles concerning American habits, social and political conditions; editor: *Portland Yankee* 1828–29; author: poems: *The Battle of Niagara* 1819, *Man of the North*, *Music of the Night*, novels: *Keep Cool, A Novel* 1817, *Otho: A Tragedy in Five Acts* 1819, *Errata, or, The Works of Will. Adams: A Tale* 1823, *Randolph, A Novel* 1823, which resulted in a challenge to a duel by Edward Pinckney, which Neal, a Quaker, declined, *Seventy-Six* 1823, *Brother Jonathan: or, The New Englanders* 1825, *Rachel Dyer* 1828, *Otter-Bag: the Oneida Chief* 1829, *Authorship: A Tale* 1830, *Down-easter* 1833, *Moose Hunters, Life in the Maine Woods* 1864, nonfiction: *Logan: A Family History* 1822, *A History of the American Revolution; Comprehending All the Principal Events Both in the Field and in the Cabinet* 1822, *City of Portland: Being a General Review of the Proceedings Heretofore Had, in the Town of Portland, On the Subject of a City Government: With Petitions and Signatures, and Remarks Thereon* 1829, *One More Word: Intended for the Reasoning and Thoughtful Among Unbelievers* 1854, *Account of the Great Conflagration in Portland, July 4th and July 5th* 1866, *Wandering Reflections of a Somewhat Busy Life* 1869, *Great Mysteries and Little Plagues* 1870, *Portland Illustrated* 1874, *Bentham's Morals and Legislation*, *True Womanhood*; an early proponent of female suffrage, for which he called in a Fourth of July oration 1838, considered, by some, as the birth of the women's rights movement; architect; opponent of capital punishment.

Neal, Josephine Bicknell 1880–1955, born: Belmont; A.B. Bates College φBK (first honors in physics), D.Sc. (Hon.) 1926, M.D. Cornell University Medical School 1910; practiced in New York, consultant in neurology from 1918, assistant in meningitis division, research laboratory, New York Department of Health 1910–14, in charge of division from 1914, instructor in medicine: Cornell University Medical School 1914–20, instructor: Columbia University College of Physicians and Surgeons 1922–27, clinical professor of neurology 1929–44; attending physician: Children's Tuberculosis Clinic and Vanderbilt Clinic 1922–27; consultant in acute infections of the central nervous system: New York Infirmary for Women and Children from 1925, Neurological Institute of New York 1936–44, director: Department of Infectious Diseases, Neurological Institute of New York 1937–39; director: William J. Matheson Survey of Epidemic Encephalitis 1927–29, executive secretary: Matheson Commission for Encephalitis Research from 1929; secretary: International Commission for Study of Infantile Paralysis 1929–32; author: chapters in Abbot's *System of Pediatrics*, Tice's *Practice of Medicine*, Barr's *Modern Medical Therapy*, first, second, and third *Reports on Encephalitis* (Matheson Commission), *Poliomyelitis* (International Commission for Study of Infantile Paralysis), *The Human Cerebral Spinal Fluid*, *Infections of the Central Nervous System*, chapter on "Viral Diseases of the Central Nervous System" in *Cyclopedia of Medicine* 1940, *Encephalitis, A Clinical Study* 1942, some seventy-five articles on acute infections of the central nervous system for medical journals.

Neptune, Clara 1831–1923, born: Indian Island, Old Town; daughter of the twin  brother of Joseph Polis, adopted at an early age by her aunt Margaret, wife of Dr. Sebatis Mitchell, known as "Sebatis Lobster"; at age fourteen married Joseph Orono, great-grandson of Chief Joseph Orono; after his death married Mitchell Neptune, grandson of John Neptune; soon after her first marriage acted in "Indian Tableaux" on vaudeville stages in Philadelphia and New York City, occasionally appearing on the same bill as John Wilkes Booth, whom she claimed would fix her hair; served as a major source of stories and anecdotes for Fanny Hardy Eckstorm's *Old John Neptune and Other Indian Shamans*.

Nescambiouit c. 1660–1727, born: Pequawket (Fryeburg); his name translates as "he who is so important and so highly placed because of his merit that his greatness cannot be attained, even in thought, his sang-froid is so great that he has never been seen to laugh," regarded by New Englanders as a bloody devil, claimed to have killed 150 men, women, and children; participated in peace negotiations at Pemaquid 1693, but soon accompanied Pierre Le Moyne d'Iberville to the siege of Fort William at Saint John's, Newfoundland, to see if the French waged war against the English better than he did himself, where he distinguished himself in the fighting 1696; he and Wenemouet, in advance of a force lead by Alexandre Leneuf de Beaubassin, approached the fort at Casco Bay, under a flag of truce, but with concealed hatchets, wounded the commander, John March, who managed to escape and hold the fort 1703; participated in ravaging the Newfoundland coast 1705, journeyed to France where he was presented to Louis XIV, who showered him with gifts, entitled him Prince of the Abenakis, some say that he was ennobled as knight commander of the Order of Saint Louis and given a life pension of eight *livres per diem* 1705; participated in an expedition against Haverhill, Massachusetts, where he did wonders with a sabre given him by Louis XIV 1708; removed to what is now Green Bay, Wisconsin, and dwelt among the Foxes 1716.

Nesmith, James Willis 1820–85, born: St. Stephen, New Brunswick, during a visit by his parents, raised in Calais, removed with his father to Claremont, New Hampshire, 1828, removed to Ohio 1838, Oregon 1843, studied law, member: Oregon bar, farmer, stockman; judge of Oregon provisional government 1845; captain of punitive expeditions against hostile Indians 1848, 1853; U.S. marshal for Oregon 1853–55; superintendent of Indian affairs for Oregon and Washington territories 1857–59; member: U.S. Senate 1861–67, unsuccessful candidate for reelection 1866; appointed U.S. minister to Austria-Hungary, but not confirmed by the U.S. Senate 1868; Polk County (Oregon) road supervisor 1868; member: U.S. House of Representatives (Democrat) 1873–75; buried on the south bank of Rickreall Creek, Polk County, Oregon; grandfather of Clifton Nesmith McArthur, cousin of Joseph Gardner Wilson, both members of the U.S. House of Representatives from Oregon.

Nevelson, Louise Barliawsky 1899–1988, born: Kiev, Russia; raised in Rockland; primarily known as a sculptor, her works are exhibited in: the Whitney Museum of American Art, Museum of Modern Art, Pace Gallery, Jewish Museum, Metropolitan Museum of Art, Brooklyn Museum, New York, the Museum of Fine Arts, Houston, Texas, Walker Art collection, Minneapolis, Albright-Knox Art Gallery, Buffalo, Tate Gallery, London, Massachusetts Institute of Technology, Cambridge, Princeton University, Art Institute of Chicago, Cleveland Museum of Art, Farnsworth Museum of Art, Rockland, Israel Museum, Jerusalem, Yale University, New Haven, Connecticut, Rijksmuseum, Amsterdam, Museum of Fine Art, Paris, many private collections.

Newell, Samuel 1785–1821, born: Durham; A.B. Harvard College 1807, graduate: Andover Theological Seminary 1810, one of the signers of the memorandum from the students at Andover that led to the formation of the American Board of Commissioners for Foreign Missions 1810; ordained foreign missionary at Salem 1812, immediately sailed for Calcutta, upon his arrival, ordered by the Bengali government to leave, removed to the Isle of France, thence to Ceylon, finally settled in Bombay, where he coauthored *The Conversion of the World, or the Claims of Six Hundred Millions* 1818.

Nichols, Charles Henry 1820–89, born: Vassalboro; graduate: Friends School, Providence, Rhode Island, taught school 1837–40, studied medicine at City University of New York, M.D. University of Pennsylvania 1843; practiced at Lynn, Massachusetts, 1843–47; assistant to Dr. Aramiah Brigham, director: New York Lunatic Asylum, Utica, 1847–49; resident physician: Bloomingdale Asylum, New York, 1847–52; largely through the moral and political suasion of Dorothea Dix, Congress appropriated funds for a model institution, a national mental hospital, under the jurisdiction of the secretary of the interior; as director, Nichols designed, constructed, and administered Saint Elizabeth's Hospital for the Insane 1852–77; in the trial of Charles Guiteau, the assassin of President Garfield, Nichols was called to testify as to Guiteau's mental state, this was the first attempt to mount a defense by reason of insanity 1881; in Civil War: volunteer surgeon, Army of the Potomac; president of the first board of school commissioners in Washington, D.C.; superintendent: Bloomingdale's Hospital, New York from 1877; president: Association of American Superintendent of Institutions for the Insane (later American Psychiatrist Association) 1873–79.

Nichols, George Ward 1831–85, born: Mount Desert; art editor and critic: *New York Evening Post* 1859–61; in the Civil War: captain, USA, *aide-de-camp* to General John C. Frémont until the battle of Cross Keys, later aide-de-camp to General Sherman, participated in the march to the sea; brevetted lieutenant colonel, USA; founder: School of Design, Cincinnati; president: Harmonic Society of Cincinnati, founding president: College of Music, Cincinnati 1879; instrumental in the founding of the Rookwood Pottery Works; author: *The Story of the Great March* 1865, *Art Education Applied to Industry* 1877, *Pottery, How It Is Made* 1878.

Nickerson, Hiram Robert 1853–1915, born: Wayne; student: Westbrook Seminary, Maine Wesleyan Seminary, Kents Hill; messenger to general manager: Atchison, Topeka & Santa Fe Railroad 1872–94, assistant general manager 1899–1903, vice president 1903–07; president: Mexican Central Railroad, Sierra Madre & Pacific Railroad, Mexican-American Steamship Co., Mexican & Northern Steamship Co., Tampico Harbor Co., El Paso Southern Railroad, South Atlantic Transcontinental Railroad, Mexican National Construction Co., United States Banking Company of Mexico.

Nicolar, Joseph 1827–94, born: Indian Island, Old Town; farmer, politician, journalist; Penobscot representative to the Maine State Legislature; author: column in the Indian Island newspaper, and the book *The Life and Traditions of the Red Man*, based on Penobscot oral tradition 1893.

Noble, William Clark 1858–1938, born: Gardiner; son of a ship captain and skilled carver who was lost at sea, along with his wife, 1869; subsequently raised by his grandfather, who appreciated Noble's early work sculpted out of local clay; apprenticed in sculpture in Boston, studied with Greenough, Hunt, and Peter Tefft, began his career in Newport, Rhode Island, later, had a studio in New York, resided in Washington after 1923; principal works include: bust of John McCullough, Actors' Society, Philadelphia, 1887, Soldiers and Sailors Monument, Newport, Rhode Island, Mothers' Memorial, Washington, D.C., William Ellery Channing statue, Newport, Rhode Island, statue of Governor Curtin, Bellefont, Pennsylvania, statue of Monsignor Duane, Newark, New Jersey, Brooks Memorial, Church of the Incarnation,

New York, statue of General Porter, van Cortland Park, New York, statue of Pierre L'Enfant, Washington, D.C., portrait busts of Longfellow, Hawthorne, Hamilton, Pierpont Morgan, Henry Cabot Lodge, David Lloyd George, Harriet Beecher Stowe, and others, designed currency and coinage for Guatemala 1925, Panama 1930, designed the national John Philip Sousa Memorial, Washington, D.C., statue of Minerva atop Maine statehouse dome; a founder: National Sculpture Society, New York Art Club; buried in South Gardiner.

Norcross, Jonathan 1808– ?, born: Orono; son of a clergyman; attended public school in Orono, learned the trade of machinist and millwright, put up a mill for sugar-making in Cuba, attended lectures on mechanics and science at the Franklin Institute in Philadelphia, taught school in North Carolina 1833, opened a school in Augusta, Georgia, 1835, took charge of lumber interests in southern Georgia for northern capitalists, removed to Atlanta 1844, where he became a leading merchant; a founder of the first bank in Atlanta; elected mayor of Atlanta 1850; secured the charter for the Air Line Railroad and the services of Lemuel Pratt Grant, served as its president from 1858; an opponent of secession, Republican nominee for governor 1876; gave twenty acres of land within Atlanta to the Baptist Convention of Georgia to found an orphanage 1888; author: *Mercantile Integrity* 1832, *The History of Democracy* 1844, wrote a second work demonstrating that democratic rule always tends to ruin the government, printed a pamphlet against state sovereignty 1875; played a vital role in the agitation that led to the creation of the Interstate Commerce Commission.

Norcross, Leonard 1798–1864, born: Readfield; millwright, mechanic; removed to Dixfield, invented a threshing and separating machine, a nail-making machine, patented 1824, an accelerated spinner for hand-woven wool, patented 1835, a stump lifter; his most important and enduring invention: a water dress or rubber diving suit, with a tightly fitting helmet and leaden shoes to overcome buoyancy, a rubber hose connecting to an air pump, patented 1834; lecturer on astronomy and temperance, preacher of the gospel, named his son "Submarinus."

Norcross, Orlando Whitney 1839–1920, born: Clinton; son of a carpenter, learned his father's trade; in the Civil War: enlisted in the 14th Regiment, Massachusetts Volunteer Infantry, later reorganized as the 1st Massachusetts Heavy Artillery, discharged 1864; with his brother James founded: Norcross Brothers Co., Salem, Massachusetts, 1866, removed to Worcester 1868, which became the premier building contractors of the late nineteenth early twentieth centuries; closely associated with the architectural firm of H. H. Richardson, later with McKim, Mead, and White; built: Trinity Church, Boston, the extension of the Massachusetts Statehouse, the Museum of Fine Arts, Boston, the Customs House tower, Boston, Hemenway Gymnasium and Sever Hall, Harvard University, the Harvard University Law School (Austin Hall), Harvard University Medical School, the Sherman house, Newport, Rhode

Island, City Hall, Albany, New York, Allegheny Court House and Jail, Pittsburgh, Pennsylvania, the Connecticut and Rhode Island statehouses, the Soldiers Monument, West Point (then the largest polished monolith in the world 1893), the Columbia University campus, Union Theological Seminary, New York, the Lawrenceville School campus, the New York Public Library, renovations of the White House and the Corcoran Art Gallery, Washington, D.C., constructed the Ames Memorial, Sherman, Wyoming, the Crane Memorial Library, Quincy, Massachusetts, &c.; the company had numerous quarries and shops, filled an order for one-half million cubic feet of granite for the Pennsylvania Station, New York; invented the flat-slab form of reinforced concrete construction, devised an innovative pneumatic caisson system for digging foundations in boggy soil, as in the new Customs House, Boston; trustee: Clark University.

North, William 1755–1836, born: Fort Frederick, Pemaquid (Bristol); son of the commander of Fort Frederick, later Fort St. George, Thomaston; in the American Revolution, served in the Arnold Expedition to Canada 1775, second lieutenant of artillery 1776, promoted to captain, assigned to Jackson's Massachusetts regiment 1777, led his company at the battle of Monmouth, aide-de-camp to Baron von Steuben 1779, sub-inspector in introducing and perfecting von Steuben's mode of discipline, attended von Steuben in the Virginia campaign, present at the surrender of Cornwallis; after the war: appointed major, 2nd United States Regiment 1786; speaker: New York Assembly 1795, 1796, 1810; member: U.S. Senate 1798 (Federalist); commanding brigadier general and adjutant general: U.S. Provisional Army 1798-1800; member: committee to report on the feasibility of connecting the Hudson River with lakes Ontario and Erie; executor of the will of his adoptive father, Baron von Steuben; buried in the crypt below Christ Episcopal Church, Duanesburg, New York.

Norton, Carol 1869–1904, born: Eastport; attended Eastport High School, began a business career in New York at age seventeen; from an early age evinced a strong and abiding interest in religion, Unitarianism, in particular; made his first public address at age sixteen, an appeal in the interests of the White Cross, earnestly urging personal purity and a single standard of morals; intensely interested in church work and reform, and in efforts for spiritual welfare of the community, especially that of young men; a severe illness at age nineteen turned his attention to Christian Science, to which he devoted his life to its service; became a reader, teacher, lecturer, and writer; after his death in a bizarre accident, it was rumored that he had been murdered by Augusta Stetson by means of malignant animal magnetism; author: *The New World* 1892, *Woman's Cause* 1896, *Poems and Verses* 1901, *Studies in Character* 1906, some of his best known poems include: *A Song of Life, Down Through the Ages, The End is Light, The Eternal Hope, The Radiant Cross, There Remaineth a Sabbath Rest, Peace;* cousin of Henry Wadsworth Longfellow.

Norton, Lillian (yclept Lillian Nordica) 1859–1914, born: Farmington;

removed, with her parents, to Boston 1864, entered the New England Conservatory of Music at age fifteen, graduated with high honors 1877; studied voice with John McNeil, sang with the Handel and Haydn Society, taking a leading part in *The Messiah* and other oratorios; the singer Tietjens, upon hearing her, introduced her to Madame Maretzek, with whom she studied; toured Europe with Gilmore's Grand Boston Band, sang at the Crystal Palace, London, and the Trocadero, Paris, remained in Europe, settled in Milan; student of François Sangiovanni (who convinced her to adopt Nordica as her stage name), made her debut at Brescia in *La Traviata*, sang the part of Marguerite in *Faust* 1880, appeared at Novara as Alice in *Roberto*, at Aquilla, Italy, appeared in thirty-five performances of *Faust*, *Rigoletto*, and *Lucia*; had her first real triumph in St. Petersburg, where she also sang for Czar Alexander II a week before his assassination 1881; appearing as Filina in *Mignon*, sang in Paris for Ambrose Thomas and the impresario Vancorbeil, who engaged her to sing at the Paris Opéra 1881, where her debut was accorded a triumph; engaged by Mapelson to make a tour of the United States, appeared at the Academy of Music, New York; met with great favor in Berlin, a city not well-disposed to American singers 1887; sang in the Drury Lane Theatre, London, where she met great acclaim, gave a command performance in Buckingham Palace, received the personal thanks of the Prince and Princess of Wales, commanded by Queen Victoria to sing in Westminster Abbey; toured the United States several times as a member of the Abbey, Schoeffel & Grau company; gradually took up Wagnerian roles, first appeared at Bayreuth as Elsa in *Lohengrin* 1894, received great acclaim as Isolde in *Tristan und Isolde*; decorated by the Duke of Edinburgh and the Duke of Saxe Coburg and Gotha, Queen Victoria presented her with a brooch composed of diamonds, pearls, and emeralds, the stockholders of the Metropolitan Opera House, New York, presented her with a diamond tiara; her first husband, Frederick Gower, disappeared while attempting to cross the English Channel in a balloon, later she married Zolton Dome, an officer in the Austro-Hungarian army, in Indianapolis; died in Batavia, Dutch East Indies, subsequent to a shipwreck.

Noyes, Crosby Stuart 1825–1908, born Minot; student: Hebron Academy, A.M. (Hon.) Bowdoin College 1887; harnessmaker, cotton mill operative; before his fifteenth birthday, began producing the *Minot Notion*, a small, handwritten, four-page sheet, that exhibited judgment and maturity far greater than his years, he also wrote for several Maine journals; his "A Yankee in a Cotton Factory" appeared in the *Yankee Blade*, Boston, and was widely copied; his "The Harp of a Thousand Strings" also attracted wide attention; removed to Washington, D.C., 1847, supplying weekly let-

ters to several New England journals, and working as a bookseller and as a route agent for the *Baltimore Sun*; ushered in a theatre; member of the staff: *Washington News* 1848; member of the Congressional press gallery, made a foot tour of Europe which he described in a series of well-received letters to the *Portland Transcript* 1855; on his return, became a reporter for the *Washington Evening Star*, his crisp, energetic style attracted wide attention, his tactful and accurate reporting secured the confidence of high government officials, including Secretary of War Stanton and President Lincoln, with whom he was on intimate terms; became a major source of news of the armies during the Civil War; became editor-in-chief and owner: *Evening Star* 1866, editor-in-chief of the most influential newspaper in Washington; of the daily which shapes more legislation than any other paper in the United States; alderman: District of Columbia 1863–64; worked incessantly for the adoption of the Organic Act of 1878, which gave practical recognition to the fact that the district is the ward of the nation; campaigned for parkland, chairman, Executive Committee for the Creation of Rock Creek Park, led the fight for street paving, filling of disease-breeding marshland, adequate sewers, and water supplies, endorsed the Shepard Plan for rebuilding the city, defended it against criticism and slander; endowed the first library, now the Noyes Library, in the district; director: District of Columbia Reform School, Newsboys Home, Foundlings Asylum; visited Japan several times, presented to the Library of Congress a large collection of Japanese art and manuscripts; endowed two scholarships to Bowdoin College and a prize in political economy.

Nye, Edgar Wilson (Bill) 1850–96, born: Shirley; brother of Frank Mellen Nye; removed with his family to Grant County, Wisconsin, 1853, later settling in St. Croix County; studied law, member: Wyoming bar 1876, justice of the peace; wrote for various western journals, co-founded the *Laramie* (Wyoming) *Boomerang* 1878, postmaster: Laramie 1882–83, moved back East 1886; member of the staff of the *New York World*; lecturer with James Whitcomb Riley 1886–90; helped make humor a distinct branch of American literature, credited with the quip "Wagner's music is better than it sounds"; author: *Bill Nye and the Boomerang* 1881, *The Forty Liars* 1883, *Baled Hay* 1884, *Bill Nye's Blossom Rock* 1885, *Thinks and Remarks by Bill Nye* 1886, *Nye and Riley's Railway Guide* 1888, *Bill Nye's History of the United States* 1894, *Bill Nye's History of England* 1895, coauthor, with James Whitcomb Riley: *Fun, Wit, and Poetry* 1891.

Oakes, Sir Harry, Bart. 1874–1943, born: Sangerville; A.B. Bowdoin College 1896, overseer 1935–43; goldminer and prospector in Africa, Australia, the western United States; discovered second largest gold deposit in Western Hemisphere: the Lake Shore Mine, in Ontario, later played a large part in the development of Nassau and New Providence Island, Bahama Islands; his unsolved murder is still a matter of intense speculation; buried in Dover.

Oaksmith, Appleton 1827–87, born: Westbrook; son of Seba Smith and Elizabeth Oaks Smith; raised in New York; became an adventurer in South America; indicted in Massachusetts for equipping a slave ship, escaped and fled to England, later served as captain of a blockade runner, member: North Carolina House of Representatives.

O'Brien, Edward 1793–1882, born: Warren; son of John O'Brien; worked on the family farm until age twenty-one, went coasting for a short time, entered the shipyard of John Counce in Warren to 1823; on his own, built a brig in Friendship, established his own yard in Warren 1825, where he built at least one vessel per year until 1854, when he removed to Thomaston, where he continued building ships until his death in 1882; began the cutting of white oak timber in Virginia and brought the first southern timber into Maine 1839, began the production of live oak frames in the Sea Islands of Georgia 1853; often owned a portion or the whole of ships built in his yard; commenced the production of lime 1843; a founder, president, largest stockholder in the Georges Bank (later Georges National Bank) 1852, personally tided the bank over the financial crisis of 1857; owned large tracts of land in the Dakota Territory; with Chapman and Flint (both originally of Thomaston) built a block of houses in Brooklyn Heights; principal in getting telegraph wires strung to Thomaston 1848; served three terms in the Maine House of Representatives, two in the Maine Senate; at the time of his death thought to be the oldest shipwright in the United States.

O'Brien, Henry D. 1842–1902, born: Calais; corporal (highest rank: major), Company E, 1st Minnesota Infantry, recipient: Medal of Honor, Gettysburg, Pennsylvania, 3 July 1863, "Taking up the colors where they had fallen, he rushed ahead of his regiment, close to the muzzles of the enemys guns and engaged in the desperate struggle in which the enemy was defeated and though severely wounded, he held the colors until wounded a second time." Buried in Bellefontaine Cemetery, St. Louis, Missouri.

O'Brien, Jeremiah 1744–1818, born: Scarborough; removed to Machias 1765, where he engaged in the lumber trade along with his five brothers; led the first naval engagement of the American Revolution, when he captured HMS *Margaretta* along with two merchant vessels 12 June 1775; commanding officer: *Machias Liberty*, later captured HMS *Diligence* and HMS *Tatmagouche*; repulsed a British attack on fortifications below Machias; while commanding officer: *Hannibal* was captured off New York 1780, held prisoner aboard the prison hulk *Jersey*, later at Mill Prison, England, from which he escaped to France; after the Revolution, served as collector of customs at Machias; there have been five naval vessels named USS *O'Brien* in his honor, the first, a torpedo boat was launched 1898, the second USS *O'Brien* (DD-51), was launched 1914, saw service in World War I, the third USS *O'Brien* (DD-415), was launched 1939, before she was sunk by a Japanese torpedo 19 October 1942, she earned one battle star in World War II, the fourth USS *O'Brien* (DD-725), was launched 1943, at Bath Iron Works, participated in the invasion at Normandy, was crashed by a Japanese suicide bomber, earned six battle stars for World War II, five battle stars for Korea, three for Vietnam, the fifth USS *O'Brien* (DD-975) was commissioned in 1976 and sunk as a target in 2006.

O'Brien, John 1750–1826, born: Scarborough; brother of Jeremiah O'Brien; a member of the party that captured HMS *Margaretta* 1775, later put in command of the detail that marched the prisoners from that fight to Cambridge, where he received the thanks of General Washington, served as second lieutenant aboard the *Diligence*, later commanding officer: *Hannibal*, commanding officer: *Holderness*, *Adventure*, *Hibernia*, captured numerous prizes, overmatched by a seventy-four-gun ship, which chased him up Long Island Sound, taking refuge in the Thames River, managed to escape through a cunning subterfuge; after the war, settled in Newburyport, later Brunswick; father-in-law of the Reverend Jeremiah Chaplin.

O'Brien, Richard 1758–1814, born: Maine; ship captain, privateer during American Revolution, lieutenant on board brig *Jefferson*; commanding officer: *Dauphin*, captured by Algerine pirates, during his captivity, corresponded with prominent Americans regarding Algerine affairs; with peace 1795, he conveyed the treaty to Lisbon to be countersigned by the U.S. Commissioner David Humphreys; he then journeyed to the United States, where he was commissioned to go to Tripoli to conclude a treaty of peace; appointed consul general to Algiers 1797, relieved by Tobias Lear 1803; assisted Edward Preble in negotiating with the pasha of Tripoli; returned to United States, member: Pennsylvania House of Representatives 1808.

Oliver, James Edward 1829–95, born: Portland, attended public schools in Lynn, Massachusetts, A.B. Harvard College φBK 1849, class poet, came under the influence of Professor Benjamin Peirce, who considered Oliver to be one of the ablest students; assistant to Peirce in the nautical almanac office, then located in Cambridge 1849–69; assistant professor of mathematics: Cornell University 1871–73, professor 1873–95; contributor of numerous papers published in mathematical journals and the transactions of scientific societies, author of several texts on algebra and trigonometry; at the time of his death, Oliver was working on treatises on non-Euclidian geometry, on the theory of functions and a new application of mathematical methods and principles to certain economic questions; fellow: American Academy of Arts and Sciences, American Philosophical Society, American Association for the Advancement of Science.

Osgood, James Ripley 1836–92, born: Fryeburg; brother of Kate Putnam Osgood, grandson of Judah Dana, cousin of John Winchester Dana, cousin of George Ripley, founder of Brook Farm, descendant of Israel Putnam and Eleazer Wheelock;

graduate: Fryeburg Academy 1848, Standish Academy 1850, A.B. Bowdoin College ΦBK 1854; studied law in Portland 1854–55, removed to Boston; clerk in the publishing house of Ticknor & Fields 1855–64, accompanied Charles Dickens on his American tour; partner in Tickner & Fields 1864–68, partner in Fields, Osgood & Co. 1868–70, partner in James R. Osgood & Co. 1871–77, partner in Houghton, Osgood & Co. 1878–80, partner in James R. Osgood & Co. 1880–85; removed to New York, author's agent with Harper & Brothers 1885–86, removed to London, agent of Harper & Brothers 1886–90; partner in James R. Osgood, McIlvaine & Co. 1891–92; among the authors he published were: Henry Wadsworth Longfellow, John Greenleaf Whittier, James Russell Lowell, Ralph Waldo Emerson, William Cullen Bryant, Henry David Thoreau, Nathaniel Hawthorne, Julian Hawthorne, Charles Francis Adams, Louisa May Alcott, Thomas Bailey Aldrich, Richard Henry Dana, Oliver Wendell Holmes, Edward Everett Hale, Thomas Wentworth Higginson, Lucy Larcom, Elizabeth Stuart Phelps, James T. Fields, John Parton, John G. Saxe, E. C. Stedman, Harriet Beecher Stowe, John T. Trowbridge, E. P. Whipple, Bret Harte, Mark Twain, Celia Thaxter, Louis Agassiz, Horace Greeley, R. H. Stoddard, Lafacadio Hearn, Edward Bellamy, William Dean Howells, Joel Chandler Harris, Robert Browning, George Eliot, C. C. Felton, John Forster, H. C. Robinson, Charles Reade, Matthew Arnold, Jane Austin, George Sand, Harriet Proctor Spofford, Thomas DeQuincey, Leigh Hunt, Coventry Patmore, Henry James, Sir Walter Scott, Alfred, Lord Tennyson, William Makepeace Thackeray, Thomas Hardy, Edward Fitzgerald, Sarah Orne Jewett; Anna H. Leonowen's *The English Governess at the Siamese Court*, became the play *Anna and the King of Siam*; extremely well-regarded by his contemporaries as a publisher willing to take up new talent; buried in London; his grandson, James Ripley Osgood Perkins, an actor, was the father of Anthony Perkins, also an actor.

Osgood, Kate Putnam 1841– ?, born: Fryeburg; sister of James Ripley Osgood; began to write at an early age, contributed prose and poetry to magazines; studied in France, Germany, and Switzerland 1867–74; her best-known poem *Driving Home the Cows* appeared in *Harper's Magazine* March 1865 and was widely reprinted, considered to be one of the few poems of merit to be suggested by the Civil War.

Packard, Alpheus Spring 1798–1884, born: Chelmsford, Massachusetts; son of Hezekiah Packard; A.B. Bowdoin College 1816, D.D. 1869; taught at Gorham and Hallowell academies 1816–19; tutor, later: professor of Latin, Greek: Bowdoin College 1824–65, rhetoric and oratory 1842-45, natural and revealed religion 1864–84, acting president 1883; his college career of sixty-five years was the longest in the country, to that date; ordained Congregational ministry 1850, in his later years, served as Bowdoin College chaplain; Bowdoin College librarian 1865–84; librarian and cabinet-keeper for the Maine Historical Society for forty-eight years; contributor to the *North American Review, Bibliotheca Sacra, Collections of the Maine Historical Society*, editor: *Zenophon's Memorabilia of Socrates with English Notes* 1839 *History of Bowdoin, with Bio-*

graphical Sketches 1882, author: *Works of Jesse Appleton, with a memoir* (two volumes) 1836-37; son-in-law of Jesse Appleton, brother-in-law to Franklin Pierce, father of Alpheus Spring Packard and William Alfred Packard.

Packard, Alpheus Spring 1839–1905, born: Brunswick; son of Alpheus Spring Packard; A.B. Bowdoin College 1861, L.L.D. (Hon.) 1901; entomologist: Maine Geological Survey, his *How to Observe and Collect Insects* attracted the attention of Professor Louis Agassiz of Harvard University, with whom he studied for three years; M.D. Harvard University Medical School 1864; in the Civil War: served briefly as an assistant surgeon with the VI Corps of the Army of the Potomac 1865; librarian and custodian: Boston Society of Natural History 1865–66, curator: Essex Institute 1866, director: Essex Institute 1867–78; a founder (along with Edward S. Morse), curator, chair of natural science: Peabody Academy of Science; Massachusetts State entomologist 1871–73; in charge of entomology for the U.S. Geological Survey, under Hayden; lecturer at Agassizs summer institute on Penikese Island 1873–74; professor of zoology and geology: Brown University from 1875; president: Zoology Congress, Paris 1889; founder and editor-in-chief: *American Naturalist*; proposed a new system of classification of insects 1863, discovered the morphology and mode of development of the ovipositor and sting of insects, the nature of the tracheae of insects, collected and described the post-pliocene fossils of Maine and Labrador and the merostomata and crustacea of the carboniferous formations of Illinois and Pennsylvania, showed the close relationship between trilobites to limulus; coined the term "neo-Lamarackianism" in order to classify his stance on evolution, his writing being one of the chief extensions of Darwinism; the author of over 400 works, they include: *Observations on the Glacial Phenomenon of Labrador and Maine* 1866, *Revision of the Fossorial Hymenoptera of North America* 1866–67, *Structure of the Ovipositor of Insects* 1868, *Development and Anatomy of Limulus Polyphemus* 1871–85, *Monograph of the Geometrid Moths* 1876, *The Brain of the Locust* 1881, *Monograph of North American Phyllopod Crustacea* 1883, *The Cave Fauna of North America* 1872, *A Guide to the Study of Insects* 1869, *Life Histories of Animals, including Man, or Outlines of Comparative Embryology* 1876, *Half-Hours with Insects* 1877, *Insects of the West* 1877, *Zoology for Students and General Readers* 1879, *First Lessons in Geology* 1882, *First Lessons in Zoology* 1886, *A Textbook of Entomology* 1898, *Lamarck, The Founder of Evolution, His Life and Work* 1901, *A Naturalist on the Labrador Coast* 1891.

Paine, John Knowles 1839–1906, born: Portland; son of the owner of a music store; student of Herman Kotzschmar, enrolled in the *Hochschule für Musik* in Berlin, studied organ and composition with August Haupt 1858–61, met and played for Clara Schumann, upon his return, lectured and introduced several organ pieces by Bach to the United States at the Music Hall, Boston, and in Portland; musical director: Harvard University 1862–73, professor from 1876; first professor of music and first composer-in-residence at an American university; founding dean: Harvard University

Music School; a founder: American Guild of Organists; among his students were: John Alden Carpenter, Frederick Converse, Arthur Foote, M. A. DeWolfe Howe, Owen Wister, and Henry Lee Higginson, the last of whom he advised in the founding of the Boston Symphony Orchestra; associated with the Harvard community for forty-three years, his presence and serious concern for music as a part of the liberal arts college awakened a regard for music among several generations of Harvard graduates; his works include: two symphonies, the first of which is considered to be the first written by an American, four symphonic poems, four cantatas, music for *Oedipus Tyrannus* 1891, an opera: *Azara* 1896–1900, numerous works for solo piano and organ, several songs, works for chamber orchestra and choral works, his oratorio *St. Peter* (the first oratorio composed by an American) was introduced in Portland 1873, the *Centennial Hymn* to Whittier's words, was the centerpiece of the opening of the Centennial Exhibition, Philadelphia 1876; Paine Hall, home of the Harvard University Department of Music, on the Harvard University campus, was named in his honor. (See *The Life and Works of John Knowles Paine*, John C. Schmidt, UMI Research Press, 1980.)

Palmer, Edward 1802–86, born: Belfast; became a printer in Boston, he became an itinerant propagandist for the abolition of money, he published his *A Letter to Those Who Think* 1840, wherein he delineated his radical philosophy that benevolence and fraternalism should be the basis for business and that requiring monetary payment for goods and services was a faith-destroying and soul-perverting practice; Palmer was highly regarded by Ralph Waldo Emerson, who ranked him, as a serious reformer, with William Lloyd Garrison and Sylvester Graham; his philosophy underlaid the philosophy of Fruitlands, New Harmony, and Brooke Farm.

Palmer, Lizzie Pitts Merrill 1838–1916, born: Portland; daughter of a major landowner in Maine and Michigan, wife of Thomas Palmer, member: U.S. Senate and ambassador to Spain, president: Chicago Worlds Columbian Exposition; donated Palmer Park to the city of Detroit, founded: Michigan Society for the Prevention of Cruelty to Animals, founder: Merrill-Palmer Institute 1916, endowed Merrill-Palmer Motherhood and Home Training School, Detroit.

Parker, Harvey D. 1805–84, born: Temple, raised in Paris; coachman in Boston, bought and operated the Tremont Restaurant, began construction of the Parker House 1854; introduced the American Plan.

Parker, Millard Mayhew 1849–1928, born: Jay; graduate: Maine Wesleyan Seminary, Kents Hill, A.B. Wesleyan University 1875, A.M. 1878; principal: North Livermore High School 1876–77, Glastonbury (Connecticut) Academy 1876–77, Holliston (Massachusetts) High School 1877–82; a founder of Pasadena, California; professor of Greek and Latin: Sierra Madre College, Pasadena 1884–86; principal: Pasadena Academy 1886–91; a founder, professor of Greek and Latin, vice president:

Throop Polytechnical Institute (later California Institute of Technology), Pasadena 1891–97; president: Pasadena City Council 1887–89, carried out temperance legislation; president and professor of civics: University of Arizona 1897–1901; retired to Pasadena; his wife, Josie Miles Parker, was the niece of General Nelson Miles, USA.

Parker, Stephen 1706–1744, born: Boston, Massachusetts; son of a tanner; A.B. Harvard College 1727, A.M. 1730; as an undergraduate, was a scholar of the house, later enjoyed a Hopkins Scholarship; ordained as a missionary 1731, supported, in part, by the Scotch Society for Propagating Christian Knowledge among the Indians, served as chaplain to the truckhouse and the garrison of Fort Richmond; learned various Indian tongues and attempted to spread the gospel up and down the Kennebec; also came to be known as a great fisherman, visiting Harvard graduates (among others) sought him out that they might be guided to favorable fishing spots; dying of consumption, he retired to Boston 1741.

Parris, Albion Keith 1788–1857, born: Hebron; son of a farmer, judge of common pleas for Oxford County, presidential elector 1812, cousin of Virgil Delphini Parris; A.B. Dartmouth College ΦBK 1806, studied law with his father-in-law, Judge Whitman in New Gloucester and in Portland; member Maine bar 1809, practiced in Paris; Oxford County, attorney 1811; member: Massachusetts House of Representatives 1813, Massachusetts Senate 1814; member: U.S. House of Representatives: 1815–18 (Republican); judge of the U.S. District Court for Maine 1818; removed to Portland; delegate, treasurer: Maine Constitutional Convention 1819; judge of probate for Cumberland County 1819–22; third governor of Maine 1822–27, resigned to fill John Holmes's unexpired term in the U.S. Senate 1827, resigned 1828 to become associate justice: Maine Supreme Judicial Court 1828–36; appointed second comptroller of the U.S. Treasury 1836–50; mayor of Portland 1852; unsuccessful Democratic candidate for governor 1854; Bowdoin College overseer 1819–21, trustee 1821–44; buried in Western Cemetery, Portland.

Parris, Alexander 1780–1852, born: Hebron (or Halifax, Massachusetts, immediately before his parents removal to Hebron); trained as a housewright, demonstrated a remarkable facility for drawing, many preserved at the Boston Athenaeum and the American Antiquarian Society; a student of the work of Bulfinch and McIntyre; his commissions in Portland include: Ingraham house 1801, Matthew Cobb house, Asa Clapp house, Richard Hunnewell house, Commodore Edward Preble house, William Pitt Preble house, McLellan-Sweat house; elsewhere in Maine: several lighthouses including Monhegan Light 1849, Saddleback Ledge Light 1839, Matinicus Rock Light, Mount Desert Light, Libby Island Light; at Portsmouth Naval Shipyard: barracks, officers' living quarters, magazine, breakwater, &c.; in Boston: Quincy Market, David Sears house (later the Somerset Club), houses for the Appleton and Parker families at 40 and 42 Beacon Street, St. Paul's Cathedral, directed the construction of

Massachusetts General Hospital; at the Charlestown (Massachusetts) Naval Shipyard, Parris designed and oversaw the construction of all the first, major buildings, including the Commandant's House, the Ropewalk (originally constructed in 1836–38, and which continued to make most of the U.S. Navy's nonferrous rope, line, and cable to 1971) and the Constitution Drydock (the oldest functioning drydock in the United States); elsewhere, he designed the Unitarian Church in Quincy (which contains, in its crypt, the remains of Presidents John and John Quincy Adams); retired to his country estate in Pembroke, Massachusetts, buried in the Briggs Cemetery in North Pembroke; after his death an obituary in a Boston newspaper contained the following: "To no other person do so large a number of imposing and substantial buildings which characterize our city, owe their distinction. His work included many, if not most of the edifices built in Boston on Beacon Street, Tremont, and Summer Streets."

Parris, Virgil Delphini 1807–74, born: Buckfield; cousin of Albion Keith Parris; attended Hebron Academy, Waterville College, A.B. Union College; member: Maine bar 1830, practiced in Buckfield; member: Maine House of Representatives 1832–38, member (2nd District 1838–39, 6th District 1839–41): U.S. House of Representatives 1838–1841 (State Rights Democrat); member: Maine Senate 1842–43, president 1843; U.S. marshal for the District of Maine 1844–48; developer and first president: Buckfield Branch Railroad; buried in Old Cemetery, Paris.

Parshley, Howard Madison 1884–1953, born: Hallowell; son of a Baptist clergyman; student: Boston Latin School 1901–05, A.B. Harvard College 1909, A.M. 1910, Sc.D. (Hon.) 1917; student: New England Conservatory of Music 1906–09; instructor in zoology: University of Maine 1911–14, researcher in zoology: Bussey Institute, Harvard University, 1914–17, assistant professor of zoology: Smith College 1917–19, associate professor 1919–25, professor 1925–52; fellow: American Academy of Arts and Sciences, American Society of Zoologists, Entomological Society of America, his primary work was the taxonomy and ecology of *Hemiptera* and the biology of sex, identified and named several species of *Hemiptera*; author: *Bibliography of North American Hemiptera Heteroptera* 1925, *Science and Good Behavior* 1928, *Science of Human Reproduction* 1933, *Survey of Biology* 1940; editor and translator: *The Second Sex* by Simone de Beauvoir, 1953, *Life and Habits of the Mammals* by F. Bourliere 1953, contributor to books and professional journals; played the double bass in the Smith College Orchestra, the Springfield Symphony Orchestra.

Parsons, John Usher 1806–74, born: Parsonsfield; grandson of Thomas Parsons, founder of the eponymous town; attended school in Effingham, New Hampshire, and Limerick, M.D. Bowdoin College 1828, graduate: Andover Theological Seminary, ordained a Congregational minister in New York City 1831, removed to Indiana where he was a frontier missionary, later served in Wisconsin, Georgia, and Kansas; founded and directed a seminary in Indiana, established numerous churches, wrote several texts on elementary education, orthography, spelling, and religious topics, founded the Southern Mutual Insurance Company, the first mutual life insurance company in Georgia; claimed to have preached in every state east of the Mississippi and three west of it; while recuperating from pulmonary disease, took to painting portraits, which are now highly prized, some of which are in the collection of the American Folk Art Collection and Bowdoin College; while in Georgia, became an abolitionist, traveled to Kansas with his son in 1855, during "bleeding Kansas"; after returning from Kansas, he preached in New Sharon, other towns in Maine, Massachusetts, and Long Island, New York.

Parsons, Usher 1788–1868, born: Alfred; son of a farmer, a descendant of Sir William Pepperrell; attended public school in Alfred and Berwick Academy, studied medicine with Dr. Abiel Hall, Alfred, later with Dr. John Warren, Cambridge, licensed to practice by the Massachusetts Medical Society 1812; in the War of 1812: commissioned surgeon's mate, USN, 1812, had charge of the sick and wounded at Black Rock, near Buffalo, New York, assigned to Captain Oliver Hazard Perry's fleet, distinguished himself greatly at battle of Lake Erie 1813; in his official dispatch, Perry wrote, "Of Dr. Usher Parsons, surgeon's mate, I can not say too much. In consequence of the disability of Drs. Horseley and Barton, the whole duty of operating, dressing, and attending near a hundred wounded and as many sick devolved upon him; and it must be pleasing to you, sir, to reflect, that of the whole number wounded, only three have died. I can only say that, in the event of my having another command, I should consider myself fortunate in having him with me as a surgeon"; attached to the USS *Java*, commanded by then Commodore O. H. Perry 1815–17; M.D. Harvard University Medical School 1818, attached to the USS *Guerrière* 1818–20; author: "A Surgical Account of the Naval Battle of Lake Erie" published in *The New England Journal of Medicine and Surgery*; professor of anatomy and surgery: Dartmouth College Medical School 1820–22, professor of anatomy and surgery: Brown University Medical School 1822-28, professor of obstetrics: Jefferson Medical College, Philadelphia 1831; founding president: Rhode Island Natural History Society, founding president: Rhode Island Medical Society; an organizer and vice president of the American Medical Association 1853; author: *The Art of Making Anatomic Preparations* 1831, *Prize Dissertations* 1843, *The Sailor's Physician* 1851, an ubiquitous work at sea for many years, *History of the Battle of Lake Erie* 1851, *Life of Sir William Pepperrell* 1855.

Parton, Sara (originally christened Grata) Payson Willis 1811–72, born: Portland; sister of Nathaniel Willis and Richard Willis, composer of *It Came Upon a Midnight Clear*; attended Catherine Beecher's school in Hartford, Connecticut; under the pen name Fanny Fern, contributor to *Youth's Companion*, wrote a weekly article for the *New York Ledger*, for the then-princely sum of $100 a column, making her the highest-paid newspaper reporter of the day 1856–72; author: *Ruth Hall* 1855, *Little Ferns for Fanny's Little Friends* 1854, *The Playday Book: New Stories for Little Folks* 1857, *A New*

Eminent Mainers

Story Book for Children 1844, *Fanny Fern* 1851, *Fern Leaves* (an international best-seller), *Rose Clark* 1855, *Folly As It Flies* 1868, *Ginger-Snaps* 1870, *Caper-Sauce; A Volume of Chit-Chat* 1872; credited with the phrase "the way to a man's heart is through his stomach."

Partridge, Donald Barrows 1917–91, born: Canton; B.S. Bates College 1938, M.Ed. 1949, postgraduate study: Harvard University Graduate School of Education, L.L.D. (Hon.) Philadelphia College of Textiles and Sciences 1974; teacher of chemistry and physics in high schools in Maine and Massachusetts 1939–45; director of guidance: Sanford public school system 1945–48; director of admissions and placement: Philadelphia College of Textiles and Sciences 1948–53, dean of students 1953–62, dean of college 1962–66, vice president 1967-76, vice president, director of development 1976–77, acting president 1977–78, president 1978–84, trustee from 1978.

Pattangall, William Robinson 1865–1942, born: Pembroke; B.S. University of Maine 1884, M.S. 1897, L.L.D. (Hon.) 1927; member: Maine bar 1893; member: Maine House of Representatives 1897, 1901, 1909; candidate for U.S. House of Representatives 1904, 1913; mayor of Waterville 1911–13, member: Democratic National Committee; candidate for governor 1922, 1924; associate justice, Maine Supreme Judicial Court 1926–30, chief justice 1930–36; author: *Great Maine Men, The Meddybemps Letters* 1903; his portrait is in the Maine Statehouse collection.

Patten, Francis Jarvis 1852–1900, born: Bowdoinham; son of Captain Jarvis Patten, first commissioner of navigation of the United States; educated abroad from age thirteen, first at a school in Bremen, then University of Bonn 1865–69, the youngest scholar registered; devoted to the study of mathematics and electricity, showed an aptitude for drawing; attended Cornell University for nearly four years, but did not take a degree, graduate: U.S. Military Academy 1877, commissioned second lieutenant, USA, posted west, participated in several Indian skirmishes, aide-de-camp to General O. O. Howard during the Nez Perce campaign; engineered the laying of the first telegraph line from Coeur d'Alene to Spokane, Washington, 1880; still very interested in electricity, on his return to the East in 1883, procured apparatus and began a series of inventions, the first was a self-recording electrical target for the army, his development of alternating current motors for synchronous multiplex telegraphy, was, by far, his most important invention; after his resignation from the army in 1889, he maintained a large laboratory from which he issued numerous papers and articles for scholarly journals, developed numerous improvements in electrical motors, a telephone repeater, and, during the Spanish-American War, a novel and highly destructive bomb utilizing acetylene gas; acted as vice president of the firm created to exploit his advances in carbide technology; at the time of his early death he was at work on his gyroscopic compass, later perfected by Elmer Sperry; buried at Arlington National Cemetery.

Patten, George Washington 1808–82, born: Houlton; son of a clergyman, great-grandson of Eleazar Wheelock; A.B. Brown University 1825, graduate: U.S. Military Academy 1830; served on frontier and garrison duty until the Seminole War 1837–42, commissioned captain, USA, 1846, in the Mexican War: lost his left hand, while storming the heights at Cerro Gordo, brevetted major, USA, for gallantry; declined a captaincy in the quartermaster's department, obtained sick leave, returned to duty on the frontier 1850, with the outbreak of the Civil War: prevented by disability from field service, served on various military commissions, promoted to lieutenant colonel, USA, 1862, retired for disability resulting from long and faithful service, and from wound and exposure in the line of duty 1864; obtained a reputation as a writer, known, by some, as the poet laureate of the army; his poems include: *The Seminole's Reply, Joys We've Tasted, Episode in the Mexican War*, author: *Army Manual* 1863, *Infantry Tactics, Bayonet Drill and Small Sword Exercise* 1861, *Artillery Drill* 1861, *Cavalry Drill and Sabre Exercise* 1863, *Voices of the Border*, a collection of poems 1867, editor: General Philip St. George Cooke's *Cavalry Tactics* 1863.

Patten, Gilbert (born George William Patten) 1866–1945, born: Corinna; son of a cooper and carpenter; student: Corinna Union Academy 1880-84; reporter: *Pittsfield Advertiser* 1883–84, founded the *Corinna Owl*, a weekly newspaper which he sold 1884, reporter: *Dexter Eastern State* 1884; marketed his first novel at age seventeen, for which he was paid six dollars, became a regular contributor to juvenile weeklies and monthly magazines, staff fiction writer for American Press Association, created the character of Frank Merriwell, under the pen name of Burt L. Standish, for the *Tip Top Weekly*, wrote weekly books about him for eighteen years, from 1896, sold well over one hundred million copies, the most widely read juvenile fiction, in its day; wrote scripts for radio program *Frank Merriwell's Adventures* 1934, wrote the lyric for patriotic song *On Freedoms Shore*, sponsored by Council Against Intolerance in America 1939; author: Merriwell Series (208 books), Rockspur Series (3 books), Cliff Sterling Series (5 books), College Life Series (6 books), Big League Series (14 books), Rex Kingdon Series (5 books), Oakdale Series (6 books), *Mr. Frank Merriwell* 1941.

Patten, Mary Brown 1837–61, born: Rockland; at age nineteen and pregnant, took over the command of the clipper ship *Neptune's Car* from her ailing husband, learned celestial navigation, suppressed mutiny, drove ship around Cape Horn and on to San Francisco; nationally acclaimed.

Payson, Edward 1783–1827, born: Rindge, New Hampshire; son a Congregational minister; A.B. Harvard College 1803, A.M. 1806, D.D. Bowdoin College 1821, overseer 1820–24, trustee 1824–27; principal: Portland Academy 1803–06, ordained Congregational minister 1807, pastor: Second Congregational Church, Portland, 1811–27; his printed sermons were read and reread throughout New England, according to Rufus Griswold, "It is more read at home and abroad than the writings of any other New England divine except Dr. Timothy Dwight"; author: *The Bible Above All Price* 1814, *Address to Seamen* 1821.

Peary, Josephine Diebitsch 1863–1955, born: Washington, D.C.; married Robert E. Peary 1888, accompanied him on his 1891–92 and 1893–94 expeditions as far as winter quarters in Greenland; first white woman to winter with an arctic expedition, gave birth to a daughter (Marie Ahnighito Peary), the most northerly born white child, to date, in the world; accompanied her husband on his arctic trip of 1897, went north to meet her husband in 1900, ship caught in ice, and she wintered with her little daughter at Cape Sabine, 78 degrees, 42 minutes North latitude, went north again 1902; vice president: Alaska Geographic Society; author: *My Arctic Journal* 1894, *The Snow Baby* 1901, *Children of the Arctic* 1903.

Peary, Robert Edwin 1856–1920, born: Cresson, Pennsylvania, of Maine par-

ents, son of a manufacturer of barrel staves and heads; after his father's death, he removed with his mother to Cape Elizabeth 1858; student: Fryeburg Academy, schools in Topsham and Gorham, graduate: Portland High School, Sc.B. Bowdoin College ΦBK 1877, overseer 1917–20, L.L.D. (Hon.) Edinburgh University, Bowdoin College; land surveyor at Fryeburg 1877–79, draftsman at the U.S. Coastal and Geodetic Survey 1879–81; commissioned lieutenant, USN, civil engineer, assistant surveyor: proposed canal route across Nicaragua 1884; a chance reading of an account of the expedition to the interior of Greenland by Adolph Erik Nordenskjold 1885, led to his consuming interest in that area; obtained six months leave 1886, went as supercargo on a steam whaler to Disco Bay in Greenland, dragged a sledge, on foot, to a point 100 miles from the edge of the ice cap and 7,500 feet above sea level, this expedition was recorded in his article "A Reconnaissance of the Greenland Inland Ice," published in the *Bulletin* of the American Geographical Society 1887; chief engineer: Nicaragua Canal project, later on engineering projects in New York and Philadelphia; obtained an eighteen-month leave from the navy 1891, organized an expedition under the auspices of the Academy of Natural Sciences, boarded the *Kite*, a chartered sealer, with his wife and a party of scientists, spent the winter at Cape Cleveland, set out with one companion and sixteen dogs 1892, reached the northern shore of Greenland, surveyed the coast, established the fact of Greenland's insularity; a lecture tour financed the next expedition, at Cape York, discovered three large meteorites 1894, from which Eskimos had chipped pieces for blades for years, eventually all three were moved to the American Museum of Natural History, New York; spent another winter in Greenland, set off the next spring 1895, explored the area subsequently known as Peary Land; after obtaining another leave from the navy, set off 1898, aboard the *Windward*, which had been presented to him by Lord Northcliffe, after hearing his address to the Royal Geographical Society in London, this expedition was the first under the auspices of the Peary Arctic Club, sledged to 84 degrees, 54 minutes, North latitude, lost eight toes to frost bite; after several more expeditions and winters in Greenland, commissioned the construction of the *Roosevelt* (at Verona) 1905, wintered at Cape Hecla, pushed to within 172 miles of the North Pole 21 April 1906, before being forced to return, sailed once more aboard the *Roosevelt*, September 1908, reached the North Pole 7 April 1909, cabled the news when he reached Battle Harbor, Labrador, on 8 September, which came five days after the electrifying, if fraudulent, announcement from Dr. Frederick Cook that he had reached the Pole on 21 April 1908; both submitted their respective claims and proofs to panels, assembled for this purpose, of the Naval Affairs Committee of the U.S. House of Representatives and the National Geographic Society (headed by Henry Gannett), which both reached the conclusion that Peary was indeed the first man to reach the North Pole; Congress promoted Peary to rear admiral, USN, on the retired list; retired to his home on Eagle Island, Casco Bay; chairman: Committee on Aeronautical Maps and Landing Places of the Aero Club of America 1913–20; author: *Northward Over The Great Ice* 1898, *Snow Land Folk* 1904, *Nearest the Pole* 1907, *The North Pole* 1910, *The Secrets of Polar Travel* 1917, numerous contributions to scientific journals; received numerous honors; buried in Arlington National Cemetery; the U.S. Navy launched a destroyer, USS *Peary* (DD-226), in 1919; she was sunk in a fierce battle off Darwin, Australia 1942, and was accorded one battle star for World War II.

Peavey, Frank Hutchison 1850–1901, born: Eastport; son and grandson of owners of extensive pinelands and sawmills in eastern Maine; set out for Chicago, at age fifteen, to seek his fortune; employed as a messenger boy, later bookkeeper for the Northwestern National Bank 1865–67; accepted a position in a general store in Sioux City, Iowa, became a grain merchant in 1875, with one elevator; founded: F. H. Peavey Co.: builder and owner of the largest number of grain elevators under one management; worldwide distributor of grain, other interests included banking, building, and shipping on the Great Lakes.

Peavey, Joseph 1838–1918, born: Old Town; blacksmith, invented, in 1858, the eponymous peavey or cant-dog, which became, rapidly, an essential logging tool; founded a company for its manufacture and of other useful devices of his invention, including the Peavey hoist for pulling stumps and raising dam gates and a hay press; buried in Mt. Hope Cemetery, Bangor.

Peirce, Hayford 1883–1946, born: Bangor; brother of Waldo Peirce; attended Maine schools, Milton (Massachusetts) Academy, Roxbury Latin School, A.B. Harvard University 1906; traveled and studied, for many years, in Europe, Asia Minor, and Egypt, making Paris his headquarters; in World War I: captain, USA, intelligence, where his linguistic ability and knowledge of Europe aided him as an interpreter and later in his studies of enemy defensive organization and camouflage; after the armistice, went to Germany as an expert with the Gherardi military mission, later attached to the American delegation at the Paris Peace Convention, aide to Royall Tyler, with whom he later collaborated in a series of learned publications in England and France on late Byzantine and early Islamic art and architecture; wriote the article "Byzantine Art" for the 1929 edition (and subsequent editions) of the *Encyclopedia Britannica*, published papers on Byzantine works of art in the Dumbarton Oakes collection, Harvard University Press 1941; at the time of the outbreak of World War II, they were at work on their *l'Art Byzantin*, having completed two volumes, with contracts signed for the publication of the third volume in French, German, and English, volume three was on the press in Paris, at the time of the occupation in 1940, plates and text survived the war and were subsequently printed.

Peirce, Waldo 1885–1970, born: Bangor; son of a lumberman, brother of Hayford Peirce, descendant of Samuel Waldo; graduate: Phillips Academy, Andover, A.B. Harvard University ΦBK 1908; subsequent to graduation, decamped for Paris, along with his friend and classmate, John Reed, originally intending to sail on the RMS *Mauritania*, Reed talked Peirce into working their passage on a cattle boat out of Boston; once aboard, Peirce found conditions deplorable, leaving his watch and papers with Reed, he dove overboard and eventually reached shore and made his way to England aboard RMS *Mauritania*, arriving in Southhampton, he heard that Reed was on trial for his murder, having been found in possession of Peirce's goods by the captain of the cattle boat; journeying to Liverpool, Peirce attended Reed's trial; Reed was subsequently released but Peirce was clapped into jail for having violated his articles, eventually both were allowed to continue onto Paris and their respective fates; painting student at Académie Julian, Paris 1910–12; ambulance driver for French army and for the American Field Service during World War I 1915–17, awarded croix de guerre; after the entry of the United States in the war, worked for the American Military Intelligence Department in Madrid; introduced Ernest Hemingway to Pamplona, who, in turn, patterned one of the characters in *The Sun Also Rises* after Peirce; painted in Tunis, southern France, Paris, Maine; his works hang in the Metropolitan and Whitney museums, New York, Pennsylvania Academy, Philadelphia, Boston Museum; several murals in various locales; illustrated several children's books, including *The Magic Bed Knob* 1943, *The Children's Hour* 1944; his portrait, by George Bellows, hangs in the Fine Art Museum of San Francisco; made a home in Searsport.

Pendexter, Hugh 1875–1940, born: Pittsfield; graduate: Nichols Latin School, Lewiston 1896, A.M. (Hon.) Bates College 1933; on staff of the *Rochester Post Express* 1900–11; writer from 1911, removed to Norway; author: *The Young Gem-hunters, or, the Mystery of the Haunted Camp* (illustrated by Charles Copeland) 1911, *The Young*

Timber-cruisers, or, Fighting the Spruce Pirates (with Charles Copeland) 1911, *Young Woodsmen, or, Running Down the Squaw-tooth Gang* (with Charles Copeland) 1912, *The Young Fisherman, or, the King of Smugglers' Island* (with Charles Copeland) 1912, *Young Trappers, or The Quest of the Giant Moose* (with Charles Copeland) 1913, *Young Sea-merchants, or, After Hidden Treasure* (with Charles Copeland) 1913, *The Young Loggers, or, the Gray Axeman of Mount Crow* (with Charles Copeland) 1917, *Gentlemen of the North* 1920, *Red Belts* 1920, *Kings of the Missouri* 1921, *A Virginia Scout* 1922, *Pay Gravel* 1923, *Old Misery* 1924, *The Wife-ship Woman* 1925, *Harry Idaho* 1926, *The Red Road: A Romance of Braddock's Defeat* 1927, *The Road to El Dorado* 1929, *The Gate Through the Mountain* 1929, *Partners* 1930, *Red Autumn* 1931, *Over the Ridge* 1931, *The Scarlet Years* 1932, *Rifle Rule* 1932, *The Trail of Pontiac* 1933, *The Flaming Frontier* 1933, *Red Man's Courage* 1934, *Log Cabin Men* 1934, *White Dawn* 1935, *The Torch-bearers* 1936, *Go-ahead Davie* 1936, *The Homesteaders* 1937.

Pepperrell, Andrew 1725–1751, born: Kittery; only son of Sir William Pepperrell, great-grandson of Chief Justice Samuel Sewall; A.B. Harvard College 1743, A.M. 1746; immediately upon his taking of his undergraduate degree, his father, being consumed with the upcoming Louisbourg campaign, turned all of his commercial affairs over to him, an area in which Andrew Pepperrell did not particularly shine, except in the construction of various ships for London merchants; became engaged to Hannah Waldo, daughter of General Samuel Waldo 1746; in preparation for the marriage, he had constructed a splendid mansion, near his father's, importing materials and labor from England; inexplicably, the engagement dragged on for four years, despite the fulminations of Waldo, Pepperrell Sr., and various relations of both the bride and groom elect; finally Pepperrell agreed that the wedding should take place in Boston on a certain date; a few days before the event, he wrote begging for another delay, Hannah said nothing, allowed the party and ministers to arrive, and took the moment to announce that she was quite done with Sir Pepperrell, six weeks later she married Thomas Flucker, secretary of the province, eventually becoming the mother-in-law of Henry Knox; tradition and Nathaniel Hawthorne have it that Pepperrell went quite mad in his grief, but in fact, he went about his business quite cheerfully until he was struck down by a fever returning from a ball in Portsmouth; with his death, the male Pepperrell line became extinct, his nephew, William Sparhawk, succeeded to the title and took the name of Pepperrell.

Pepperrell, Sir William 1696–1759, born: Kittery; son of a ship owner and dealer in fish, naval stores, and lumber, proprietor of the town of Saco; assisted his father in business matters, purchased an adjoining tract next to his father's land in Saco, oversaw the construction of vessels on the Piscataqua and Saco rivers; commissioned justice of the peace and captain of militia 1716, rose quickly in rank to command: Maine militia 1726; member: Massachusetts General Court 1726–59, member: Massachusetts Council 1727–59, president for ten years; chief justice: court of common pleas 1730–59; commander in chief: New England volunteers 1744, led a force of 4,000 (one-third from Maine) to Louisbourg citadel, on Cape Breton Island, Nova Scotia, and directed its reduction, after a siege of 49 days 1745, the news of which was greeted both in the colonies and in Great Britain, with the greatest of joy, made baronet 1746; active in raising troops for the French and Indian War, commissioned major general of the British army 1755; acting royal governor of Massachusetts 1756–58; lieutenant general commanding British Army forces in America 1759; at his death, was considered to be New England's wealthiest man; buried in Kittery.

Percy, George Washington 1847–1900, born: Bath; after attending public schools in Bath, began as an apprentice to the architect Francis Fassett in Portland, later served in the office of Bradlee & Winslow in Boston; removed to San Francisco and in partnership with F. F. Hamilton, established the firm of Percy & Hamilton 1876; among their commissions were: the old Academy of Science building, the Children's Playhouse and grounds at Golden Gate Park, the First Unitarian Church, the Kohl Building (a very early example of reinforced-concrete construction), the Alameda City Hall, the museum, library, and assembly hall at Stanford University, the Lick Observatory on Mt. Hamilton; his daughter, Isabelle Clark Percy (1882–1976) was a prominent painter and co-founder of the California College of Arts and Crafts.

Perham, Josiah 1803–68, born Wilton; storekeeper, woolen manufacturer in Wilton, merchant in Boston, set up a moving panorama of the Great Lakes in Melodeon Hall; organized the first excursion trains in United States; secured the charter for the Northern Pacific Railroad from the United States government, along with land grants, along the projected right-of-way, totaling 47 million acres of land (more than the size of New England), served as first president; only after Perham's death, did it and its chief financial agent, Jay Cooke & Co., become involved in what was to become one of the most notorious railroad financing scandals of the nineteenth century.

Perham, Sidney 1819–1907, born: Woodstock; son of a farmer; graduate: Gould Academy, taught school in the winter and farmed in the summer for fifteen years, after acquiring his father's homestead, specialized in raising sheep; member: Woodstock Board of Selectman 1841; member: Maine Board of Agriculture 1853–54; advocate of temperance, spoke to the question in some 200 towns advocating the reenactment of the repealed Prohibition laws; member: Maine House of Representatives 1854, 1858, upon election, was immediately chosen as speaker; an organizer of the Republican party in Maine, Republican presidential elector for Frémont 1856; clerk of the supreme court of Oxford County 1858–63; member from the Second District: U.S. House of Representatives (Republican) 1862–70, chairman: Pensions Committee; when President Andrew Johnson was brought up for impeachment, it fell to Perham to do the arraignment; elected twenty-seventh governor of Maine 1870–74, advocated the establishment of shops within the prison system so that prisoners might do and learn something useful, while incarcerated, the establishment of an industrial school for girls, the adoption of biennial elections and sessions of the legislature, all of which were adopted; president, board of trustees: Maine State Industrial School, Westbrook Seminary, Universalist National Convention; appraiser of the port of Portland 1877–85; appointed by President Harrison to a committee for choosing the site of a drydock on the Gulf of Mexico; buried in Lakeside Cemetery, Bryant Pond.

Perham, William Sidney 1905–68, born: Augusta, son of a power plant engineer; attended public schools in Augusta, University of Maine 1924–26, B.S. University of Michigan 1928, M.D. University of Michigan Medical School 1932; interned at University Hospital, Ann Arbor, Michigan, resident in orthopedic surgery; practiced in New Haven, Connecticut, from 1937, chief orthopedic surgeon: Yale University Department of University Health, attending orthopedic surgeon: Yale-New Haven Hospital 1937–68, assistant clinical professor of orthopedic surgery: Yale University Medical School 1937, associate professor 1955–68; author: *Study of the End Results in 113 Cases of Septic Hips* 1936, *Multipole Cystic Tuberculosis of the Bones in Children* 1938, *A Compound Fracture of the Shaft of the Humerus with One Hundred and Eighty Degrees Rotation of the Lower Fragment within the Elbow Joint* 1940; his thirty years of caring for the major and minor ills of all undergraduate and graduate athletes and nonathletes at Yale were credited with setting the standard, his philosophy in the area underlay the book *The Athlete and the Doctor* 1967, by Isao Hirata, who worked under Perham; in World War II: lieutenant colonel, USA Medical Corps, chief of orthopedic surgery with the Yale unit, the 39th General Hospital, in New Zealand and the Mariannas, later with the 148th General Hospital at Iwo Jima and Okinawa.

Perkins, Francis (born Fannie Coralie Perkins) 1880–1965, born: Boston, of Maine parents; graduate: Worcester Classical High School, A.B. in physics and chemistry: Mount Holyoke College 1902, while at Mt. Holyoke, established a chapter of the National Consumers League, an organization for the abolition of sweatshops and child labor; teacher at Ferry Hall, Lake Forest, Illinois, 1904–07, concluded that settlement work was personally more satisfying, became general secretary of the Research and Protective Association, Philadelphia, while studying sociology and economics at the University of Pennsylvania; a Russell Sage Foundation fellowship made it possible for her to study at the New York School of Philanthropy 1909, her study of childhood malnutrition became the basis for her master's thesis at Columbia University; executive secretary of the New York Consumers League, also taught sociology at Adelphi College; resigned to become executive secretary of the State Investigating Commission, established in the wake of the Triangle Shirtwaist Co. fire, associated with Robert F. Wagner, Al Smith, and Samuel Gompers; retired from active life for a several years, in order to raise her children, she became the first woman to be appointed to the Industrial Commission of the State of New York 1919–20, 1923–26,

Eminent Mainers

chairman from 1926, campaigned for factory inspection, minimum wages, reduction in working hours, abolition of child labor, workmen's compensation, &c.; subsequent to the stock market crash, became vocal in her condemnation of the policies of Herbert Hoover, persuaded Governor Franklin Roosevelt to form the Committee on Stabilization of Industry for the Prevention of Unemployment; secretary of labor under presidents F. D. Roosevelt and Truman 1933–45, first female cabinet member; played a significant role in the creation of the Civilian Conservation Corps, formulating the Social Security Act, the Fair Labor Standards Act, &c.; after her resignation, 1 July 1945, appointed by President Truman to the Civil Service Commission 1945–53; author: *The Roosevelt I Knew* 1946, her *Al Smith: A Political Portrait Drawing Upon the Papers of Francis Perkins* was published posthumously in 1970; lived for many years in Newcastle and is buried there in the Glidden Cemetery.

Perkins, George Clement 1839–1923, born: Kennebunkport; reared on a farm, went to sea at age twelve, as cabin boy on the *Golden Eagle*, to New Orleans; did not return home but began the life of an itinerant seamen, made voyages to England, Ireland, Wales, France, Norway, Sweden, and Russia; returned home at age fourteen when he attended district school for six months; shipped out for New Orleans, where he contracted yellow fever, after his recovery, made three more voyages to Europe from New Orleans, also from Maine to Cork, Ireland; on the last voyage, the crew mutinied and the officers put him at the wheel until the mutiny was suppressed 1855; hearing of the riches of California, shipped out around the Horn to San Francisco, made his way to Oroville, where he engaged in mining for two years without much profit, found employment as a drover, later as a porter in a store, later clerk, then partner, also engaged in banking, milling, mining, and sheep-raising; during a flood in 1862 made a perilous journey by skiff from Oroville to Marysville, where he chartered a steamer for the relief of his fellow townspeople; member: California Senate 1869–76, removed to San Francisco; president: Merchants Exchange; director: First National Bank of San Francisco; founder and president: Pacific Coast Steamship Co., which acquired most of the coastal steamers plying the waters between California, Oregon, Washington, British Columbia, and Alaska, acquired the Oregon Railway and Navigation Co., introduced steam whalers to the Arctic; president: San Francisco Chamber of Commerce, San Francisco Art Association; trustee: California Academy of Sciences, California State Mining Bureau, State Institution for the Dumb and Blind, acting president of the Boys' and Girls' Aid Society for thirty years; elected fourteenth governor of California (Republican) 1879–83, founder: University of Southern California; unsuccessful candidate for U.S. Senate 1886; member: U.S. Senate (Republican) 1893–1915; ardent opponent of Japanese immigration; chairman: Committee on Fisheries, Committee on Civil Service and Retrenchment, Committee on Railroads, chairman of Naval Affairs Committee, subsequent to Eugene Hale; buried in Mountain View Cemetery, Oakland.

Perkins, John Carroll 1862–1950, born: Auburn; A.B. Bates College ΦΒΚ 1882, A.M. 1885, student: universities of Berlin and Marburg 1886–87, A.M., S.T.B. Harvard University Divinity School 1891, D.D. Bowdoin College 1904, Bates College 1932; principal: West Lebanon Academy 1882–83, teacher: Roxbury Latin School 1883–86; ordained Unitarian ministry 1891, pastor: First Parish, Portland 1890–1913, University Church, Seattle 1914–26, minister: Kings Chapel, Boston 1927–33, author: *Annals of Kings Chapel* (volume three) 1940.

Perkins, Walter Eugene 1870–1925, born: Biddeford; began stage career at Boston Museum 1885, later with Theatrical Doll Stock Company in Winnipeg and repertoire with John Jack, Maggie Mitchell, in *Held by the Enemy* with James A. Herne, in *Drifting Apart* with Charles Froman's stock company, in *Lost Paradise* and *Men and Women, The Country Fair, Barrel of Money, All the Comforts of Home, Charley's Aunt, The New Boy* 1896–1900, *My Friend from India, My Wife's Step-Husband, The Man from Mexico*; starred in *Jerome, A Poor Man* 1902–03, stock star 1903–04, starred in *Who Goes There?* 1904–05.

Peters, John Andrew 1822–1904, born: Ellsworth; A.B. Yale College ΦΒΚ 1842,  member: Skull and Bones Association, student at Harvard University Law School 1843–44, L.L.D. (Hon.) Colby College 1884, Bowdoin College 1884, Harvard University 1885, Yale University 1893; member: Maine bar 1844, practiced in Ellsworth, later Bangor; member: Maine Senate 1862–63, Maine House of Representatives 1864; Maine attorney general 1865–68; member from the Fourth District: U.S. House of Representatives 1868–73 (Republican), chairman: Joint Committee on the Library of Congress, member: committees on patents, public expenditures; associate justice, Maine Supreme Judicial Court 1873–83, chief justice 1883–1904; Bowdoin College trustee 1891–1904; buried in Mount Hope Cemetery, Bangor; uncle of John Andrew Peters.

Peters, Lulu Hunt 1873–1930, born: Milford; A.B. Maine State Normal School, Castine, M.D. University of California Medical School 1909, A.B. University of Southern California 1911; practiced medicine in Los Angeles from 1911; nationally syndicated columnist on health and diet; awarded Order of St. Sava (Serbia), Order of Scanderberg (Albania) for Red Cross work in the Balkans following World War I; author: *Diet and Health with Key to Calories* 1918 (a bestselling book, Peters is credited with being the first dietician to use "calories" as a means to calculate diet intake and the means for weight loss), *Diet for Children* 1924.

Pettygrove, Francis William 1812–87, born: Baileyville; raised in Calais, lived for a time in Portland; removed to Galveston, Texas, where he kept a store; set out for Oregon 1842, kept a general store in Oregon City, became known by the local Indians as a medicine man due to his flute playing; purchased half of the Stumptown claim, he and his partner, Asa Lovejoy, flipped a coin to determine the new name for settlement, Pettygrove won and called it Portland, Oregon; built the first house, first warehouse, and first road, later sold up and removed to San Francisco, later removed to Port Townsend, Oregon, where he settled for good.

Phelps, Thomas Stowell 1822–1901, born: Buckfield; appointed midshipman, USN, 1840, graduate: U.S. Naval Academy 1846; commissioned passed midshipman, USN, 1846, master, USN, 1845, lieutenant, USN, 1855, served in the war with Mexico, Indian War on the northwestern coast 1855–56, where he played a prominent part in the bloody battle of Seattle; Paraguay Expedition 1858–59; commanding officer: USS *Vixen*, extensive service with the U.S. Coast Survey; in the Civil War: joined the expedition to relieve Fort Sumter, March 1861; because of his knowledge of surveying, was employed in charting Confederate waters, often in disguise; as commander of USS *Corwin*, charted five inlets in North Carolina, often had skirmishes with Confederate forces, for which he received the thanks of the secretary of the navy; ordered to join the North Atlantic squadron, assigned to the command of a division operating in the rear of Gloucester Point, Virginia, three times engaged Confederate batteries at Gloucester Point and Yorktown, captured five and destroyed two Confederate vessels, prevented the destruction of White House Bridge, ascended the Mattapony River and engaged a large Confederate force advancing to aid the main army; commissioned lieutenant commander, USN, 1862, commenced a thorough survey of the Potomac River, often engaging Confederate forces; later made extensive surveys of waters in anticipation of military movements; commissioned commander, USN, 1865, commanding officer: USS *Juniata* in the assault on Fort Fisher; after the war: promoted to captain, USN, 1871, commanding officer: Mare Island Navy Yard, California; promoted to commodore, USN, 1879, rear admiral, USN, 1884, commanding officer: South Atlantic Squadron 1883–84; author: *Sailing Directions for the Straits of Magellan, Memories of Seattle, Reminiscences of Washington Territory* 1882; buried in Arlington National Cemetery; his son Thomas Stowell Phelps, Jr., also obtained the rank of rear admiral, USN; USS *Phelps* (DD-360), a destroyer, was named in his honor; she received twelve battle stars during World War II.

Phenix, George Perley 1864–1930, born: Portland; graduate: Hebron Academy, A.B. Colby College ΦBK 1886, Sc.D. (Hon.) 1911; instructor: Hebron Academy 1886–88, science teacher: New Britain (Connecticut) State Normal School 1888–93, principal: Willimantic (Connecticut) State Normal School 1893–1904, head of the academic department and training school: Hampton (Virginia) Institute 1908–30, vice principal from 1909, principal and first president 1930; deeply interested in the education of the Negro and regarded as an authority on the subject; organized and directed the summer school of Hampton Institute for the benefit of teachers and principals of Negro schools; in World War I: director of Negro training in the War Department in Washington.

Phips, Sir William 1651–95, born: Woolwich; one of twenty-two children, shepherd, shipwright, removed to Boston, became interested in sunken Spanish treasure, made three trips to the Caribbean, on third trip, made a spectacular recovery, off Puerto Plata, Dominican Republic, 1684–87; first American to be knighted 1687; appointed by James II: provost marshal general of the short-lived Dominion of New England; major general and commanding officer: of an expedition to reduce Port Royal, Nova Scotia, which surrendered without a shot 1690; commanding officer: of an expedition against Québec, which ended badly and forced the colony to issue the first paper money in the British Empire; appointed first royal governor of Massachusetts 1690; brought the witch trials to an end, rebuilt the fort at Pemaquid, collided with rival authorities to the point of physical violence, summoned to England to defend himself before the Privy Council, where he died of malignant fever, buried in Woolnoth churchyard.

Pickard, Greenleaf Whittier 1877–1956, born: Portland; son of Samuel Pickard, editor and a proprietor of the *Portland Transcript*, brother of Frederick William Pickard; graduate: Westbrook Seminary, B.S. Lawrence Scientific School, Harvard University, student: Massachusetts Institute of Technology; began his first experiments in radio communication while an assistant at the Blue Hill Observatory, Milton, Massachusetts, 1898, for the Smithsonian Institution; his first work was the characteristics of very high antennae; subsequently associated with the Huff Electrostatic Separator Co., Boston; was the second person to transmit human speech via radio waves; chief engineer: American Wireless Telephone & Telegraph Co., Philadelphia; installed complete wireless telegraph plants in Baltimore, Washington, and Galilee, New Jersey; joined the engineering staff of the American Telephone & Telegraph Co., Boston 1902, took entire charge of its wireless telephony investigations; developed the crystal detector, which he patented in 1906, which supplanted all other detectors and was used exclusively until the invention of the audion or tube detector; devised methods and apparatus for the protection of telephone circuits, simultaneous telegraphic and telephonic communication over telegraph wires, invented and patented the radio compass (or radio direction finder) 1908; consulting engineer: Wireless Specialty Apparatus Co., Boston 1906–31; consulting engineer: RCA Victor Co. 1930–31; independent consultant, with offices in Boston 1932–42; director of research: American Jewels Corp., Attleboro, Massachusetts, 1942–45; president: Pickard and Burns, Inc., Needham, Massachusetts, 1945–52, chairman of the board from 1952; devised methods of measuring the sensitivity of wireless detectors, measuring the received energy of wireless stations, and for receiving

Eminent Mainers

radio signals by use of an ungrounded closed loop of wire; during the World War I: assisted in designing and producing radio apparatus and in solving the vital problem of static interference with transatlantic radio communication, installed the first successful static eliminator at the U.S. Navy Radio Station at Otter Cliffs, Maine; held over one hundred patents; member: American Academy of Arts and Sciences, American Association for the Advancement of Science; president: Institute of Radio Engineers 1913; awarded the Medal of Honor of the Institute of Radio Engineers 1926.

Pierce, Edward Allen 1874–1974, born: Orrington; L.L.D. (Hon.) Bowdoin College, Brown University; director, vice president: Merrill Lynch, Pierce, Fenner, and Beane, Inc., New York, when he died at the age of one hundred, he was last surviving partner; director: Dictaphone Corp.

Pike, Frederick Augustus 1816–86, born: East Machias; brother of James Shepard Pike; graduate: Washington Academy, A.B. Bowdoin College 1837; practiced law in Calais from 1840; mayor of Calais 1852–53; member: Maine House of Representatives 1858–60, 1870–71, speaker 1860; member (Sixth District 1861–63, Fifth District 1863-69): U.S. House of Representatives 1861–69 (Republican); in a speech, delivered on the floor of the U.S. House of Representatives, he closed with the words, "tax, fight, emancipate," which became watchwords of the Republican party; chairman: Committee on Expenditures in the State Department, chairman: Committee on Naval Affairs, a member of the national committee appointed to conduct the remains of President Lincoln to Springfield, Illinois; delegate: Maine Constitutional Convention 1871; buried in Calais Cemetery.

Pike, James Shepard 1811–82, born: Calais; brother of Frederick Augustus Pike; attended public school in Calais until age fifteen, clerked for a merchant, became a journalist; editor: *Boundary Gazette* and *Calais Advertizer*, correspondent: *Portland Advertizer*; influential in strengthening the abolitionist sentiment in Maine; invited by Horace Greeley to be the regular Washington, D.C., correspondent for the *New York Tribune* 1850–60; United States minister to the Hague 1861–66; supported Greeley for the presidency in 1872; author: *The Restoration of the Currency* 1868, *The Financial Crisis* 1869, *Horace Greeley in 1872* 1873, *A Prostrate State, South Carolina under Negro Government* 1876, *The New Puritan* 1878, *The First Blows of the Civil War* 1879; the twelve granite milestones that he installed along what is now U.S. Route 1, in Robbinston, are on the National Register of Historic Places.

Pike, Mary Hayden Green 1824–1908, born: Eastport; raised in Calais, graduate: Charlestown (Massachusetts) Female Seminary 1843; married Frederick Augustus Pike, became close to Hannibal Hamlin and James G. Blaine; fervent abolitionist; author: *Ida May* 1854, a novel of slavery and life in the South, that sold 60,000 copies in a matter of months, *Caste* 1856, *Agnes* 1858, *Bond and Free* 1858.

Pike, Sumner Tucker 1891–1976, born: Lubec; A.B. Bowdoin College ΦBK 1913, L.L.D. (Hon.) 1941, Bates College 1945, Colby College 1948, S.C.D. Centre College 1947; clerk in public utility companies: Boston, Savannah, Lowell, Beaumont, Texas, 1913–19; vice president: Equipment Sales Co., Dallas, Texas, Kansas City, Missouri, 1920–23; assistant to president: G. Amsinck & Co., New York 1923; financial employee and secretary: Continental Insurance Co., New York, 1923–28; vice president, director: Case Pomeroy & Co., New York, 1928–39; business adviser to U.S. secretary of commerce, Washington, 1939–40; member: Temporary National Economic Committee 1940–41; commissioner of Securities and Exchange Commission, Philadelphia, 1940–46; director: Fuel Price Division, Office of Price Administration, Washington, 1942–46; member: Atomic Energy Commission 1946–51; chairman: Maine Public Utilities Commission 1953–56; member: Maine House of Representatives 1959–76; chairman: Governor's Commission on Passamaquoddy Tidal Power from 1959; Bowdoin College overseer from 1939; member: American Association of Petroleum Geologists.

Pillsbury, Albert Freeman 1864– ?, born: Rockland; son of a master mariner; attended public schools in Rockland before shipping out at age fifteen, became master at age nineteen, commanded both sailing and steamships in all parts of the world; ship captain for the Pacific Mail Steamship Co., San Francisco 1897–1903, commanding officer: *City of Sydney*, which carried the first American troops to the Philippines 1898, retired from the sea 1903; in San Francisco, was surveyor for the board of marine underwriters 1903–12; marine surveyor, consulting engineer, and salvage expert 1912–17; representative of Lloyd's of London for a number of years; in World War I: California manager of the U.S. Shipping Board, which compiled a remarkable record for war production and efficiency; founder, president of the firm of Pillsbury & Curtis (later Pillsbury & Curtis Corp.) from 1919, consulting engineers, marine surveyors, ship designers, and shipbuilders.

Pinette, Mattie 1903–99, born: New Canada Plantation; graduate: Madawaska Training School, later attended George Washington University, American University; began as a secretary with the Bureau of Weights and Measures, Washington; later she worked for the Bureau of Aeronautics, during the period of the *Hindenburg* investigation; in World War II: enlisted in the Women's Army Corps (WAC), eventually obtaining the rank of lieutenant colonel; in the military, she served as liaison officer with the Army Air Corps, determining which jobs could be assigned to women; later because of her knowledge of French, detailed to North Africa; while en route, her ship was torpedoed, she spent ten hours in a lifeboat, before being rescued; in Algiers, she served on the staff of the Casablanca Conference, attended by President Roosevelt, Winston Churchill, Charles DeGaulle, among others; after the conference, she was detailed to London, where she served as General Eisenhower's personal and confidential secretary during the planning of the Normandy invasion and later, in Europe;

after the war and her discharge in 1946, she worked for the Atomic Energy Commission until her retirement in 1964.

Pingree, Hazen Stuart 1840–1901, born: Denmark; cousin of Samuel Everett Pingree, governor of Vermont 1884–86; worked on his father's farm, removed to Saco at age fourteen, where he was an operative in a textile mill, removed to Hopkinton, Massachusetts, 1860, where he learned the trade of cutter in a shoe factory; in the Civil War: enlisted as a private in Company F, 1st Massachusetts Heavy Artillery, participated the battles of second Bull Run, Spotsylvania Court House, Cold Harbor; while in the escort of wagon train bound for Front Royal, Virginia, was captured by Mosby's men, confined to Andersonville prison, exchanged six months later; rejoined his regiment at Petersburg, took part in the Weldon Railroad Expedition, in the battles of Boydon Road, Saylers Creek, Farmville, and Appomattox; removed to Detroit, employed in a shoe factory; with C. H. Smith, purchased a small shoe factory, styled Pingree & Smith and Co., which, in time, grew to be largest in the West and the third largest in the country; mayor of Detroit 1889–97, immediately introduced reforms to curb the power of the various rings that controlled municipal affairs; attracted national attention, when, during a severe recession, turned over vacant city-owned land to the poor for vegetable gardens, which came to be known as Pingree's Potato Patches, refused to prosecute strikers that dumped a trolley car into the Detroit River, had the entire Detroit Board of Education arrested, describing it as a pack of thieves, grafters, and rascals; governor of Michigan 1897–1901, although a Republican, he advocated an eight-hour day, graduated income tax, municipal ownership of traction lines, direct election of U.S. senators; laid the groundwork for the Progressive movement in Michigan; died in London, England, returning from a African safari with Theodore Roosevelt; buried in Woodlawn Cemetery, commemorated in Grand Circus Park with a heroic-sized bronze statue.

Piston, Walter Hamor 1894–1976, born: Rockland; grandson of an Italian immigrant stone cutter, taught himself violin and piano; graduated from the Mechanic Arts High School, Boston; worked as a draftsman for the Boston Elevated Railway Co.; played violin in theatre orchestras and dance bands; graduate: Massachusetts Normal Art School 1916, where he studied architectural drawing, his skill is evident in his published scores, most of which are facsimiles of his manuscripts and have the clarity of engraved music, all but one of the detailed drawings of instruments in his *Orchestration*, are his work; in World War I: volunteered to play the saxophone in a U.S. Navy band after learning the instrument in a few days; after the war played in dance halls and restaurants; became a special student in counterpoint at Harvard University 1919, A.B. *summa cum laude* Harvard College ΦBK 1924, D.Mus.; a John Knowles Paine traveling fellowship enabled him to study in Europe with Nadia Boulanger and Paul Dukas at the École Normale de Musique Paris; assistant professor of music: Harvard University 1926, professor 1944, chairman of the music department, Walter Naumberg professor of music 1951-60; author: *Principles of Harmonic Analysis* 1933, *Harmony* 1941, *Counterpoint* 1947, *Orchestration* 1955; among his students were Leonard Bernstein, Elliot Carter, Irving Fine; received eight honorary doctorates, a Guggenheim Fellowship 1935, Pulitzer Prizes for his third (1948) and seventh (1961) symphonies; member: American Academy of Arts and Sciences, officer dans l'Ordre des Arts et des Lettres, France 1969; composer of numerous works, including eight symphonies, a ballet: *The Incredible Flutist* 1938, *Three New England Sketches* 1959, five string quartets, two concerti for violin, &c.

Pitts, Hiram Avery 1799–1860, born: Winthrop; after attending public school, worked in his father's blacksmith shop, where he early showed signs of mechanical ability; developed an improved chain type of hand pump, invented a chain band for horse-powered treadmill, patented 1834; built a portable combined thresher and fanning mill 1834, patented 1837, these machines were capable of threshing 300 to 500 bushels of wheat per day; manufactured threshers in Alton, Illinois, 1847–52, Chicago 1852–60; invented a machine for breaking hemp stalk from fiber, several corn and cob mills; his twin brother, John Abiel Pitts 1799–1859, was also involved in thresher improvements, later removed to Buffalo, New York, where he organized the Pitts Agricultural Works 1837, later incorporated as Buffalo Pitts Co., which, for many years, was the oldest thresher manufacturing company in the country; invented an attachment for measuring and registering the number of bushels threshed and bagged, for which he won a gold medal at the Paris Exposition of 1855.

Plaisted, Harris Merrill 1828–98, born: Jefferson, New Hampshire; son of a

farmer; attended district schools, academies in Lancaster and New Hampton, New Hampshire, and St. Johnsbury, Vermont; A.B. Waterville College 1853, L.L.B. Albany (New York) Law School 1855; member: Maine bar 1858, practiced in Bangor; in the Civil War: enlisted in the 11th Maine regiment, USV, commissioned lieutenant colonel, USV, 1862, colonel, USV, 1862, commanding officer: 11th Maine regiment, USV, participated in the siege of Yorktown, the battles of Williamsburg, Fair Oaks, the Seven Days 1862, the siege of Charleston 1863, the Petersburg campaign 1864–65; brevetted brigadier general, USV, for meritorious conduct, promoted to major general, USV, 1865; returned to practice in Bangor; member: Maine House of Representatives 1867–69; delegate: Democratic National Convention 1868; Maine attorney general 1873–75, resigned to become member from the Fourth District: U.S. House of Representatives (Democrat) 1875–76, declined renomination; elected thirty-second governor of Maine 1881–83; unsuccessful candidate for re-

election 1882; unsuccessful candidate for U.S. Senate 1882, 1888; editor and owner: *The New Age* magazine 1863–89; buried in Mount Hope Cemetery, Bangor.

Plaisted, Samuel 1696–1731, born: Berwick; scion of a line of Indian fighters, his grandfather was scalped, his father was Colonel Ichabod Plaisted; A.B. Harvard College 1715; as an undergraduate known primarily for his prodigious appetite; at the time of his father's death, inherited considerable real estate in Berwick and Greenland and one Negro slave; settled in Portsmouth, married the daughter of Governor John Wentworth, who was not well-pleased; often faced difficulties with his creditors, one of whom had him jailed briefly; appointed, at some time, as justice of the peace of York County, removed from that position by the provincial council for profane and immoral behavior 1728; elected by Berwick to the Massachusetts House of Representatives 1731; died of a stroke and buried on his farm, in what is now South Berwick, next to his scalpless grandfather.

Plant, Thomas Gustave 1859–1941, born: Bath; son of a French-Canadian immigrant sailor and day laborer, who fought in the Union Army during the Civil War; attended public school in Bath to the age of fourteen, worked as a rope maker, boiler aker, ice cutter, shoemaker in Lynn, Massachusetts, 1880, later in New Bedford; investor and salesman: Co-operative Shoe Co., Lynn, 1886, a founder: Williams, Plant & Co. 1887, founder Thomas G. Plant Co. 1891, after protracted labor disputes, removed the company to Roxbury 1897, began the manufacture of his Queen Quality brand shoe, which were accorded a gold medal at the Pan American Exhibition, Buffalo, New York, 1901; by 1910 the company possessed the largest shoe factory in the world; irked by the monopolistic control exerted by the United Shoe Machinery Co., began the production of his own brand of shoe machinery, styled Wonder Worker, eventually came to hold fifty-five U.S. patents; eventually sold all his interests to United Shoe Machinery Co. and retired to the Ossipee hills of New Hampshire where he constructed his home, originally styled Lucknow, but now known as the Castle in the Clouds; donated to Bath what was originally called the Old Folks' Home, but now known as the Thomas G. Plant Memorial Home.

Plumer, William Henry 1830–64, born: Addison; consumptive, joined gold rush 1852, worked in a San Francisco bookstore, bought a ranch and mine in Nevada City, elected manager marshal 1856; candidate: California House of Representatives; while protecting a woman from her abusive husband, returned fire and killed the husband, sentenced to San Quentin Prison for second-degree murder 1859, pardoned; slashed by a San Quentin escapee, in turn, shot and killed him, in light of his previous conviction, the authorities advised him to flee; in Washington Territory became a camp leader, thwarted a lynching in Bannock, Montana, organized courts, built the first jail in Montana, appointed U.S. marshal 1863, lynched by a vigilance committee 1864.

Poland, John Carroll 1847–1927, born: Lovell; while an employee of Bates Mill, Lewiston, invented a shuttle binder 1868; worked in a shoe factory, established a heating and ventilation manufacturing and installation company, installed heating systems in the Union League Club and Columbia University, New York, the New York State Capitol Building in Albany; became interested in laundry machines, co-founded the Poland Laundry Machinery Co., Boston, had sales offices in the principal cities of the United States and in Great Britain; invented the centrifugal wringer 1884, an automatic reversing mechanism 1885, the mangle ironing machine, originator of the wet-wash system now in universal use; summered on his large farm in Lincolnville.

Poole, William B. 1833–1904, born: Cape Elizabeth; quartermaster, USN, recipient: Medal of Honor, "Service as quartermaster on board the USS *Kearsarge* when she destroyed the CSS *Alabama* off Cherbourg, France, 19 June 1864. Stationed at the helm, Poole steered the ship during the engagement in a cool and most creditable manner and was highly commended by his divisional officer for his gallantry under fire." Buried in Pine Grove Cemetery, Lynn, Massachusetts.

Poor, Henry Varnum I 1812–1905, born: Andover; son of a physician, brother of John Alfred Poor, nephew of Moses Greenleaf; A.B. Bowdoin College 1835; studied law, practiced in Portland; removed to New York, along with brother John, in 1849, editor: *American Railroad Journal*, the first American trade journal devoted exclusively to railroads 1849–63; author: *History of the Railroads and Canals of the United States of America*, a compilation of an enormous quantity of data on railroads and canals, generally regarded as the country's first investment manual 1860; on editorial staff of the *New York Times* 1863–67; original secretary of the Union Pacific Railroad Co. 1864; formed, along with his son, Henry William Poor, H. V. & H. W. Poor Co., dealers in rails and railroad equipment 1867, compiled annual reviews of railroad statistics and financial conditions, entitled *Manual of Railroads of the United States* 1868–1924; also produced *Directory of Railway Officials* 1886–95, *Poor's Handbook of Investment Securities* from 1890; numerous other works on the tariff, monetary policy, government railroad regulations, &c.

Poor, Henry Varnum II 1880–1931, born: New York; son of Henry William Poor, grandson of Henry Varnum Poor; graduate: Cutler School, New York, A.B. *cum laude* Harvard College 1901, L.L.B. *cum laude* Harvard University Law School 1904; member: New York bar, member: Joline, Larkin & Mynderse, later Joline, Larkin & Rathbone and Larkin, Rathbone & Perry, partner from 1910; counsel: Central Hanover Bank and Trust Co.; specialist in corporate and railroad finances and reorganization, held a national reputation; in charge of the foreclosure of the Père Marquette Railway Co.'s refunding mortgage, counsel for a committee of refunding bondholders 1915, chief counsel for the reorganization of the company until it was acquired by the Chesapeake & Ohio Railway Co. 1929; attorney for bondholders in the reorganization of the Minneapolis & St. Louis Railroad Co. 1917; general counsel, director: Gulf States Steel Co.; chairman of the board: Poor's Publishing Co.; treasurer: Lambert & Co.; a student of Greek, Arabic, and Icelandic languages; close friend and associate of Stanford White, whom he employed as architect for the renovation of the family home in Andover, where he subsequently died.

Poor, Henry William 1844–1915, born: Andover; son of Henry Varnum Poor I; removed with his family to New York 1851, attended public schools in New York, Mount Washington Collegiate Institute, graduate: Boston Latin School, A.B. Harvard College 1865, A.M. 1872; with father, organized H. V. and H. W. Poor & Co. 1867, for dealing railroad securities, became interested in the importation of railroad iron, a business that made desirable a careful record of all railroad companies and the extension work they were doing, that he might be the first in the field to negotiate the sale of rails, the resulting *Poor's Railroad Manual* was an exhaustive compilation of railroad statistics, first published in 1868 and updated on a yearly basis, came to be regarded as the foremost authority on American railroads; publisher: *Poor's Manual of Public Utilities, Poor's Handbook of Investors' Holdings*; a student of language, proficient in Greek, Latin, Sanskrit, Hebrew, Icelandic, and Russian; member: New York Stock Exchange.

Poor, John Alfred 1808–71, born: Andover; brother of Henry Varnum Poor,

nephew of Simon, Jonathan and Moses Greenleaf; A.M. (Hon.) Bowdoin College 1845; member: Maine bar 1832; a founder of the Bangor Lyceum, Bangor Social Library; removed to Portland, edited *The State of Maine*, a daily newspaper for several years, member: Maine House of Representatives; announced plans for two railroads, one to connect Portland and Halifax, Nova Scotia, and the other to connect Portland and Montréal, Québec, 1844, secured charters for both 1845; founded *American Railroad Journal*, New York 1849; secured charter for the European & North America Railroad 1850, built the Saint Lawrence & Atlantic Railroad, which made Portland Canada's winter seaport, which contributed enormously to Portland's prosperity and wealth; chaired a commission to represent Maine in the War Department in Washington, so as to acquire federal monies for the improvement of military infrastructure within the state 1861–62; author: *Commercial Railways and Shipbuilding Statistics of the City of Portland and the State of Maine* 1855, *A Vindication of the Claims of Sir Fernando Gorges as the Founder of English Colonialism in America* 1862.

Pope, Everett Parker 1919–44, born: Belgrade; captain, U.S. Marine Corps, Company C, 1st Battalion, 1st Marines, 1st Marine Division, recipient: Medal of Honor (posthumous), "For conspicuous gallantry and intrepidity at the risk of his life above and beyond the call of duty while serving as commanding officer of Company C, 1st Battalion, 1st Marines, 1st Marine Division, during the action against enemy Japanese forces on Peleliu Island, Palau group, on 19-20 September 1944. Subjected to point blank cannon fire which caused heavy casualties and badly disorganized his company while assaulting a steep coral hill, Captain Pope rallied his men and gallantly led them to the summit in the face of machine gun, mortar, and sniper fire. Forced by widespread hostile attack to deploy the remnants of his company thinly in order to hold the ground won and with his machine guns out of order and insufficient water and ammunition, he remained on the exposed hill with twelve men and one wounded officer, determined to hold through the night. Attacked continuously with grenades, machine guns and rifles from three sides, he and his valiant men fiercely beat back or destroyed the enemy, resorting to hand-to-hand combat as the supply of ammunition dwindled and still maintained his fire and he was ordered to withdraw. His valiant leadership against odds while protecting the units below from heavy Japanese attack reflects the highest credit upon Captain Pope and the U.S. Naval Service. "

Pope, John 1820–80, born: Gardiner, studied painting in Boston, exhibited at Boston Atheneum 1843; joined gold rush 1849; returned to Boston, later removed to Europe, maintained studio in New York City 1857–80; member: National Academy of Design; father of the eminent architect John Russell Pope.

Popham, George 1550–1608, born: Somersetshire, England; nephew of Lord Chief Justice Sir John Popham; post captain in Robert Dudley's expedition to Guiana and West Indies 1594–95; among those who petitioned King James for patent of land in America, named in patent for Northern Virginia 1606; member: governing council for Northern Virginia; commanding officer: ships *Gift of God* and *Mary and John*; reached mouth of Kennebec July 1607; governor of colony; his death that winter contributed greatly to the abandonment of the colony.

Porter, Fitz-John 1822–1901, born: Portsmouth, New Hampshire; son of John Porter, master commandant, USN, executive officer: Portsmouth Naval Shipyard, Kittery, and later, when in the service of the Confederate states, rebuilt the USS *Merrimac* into the CSS *Virginia*, to a design of his own, cousin of Admiral David Dixon Porter and Commodore William D. Porter; raised in the navy yard, attended school in Kittery; graduate: U.S. Military Academy 1846, commissioned second lieutenant, USA; assigned to the 4th Artillery; in the Mexican war: engaged at the siege of Vera Cruz, promoted to first lieutenant, USA, 1847; saw service at the battle of Cerro Gordo, Contreras, Molino del Rey, brevetted captain, USA, for gallant and meritorious conduct in the battle of Molino del Rey, Mexico, 1847, Chapultepec, brevetted major, USA, 1847, assault on Mexico City, wounded at the Belen Gate; on garrison duty at Fortress Monroe, Virginia, and Fort Pickens, Florida; assistant instructor of artillery: U.S. Military Academy 1849–53, adjutant 1853–54, instructor in artillery and cavalry 1854–55; assistant adjutant general of the department of West, Leavenworth, Kansas, during the troubles in that state 1856; assistant adjutant general and chief of staff of the Utah Expedition, during which he detected a plot, on the part of Mormon authorities, to counterfeit a large amount of U.S. Treasury checks; eventually secured the conviction of the engraver 1857–60; on special duty in the Gulf of Mexico, saved several companies of artillery from surrender to Texas authorities, February 1861; in the Civil War: chief of staff of the department of Pennsylvania 1861, colonel, USA, commanding officer: 15th Infantry, USA, served under Patterson and Banks in the Shenandoah Valley; in command of the division of defenses of Washington 1861–62, promoted to brigadier general, USV, 1861; led his division in the Peninsula campaign, commanding officer: V Corps, served as director of the siege at Yorktown, later, saw action at Mechanicsville, Gaines' Mill, Malvern Hill, brevetted brigadier general, USA, for gallant and meritorious conduct at the battle of Chickahominy, Virginia; led the division at the second battle of Manasses and at the battle of Antietam 1862; for his failure to engage the enemy, at the second battle of Bull Run, Porter was cashiered and forever disqualified from holding any office of trust or profit under the government of the United States for violation of the 9th and 52nd sections of the Articles of War, January 1863; President Hayes appointed a commission to review the case and hear evidence presented by Confederate leaders, General Longstreet, in particular, Porter was found to be not guilty of the charges 1872, and eventually reinstated as colonel, USA, 1886, it was also found that he had, quite possibly, saved the Army of the Potomac from a disaster; subsequent to his dismissal, he worked as a mining superintendent in Colorado, where he ran afoul of Benjamin Franklin Smith 1864–65, a merchant in New York 1865–71, superintendent of the erection of the New Jersey State Asylum for the Insane, Morristown, 1872–75, New York (city) commissioner of public works 1875–76, assistant receiver: Central Railway of New Jersey 1877–82, New York (city) police commissioner 1884–88, fire commissioner 1888–89, merchant 1889–93, cashier: New York (city) post office 1893–97; author: "Hanover Court House and Gaines Mill," "Battle of Malvern Hill," both originally appeared in *Century Magazine*, later reprinted in *Battles and Leaders of the Civil War* 1887.

Porter, Florence Collins 1853–1930, born: Caribou; niece of Wallace Hardison, cousin of Charles C. Teague, Chester Brown; first female to serve on a Maine school committee, first female Maine school superintendent (in Caribou); founder: National Women's Republican Club, New York, 1888; owner and editor: *Caribou Republican*; removed to Los Angeles 1900, staff: *Los Angeles Herald*; prominent in suffrage movement, president: Los Angeles County Equal Suffrage League 1909; vice president: Roosevelt Progressive League of Los Angeles County, first female delegate: Republican National Convention 1912, first female presidential elector 1912, delegate: Republican National Convention 1924, made seconding speech nominating Calvin Coolidge; member: Women's National Executive Committee, president: Republican Women's Federation of California; author: *Maine Men and Women in Southern California* 1913, *Our Folks and Your Folks* 1919.

Porter, Henry H. 1835–1910, born: Machias; entered railroad service as station agent: Galena & Chicago Union Railroad, later, paymaster and general freight agent; general superintendent: Michigan & Northern Indiana Railroad; director: Chicago, Rock Island & Pacific Railroad from 1879, director: Chicago & Northwestern Railroad 1870–78; general manager and director: Union Pacific Railroad 1873–77; engaged in consolidating various lines into the Chicago, Saint Paul, Minneapolis & Omaha Railroad; president and chairman of the board: Chicago & Eastern Railroad.

Porter, Rufus 1792–1884, born: West Boxford, Massachusetts; removed to West Baldwin in 1801, attended Fryeburg Academy, supported himself playing fife and fiddle in Portland, as a sign painter, painting gunboats, drum teacher, school teacher in Baldwin and Waterford; builder of a wind-powered gristmill in Portland; author: *The Martial Musician Companion*; constructed a camera obscura, with which he did portraits, painter of numerous murals, invented a revolving almanac, a horse-driven flatboat; in 1816 removed to New Haven, Connecticut, portrait painter, dancing master, took voyage to the Northwest and Hawaii; invented an aerial locomotive, floating drydock, a steam carriage, corn-sheller, a washing machine, a signal telegraph, a fire alarm, &c.; in 1840 became editor of *New York Mechanic*, removed to Boston and renamed it *American Mechanic*, gave up editing to devote himself to the new art of electrotyping; devised a revolving rifle which he sold to Samuel Colt; in 1845 founded: *Scientific American* magazine; buried in Oak Grove Cemetery, West Haven, Connecticut.

Potter, Charles Lewis 1864–1928, born: Lisbon Falls; graduate: U.S. Military Academy 1886; commissioned second lieutenant, USA, assigned to 5th Cavalry, transferred to engineers, promoted through the ranks to brigadier general, USA, Spanish-American War and Philippine Insurrection 1898–1900, river and harbor work: Memphis 1900–03, Duluth 1903–06, Puerto Rico 1907–10, Saint Louis 1910–12, Saint Paul 1912–15, Portland, Oregon, 1915–16, Boston 1916–17, San Francisco 1918–20; president: Mississippi River Commission from 1920, played a prominent part in events surrounding the great flood of the Mississippi 1927; the *Potter*, named in his honor, is the oldest dredge operated by the Corps of Engineers.

Potter, John Fox 1817–99, born: Augusta; graduate: Phillips Academy, Exeter, New Hampshire; studied law in Augusta, removed to Wisconsin 1836; acquired a piece of forest land, twenty-five miles west of Milwaukee, cleared the land and built a log house with his own hands; member: Wisconsin bar 1839, Walworth County probate judge 1837–51; member: Wisconsin House of Representatives 1852–56; attended the first Republican National Convention, Philadelphia 1856, as well as subsequent conventions in 1860 and 1864; member: U.S. House of Representatives 1857–63 (Republican), chairman: Committee on Revolutionary War Pensions, member: Committee on Public Lands; while in Congress, was challenged to a duel by Representative Roger Pryor of Virginia (who had been the intermediary in the duel where Jonathan Cilley was killed), Potter quickly accepted and named Bowie knives as the weapons to be used, the duel was to be held in a closed room in the district, that each would be both accompanied by two friends, also armed, and that only the victor would emerge, alive, Pryor was horrified and declined to fight, the story quickly spread throughout the nation, making both Pryor and the institution of dueling appear ridiculous; introduced the Homestead Bill 1861; chairman of the investigating committee for unearthing treason and disloyalty in government officers and departments, was the only member to remain in Washington through the summer; unsuccessful candidate for reelection 1862; appointed by President Lincoln as U.S. consul general in British North America 1863–66; at the Republican National Convention 1864, steadfastly opposed the nomination of Andrew Johnson as vice president; declined appointments as governor of Dakota Territory, minister to Denmark; an abolitionist member of the Clay Battalion, his first wife died as a result of contracting a fever caught while nursing wounded soldiers; buried in Oak Ridge Cemetery, Troy, Wisconsin.

Pottle, Frederick Albert 1897–1987, born: Center Lovell; A.B. *summa cum laude* Colby College ΦBK 1917; in World War I: surgical assistant, medical evacuation hospital, France; A.M. Yale University 1921, Ph.D. 1925; assistant professor of English: University of New Hampshire; author: *Shelley and Browning: A Myth and Some Facts* 1923; recipient: John Addison Porter Prize for his dissertation on James Boswell; assistant professor of English: Yale University 1926, chairman: department of English 1932–33, Sterling Professor of English from 1944; recipient: Wilbur Cross Medal 1967, William Clyde DeVane Medal 1975, Lewis Prize: American Philosophical Society 1975; editor: *Catalogue of the Papers of James Boswell, from Malahide Castle, at Yale University: For the Greater Part, Formerly the Collection of Lieut. Ralph Heyward Isham* 1930–34 , *Boswell's Journal of a Tour to the Hebrides with Samuel Johnson, L.L.D.* 1936, *Boswell and the Girl From Botany Bay* 1937, *Boswell's London Journal 1762–63* 1950, *Boswell on the Grand Tour: Germany and Switzerland 1764* 1953, *Boswell on the Grand Tour: Italy, Corsica, and France 1765–66* 1955, *Boswell for the Defense 1769–74* 1959, *Boswell in Search for a Wife 1766-1769* 1956, *Boswell, the Ominous Years 1774–76* 1963, *Boswell in Extremes 1769–1774* 1970, *Boswell, Laird of Auchinleck 1778–82* 1977, *Boswell, the Applause of the Jury 1782–85* 1981, *Boswell, the English Experiment 1785–89* 1986, author: *Stretchers: The Story of a Hospital Unit on the Western Front* 1929, *The Idiom of Poetry* 1941, *The Literary Career of James Boswell, Esq.: Being Biblio-*

graphical Materials for a Life of Boswell 1967, *Pride and Negligence: The History of the Boswell Papers* 1982.

Powers, Llewellyn 1838–1908, born: Pittsfield; son of a farmer, brother of Frederick Alton Powers; graduate: Coburn Academy, attended Waterville College, L.L.B. Albany (New York) University Law School; member: New York bar, Maine bar 1860; practiced in Houlton; Aroostook County prosecuting attorney 1865–71; U.S. collector of customs 1868–72; member: Maine House of Representatives 1874–76; member: U.S. House of Representatives 1877–79 (Republican); defeated for reelection in the Greenback craze; member: Maine House of Representatives 1892–96, speaker 1895; governor of Maine 1897–1901; member from the Fourth District: U.S. House of Representatives 1901–05; at his death Powers was one of the largest timber landowners in New England; buried in West Pittsfield Cemetery.

Pratt, William Veazie 1869–1957, born: Belfast; son of a ship captain, grandson of General Samuel Veazie; attended schools in Shanghai, China, the Abbot School, Farmington, and public schools in Belfast, graduate: U.S. Naval Academy 1889, L.L.D. (Hon.) Bowdoin College 1929, University of Maine 1936; passed midshipman 1889-91, commissioned ensign, USN, 1891, rose through ranks to rear admiral, USN, 1921; served aboard USS *Atlanta* and USS *Chicago* 1889–91, USS *Petrel* 1891–95, saw active service in the Spanish-American War, the Philippine Insurrection, and the Boxer Rebellion; navigator: USS *Kearsarge*, flagship of the Atlantic Fleet 1902–05, USS *Newark* 1906, executive officer: USS *St. Louis* 1908–10, USS *California* 1910; tours of duty at the U.S. Naval Academy 1895–97, 1900–02, 1905–06, 1906–08, at Naval War College 1911–13; commanding officer: USS *Birmingham* 1913–15; on duty: Panama Canal Zone 1916, Army War College, Washington, 1917; assistant chief of naval operations 1917–19, accompanied Woodrow Wilson to France as naval adviser 1919; commanding officer: USS *New York* 1919–20, commanding officer: Destroyer Force, Pacific 1920–21; naval expert at the Washington Conference on the Limitation of Armaments 1921–22; commanding officer: Battleship Division Four 1923–25; president: Naval War College 1925–27, commanding officer: Battleship Divisions, Battle Fleet, with rank of vice admiral 1927, commanding officer: Battle Fleet 1928-29, commander in chief, U.S. Fleet (CINCUS) 1929–30, with rank of admiral; naval adviser to the American delegation to the London Conference on the Limitation of Naval Armament 1930; chief of naval operations 1930–33; recalled during World War II by President Roosevelt to serve in expediting the development of escort carriers for anti-submarine warfare; columnist for *Newsweek* magazine 1940–46; trustee: National Geographic Society; received Distinguished Service Medals from both the USA and USN, 1917; named grand officer: French Legion of Honor 1931; retired to Belfast, where he is buried; the USS *William V. Pratt* (DLG-13, later DDG-44), a guided missile frigate, named in his honor, was launched 1958, earned one battle star for service in Vietnam.

Eminent Mainers

Pray, Publius Rutilius Rufus 1795–1840, born: Maine; removed to Hancock County, Mississippi, member: Mississippi House of Representatives 1828, president of the convention that ratified the revised constitution 1832, appointed by the Mississippi legislature to revise the laws of the state 1833, judge of the high court of errors and appeals 1837–40; author: *Revised Statutes of the State of Mississippi* 1836.

Preble, Edward 1761–1807, born: Portland; son of Jedidiah Preble; attended Dummer Academy, Newbury, Massachusetts, 1775–78; during the American Revolution, contrary to his father's wishes, shipped out on a privateer 1778, made a voyage to Europe, midshipman aboard the Massachusetts naval militia vessel *Protector*, which was, after several successful cruises, captured, Preble was held prisoner in England, later aboard the prison ship *Jersey*, from which he was exchanged; served first lieutenant, aboard *Winthrop* (a captured English brig) to 1783; after the peace, acted as a merchant captain for several years; lieutenant in command: brig USS *Pickering*, cruised West Indies to 1798; promoted to captain, USN, commanding officer: frigate USS *Essex* 1799, first American warship to sail east of the Cape of Good Hope, convoyed American merchantmen to and from the East Indies; as commodore, USN, commanding officer: USS *Constitution* directed the war against Tripoli 1803–04, Congress voted him thanks and a gold medal; built gunboats for U.S. Navy 1805–07; declined the offer of President Jefferson to be his secretary of the navy 1806; buried in the Eastern Cemetery, Portland; five naval vessels have been named in his honor, the first USS *Preble*, a sloop was acquired on Lake Champlain 1813, participated in the battle of Lake Champlain, the second USS *Preble*, a sloop of war was launched at Kittery 1839 and served in the Civil War, the third USS *Preble* (torpedo boat destroyer No. 12) was launched 1899, the fourth USS *Preble* (DD-345, later DM-20) was launched at Bath Iron Works 1919, present at the attack on Pearl Harbor, earned eight battle stars for World War II, the fifth USS *Preble* (DLG-15), was launched at Bath Iron Works 1959, saw extensive service in Vietnam.

Preble, George Henry 1816–85, born: Portland; nephew of Edward Preble, grandson of Jedidiah Preble; commissioned midshipman, USN, 1835, cruised the Mediterranean and West Indies, passed midshipman 1841, took part in the Florida war 1841–42, circumnavigated the globe aboard USS *St. Louis* 1843–45, commanding officer: first U.S. landing force in China; in the war with Mexico: executive officer of USS *Petrel*, participated in the capture of Alvarado, Laguna, Tampico, and Panuco, the siege of Vera Cruz; promoted to master, USN, 1847, with Commodore M. C. Perry on USS *Macedonian* to Japan 1852, operated against Chinese pirates, for which he received the thanks of the English authorities, surveyed the Wee Sung River below Shanghai; in the Civil War: executive officer: USS *Narragansett*, Pacific squadron, commanding officer: USS *Katahdin* with Farragut at New Orleans, Grand Gulf, and Vicksburg; promoted to commander, USN, 1862, on blockade duty in the Gulf, engaged and disabled CSS *Oreto*, which managed to get to shallow water, where Preble could not pursue, as a result, was summarily dismissed from the service, promptly restored by President Lincoln; given command of USS *St. Louis*, in command of the fleet brigade, cooperating with General W. T. Sherman 1864-65; promoted to captain, USN, 1867, commodore, USN, 1871, rear admiral 1876, vice admiral; commanding officer: Pacific squadron; commandant: Philadelphia Navy Yard, retired 1878; author: *The Chase of the Rebel Steamer of War Oreto* 1862, *The Opening of Japan* 1862, *The First Cruise of the United States Vessel Essex* 1870, *A Complete History of Vessels of the United States Navy from 1797 to 1874* 1874, *Henry Knox Thatcher, Rear Admiral, U.S. Navy* 1882, *A Chronological History of the Origin and Development of Steam Navigation* 1883, *History of the United States Navy Yard, Portsmouth, New Hampshire* 1892, *History of the Flag of the United States of America: Symbols, Standards, Banners and Flags of Ancient and Modern Nations* 1880, *Origin and History of the American Flag* (two volumes) 1907; buried in Evergreen Cemetery, Portland.

Preble, Jedidiah 1707-84, born: York; master and owner of various trading vessels; in King George's War, rose from ensign to brigadier general, an important principal in the reduction of Louisbourg citadel 1745; highly regarded by regular British Army; in French and Indian War, participated in Fort Ticonderoga Expedition; commanding officer: Fort Pownall 1759; removed to Falmouth (Portland), served for twelve years as representative to the Massachusetts General Court, became councilor 1773; refused the offer of a commission as major general in the Continental Army, due to advancing age; member: Massachusetts Senate 1780; owner of ships, wharves, farms; father of Edward Preble; generally credited with being the first to climb what is now Mount Washington.

Preble, William Pitt 1783-1857, born: York; son of captain in the Revolutionary Army and dissident member of the Massachusetts Constitutional Convention; A.B. Harvard College φΒΚ 1806, A.M. 1809, L.L.D. (Hon.) Bowdoin College 1829; tutor in mathematics: Harvard University 1809-11; studied law, practiced in York, Alfred, and Saco; appointed U.S. district attorney by President Madison 1813; settled in Portland, active in the separation of Maine from Massachusetts; member: Maine Constitutional Convention 1819; judge: Maine Supreme Judicial Court 1820-28; appointed by President Jackson as minister plenipotentiary to the Hague 1829, resigned in protest of the arbitration award of lands in the north of Maine to Canada by the king of the Netherlands 1831; one of four commissioners, appointed by Congress, to adjust the final settlement of the boundary 1842; one of two commissioners appointed to further the building of a railroad, linking Portland with the Great Lakes; author: *Address to the Citizens of Montréal* 1845, *Address to Mr. Gladstone, the English Colonial Secretary* 1846, *Memorial to the Governor General of Canada* 1847; first president: Atlantic & St. Lawrence Railroad Co. 1845-48; Bowdoin College overseer 1820-21, trustee 1821-42.

Prentiss, Elizabeth Payson 1816–78, born: Portland; daughter of Edward Payson; beginning at age sixteen, began to make contributions to *Youth's Companion*; teacher at Mr. Persico's young ladies seminary, Richmond, Virginia, 1840–44; married George Prentiss 1845, accompanied her husband to New York 1851, where she remained the rest of her life; lost two children in a matter of weeks 1852, the eldest of whom, she immortalized in her *Susy-Books*; author: *Little Susy's Six Birthdays* 1853, *The Flower of the Family* 1854, *Only a Dandelion* 1854, *Henry and Bessie* 1855, *The Little Preacher* 1867, *Little Lou's Sayings and Doings* 1868, *Little Threads* 1868, *Fred, Maria, and Me* 1868, *Old Brown Pitcher* 1868, *Stepping Heavenward* 1869 (her most popular work, selling 150,000 copies in this country and translated into French, German, Norwegian, Swedish, and Italian), *Nidworth* 1869, *The Percys* 1870, *The Story of Lizzie Todd* 1870, *Aunt Jane's Hero* 1871, *Six Little Princesses* 1871, *Golden Hours* 1873, *Urbane and His Friends* 1874, translator of *Griselda* 1876, author: *At Home in Greylock* 1876, *Pemaquid* 1877, *Gentleman Jim* 1878, *Avis Benson* 1879, her *Life and Letters*, edited by George Prentiss, was published posthumously.

Prentiss, John Wing 1875–1938, born: Bangor; son of a woodland operator; student: Belmont School, San Francisco, Phillips Academy, Andover, A.B. Harvard College 1898; messenger: Devins, Lyman, and Co., stockbrokers, Boston, bond salesman: Hornblower & Weeks, investment bankers, Boston 1904, later transferred to the New York office, made partner 1906, senior partner from 1936; internationally recognized figure on Wall Street, a pioneer in the movement to make common stocks available to the public; appeared, on numerous occasions, before governmental investigating agencies as an expert on financial matters; offered Henry Ford, on behalf of Hornblower & Weeks, $1 billion for his holdings in Ford Motor Co. 1924, the offer was repeated in 1925 and 1927; aided in settling the Stutz Motor Co. pool controversy 1929; member, board of trustees: Phillips Academy, Andover 1938; national champion squash player 1913.

Prentiss, Seargent Smith 1808–50, born: Portland; son of a ship captain, brother of George Prentiss; crippled from an early age; graduate: Gorham Academy, A.B. Bowdoin College 1826, studied law with Judge Pierce of Gorham for a year; settled in Natchez, Mississippi, found employment as a tutor; member: Mississippi bar 1829, early obtained a reputation as a skilled orator and advocate, appeared before the U.S. Supreme Court at age twenty-four; member: Mississippi House of Representatives 1836, member: U.S. House of Representatives (Whig) 1837, the result of the election was contested by Claiborne, his Democratic opponent, Prentiss spoke in defense of his claim to election for three days, before the U.S. House of Representatives, as word spread of his eloquence, the galleries and floor filled to overflowing, earned the admiration of Daniel Webster and Henry Clay; his claim rejected by the vote of Speaker Polk, the election was returned to the people, Prentiss was triumphantly reelected; a later speech at a banquet in Boston, held the critical audience spellbound and earned the plaudits of Edward Everett; fought two duels with the same man; defeated Jefferson F. Davis in a contest for a seat in the Mississippi House of Representatives 1843; having lost his extensive property in Natchez due to an adverse decision of the U.S. Supreme Court, removed to New Orleans; consorted with whores, and drank himself to death; buried in the private cemetery of Longwood Plantation, near Natchez; Prentiss County, Mississippi, was named in his honor.

Prescott, Mary Newmarch 1847–88, born: Calais; daughter of a lumber merchant and lawyer, younger sister of Harriet Prescott Spofford; removed with her family to Derry, New Hampshire, later Newburyport, Massachusetts, where she spent her life; a leading contributor to magazines, such as *Harper's Magazine*; author: *Letters from Switzerland* 1860, *Memoirs of Mrs. Joanna Bethune, Kirwan* 1862, *Fifteen Years of Prayer,* *W--¹ ,g with God* 1872, *The Alhambra and the Kremlin, Matt's Follies* 1873, *Songs of the Soul* 1874, *Life of S. F. B. Morse, L.L.D.* 1875, *Irenaeus Letters* 1882, *Prayer and its Answer* 1882, her *Power of Prayer* sold 175,000 copies, translated into French and Tamil.

Procter, Fred Francis 1851–1929, born: Dexter; professional acrobat, as Fred Levantine made circuit of European music halls, bought an interest in a theatre in Albany, New York, 1886, became the sole proprietor 1889, removed to New York; in alliance with Charles Frohman opened a legitimate theatre on 23rd Street, turned to vaudeville, originated continuous entertainment, from noon to midnight, appealed to women and children, made his theatres refrain from vulgarity, came to own twenty-five houses, retired in 1929; his theatres were taken over by RKO.

Pullen, Elisabeth Cavazza Jones 1849–1926, born: Portland; daughter of Charles Jones, a prominent merchant; received a thorough private education in pianoforte, singing, and theory of music; while still a schoolgirl, reviewer and musical critic: *Portland Daily Press*, editorial contributor to *Literary World*, Boston; her parody of Swinburne's *Atalanta* so amused members of New York's Century Association that they sent her a card of admission to the club, supposing that she was male; fluent in Italian from an early age, chose to illustrate the manners and customs of Calabria and Sicily, in fiction; author (under the name of E. Cavazza): *Don Finimondone* (collection of short stories), *The Man from Aidone, Rocco and Sidora,* (under her own name) *Mr. Whitman* 1902, contributor to magazines of short stories, critiques, verse, and translation from French and Italian; her first husband, Signor Nino Cavazza, died soon after their marriage in 1885, her second husband was Stanley Pullen, owner and editor of the *Portland Press*.

Putnam, George Palmer 1814–73, born: Brunswick; grandnephew of General Israel Putnam, cousin of Judah and John Winchester Dana, Kate Putnam, and George Ripley Dana; attended school in Brunswick to age eleven, apprenticed to a carpet manufactory in Norwich, Connecticut, for four years; removed to New York, where he clerked for the bookstore of G. W. Bleecker for $25 per annum and board; later clerked for the bookstore of Daniel & Jonathan Leavitt 1830; compiled his *Index to Universal History* 1833, later entitled *The World's Progress* and which remained in print for many years; started a trade newspaper *Book-seller's Advertiser*, the first of its kind; entered the firm of Wiley & Long, later junior partner: Wiley & Putnam, importers of foreign books 1836; soon was dispatched to London, where he looked after the firm's interests and became friends with Giuseppe Mazzini and Louis Napoleon (later Napoleon III), among others; compiler of *American Facts* (designed to improve Anglo-American relations) 1840; returned to New York and dissolved his connection with Wiley 1848; began publishing on his own; publisher: *Putnam's Monthly* 1853–70; founder: G. P. Putnam & Company, later G. P. Putnam & Sons 1854; first to publish Edgar Allen Poe, William Cullen Bryan, James Fenimore Cooper, James Russell Lowell, Bayard Taylor, and others; appointed U.S. collector of internal revenue 1863–66; a founder, honorary superintendent: Metropolitan Museum of Art, New York; author: *Tours in Europe: A Concise Guide with Memoranda of a Tour in 1836 1838, American Book Circular with Notes and Statistics* 1843, *A Pocket Memorandum Book in France, Italy, and Germany in 1847* 1848; among the first Americans to speak for the creation of international copyright, published the first argument for it in 1837; his posthumous memoir was published by his son, George Haven Putnam, in 1912; his grandson, George Haven Putnam, Jr., was the promoter and husband of Amelia Earhart.

Quimby, Phineas Parkhurst 1802–66, born: Lebanon, New Hampshire; son of

a blacksmith; removed, with his family, to Belfast 1804; apprenticed to a watch and clockmaker; devised several mechanical devices: a vise, a method for steering vessels, an endless chainsaw, and a clock movement, also engaged in amateur daguerreotyping; his interest in hypnotism was sparked by a Doctor Collyer, a traveling hypnotist, who gave a series of lectures in Belfast; gave the process much thought, acquired considerable proficiency, his influence upon a young man named Burkmar was considered so remarkable that the two toured Maine and New Brunswick for several years, giving displays that sore astonished the beholders; using his talents to diagnose diseases, made the discovery that some illness could be cured by post-hypnotic suggestion, felt that he had discovered the method of Christ; founded the New Thought movement; used the term "Christian science" in an article of 1863; longtime patient Mary Baker Eddy essentially appropriated, after his death of an erroneous tumor, Quimby's thinking and produced what came to be known as Christian Science, refusing, in the process, to properly credit Quimby.

Quinby, William Emory 1835–1908, born: Brewer; removed to Michigan at

age thirteen, with his family, where his father published the *Literary Miscellany*; A.B. University of Michigan 1858, studied law, member Michigan bar 1859; took a temporary position with the *Detroit Free Press* 1861, managing editor 1863, editor in chief and principal owner from 1872; U.S. minister to the Hague 1893–97.

Râle, Sébastien 1654–1724, born: Pontarlier, Franche-Comté, France; became Jesuit priest 1675; instructor at Carpentras and Nîmes 1677–84; to Canada to do missionary work 1689; succeeded Marquette at Illinois mission; sent to Abenaki mission at Norridgewock, converted whole tribe of Malecites, killed in English attack.

Ralston, Esther 1900–94, born: Bar Harbor; a vaudevillian from the age of two, made screen debut at age fourteen; known as "the American Venus," her films include: *Phantom Fortunes* 1916, *Huckleberry Finn* 1920, *Crossing Trails* 1921, *Pals of the West, Remembrance, Oliver Twist* 1922, *The Wild Party, Pure Grit* 1923, *The Marriage Circle, The Heart Buster* 1924, *Peter Pan, The Goose Hangs High, The Little French Girl, Beggar on Horseback, The Lucky Devil, The Trouble with Wives, The Best People, A Kiss for Cinderella, Woman Handled* 1925, *The American Venus, The Blind Goddess, The Quarterback, Old Ironsides* 1926, *Fashions for Women, Children of Divorce, Ten Modern Commandments, Figures Don't Lie, The Spotlight* 1927, *Love and Learn, Something Always Happens, Half a Bride, The Sawdust Paradise* 1928, *The Case of Lana Smith, Betrayal, The Wheel of Life, The Mighty* 1929, *Lonely Wives, The Prodigal* 1931, *After the Ball, Black Beauty, To The Last Man* 1933, *Sadie McKee, Romance in the Rain, The Marines Are Coming* 1934, *Strange Wives, Mr. Dynamite, Ladies Crave Excitement* 1935, *Hollywood Boulevard, Reunion* 1936, *As Good as Married, Shadows of the Orient* 1937, *Letter of Introduction* 1938, *Tin Pan Alley* 1940, *San Francisco Docks* 1941.

Reed, Axel Hayford 1835–1917, born: Hartford; sergeant (highest rank: captain), USV, Company K, 2nd Minnesota Infantry, recipient: Medal of Honor, at Chickamauga, Georgia, and Missionary Ridge, Tennessee, 19 September & 15 November 1863, "While under arrest at Chickamauga, Georgia, left his place in the rear and voluntarily went to the line of battle, secured a rifle, and fought gallantly during the two day battle; was released from arrest in recognition of his bravery. At Missionary Ridge, Reed commanded his company and gallantly led it, being among the first to enter the enemy's works; was severely wounded, losing an arm, but declined a discharge and remained in active service to the end of the war." Buried at Mount Auburn Cemetery, Glencoe, Minnesota.

Reed, Thomas Brackett "Czar" 1839–1902, born: Portland; son of a ship captain; A.B. Bowdoin College 1860, removed to California, where he taught school and was admitted to the bar; in the Civil War: assistant paymaster, USN, 1864–65; served aboard the tin clad USS *Sybil*, patrolled uneventfully on the Tennessee, Cumberland, and Mississippi Rivers; member: Maine House of Representatives 1867–69; Maine Senate 1869–70; Maine attorney general 1870–73; Portland city solicitor 1873–76; member: U.S. House of Representatives 1877–99 (Republican), chairman: Judiciary Committee, member: Ways and Means Committee; speaker 1889–91,

1895–99, minority floor leader 1891–95; unsuccessful candidate for the Republican nomination for president of the U.S. 1896; for his absolute control of the often fractious chamber, he was dubbed "Czar"; known for his dry wit and skill in debate, an outspoken opponent of neo-imperialism, used all his powers to avert the war with Spain and the subsequent annexation of Puerto Rico and the Philippines, resigned his seat and the speakership in disgust; became head of the law firm of Reed, Simpson, Thatcher, and Barnum, New York; author of *Reed's Rules*, the manual of procedure and parliamentary law, used in the U.S. House of Representatives; buried in Evergreen Cemetery, Portland.

Reid, Walter E. 1869–1955, born: Harmon Harbor, Georgetown; dropped out of school at age eight, bound out to a farmer, shipped out on a coastal schooner, employed as an actor in Worcester, Massachusetts, employed as a clerk in a grocery in Bath, fireman aboard the *Cottage City*, a steamer in the Portland and New York line, opened a Fleischman's Yeast office in Waterville, later, cattle buyer for Armour and Co.; associated with Charles W. Morse, whom he had known as a boy; director: Eastern Steamship Co., president: Northern and Southern Shipping Co.; Waterville alderman, unsuccessful candidate for mayor; became the single largest stockholder in Mack Truck Co., member: board of directors 1927–51, chairman of the board; financed a private investigation into the Maine Liquor Commission 1948; donor of 1,200 acres in Georgetown to the state, named Reid State Park, in his honor 1946.

Rice, Richard Henry 1863–1922, born: Rockland; M.E. Stevens Institute of Technology, Hoboken, New Jersey, 1885, D.Eng 1921; apprentice: Cleveland, Cincinnati, Chicago & Saint Louis Railroad 1885–86, draftsman and designer: Bath Iron Works 1886–87, designer and chief draftsman: E. D. Leavitt Co. (engineers of Calumet and Hecla Mining Companies), Cambridgeport, Massachusetts, 1887–91, general superintendent: William A. Harris Steam Engine Co., Providence, Rhode Island, 1891–94, superintendent and treasurer: Rice and Sargent Engine Co. 1894–99, merged with Providence Engine Works 1899–1903, with engine and turbine department: General Electric Co., Lynn, Massachusetts, 1903–18, general superintendent from 1918, devoted himself to perfecting the General Electric steam turbine, held a total of over fifty patents on devices using steam, water, and air pressure, including: mechanical valve gears, a multivalve controller for turbine speed, cast-in diaphragms, through-point support for turbine generator sets, a constant volume governor, a vertical condenser, the G-form bucket dovetail; first president: Associated Industries of Massachusetts, president: National Conference of State Manufacturers' Associations, member: American Society of Mechanical Engineers, Appalachian Mountain Club; in his memory, General Electric endowed the Richard H. Rice Scholarship at Stevens Institute of Technology 1924.

Rice, Thomas 1734–1812, born: Westborough, Massachusetts; A.B. Harvard College 1756, A.M. 1759, as an undergraduate, kept school in Chelmsford, candidate for the pulpit in Templeton, but declined the call to study medicine with Dr. Oliver Prescott in Groton, Massachusetts; practiced medicine in Pownalborough, first trained physician in the area, preached for a time at Wiscasset Point, helped build the first meetinghouse; first moderator of the town meeting of the North Parish; justice: court of common pleas, later chief justice; Lincoln County registrar of deeds; served on the committee formed to reply to the Boston Committee of Correspondence 1773; served regularly on the Pownalborough Committee of Correspondence, chairman: Committee on Inspection; on one occasion, his life and property were threatened by a mob incited by Thomas Bowman, who was jealous of Rice's position as registrar of deeds; elected to the Provincial Congress 1774, the first representative from east of the Kennebec, the next year, his reelection was contested, but the protest was decided in his favor by the Provincial Congress, which appointed him to sign provincial paper currency and reappointed him to the court of common pleas 1775; Timothy Langdon and Timothy Parsons carried the case against Rice to the Boston newspapers, which charged that Rice, as chairman of the Committee of Inspection, had connived with Abiel Wood, a notorious Tory, to export desperately needed food to Nova Scotia; elected to the Lincoln County Congress and to the Massachusetts House of Representatives, with instructions to vote for independence 1776; he was carried away to Machias, in order to guarantee the good conduct of the inhabitants of Pownalborough, Sir George Collier, who had come up the Sheepscot aboard HMS *Rainbow*, to seize a provincial ship, its gear, and all the mast timbers on the river 1777; elected to the Massachusetts Constitutional Convention 1779; member: Massachusetts Senate 1781–83; sent by the town to the convention called to consider the United States Convention, with instructions to vote against ratification, which he ignored 1783; along with Benjamin Lincoln and Rufus Putnam, negotiated the treaty at Bangor with the Penobscots 1786; president: Hallowell Academy Board of Trustees; Bowdoin College trustee 1794–99; as a Pownalborough selectman, led the movement to divide the town into Dresden, New Milford (later Alna), and Wiscasset 1794; Federalist presidential elector 1792, 1796, 1800.

Richards, Ellen Henrietta Swallow 1842–1911, born: Dunstable, Massachusetts; daughter of schoolteachers, who also farmed and kept a general store; educated at home, began to teach as a teenager, entered Vassar College at the age of twenty-five, paid for her tuition and board by tutoring her classmates, A.B. Vassar College 1870; the first female graduate of Massachusetts Institute of Technology (B.S. 1873), remained at M.I.T. as assistant in chemistry, engaged mostly in water analysis for the city of Boston; married Robert Hallowell Richards 1875; instructor in chemistry and mineralogy in the Woman's Laboratory (of which she was a founder) at Massachusetts Institute of Technology 1878, founder: Society to Encourage Studies at Home; founder: New England Kitchen, where the diets of working class families were analyzed and demonstration given so that these people might prepare more nutritious, less costly meals, as such, Richards is considered to be the founder of the home economics movement in the United States, through her prodding, many land grant colleges began to offer courses in domestic science; founder: National Household Economics Association, called for the elimination of heavy carpets (which collect dust), the adoption of many, new labor-saving devices, the adoption of home economics courses in high schools; instructor in sanitary chemistry 1885, as such, Richards was the first professional female scientist in the United States; first female to be elected to the American Institute of Mining; author of many works, papers, including: *Chemistry of Cooking and Cleaning* 1882, *Food Materials and Their Adulterations* 1885, *First Lessons in Mineralogy* 1885, coauthor: *Home Sanitation* 1887; buried in Christ Churchyard, Gardiner.

Richards, Henry 1848–1949, born: Gardiner; son of an agent of Baring Brothers, London, and founder of Richards Paper Co., Gardiner, brother of Robert Hallowell Richards; attended Temple School, Brighton, England, Wellington College, Hampshire, England, Dr. Humphrey's School and Miss Dixwell's School, Cambridge, Massachusetts; A.B. Harvard College 1869, postgraduate study at Massachusetts Institute of Technology; employed by the architectural firm of Ware & Van Brunt, Boston, to 1876; returned to Gardiner, where he practiced independently; took over the management of the Richards Paper Co. 1885, continuing until 1900, when it was sold to International Paper Co.; designed private residences in Bar Harbor, Beverly, Massachusetts, three master's houses for Groton Academy, the Jacobean house for William Amory Gardner which became College Hall of Endicott Junior College, Prides Crossing, Massachusetts, the public library and grammar school in Gardiner, the monument for the 19th Maine Volunteers at Gettysburg; founded, with his wife, Laura Richards, Camp Merryweather, one of the first summer camps in the country, at North Belgrade 1900, active in its management to 1933; illustrated *Sketches and Scraps* by Laura Richards; on his one hundredth birthday had his first exhibition of his paintings, at the Gardiner Public Library, later, the paintings were exhibited at Bowdoin College; author: *Ninety Years On* 1940, several pamphlets, including: *The First Slow Sand Filter in Maine, The League of Nations*; president: Maine Public Health Association 1924–39, vice president, president: Gardiner General Hospital, chairman: Gardiner Water District, member: Gardiner School Committee; husband of Laura Richards, brother of Robert Hallowell Richards, who also lived to be 101 years old.

Richards, Laura Elizabeth Howe 1850–1943, born: Boston, Massachusetts;  daughter of Samuel Gridley and Julia Ward Howe, the author of the words to the patriotic song *The Battle Hymn of the Republic*; educated privately, Litt.D. (Hon.) Bates College, University of Maine; married Henry Richards 1871, removed, with him to Gardiner 1876; first published in *St. Nicholas Magazine*, first female to receive a Pulitzer Prize; author: *Sketches and Scraps* 1881, *The Joyous Story of Toto* 1885, *Hildegarde; A Story for Girls* 1889, *In My Nursery* 1890, *Hildegard's Home* 1892, *Melody* 1893, *Glimpses of the French Court; Sketches from French History* 1893, *When I Was Your Age* 1893, *Narcissa* 1894, *Marie* 1894, *Five Minute Stories* 1895, *Nautilus* 1895, *Hildegarde's Neighbors: A Story for Girls* 1895, *Jim of Hellas; or, In Durrance Vile: Bathesda Pool* 1895, *Isla Heron* 1896, *Some Say: Neighbors in Cyprus* 1896, *Three Margarets* 1897, *Hildegarde's Harvest* 1897, *Love and Rocks* 1898, *Rosin the Beau: A Sequel to Melody and Marie* 1898, *Margaret Montfort* 1898, *Quicksilver Sue* 1899, *Peggy* 1899, *Chop-Chin and the Golden Dragon* 1899, *For Tommy, and Other Stories* 1900, *Snow-White: or, The House in the Wood* 1900, *Rita* 1900, *Geoffrey Strong* 1901, *Fernley House* 1901, *The Hurdy-Gurdy* 1902, *Captain January* 1902, which later became a movie with Shirley Temple, *Mrs. Tree* 1902, *The Golden Windows: A Book of Fables for Young and Old* 1903, *The Green Satin Gown* 1903, *More Five Minute Stories* 1903, *The Merryweathers* 1904, *Mrs. Tree's Will* 1905, *The Armstrongs* 1905, *The Pico* 1906, *The Silver Crown: Another Book of Fables* 1906, *Grandmother: The Story of a Life That Never Was Lived* 1907, *Five Mice in a Mouse-Trap* 1908, *The Wooing of Calvin Parks* 1908, *The Pig Brother, and Other Fables and Stories; A Supplementary Reader for the Fourth School Year* 1908, *A Happy Little Time: A Partly True Story for Children of Betty's Age* 1910, *Up to Calvin's* 1910, *On Board the Mary Sands* 1911, *Miss Jimmy* 1913, *Three Minute Stories* 1914, *Julia Ward Howe, 1819–1910* (for which Richards was accorded the Pulitzer Prize) 1915, *The Pig Brother Play-Book* 1915, *Elizabeth Fry: The Angel of the Prisons* 1916, *Abigal Adams and Her Times* 1917, *To Arms!: Songs of the Great War* 1917, *Pippin: A Wandering Flame* 1917, *A Daughter of Jehu* 1918, *Joan of Arc* 1919, *Honor Bright: Story for Girls* 1920, *In Blessed Cyrus* 1921, *The Squire* 1923, *The Beginnings of Maine* 1924, *Star Bright: A Sequel to Captain January* 1927, *Laura Bridgman: The Story of an Opened Door* 1928, *Stepping Westward* 1931, *Tirra Lirra, Rhymes Old and New* 1932, *Merry-Go-Round: New Rhymes and Old* 1935, *Please! Rhymes of Protest* 1936, *Harry in England: Being the Partly True Adventures of H.R. in the Year 1857* 1937, *My Boston* 1937, *I Have A Song To Sing You: Still More Rhymes* 1938, *What Shall the Children Read?* 1939, *Laura E. Richards and Gardiner* 1940; founder of the Gardiner chapter of the American Red Cross, the first in Maine; founded the Gardiner Public Library

1884; founder, chairman: Women's Philanthropic Union 1895–1921; volunteer visitor: Maine State Hospital for the Insane, Maine State Prison, Thomaston, Soldiers' Home, Togus.

Richards, Robert Hallowell 1844–1945, born: Gardiner; son of an agent for Baring Brothers, brother of Henry Richards; B.S. Massachusetts Institute of Technology (first graduating class) 1868, L.L.D. (Hon.) University of Missouri 1908; assistant in chemistry: Massachusetts Institute of Technology 1868–69, instructor in assaying and qualitative analysis 1869–70, assistant professor: analytical chemistry 1870–71, professor of mineralogy and assaying; developed mining and metallurgical laboratories 1871–72, professor of mining engineering 1873–84, professor of mining engineering and metallurgy 1884–1914; invented: a jet aspirator for chemistry and physical laboratories 1873, a prism for stadia surveying 1890, an ore separator for the Great Lakes copper mills 1881, an iron ore separator 1900, designed and installed apparatus for Massachusetts Cremation Society; fellow: American Academy of Arts and Sciences; author: *Ore Dressing* (volumes one and two) 1903, *Ore Dressing* (volumes three and four) 1909, an autobiography *Robert Hallowell Richards His Mark* 1936; husband of Ellen Henrietta Swallow Richards; buried in Christ Churchyard, Gardiner.

Ricker, Hiram 1809–1893, born: Poland Spring; grandson of Jabez Ricker, who, in 1794, purchased 300 acres in Poland, from the Shakers; son of Wentworth Ricker, who opened the Wentworth Ricker Inn, later Mansion House on the road from Portland to Montréal 1797; Hiram Ricker began his career in a clothing store in Boston but was obliged by his father's failing health to return to Poland; the Mansion House had a natural spring which became famous as the purest natural water known, and the most efficient natural diuretic known for its wonderful stimulating effect upon the kidneys, began shipping three-gallon demijohns of water, via stage, to Portland, for which he received fifteen cents 1859; when the Mansion House grew too small, Ricker erected the Poland Spring House 1872, a sprawling Victorian confection and increased the acreage to 4,000 acres; father of Hiram Weston Ricker.

Ricker, Hiram Weston 1857–1930, born: Poland; son of Hiram Ricker; attended local public school, Hebron Academy and Maine Wesleyan and Westbrook seminaries, A.M. Bates College 1927; during his summers, drove a team and wagon into Lewiston and Auburn every other day to sell jugs of Poland Spring water; after completing his education, joined his father and brothers in the management of Poland Spring, treasurer 1894–1912, 1919–23, vice president 1923–30; as soon as time would allow, began promoting Maine as a summer resort, organized the Maine Publicity Board and the New England Council 1922; active in the affairs of the Maine and New Hampshire hotel associations, the Maine Automobile Association, the Maine Historical Association, and the American Forestry Association; actively opposed the spoilation of Maine's natural resources, i.e., the cutting of forests, the erection of dams, the construction of odorous paper mills, &c.; politically allied with Bert Fernald and Percival Baxter; vice president: Manufacturers National Bank, Lewiston, from 1896; at the request of the governor of Maine, reorganized and rebuilt the Maine Reformatory for Boys, removing, in the process, all barred windows and other physical aspects that resembled a prison, put the boys on their honor to stay put, and despite intense criticism, the results proved gratifying; reorganized and put on a sound financial footing the Maine State Sanitarium for Tuberculars, whose condition had become deplorable 1900–10.

Ricker, Nathan Clifford 1843–1924, born: Acton; son of a farmer, attended high school in Springvale, taught school for a few terms; learned the carpenter's trade; learning that a state university had opened in Urbana, Illinois, that offered certificates in architecture, he journeyed west, B.S. University of Illinois 1872 (as such, was the first certified college-trained architect in the United States), M.Arch. 1878, D.Arch (Hon.) 1909; after receiving his undergraduate degree, traveled to Germany where he was a student at the Prussian College of Architecture, later traveled extensively on the continent; as instructor, completely reorganized the curriculum of the department, assistant professor, professor in charge of Department of Architecture, University of Illinois 1873–1911; dean: College of Engineering 1878–1905; served as architect of the university; chairman: Illinois State Commission on Building Rules; author: *Elemental Graphic Statics and Construction of Trussed Roofs* 1885, *Roofs* 1911, *Simplified Formulas* 1913.

Ricker, Robert Edwin 1828–94, born: Portland; left school at age sixteen and became a surveyor on the Atlantic & St. Lawrence Railroad line 1845; located and constructed the Great Falls & Conway Railroad 1849; in charge of construction of extension of railroad from Portland to Yarmouth; located and constructed the White Mountain carriage road; surveyed the Utica to Binghamton line 1854; superintendent: Detroit, Toledo, and Monroe line 1856; superintendent and chief engineer: New Albany & Chicago Railroad to 1861; superintendent: Terre Haute & Indianapolis Railroad; in the Civil War: colonel, USA, military supervisor of Indiana railroads; superintendent: Pennsylvania Railroad 1866; superintendent and chief engineer: New Jersey Central Railroad 1867; judge of machinery: Philadelphia Exposition 1876; general manager: Gilbert and Rush locomotive works, Troy, New York, 1884; general superintendent and chief engineer: Denver & Rio Grande Railroad, superintendent: St. Louis, Iron Mountain & Southern Railroad Co. 1888–93.

Roberts, Kenneth  1885–1957, born: Kennebunk; son of a businessman; A.B. Cornell University 1908, Litt.D. and honorary membership in ΦBK Dartmouth College 1934, Colby College 1935, Middlebury College 1938, Bowdoin College 1938, Northeastern University 1945; editor in chief : *Cornell Widow* 1905–08, reporter: *Boston Post* 1909-17; member: editorial staff of *Life* 1915–18, *Puck* 1916–17, foreign correspondent *Saturday Evening Post* 1921–26; in World War I: captain, USA, intelligence section, Siberian Expedition 1918–19; author: *The Brotherhood of Man* (a play) 1919, *Europe's Morning After* 1921, *Why Europe Leaves Home* 1922, said to be partially responsible for the passage of more restrictive immigration laws, *Sun Hunting* 1923, *Black Magic* 1924, *Concentrating New England: A Study of Calvin Coolidge* 1924, *Florida Loafing* 1925, *Florida* 1926, coauthor, with Booth Tarkington: *The Collector's Whatnot* 1926, author: *Antiquamania* 1928, *Trending into Maine* 1935, *For Author Only and Other Gloomy Essays* 1935, *It Must Be Your Tonsils* 1936, *March to Quebec* 1939, *The Kenneth Roberts Reader* 1945, *I Wanted to Write* 1949, *Don't Say That About Maine* 1950, *Henry Gross and His Dowsing Rod* 1951, *The Seventh Sense* 1953, *Water Unlimited* 1957, *The Battle of Cowpens* 1958; with his wife, translated Moreau de St. Mery's *American Journey 1793–98* 1947; his historical novels, noted for their historical accuracy, and for which he is best known, composed in Porto Santo Stefano, Italy: *Arundel* 1930, *Rabble in Arms* 1933, *Captain Caution* 1934 (made into movie), *Northwest Passage* 1937 (made into movie), *Oliver Wiswell* 1940, *Lydia Bailey* 1947 (made into movie).

Robinson, Edwin Arlington 1869–1935, born: Head Tide, Alna; descendant of the colonial poetess Anne Bradstreet; son of a lumber dealer, banker, postmaster, and member of the Maine legislature; removed, with his family, at an early age, to Gardiner, began to write verse at age eleven; graduate: Gardiner High School, attended Harvard College 1891–93; printed, at his own expense, *The Torrent and the Night Before* 1896, which received some positive reviews but no financial gain, later, with the addition of sixteen new poems, reprinted as *Children of the Night* 1897, obtained a clerkship at a Harvard University office but left after a few months and made his way to New York, where he held a number of menial jobs; published *Captain Craig* 1902, a searching story of an old derelict rescued by a group of young men in Tilbury Town to whom he gave philosophical advice; while working as a timekeeper on a subway construction job in New York, his work came to the attention of Theodore Roosevelt, through his son, a student at Groton Academy, where a teacher, Henry Richards, son of Laura Richards of Gardiner, had assigned the poems of his friend, Robinson, to the president's son; Roosevelt wrote a favorable review in *The Outlook*, invited the somewhat startled Robinson to the White House, offered him a foreign service appointment in either Canada or Mexico, which Robinson declined but agreed to accept a position in the office of collector of U.S. customs, in New York 1905; this tranquil period produced his *The Town Down the River* 1910, which contains his poem *Miniver Cheevey*; much against his will, he agreed to visit the MacDowell Colony in Peterborough, New Hampshire, 1911, which he found so congenial that he returned every summer of his life; in this period he produced two plays *Van Zorn* 1914, and *The Porcupine* 1915, later returned to poetry with *The Man Against the Sky* 1916, *Merlin* 1917, *Lancelote* 1920; his fiftieth birthday in 1919 was celebrated across the United States, one of the few occasions in history where an American poet had a nationwide commemoration during his lifetime; his *Collected Poems* 1921, received the Pulitzer Prize, as did *The Man Who Died Twice* 1924, as did *Tristram* 1927, another presentation of the Arthurian legend, which many consider his best work; his other works include: *The Three Taverns* 1920, which portrays a group of historical characters including Saint Paul, Lazarus, Aaron Burr, and John Brown, *Avon's Harvest* 1921, which he called his dime novel in verse, *Roman Bartholow* 1923, *Dionysius in Doubt* 1925, *Sonnets* 1928, *Cavender's House* 1929, for which the National Institute of Arts and Letters awarded him its gold medal, *The Glory of the Nightingales* 1930, *Matthias at the Door* 1931, *Nicodemus* 1932, *Taliter* 1933, *Amaranth* 1934, *King Jaspar* 1935; received honorary doctorates from Yale University in 1922 and Bowdoin College in 1924, refused to be doctored further, declining to accept similar honors from many colleges and universities; buried in the Robinson family plot, Oak Grove Cemetery, Gardiner.

Robinson, Frank Mason 1843– ?, born: Corinth; after service in Union Army during the Civil War, returned to Maine where he was associated with D. D. Doe in the management of a department store; removed to Iowa, where he built the first house in Sibley; later, representing a chromatic printing machine manufacturer, approached John Pemberton, of Atlanta, inventor of Pemberton's Coca Wine; in 1886, Robinson purchased a part of the company, served as bookkeeper; devised the name Coca-Cola and, because of his flowing penmanship, created the now-familiar script logo; approached Asa Candler (later president and CEO of Coca-Cola, Inc.) and advised him to purchase the company, remained with the company for many years; under Candler, became chief of advertising; devised the first direct-mail campaign for a beverage.

Robinson, Franklin Clement 1852–1910, born: East Orrington; A.B. Bowdoin College 1873, A.M. 1876, student in chemistry: Harvard University 1876–78, L.L.D. Bowdoin College 1903; instructor in chemistry: Bowdoin College 1874–78, Josiah Little professor of natural science 1878–85, professor of chemistry and mineralogy from 1885; Maine state assayer 1877–1909, Maine state geologist from 1908; author: *The Metals* 1878, *Qualitative Analysis* 1897, contributor of numerous papers to proceedings of the American Public Health Association, the Maine Medical Association, the American Association for the Advancement of Science, U.S. government reports, *American Chemical Journal,* &c.; president: American Public Health Association 1906; his researches in chemistry were along the lines of the improvement of public health, such as the adulteration of foods, disinfectants, sanitary work, he was considered to be the leading expert on disinfectants in the country, originated a method of disinfection that became ubiquitous, appeared as chemical witness in numerous murder and civil trials in Maine.

Robinson, George Foster 1832–1907, born: Island Falls; in the Civil War: enlisted as a private in the 8th Maine Volunteer Infantry 1863, after becoming invalid, detailed to act as nurse and guard to Secretary of State William Seward, who had been badly injured in a carriage accident 1865, foiled the attack of Lewis Powell (a co-conspirator of John Wilkes Booth) on the night of 14 April 1865; after Powell stabbed two others upon entering Seward's residence, Robinson made a determined attempt to prevent Powell from entering Seward's room, despite being stabbed several times with Powell's Bowie knife, he managed to thwart Seward's murder; subsequent to the court martial of the conspirators, the court gave to Robinson the knife used in the attack, later, he was awarded a Congressional Gold Medal in 1871; commissioned major, USA, served as paymaster 1879–96, promoted to lieutenant colonel on the retired list 1904.

Robinson, Helen Ring ?–1923, born: Eastport; student at Wellesley College; editor: *Rocky Mountain News* 1906–12; member: Colorado Senate 1913–17, first female elected to the Colorado Senate, second female in the United States elected to a state senate, drafted legislation to allow for female jurors, also a bill to allow for a minimum wage for women; appointed by Secretary of the Navy Josephus Daniels to Navy Department Commission of Training Camp Activities 1917; member: Women's Council Defense for Colorado 1917–19; author: *Uncle Tom's Cabin for Children* 1907, *Preparing Women for Citizenship* 1918.

Robinson, Thomas Pendelton 1878–1954, born: Calais; son of a logger; attended Chauncey Hall School, Boston; studied architecture at Massachusetts Institute of Technology with the class of 1899; associated with several architectural firms in Boston, including Sawyer & Sylvester, Coolidge & Carlson, Guy Lowell, Fox & Gale to 1908; formed a partnership with Richard Derby, styled Derby & Robinson, Boston, to 1929; specialized in the design of residences in early American style, notably the house in Cambridge, Massachusetts, that came to house the Harvard University Press and the headmaster's house at Milton Academy; restored the Governor Winslow House in Marshfield; prepared designs for the New England Sanatorium, Rutland, Massachusetts, the Henrietta D. Goodall Hospital, Sanford, First Church of Christ, Scientist, Concord, Massachusetts, schools in Winchester, Hingham, Sandwich, and Bedford, Massachusetts; after the dissolution of his partnership, devoted himself to writing; studied drama with George P. Baker at Harvard University 1912–24, joined his famous 47 Workshop, where he was technical director of stage management, design, costumes, and lighting; his first play produced was *The Rebound* put on by the 47 Workshop and later produced in New York under the title of *Artistic Temperament* 1924, three other of his plays had New York productions: *Skylark* produced by Richard Herndon at the Belmont Theatre 1921, starring Gene Lockhart, *Brook*, produced by John Mckee at the Greenwich Village Theatre 1926, *Be Your Age*, produced by Herndon at the Belmont 1929, starring Spring Byington, *The Hunchbuckle* produced by the 47 Workshop 1920; also contributed many articles on architecture, published seventeen books, including a number for children, two of his published plays were: *Darick Clausen* 1931, *The Wing in on the Bird* 1943, coauthor (with his wife) *Houses in America* 1936, *Your Own House* 1941, both of which were illustrated with his own pencil drawings, his children's books included: *Trigger John's Son* 1934, *Buttons* 1938, *Mr. Red Squirrel* 1943, *Greylock and the Robins* 1946, *Lost Dog Jerry* 1952; under the general title of *Players' Shakespeare* he edited, with notes, glossary, and drawings for settings and costumes, *As You Like It*, *A Midsummer's Night Dream*, *The Taming of the Shrew* 1941, *Julius Caesar*, *The Tempest*, and *MacBeth* 1942; prepared editions of several other Shakespeare plays that remained unpublished at his death, as were many of his own plays, libretti, lyrics, and articles; received an award from the Boston Park Commission for his design of the Parkman Bandstand in Boston Common 1910, the Harvard-Morosco Award for his play *The Copy* 1921, the American Drama League Award for his play *Darick Clausen* 1931, *New York Herald-Tribune* Spring Festival Award for his book *Pete* 1941.

Rockefeller, Nelson Aldrich 1908–79, born: Bar Harbor; A.B. Dartmouth College ΦBK 1930; director: Rockefeller Center, Inc. 1931–58, president 1938–45, 1948–53, chairman 1945–53, 1956–58; president and chairman of the board: Museum of Modern Art, New York 1932–75; director: Office of Inter-American Affairs 1940–44; assistant secretary of state for Latin American Affairs 1944-45; chairman: Presidential Advisory Commission on Governmental Organization 1953–58; undersecretary of the Department of Health, Education, and Welfare 1953–54; special assistant to the president for foreign affairs 1954–55; governor of New York (Republican) 1959–73; unsuccessful candidate for the Republican nomination for president 1964, 1968, 1972; vice president of the United States 1974–77; author: *The Future of Federalism* 1962, *Unity, Freedom and Peace* 1968, *Our Environment Can Be Saved* 1970; buried in the Rockefeller Cemetery, adjacent to Sleepy Hollow Cemetery, North Tarrytown, New York.

Rockwell, George Lincoln 1918–1967, born: Bloomington, Illinois; son of Doc Rockwell, a vaudevillian; raised in Southport; graduate: Hebron Academy, A.B. Brown University 1940; during World War II, served in USN as an anti-submarine pilot in the South Atlantic and Pacific, discharged as lieutenant commander; founded

Lady magazine 1954; founded: World Union of Free Enterprise Socialists 1956, founded: National Committee to Free America from Jewish Domination, which shortly became the American Nazi Party 1959; author: *The World This Time* 1962, advocated the sterilization of all Jews, confiscation of their property, and the deportation of American blacks to Africa; assassinated by a member of his coterie.

Rogers, Edith Nourse 1881–1960, born: Saco; daughter of a woolen manufacturer; student: Rogers Hall School, Lowell, Massachusetts, Madame Julien's School, Paris, France, A.M. (Hon.) Bates College, Tufts University, L.L.D. George Washington College of Law, Lowell Technological Institute; married John Jacob Rogers 1907, a lawyer who was elected to the U.S. House of Representatives representing the Fifth District of Massachusetts 1912; during World War I, joined the Women's Overseas Service League, representative in France, inspector of field hospitals; President Harding named her his personal representative in charge of assisting disabled veterans, continued to serve under Presidents Coolidge and Hoover, visited every military hospital in the United States; on her recommendation, a number of reforms and improvements were made; Republican presidential elector 1924; with the death of her husband in 1925, she ran for his seat and won, becoming the first female representative from New England, served 1925–60 (Republican), twice chairman: Committee on Veterans Affairs, helped draft and a prime sponsor of the G.I. Bill of Rights, introduced the legislation establishing the Women's Army Corps 1942; early appalled by Nazi persecution of minorities, broke with her party over the Neutrality Act 1937, voted for the Selective Service Act 1941, supported the establishment of the United Nations; reelected nineteen times, often unopposed, even in the depth of the Great Depression; on several occasions, her only campaign expense was her filing fee; her thirty-five years in the House of Representatives is the longest term for any female to date; enormously popular with veterans' groups, she was the subject of a nose artist on a B-17 bomber; buried in Lowell (Massachusetts) Cemetery; the Edith Nourse Rogers Memorial Veterans Hospital, in Bedford, Massachusetts, was named in her honor.

Rogers, John Rankin 1838–1911, born: Brunswick; clerk/apprentice in a drugstore in Boston 1852-56, manager of a drugstore in Jackson, Mississippi, 1856, schoolteacher and farmer in Illinois 1860–66, farmer and druggist 1866–76, removed to Burton, Kansas, 1876, farmer, became a deeply committed Populist, organizer: Farmers' Alliance, left the Republican party for the Greenback party, in which he subsequently held local offices 1884, left the Greenback party for the Union Labor party 1887, founder, editor: *Kansas Commoner*, Newton, a newspaper founded to support the Farmers' Alliance; after he became insolvent and lost his farm, removed to Washington State, settled in Puyallup, where he became a real estate broker and merchant; organized the Farmers' Alliance in Washington, wrote articles and pamphlets in support of the People's party, opened a grocery which became a center of Populist activity; member: Washington House of Representatives 1894-96; championed the rights of miners, who sought a proper ventilation law, author of the measure known as the Barefoot Schoolboy Law, requiring a tax of six dollars for each child of school age; elected fourth governor of Washington (Populist) 1896–1901, succeeded John Harte McGraw; died in office, buried in Puyallup; author: *The Irrepressible Conflict, or An American System of Money* 1892, *Reformers I Have Known* 1894, *Home for the Homeless* 1895, *Free Land: The Remedy for Involuntary Poverty, Social Unrest and the Woes of Labor* 1897, *Looking Forward; or the Story of an American Farm* 1898, *Life* 1899, *The Inalienable Rights of Man* 1900, "The Source of Strength" left in manuscript at the time of his death.

Rollins, Charles Cogswell 1832–1914, born: Lebanon; graduate: Parsonfield Academy, apprenticed to a machinist in Somersworth, New Hampshire, later was employed by the Great Falls Manufacturing Co., Somersworth; received part of his salary in castings for his first steam engine, the profits from which he employed in establishing his own company, in Boston, where he manufactured steam equipment, primarily hoists; first to employ steampower for stevedore work on the wharves of Boston, also devised a steam wood-sawing machine.

Rollins, Weld Allen 1874–1928, born: Portland; son of an insurance man; A.B. Dartmouth College 1897, L.L.B. Harvard University Law School 1900; practiced in Boston from 1900, partner: Currier, Rollins, Young, and Pillsbury to 1914; counsel for the Old Colony Trust Co., the American Trust Co., United States Trust Co. of New York, Boston counsel for the General Motors Corp.; an organizer of the Five Cent Savings Bank of Boston; author: *The Fertility of College Graduates* 1929; secretary: Dartmouth class of 1897; treasurer: Dartmouth Loan Association; introduced the sport of skiing to Dartmouth, had several sets of skis made in Portland, from specifications derived from a book on the subject; member: Appalachian Mountain Club.

Ropes, Hannah Chandler 1809–63, born: New Gloucester; daughter of Peleg Chandler; married William Henry Ropes, principal of Foxcroft Academy 1832–35, 1834; principal: Milton (Massachusetts) Academy, later Waltham (Massachusetts) High School; after her husband left for Florida in 1847, she was left to her own devices; removed to Lawrence, Kansas, where her son, Edward Ropes, had homesteaded and was a supporter of the Free Soil movement; living there in a period of great unrest, she often kept loaded firearms at the ready in case of attack by pro-slavery mobs; soon after her return to Maine, Lawrence was sacked; her book *Six Months in Kansas* 1857, was a compilation of her letters home and was well-received by the Abolitionist movement; during the Civil War, worked as a nurse in Washington, until she died of pneumonia; eulogized by Senator Charles Sumner, who also arranged for the return of her body to the family plot in New Gloucester.

Eminent Mainers

Rose, Daniel 1772–1833, born: Branford, Connecticut; A.B. Yale College 1791; settled in Alna, practiced medicine in Boothbay, later in Wiscasset; member: Massachusetts House of Representatives 1808, 1815; during the War of 1812, served as an engineer in the USA; delegate: Maine Constitutional Convention 1819; member: Maine Senate 1820–24, president 1822–24, became acting governor when Governor Benjamin Ames resigned 2 January 1822, served until 5 January 1822, when the governor-elect, Albion Parris, took office; first warden of the Maine State Prison, Thomaston 1823–28; Maine state land agent 1828–31; Bowdoin College overseer 1815–31.

Ross, John Alexander, Jr. 1878– ?, born: Belfast; B.S. Massachusetts Institute of Technology 1901, Sc.D Clarkson College of Technology, Potsdam, New York, 1933, L.L.D. St. Lawrence University 1942; ship draftsman: Bureau of Construction and Repair, U.S. Navy 1901–05; instructor, warship design: Massachusetts Institute of Technology 1905–07, instructor, architecture: University of Michigan 1907–08, instructor in mechanical engineering: Case School of Applied Science 1908–09, machine design: Cornell University 1909–10, professor of mechanical engineering: Lafayette College 1910–11, in charge of Department of Engineering, Clarkson University 1911-40, dean of administration 1929–40, president 1940–48; member: American Society of Mechanical Engineers, The Newcomen Society.

Ross, Lewis H. 1901–69, born: Auburn, son of a merchant; attended public schools in Lewiston, Bowdoin College 1919–21, A.B. Dartmouth College φBK 1923, M.B.A. 1924; associated with Merchandising Corp., New York, a central purchasing and research association for a group of leading department stores to 1926; partner: E. M. Chase Co., Manchester, New Hampshire, the state's largest furniture store, sole owner 1937, president 1938–65, sales were mainly by house-to-house salesmen throughout New England, often selling on credit extended by the company; an incorporator: Amoskeag Savings Bank, Manchester; sponsor of the New Hampshire Symphony Orchestra; president: Manchester Jewish Committee; his lifelong interest in music began at an early age, had his own orchestra while in high school, active in Dartmouth musical clubs, concert pianist for the Dartmouth Glee Club.

Ross, Louis 1859– ?, born: Bangor; student: English High School, Boston; removed to Mexico to work in the mines of Cuishuiriachic and Santa Eulalia, controlled by Kidder, Peabody & Co., Boston 1881; also employed by Thomas Nickerson, builder of the Mexican Central Railroad; managing director: San Luis Co., Durango, a mine with 1,200 operatives 1902–06; associated with Albert C. Burrage of Boston, delegated to investigate mining potential in Chile and Peru 1910; discovered the atacamite deposit of copper at Chuquicamata, Chile, 1911, the largest copper deposit in the world, capitalized by the Guggenheims as the Chile Copper Co.; member: American Institute of Mining Engineers, frequent contributor to scholarly and popular literature on mining.

Ross, Morrill 1895–1960, born: Portland; commissioned second lieutenant, USA, field artillery 1917, in World War I: served with the 17th Field Artillery, American Expeditionary Forces 1917–19; served as an instructor at the Field Artillery School 1923–27, graduate: Command and General Staff School 1936, commanding officer: 66th Field Artillery 1941–42, promoted to brigadier general, USA, 1942; assigned to the 10th Armored Division 1942–43, commanding general: 26th Infantry Division Artillery 1943–45, retired 1950; decorations include: two Silver Stars, the Legion of Merit, two Bronze Stars.

Rowse, Samuel Worcester 1822–1907, born: Bath; removed, with his family, to Augusta; apprenticed to an engraver, his first work was for bank notes; removed to Boston to learn lithography in the shop of Tappan & Bradford, settled in Boston 1852–80, kept a studio on Tremont Street; his first identified work is a portrait of Richard Fletcher, did the illustrations for *This, That, and the Other* by Louise Chandler Moulton 1856, his budding career on the stage met with failure, redirected his efforts to portraiture, boarded with the Thoreaus during the summer of 1854, became Henry David Thoreau's constant companion on his rambles and produced the now-famous drawing of him during this period; hired by Charles Eliot Norton to do a portrait of Ralph Waldo Emerson, which received high praise and which now hangs in Emerson's house in Concord; grew to have an international reputation for his portraits and drawings of James Russell Lowell, Henry Wadsworth Longfellow, Nathaniel Hawthorne, and others; journeyed to England and spent time with John Ruskin 1872; closest friend and adviser of Eastman Johnson; removed from Boston to New York in 1880, died in Morristown, New Jersey.

Ruggles, John 1789–1874, born: Westboro, Massachusetts; A.B. Brown University 1813; member: Massachusetts bar, practiced in Skowhegan 1815, Thomaston 1817; member: Massachusetts House of Representatives 1813–20, speaker: Maine House of Representatives 1825–29, 1831; associate justice: Maine Supreme Judicial Court 1831–34; member: U.S. Senate 1835–41 (Jacksonian), chairman: Committee on Patents, framer of bill for reorganization of U.S. Patent Office; after term: inventor (his patent for an improvement on railroad traction bears the number 1, that is, the first patent issued after the disastrous fire of 1836 destroyed the U.S. Patent Office), orator, writer; buried in Elm Grove Cemetery, Thomaston.

Ruohomaa, Kosti 1914–61, born: Quincy, Massachusetts, raised from an early age on Dodge Mountain, Rockland; after graduating from Rockland High School migrated to Boston to study art; commercial artist in Boston and New York City; animator for Walt Disney; photographer for *Life* magazine and others; his portraits of mid-century Maine life a singular achievement; buried in Achorn Cemetery, Rockland.

Russell, Helen Gertrude 1901–68. born: Gorham; A.B. Wellesley College ΦBK 1921, A.M. Columbia 1924, Ph.D. Radcliffe College 1932; teacher in Mt. Holly, New Jersey, High School 1921–23, Horace Mann School for Girls, New York 1923–27, instructor in mathematics: Wellesley College 1928–29, 1932–36, assistant professor 1936–45, associate professor 1945–51, professor 1951–68, Helen Day Gould professor of mathematics; buried in Gorham.

Russell, Osbourne 1814–65, born: Hallowell; fur trapper in Wisconsin and Minnesota 1830–33, joined Nathaniel J. Wyeth's second expedition to the Rockies, participated in the building of Fort Hall, Idaho, 1834, went to Oregon with Dr. Elijah White's emigrant party 1842; member: executive committee, Oregon provisional government 1844; gold prospector in California 1848–49; operated two trading vessels between Sacramento and Portland, Oregon, 1855; his journal published as *A Journal of a Trapper or Nine Years in the Rocky Mountains 1834–43* 1914.

Russell, Sol Smith 1838–1902, born: Brunswick; named for his uncle, Sol Smith, the actor; attended public schools in St. Louis, Missouri, and Jacksonville, Illinois; drummer boy in Union Army, which he left in Cairo, Illinois, where he sang in a theatre, acted small parts, and beat the drum in the orchestra, attempted to become a slack wire walker, but a fall decided him in favor of remaining an actor, secured an engagement in St. Louis as second low comedian at De Bars Theatre, made a western tour with the Berger family, later, he was a member of a stock company at the Chestnut Street Theatre, Philadelphia; appeared first in New York 1871, at Lina Edwins Theatre, returned to New York 1874, played for more than six months at the Olympic Theatre as a variety of characters, joined Augustin Daly's company, won particular praise for his Trip in *School for Scandal*; with Frederick Berger as his manager and with his own company, became a star in *Edgewood Folks*, which ran for 1,500 performances over a period of five years; in each performance, sang seven songs and made ten costume changes; he starred again in *Country Editor* and *Felix McCusick* 1887, *Pa* and *Bewitched* 1890, *A Poor Relation* by Edward Kidder, *The Tale of a Coat* by Dion Boucicault, remodeled into *April Weather* by Clyde Fitch, *Peaceful Valley*, *Uncle Dick*, *A Bachelor's Romance*, *Hon. John Grigsby*, *The Heir-at-Law*, *The Rivals*; a collector of books and autographs; member: Players Club, Century Association, New York.

Russwurm, John 1799–1851, born: Port Antonio, Jamaica; the son of a white planter and a black former slave, removed with his father to Back Cove (Westbrook) 1812; graduated from Hebron Academy 1819; teacher at a school for black children operated by Primus Hall, Boston, 1819–24; A.B. Bowdoin College 1826, Russwurm was the second black graduate of an American College, invited to join the Athenean Society by its president, Nathaniel Hawthorne, he was the first black to join an American college fraternity; founded and edited *Freedom's Journal*, the first black-owned newspaper in the United States 1827–29; secretary of the African Dorcas

Associates; superintendent: public schools of Liberia 1829–36, published and edited Liberia's first newspaper *Liberia Herald* 1830–36, secretary of Liberia 1830–36, governor of the Maryland Colony 1836–51.

Ryder, Calvin 1810–90, born: Orrington; architect; master of the Greek Revival style, his work includes the John P. White House and Williamson House, both in Belfast; the Blake House in Bangor is the first building in the Mansard style in Maine; later practiced in Boston.

Sabine, Lorenzo 1803–77, born: New Concord (later Lisbon), New Hampshire; removed with his parents to Boston 1811, later Hampden 1814; removed to Eastport 1818, employed as a clerk, later pursued mercantile activities; editor: *Eastport Sentinel*, founder: Eastport Lyceum; incorporator of Eastport Academy, Eastport Atheneum; member: Maine House of Representatives 1833, 1834; deputy collector of customs in Eastport 1841–43; removed to Framingham, Massachusetts, 1848; member from the Ninth District of Massachusetts: U.S. House of Representatives 1852–53; removed to Roxbury, Massachusetts; secretary: Boston Board of Trade, special agent: U.S. Treasury Department; buried in Hillside Cemetery, Eastport.

Salm-Salm, Princess, née Agnes Elisabeth Winona Leclerque Joy 1840–1912, born: Madawaska (some sources suggest Thetford, Vermont, or Québec); first achieved notoriety as a circus performer, riding a galloping horse, while standing on its back, playing an accordion; later served as a nurse in Washington, D.C., during the Civil War; attracted the attentions of Felix Constantin Alexander Johann Nepomuk, Prince Salm-Salm, a Prussian cavalry officer who had come to the United States to obtain a commission in the Union Army; after their marriage 20 August 1862, she assisted him in becoming colonel of the 68th New York Volunteer Infantry; accompanied him to the headquarters of the Army of the Potomac where she quickly became a great favorite, due, in part, to her extraordinary horsewomanship and also to her musicality, some sources suggest that she was capable of even coaxing the very-bad tempered General George Gordon Meade into song, later Prince Salm-Salm served under General William T. Sherman in the Atlanta Campaign, where he was brevetted brigadier general, USV, later served as military commander of the District of Atlanta; after the end of the Civil War, journeyed with her husband to Mexico, where he entered the service of the Emperor Maximilian, becoming chief military aide 1866, after he was captured by Mexican forces at the battle of Queretare, the princess made her way to Jaurez, met with the Mexican leader and successfully begged for her husband's life, also attempted to bribe the authorities for the release of Maximilian, this incident has become part of Mexican folk mythology, as well as the subject a giant painting by Manuel Ocaranza; making their way to Germany, the prince served as major in the Queen Augusta Regiment of the Prussian Army, in the Franco-Prussian

War, killed at the battle of Gravelotte 18 August 1870; after her husband's death, the (now dowager) princess continued in work as a nurse, attracting the attention of Prince Otto von Bismarck, she was the first female to be awarded the Prussian Medal of Honor, she was also pensioned by Franz Joseph, emperor of Austria; after the war concluded, she journeyed to Rome to ask the pope's advice, the pope advised her that the contemplative life of a nunnery was probably not the best place for her; living in Germany for the remainder of her life, she visited the United States in 1900 to stir up support for the Boers of South Africa, dogging Winston Churchill, who had come to speak against the Boers; inducted into the New Jersey chapter of the Daughters of the American Revolution; she became a subject in several novels, as well as a figure in Franz Werfel's play *Juarez and Maximilian*; author: *Zehn Jahre Aus Meinem Leben* (English translation: *Ten Years in My Life*), two volumes, 1876.

Salzédo, Leon Carlos 1885–1961, born: Arcachon, France; studied music at the Bordeaux Conservatory 1891–94, winning first prize in piano, entered the Paris Conservatory, where his father was professor of voice; studied piano with Charles de Bériot in piano, winning first prize in 1901, also studied harp with Hasselmans; began his career as a concert harpist upon graduation, after playing in many European places, settled in New York city, serving as first harp in the Metropolitan Opera orchestra 1909–13; formed the Trio de Lutèce 1913; co-founder (with Edgar Varèse) of the modern music magazine *Eolian Review* 1923; became an American citizen 1923; held teaching positions at Curtis Institute and Juilliard Graduate School of Music; founded, in Camden, the Salzedo Harp Colony for teaching and performance 1931; designed a Salzedo model harp, capable of producing many hitherto unknown effects; author: *Modern Study of the Harp* 1921, *Method of the Harp* 1929, *The Art of Modulating* 1950; his compositions include numerous works for solo harp, multiple harps, harp and orchestra, &c.; died in Waterville.

Samoset c. 1590–c. 1653, born: Bristol; learned English from fishermen, befriended Pilgrims, introduced them to Squanto, who probably came from the Muscungus region, captured by Waymouth and returned to Maine by John Smith; Samoset made the first transfer of land in Maine: 12,000 acres to John Brown of New Harbor.

Sampson, Alden 1853–1925, born: Manchester; A.B. Haverford College 1873, A.M. 1876, A.B. Harvard College 1876, A.M. 1877, student at Harvard University Law School 1878–80; artist, explorer, game preserve expert: U.S. Biological Survey 1907; spoke for establishment of game refuges in national forests, lecturer on archaeology, literature, art, mountaineering, and life in the forest; prominent in the fight to preserve Hetch Hetchy; author: *Milton's Sonnets* 1886, *A Bear Hunt in the Sierras* 1895, *The Establishment of Game Refuges* 1900, *Essay on the Wild Life* 1905, *Sketches on Milton and an Essay on Poetry* 1912.

Sampson, Sarah Smith 1830–1907, born: Bath; wife of Charles A. L. Sampson, a ship carver, who, in the Civil War, enlisted in the 3rd Maine Volunteer Infantry Regiment (commanding officer: O. O. Howard); accompanying her husband, she worked as a nurse, first in hospitals in the Washington area, later, journeyed by boat to Fort Monroe, where she spent considerable time ministering to the wounded, subsequent to the Peninsula campaign; at White House Landing, found herself cut off by Confederate advances, losing all her supplies and personal goods; commissioned to operate the Maine Soldiers' Relief Association, often associated with the Maine Camp Hospital Association; nursed incessantly at Gettysburg for a month after the battle; her report is contained in *Report of the Adjutant General of the State of Maine 1864–65*; after the war, established the Bath Military and Naval Orphan Asylum, which after it came under Maine state control became the Bath Children's Home in 1919; often attended reunions of the 3rd Maine Volunteers; buried in Arlington National Cemetery.

Sanborn, James Solomon 1835–1919, born: Wales; with Caleb Chase formed Chase and Sanborn: importers, roasters and wholesalers of tea and coffee; bred coach horses on his farm in Poland.

Sanborn, John Albert 1901–66, born: Norway; B.S. University of Maine 1926, certificate of proficiency in electrical engineering, Westinghouse Electrical and Manufacturing Co. 1927, student: George Washington University law school 1928–29, L.L.B. New York University 1932, J.S.D. 1933, student: School of Accounting and Business Administration 1934–35; with Central Maine Power Co., Augusta 1922–25; apprentice: Department of General Engineering, later, graduate student, Science Research Laboratory, Westinghouse Electrical & Manufacturing Co., Pittsburgh 1926–27; assistant examiner: U.S. Patent Office 1928; Office of Judge Advocate General, War Department; technical advisor relative to aircraft and radio: German-Austrian Patent Claims Commission (Berlin, Vienna, Prague, Budapest, Amsterdam, London, Paris) 1928–29; director: patent research: Manufacturers' Aircraft Association, Inc., New York 1929–37, general manager from 1937, vice president from 1948; arbitrator for aircraft industry in proceedings under Patent Cross-License Agreement from 1931; consultant on patents and related subjects to Federal Aviation Commission 1935; president: Air Policy Commission 1947; fellow: Institute of Aeronautical Sciences.

Sanders, Henry Arthur 1868–1956, born: Livermore; A.B. University of Michigan φBK 1890, A.M. 1894, student: University of Berlin 1895–96, University of Munich 1896–97, Ph.D. 1897, L.H.D. Colby College 1940; instructor in Latin: University of Michigan 1893–95, University of Minnesota 1897–99, University of Michigan 1899–1902, assistant professor 1902–08, junior professor 1908–11, professor 1911–39, chairman, Department of Speech and General Linguistics 1932–39; president: American Philological Association 1936–37; member: American Philosophical Society, American Oriental Society, American Academy of Arts and Sciences; author: *The Old Testament Manuscripts in the Freer Collection, Part I* 1910, *Part II* 1917, *The New Testament Manuscripts in the Freer Collection, Part I* 1912, *Part II* 1917, *The Papyrus of the Minor Prophets in the Freer Collection* 1927, *The Berlin Papyrus of Genesis* 1927, *Beati in Apocalipsin Libri Duodecim, Papers and Monographs of the American Academy in Rome, Vol. III* 1930, *A Third-Century Papyrus Codex of the Epistles of Paul, Vol. XXXVIII* 1935, *Latin Papyri in the Michigan Collection, Vol. XLVIII* 1947, editor: *University of Michigan Studies*, contributor of numerous articles to archaeological and philological journals, acting director: School of Classical Studies of American Academy in Rome 1915–16, professor in charge 1928–31.

Sands, George Lincoln 1845–1919, born: Brunswick; brakeman, conductor, assistant supervisor, and division supervisor on various railroads 1865–79; resident engineer and division superintendent: Great Northern Railroad 1879–80; division superintendent: Texas & Pacific Railroad 1880–82; division superintendent: Atchison, Topeka & Santa Fe Railroad 1882–87; superintendent: Atlantic & Pacific Railroad 1887; general superintendent: Atchison, Topeka & Santa Fe Railroad 1887–91; superintendent of transportation and general superintendent: San Antonio & Arkansas Pass Railroad 1891–92; assistant manager: Wiggins Ferry Co., East Saint Louis Connecting Railroad 1892–94, manager from 1892; vice president: Saint Louis & West Arkansas Railroad, vice president: Kansas City & Colorado Railroad.

Sands, Merrill Burr 1884–1951, born: Portland; A.B. Yale College 1906; president and director: Dictaphone Corp., chairman, board of trustees: International Business Machines, Inc.

Sanger, Eugene Francis 1829–97, born: Bangor; student: Waterville College 1849, Medical School of Maine 1853; in the Civil War: surgeon with rank of major, USV, 6th Maine Volunteer Infantry, later brigade surgeon, regional medical director; chief medical officer: Elmira (New York) Prison Camp 1864, excoriated in the South for the miserable, deadly conditions in that camp; brevetted lieutenant colonel, USV; after the war, served as Maine surgeon general and president of the Maine Medical Association.

San Souci, Emery John 1857–1936, born: Saco; son of a mill worker, who was killed in the Civil War; began as a back boy at age eleven in the Laconia Cotton Mill, Biddeford, apprentice machinist: Saco Water Power Co., began working as a clerk in shoe stores in Greenfield, Massachusetts, 1875, traveling salesman for the Clark Holbrook Manufacturing Co., manufacturers of women's shoes, Hartford, Connecticut, 1877–88; partner: Foller & San Souci & Co., Hartford 1888–90, remained as manager after the company was sold to his brothers J. O. and A. G. San Souci

1890; removed to Providence, where he was put in charge of the family retail store 1892, the brothers consolidated their interests with a men's clothing concern, incorporated as J. O. San Souci & Co. 1900, came to be one of the more successful of Providence's larger stores, San Souci served as secretary-treasurer until his retirement in 1919; trustee: Old Colony Cooperative Bank, director: Union Trust Co.; member: Company K, 1st Connecticut National Guard; aide-de-camp, with rank of colonel on the staff of Governor Aren Pothier 1909–15; member: Providence City Council 1901–07; lieutenant governor of Rhode Island 1915–20, governor 1921–22, during his tenure as governor, he adopted a strong program of social amelioration, including aid to disabled veterans, vocational rehabilitation of disabled persons, increased benefits under workman's compensation laws, stricter measures for the control of social diseases, and higher standards for the sanitation of milk; because he was forced to call out the militia to quell the most violent strikes in Rhode Island history, he was denied renomination by the Republican party; after his term as governor, he was appointed collector of customs of the port of Providence by President Harding, reappointed by Presidents Hoover and Roosevelt 1923–35; buried in Saint Benedict's Cemetery, Hartford, Connecticut.

Sargent, Dudley Allen 1849–1924, born: Belfast; attended public schools in Belfast; invited to become director of the gymnasium at Bowdoin College 1869; A.B. Bowdoin College 1875, Sc.D. 1894, M.D. Yale University Medical School 1878; while at Yale developed the new system of physical culture that became ubiquitous; first to conceive of the idea of individual achievement in physical education; developed an anthropometric system; director: Hemenway Gymnasium, Harvard University, 1879–1919; first professor of physical education in the United States; inventor of modern gymnastic apparatus, such as the horse, the parallel bars, the rings, &c.; generally known as the father of physical education; author of numerous works, papers, and articles concerning aspects of physical education, including *Handbook of Developing Exercises* 1889, *Anthropometric Charts* 1893, his article "Military Drill in Public Schools" was published by the American National Education Association 1896; as examining physician for Harvard College, advised the then-young Theodore Roosevelt that, because of suspected heart problems, he should lead a quiet, retired existence.

Sargent, Nathaniel 1686–1762, born: Saco; son of a tavernkeeper and ferryman; A.B. Harvard College 1707, A.M. 1710; first Mainer to graduate from Harvard; apprenticed as a physician with Dr. Thomas Packer, of Portsmouth, New Hampshire, practiced in Hampton, New Hampshire, from 1712 made justice of the peace 1717, Governor Belcher suggested that he be given a temporary appointment to the bench of superior court, also sat as a special justice of the inferior court 1735; his son, Nathaniel Jr., also a physician, attended the Louisbourg Expedition, the father remained at home, treating veterans of that campaign; removed to Portsmouth 1748, in time entered into partnership with Dr. Benjamin Dearborn, became the most respected physician in that place; father-in-law of Thomas Cutts.

Sarton, May 1912–95, born: Wodelgem, Belgium; came to the United States 1912, naturalized 1916; graduate: Cambridge High and Latin School 1929; settled in York; Litt.D. (Hon.) Russell Sage College, Troy, New York, 1959, Clark University 1975, University of New Hampshire 1976, Bates College 1976, Colby College 1976, Thomas Starr King School of Ministry 1976, University of Maine 1981, Bowdoin College 1983, Centenary College 1990, Bucknell University 1985; lecturer on poetry: University of Chicago, Harvard University, University of Iowa, Colorado College, Wellesley College, Beloit College, University of Kansas, Denison University; Briggs-Copeland instructor in composition: Harvard University 1950–52; author: *The Single Hound* 1938, *The Bridge of Years* 1946, *Shadow of a Man* 1950, *A Shower of Summer Days* 1952, *Faithful Are the Wounds* 1955, *The Birth of a Grandfather* 1957, *The Fur Person* 1957, *The Small Room* 1961, *Joanna and Ulysses* 1963, *Mrs. Stevens Hears the Mermaids Singing* 1965, *Miss Pickthorne and Mr. Hare* 1966, *The Poet and the Donkey* 1969, *Kinds of Love* 1970, *Journal of a Solitude* 1973, *As We Are Now* 1973, *Punch's Secret* 1974, *Crucial Conversations* 1975, *A Walk Through the Woods* 1976, *A Reckoning* 1978, *Anger* 1982, *The Magnificent Spinster* 1985, *The Education of Harriet Hatfield* 1989, poems: *Encounter in April* 1937, *Inner Landscape* 1939, *The Lion and the Rose* 1948, *The Leaves of the Tree* 1950, *The Land of Silence* 1953, *In Time Like Air* 1957, *Cloud, Stone, Sun, Vine* 1961, *A Private Mythology* 1966, *As Does New Hampshire* 1967, *A Grain of Mustard Seed* 1971, *A Durable Fire* 1972, *Collected Poems* 1974, *Selected Poems of May Sarton* 1978, *Halfway to Silence* 1980, *A Winter Garland* 1982, *Letters from Maine* 1984, *The Phoenix Again* 1988, *The Silence Now* 1988, *Collected Poems* 1993, *Coming Into Eighty* 1994, autobiographies: *I Knew A Phoenix* 1959, *Plant Dreaming Deep* 1968, *A World of Light* 1976, *May Sarton: A Self Portrait* 1986, *Honey in the Hive* 1988, journals: *The House by the Sea* 1977, *Recovering* 1980, *After the Stroke* 1988, *Endgame* 1992, essays: *Writings on Writing* 1981, play: *The Underground River: A Play in Three Acts* 1947, anthology: *Sarton Selected: An Anthology of Novels, Journals and Poetry* 1991, editor: *Letters to May* 1986; recipient: Golden Rose Award for Poetry 1945, Ministry to Women Award, Universalist Women's Federation 1982, Avon/COCOA Pioneer Woman Award 1983, Fund for Human Dignity Award 1984, American Book Award 1985, Maryann Hartman Award: University of Maine 1986, New England Author Award, New England Booksellers Association 1990; Bryn Mawr fellow in poetry 1953–54, Guggenheim Foundation fellow 1954–55, National Foundation of Arts and Humanities grantee 1967, fellow: American Academy of Arts and Sciences, member: New England Poetry Society, recipient: Reynolds Lyric Award: Poetry Society of America 1953.

Savage, Auzella 1846–82, born: Anson; common seaman, USN, recipient: Medal of Honor, "On board the USS *Santiago de Cuba* during the assault on Fort Fisher, 15 January 1865. When the landing party to which he was attached charged on the fort with a cheer and the determination to plant the colors on the ramparts, Savage remained steadfast when more than two-thirds of the marines and sailors fell back in panic during the fight. When enemy fire shot away the flagstaff above his hand, he bravely seized the remainder of the staff and brought his colors safely away." Later lost at sea in the Atlantic.

Savage, Boutelle 1910–70, born: Bangor, attended the Somerset School in Bangor, graduate: Hotchkiss School, Lakeville, Connecticut, A.B. Yale College 1932; associated with the T. R. Savage Co., Bangor, a family wholesale food distributing firm, first as a salesman, then president and treasurer; subsequent to his father's death, merged his firm with Hannaford Brothers Co. 1955; vice president: Hannaford Brothers Co. 1955–57, executive vice president 1957, chairman of the board 1960–70; president: Bangor Real Estate Development Co. 1945–65, director: Merrill Trust Co.; at Yale he was a Whiffenpoof and member of Skull and Bones.

Savage, Minot Judson 1841–1918, born: Norridgewock; ill health forced him to withdraw from Bowdoin College, graduate: Bangor Theological Seminary 1864, D.D. Harvard University 1896; Congregational home missionary in San Mateo and Grass Valley, California, 1864–67, pastor: Framingham, Massachusetts, 1867–69, Hannibal, Missouri, 1869–73; his constant study of science had convinced him of the validity of the theory of evolution, which caused him to be labeled as a heretic in Hannibal; converted to Unitarianism, pastor: Third Church, Chicago, 1873–74, Church of the Unity, Boston, 1874–96, Church of the Messiah, New York, 1896–1906; regarded as the first minister in either England or the United States to embrace Darwinism and to attempt to synthesize such with Christian dogma; convinced Mrs. Brewster Hackley to found the Hackley School, where the first academic building constructed was named in his honor; author: *Life Questions* 1879, *The Morals of Evolution* 1880, *Religion of Evolution* 1876, *Bluffton, a Story of Today* 1878, *Belief in God* 1881, *Beliefs About Man* 1882, *Poems* 1882, *Beliefs About the Bible* 1883, *The Modern Sphinx* 1883, *The Religious Life* 1886, *Social Problems* 1886, *My Creed* 1887, *Science and the Church*, *The Minister's Hand Book*, *True Christianity*, *Life's Dark Problems* 1905, *Life Beyond Death* 1901, *The Passing and the Permanent in Religion* 1901, *Living by the Day* 1901, *Men and Women* 1902, *Poems* 1905; editor: *Sacred Songs for Public Worship* (the Unitarian hymnal), author of the Unitarian catechism.

Sawtelle, Charles Greene 1834–1913, born: Norridgewock; son of Cullen Sawtelle; student: Phillips Academy, Andover, graduate: U.S. Military Academy 1854; participated in the Sioux Expedition 1854–55, second lieutenant, 6th Infantry, USA, 1855, with his regiment in quelling disorder in Kansas 1857–58, Utah Expedition and march to California 1858, quartermaster: Mojave Expedition 1859, promoted captain 1861; during the Civil War, held various quartermaster positions, chief quartermaster of the Army of the Potomac; chief quartermaster, Cavalry Bureau, Washington; ordered to Texas, built a bridge 900 feet long across the Atchafalaya River using 21 steamers as pontoons, for the crossing of General Banks's army 1864; received brevet appointments as major, lieutenant, and brigadier general, USV, for faithful and meritorious service May 1865; after the war, served as chief quartermaster of various departments, districts, and posts on the Atlantic and Pacific coasts; promoted, in the regular army to major 1867, lieutenant colonel 1881, colonel 1894, quartermaster general of the army with rank of brigadier general, USA, 1896, retired 1897; buried in Arlington National Cemetery.

Sawtelle, Cullen 1805–87, born: Norridgewock; A.B. Bowdoin College 1825; member: Maine bar 1828; practiced in Norridgewock to 1841, register of probate 1830–38; member: Maine Senate 1842–44; member: United States House of Representatives 1845–47, 1849–51 (Democrat), chairman: Committee on Revisal and Unfinished Business, Committee on Revolutionary War Claims; attorney and credit manager for several mercantile firms in New York 1852–82; buried in Brookside Cemetery, Engelwood, New Jersey.

Sawtelle, Franklin H. 1846–1911, born: Norridgewock; attended public schools in Norridgewock, served as apprentice to Francis Fassett in Portland, won a Traveling Scholarship, which enabled him to travel and study in France and Great Britain for a period of two years; became a draftsman for Alfred Stone in Providence, Rhode Island; began independent practice in 1880; designed a building on the campus of Miss Wheeler's School, several public schools, the Bates Opera House; associated with the firm of Carrière & Hastings in supervising a number of their buildings in Rhode Island and Connecticut; president: Rhode Island chapter of the American Institute of Architects.

Sawtelle, William Otis 1874–1939, born: Bangor; graduate: Bangor High School, B.S. Massachusetts Institute of Technology ΦBK 1899, M.S. Harvard University 1907, L.H.D. University of Maine 1933; instructor in mathematics: Bangor High School, instructor: Massachusetts Institute of Technology, Harvard University, professor of physics: Haverford College; achieved distinction in field with his spectroscopic studies of electric sparks as published in *Astrophysical Journal*, October 1915; fellow: American Academy of Arts and Sciences; removed to Islesford, Cranberry Islands; scholar in early Maine history, opened the Black Mansion in Ellsworth to public, established Islesford Historical Society; author: "Mount Desert Papers" published in Sprague's *Journal of Maine History*, *Acadie: the Pre-Loyalist Migration and the Philadelphia Plantation* 1926, *Acadia National Park: Random Notes on the Significance of the Name* 1929, *Thomas Pownall, Governor and Some of His Activities in the American Colonies* 1931, *Historic Trails and Waterways of Maine* 1932, *William Bingham of Philadelphia and His Maine Lands, Mt. Desert: the Story of Saint Sauveur.*

Sawyer, Antonia Savage 1863–1913, born: Waterville, inherited a musical talent from her mother, Adaline Chase Savage, a singer of note; studied music in Boston with Charles R. Adams and Warren Davenport, removed to New York 1880; professional singer at the old First Presbyterian Church for twelve years and Temple Beth El for eight years; studied in London, sang with George Henschel, Sir Joseph Barnby, and in Paris with Anne de la Grange; toured the United States with Anton Seidl 1894, from whom she acquired a knowledge of Wagner arias; became a manager of professional musicians in New York.

Sawyer, Lucy Sargent 1840– ?, born: Belfast; one of the first American women to recognize the scope of possibilities for women in the missionary field; organized the Women's Foreign Missionary Society 1870, president from 1870; built a training school for black women in Greensboro, North Carolina.

Scammon, Charles Melville 1825– ?, born: Pittston; brother of Eliakim and Jonathan Young Scammon; became a sailor, shipped out for California 1850, engaged in the whale fishery, discovered the habitat of the gray whale in a bay on the California coast, later named Scammon Lagoon in his honor; in the Civil War: became the commanding officer of a revenue cutter in San Francisco Bay, subsequently obtained the rank of captain; author: *The Marine Mammals of the Northwest Coast of America and the American Whale Fishery* 1874.

Scammon, Eliakim Parker 1816–94, born: Whitefield; son of Eliakim Scammon, surveyor, first first selectman of Whitefield after incorporation 1809, brother of Charles Melville and Jonathan Young Scammon; A.M. (Hon.) Bowdoin College 1843, Trinity College; graduate: U.S. Military Academy 1837; commissioned second lieutenant, USA, assigned to the artillery/engineers; assistant professor of mathematics: U.S. Military Academy 1837–38, assistant topographical engineer in the Seminole War 1838–40, engaged in mapping of western territories 1840–41, returned to the U.S. Military Academy, as assistant professor of history, geography, and ethics 1841, principal assistant professor 1841–46, supervising topographical engineer on survey of New Bedford (Massachusetts) Harbor 1846, promoted to first lieutenant, topographical engineers, USA, 1846; in Mexican War, aide-de-camp to General Winfield Scott, performed a survey of Vera Cruz, while under fire 1847; as assistant topographical engineer, performed survey duty on the Great Lakes 1847–55, promoted to captain, topographical engineers, USA, 1855, detailed to construct military roads in New Mexico Territory 1855–56, dismissed for Conduct to the Prejudice of Good Order and Military Discipline and Disobedience of Orders 1856; professor of mathematics: Mount St. Mary's College, Cincinnati 1858–59, president: Polytechnic College of the Catholic Institute, Cincinnati 1860–61; in the Civil War: commissioned colonel, USV, commanding officer: Scammon's Brigade, Army of Occupation, West Virginia 1861–62; commanding officer: 3rd Brigade, Kanawha Division, IX Corps, led bayonet charge at South Mountain, saw his brigade at Antietam 1862; promoted to brigadier general, USV; commanding officer: Scammon's Division, commanding officer: District of Kanawha, captured 3 February 1864, sent to Libby Prison, exchanged 3 August 1864; commanding officer: 1st Separate Brigade during siege of Charleston, captured, released; commanding officer: 3rd Separate Brigade at Hilton Head and Florida, commanding officer: District of Florida; after the war: U.S. consul at Prince Edward Island 1866–70; U.S. engineer for New York Harbor 1870–75; professor of mathematics: Seton Hall College 1875–85; buried in Calvary Cemetery, Long Island City.

Scammon, John Fairfield 1786–1858, born: Wells; member: Massachusetts House of Representatives 1813, member: Maine House of Representatives 1823–41; member from the First District: U.S. House of Representatives 1845–47 (Democrat), chairman: Committee on Expenditures in the Department of the Treasury; member: Maine Senate 1855; buried in Laurel Hill Cemetery, Saco.

Scammon, Jonathan Young 1812–90, born: Whitefield; son of a surveyor, brother of Eliakim Parker Scammon; attended Waterville College 1830–31; member: Maine bar 1835, member: Illinois Bar 1836; reporter: Illinois Supreme Court 1840–44, prepared a new edition of Illinois laws, published *Scammon's Reports* (four volumes) 1832–43; founder: *Chicago Journal* 1844; president: Chicago Board of Education 1845–48; member: Illinois Senate; founder and president: Marine Bank 1851; organizer and president of the Galena and Chicago Railroad, later the Chicago and Northwestern Railroad, the first railroad west of Chicago, employed Abraham Lincoln as corporate lawyer, later served as pallbearer at his funeral in Springfield, Illinois; delegate: Republican National Convention 1864, 1872; founder and first president of the Chicago Astronomical Society, maintained, at his own expense, the Dearborn Observatory; lost much of his fortune in the Great Fire of 1871 and the Panic of 1873; a Swedenborgian, established the first Society of the New Jerusalem in Chicago, served for ten years as vice president of the general convention of that denomination in the United States; introduced homeopathy to Chicago, founded the Hahnemann Hospital and Hahnemann Medical College; a founder: University of Chicago, Chicago Historical Society.

Schonland, Herbert Emery 1900–84, born: Portland; student: Severna Academy, Severna, Maryland; B.S. U.S. Naval Academy 1925; student: Massachusetts Institute of Technology 1925; commissioned ensign, USN, 1925, advanced through the ranks to rear admiral, USN, 1947; served aboard USS *Utah* 1925, USS *Lawrence* 1926–29, USS *Camden* 1930, USS *Bushnell* 1931, shore duty at Naval Torpedo Station, Newport, Rhode Island, 1931–33, aboard USS *Milwaukee* 1934, USS *Argonne* 1935–37, at Naval Training Station, Newport, Rhode Island, 1937–39, aboard USS *San Francisco* 1939–42, executive officer 1942, recipient: Medal of Honor, Savo Island, 12–13 November 1942, as lieutenant commander, "For extreme heroism and courage above and beyond the call of duty as damage control officer of the USS *San Francisco* in action against greatly superior enemy forces in the battle off Savo Island. In the same violent night engagement in which all of his superior officers were killed or wounded, Lieutenant. Comdr. Schonland was fighting valiantly to free the USS *San Francisco* of large quantities of water flooding the second deck compartments through numerous shell holes caused by enemy fire. Upon being informed that he was commanding officer, he ascertained that the conning of the ship was being efficiently handled, then directed the officer who had taken over that task to continue while he himself resumed vitally important work maintaining the stability of the ship. In water waist deep, he carried on his efforts in darkness illuminated only by hand lanterns until the water in the flooded compartments had been drained or pumped off and watertight integrity had again been restored to the USS *San Francisco*. His great personal valor and gallant devotion to duty at great peril to his own life were instrumental in bringing his ship back to port under her own power, saved to fight again in the service of her country." At Damage Control School, San Francisco 1944; chief staff office: U.S. Naval Training and Distribution Center, Treasure Island, California 1945–46, retired 1947; assistant professor of mathematics: University of Santa Clara from 1947; awarded: Presidential Unit Citation, Asiatic-Pacific ribbon with nine stars, American Defense Medal with fleet clasp, American Theatre ribbon; retired to New London, Connecticut, buried in Arlington National Cemetery.

Scribner, Fred Clark, Jr. 1908-94, born: Bath; A.B. Dartmouth College ΦBK 1930, L.L.D. 1959, L.L.B. Harvard University Law School 1933, L.L.D. Colby College 1959, Bowdoin College 1959, University of Vermont 1960, D.D. General Theological Seminary 1984; member: Maine bar 1933, Massachusetts bar 1933, District of Columbia bar 1961; associate: Cook, Hutchison, Pierce, and Connell, Portland, 1933–35, partner: Cook, Hutchison, Scribner, Allen, Smith, and Lancaster, Portland, 1961–94, Scribner, Hall & Thompson, Washington, D.C., 1961–94; director, general counsel, vice president, treasurer: Bates Manufacturing Co., Lewiston 1946–55; general counsel: U.S. Department of the Treasury 1955–57; assistant secretary of the U.S. Treasury 1957, undersecretary 1957–61; director: Sentinel Groups Funds, Inc.; member: Commissioner's Advisory Committee on Exempt Organizations, Internal Revenue Service; chairman: ad hoc advisory group on presidential vote for Puerto Rico; president: Maine Constitutional Commission 1963–64; chairman: Portland Republican City Committee 1936–40; member: Maine Republican State Committee 1940–50, chairman: Executive Committee 1944–50, Republican national committeeman from Maine 1948–56, delegate: Republican National Convention 1940, 1944, 1948, 1952, 1956, 1960, 1964, 1968; counsel: Republican National Committee 1952-55, 1961–73; general counsel, Arrangements Committee, Republican National Convention 1956-72; presidential elector 1976; trustee: Maine Medical Center, American Council Capitol Formation; president, board of trustees: Bradford College, Haverhill, Massachusetts; trustee: Cardigan Mountain School, Canaan, New Hampshire; recipient: Alexander Hamilton Award, U.S. Department of the Treasury, Silver Beaver Award: Boy Scouts of America.

Seeley, William Henry 1840–1914, born: Topsham; at age fourteen, shipped out, deserted in Chinese waters, joined the Royal Navy; recipient: Victoria Cross, "On 6 September 1864, at Shimonoseki, Japan, during the capture of the enemy's works Ordinary Seaman Seeley of HMS *Euryalus* distinguished himself by carrying out a daring reconnaissance to ascertain the enemy's position, and he, although wounded, continued to take part in the final assault on the battery. Seeley led a charge there, and while in a wounded condition, carried back to his vessel a wounded companion, doing so while they were under fire." After leaving the Royal Navy retired to Stoughton, Massachusetts, where he farmed.

Seltzer, Leon Eugene 1918–88, born: Auburn; A.B. Columbia University 1940, J.D. Stanford University 1974; member: California bar 1974; assistant editor: Columbia University Press 1939–41, editor 1946–52, sales promotion manager 1952–56; director: Stanford University Press 1956–83; assistant editor: *Columbia Encyclopedia* 1946–50; editor: *Columbia Lippincott Gazeteer of the World* 1946–52; scholar-in-residence: Center for Advanced Study in Behavioral Sciences 1975–76; contributor of short stories, articles, and verse; author: *Exemptions and Fair Use in Copyright* 1977; vice president: Santa Clara County Board of Education 1966–71; Guggenheim fellow 1975–76; president: Association of American University Presses 1968–69.

Severance, Luther 1797–1855, born: Montague, Massachusetts; learned the printer's trade in Peterboro, New York, worked in Washington, Philadelphia, settled in Augusta, founder and editor: *Kennebec Journal* 1825; member: Maine House of Representatives 1829, 1839–40, 1842, 1848, Maine Senate 1835–36; member from the Third District: U.S. House of Representatives 1843–47 (Whig); vice president: Whig National Convention, Philadelphia 1848; U.S. commissioner to the Sandwich Islands (Hawaii) 1850–54; buried in Forest Grove Cemetery, Augusta.

Sewall, Arthur 1835–1900, born: Bath; descendant of Samuel Sewall, great nephew of David Sewall, brother of Frank Sewall, son of a shipwright who built the *Rappahannock* 1841, then the largest ship afloat; attended public school in Bath, apprenticed in father's shipyard, with brother formed E. & A. Sewall, Shipbuilders 1854, later as Arthur Sewall & Co., the firm was the largest manager and owner of sailing tonnage in United States, builder of the last and largest wooden ships in the world, later turned to building steel vessels; president: Bath National Bank 1871–1900; director, president: Maine Central Railroad 1884–93; president: Eastern Railroad Co., Boston & Maine Railroad Co.; delegate: Democratic National Convention 1872, 1880, 1884, 1888; elected member of the Democratic National Committee, 1892, 1900; Democratic party nominee for vice president of the United States 1896; father of Harold Marsh Sewall.

Sewall, David 1735–1825, born: York; son of a tanner, brother of Stephen Sewall; A.B. Harvard College 1755 (classmate and friend of John Adams), A.M. 1757, L.L.D. Bowdoin College 1812; while an undergraduate, acquired a flageolet, upon which he was considered a virtuoso; studied law in Portsmouth, published a series of astronomical almanacs; member: Massachusetts bar, practiced in York; collector of liquor excise 1763, registrar of probate 1766, justice of the peace 1767; delegate: York County Congress 1774, chairman: committee that drafted instructions to delegate to Second Provincial Congress 1775; member: York County Committee of Correspondence; elected by the Massachusetts House of Representatives to the council which exercised executive authority, in lieu of the governor 1776–77; justice: Massachusetts Superior Court 1777–78; delegate: Massachusetts Constitutional Convention 1779–80, member: drafting committee to revise Massachusetts laws; justice: Massachusetts Supreme Judicial Court 1781–89; Federalist presidential elector 1789; judge: U.S. District Court for District of Maine 1789–1818; presided over trial of Thomas Bird for mutiny and murder on the high seas, first capital proceedings in the federal court system; member: Massachusetts House of Representatives 1790; a founder: American Philosophical Society 1790; founding member: Massachusetts Historical Society 1822; Berwick Academy overseer, Bowdoin College overseer 1794–1815, president of the board 1794–1815; Harvard College overseer, contributed Sewall Prize (which continues to be awarded); being the seventh son of a seventh son, children would often come to him to have their warts stroked away; buried in the Old Burying Ground, York Village.

Sewall, Dummer 1737–1832, born: York; served as a lieutenant in the French and Indian War, colonel in the Revolutionary War; merchant in Bath; delegate: Massachusetts Constitutional Convention 1788; member: Massachusetts Senate 1788, 1790; Bowdoin College overseer 1794–99, 1805–10.

Sewall, Frank 1837–1915, born: Bath; brother of Arthur Sewall; A.B. Bowdoin College 1858, A.M. 1862, studied at universities of Tübingen, Berlin, and the Sorbonne; ordained New Church (Swedenborgian) minister 1863, pastor: Glendale, Ohio, Urbana, Ohio; president: Urbana College for sixteen years; Glasgow, Scotland, and Washington, D.C.; general pastor: Maryland Association from 1890; president: Swedenborgian Scientific Association from 1898; author: *The New Metaphysics* 1888, *Dante and Swedenborg and Other Essays in the New Renaissance* 1893, *Swedenborg and Modern Idealism* 1902, *Pulpit and Modern Thought* 1905, *Reason and Belief* 1906, *Being and Existence—A Philosophical Discussion* 1909, *Swedenborg and the Sapienta Angelica* 1910, *Life on Other Planets, According to Swedenborg* 1911, *Spirit As Object* 1912,

Ericken and Borgeson: Have Their Teachings a Spiritual Content? 1913.

Sewall, Harold Marsh 1860–1924, born: Bath; son of Arthur Sewall; A.B. Harvard College 1882, L.L.B. Harvard University Law School 1885; U.S. consul in Samoa during the Samoa crisis, stood up to German attempts at intimidation 1887; attaché to American Commission to Berlin which negotiated the tripartite treaty giving the United States, Britain, and Germany joint control of the Samoan Islands; while in Pago Pago, obtained the site for the U.S. naval station; member: Maine bar 1892; delegate: Republican National Convention 1896, 1916; U.S. minister to Hawaii 1897, presided over the transition to United States territory, personally raised the Stars and Stripes over the new territory 1900; member: Maine House of Representatives 1897–98, 1903–07, Maine Senate 1907–09; a reformer, fought and often won fights over fees, reimbursements, contracts; unsuccessful candidate for the U.S. House of Representatives 1914; in World War I: chairman: Maine Committee of Public Safety; member: Advisory Committee, Washington International Conference on the Limitation of Armaments 1921–22; member: Republican National Committee from 1923; Bath city forester for many years, devoted particular attention to the health and beauty of Bath's trees; his collection of maritime pictures, models, figureheads, and logs form the core of the collection of the Bath Marine Museum.

Sewall, Harriet Winslow List 1819–89, born: Portland; daughter of Comfort Hussey Winslow, a noted female Quaker preacher; attended the Friends School, Providence, Rhode Island; married Charles List, an immigrant German journalist and reformer 1848; after his death, married Samuel E. Sewall 1856; active in abolitionism, transcendentalism, women's suffrage, and educational works; editor: *The Letters of Lydia Marion Child* 1883, author of a collection of poems, published posthumously in 1889.

Sewall, John Smith 1830–1911, born: Newcastle; grandson of Jotham Sewall; A.B. Bowdoin College 1850, A.M. 1855, graduate: Bangor Theological Seminary 1858; clerk to Commodore Mathew Calbraith Perry, USN, 1850–54, member: Perry Expedition to Japan; ordained Congregational minister 1859, pastor: Wenham, Massachusetts, 1859–67; professor of rhetoric, oratory, and English literature: Bowdoin College 1867–75, overseer 1875–85, trustee 1885–1911; professor of homiletics and sociology: Bangor Theological Seminary 1875–1903; author: *The Captain's Clerk, Adventures in the China Seas* 1906, regarded by Samuel Eliot Morrison as the best firsthand account of the Perry Expedition.

Sewall, Joseph Addison 1830–1917, born: Scarborough; M.D. Harvard University Medical School 1852, practiced in Bangor, removed to Illinois; principal: Princeton High School, practiced medicine in LaSalle County; returned to Cambridge, where he was awarded his Ph.D. at Harvard University 1860, L.L.D. Knox College

1877, University of Colorado 1914; professor of natural science: State Normal University of Illinois, Normal (later University of Illinois) 1861–76, hired John Wesley Powell as an assistant; founding president: University of Colorado 1877–88, chair of natural science: University of Denver 1888–92, professor of medicine from 1892; later had charge of the U.S. Experimental Grass and Forage Station, Garden City, Kansas; author: *A Condensed Botany* 1872.

Sewall, Joseph Wingate 1884–1946, born: Old Town; A.B. Bowdoin College ΦBK 1906; forester with David Pingree, Bangor and Salem, Massachusetts, 1906–09; member: Appleton and Sewall, foresters, Old Town and New York 1910–12, after the death of his partner, practiced under his own name from 1912; valued and mapped over 35 million acres of land in the United States and Canada; acting forester in charge of Maine state camps 1933–36; postmaster of Old Town 1915–21; Democratic candidate for U.S. House of Representatives 1922.

Sewall, Jotham 1760–1852, born: York; nephew of Stephen Sewall; a stone mason, by trade, ordained Congregational ministry 1800; itinerant minister in Maine, New Brunswick, and eleven other states; pastor in Chesterville 1820–50, established many new churches, often preached four times a week.

Sewall, Rufus King 1814–1903, born: Edgecomb; grandnephew of Jotham Sewall; A.B. Bowdoin College 1837, A.M. Bangor Theological Seminary 1841; preached for five years but ill health forced retirement to Saint Augustine, Florida; studied law in Mobile, returned to Maine, practiced in Wiscasset; member: U.S. Supreme Court bar, examining counsel: Lincoln County bar; vice president: Maine Historical Society; author: *Memoir of Joseph Sewall, D.D.*, *Lectures on the Holy Spirit*, *Sketches of Saint Augustine*, *The Views of John McKeen, Esq. On the Voyage and Discoveries of George Weymouth* 1857, *Ancient Dominions of Maine: Embracing the Earliest Facts, The Recent Discoveries, With the Religious Developments of Society within the Ancient Sagadahoc, Sheepscot, and Pemquid Precincts and Dependencies* 1859, *History of the Lincoln Lodge at Wiscasset* 1863, *Popham's Town of Fort Saint George* 1876, *Wiscasset Point, the Old Meeting House and Interesting Incidents Connected with Its History* 1883, *Ancient Voyages to the Western Continent: Three Phases of History on the Maine Coast* 1895, *Pemaquid, Its Genesis, Discovery, Name, and Colonial Relations to New England* 1896, *Centennial Memorial Services of the Old Alna Meetinghouse, Alna, Maine, September 11, 1889* 1896, *Memorials of the Bar of Lincoln County, Maine 1760–1900* 1900.

Sewall, Samuel 1724–1815, born: York; the inventor of numerous devices, is credited with the invention of the pile driver, with which he constructed several notable bridges, including Sewall's Bridge in York 1761 and the Charlestown, Massachusetts, Bridge 1786.

Sewall, Samuel Swanton 1858–1935, born: Bath; son of a shipbuilder; A.B. Yale College 1880; employed by Van Vliek & Co., New York, proprietors of a line of sailing ships serving Atlantic and Pacific ports 1880–82; junior partner: Arthur Sewall & Co., Bath, which was reequipping itself to produce steel vessels, notably *Dirigo*, the first steel sailing vessel built in the United States 1894; after the death of his uncle Arthur in 1900, became senior partner, retiring in 1919; one of his vessels, the *William P. Frye* was the first American ship sunk by the Germans in World War I, January 28 1915; vice president, director: Bath National Bank, trustee: Bath Savings Institution, member: Bath City Council; passed his winters in Redlands, California, where he owned an orange grove; Swedenborgian in religion, Republican in politics.

Sewall, Stephen 1734–1804, born: York; son of a tanner, brother of David Sewall; apprenticed to a joiner, received instruction in the classics from a clergyman, A.B. Harvard College 1761, while an undergraduate, served as a waiter, monitor, clock-keeper; instructor in Hebrew: Harvard College 1761–64, also served as library-keeper and as an instructor at Cambridge Latin School; asked by the Harvard Corporation to prepare a new text, which was entitled *Hebrew Grammar, Collected Chiefly from those of Mr. Israel Lyons…and the Reverend Richard Grey…with a Sketch of the Hebrew Poetry, as Retrieved by Bishop Hare* 1763, the excellence of which was considered to be so great that he was named first Hancock Professor of Hebrew and Oriental Languages 1765–85, completely revamped the study of the classics at Harvard and thus, in the United States, came to be regarded as the most distinguished scholar of his generation; maintained a wide correspondence with European scholars as to the meaning of the inscriptions on Dighton Rock and other matters; still a skilled carpenter, oversaw the carpentry involved in the rebuilding of Massachusetts Hall, as well as that of his own home; when, during the Revolution, Harvard College removed to Concord, he took over the instruction of the freshmen class and returned to Cambridge to rescue the library, museum, scientific apparatus, and the college fire engine; represented Cambridge in the Massachusetts House of Representatives 1777; a founding member and president: American Academy of Arts and Sciences; after the death of his wife in 1783, Sewall began a downward spiral into acute alcoholism that only ended in his death; author: his works include a funeral oration, in Latin, on the death of Edward Holyoke 1769, a volume of Greek and Latin poetry *Pietas et Gratulatio* 1761, *Carmina Sacra Quæ Latine Græceque Condidit America* 1789, *The Scripture Account of the Shechinah* 1794, *The Scripture History Relating to the Overthrow of Sodom and Gomorrah, and to the Origin of the Salt Sea* 1796, a dictionary in Chaldee and English, left in manuscript at his death.

Sewall, Sumner 1897–1965, born: Bath; son of William Dunning Sewall; attended public school in Bath and Harvard College, withdrew to enlist in the American Ambulance Field Service and served in France 1916, later, served in U.S. Army Air Corps, member: Squadron 95, first pursuit group, aviation section of the Army

Signal Corps 1917, became an ace by shooting down seven German aircraft and two observation balloons, decorated: Distinguished Service Cross with oak leaf cluster, the French Legion of Honor, the croix de guerre, and the Order of the Crown of Belgium; after the war, attended Yale College for a year, worked on oil-drilling rigs in Mexico, clerked in a bank in Spain, worked on a sugar plantation in Cuba, worked as a riveter at the Ford Motor Co. in Michigan; with Juan Trippe, organized Colonial Air Transport, the first commercial airmail carrier, served as traffic manager; Bath alderman 1933, member: Maine House of Representatives 1934–36; Maine Senate 1936–40, president 1938–40; governor of Maine (Republican) 1941–45; president: American Overseas Airlines; military governor of Wurttemberg-Baden 1946.

Sewall, Thomas 1786–1845, born: Augusta; cousin of Jotham Sewall; M.D. Harvard University Medical School 1812, practiced in Essex, Massachusetts, to 1820, removed to Washington, appointed professor of anatomy at the National Medical College of Columbian University from 1821; author: *The Pathology of Drunkenness,* which was translated into German and established his reputation as an original investigator.

Seward, Richard Henry 1840–99, born: Kittery; paymaster's steward, USN, recipient: Medal of Honor, Ship Island Sound, Louisiana, 23 November 1863, served as paymaster's steward on board the USS *Commodore*. "Carrying out his duties courageously, Seward volunteered to go on the field amidst a heavy fire to recover the bodies of two soldiers which he brought off with the aid of another; a second instance of personal valor within a fortnight." Promoted to acting master's mate; buried in First Christian Church Cemetery, Kittery Point.

Sharpe, Philip Burdette 1903–61, born: Portland; B.C.S. Portland University 1924; began as a feature writer with *Portland Sunday Telegram* 1919–25, reporter: *Portland Evening News* 1927–31, specializing in subject of firearms from 1919; firearms editor: *Michigan Sportsman, Outdoors, National Sportsman, Hunting & Fishing*; firearms technician and consultant from 1930; owner: Philip B. Sharpe Research Laboratories, Fairfield, Pennsylvania, Emmitsburg, Maryland, from 1947; president, treasurer: Sharpe and Hart Associates, Inc. (Maryland, Pennsylvania, California); in World War II: captain of ordnance, USA, 1942–46, chief: small arms historian, Office of Chief of Ordnance 1942–44, proof officer, Foreign Materiel (research and development section), Aberdeen proving ground 1944, chief, small arms unit, Ordnance Technical Intelligence, Enemy Equipment Unit, European Theatre of Operations 1945; author: *This Handloading Game* 1934, *The Complete Guide to Handloading* 1937, *The Rifle in America* 1938; designer (with Douglass B. Wesson): the Smith & Wesson .357 magnum revolver and cartridge, the 7x61 Sharpe & Hart cartridge 1949–54; buried: Arlington National Cemetery.

Shaw, George Russell 1848–1937, born: Parkman; brother of Robert Gould Shaw; A.B. Harvard College 1869, studied architecture in Paris; practiced in Boston, in association with Henry Hunnewell, as Shaw & Hunnewell; among his designs were: Pierce Hall and the Jefferson Physics Building on the Harvard campus, the library at Wellesley College, the Eye and Ear Hospital, Boston; after his retirement, wrote several books, including: *The Pines of Mexico* 1909, *Genus Pinos* 1914.

Shaw, Howard Burton 1869–1943, born: Winslow; A.B. University of North Carolina 1891, A.M. Harvard University 1894; instructor in mathematics: Harvard University 1889–90; professor of math, surveying, and drawing: University of North Carolina 1891–93; assistant professor: electrical laboratory, Lawrence Scientific School, Harvard University 1894–96, assistant professor electrical engineering 1896–99, professor 1899–1913, dean: school of engineering, Harvard University 1907–13; author: *Dynamo Laboratory Manual*, volume one 1906, volume two 1910.

Shaw, Reta 1912–82, born: Paris; graduate: South Paris High School 1929; as a young woman, member of her father's dance band: Shaw's Snappy Syncopaters, later, studied stage at Leland Power's School of Theater in Boston; played piano and sang in various cocktail lounges in New York; in World War II: served with the Red Cross, entertaining troops in England, France, Belgium, and Germany; got her start on Broadway in *Annie Get Your Gun*, later appeared in *Gentleman Prefer Blonds* and *Pajama Game*; removing to Hollywood, she appeared in the movies: *Pajama Game* 1957, *The Lady Takes a Flyer* 1958, *Pollyanna* 1960, *Mary Poppins* 1964, *The Ghost and Mr. Chicken* 1966, *Guess Who's Sleeping in My Bed?* 1973, *Escape to Witch Mountain* 1975, *Husbands, Made in Paris, That Funny Feeling, Marriage on the Rocks, A Global Affair, Bachelor in Paradise, Sanctuary, Man Afraid, All Mine to Give, Picnic*; appeared on television in: *The Girl Who Came Gift-Wrapped, Guess Who's Been Sleeping in my Bed?, Murder Once Removed, The Tab Hunter* Show, *The Man From U.N.C.L.E., The Ghost and Mrs. Muir, I Dream of Jeannie, The Andy Griffith Show, The Ann Sothern Show, The Betty White Show, Annie Get Your Gun, Mr. Peepers, The Betty White Show, The Carla Williams Show, Ichabod and Me, Oh, Those Bells!, Happy Days, Emergency!, Here's Lucy, The Odd Couple, Bewitched, Please Don't Eat the Daisies, I Spy, Lost in Space, The Dick Van Dyke Show*, &c.; buried in Forest Lawn Cemetery, Los Angeles.

Shaw, Robert Gould 1776–1853, born: Gouldsborough, son of Francis Shaw, proprietor of Gouldsborough; removed to Boston, apprenticed himself to his uncle 1789, became a prominent merchant in Boston and in London; at his death left a large sum of money to be used to support an asylum for mariners' children.

Shaw, Robert Gould 1850–1931, born: Parkman; grandson of Robert Gould Shaw; attended the local schools, A.B. Harvard College 1869; entered the business office of Horatio Harris & Co., Boston; after several trips to Europe, including study at the universities of Stuttgart and Heidelberg, undertook the study of architecture at the Royal Polytechnic School in Munich 1871–74, draftsman in the office of A. C. Martin, Boston; later associated as an architect with his brother George Russell Shaw, gave up the profession after three years and devoted his attention, as a trustee, to the management of various properties, including that of his father-in-law Horatio Hollis Hunnewell; interested from an early age in the theatre, began collecting memorabilia and data, which came to be the largest in the world, eventually housed in the Widener Library at Harvard University, appointed curator of the Widener Theatre Collection 1915; first cousin of Robert Gould Shaw, who was killed leading his troops, at the assault on Battery Wagner, near Charleston, South Carolina, 1863.

Shaw, William Tuckerman 1822–1909, born: Steuben; a member of the family that settled Gouldsboro, cousin to Robert Gould Shaw; attended Maine Wesleyan Seminary, Kents Hill, removed to Indiana where he taught at the private academy that later became DePauw University; removed to Kentucky, where he taught school and studied law; enlisted for the Mexican war in Harrodsburg, Kentucky, 1845; at the battle of Buena Vista, all the commissioned officers in his unit were killed; later captain of a group that crossed the plains and mountains to California 1849; engaged in the lumber business, returned to Iowa; built the Fisher House at Anamosa 1855, instrumental in building the Dubuque Southwestern Railroad 1857; in the Civil War: organized the 14th Iowa Volunteers, later commanding officer: 2nd Brigade, 3rd Division, 16th Corps, led his troops at Fort Donelson and Shiloh, where he and his command distinguished themselves, spent six months campaigning in Alabama and Georgia, detailed to investigate the loyalties of certain individuals in St. Louis, with the result that several were sent South, rejoined his regiment, but was again detached to preside over a court martial at Columbia, Kentucky, later, commanding officer of the post; with his regiment, served in the Meridian campaign and at the battle of Fort DeRussey 1864; subsequently with General Banks, bore the brunt of the battle of Pleasant Hill, where his regiment lost heavily; commanding officer: 16th Division, 16th Corps, with General Price's army in Missouri; after the war, returned to Anamosa; president: Midland Railroad Company 1870–73; member: Iowa House of Representatives 1875–76; built a number of buildings; senior member: Shaw & Schoonover Bank.

Sheldon, David Newton 1807–87, born: Suffield, Connecticut; son of a farmer; graduate: Westfield (Massachusetts) Academy, A.B. Williams College 1830, first in his class, student at Newton Theological Institution 1831–34, D.D. Brown University 1847; ordained Baptist minister 1835, missionary to Paris 1835–37, minister in Halifax, Nova Scotia 1840–42, settled in Waterville 1842; fifth president: Waterville College 1843–53; pastor: Baptist Church in Bath 1853–56, converted to Unitarianism 1856; minister in Bath 1856–62, Waterville 1862–78; author: *Sin and Redemption* 1856; father of Edward Stevens Sheldon.

Sheldon, Edward Stevens 1851– ?, born: Waterville; son of David Newton Sheldon; student: Colby College 1867–68, A.B. *summa cum laude* Harvard College 1872, proctor 1872–73, recipient: Parker Fellowship 1873–77, which facilitated travel and study in Germany, Switzerland, and Italy; instructor in modern languages: Harvard University 1877, tutor in German 1878, assistant professor and professor: Harvard University 1884–94, professor of philology from 1894; organizer, secretary: American Dialect Society, president 1889–93; contributor of numerous papers on philology, including: "Some Specimens of a Canadian French Dialect Spoken in Maine," "The Origin of the English Names of the Letters of the Alphabet"; prepared the etymologies for *Webster's International Dictionary*; author: *Short German Grammar for High Schools and Colleges* 1879.

Shepley, Ether 1789–1877, born: Groton, Massachusetts; descendent of John  Shepley, who as a small boy was captured by the Indians in a massacre at Groton, Massachusetts, and held captive until he escaped at age sixteen; A.B. Dartmouth College ΦBK 1811, A.M. 1811, L.L.D. 1845, Waterville College 1842; studied law in South Berwick, member: Massachusetts bar 1814, practiced in Saco, later Portland; member: Massachusetts House of Representatives 1819; delegate: Maine Constitution Convention 1819; U.S. district attorney for Maine 1821–33; Bowdoin College trustee 1829–66; member: Maine Senate 1833–36; member: U.S. Senate 1833–36 (Jacksonian), chairman: Committee on Engrossed Bills; judge: Maine Supreme Judicial Court 1836–48, chief justice 1848–55; sole commissioner to revise and print the laws of Maine 1856; published: *Revised Statutes of the State of Maine* 1857, *Speech in Congress on the Removal of the Deposits*, a vindication of President Jackson 1857; Bowdoin College overseer 1821–29, trustee 1829–66; father of George Foster Shepley and John Rutledge Shepley; buried in Evergreen Cemetery, Portland.

Shepley, George Foster I 1819–78, born: Saco; son of Ether Shepley; A.B. Dartmouth College 1837, L.L.D. 1878, attended the Dane Law School, Cambridge 1839; member: Maine bar 1840, practiced in Bangor from 1840; U.S. district attorney for Maine 1848–49, 1853–61; argued cases before the U.S. Supreme Court on several occasions; delegate to Democratic National Convention in Charleston, South Carolina, and later to the rump session in Baltimore 1860; in the Civil War: commissioned colonel, USV, commanding officer: 12th Maine Volunteer Infantry, took part in General Butler's expedition against New Orleans, as acting brigadier general, USV, led the 3rd Brigade in the capture of that city, appointed military commandant of New Orleans 1862–64, commanding officer: defenses of New Orleans, promoted to brigadier general, USV, military governor of Louisiana 1862–64, commanding officer: District of Eastern Virginia, military governor of Richmond 1865; after being mustered out, refused the offer of a seat on the U.S. Supreme Court; appointed U.S. Circuit Court judge 1865–78; died of Asiatic cholera, buried in Evergreen Cemetery, Portland.

Shepley, George Foster II 1860–1903, born: Portland; son of John Rutledge Shepley; A.B. Washington University, St. Louis 1880, student of architecture, Massachusetts Institute of Technology 1880–82; employed by Henry Hobson Richardson in his architectural office from 1884, married Julia Hayden Richardson, daughter of H. H. Richardson, after whose death, Shepley formed the architectural firm of Shepley, Rutan, and Coolidge 1886; among his designs are the Ames Building, Boston, the Art Institute of Chicago, the original campus of Stanford University, Harvard University Medical School, several buildings for the University of Chicago, Massachusetts General Hospital, the John Hay Library, Brown University, the chapel at Vassar College, several buildings for St. Elizabeth's Hospital, Washington, D.C..

Shepley, John Rutledge 1817–1884, born: Saco; son of Ether Shepley; A.B. Bowdoin College 1837, L.L.B. Harvard University Law School 1839, practiced in Portland 1839–41, removed to St. Louis, Missouri, 1841, entered the law office of Spalding & Tiffany, later, partner; partner: Glover & Shepley 1861; among his more important cases were: *St. Louis Railroad Co.* v. *Northwestern St. Louis Railroad Co.*, *Kitchen et al* v. *St. Louis, Kansas City & Northern Railroad Co.*, *Buford* v. *Keokuk Northern Line Packet Co.*, *City of St. Louis* v. *St. Louis Gas Light Co.*, *Chouteau* v. *Allen*, *Wiggins Ferry Co.* v. *Chicago & Alton Railroad Co.*; father of George Foster Shepley II.

Sherman, Frank Asbury 1841–1915, born: Knox; son of a farmer and school teacher, became a farmer, until the outbreak of the Civil War: enlisted in Company R, 4th Maine Regiment, USV, 1862–65, wounded several times, lost left arm at the battle of the Wilderness 1864; graduate: East Maine Conference Seminary, Bucksport, B.S. Dartmouth College 1870, M.S. 1875; instructor in mathematics: Worcester Polytechnical Institute 1870–71, associate professor of mathematics: Dartmouth College 1871–72, professor 1872–1911.

Sherwood, Grace Mabel 1886– ?, born: Buxton; A.B. Pembroke College 1906, Litt.D. Rhode Island College of Education, L.H.D. Brown University 1951; director: legislation reference bureau, Rhode Island State Library 1907–37, Rhode Island state librarian, state record commissioner from 1937; director: state library book pool for the fighting services 1941; writer of digests of legislation, history, verse, law drafting for Rhode Island General Assembly; author: *Gifts*, *Navigators*; musical plays; president: National Association of State Libraries 1952–53; during World War I: served in leave areas as writer, director of soldier shows in France and England.

Sibley, John Langdon 1804–85, born: Union; graduate: Phillips Academy, Exeter, A.B. Harvard College 1825, student: Harvard University Divinity School, A.M. (Hon.) Bowdoin College 1856; ordained Congregational minister 1829, pastor: Unitarian Church, Stow, Massachusetts, removed to Cambridge 1833; engaged in literary work, editor: *American Magazine of Useful and Entertaining Knowledge* 1833–41; assistant librarian: Harvard University 1825–26, 1841–56; librarian 1856–77; introduced a novel and useful means of cataloging books, in general use until the Dewey Decimal System superseded it, quadrupled the number of volumes in the Harvard University library; editor of the annual catalogs 1850–70; author: *History of the Town of Union, Maine* 1851, *Index to the Works of John Adams* 1853, *Notices of the Triennial and Annual Catalogue of Harvard University, with a Reprint of the Catalogue of the Catalogues of 1674, 1682, and 1700* 1865, *Bibliographical Sketches of Graduates of Harvard University* (3 volumes)1873–85, *Index to the Writings of George Washington* 1887, *Shubael Dummer* 1898; he left a large mass of materials accumulated over half a century, arranged chronologically and bound, as well as a large collection of newspaper clippings, containing biographical material on Harvard graduates.

Sills, Kenneth Charles Morton 1879–1954, born: Halifax, Nova Scotia; A.B. Bowdoin College ΦBK 1901, A.M. Harvard University 1903, L.L.D. (Hon.) University of Maine 1916, Bates College 1918, Dartmouth College 1918, Colby College 1920, Williams College 1927, Bowdoin College 1934, Dalhousie University 1939, Yale University 1941, Tufts University 1847; assistant in English: Harvard University 1901–03, instructor in classics and English 1903–04, tutor in English: Columbia University 1904–05, student: Columbia University graduate school 1905–06, adjunct professor of Latin language and literature: Bowdoin College 1906–07, Winkley professor of Latin language and literature 1907–46; secretary of the Bowdoin faculty 1906–10, dean 1910–18, acting president 1917–18, president 1918–1954; member, board of visitors: U.S. Military Academy 1917–21, 1934-35, president of the board 1920–21; trustee: Wellesley College 1927–46, Athens College, Greece, 1927–47, chairman of the board 1944–47, Worcester (Massachusetts) Academy 1938–43, Episcopal Theology School 1938–47, Waynflete School 1939–47, Carnegie Foundation 1933–47, chairman of the board 1939–41; Northeast representative: War Labor Board 1943–45, recipient: Medal of Liberation, Kingdom of Denmark 1946; trustee, overseer ex officio: Bowdoin College 1918–47.

Silver, Arthur Elmer 1879–1975, born: Dexter; son of sawmill owner; attended public schools in Dexter, B.S. University of Maine 1902, D.Eng. 1954; student engineer: General Electric Co., Schenectady, New York, 1902–04; in charge of meter department: Raleigh Electric Co. 1904–05; operating engineer, chief engineer: Carolina Power & Light Co., Raleigh, North Carolina, 1905–10; electrical engineer: design and construction, Electric Bond & Share Co., New York 1910–14; assistant chief engineer: Ebasco Services, Inc. 1914–20, consulting electrical engineer 1920–48, in charge of planning and design of power plants, transmission lines, substations, and distribution systems, head of the electrical engineering division, designed the first complete high-voltage substation (100,000 volts) near Raleigh in 1911, made the designs for systems capable of transmitting 220,000 volts 1919, other applications to which he contributed innovative designs included system interconnections, application of controls to equipment and lines, rural electrification, standardization of equipment, simplification of wiring systems, cathodic protection, induction interference; co-recipient of award for best national paper in engineering field: American Institute of Electrical Engineers 1931–32, Lamme Medalist 1951; fellow: American Academy of Arts and Sciences, American Institute of Electrical Engineers; retired to Montclair, New Jersey.

Simmons, Franklin 1839–1913, born: Lisbon (that portion that is now Webster);  removed with his parents to Bath, where he attended public school, A.B. Bates College 1860, A.M. (Hon.) Bowdoin College, Colby College, Bates College; opened a sculpture studio in Portland, produced his first statue, that of General Hiram Berry for the city of Rockland; spent 1864–65 in Washington, D.C., modeling Admirals Farragut and Porter, Generals Grant, Meade, Sherman, Hooker, Burnside, Banks, Butler, and Custer, Secretaries Seward, Chase, and Wells for life-sized medallions, cast in bronze, in Rome, 1868–72; his work includes over one hundred portrait busts in marble, fifteen public monuments, including the *Soldiers and Sailors Monument* and *Henry Wadsworth Longfellow Monument,* both in Portland, General Grant in the United States Capitol, Roger Williams in Providence; knighted and decorated three times by king of Italy, including: Commendatore of the Crown.

Simons, Manley Hale 1879–1963, born: Portland; B.S. U.S. Naval Academy 1903, graduate: U.S. Naval War College 1924; commissioned ensign USN, 1903, advanced through the grades to rear admiral 1934, retired 1943; in World War I: commanding officer: transport *Kroonland* and 3rd Division, U.S. Battle Fleet; director of fleet training and chief of staff to Vice Admiral Laning, cruisers, U.S. Fleet; commanding officer: 5th Naval District and Sea Frontier, and U.S. Naval Yard, Portsmouth, Virginia; president: Simondale Corp. 1940–41; decorated: Navy Cross and citation for hazardous duty in World War I, Legion of Merit for German submarines in World War II; retired to Pasadena, California.

Skelton, Thomas Reginald, Jr. 1927–94, born: North Bridgton; A.B. Middlebury College 1950; associate director, member, Executive Committee: Ohio Ballet; associate professor: Yale University School of Drama 1978–81; lighting designer: Joffrey Ballet, New York; lecturer, trustee: Studio and Forum of Stage Design, New York; guest lecturer: University of Washington, University of Ohio, New York University, University of Akron; member, board of visitors: North Carolina School of the Arts; lighting designer, Broadway productions: *Oh Dad, Poor Dad, Mom's Hung You In The Closet And I'm Feeling So Sad*, *Come Summer*, *Indians*, *Coco*, *Mahogany*, *Bob and Ray*, *Purlie*, *Gigi*, *Shenandoah*, *All God's Chillun Got Wings*, *Guys and Dolls*, *Richard III*, *The King and I*, *Camelot*, *Oklahoma!*, *Peter Pan*, *Brigadoon*, *West Side Waltz*, *Lena Horne*; repertory productions: Boston Opera Company, Yale Repertory Theatre, American Shakespeare Festival, National Opera of Belgium, Circle in the Square, National Opera of Holland, American Dance Festival, American Spoleto Festival; dance productions: José Limon Dance Company, Dancers of Bali, Inbal, Escudero, Mary Anthony Dance Theatre, Paul Taylor Company, The Joffrey, Ballet Folklorico de Mexico, Pearl Lang Company, Merce Cunningham Company, Shankar, Peral Primus Company, The Royal Ballet, Eliot Field Company, American Ballet Theatre, Pennsylvania Ballet, National Ballet of Australia, Nureyev and Friends, Narkarove Company, Ohio Ballet; ballets: *Parade* (Massene), *The Green Table* (Joos), *Astarte* (Joffrey), *Dancers at a Gathering* (Robbins), *Scenes from a Childhood* (Poll), *Aurole* (Taylor), *The Poor's Pavane* (Limon), *Kettentanz* (Arpino), *Tiller of the Fields* (Tudor), *Rodeo* (DeMille), *Rooms* (Sokolow), *Concerto Barocco* (Ballanchine), *A Footstep of Air* (Feld); designer of decor and lighting: *The Beautiful Bait, Astarte* (Joffrey), *Sleeping Beauty* (Pennsylvania Ballet), *The Medium and the Telephone, The Passion Play, Dancers of Bali, Compulsions* (Poll); staging designer: *Bacalor* Haiti, *Anrang* Korea, *Feux Follet* Canada, *Foo Hsing* Formosa; director of productions: *Turn of the Screw* San Francisco Opera, *The Old Maid and the Thief* Comic Opera Players, *Come Slowly Eden* Anta Matinee Series, *Faces* Berghoff Studio, *Carmen* Theatre de la Monaie; author: *Handbook of Dance Stagecraft and Lighting* 1955–57; recipient: Tony Award nomination for *Indians* 1969–70, *All God's Chillun Got Wings* 1971-72, *The Iceman Cometh* 1985–86; recipient: Carbonell Award for *Peter Pan* 1981.

Skidgel, Donald S. 1948-1969, born: Caribou; sergeant, U.S. Army, Troop D, 1st Squadron, 9th Cavalry, 1st Cavalry Division, recipient: Medal of Honor (posthumous), near Song Be, Republic of Vietnam, 14 September 1969 for conspicuous gallantry and intrepidity in action at the risk of his life above and beyond the call of duty. "SGT Skidgel distinguished himself while serving as a reconnaissance section leader in Troop D. On a road near Song Be in Binh Long Province, SGT Skidgel and his section with other elements of his troop were acting as a convoy security and screening force when contact occurred with an estimated enemy battalion concealed in tall grass and in bunkers bordering the road. SGT Skidgel maneuvered off the road and began placing effective machine gun fire on the enemy automatic weapons and rocket propelled grenade positions. After silencing at least one position, he ran with his machine gun across sixty meters of bullet-swept ground to another location from which he continued to rake the enemy positions. Running low on ammunition, he returned to his vehicle over the same terrain. Moments later he was alerted that the command element was receiving intense fire from automatic weapons and rocket-propelled grenades. Ignoring his extremely painful wounds, he staggered back onto his feet and placed effective fire on several other enemy positions until he was mortally wounded by hostile small arms fire. His selfless actions enabled the command group to withdraw to a better position without casualties and inspired the rest of his fellow soldiers to gain fire superiority and defeat the enemy. SGT Skidgel's gallantry at the cost of his life were in keeping with the highest traditions of the military service and reflect great credit upon himself, his unit and the U.S. Army." Buried in Sawyer Cemetery, Plymouth.

Sleeper, Jacob 1802–89, born: Newcastle; student: Lincoln Academy, orphaned at age fourteen, lived with an uncle in Belfast, in whose store he clerked; removed to Boston 1825, worked as a bookkeeper, became a wholesale clothier 1835–50; amassed a great fortune and retired, visited England, where he studied at the universities of Oxford and Cambridge, aided in the founding of an evangelical College at Belfast, Ireland, assisted in organizing the New England Education Society 1855, member: board of directors 1855–69; member: Massachusetts House of Representatives 1851–52, member: Massachusetts Executive Council 1859–61, Boston alderman 1852–53; founder, treasurer, and president of the board of trustees: Boston University 1869; a founder: New England Conservatory of Music, which named its hall in his honor; Harvard University overseer 1857–69; president, board of trustees: Wesleyan University.

Small, Albion Woodbury 1854–1926, born: Buckfield; son of a prominent Baptist minister and trustee of Colby College; graduate: Portland High School, A.B. Colby College 1876, A.M. 1879, S.T.D. Newton Theological Institution 1876–79, student at the universities of Berlin and Leipzig 1879–81, Ph.D. Johns Hopkins University 1889; professor of history and political economy: Colby College 1881–88; reader in history: Johns Hopkins University 1889; fourth president: Colby College 1889–92; professor and head of Department of Sociology: University of Chicago from 1892, dean: graduate school of arts and literature from 1905; editor: *American Journal of Sociology* from 1895; vice president: University of Chicago 1905–23; author: *General Sociology* 1907, *The Cameralists* 1909, *The Meaning of Social Science* 1910, *Between Eras from Capitalism to Democracy* 1913.

Small, Alvah Randall 1882– ?, born: South Portland; B.S. University of Maine 1904, C.E. 1929; inspector: New York Fire Insurance Exchange 1904–06; with Underwriters Laboratories, Chicago, Illinois, from 1906, assistant engineer, assistant electrical engineer 1906–07, special agent 1908–09, superintendent: label service 1910–16, vice president 1916, president 1935–48, vice chairman of the board from 1948; trustee, director, president: Underwriters Laboratories of Canada 1935–38; expert, fire protection section: War Industries Board 1917–18; fellow: American Institute of Electrical Engineers, member: American Society for Testing Materials, director: American Standards Association.

Small, Alvin Edmund 1811–86, born: Wales; graduate: Monmouth Academy; principal: Bath grammar school, studied medicine in Bath with Dr. Israel Putnam; M.D. Pennsylvania Medical College 1842, practiced physiology and pathology: Homeopathic Medical College of Pennsylvania 1848–56; professor of theory and practice of medicine: Hahnemann Medical College (Chicago) 1856–69, first dean 1859, president 1869–1885; life member: Chicago Historical Society, general secretary: American Institute of Homeopathy, president 1850; co-editor: *Philadelphia Journal of Homĺopathy* 1854–60, *U.S. Medical and Surgical Journal* 1870–74; made an enormous contribution to medical literature; author: *Manual of Homaeopathic Practice* 1854 fifteen editions, *Diseases of the Nervous System* 1856, *A Systematic Treatise on the Practice of Medicine* (900 pages) 1886.

Small, Frederick Percival 1874–1958, born: Augusta; L.L.B. Cornell University School of Law; began with Merchants Dispatch Transportation Co.; with American Express Co. from 1896, director from 1918, president 1923–44; director: Chase Manhattan Bank, Continental Insurance Co., Remington Rand division of Sperry-Rand Corp., American Surety Co. of New York; member: Maine Society, Sons of the Revolution.

Small, Vivian Blanche 1875–1946, born Gardiner; A.B. Mount Holyoke College 1896, Litt.D. 1912, A.M. University of Chicago 1905, L.L.D. (Hon.) Western Reserve University 1913; assistant in Gorham High School 1896–98, Howe School, Billerica, Massachusetts 1898–1901, assistant in Latin: Mount Holyoke College 1901–02, instructor 1902–08, associate professor 1908–09, head of Mead Hall 1907–08, president: Lake Erie College from 1909.

Smiley, Albert Keith 1828–1912; born: Vassalboro; brother of Daniel and Sarah Frances Smiley; A.B. Haverford College 1849; A.M. (Hon.) 1859, Brown University 1875, L.L.D. Haverford College 1906; instructor: Haverford College 1848–53; founder and principal: English and Classical Academy, Philadelphia 1853–57; principal: Oak Grove Seminary 1858–59, Friends Boarding School (later Moses Brown School), Providence, 1860–70; in 1869, began construction of the Mohonk Mountain House, in the Shawangunk Mountains of New York, a large park and hotel widely known for its Quaker gentility, the silent rule forbade card playing, dancing, Sabbath breaking, and consumption of alcohol; as member of the Board of Indian Commissioners, from

1879, brought major reforms, began hosting yearly convocations at Mohonk 1883, which became known as the Lake Mohonk Conference of Friends of the Indian, to discuss the state of Indian affairs and those of other dependent peoples, and possible reforms; began a similar convocation on international arbitration; original member of the board of trustees: Bryn Mawr College, president, board of trustees: New Paltz State Normal School, member: board of trustees, Brown University from 1875.

Smiley, Daniel 1855–1930, born: Vassalboro; brother of Albert and Sarah Frances Smiley; A.B. Haverford College 1878; instructor in Greek and Latin: William Penn Charter School, Philadelphia 1878–81; joined brother Albert in the management of Lake Mohonk, succeeding to ownership 1912; president: Conference on International Arbitration, Conference of Friends of the Indians and Other Dependent Peoples; member: U.S. Board of Indian Commissioners from 1912; trustee: Vassar College 1902–22, chairman 1920–22; trustee: Haverford College, New Paltz State Normal School, University of Redlands.

Smith, Amos 1871–1937, born: Eastport; pugilist, known as Mysterious Billy Smith, became first welterweight champion 1892–1900; was the subject of two oil portraits by Thomas Eakins: *Between the Rounds* (now at the Philadelphia Museum of Art), and *Salutat,* (now at the Addison Museum of Art, Andover, Massachusetts); became a close companion of Eakins before the artist's death; later operated a hotel in Tacoma and a bar and grill in Portland, Oregon.

Smith, Benjamin Franklin 1830–1927, born: South Freedom; brought up on his father's farm, after teaching for a year (1849), joined his brothers George, Francis, and David, in the business of publishing lithographic prints and steel engravings, such as portraits of presidents of the United States and other eminent men, and views of the principal cities of the United States, many of which were of his devising; after the financial panic of 1857, established a small bank in Omaha, Nebraska; gold having been discovered in Colorado, he proceeded to Mountain City with five wagonloads of merchandise, purchased a quartz claim near Mountain City that proved rich in gold; was involved in a number of exciting adventures, including a dispute with General Fitz-John Porter, who had attempted to tap Smith's claim by sinking a shaft on an adjoining claim; founded Smith & Parmalee Gold Mining Co. with offices in New York 1864; after selling the mine in 1865, spent three years in bond investment in New York, returned to Omaha, acquired a large amount of real estate as well as mining properties elsewhere, purchased 2,000 acres in South Omaha 1882, organized the South Omaha Stockyards, Inc., which became the second largest stockyard and meatpacking center in the United States; founder and first president: U.S. National Bank of Omaha; purchased Warrenton Park on Penobscot Bay and developed it into one of the noted estates on the coast.

Smith, Charles H. 1826–98, born: Standish; coxswain, USN, recipient: Medal of Honor, "On board the USS *Rhode Island* which was engaged in saving the lives of the officers and crew of the USS *Monitor*, off Cape Hatteras, North Carolina, 30 December 1862. Participating in the hazardous rescue of the officers and crew of the sinking *Monitor*, Smith, after rescuing several of the men, became separated in a heavy gale with other members of the cutter that had set out from the *Rhode Island*, and spent many hours in the small boat at the mercy of the weather and high seas until finally picked up by a schooner fifty miles east of Cape Hatteras." Buried in Arlington National Cemetery.

Smith, Charles Henry 1827–1902, born: Salmon Falls (Buxton); graduate: Limerick Academy, A.B. Waterville College 1856; taught at Eastport High School for several years; studied law in the office of Aaron Hayden; in the Civil War: commissioned captain, USV, assigned to the 1st Maine Cavalry, conducted a reconnaissance from Front Royal to Martinsburg and Williamsport, behind enemy lines; participated in the battles of Cedar Mountain (after which he was detailed, under flag of truce, to collect the wounded and dead), Raccoon Ford, second Bull Run; promoted to major, USV, lieutenant colonel, USV, participated in Stoneman's Raid, Brandy Station, Aldie, Middleburg, during which, he had two horses shot from beneath him, promoted colonel, USV, Gettysburg, Shepardstown, Bristoe Station, Mine Run, Todd's Tavern, South Anna, Haw's Shop, Trevilian's Station, St. Mary's Church (wounded, recipient: Medal of Honor, remained in the fight to the close, although severely wounded); commanding officer: 3rd Brigade, Maine Cavalry: Rowanty Creek, Gravelly Run, Boydtown Plank Road, Dinwiddie Court House, where he was wounded in the leg by the bullet that killed his horse, brevetted major general, USV, Appomattox, after being mustered out 1865, appointed aide-de-camp to the governor of Maine, to aid in suppressing a Fenian outbreak; member: Maine bar; member: Maine Senate 1866; rejoined the regular army, appointed colonel of the 28th Infantry, USA, brevetted brigadier general, USA, 1867, commanding officer: 19th Infantry, USA, retired 1891; buried in Arlington National Cemetery.

Smith, Clyde Harold 1876–1940, born: Harmony; graduate: Hartland Academy; taught school; member: Maine House of Representatives 1899–1903; removed to Skowhegan, sheriff of Somerset County 1905–09; sold automobiles, hardware, and plumbing, newspaper publisher; member: Maine Senate 1923–29; chairman: Maine State Highway Commission 1928–32, member: executive council 1933–37; member from the Second District: U.S. House of Representatives 1937–40 (Republican), died in office, succeeded by his wife Margaret Chase Smith; buried in Pine Grove Cemetery, Hartland.

Smith, Daniel Appleton White 1840–1921, born: Waterville; son of Samuel Francis Smith; A.B. Harvard College 1859, graduate: Newton Theological Institution

1863; ordained Baptist minister 1863, missionary from 1863; president: Karen Theological Seminary, Inselin, Burma, 1876–1916; editor: *The Morning Star*, a monthly in Karen from 1868; author: *Sermonizing and Preaching* 1904, *Sketch of the Life of Edward Abiel Stevens* 1886, *Sound Principles of Interpretation* 1902, translator: *Wayland's Moral Science* 1885, annotations of the *Annotationed Para Bible of the London Tract Society* 1887.

Smith, Earl Baldwin 1888–1956, born: Topsham; son of a merchant; graduate: Pratt Institute, Brooklyn 1906, A.B. Bowdoin College ΦBK 1911, A.M. 1912, L.H.D. (Hon.) 1931, A.M. Princeton University 1912, Ph.D. 1915; instructor, assistant professor, associate professor of art and archaeology: Princeton University 1916–26, professor 1926–31, first Howard Crosby Butler memorial professor of history of architecture 1931–54, chairman of department 1945–54; an excellent freehand draftsman, taught a graduate course in the history of ornament; first chairman of the special program in the humanities, established 1936; belonged to the faculty committee that formulated the four-course plan of study, instituted in 1924, which reduced the number of courses taken in the senior and junior years to four, giving additional time for independent study; chairman of the faculty committee that formulated the design of the Firestone Library, completed in 1949; chief marshal at all Princeton convocations, for many years; in World War I: captain, USA, served with the 312th Regiment, 78th Division, in France, where he was wounded, in World War II: instructor at the Naval Air Intelligence Officers School, Quonset Point, Rhode Island; author: *Early Christian Iconography* 1918, *Early Churches in Syria* 1929, *Egyptian Architecture* 1938, *The Dome* 1950, *Architectural Symbolism of Imperial Rome and the Middle Ages* 1956; contributor: *American Journal of Archaeology*, *Art Studies*, *Art and Archaeology*, *The Art Bulletin*; director: American Institute for Iranian Art and Archaeology, College Art Association.

Smith, Edward Staples Cousens 1894–1971, born: Biddeford, attended public schools in Biddeford, B.S. Bowdoin College 1918; in World War I: employed as a chemist with Hercules Powder Co., Wilmington, Delaware; graduate student at Massachusetts Institute of Technology 1918–19, A.M. Harvard University in geology 1920; instructor in geology: Radcliffe College 1921–23, instructor in geology: Union College 1923–25, assistant professor 1925–29, associate professor 1929–32, professor 1932–60, chairman of the department 1925–60; responsible for the creation and furnishing of the geological laboratories and the installation of the Wheatley Cabinet, a notable early collection of minerals, established in 1858; director: Union College's Summer Institute of Earth Sciences 1958–60; instrumental in the making of Union College's first movie: *George Goes to College* 1936; professor on the faculty of the National Science Foundation's Institute of Science and Mathematics 1959–60; Smith's special interest was in fluorescent and radioactive minerals, meteorites, and hydrology; an early advocate of conservation of water resources; coauthor: *An Annotated Bibliography* *of Katahdin* 1946, *Applied Atomic Power* 1946; contributed the chapter "Why Do Ice Ages Occur?" to *Science Marches On* 1927; author of numerous articles for scientific journals on the geology of Maine and other subjects; for many years, a speaker on the General Electric Company's *Science Forum* broadcast over radio station WGY, Schenectady; presented his valuable collection of minerals to Bowdoin College 1960; after his retirement, his former students established the Edward S. C. Smith Prize, awarded annually to the student demonstrating high professional potential in geology; president: New York State Geological Society 1930, life member of the Appalachian Mountain Club.

Smith, Elizabeth Oakes Prince 1806–93, born: North Yarmouth; married to Seba Smith, to whose career she devoted her time; editor: *Mayflower*, an annual published in Boston 1839–42; removed with her husband to New York 1842, became one of the first American women to appear on the lecture platform; ardent advocate of women's rights, preached at an independent congregation in Canistota, New York; first white woman to climb Katahdin 1849; after her husband's death in 1868; removed to Hollywood, South Carolina; author: *Riches Without Wings* 1838, a collection of poems, *The Sinless Child, and Other Poems* 1843, *Stories for Children* 1847, *The Roman Tribute* 1850, a tragedy in five acts, *Woman and Her Needs* 1851, *Jacob Ziesler* 1853, a drama, *Hints on Dress and Beauty* 1852, *Bald Eagle; or, the Last of the Ramapaughs* 1867, *The Newsboy*, *Sagamore of the Saco*, *The Two Wires*, as well as sketches and contemporary journals, social and moral issues dominated her work, especially female suffrage, her autobiography was published in 1924; mother of Appleton Oaksmith.

Smith, Eugene Hanes 1853–1925, born: Old Town; D.M.D. Harvard University Dentistry School 1874, A.M. Howard University; professor of clinical dentistry and dean: Harvard University Dentistry School from 1895.

Smith, Francis Ormand Jonathan 1806–76, born: Brentwood, New Hampshire; attended Phillips Academy, Exeter; studied law in Portsmouth, entered the law office of Samuel Fessenden and Thomas Amory Deblois, Portland 1826; editor: *Portland Argus* 1827; division advocate of the fifth division of the circuit court martial in Maine 1829–34; member: Maine House of Representatives 1831, unsuccessful candidate for reelection; editor: *Augusta Age* 1831; member, president: Maine Senate 1832, member: U.S. House of Representatives: 1833–39 (Jacksonian), chairman: Committee on Commerce; unsuccessful candidate for reelection 1838; member: Maine House of Representatives 1863–64; agent of Secretary of State Daniel Webster's campaign to sway public opinion in favor of the Webster-Ashburton Treaty; instrumental in establishing the Portland gasworks, the York and Cumberland Railroad and Portland and Oxford Central Railroad companies, president of the latter, as well as of the Androscoggin Navigation Co., which he created to connect Canton and Rumford Falls by steamboats (it was during his presidency that the Portland & Oxford Central Railroad's passenger trains acquired such a reputation for slowness and uncertainty of schedule that it was suggested that cattle guards be placed, not only on the front of railroad trains, but also on their rear, to prevent cattle from entering the cars and annoying the passengers); patron and early supporter of Samuel F. B. Morse and his telegraph, from which he made a fortune; a copperhead during the Civil War, regarded by many to be a complete scoundrel; author: *Reports of Decisions in the Circuit Courts-Martial of Maine* 1831, *Laws of the State of Maine* (two volumes) 1834, *Secret Corresponding Vocabulary: Adopted for Use to Morse's Electro-Magnetic Telegraph* 1845; buried in Evergreen Cemetery, Portland, where his tomb, in the Egyptian Revival mode, is on the National Register of Historic Places.

Smith, George Otis 1871–1944, born: Hodgdon; son of Joseph Smith, Maine attorney general 1881–84; A.B. Colby College ΦBK 1893, A.M. 1896, Ph.D. Johns Hopkins University 1896, Sc.D. (Hon.) Case Institute of Technology 1914, Colorado School of Mines 1928, L.L.D. Colby College 1920; assistant geologist: U.S. Geological Survey, engaged in geologic work in Michigan, Utah, Washington and the New England states 1896–1901, geologist 1901; director: U.S. Geological Survey 1907–30, oversaw investigations in all parts of the United States, work in mining and geology, geologic land classification and valuation, investigations and mapping of Alaskan mineral resources, both surficial and below ground; instrumental in the creation of the Federal Oil Conservation Board; appointed chairman by Calvin Coolidge: Technical and Advisory Commission 1924–31; appointed by Herbert Hoover as chairman: Federal Power Commission 1930–33; devoted himself to studies of coal, oil, and waterpower; appointed by Warren Harding to the U.S. Coal Commission 1922–23, chairman: Naval Oil Reserve Commission 1924; it was Smith's observations of attempts to defraud the government that led directly to the so-called Tea Pot Dome scandals; author of numerous works, including *World Atlas of Commercial Geology*; generally considered to be the foremost expert on hydroelectric power in United States; director: Central Maine Power Co., trustee: National Geographic Society, University of Chicago, Coburn Classical Institute, Bloomfield Academy, chairman, board of trustees: Colby College, president: American Institute of Mining and Metallurgical Engineers 1928–29.

Smith, Joseph Adams 1837–1907, born: Machias, graduate: Bucksport Seminary, L.L.D. Harvard University Law School; USN, 1861; on board USS *Kearsarge* during her fight with the CSS *Alabama*, commanding officer: powder division; paymaster 1862, pay inspector 1879, paymaster general 1882–86, retired as rear admiral, USN, 1899; buried in Arlington National Cemetery.

Smith, Joseph Sewall 1836–1919, born: Wiscasset; in the Civil War: Sergeant, 3rd Maine Volunteers, June 1861, first lieutenant, USV, August 1861, captain, USV

Commissary of Subsistence Volunteers, November 1861, brevetted brigadier general, USV, July 1865, recipient: Medal of Honor, at Hatcher's Run, Virginia, 27 October 1864, led a part of a brigade, saved two pieces of artillery, captured a flag, and secured a number of prisoners.

Smith, Margaret Chase 1887–1996, born: Skowhegan; wife of Clyde Smith; member from the Second District: U.S. House of Representatives 1940–49 (Republican); member: U.S. Senate 1949–1973, chairman: Committee on Rates of Compensation; first woman to serve in both houses of Congress, first woman to break the sound barrier, first woman to be nominated for president of the United States by a major political party, her stance against Senator Joseph McCarthy, in her "Declaration of Conscience" speech signaled the turning of the tide in that dismal period, awarded the Presidential Medal of Freedom 1989; interred at the Margaret Chase Smith Library, Skowhegan.

Smith, Mathew Hale 1816–79, born: Portland; son of a minister and publisher of the first religious newspaper in the United States, entitled *The Herald of Gospel Liberty* 1808; ordained Universalist minister 1834, converted to Calvinism, ordained Congregational minister, Malden, Massachusetts, 1842, began the study of law 1850, removed to New York, correspondent: *Boston Journal*, his "Burleigh Letters" attracted considerable attention and were reprinted in newspapers across the country; occasionally lectured from pulpits in Dutch Reformed, Methodist, and Presbyterian churches; author: *Text-Book of Universalism* 1836, *Universalism Examined, Renounced and Exposed* 1842, *Universalism not of God* 1847, *Sabbath Evenings* 1849, *Mount Calvary* 1866, *Marvels of Prayer, Sunshine and Shadow in New York* 1869, *Successful Folks*; made extensive lecture tours around the country, spent six months in California, his lecture topics included: "From the Thames to the Tiber," "Old Times and Our Times," "Wit and Humor"; in the Civil War: chaplain, 12th New York Volunteers from 1861; married to the grandniece of President John Adams.

Smith, Orland Francis 1905–74, born: Gorham, son of a merchant; attended public schools in Gorham and Brockton, Massachusetts, Ph.B. Brown University 1927, M.D. Boston University 1931; interned at Somerville Hospital 1931–32, resident at Rhode Island Hospital, Providence, 1932–33, Providence Hospital 1933–34; to help finance his medical education, played professional football with the Providence Steamrollers 1927–29, assisted that team when it won the world championship in 1928, also worked nights as an ambulance driver; practiced in Pawtucket 1934–71, Providence 1947–75, assistant surgeon: Rhode Island Hospital, senior assistant surgeon: Memorial Hospital, Pawtucket, chief of surgery 1954–64, chief of surgery: Notre Dame Hospital, Central Falls, Rhode Island, 1971–75, consultant in surgery: Cape Cod Hospital, Hyannis, South County Hospital, Wakefield, Rhode Island; author: *Intersusception: Diagnosis and Treatment* 1945, *Multiple Transfusions* 1946, *Colovesical*

Fistula: A Complication of Diverticulitis 1960, *Spontaneous Rupture of the Normal Spleen; A Case Report* 1962, *The Cost of Doing Business* 1962; in World War II: lieutenant commander, USN Reserve, served aboard USS *Bountiful*, a hospital ship as chief surgeon, which lay just offshore during the battles of Guam, Saipan, Leyte, Iwo Jima, Okinawa; alumni trustee: Brown University.

Smith, Peter Thacher 1731–1826, born: Falmouth (that portion that later became Portland); son of Thomas Smith; all the married women upon the Neck were present at his birth, and their husbands were entertained with a supper on the occasion; A.B. Harvard College 1753, A.M. 1756, as an undergraduate, waited on tables, worked as a scholar of the house and held a Hollis Scholarship; after teaching school for a time in Falmouth, returned to Harvard College as library-keeper 1755; that same year, agreed to remove to New Marblehead (now Windham) and to preach to the congregation of the deceased John Wight, which was in the thrall of an illiterate exhorter named Ebenezer Townsend; the activities of hostile Indians drove Smith back to Harvard College a year later; after qualifying for his master's degree, he studied theology, supported by Hopkins and Saltonstall Scholarships, for five years; as candidate preacher, preached in Plymouth and Weymouth, Massachusetts, whose call he refused; preached for a term in New Marblehead, served as probationer in Shrewsbury 1761; after an ardent call from New Marblehead, returned to that place 1762 and was installed with great pomp, preaching without major incident to 1787; running afoul of his own parishioners, Baptists, and Quakers, he was illegally dismissed by the vote in town meeting, after which disgruntled citizens attempted to steal the schoolhouse, which had also served as the meetinghouse of the First Parish, which they abandoned in the road; after holding meetings in his home, he agreed to dismissal, given his continued use of the ministry lot; continued his role as intermediary with the town's proprietors; appointed justice of the peace and quorum for Cumberland County 1795; member: Massachusetts House of Representatives 1804; left, at his death, a very large number of descendants.

Smith, Samantha Reed 1972–85, born: Houlton; daughter of a school teacher and an employee of the Maine Department of Human Services; at age ten wrote a letter to the Soviet leader at the Kremlin in Moscow questioning why the Soviet Union wanted to dominate the United States, newly elected Soviet President Yuri Andropov responded with a letter indicating that that was not his wish and invited Samantha to the Soviet Union, so that she could make her own appraisal; this visit was accorded international attention; subsequently she was offered and accepted a role in a television series; returning from London with her father, she was killed in an airplane crash in Auburn; her letter to Andropov is credited, by some, as the turning of the tide in the Cold War.

Smith, Samuel Emerson 1788–1860, born: Hollis, New Hampshire; son of a chaplain in the Revolutionary Army and, subsequently, a lawyer in Wiscasset; graduate: Groton Academy, A.B. Harvard College φBK 1808; studied law with Samuel Dana, in Groton; member: Massachusetts bar 1812, removed to Wiscasset; member: Massachusetts House of Representatives 1819, member: Maine House of Representatives 1820; chief justice of the court of common pleas 1821, judge: Maine Supreme Judicial Court 1822–30; seventh governor of Maine (Republican) 1830–34; first chief executive to preside in Augusta; member: commission to codify and revise Maine public law 1835–37; Bowdoin College overseer 1821–31, trustee ex-officio 1831–34; his home, on Federal Street in Wiscasset, is extant and is on the National Register of Historic Places.

Smith, Samuel Francis 1808–95, born: Boston, Massachusetts; graduate: Boston Latin School, recipient: Franklin Medal for primacy in scholarship, A.B. Harvard College 1829, S.T.D. Andover Theological Seminary 1832; while a student at Andover, composed the words for the patriotic hymn *America*, originally for a children's Fourth of July festival at the Park Street Church, Boston, 1831; pastor of the Baptist church in Waterville and professor of modern languages at Waterville College 1833–41; pastor of the Baptist church in Newton Center, Massachusetts, and editor of *The Christian Review*, later editorial secretary of the Missionary Union; his classmate at Harvard, Oliver Wendell Holmes, referred to him in a reunion poem:

> And theres a nice youngster of Excellent pith;
> Fate tried to conceal him by naming him Smith!
> But he chanted a song for the brave and the free,
> Just read on his medal, "My country, tis of thee!"

Buried in Newton (Massachusetts) Cemetery; father of Daniel Appleton White Smith.

Smith, Sarah Perry 1836–1914, born: Norridgewock; a relation of Commodores Oliver Hazard and Matthew Calbraith Perry; married Lieutenant Hillman Smith, USV, Company K, 8th Maine Volunteer Infantry, later Androscoggin County sheriff, mayor of Auburn, and warden of the Maine State Prison; accompanied her husband to Hilton Head, South Carolina, where she was under near-constant artillery fire; on at least two occasions, found herself behind Confederate lines and was able to extricate herself, one source suggests that she observed the assault on Battery Wagner, in which Robert Gould Shaw was killed; finally ordered to remove herself from the scene of the war by General Quincy Adams Gilmore; she settled in Auburn.

Smith, Seba 1792–1868, born: Buckfield; A.B. Bowdoin College 1818; editor: *Eastern Argus*, Portland, founded Maine's first daily newspaper, the *Portland Daily Courier* 1829, removed to New York 1842; during the Jackson Administration, created the character of Major Jack Downing, the subject of numerous columns, widely reprinted, and a book: *My Thirty Years Out of the Senate*, the importance of Major Jack

Downing to the country can be measured by his obituary, which was widely reprinted: "The *Portland Courier* announces the death of Maj. Jack Downing. His funeral was the largest that ever took place in Downingville—all were mourners, but the company dispensed with *weeds* it being too early in the season for green vegetables. His funeral service was performed by Elder Pennyroyal, of the Mormon connexion [*sic*], who for his text that celebrated passage in the Book of Jasher—he lifted up his voice like a loon; lo! Like a loon he lifted up"; his other works are: *Powhatan, A Metrical Romance*, in seven cantos 1841, *Way Down East, or Portraitures of Yankee Life* 1855, *New Elements of Geometry, Dew Drops of the Nineteenth Century*; husband of Elizabeth Oakes Prince Smith, with whom he edited *Emerson's Magazine* and *Putnam's Monthly*, father of Appleton Oaksmith; retired to Patchogue, Long Island, New York, where he subsequently died and is buried.

Smith, Sidney Irving 1843–1926, born: Norway; Ph.B. Sheffield School, Yale University 1867, A.M. Yale University 1887; assistant in biology: Yale University 1867–75, professor of comparative anatomy 1875–1906, professor emeritus from 1906; had charge of deep water dredging in Lake Superior for the U.S. Lake Survey 1871, U.S. Coast Survey, Georges Bank, 1872; associated for many years with the U.S. Fish Commission; member: National Academy of Arts and Sciences; author of numerous papers on marine zoology; brother-in-law and colleague of Addison Emery Verrill.

Smith, Theodate Louise 1859–1914, born: Hallowell; A.B. Smith College 1882, A.M. 1884, Ph.D. Yale University 1896, student at Clark University 1895–96 (first female student at Clark); while psychologist, worked with Granville Stanley Hall 1902–09, lecturer and librarian 1909–14, assisted Hall in his pioneer studies in genetic psychology, as librarian brought together the largest collection on child welfare in world; contributed to: *Pedagogical Seminary, American Journal of Psychology*; coauthor: *Aspects of Child Life* 1907, author: *The Montessori System in Theory and Practice: An Introduction to the Pedagogical Methods of Mme. Montessori* 1912, the first work in English detailing the Montessori system.

Smith, Winford Henry 1877–1961, born: West Scarborough; A.B. Bowdoin College 1899, Sc.D. 1918, M.D. Johns Hopkins University Medical School 1903; intern and resident gynecologist: Lakeside Hospital, Cleveland, 1903–05; hospital physician, New York City Health Department 1905–06, superintendent: Hartford (Connecticut) Hospital 1906–09, general medical superintendent of Bellevue and allied hospitals, New York 1909–11; director: Johns Hopkins University Hospital, Baltimore 1911–46; in World War I: chief of hospital division, staff of surgeon general, Washington, D.C.; president: American Hospital Association 1916, awarded gold medal for outstanding achievement in hospital administration; author of numerous papers and articles on hospital administration.

Smyth, Egbert Coffin 1829–1904, born: Brunswick; son of William Smyth, brother of Newman Smyth; A.B. Bowdoin College 1848, D.D. 1866, L.L.D. (Hon.) 1902, D.D. Harvard University 1886, graduate: Bangor Theological Seminary 1853; professor of rhetoric: Bowdoin College 1854–56, professor of natural and revealed religion: Andover Theological Seminary 1856–63, professor of ecclesiastical history from 1883, president of the faculty 1876–96; leader of the Andover movement that sought to reform dogmatic theology; a complaint was lodged in 1886 that Smyth, Samuel Harris, and two other members of the faculty had inculcated beliefs inconsistent with the creed of the seminary, in particular, that they had denied the infallibility of the Bible, had taught that a previous knowledge of Christ was not necessary to repentance, and that there is a probation, after death, for those who have not known of and decisively rejected Christ; the trustees of Andover Theological Seminary sustained Smyth and the others, and they were eventually vindicated by the Massachusetts Supreme Court, which found for Smyth 1892; Bowdoin College overseer 1874–77, vice president of the board 1876–77, trustee 1877–1904; founder and editor: *Andover Review*, author: *Three Discourses on the Religious History of Bowdoin College* 1858, translator of Uhlhorns *Conflict of Christianity and Heathenism* 1879, furnished introduction and appendix to *Observations Concerning the Scriptural Economia of the Trinity* by Jonathan Edwards 1880.

Smyth, Samuel Phillips Newman 1843–1925, born: Brunswick; son of William Smyth, brother of Egbert Smyth; A.B. Bowdoin College 1863, A.M. 1866; graduate: Andover Theological Seminary 1867, D.D. New York University 1881, Yale University 1895, Bowdoin College 1921; after teaching at the U.S. Naval Academy, then located in Newport, Rhode Island, commissioned first lieutenant, 16th Maine Volunteers, rose in rank to acting quartermaster 1864–65; ordained Congregational minister 1868, pastor: Mission Chapel, Providence, 1867–70, First Congregational Church, Bangor, 1870–75, First Presbyterian Church, Quincy, Illinois, 1876–82, First Congregational Church, New Haven, 1882–1907; Yale fellow from 1899; author: *The Place of Death in Evolution* 1897, *Personal Creeds* 1890, *Christian Ethics* 1892, *Through Science to Faith* 1902, *Passing Protestantism and Coming Catholicism* 1908, *Modern Belief in Immortality* 1910, *Constructive Natural Theology* 1913, *The Meaning of Personal Life* 1916, *Approaches Toward Church Unity* 1919, *Story of Church Unity* 1924; in his later years, devoted himself to religious unity, perceiving that the two great branches of Christianity—Protestantism and Roman Catholicism—would be reunited in one communion, he maintained that while Protestantism has won the victory forever for the spiritual liberty of the individual man, which was its crowning victory, it was losing mastery over the controlling forces of modern life and its authority was disappearing, the solution to which was the restoration of a single Christian society, the first step being the union of the Congregational and Episcopal churches, to which he devoted much effort; founder and chairman: New Haven Good Government Club, New Haven Law and Order League.

Smyth, William 1797–1865, born: Pittston; grandson of Reuben Coburn; orphaned at age seventeen, the care of his siblings fell to him; served in the army during the War of 1812; clerked for a Wiscasset merchant, assistant to the principal of Gorham Academy; A.B. Bowdoin College 1822, D.D. 1863, attended Andover Theological Seminary 1822–23; instructor in Greek and mathematics: Bowdoin College 1823–28, professor of Greek 1828–68, adjunct professor of natural philosophy 1845–68; conductor on the underground railroad; raised money required to build Memorial Hall to honor Bowdoin men who had fought in the Civil War; member of the Brunswick School Committee for seventeen years, introduced a system of graded schools at Brunswick, considered revolutionary, at the time; author of a series of textbooks, including *Plane Trigonometry* 1830, *Elements of Algebra* 1830, *Elements of Analytic Geometry* 1830, *Elementary Algebra for Schools* 1833, *Treatise on Algebra* 1852, *Plane Trigonometry, Surveying and Navigation* 1855, *Analytical Geometry* 1855, *Elements of the Differential and Integral Calculus* 1856, editor: *Advocate of Freedom*, the earliest antislavery newspaper in Maine; father of Egbert and Newman Smyth.

Snow, Albert Sydney 1845–1932, born: Rockland; graduate: U.S. Naval Academy 1865; aboard USS *Marblehead* during her pursuit of the Confederate raiders CSS *Florida* and CSS *Tallahassee*, stationed at Pensacola 1866–69, Alaska 1870–73, aboard USS *Congress* 1874–76, executive officer: USS *Portsmouth*; coastal survey 1883–87, commanded the geodetic survey ship *Patterson* in Alaska, where he surveyed some particularly difficult stretches of coast; duty at U.S. Naval Academy 1893–94; inspector of lighthouses 1895–98; commanding officer: USS *Badger* during the Spanish-American War, later commanding officer: of USS *Vermont*, USS *Columbia*, USS *Hancock*; retired as rear admiral, USN, 1907.

Snow, Charles Wilbert 1884–1977, born: Whitehead Island, Saint George; son of a coast guardsman; attended public schools in Spruce Head and Thomaston, A.B. Bowdoin College φBK 1907, A.M. 1925, A.M. Columbia University 1910, L.L.D. (Hon.) Wesleyan University 1945, D.Litt. Marietta College 1945; for three years before entering high school, worked as a lobsterman, completed high school in two years, boxed stone at the Spruce Head Island Quarry, taught at the Bussick School, Spruce Head, Timber Hill School, Owl's Head, while attending Bowdoin College was employed as the college bell ringer; instructor in English: New York University 1907–08, Bowdoin College 1908–09, Williams College 1909–10; Eskimo school teacher and reindeer agent, Council, Alaska, 1911–12; instructor in English: University of Utah 1913–16, Indiana University 1916–17, Reed College 1918–19, Indiana University 1919–21, assistant professor: Wesleyan University 1921–26, associate professor 1926–29, professor 1929–52; in World War I: first lieutenant, Field Artillery, USA, 1917–18; president: Connecticut Association of Education 1940; special lecturer for the U.S. Department of State in Europe, Asia, and the Near East 1951–52; lieutenant governor of Connecticut 1945–46, governor of Connecticut 1946–47; fellow: Yale Corporation; author: *Maine Coast* 1923, *The Inner Harbor* 1926, *Down East* 1932, *Selected Poems* 1936, *Before the Wind* 1938, *Maine Tides* 1940, *Sonnets to Steve and Other Poems* 1957, *Spruce Head: Selections from His Poetry* 1958, *The Collected Poems of Wilbert Snow* 1963, *Autobiography* 1973.

Sockelexis, Louis 1873–1917, born: Indian Island; played baseball for a variety of college teams: Harvard, Holy Cross, Ricker, Notre Dame to 1897, attracted the attention of the Cleveland Spiders, his father, outraged, traveled to Washington, D.C., and asked President Cleveland to prevent his son from playing a child's game with sticks and balls, Cleveland declined and Sockelexis went on to be a superlative ball player; later, the Cleveland team adopted the name Indians in his honor, cousin of Andrew Sockelexis, runner in the 1912 Olympics; buried in Old Town Cemetery.

Somers, Frederic Maxwell 1850–94, born: Portland; B.S. Massachusetts Agricultural College 1872; while an undergraduate: president of the Union Literary Society, correspondent for the *Springfield Republican*, rowed on the crew, which won the first race under the auspices of the Regatta Association of American Colleges; taught school for a year in Fairmount, Kansas; assistant editor: *Leavenworth* (Kansas) *Daily Times, Daily Commercial*; organizer, secretary: Kansas Academy of Arts and Sciences; editorial writer and political correspondent: *San Francisco Chronicle* from 1875, founded: *The Argonaut* 1877, a weekly political, satirical, and society journal, the first of its kind on the Pacific Coast and so original in its makeup and methods as to establish a type and style for this form of journalism throughout the country; publisher: *The Californian* from 1880; founded the enormously influential: *Current Literature* 1888; founded: *Short Stories* 1890; a founder and member: The Bohemian Club; died on his way to England, where he intended to found a literary magazine.

Sorenson, Lloyd Raymond 1897– ?, born: Calais; B.S.E.E. Massachusetts Institute of Technology 1919; with Newport News Shipbuilding & Dry Dock Co. from 1918, assistant naval architect 1930–42, cost engineer 1942–54, production engineer 1954–56, vice president, production manager 1955–57, vice president from 1957, general manager 1957–64; president, director: Newport News Building and Loan Association.

Soule, Gideon Lane 1796–1879, born: Freeport; son of a farmer, ship caulker, and schoolteacher; left school to become an errand boy for Jacob Abbott, through him, gained admittance to Phillips Academy, Exeter, New Hampshire, 1813, graduating in 1816, A.B. Bowdoin College 1818, having entered as a junior, L.L.D. (Hon.) Harvard University 1856; professor of ancient languages: Phillips Academy, Andover, Massachusetts, 1822–38, second principal 1838–73, during his long administration, Abbot, Gorham, and the New Academy buildings were built.

Soule, Joshua 1781–1867, born: Bristol; son of a ship captain; admitted on trial, New England Methodist Episcopal Conference 1799, ordained elder 1802, itinerant preacher in New England 1803–16, known as a vocal and resourceful enemy of Calvinism, Unitarianism, and Universalism; presiding elder: Maine District 1804, proposed the plan for a general conference of delegates, which was adopted at Baltimore 1808, member of the conferences 1812, 1816; book agent and first editor: *Methodist Magazine* 1818–22; elected bishop, but declined 1820; pastor: Methodist churches in New York and Baltimore conferences 1820–24; ordained bishop, assigned to western and southern conferences 1820–44, living part of the time in Lebanon, Ohio; senior bishop, southern branch, with offices in Nashville, Tennessee, from 1846, faced many problems with the coming of the Civil War.

Southgate, Horatio 1812–94, born: Portland; A.B. Bowdoin College 1832, graduate: Andover Theological Seminary 1835, S.T.D. Columbia University 1845, Trinity College 1846; ordained Episcopal minister 1834, sent to Turkey and Persia by Board of Foreign Missions 1835–38, missionary to Constantinople 1840, consecrated missionary bishop 1844, involved in dispute with other missionaries, returned to United States 1849, declined election as bishop of California 1850, Haiti 1870; organized and served as rector: Saint Luke's, Portland 1851, Church of the Advent, Boston, 1852–58, involved in controversy with local bishop over high church ritual, rector: Zion Church, New York 1859–72; author: *Narrative of a Tour Through Armenia, Kurdistan, Persia, and Mesopotamia* (two volumes) 1840, *Narrative of a Visit to the Syrian (Jocobite) Church of Mesopotamia* 1844, *A Treatise on the Antiquity, Doctrine, Ministry, and Worship of the Anglican Church* (in Greek) 1849, *Practical Directions for the Observance of Lent* 1850, *The War in the East* 1855, *Parochial Sermons* 1859, *The Cross above the Crescent, a Romance of Constantinople* 1877.

Spalding, John Franklin 1828–1902, born: Belgrade; son of a farmer; attended North Yarmouth Academy, Maine Wesleyan Seminary, Kents Hill, A.B. Bowdoin College 1853, graduate: General Theological Seminary 1857, D.D. Trinity College 1874; ordained dean, St. Stephen's Church, Portland, 1857, priest, Christ Church, Gardiner, 1858, rector: Saint James' Episcopal Church, Old Town, 1859–60, Saint George's Church, Lee, Massachusetts, assistant rector: Grace Church, Providence, rector: Saint Paul's Church, Erie, Pennsylvania, 1862–73; member: general board of missions 1865–74, dean of the Erie convocation 1866–74; first Episcopal bishop of Colorado, New Mexico, and Wyoming from 1873, founded St. Luke's Hospital, Denver, 1881, rebuilt Mathews Hall, the divinity school 1882, rebuilt Wolfe Hall, the seminary for girls 1888, rebuilt St. John's military school 1888, president: St. John, the Evangelist College, built thirty churches; author: *Modern Infidelity* 1862, *Hymn from the Hymnal with Tunes Indicated* 1872, *The Cathedral System* 1880, *The Higher Education of Women* 1886, *A Manual for Mothers' Meetings*, *The Church and Its Apostolic Ministry* 1887, *The Three-Fold Ministry of the Church of Christ, The Pastoral Office, The Best*

Mode of Working a Parish 1889, *Jesus Christ—the Proof of Christianity* 1890.

Spaulding, Frederic Henry 1892–1974, born: Norridgewock; A.B. Bates College 1916, Ed.M. Harvard University 1926, Ed.D. University of Tampa 1936; principal: Massachusetts High School 1916–20, teacher and principal: Hillsborough Senior High School, Tampa, Florida, 1921–33, founder and president: University of Tampa, president: Edgewood Park School, Briarcliff, New York, founder: Tampa Junior College 1931, founder and president: Florida State Music Festival Association; in World War I: chemist: Chemical Warfare Service, USA, 1918; Florida state delegate: World Federation of Educational Associations, Geneva, Switzerland, 1928; founder, president: Hillsborough Schoolmasters Club; author: *The Teaching of English.*

Spaulding, Nathan Weston 1829– ?, born: North Anson; grandson of Nathan Weston, cousin of Nathan Weston Blanchard, Melville Weston Fuller; educated in public schools in North Anson 1833–47, going to school part-time and working as a carpenter, millwright; attended night school in Boston, while working in a saw factory; like his cousin, N. W. Blanchard, removed to California 1851, constructed the first quartz mine in California, on Mokeluma River; operated several sawmills in mining camps, established a saw manufacturing firm 1856, first west of the Mississippi; inventor of adjustable sawteeth 1861, which worked a revolution in the trade; holder of many patents for saws, sawteeth, and manufacturing machines, copyrighted the Spaulding log-scale, a scale for the measurement of logs which became the standard in United States; appointed by President Garfield as assistant U.S. treasurer, city of San Francisco 1881–85, twice mayor of Oakland (California), donated his salary to charitable causes; trustee: Stanford University; founder and director: Mechanics Institute, Oakland.

Spear, Albert Moore 1852–1929, born: Madison; graduate: Coburn Classical Institute, A.B. Bates College 1875; member: Maine bar 1878; practiced in Hallowell 1879–85, chairman: Hallowell School Board; Hallowell city solicitor; member: Maine House of Representatives 1883–85; removed to Gardiner, mayor of Gardiner 1889–93; member: Maine Senate 1891–95, president 1893–95; associate justice: Maine Supreme Judicial Court 1902–23, his decisions on waterpower attracted much attention, won the confirmation in the British House of Lords on the correct interpretation of common law.

Spear, Ellis 1834–1917, born Warren; A.B. Bowdoin College 1858, overseer 1912–17; school teacher at Wiscasset Academy; commissioned captain, USV, 1862, assigned to the 20th Maine Regiment, which was assigned to the 3rd Brigade, 1st Division, 5th Corps, served in that division to the close of the war; promoted to major, USV, after Fredericksburg, USV, after Gettysburg, at Peeble's Farm: commanding officer: of the brigade while only a major; brevetted brigadier general USV, for

Peeble's Farm 1865; assistant examiner: U.S. Patent Office 1865–68, examiner 1868–72, examiner in chief 1872–74; civil service examiner: U.S. Department of the Interior and assistant commissioner of patents 1874–76, resigned 1876; U.S. commissioner of patents 1877–78; practiced patent law and was solicitor of patents from 1878; trustee of Washington Public Schools, director: Washington, D.C., Board of Trade; commander of the military order of the Loyal Legion of the District of Columbia; second vice president: Washington Loan & Trust Co.; vice president: Equitable Co-Operative Building Association; president: Congregational Society of Mount Pleasant.

Spencer, Percy LeBaron 1894–1970, born: Howland; orphaned at an early age,
dropped out of school in the third grade; student: Naval Wireless and Electricians School, Brooklyn, New York, D.Sc. (Hon.) University of Massachusetts 1950, Nasson College 1959, University of Maine 1961; superintendent of operations: American Radio and Research Corp., superintendent: Wireless Specialty Co. 1915–18; manager: field engineering, Submarine Signal Co. 1920–25; director of development and engineering: Raytheon Manufacturing Co., Waltham, Massachusetts, 1925–40, manager and chief engineer: microwave and power tube division, Raytheon 1940–55, senior vice president, director: Raytheon 1955–65, director, consultant to 1970; assisted in development of photocell and gaseous rectifier tubes, mercury pool-type tubes for welding, subminiature tubes, holder of over 200 patents on electronic tube processes; when he noticed while standing next to a magnetron that the chocolate bar in his pocket had melted without heat, he realized the cooking potential of microwaves, further experimentation earned him the title of "Father of the Microwave Oven" 1945; recipient: Naval Ordnance Award for Exceptional Service Bureau of Ordnance, USN, 1942; fellow: American Academy of Arts and Sciences; buried in Newton (Massachusetts) Cemetery.

Spofford, Harriet Prescott 1835–1921, born: Calais; removed with her parents
to Newburyport, Massachusetts; attended Putnam Free School, Newburyport, graduate: Pinkerton Academy, Derry, New Hampshire; while still in Newburyport, her essay on *Hamlet* attracted the attention of Thomas Wentworth Higginson, who became her friend and gave her wise counsel and encouragement; with the debility of her parents, being the oldest child, she felt it necessary for her to become useful; began publishing in *Frank Leslie's Monthly Magazine*, later in *Atlantic Monthly* and other high-quality periodicals; author: *Sir Rohan's Ghost: A Romance* 1860, *The Amber Gods, and Other Stories* 1863, *Azarian: An Episode* 1864, *Art Decoration Applied to Furniture* 1877, *The Servant Girl Question* 1881, *Poems* 1882, *The Marquis of Carabas* 1882, *Hymn for the One Hundredth Anniversary of the Birth of Sarah Balch Braman* 1890, *The Maid He Married* 1891, *A Lost Jewel* 1891, *Three Heroines of New England Romance: Their True Stories Herein Set Forth* 1894, *A Master Spirit* 1896, *In Titian's Garden: and Other Poems* 1897, *Harriet Stanley's Friends* 1898, *Priscilla's Love-Story* 1898, *Old Madame: and Other Tragedies* 1899, *That Betty* 1903, *Old Washington* 1906, *The Making of a Fortune: A*

Romance 1911, *A Little Book of Friends* 1916, *The Thief in the Night, House and Hearth, An Inheritance, The Great Procession, A Scarlet Poppy, and Other Stories.*

Spotted Elk, Molly (born Mary Alice Nelson) 1903–73, born: Indian Island; a member of the Penobscot tribe, at age fourteen, began performing in vaudeville; in New York: artist's model, dancer, chorus girl, cover girl (*Collier's*); in Chicago: dancer for Texas Guinan; movie actress: *Silent Enemy*, critically acclaimed; member: Provincetown Players; to Paris 1932, performed at International Exhibition with the United States Indian Band; danced at the Ritz, Salle Pleyel; escaped Nazi invasion of France on foot over the Pyrenees mountains with her small child; retired to Indian Island.

Sprague, Ezra Kimball 1866–1943, born: Milo; A.B. Bates College 1887, M.D. College of Physicians and Surgeons, Boston, 1890, postgraduate work: Harvard University Medical School; commissioned assistant surgeon: U.S. Public Health Service 1893, promoted through the ranks to colonel, USPHS 1931, served in the United States, Belgium, and Calcutta; professor of tropical medicine: Detroit Medical College 1901–02; made a study of bubonic plague, Calcutta, 1903–04, chief medical officer: Ellis Island 1925–28, director: North Atlantic District, USPHS, 1928–32, medical director: USPHS from 1932; brought about installation of water filtration plant at Washington, D.C., 1898; author: numerous articles, addresses, and reports on public health.

Spurling, Andrew Barclay 1833–1906, born: Cranberry Isles; son and grandson of ship captains, dropped out of school at age twelve and went to sea, at age eighteen went to California to prospect for gold, became a farmer and hunter; his antislavery opinions occasioned a duel with Bowie knives; returned to Maine in 1855 where he served as a ship captain; in the Civil War: commissioned first lieutenant, assigned to Company D, 1st Maine Cavalry, October 1861; promoted to captain, USV, February 1863; major, USV, January 1864; lieutenant. colonel, USV, June 1864; brevetted brigadier general, USV, March 1865; distinguished himself at Brandy Station and was wounded in the fierce hand-to-hand combat at Upperville; brevets for Mobile (2) and Pollard, Alabama; recipient: Medal of Honor, at Evergreen, Alabama, 23 March 1865, "advanced alone in darkness beyond the picket line, came upon three of enemy, fired upon them (his firing being returned), wounded two and captured the whole party." Upon being mustered out, returned to the sea, survived one shipwreck; sheriff of Hancock County for four years; removed to Chicago, where he served as an inspector for the U.S. Postal Service; with two other investors, founded and presided over the Chicago Rawhide Manufacturing Company; built the Spurling Block, the first steel-framed structure in Elgin; after losing his fortune in the Panic of 1893, returned to Chicago where he subsequently died; buried in an unmarked grave in Rose Hill Cemetery, Chicago.

Stanley, Francis Edgar 1859–1940, and **Freelan Oscar** 1859–1918, born: Kingfield; twin brothers of Chansonetta Stanley Emmons; graduates: Farmington State Normal and Training School, removed to Lewiston 1874–83, became leading portrait photographers, organized the Stanley Dry Plate Co. (inventors of an improvement in dry plate photography 1883, sold to Kodak 1905), invented the air brush, made violins, produced the first successful steam-operated automobile in New England 1897, drove the first motorized vehicle to reach the top of Mount Washington 1899, organized the Stanley Motor Carriage Co., Watertown, Massachusetts, 1902; a Stanley was driven at a speed of over 120 miles an hour, a world record, on Ormond Beach, Florida, 1906, later, the same vehicle was approaching a speed of 197 miles an hour when it became airborne and crashed; developed Estes Park, Colorado, built the Stanley Hotel (the inspiration for and the setting of Stephen King's *The Shining*); author (Freelan Edgar Stanley): *Theories Worth Having* 1919; F. E. Stanley is buried in Newton (Massachusetts) Cemetery, F. O. Stanley is buried in Riverside Cemetery, Kingfield.

Stanley, Robert William "Bigfoot" 1954– , born: Portland; son of a lobsterman; removed with his family to Kerney, New Jersey, as a child; demonstrated great athletic ability in Kearney High School, upon graduation, drafted by the Los Angeles *Dodgers*, but chose to attend Newark State College instead, dropped out after one month and was signed by the Boston *Red Sox*, playing first for the Elmira, New York, team 1974 and then with the Winter Haven, Florida, team 1975, at Bristol, Connecticut, compiled an impressive record and was advanced to the Boston *Red Sox* home team in 1977, playing as starting and relief pitcher; compiling an impressive record as starting, middle relief, and closing pitcher; became the subject of intense fan booing after his disastrous ninth inning wild pitch in the pivotal sixth game of the World Series game 1986, retired after the 1989 season to landscaping and sporting goods businesses in Wenham, leaving behind Red Sox records as all-time leader in saves (132) and games pitched (637).

Stanwood, Daniel Caldwell 1869–1951, born: Augusta; son of Isaac Augustus Stanwood; attended public schools in Brooklyn, New York, L.L.B. New York University 1890, practiced law in Boston 1890–1908, A.B. Oxford University 1914, A.M. 1915; in World War I: chosen by the British War Office to oversee the transfer of 40,000 Americans serving in British forces to the forces of the United States; lecturer in international law: Bowdoin College 1918–19, professor 1919–36; sent by the Carnegie Endowment for International Peace to study agencies of international cooperation 1926; member: the Research in International Law Committee organized by Harvard University Law School and the Carnegie Endowment 1927, to carry on intensive preparatory work in anticipation of the Hague Codification Conference, of which he was also a member 1930; honorary fellow: University College, Oxford University, 1921; known for his scholarship in the field of the origins of the New Testament; in his spare time, engaged in woodworking and the making of crystal chandeliers.

Stanwood, Edward 1841–23, born: Augusta; son of a papermaker, brother of Isaac Augustus Stanwood, cousin of Mrs. James G. Blaine (née Harriet Stanwood); A.B. Bowdoin College 1861, Litt. D. (Hon.) 1894, overseer 1886–1904, trustee 1904–23; assistant editor: *Boston Daily Advertiser* 1867–82, editor 1882–83, managing editor: *Youths Companion* 1887–1911; Bowdoin College overseer; member and recording secretary: Massachusetts Historical Society from 1905; secretary: Arkwright Society from 1881; author: *History of Presidential Elections* 1884, *History of the Presidency* 1898, *History of the Class of 1861 of Bowdoin College* 1897, *American Tariff Controversies in the Nineteenth Century* 1903, *James Gillespie Blaine* 1905, *The Separation of Maine from Massachusetts: A Study of the Growth of Public Opinion (1784–1820)* 1907, *History of the Presidency (1897–1909)* 1912 .

Stanwood, Isaac Augustus 1839–1914, born: Augusta, son of a papermaker, Augusta city clerk and member: Maine House of Representatives, brother of Edward Stanwood; attended public schools in Augusta, having learned the paper trade from his father, formed a partnership with William Tower 1861, as Stanwood & Tower, successors to Cushnoc Manufacturing Co., Brown's Corner (now Riverside), Vassalboro; began experimenting with wood as a source of paper, Stanwood having observed hornets making a paper-like substance for their nests from the wood of fence posts, some consider this to be the birth of the wood pulp-based paper industry; by 1863 the company was producing excelsior, by 1867 groundwood pulp-derived paper was being produced; another story, associated with Stanwood, is that, because of the cotton embargo during the Civil War, rags (then the primary source of paper) became very expensive, learning that the Egyptian government was mining mummies, by the million to fuel the Egyptian state railroad, Stanwood contracted for shiploads of mummy-wrappings to be delivered to his mill in Gardiner, to be turned into butcher paper; removed to New York 1875, employed in the U.S. customs house there to 1888; practiced law before the U.S. Supreme Court and U.S. District Court 1888–92, where he tried revenue cases; clerk in the Brooklyn Police Department from 1895; deacon: Plymouth Church, Brooklyn; father of Daniel Stanwood.

Stapleton, Patience Tucker 1861–93, born: Wiscasset; daughter of a ship captain, sister of Richard Hawley Tucker; graduate: Moravian Seminary, Bethlehem, Pennsylvania; showed a talent for literature from an early age; attracted the attention of James Fields, her first published effort, written under the pseudonym Patience Thornton, was "Jim," a sketch published in *Youth's Companion* 1878, removed to Denver, Colorado, 1881, married William Stapleton, editor of the *Rocky Mountain News*, later *Denver Republican*, published several hundred short stories in a very short time, many of which were very highly regarded, including her "Byer's Folly," which was awarded a prize by the editors of *Youth's Companion*, as the best story by a girl, which carried with it the commitment to publish anything she might submit; her novels include: *My Jean* 1885, *Kady* 1889, *My Sister's Husband* 1890, *Babe Murphy* 1891, *Rose-Geranium*, a tragedy in blank verse 1892, her last work was a series of editorial articles for the *Denver Republican* favoring equal suffrage, said to have exerted considerable influence in the passage of the bill extending the vote to women in Colorado 1893.

Starkey, George R. 1823– ?, born: Kennebec County; orphaned at an early age, sent by Sybil Jones to the Friends School, Providence, Rhode Island, taught for a year after graduation, A.B. Waterville College 1846, first in his class, taught mathematics and classics at the Friends School, Providence, M.D. Hahnemann College, Philadelphia, 1855, practiced in Reading 1856–58, professor of anatomy: Hahnemann Medical College 1859–64, professor of surgery 1860–64, first physician to administer oxygen 1869, originated the Compound Oxygen home treatment 1875.

Starrett, Laroy S. 1836–1922, born: China; worked on a stock farm in Vassalboro and later Newburyport, Massachusetts, acquired a stock farm in Newburyport; invented a meat chopper, washing machine, and butter worker, all patented; superintendent: Athol Machine Co., invented combination square and ruler with sliding head 1879, a ubiquitous device still in use, a center tri-square, a bevelling instrument, a surface gauge, a micrometer caliper square, came to employ a thousand people in Athol; president: L. S. Starrett and Co., manufactured bevels, surface and depth gauges, steel tapes, plumb bobs, and a number of other unique instruments, held a total of one hundred patents; his son, William Starrett, was the chief constructor of the Empire State Building, among others.

Stearns, Carl Leo 1892–1972, born: Westbrook; A.B. Wesleyan University ϕBK 1917, Ph.D. Yale University 1923; assistant: Dudley Observatory, Albany, New York 1917–18; instructor in mathematics: Wesleyan University 1918–19, instructor in astronomy: Yale University 1919–20, research assistant: Yale University Observatory 1920–25, research associate in astronomy: Van Vleck Observatory, Wesleyan University 1925–42, director of observatory, associate professor of astronomy 1942–44, professor from 1944; instructor in navigation: Wesleyan University Naval Flight Preparatory School 1943, visiting instructor: Trinity College, Hartford 1940–41; awarded Donohoe Comet Medal by the Astronomical Society of the Pacific 1927; Stearns Comet named in his honor; fellow: Royal Astronomical Society, American Academy of Arts and Sciences; author: *Stellar Parallaxes from Photographs Made with the Twenty Inch Refractor of the Van Vleck Observatory* 1938, contributor of articles on stellar distances, solar eclipses, solar parallax, &c. to *Astronomy Journal*.

Stearns, Frederic Pike 1851–1919, born: Calais; cousin of John Barker Stearns and Thomas Stearns Eliot; attended public schools in Calais; A.M. (Hon.) Harvard University 1905, Sc.D. University of Pennsylvania 1906; clerked in a store in Calais for two years, studied civil engineering in Boston with Hiram Mills, engaged in building the Sudbury River water supply for Boston 1872, division engineer for sewerage tunnel under Dorchester Bay 1880; chief engineer: Massachusetts Board of Health 1886, his approach to water and sewerage became the model for many others state facilities; built a sewerage and water system for the Mystic and Charles River drainage areas, constructed the dam between Boston and Cambridge, which turns the lower Charles River into a freshwater lake, oversaw the construction of the Boston Metropolitan Waterworks, an immense undertaking consisting of works in earth, masonry, and metal, reservoirs, aqueducts, pumping stations, and pipe systems, built the Wachusetts Reservoir, then the largest artificial lake in the world, planned the Quabbin Reservoir, which was not finished until after his death, utilized the fall of water in the Nashua aqueduct to generate power, a first; consultant on New York, Baltimore, Los Angeles, Hartford, Winnipeg, Chicago, Pittsburgh water and sewerage systems; member, Board of Consulting Engineers: Panama Canal, 1905–06, one of the minority members that supported Chief Engineer J. F. Stevens in his plan involving locks, dams, and a lake; member of another board which traveled with Secretary of War Taft to Panama in 1907 and passed on the stability of the foundations of the proposed locks; author: *Description of Some Experiments on the Flow of Water for Conveying the Water of Sudbury River to Boston* 1883, *The Current Meter* 1883, *On the Flow of Water in a Forty-Eight-Inch Pipe* 1885, *Disposal of Sewerage in Massachusetts* 1888, *The Effects of Storage Upon the Quality of Water* 1892, *The Development of Water Supplies and Water Supply Engineering*; president: American Society of Civil Engineers; eventually retired to his home, Nurembega, in Camden.

Stearns, Joseph Barker 1831–95, born: Weld; after receiving a common-school education and working on the family farm, Stearns became a telegraph operator, superintendent: Boston Fire-Alarm Telegraph Co. 1855–67, during that time, he made several inventions relevant to the fire alarm; in 1868, he invented and patented the duplex system of telegraphy, an invention of enormous importance and for which he received royalties from many countries around the world and all major undersea cable companies; employed by the Mexican Telegraph Co. in the laying of an undersea cable linking Galveston, Texas, and Vera Cruz, Mexico, 1879–80, similarly employed by the Central & South American Telegraph Co. in laying cable between the Isthmus of Tehuantepec, in Mexico, to Callao, Peru, a distance of 5,000 miles 1880–82; lived in retirement in Camden; his extensive collection of Chiriqui pottery was given to the Smithsonian Institution and his collection of carved ivory, the largest in the world at that time, was bequeathed to the Metropolitan Museum of Art, New York.

Stearns, Marcellus Lovejoy 1829–91, born: Center Lovell; son of a farmer and merchant; graduate: Waterville Academy (later Coburn Classical Institute), entered Waterville College 1859, withdrew in his junior year to enlist in the Civil War, later granted an honorary A.B. degree by Colby College 1877; private, USV, 12th Maine Volunteer Infantry, later orderly sergeant, promoted to second lieutenant, USV, 1862, first lieutenant, USV, 1863, one of the forlorn hope at the siege of Port Hudson, on the Red River Expedition, lost arm at the battle of Winchester, commissioned second lieutenant, USV, 20th Regiment of the Veteran Reserve Corps 1865; studied law in the office of Josiah Drummond in Portland; served under General O. O. Howard at Freedman's Bureau, sent to Wheeling, West Virginia, later to Quincy, Florida, where he was mustered out 1868; practiced law in Quincy, active in organizing Negroes into the Republican party in Florida; member: Florida Constitutional Convention 1868; member, speaker: Florida House of Representatives 1868; appointed U.S. surveyor general of Florida by President Grant 1869–73; elected lieutenant governor 1872, upon the death of Ossian Hart, became the tenth governor of Florida 1874–1877; unsuccessful candidate for reelection in the election of 1876, wherein the Florida electoral votes for president were disputed and were, ultimately, given to Rutherford B. Hayes, the gubernatorial election was decided by the Florida Supreme Court, which assigned the election to Stearns's Democratic opponent by the narrowest of margins; Lake Stearns, in Florida, was named in his honor, but the name was later changed to Lake Placid, at the insistence of Melvil Dewey; appointed U.S. commissioner at Hot Springs 1877–80, commissioned by the secretary of the interior to inspect certain public works in Florida, removed to Atlantic, Iowa, 1887, where he engaged in banking, died in Palantine Bridge, New York, buried in Center Lovell.

Stephens, Charles Asbury 1847–1931, born: Norway; born Stevens, later adopted Stephens, cousin of Addison Verrell; A.B. Bowdoin College 1869, completed the undergraduate course in two years, heavily influence by Elijah Kellogg at Bowdoin College to become an author while still an undergraduate, was a contributor to *Ballou's Magazine*, later a contribution to *Youth's Companion* so pleased the editor that Stephens was engaged to write exclusively for that magazine, his connection lasted over sixty years, during which period the circulation increased from 5,000 to over 300,000, due in no small part to the popularity of Stephens's work; encouraged by the editor, he completed his M.D. at Boston University Medical School 1887; author of some 3,000 articles and numerous books, including *The Young Moose Hunters* 1874, *Camping Out, Off to the Geysers, Fox Hunting* 1872, *Lynx Hunting, On the Amazon* (where he first proposed the concept of a floating university) 1873, *Left On Labrador* 1873, *The Knockabout Club Along Shore* 1883, *The Knockabout Club in the Tropics* 1884, *The Knockabout Club in the Woods* 1885, *Katahdin Camps* 1892, *Three Boys Afloat on the Mississippi* 1882, *When Life Was Young, A Great Year Of Our Lives* 1912, *Under The Sea in the Salvador* 1920, *A Busy Year at the Old Squires* 1922, *Molly's Baby* 1924, *Haps and Mishaps* 1925, *The Story of My Home Folks* 1926; established a home on Lake Pennesseewasee in Norway, where he constructed a large laboratory for the systematic study and research into cell life, developed a theory of the possibility of indefinite extension or maintenance of cell life by systematic renewal of the biogen transmitted through the ovum by inheritance, about which he wrote: *Living Matter* 1888, *Pluricellular Man* 1892, *Long Life* 1896, *Natural Salvation* 1903, *Salvation by Science* 1913, *Immortal Life, How It Will Be Achieved* 1920.

Stetson, Augusta Simmons 1842–1928, born: Waldoboro; attended Lincoln Academy, Newcastle; married Captain Frederick Stetson of Damariscotta 1864, removed to Havre, France, where Frederick Stetson was a ship broker, traveled extensively in Europe, India, and Burma; took up the study of Christian Science, began to practice healing 1884, preached in the Mother Church in Boston, alternating with Mrs. Eddy; sent to organize First Church of Christ, Scientist, in New York, in part, because of her talent as a singer and organist 1887; led Christian Science movement in New York City, came to rival Mrs. Eddy in influence; awarded a doctorate in Christian Science by Mrs. Eddy; considered by most to be Mrs. Eddy's successor but was later excommunicated by her; from her magnificent apartment on Fifth Avenue controlled an early radio station in New York whose programming alternated between classical music and proto-fascistic propaganda; author: *My Spiritual Aeroplane, Reminiscences, Sermons and Correspondence* 1914, *Vital Issues in Christian Science, with Facsimile Letters of Mary Baker Eddy* 1914, *Sermons and Other Writings* 1924; buried in Hillside Cemetery, Damariscotta.

Stetson, William Wallace 1849–1910, born: Greene; son of a mariner, brother of Herbert Lee Stetson; graduate: Greene Academy, A.M., L.L.D. Colby College, L.L.D. Monmouth (Illinois) College; at age fifteen, was a teacher in a district school, struck out west at age sixteen, clerk in a book and drug store in Peoria, superintendent of schools: Rockford, Illinois, 1880–84, reorganized city schools, effected reforms in pedagogy; principal: Webster School, Auburn, 1884, superintendent of schools 1885, established modern courses of study, improved equipment, rewarded schools 1885–95; president: Maine Pedagogical Society 1890–91; president: American Institute of Instructors 1894–95; superintendent of Maine schools 1895–1907, abolished district system, mandated the adoption of free textbooks, free tuition, state certification of teachers; his annual reports were widely reprinted and translated into French, German, and Spanish; lectured widely; president: National Educational Association 1905; author: *History of Civil Government of Maine* 1890, *Ideals and Essentials* 1911.

Stevens, Albert William 1886–1949, born: Belfast; B.S. University of Maine 1907, M.S. 1909, D.Eng. (Hon.) 1932, Norwich University 1936, D.Sc., South Dakota School of Mines 1935; spent several years as an electrical and mining engineer in the gold fields of Montana, Idaho, Alaska, and California; experimented with photography and developed an individual technique, making it possible to take photographs of distant objects obscured by haze; in World War I: enlisted in Signal Corps, USA, 1917, commissioned first lieutenant, USA, at Cornell University, attached to photographic section in France, 88th Observation Squadron, 1st Army, participated in most major engagements of U.S. troops; captain, chief photographic officer, 1st Army 1918, after armistice photographed battlefronts and part of France and Germany with 24th Airplane Observation Squadron, assisted in making the first large photographic mosaics in the United States 1919, made a world-record parachute jump at 24,200 feet 1922, joined Rice Expedition to South America 1924, made extensive air maps of the upper Amazon, made photographic survey of large areas of South America for the National Geographic Society 1930; balloonist; made first photograph showing earth's curvature 1930, took the first picture showing the shadow of the moon on the earth from an airplane, five miles over the Peruvian coast, during a total eclipse 1932; made first natural color photograph of the stratosphere, made first photograph of the division of troposphere from stratosphere; made first nonstop flight across the United States; made a record flight to 60,000 feet, balloon exploded, barely escaped with his life 1934; later, made another record flight to 72,335 feet 1935 (this flight was commemorated by the United States Post Office with a 20-cent stamp 1983); these high altitude flights provided enormously important data to the U.S. Army Air Corps in its construction of high altitude bombers and fighters and equipping their pilots and crews; long-time writer and photographer for the *National Geographic* magazine; his adventures were depicted in Action Comics; the Albert W. Stevens Alumni House at the University of Maine was named in his honor; recipient: Hubbard Medal, Franklin Burr Prize, Purple Heart, Distinguished Flying Cross with oak leaf cluster.

Stevens, Alzina Ann Parsons 1848–1900, born: Parsonsfield; worked in a textile mill in Somersworth, New Hampshire, prior to 1864; removed to Chicago 1871, apprenticed to a printer; founder and president: Working Women's Union No. 1 1878; received financial aid from the Chicago Typographical Union; outspoken advocate of the rights of women and working people; member: Chicago Typographical Union 1879, journeyman printer in Toledo 1881, proofreader and copy editor for H. H. Hardesty, publisher of local histories and atlases; author: *Military History of Ohio* 1887, contributor of articles to labor press, *i.e. John Swanton's Paper*; writer for *Toledo Bee;* member: Knights of Labor 1883; head: district assembly of Northwestern Ohio, led the Joan of Arc Assembly, organized women in outlying areas; co-editor: Populist newspaper *Vanguard*, Chicago 1892; Knights of Labor representative at World's Congress Auxiliary; appointed by Illinois Governor John Altgeld: assistant factory inspector, enforced child labor and women's hours laws; resident of Hull House, established labor unions in women's trades, headed Dorcas Federal Labor Union.

Stevens, Greenleaf Thurlow 1831–1918, born: Belgrade, attended Belgrade

Left to right: E. N. Whittier, G. W. Woodbury, G. T. Stevens, D. I. Black, C. O. Hunt.

Academy, graduate: Litchfield Liberal Institute, taught school for several years; read law under Samuel Titcomb, Augusta; member: Maine bar 1860, L.L.B. Harvard University Law School 1861; in the Civil War: commissioned first lieutenant, USV, 5th Mounted Artillery, served under Generals McDowell, Pope, McClellan, Burnside, Hooker, Meade, Grant, and Sheridan; commanded his battery at Fredericksburg, Chancellorsville, where he was wounded, promoted to captain, USV, played an important role on the first day at Gettysburg, where his battery, as part of the 1st Division of the 1st Corps, was instrumental in stopping the Confederate advance on Culp's Hill, wounded on the second day at what came to be known as Stevens Knoll, where the government placed a bronze marker, in commemoration, later served in the battles of the Wilderness, Spotsylvania Courthouse, Cold Harbor, actions in front of Petersburg and in the Shenendoah Valley; at the battle of Cedar Creek, he and his battery were singled out for recognition, brevetted major, USV, for gallant and meritorious conduct at the battles of Cold Harbor, Winchester, and Cedar Creek 1865; returned to the law in Maine; member: Maine House of Representatives 1875, member: Senate 1877–78, chairman of the Judiciary Committee; sheriff of Kennebec County 1888–92, Kennebec County judge of probate 1892–1908; buried in Woodside Cemetery, Belgrade.

Stevens, John Calvin 1855–1940, born: Boston of Maine parentage; his father was a cabinetmaker and farmer in Standish; graduated from Portland High School 1873, in same year, entered the architectural office of Francis Fassett, made partner 1883, withdrew and formed a partnership with Albert W. Cobb 1884–91, styled Stevens & Cobb, coauthors of *Examples of American Domestic Architecture* 1888; practiced independently until his son, John Howard Stevens, joined him; among his designs were: the Maine Insane Hospital, Bangor, 1888, the L. D. M. Sweat Memorial

Art Gallery, Portland, 1909, Portland City Hall (in collaboration with Carrière and Hastings) 1911, State Sanitarium, Hebron, numerous residences, &c.; president: Maine chapter of American Institute of Architects, Portland Society of Art.

Stevens, John Frank 1853–1943, born: West Gardiner; attended Maine Normal School, Farmington; L.L.D. (Hon.) Bates College 1920, D.Eng. University of Michigan 1926, University of North Carolina 1926, Brooklyn Polytechnic Institute 1937; assistant city engineer: Minneapolis, Minnesota, 1874–76, surveyor on location with the Sabine Pass & North Western Railroad Co. in Texas, later chief engineer: Denver & Rio Grande Railroad Co. 1879–80; locating engineer: Chicago, Milwaukee & St. Paul Railroad Co. 1880–82; assistant and division engineer: Canadian Pacific Railroad Co. 1882–85; assistant engineer: Chicago, Milwaukee & St. Paul Railroad Co. 1886; principal assistant engineer in charge of locating and building the Duluth, South Shore & Atlantic Railroad Co. 1887–89; assistant engineer: Spokane Falls & Northern Railroad Co. 1889; principal assistant engineer: Great Northern Railroad Co. 1890, directed the extension of the railroad from Montana to the Pacific Coast; personally, in the dead of winter, found Marias Pass, through the continental divide in Montana, found what was later called Stevens Pass through the Cascade Mountains, where he constructed the Cascade tunnel; appointed chief engineer 1895, general manager and chief engineer 1902; chief engineer: Chicago, Rock Island & Pacific Railroad Co. 1903, named second vice president, in charge of operations 1904; on the advice of J. J. Hill, Stevens was appointed by William Howard Taft, U.S. secretary of war, chief engineer: Panama Canal; brought order out of chaos, stopped all work on the canal until the problem of malaria and yellow fever was controlled by the efforts of William C. Gorgas, devised the basic construction solution with a system of locks and a lake, obtained congressional approval for this solution, completely reorganized the disposal of spoils, began the digging of the Culebra (later Gaillard) Cut, provided adequate housing and supplies for workers, rebuilt the Panama Railroad; appointed chairman of the Canal Commission 1907, abruptly resigned one month later, much to the ire of Theodore Roosevelt; vice president in charge of operations: New York, New Haven & Hartford Railroad Co. 1907–09; president: Spokane, Portland & Seattle Railroad Co., Oregon Trunk Railroad Co., Oregon Electric & United Railroad Co., Pacific & Eastern Railroad Co., all Hill lines 1909–11; removed to New York 1911, made a complete survey of Spanish railroads for the National City Bank, Kuhn, Loeb and Company and J. P. Morgan & Co.; consultant on the New York subway system; with the entrance of the United States into World War I, sent by Woodrow Wilson to Russia as chairman of the American Railroad Commission; after he had completed a study of Russian railroads, he was asked to remain by the Russian minister of railways as special advisor; with the outbreak of the Russian Revolution, appointed by the United States, Japan, Great Britain, Italy, China, and France as president of the Interallied Technical Board, charged with the general supervision and management of that portion of the Trans Siberian Railroad and other railroads under Allied control

1919–22; managed, in a period of great tumult, to keep the railroads functioning; decorated by the United States government with the Distinguished Service Medal, recipient: officer of the Légion d'Honneur by France, Order of the Rising Sun by Japan, the Order of the Golden Grain by China; director: Baltimore & Ohio Railroad Co., received the Gold Medal of the Franklin Institute, the Northern Pacific Railroad Co. erected an heroic statue of him at Marias Pass 1925, a copy of which Stevens later presented to the Maine State Library.

Stevens, John Leavitt 1820–95, born: Mount Vernon; student: Waterville Liberal Institute, Maine Wesleyan Seminary, Kents Hill, L.L.D. Tufts University 1883; ordained Universalist minister, pastor in Sharon, Biddeford, Norway; co-owner, with James G. Blaine, and editor: *Kennebec Journal* 1855, Blaine sold his interest and Stevens became chief editor 1857–70; an organizer of the Republican party in Maine, chairman: Republican State Committee 1855–60; member: Maine House of Representatives 1865–68, Maine Senate 1868–70; U.S. minister to Paraguay and Uruguay 1870–73, Norway and Sweden 1877–83; author: *History of Gustavus Adolphus* 1884; minister to Hawaii 1889–90, envoy extraordinaire and minister plenipotentiary to Hawaii 1889–93; Queen Liliuokalani, having succeeded to the throne and showing contempt for the constitution of 1887, proclaimed a new constitution, giving herself arbitrary powers, overturning the supreme court and reserving to herself the appointment of judges 1893; a provisional government was formed, with Judge Sanford Dole as president, until terms of union with the United States of America could be negotiated and agreed upon, the provisional government asked for protection from the United States government, fearing that the queen's supporters would commit excesses, Stevens summoned a force of marines from aboard the USS *Boston*, which was lying in Honolulu Harbor, recognized the provisional government, and sent a strong plea for annexation to President Harrison; his successor, Grover Cleveland, withdrew the annexation treaty, recalled Stevens, and began negotiations for the restoration of the queen; the queen's vindictiveness and statements about what she was going to do to the revolutionaries made reconciliation impossible and, on 4 July 1894, the Hawaiian Republic was declared, with Sanford Dole as president; later, during the Spanish-American War, negotiations for annexation were renewed with Harold Sewall, U.S. minister; Stevens' recommendations were incorporated into a Treaty of Annexation, 12 August 1898; author: *Picturesque Hawaii* 1894; buried in Augusta.

Stevens, Lillian Marian Nancy Ames 1844–1914, born: Dover; attended Foxcroft Academy, graduate: Westbrook Seminary, teacher in various schools; associated with the Woman's Christian Temperance Union from 1874, assisted Emma Willard, at Old Orchard Beach, in organizing the Maine union, of which she was president and treasurer; vice president: national Woman's Christian Temperance Union 1894–98, president from 1898, subsequent to the death of Emma Willard; saw the Woman's Christian Temperance Union become the largest society of women in the United States; a vocal proponent of scientific temperance education in schools, saw securing the vote for women as the most efficient way to obtain prohibition of alcohol; adopted a knot of white ribbon as an identifying badge; established temperance missions to loggers, paupers, prisoners, soldiers, and miners, initiated reform laws to protect women and children; treasurer: National Council of Women; in Portland, she was a familiar figure and friend of the unfortunate whether at the police station, the Friendly Inn, the Erring Women's Refuge, or the jail.

Stevens, William Bacon 1815–1887, born: Bath; attended public school in Bath, graduate: Phillips Academy, Andover; his health impaired, traveled in Europe for two years; attended the Medical College of South Carolina, M.D. Dartmouth College Medical School 1837, D.D. University of Pennsylvania 1848, L.L.D. Union College 1862; orphan asylum physician, Savannah; founder: Georgia Historical Society 1839, appointed Georgia state historian 1841, port health officer, Savannah; wrote editorials for various newspapers; ordained deacon in the Episcopal church 1843, missionary: Athens, Georgia; ordained priest 1844, rector: Emmanuel Church, Athens; professor of oratory and literature: University of Georgia 1844–48; rector: St. Andrew's Church, Philadelphia, 1848, assistant bishop in Philadelphia 1862, Bishop of Pennsylvania 1865; in charge of American Episcopal church in Europe 1868–74, attended the Pan-Anglican Council and preached the final sermon in St. Paul's Cathedral, London, 1878; founder: Lehigh University; author: *Discourses Before the Historical Society of Georgia* 1841, *History of the Silk-Culture in Georgia* 1841, *A History of Georgia from Its First Discovery by Europeans to the Adoption of the Present Constitution* (two volumes) 1847, *Parables of the New Testament Unfolded* 1855, *The Bow in the Cloud* 1855, *Home Service* 1856, *The Lord's Day* 1857, *The Past and Present of St. Andrews* 1858, *Sabbaths of Our Lord* 1872, *Early History of the Church in Georgia* 1873, *Sermons* 1873.

Stilphen, Charles Augustus 1877–1956, born: Pittston, son of a farmer; graduate: Bridge Academy, Dresden, B.S. University of Maine 1902, student: Massachusetts Institute of Technology 1903–04; draftsman, chief draftsman: B. F. Sturtevant Co., Boston 1902–10, sent by the company to Salt Lake City to manage their branch office 1910, designed and supervised the installation of heating and ventilation facilities for various buildings in Utah, supplied fans and engineered cement drying at the Hoover and Grand Coulee Dams, installed ventilation facilities in mines throughout the West, sent to Denver, Colorado, 1926 to manage the Sturtevant office in that city; founded his own company: C. A. Stilphen Engineering & Manufacturing Co., Denver, 1935; invented the Stil-Blade fan 1935, the company also manufactured exhaust fans, furnace fans, unit heaters, unit coolers, a centrifugal multi-blade fan especially designed for use in connection with the firm's air-conditioning equipment; after his retirement in 1945, removed to Gardiner where his hobby of repairing watches and clocks became a business, the heating system that he built and donated to Christ Episcopal Church, Gardiner, was considered to be the most advanced of its type in the world.

Stinchfield, Augustus White 1842–1917, born: Phillips; son of a farmer; graduate: Phillips Academy, Andover, M.D. Medical School of Maine 1868, postgraduate study: University of Michigan 1869; practiced in Mount Vernon, Missouri, 1870–72, removed to Minnesota, practiced in Dundas 1872–73, Eyota 1873–92, Rochester, with Mayo & Stinchfield 1892–1908, this firm included Charles and William Mayo and eventually became the Mayo Clinic; Stinchfield served as diagnostician, medical adviser, specialized in diseases of the heart and lungs; chief of staff: St. Mary's Hospital, Rochester; president: First State Bank of Rochester, First National Bank of Eyota, First National Bank of Dover (Minnesota), Farmers & Merchants Bank, Grandville, North Dakota, vice president: Rochester Loan & Trust Co., the State Institution for Savings, Minneapolis, Bank of Balfour (North Dakota).

Stockbridge, Francis Brown 1826–94, born: Bath; after attending public school in Bath; clerked in a wholesale house in Boston for four years; removed to Chicago where he operated a lumber yard 1847; removed to Kalamazoo, Michigan, where he became a lumberman and sawmill owner on the Black and St. Ignace Rivers; member: Michigan House of Representatives 1869, Michigan Senate 1871; declined appointment as minister to the Hague and nomination for Republican candidate for governor; member: U.S. Senate 1887–94 (Republican), chairman: Committee on Fisheries; buried in Mountain Home Cemetery, Kalamazoo.

Stockbridge, Frank Parker 1870–1940, born: Gardiner; student: medical department, George Washington University 1888–91, learned printer's trade, reporter; editorial writer: *Buffalo Express* 1894–1901, editor and publisher: official program, Pan-American Exposition 1901; founder and editor: *American Home Magazine* 1901–02; reporter, staff correspondent: *New York American* 1902–04; money editor: *History of Universal Exposition*, *St. Louis* 1904–05; city editor: *New York Globe* 1905–07, reporter: *New York Herald* 1907–08, political editor: *Cincinnati Times-Star* 1908–11; with Walter Hines Page, launched the public campaign for the nomination of Woodrow Wilson for president of the United States; editor: *Town Development Magazine* 1911–12, editor: *Popular Mechanics* 1915–17, editor: *Old Colony Magazine* 1919, editor and publisher: *Co-operative Commonwealth* 1921–22; author: *The School of Tomorrow* 1911, *Yankee Ingenuity in the War* 1919, *Measure Your Mind* 1920, *Florida in the Making* 1926, *So This Is Florida* 1938, *Hedging Against Inflation* 1939.

Stone, Thomas Treadwell 1801–1895, born: Waterford, nephew of Henry Varnum and John Alfred Poor; A.B. Bowdoin College 1820, D.D. 1855; pastor: Congregational Church, Andover 1824–30; principal: Bridgton Academy 1830–32; pastor: Congregational Church, East Machias 1832–46, First Unitarian Church, Salem, Massachusetts, 1846–52, First Congregational Church, Bolton, Massachusetts, 1852–60, First Ecclesiastical Society, Brooklyn, Connecticut, 1863–71; an early and important member of the Transcendentalist school, while in East Machias developed into a superior literary scholar, an eloquent and erudite preacher, espoused the causes of temperance, pacifism, women's suffrage, and abolitionism, the last of which became his passion; close friend of the martyred abolitionist newspaper editor Elijah Lovejoy, closely associated, in the antislavery cause, with John Greenleaf Whittier, William Lloyd Garrison, Wendell Phillips, Theodore Parker, and John Quincy Adams, and others; met Ralph Waldo Emerson in Waterford, summer of 1832, kept in touch through Emerson's aunt, Mary Moody Emerson, and periodically each visited the other in their respective homes; Bronson Alcott listed Stone as a member of the Transcendental Club; while serving in Salem his home became a central gathering point for transcendental discussion, the origins of Brook Farm can be traced to a conversation between George Ripley and Charles Dana in his parlor; his ministry in Salem came to an abrupt halt when he leased a pew to a free Negro and was subsequently voted out by his parishioners 1852; lectured extensively at various lycea, delivered an important address before the senior class of Harvard Divinity School that was published as *The Preacher* 1856, contributed numerous articles to religious magazines, as well as *The Dial*, author: *Sermons on War* 1829, *Sketches of Oxford County, Maine* 1830, *Sermons* 1854, *The Rod and the Staff* 1856; at the time of his death, he was the oldest living alumnus of Bowdoin College.

Storer, Bellamy 1796–1875, born: Portland; son of a shipowner, merchant, and collector of customs in Portland, brother of David Humphreys Storer; student at Bowdoin College, L.L.D. 1841, in his early life, member of the Flying Artillery, a religious band of young men, who went from town to town promoting religious revival; studied law with Chief Justice Parker of the Massachusetts Supreme Court; member: Portland bar 1817, removed to Cincinnati 1817; editor: *The Crisis* 1824, which advocated the election of John Quincy Adams to the presidency; member: U.S. House of Representatives 1835–37 (Whig); Whig presidential elector 1844; professor: Cincinnati Law School 1854–74; judge: Superior Court 1854–72; buried in Spring Garden Cemetery, Cincinnati; father of Bellamy Storer, U.S. ambassador to Belgium, Spain, and Austria-Hungary.

Storer, David Humphreys 1804–91, born: Portland; son of a shipowner, merchant, and collector of customs in Portland, brother of Bellamy Storer; A.B. Bowdoin College 1822, L.L.D. 1876; studied medicine with Dr. John Warren in Boston, M.D. Harvard University Medical School 1825; with Oliver Wendell Holmes, Jacob Bigelow, and Edward Reynolds founded the Tremont Street Medical School 1837, which was eventually merged with Harvard University Medical School, where he served as professor of obstetrics and medical jurisprudence 1854–68, dean 1855–64, built the medical library; physician to Massachusetts General Hospital 1849–58;

chairman: Department of Zoology and Herpetology, Massachusetts Geological Survey 1837; a founder of the Boston Society of Natural History; president: American Medical Association 1866; member: American Philosophical Society, frequent contributor to its *Proceedings*, writings on medical ethics and the law; collected and described *Mollusca* of Massachusetts; author: *A History of Fishes in Massachusetts* 1867, *Report on the Ichthyology and Herpetology of Massachusetts* 1839, *Synopsis of the Fishes of North America* 1846.

Storer, Seth 1702–74, born: Wells; son of Joseph Storer, an Indian fighter; his older sister Mary was carried off to captivity in Québec in the Indian raid of 1703; sent to Cambridge Latin School 1713; A.B. Harvard College 1720, A.M. 1723; called to the vacant pulpit in the east precinct of Watertown, Massachusetts, 1723; known as a diligent, quiet scholar and preacher, he served as an overseer of Harvard College; did not participate in the Great Awakening and did not allow George Whitefield to preach from his pulpit; his sister, Mary, married and converted to Catholicism, returned for a visit, but refused his overtures to return to the Puritan fold.

Stover, Elias Steever 1836–1927, born: Rockland; studied navigation with Professor Andrews; went to sea, served as a captain for eight years; removed to Kansas 1858, became a Republican; with the outbreak of the Civil War: enlisted in Company B, 2nd Kansas Regiment, USV, promoted to sergeant, served with General Lyons in the Missouri campaign, promoted to captain, served with distinction as the commander of an independent battery at the battles of Cane Hill, Prairie Rose; returned to Kansas, engaged in business in Junction City; member: Kansas House of Representatives 1866, Kansas Senate 1870; elected lieutenant governor 1872; associated with the temperance movement, procured the charter for the First National Bank of Council Grove; removed to Albuquerque, New Mexico 1876, engaged in business, an incorporator: First National Bank of Albuquerque 1881, Bernalillo County commissioner 1881–83; with the establishment of the University of New Mexico, he was named a member of the board of regents 1889, elected president 1891, served to 1897; member: New Mexico Constitutional Convention 1889.

Stowe, Harriet Elizabeth Beecher 1811–96, born: Litchfield, Connecticut; daughter of Lyman Beecher; at age four, her mother died, raised by relatives in Guilford, Connecticut, entered the Ladies Seminary in Hartford, Connecticut, run by her sister Catherine, removed to Cincinnati 1832, where her father served as president of Lane Theological Seminary, a hotbed of abolitionism; married Calvin Stowe, professor of sacred literature at the seminary 1836, while husband Calvin Stowe taught at Bowdoin College, she conceived of and wrote *Uncle Tom's Cabin; or, Life Amongst the Lowly* 1851; during her life, wrote several other works, including *The Mayflower; or, Sketches of Scenes and Characters among the Descendants of the Puritans* 1843, *Earthly Care, a Heavenly Discipline* 1850, *Key to Uncle Tom's Cabin* 1853, *Dred, a Tale of the*

Dismal Swamp 1856, *The Minister's Wooing* 1859, *Pearl of Orrs Island: A Story of the Coast of Maine* 1862, *Old Town Folks* 1869, *Lady Byron Vindicated* 1870, *Palmetto-Leaves* 1873, *Poganuc People: Their Loves and Lives* 1878, contributor to the *Atlantic Monthly, Independent, Christian Unity,* editor: *Hearth and Home* 1868; when she met Abraham Lincoln in 1863, he greeted her as "the little lady who made this big war"; enjoying immense popularity in Great Britain, her article "The True Story of Lady Byron's Life," suggesting that Lord Byron had an incestuous relationship with his sister, caused the public there to turn against her; as an elderly and quite dotty old lady, she was known to creep into her neighbor Mark Twain's home in the middle of the night, stand over his bed, and startle him awake with war-whoops; buried in Andover (Massachusetts) Chapel Cemetery.

Stowe, Lyman Beecher 1880–1963, born: Saco; son of Charles Stowe, grandson of Calvin and Harriet Beecher Stowe; attended public schools in Hartford, Connecticut, A.B. Harvard College 1904, associated with the publishers of *Outlook* magazine 1904, Unit Book Co. 1905–06, publicity manager: Frederick A. Stokes Co., publishers 1908–09, assistant editor: *The Circle Magazine* 1909–10; secretary, vice chairman: New York Public Service Commission 1910–13; secretary: National Association of George Junior Republics 1913–15; member, editorial staff: Doubleday, Page & Co., publishers, Garden City, New York, 1918–21, manager of the book department 1921–30; a founder: National Self Government Committee 1906; author: *Saints, Sinners, and Beechers* 1934, coauthor: *Harriet Beecher Stowe—The Story of Her Life* 1911, author: *Citizens Made and Remade* 1912, *Booker T. Washington, Builder of a Civilization* 1916, *The Inside Story of Austro-German Intrigue* 1919.

Stuart, James Everett 1852–1941, born: Dover; grandson of the painter Gilbert Stuart, migrated to California, with his parents, via the Isthmus of Panama, student: San Francisco School of Design; discovered a process for painting on aluminum, by which pigments could be made to attach themselves to the surface and practically become a portion of the metal, which time could not efface (in this, he was wrong); began making sketches along the Sacramento and San Joaquin Rivers before levees were built; spent summers of 1891 and 1907 in Alaska, painted Donner Lake, Lake Tahoe, Yosemite Valley, the mountains of the high Sierras, Halfmoon Bay; his works are displayed at: Society of Liberal Arts, Joselyn Memorial, Omaha, Exposition Park Museum, Los Angeles, Doheny Library, Sacramento, Northwestern University; member: Bohemian Club; said to have left over 5,000 paintings.

Sturtevant, Benjamin Franklin 1833–90, born: Martin's Stream; invented a shoe-pegging machine 1857; invented pegwood lathe; invented rotary fan; his factory in Jamaica Plain, Massachusetts, largest, of its type, in world.

Sukeforth, Clyde L. 1902–2000, born: Washington; graduate: Coburn Classical Institute, Waterville, attended George Washington University; played semiprofessional baseball in Millinocket, during summer vacations; signed with the Cincinnati Reds in 1925, played until a hunting injury of his eye 1934, traded to the Brooklyn Dodgers, where he spent three seasons as a backup, later coached and scouted; originally scouted Negro League short-stop Jackie Robinson in 1945, when Robinson (the first black to play major league baseball) was signed in 1947, Sukeforth acted as his manager, later returned to coaching; in 1951, he sent pitcher Ralph Branca, rather than Carl Erskine, to face the New York Giants batter Bobby Thomson in the ninth inning of the pennant play-off, on the second pitch, Thompson hit the shot heard round the world, winning the pennant for the Giants; on display, in the Baseball Hall of Fame in Cooperstown, New York, is the Norman Rockwell painting *Bottom of the Sixth*, showing Sukeforth, Pittsburgh manager Billy Meyer, and three umpires looking skyward at an approaching rainstorm.

Sullivan, Alexander 1847–1912, born: Waterville; son of Irish immigrants; removed to Michigan, acquired the reputation of an orator before he reached his majority, later removed to Chicago, shot and killed Francis Hanford, the author of an anonymous letter that libeled Sullivan's wife, and who later physically assaulted both Sullivan and his wife, tried and was acquitted; member: Illinois bar 1878; first president: Irish National League of America, whose purpose was the establishment of home rule in Ireland 1883–84; in an address to President Arthur, he pointed out that the British government was reducing evicted Irish persons to pauperism and then shipping them to the United States through a system of assisted emigration laws; subsequently, President Arthur directed the commissioners of emigration at New York to enforce the statute against the admission of paupers; Charles Stewart Parnell, the leader of the home rule movement in Ireland, pronounced this to be the worst blow England had received since the War of 1812; put on trial with two others for the murder of a Doctor Cronin, who had allegedly accused Sullivan of peculation, he was found to be not guilty but his associates were convicted; deeply implicated in the Fenian attempt to destroy a lock of the Welland Canal in Ontario, he was also implicated in another Fenian plot to blow up Queen Victoria.

Sullivan, James 1744–1808, born: Berwick; son of Owen Sullivan, an immigrant from Ireland and a teacher, who lived to be 105 years old; brother of John Sullivan; lamed for life by an accident; L.L.D. (Hon.) Harvard College 1780; studied law with his brother John, member: Massachusetts bar *c.* 1782, practiced in Biddeford, where he served, for some time, as king's attorney for York County; member: Committee of Public Safety 1774–75, delegate: Massachusetts General Court 1775–76; accompanied the Ticonderoga Expedition; justice: Massachusetts Supreme Court 1776–82; delegate: Massachusetts Constitutional Convention 1779; delegate: Continental Congress 1784, 1785; member: Massachusetts Executive Council 1787; Suffolk County judge of probate 1788–90; Massachusetts attorney general 1790–1807; a proprietor of Limerick, which he named for his father's birthplace in Ireland; agent of the Halifax conference to settle the Maine boundary dispute 1796; unsuccessful candidate for governor 1797, 1798, 1804, 1805, 1806; elected fifth governor of Massachusetts 1807–08, caused considerable controversy when he suggested that the people be allowed to elect presidential electors, rather than by the general court, as was then the manner; died in office, buried in Central Boston Common Cemetery; member: American Academy of Arts and Sciences, a founding member, president: Massachusetts Historical Society; author: *Observations on the Government of the United States* 1791, *The Path of Riches: An Inquiry into the Origin and Use of Money; and into the Principles of Stocks and Banks* 1792, *The History of the District of Maine* 1795, *The Altar of Baal Thrown Down, or, The French Nation Defended* 1795, *Impartial Review of the Causes of the French Revolution* 1798, *History of Land-Titles in Massachusetts* 1801, *A Dissertation on the Constitutional Liberty of the Press* 1801, *Correspondence with Col. Pickering* 1808, History of the Penobscot Indians in *Massachusetts Historical Collections*.

Sullivan, John 1741–95, born: Berwick (or possibly Somersworth, New Hampshire), brother of James Sullivan; studied law, practiced in Durham, New Hampshire; delegate: First Continental Congress 1774; led mob that took Castle William and Mary, Portsmouth; one of eight brigadier generals in the Continental Army, served through siege of Boston, assigned to army invading Canada, after an abortive thrust toward Trois-Rivière, retreated to Crown Point; at battle of Long Island, it was Sullivan that left unguarded the road used by British troops to encircle Brooklyn Heights, Sullivan was captured, carried proposals from Lord Richard Howe to certain delegates of the Continental Congress; exchanged 1776; commanded a large division at the victories of Trenton and Princeton, Washington prevented Sullivan from being removed from command and rebuked; commanded one wing of army at Germantown, spent the winter at Valley Forge, given command in Rhode Island, later commanded the army that laid waste to the lands of the Iroquois, routed the Iroquois at Newtown (Elmira) 1777, resigned commission; represented New Hampshire in Congress 1780–81; president (governor) of New Hampshire 1786, 1787, 1789; New Hampshire attorney general 1782–86; his support of the new constitution was decisive in the New Hampshire Constitutional Convention 1788; judge: Federal District Court of New Hampshire from 1789; buried in the Sullivan family cemetery, Durham.

Sullivan, John Langdon 1777–1865, born: Saco; son of James Sullivan; after engaging in mercantile interests, traveled in Europe, studied canal construction in England and France; appointed agent and engineer of the Middlesex Canal, which ran between Boston and Concord, New Hampshire, 1804; invented a stream towboat, for which he received a patent, in preference to Robert Fulton, who had made a similar application at the same time 1814; appointed by President Monroe as associate civil engineer of the Board of Internal Improvements 1824, resigned after reporting on the practicality of a canal across the Allegheny Mountains 1825; M.D. Yale University Medical School 1837, practiced homeopathy in New Haven; removed to New York 1847; made several more inventions and discoveries in medicine and surgery, published pamphlets on steamboat navigation.

Sullivan, Louis Robert 1892–1925, born: Houlton; brother of Walter Edward Sullivan; A.B. Bates College ΦBK 1914, Ph.D. Columbia University 1922; assistant in biology: Brown University, assistant curator of physical anthropology: American Museum of Natural History, New York, 1917, associate curator 1924, specialized in race differences in lower jaws; in World War I, first lieutenant Anthropology Division, Office of the Surgeon General, USA, assisted in the compilation of the reports on defects found in drafted men, and army anthropology, began study of standard population areas of United States according to homogeneity in national and racial origins, fundamentally basic to geographical distribution of anthropological types, of particular, enduring importance is his determination of the 156 standard population sections, based on the census returns of 1910; after this task, he was assigned to Camp Grant where he made an anthropometric survey of the recruits stationed there, while there, suffered an attack of influenza, from which he never fully recovered, after the war, placed in charge of the anatomical exhibits at the American Museum of Natural History, invited to join the Bishop Museum of Honolulu in an anthropological study of the Polynesian Islands; during his eighteen months on Hawaii, made measurements and photographs of a large portion of the Native population, later he published his *Marquesan Somatology with Comparative Notes on Samoa and Tonga* wherein he made a general comparative study of the races of the Pacific and formulated a working hypothesis as to the original elements entering into the mixture; published twenty-five papers in his short life, several of considerable importance, sought to uncover genetic connections between known divisions of human race, had a genius for setting up rating scales.

Svedsen, Louise Averill 1915–94, born: Old Town; A.B. Wellesley College 1937, A.M. Yale University 1941, Ph.D. 1949; docent: Metropolitan Museum of Art, New York 1941–42, lecturer, Department of Education: Boston Museum of Fine Arts 1942–43, instructor in history of art: Duke University, Durham, North Carolina, 1943–45, instructor, assistant professor: Goucher College, Baltimore, 1945–50, assistant professor: American University, Washington, 1950–51, lecturer: Solomon R. Guggenheim Museum, New York, 1954, assistant curator 1962–66, curator 1966–78, senior curator 1978–82; consultant, Impressionist Department: Sotheby's, New York, 1983–94; decorated: Knight, First Class, Royal Norwegian Order of St. Olaf, Swedish Order of the Polar Star; director: International Foundation for Art Research.

Swanton, John Reed 1873–1958, born: Gardiner; A.B. Harvard College 1896, A.M. 1897, Ph.D. 1901 in anthropology; worked with Franz Boas at Columbia University and the American Museum of Natural History, New York 1898–1900, joined the Bureau of American Ethnology, Smithsonian Institution 1900–44, devoted himself to field research and reports on North American Indians; author of 167 publications, full-length monographs, collections, and dictionaries, published chiefly in *Annual Reports and Bulletins* of the Bureau of American Ethnology, *Journal of American Folklore, International Journal of Linguistics*; author: *Indian Tribes of the Lower Mississippi Valley and Adjacent Coast of the Gulf of Mexico* 1911, *Indian of the Southeastern U.S.* 1946, *Myths and Tales of the Southeastern Indians* 1929, *Social Conditions, Beliefs, and Linguistic Relationship of the Tlingit Indians* 1908, *Source Material on the History and Ethnology of the Caddo Indians* 1942.

Sweat, Lorenzo De Medici 1818–1898, born: Parsonsfield; A.B. Bowdoin College 1837, L.L.B. Harvard University Law School 1840; member: Louisiana bar 1841, practiced in New Orleans, removed to Portland; city solicitor 1856–60, member: Maine Senate 1862; member from the First District: U.S. House of Representatives 1863–65; member: Democratic National Committee 1872–76; husband of Margaret Mussey Sweat; buried in Evergreen Cemetery, Portland.

Sweat, Margaret Jane Mussey 1823–1908, born: Portland; daughter of the merchant, John Mussey, wife of Lorenzo De Medici Sweat from 1849; grew up in the Mussey family mansion, The Elms, at the corner of High and Danforth Streets; vice regent for Maine: Mount Vernon Ladies' Association, author: *Ethel's Love Life* (regarded, by some, as the first lesbian love story) 1859, *Highways of Travel; or, A Summer in Europe* 1859, numerous articles and reviews for the *North American Review, Portland Transcript, Boston Courier, New York Saturday Press, New Orleans Picayune,* &c.; her acquaintances included William Randolph Hearst, Admiral George Dewey, Susan B. Anthony, George Sand, and others; donated the McLellan-Sweat Mansion, along with the L. D. M. Sweat Memorial Gallery, to the Portland Museum of Art.

Swett, Leonard 1825–99, born: Turner; graduate: North Yarmouth Academy, attended Waterville College, but did not graduate; read law in Portland; served as a common soldier in the Mexican War, settled in Bloomington, Illinois, 1848; traveled the circuit and became intimate friends with Abraham Lincoln, David Davis, and Henry Clay Whitney; took an active part in politics 1852–61, canvassed the state several times; at the request of Lincoln, Republican candidate for the Illinois House of Representatives, a race he won with a large majority 1858; after the election of Lincoln to the presidency, Swett was employed often as solicitor by the U.S. government, most important was the case involved in the government acquisition of mercury mines in California 1863; as a private lawyer, defended twenty men accused of murder, secured acquittal for nineteen and a light sentence for one; retained for criminal and civil cases in nearly every part of the country, did much *pro bono* work for the poor, represented Speis and other Haymarket anarchists in their appeal; gave the dedicatory speech for the statue of Lincoln by Augustus Saint Gaudens in Lincoln Park, Chicago, arranged for and participated in the hearing that declared Mary Lincoln to be insane; as delegate to the Republican National Convention, in Chicago 1888, nominated Walter Q. Gresham for the presidency.

Talbot, Emily Fairbanks 1834–1900, born: Winthrop; at age sixteen, began teaching in Augusta, removed to Baltimore 1854, met and married Israel Talbot, graduate of the Homeopathic Medical College of Pennsylvania and Harvard University Medical School, first dean and professor of anatomy: Boston University Medical School 1873; editor: *New England Medical Gazette*; intimate of Julia Ward Howe, Louisa May Alcott, persisted in attempting to enter her daughters in the Boston Latin School, established Latin School for Girls 1877, formed a vision of female college graduates uniting to promote their common interests, formed Association of Collegiate Alumnae 1881, the predecessor of the American Association of University Women, organized the Massachusetts Society for the University Education of Women, which provided funds for women who could not otherwise afford college tuition, Talbot aimed to reform education from primary to advanced schooling, remove gender bias, advocated the study of children, corresponded with Charles Darwin, provided the catalyst for the advancement of child studies, first female trustee of the Massachusetts State Insane Hospital, Westboro.

Tapley, Rose 1883–1957, born: Bridgewater; originally appeared on the stage with such actors as Richard Mansfield, Chauncey Olcott, E. H. Sothern, J. H. Stoddard, and others; received critical acclaim in *The Sign of the Cross*; began her film career with Thomas Edison in his *Wanted: A Wife* 1905, later appeared in the first two-reeler *Money Kings*; signed with Vitagraph Co. and became the first film leading lady, sometimes referred to as "Mother of the Movies" 1911, later with Famous Players and Fox Productions; toured the United States as representative of the motion picture industry, appeared before sundry state legislatures, women's and business clubs, promoting film betterment 1916–17, also served as official hostess at various motion picture expositions; her films include: *Vanity Fair* 1911, *As You Like It* 1912, *The Sign of the Cross, The Christian Cross* 1914, *Rose of the South, The Victoria Cross, Susie, the Sleuth* 1916, *Rip Van Winkle, Memories That Haunt* 1921, *Vanity Fair, Java Head* 1923, *It* 1927, *The Charlatan* 1929, *Sex Madness* 1938; died at the Motion Picture Country Hospital, Woodland Hills, California, buried in San Fernando Mission Cemetery.

Tate, George II 1746-1824, born: Rotherhithe, England; son of George Tate, royal mast agent, whose home in Stroudwater is extant; after a boyhood spent in Stroudwater, journeyed to Portsmouth, England, and enrolled in the Russian Imperial Navy 1770, served as a lieutenant aboard the *Count Orlov*, saw intense fighting off Napoli di Romagna and Chesme; commanding officer: *Patriarch John*, fought gallantly against Sweden in the battles of Hogland and the Olands 1788, sailed provocatively along the Swedish coast, made possible the defeat of the Swedish squadron off Revel; participated in the siege of the Turkish fort of Ismail, wounded and presented with a gold and diamond likeness of the Empress Catherine 1790, after taking a Swedish frigate at the battle of Vyborg, promoted to captain-major general, later rear admiral, took charge of several frontline Baltic squadrons, led the blockade of Holland 1788–90, appointed admiral of the Blue Division by the Emperor Paul, commanded the Russian North Fleet off Holland 1812–13, made imperial senator 1816, first lord of the admiralty; decorated with the orders of St. John, Alexander Nevski, and St. Vladimir; presented with a gold sword by King George III of England.

Taylor, Stewart Munn 1884–1960, born: Cape Elizabeth, son of a farmer and steamboat inspector; attended public schools in Cape Elizabeth and South Portland, L.L.D. University of Maine 1956; worked on the family farm to age twenty-one, clerked in a shoe store in Cape Elizabeth, associated with Hannaford Brothers Co., wholesale grocers in Portland from 1906, salesman, general manager, vice president, elected president 1941–60, chairman of the board; the company acquired the Red and White Food Stores, a voluntary franchise organization of some 135 stores in Maine and New Hampshire 1939; president: Taylor Dow Co., a supplier of fresh produce, Otto Produce Co., a potato producer, Bessey Foods, Inc., a cider vinegar manufacturer; director: Federal Loan Co., Portland Savings Bank; chairman of the board: Portland Salvation Army, instrumental in setting up the collection of funds for that organization, a recreation building on the Salvation Army's children's camp on Sebago Lake was named Taylor Hall in his honor.

Taylor, Thomas 1834– ?, born: Bangor; coxswain, USN, recipient: Medal of Honor, "Served on board the USS *Metacomet* during the action against rebel forts and gunboats and with the rebel ram CSS *Tennessee* in Mobile Bay, 5 August, 1864. Despite damage to his ship and the loss of several men on board as enemy fire raked her decks, Taylor encouraged the men of the forward pivot gun when the officer in command displayed cowardice, doing honor to the occasion."

Teague, Charles Collins 1873–1950, born: Caribou, nephew of William Wallace Hardison, cousin of Allen Crosby Hardison; removed with his family to Kansas, student: St. John's Military Academy, Salina; L.L.D. (Hon.) University of California 1924, University of Maine 1930; found work in 1893 as a laborer to a horticulturist in Santa Paula, California; with borrowed capital, planted a small lemon grove which did so well he was engaged to manage groves for other growers; general manager: Limoneira Co. 1897, later acquired an interest in same, president from 1917–47, at the time of his retirement, Limoneira was the largest lemon grove in the world, producing, annually, 525,000 field boxes of lemons, 200,000 field boxes of Valencia oranges, 10,000 100-pound sacks of lima beans, with 500 full-time employees, a ranch of some 2,000 acres and 500 homes; devised the Teague method of washing and curing fruit, constructed the earliest washing machine for lemons; president: Santa Paula Waterworks from 1917, president: La Cuesta from 1923, founder and president California Fruit Growers Exchange (largely responsible for the transition of oranges from an occasional treat to a staple, popularized the concept of drinking orange juice by sending carloads of oranges into the hinterlands and offering up fresh-squeezed juice), originated the name Sunkist, founder and president: California Walnut Growers Association, originated the trade name Diamond Brand; appointed by President Hoover to the U.S. Farm Board 1929, chaired Hoover's reelection campaign in California 1932; president: California Chamber of Commerce, associated with William May Garland in the campaign to defeat Upton Sinclair's bid for the California governorship 1936, invited by his close friend Herbert Hoover to level a broadside at Sinclair in the *Los Angeles Times*, later, directed the campaign, styled United for California, to raise millions of dollars from the largest California companies and corporations, hire an advertising agency to churn out propaganda, hire (if necessary) prominent literary and movie figures to speak out against Sinclair, commission a search of Sinclair's writing to find embarrassing quotes, generate radio programs and newspaper copy, create nonpartisan front groups, &c., some scholars consider this to be the first modern political campaign; regent: University of California 1930–50, member: national advisory board: Stanford University, also professor of marketing, graduate school of business, author: *Fifty Years a Rancher*; his introduction of modern marketing methods to political campaigns was then thought radical, now accepted as the norm.

Thatcher, Benjamin Bussey 1809–40, born: Warren; son of Samuel Thatcher, cousin of Henry Knox Thatcher; graduate: Warren Academy, A.B. Bowdoin College 1826, studied law and practiced in Boston; a prolific author, contributed to the *North American Review*, essayist; editor: *Colonizationist and Journal of Freedom*, organ of Young Men's Colonization Society 1833; author: *Memoir of S. Osgood Wright* 1834, sought to restrain his organization from the extremes of William Lloyd Garrison; his *Prayer for the Blind*, printed on satin, was sold widely to raise funds for good works; author: *Indian Biography* (two volumes) 1832, unusually accurate depiction for the time, *Indian Traits* (two volumes) 1835, *Traits of the Deity* 1835, *The Boston Book* 1837.

Thatcher, Henry Knox 1806–80, born: Thomaston; grandson of Henry Knox, nephew of Samuel Thatcher, cousin of Benjamin Bussey Thatcher; attended U.S. Military Academy 1822–23, appointed midshipman, USN, 1823, served in ship USS *United States* 1824–27, promoted to passed midshipman, USN, 1829, promoted to lieutenant, USN, 1833, made cruise in West Indies as acting commanding officer: USS *Erie* 1833, commanding officer: storeship USS *Relief*, Brazilian Squadron 1851–52, promoted to commander, USN, executive officer: Naval Asylum, Philadelphia, 1855–57, commanding officer: USS *Decatur* 1857-59, executive officer: Boston Navy Yard 1861, commanding officer: USS *Constellation*, promoted to commodore,

USN, 1862, flagship USS *Colorado*, commanding officer: North Atlantic Squadron 1863, commanding officer: 1st Division of Porter's fleet and served with distinction at the attack on Fort Fisher, commanding officer: West Gulf Blockading Squadron, captured Mobile, Galveston, commanding officer: North Pacific Squadron 1865–68, promoted to rear admiral, USN, 1866, post-admiral: Portsmouth Navy Yard, Kittery 1869–71; member: Society of the Cincinnati; the U.S. Navy has commissioned two destroyers, named in his honor: USS *Thatcher* (DD-162) was launched in 1918, later saw service in World War II as HMCS *Niagara*; a second USS *Thatcher* (DD-514) was launched at Bath Iron Works in 1942, she was accorded twelve battle stars for World War II.

Thaxter, Celia Leighton 1835-1894, born: Portsmouth, New Hampshire, removed with her father to Appledore Island (Maine) at age five, married Levi Lincoln Thaxter 1851; her first published work was a series of articles in the *Atlantic Monthly* 1867-68, her works include: *Poems* 1872, *Among the Isles of Shoals* 1873, *Driftweeds* 1879, *Poems for Children* 1884, *Idyls and Pastorals* 1884, *Cruise of the Mystery and Other Poems* 1886, *An Island Garden* 1894; her garden was an inspiration for several American impressionist painters; buried in Appledore Island Cemetery.

Thelberg, Elizabeth Burr 1860–1935, born: Brewer; M.D. Women's Medical College of the New York Infirmary 1884; assistant professor: eye, ear, and children's diseases, Women's Medical College of the New York Infirmary 1885–86, resident physician: Infant Asylum and Nursery, Children's Hospital, New York, 1885–87, resident physician, professor of physiology and hygiene: Vassar College 1887–1930; studied in Vienna with Dr. Joseph Schreiber and in Paris with Dr. Louis Pasteur 1889; member: board of American Women's Hospitals, visited its hospitals in Serbia, the Caucasus, and Turkey; decorated by Serbia: Order of St. Sava 1928; corresponding secretary: International Association of Medical Women, chairman, Public Health Committee: U.S. Council of Women, member, Women's Advisory Council: U.S. Public Health Service, president: Medical Women's National Association 1926.

Thomas, William Widgery, Jr. 1839–1927 born: Portland; descendant of  George Cleeve, son of W. W. Thomas, mayor of Portland, brother of Henry G. Thomas; A.B. Bowdoin College ΦBK 1860, A.M. 1866, L.L.D. 1913, Bethany College 1901; taught school, studied law in Portland; appointed U.S. bearer of dispatches 1862, carried a treaty to Turkey, vice consul general: Constantinople, acting consul: Galatz, Moldavia; sent by President Lincoln as a war consul to Gothenburg, Sweden, where he learned the Swedish language, translated Rydberg's *Last Athenian*, received the thanks of

Secretary Seward and the Department of State; returned to Portland 1865, L.L.B. Harvard University 1866, member: Maine bar 1866; as commissioner of the settlement of Maine public lands, began to advocate for Swedish migration, submitted a plan to the legislature, which passed it and dispatched Thomas to Sweden, where he recruited 51 Swedes, Thomas returned with the group and dwelt in their midst for four years, until the success of their venture was assured; member: Maine House of Representatives 1873, 1874, 1875, speaker 1874–75, member: Maine Senate 1879; president: Maine Republican Convention 1875; delegate: Republican National Convention 1880; appointed minister resident to Sweden and Norway 1883–85, first American ambassador to address the Swedish king in Swedish, appointed envoy extraordinary and minister plenipotentiary to Sweden and Norway 1888–92, delivered an eloquent speech, in Swedish, upon the occasion of the return of the remains of John Ericsson to Sweden from the United States 1890, reappointed by President McKinley 1897–1903; chosen by Swedish Americans to be the orator at the celebration of the 250th anniversary of the landing of the first Swedish settlers in America, in Minneapolis 1888; author: *Sweden and the Swedes* 1892.

Thomes, William Henry 1824–95, born: Portland; shipped out on the *Admittance* for California hides 1842; author: *On Land and Sea* 1882; deserted, knocked around, saw some military service during the conquest of California, gathered material that would eventually see light in *Lewey and I* 1884; served as a reporter and printer for the *Boston Daily Times*, got gold fever, joined the Boston and California Joint Stock Mining and Trading Co. which sailed on the *Edward Everett* 1849, after prospecting at Bidwell's Bar, became a caretaker aboard ship in San Francisco Bay, sailed to the Hawaiian Islands, on to Guam and the Philippines, China, and the gold mines of Victoria, Australia; author: *The Gold Hunter's Adventures or Life in Australia* 1864, a long, lurid tale: *The Bushrangers* 1866, *The Gold Hunters in Europe* 1868, *The Whaleman's Adventures* 1872, *Life in the East Indies* 1873, *A Slaver's Adventures* 1872, *Running the Blockade* 1875, *The Belle of Australia* 1883, *The Ocean Rovers* 1896, *Daring Deeds* (sold more than 500,000 copies).

Thompson, Augustin 1835–1903, born: Union; in the Civil War, rose to lieutenant, USV, assigned to the 28th Maine Infantry; graduate: Hahneman Homeopathic College, Philadelphia, 1857; physician in Lowell, Massachusetts, concocted the formula for Moxie (originally Moxie Nerve Food) 1884, the oldest carbonated beverage continuously manufactured in the United States.

Thompson, Francis Edward 1864–1939, born: Union; son of Augustin Thompson; student: Lowell, Massachusetts, public schools, sent by father to manage an orange grove in Florida 1884, returned and was associated with father in manufacture of Moxie, incorporated in Maine as Moxie Nerve Food 1885; treasurer, secretary, named changed to Moxie Nerve Food of New England 1893, president from 1903, expanded business from New England to the rest of the country and internationally, became the fifth largest producer of soft drinks in the world, representing the production of 80 million bottles a year; widely known for liberality, among the first companies to offer two weeks of paid vacation a year and a five-day work week.

Thompson, Richard Edward 1848–1914, born: Union; removed with his family to Providence, Rhode Island, enlisted at age fourteen in the Providence Marine Light Artillery, entered the U.S. Military Academy 1864, graduating 1868, commissioned second lieutenant, USA, assigned to the 6th Infantry, which he joined at Charleston, South Carolina, saw action in the West against the Kiowas and Cheyennes at Bear Creek, Oklahoma Territory, 1872, topographer of the expedition under Ludlow, which explored and mapped the Yellowstone National Park, after a tour at West Point as tactical officer, ordered West, chief commissary to General Alfred Terry in his expedition against Sitting Bull 1876, appointed first lieutenant, USA, 1880, regimental adjutant to General Hazen, served with his regiment in Colorado, Utah, and Dakota Territory, assigned to the school of instruction, Fort Myer, Virginia, 1886, ordered to Washington to make weather predictions for the U.S. Signal Corps, captain, USA, 1891, served at the World's Fair, Chicago, 1892–93, Texas 1893–95, St. Paul, Minnesota, 1895–98; in the Spanish-American War: ordered to Tampa and Key West, military censor and acting chief of the signal corps forces, subsequently sent to the Philippines, on General Wesley Merritt's staff as chief signals officer of the 8th Corps; distinguished himself at the capture of Manila, recommended for brevet rank of lieutenant colonel, USV, for gallantry at Manila Bay, 13 August 1898, commended in the dispatches of Major General T. M. Anderson, particularly for a task of great difficulty and danger when Major Thompson, on the evening of August 12, came through the surf in a small native boat during a raging storm to bring orders and instructions of extreme importance to General Anderson from General Merritt on the USS *Newport*, that is., the definite orders for the attack on Manila the following day and also orders to request the insurgent Chief Aguinaldo to prevent his soldiers joining in the attack and entering the city; in action against the insurgents in Manila and near Caloocan in February 1899 and in the capture of Malolos, March 1899, in the following month appointed major in the regular army, he was also military censor during his entire tour in the Philippines, returned to the United States with impaired health, stationed in Washington, for two years; commanding officer: the signal corps post at Fort Myer 1902-03, promoted to lieutenant colonel, USA, Vancouver Barracks, Washington, 1903–04, Seattle 1904; in the fall of 1904, ordered to the Philippines, where he was chief signal officer of the division; promoted to colonel, USA, 1906, stationed at the Presideo, San Francisco, 1906–07, Seattle 1907–11, where he was in command of the cable and telegraph system of Alaska; retired 1912.

Thompson, Samuel 1735–98, born: Brunswick; innkeeper in Topsham, active and ardent member: Sons of Liberty, led armed bands that swept the lower Kennebec River Valley, threatening suspected Tories 1774; commissioned colonel, sent by Provincial Congress of Massachusetts to the mouth of the Kennebec to prevent British forces from loading naval stores 1775; learning that HMS *Canceaux,* commanding officer, Lieutenant Henry Mowatt, was lying off Falmouth (Portland), Thompson laid plans for its capture, which were betrayed to Mowatt and the Friends of Government; landed fifty armed men in Back Bay and began what was termed Thompson's War, captured Mowatt who was released; with the capture of the *Margaretta* in Machias and the furor caused by Thompson's War, the British decided to chastize the coast, dispatched Mowatt and a force of three naval vessels to Falmouth, which he subjected to a bombardment 18 October 1775, leaving two-thirds of Falmouth in ruins; Thompson commissioned brigadier general, mustered the Cumberland County Second Regiment for the ill-fated expedition against Castine, where Mowatt commanded the naval forces; member: all three provincial congresses, removed to Topsham, and worked for Maine's separation from Massachusetts 1784; member: Massachusetts Constitution Convention 1788, to which he was opposed because of the lack of a bill of rights and its recognition of slavery; delegate: Massachusetts General Court 1784–98; attended first meeting of Maine leaders of separation movement 1784; donated the land that became the Bowdoin College campus, endowed a chair of mathematics and experimental philosophy, served as overseer 1794–98; member: Massachusetts Senate 1798.

Thorndike, Ashley Horace 1871–1933, born: Houlton; son of a Methodist minister; attended public schools in Lowell, Massachusetts, and the Roxbury Latin School, Boston, A.B. Wesleyan University 1893, A.M. Harvard University 1896, Ph.D. 1898, L.H.D. Wesleyan University 1909, Litt.D. Columbia University 1929; instructor in English: Boston University 1895–98, instructor and assistant professor: Western Reserve University 1898–1902, professor of English literature: Northwestern University 1902–06, professor of English and executive officer of the department: Columbia University from 1906; author: *The Influence of Beaumont and Fletcher on Shakespeare* 1901, *Elements of Rhetoric and Composition* 1905, *Tragedy* 1908, *Everyday English* 1913, *Facts About Shakespeare's Prose* 1915, *Shakespeare's Theatre* 1916, *Literature in a Changing Era* 1920, *A History of English Literature* 1920, *English Comedy* 1929, *The Outlook for Literature* 1931; editor: *Tudor Shakespeare, Everyman's English Classics, Everyday Classics*; Thorndike was internationally known as one of the outstanding authorities in the general field of English literature, drama, and nineteenth-century poetry, in particular, literary adviser to the MacMillan Co.; president: Modern Language Association of America 1927, Shakespeare Association of America 1923–33.

Thrasher, John Sidney 1817–79, born: Portland; removed to Cuba, at age sixteen with parents 1833; at first worked as a clerk, became revolutionary agitator and propagandist, assisting Narcisso Lopez and others; well-known for his annotated edition of Baron Humboldt's study of Cuba, *Personal Narrative of Travels,* 1856; editor of the anti-Spanish newspaper *El Faro Industiel de La Habana,* imprisoned by Spanish authorities, deported back to United States 1852; removed to New Orleans where he allied himself with John Quitman and other Spanish revolutionary forces who wished to see Cuba become a slave state in the United States and who were preparing a filibustering expedition to that end; reporter for *New York Herald* in South America and Mexico; editor: *Illustracion Americana, Noticioso de Nuevo York, Beacon of Cuba, Times-Picayune*; married a propertied lady in Texas and died in Galveston.

Thurston, Jane Plummer 1814–99, born: Portland; daughter and sister of military officers; employed as a teacher before her marriage to Henry Thurston, a ship captain, 1846; lived in a large house on Tyng Street; on a voyage to Marseilles, France, one son died and her husband became so ill that she had to take over command of the ship; finding herself a widow in reduced circumstances, she began a legal campaign to recover lands that she claimed had been illegally taken by the Atlantic & St. Lawrence Railroad 1861; began writing and selling pamphlets addressing the sources of conflict in the Civil War and possible modes of restoring the peace, one was entitled *The Union of the States and the Union of Families of the United States and Great Britain: How They May be Preserved*, a later pamphlet, entitled *The Plan to Close the Rebellion and Unite the States in Six Months*, offered for a fee of $500 a plan for ending the Civil War—remarkably like the platform later adopted by the Democratic party at their convention in 1864; after the war she continued her campaign to recover her lands from the Atlantic & St. Lawrence Railroad; feeling both the state of Maine and the United States government had breached their respective pledges, in re: the taking of private property, she proclaimed herself to be proprietor of the State of Maine and proprietor of the United States; in 1870, she appeared in the Maine House of Representatives chamber, before the beginning of a session and, mounting the podium, proceeded to auction off the state, receiving bids of upwards of $20 million before being put out the chamber; she later deeded the state back to Governor Joshua Chamberlain and the country back to President Ulysses Grant; whether or not she had communication with Norton I of San Francisco, who was advancing similar claims at the same time, is unknown to the compiler; at her death, her tombstone reportedly read "Empress of America."

Thwing, Charles Franklin 1853–1936, born: New Sharon; son of a tanner; encouraged by Jacob Abbott to seek a good education; graduate: Phillips Academy, Andover, A.B. Harvard College ΦBK (elected in his sophomore year) 1871, first in his class; author: *Homeward*, a novel 1871; S.T.D. Andover Theological Seminary 1879, S.T.D. Chicago Theological Seminary 1889, L.L.D. Marietta College, Illinois College 1891, Waynesburg College 1901, Washington and Jefferson College 1902, Kenyon College 1910, Litt.D. University of Pennsylvania 1917, D.Litt. Western Reserve University 1926; Congregational minister in Cambridge, Massachusetts, and Minneapolis, Minnesota; sixth president: Western Reserve University and Adelbert College (the youngest college president in the United States, at that time) 1890–1921, during his tenure raised the enrollment from 246 to 2,242, increased the faculty from 37 to 415, added schools of law, dentistry, pharmacy, applied social science, a graduate school, a library school, a school of business administration, built eighteen buildings; after his retirement, the university library was renamed Thwing Hall; president: ΦBK 1922–28; member: American Academy of Arts and Sciences; author of over 1,000 works, including: *American Colleges; Their Students and Work* 1878, a statistical work, the first of its kind, became a standard reference, *Within College Walls* 1893, *The American College in American Life* 1897, *Carrie F. Butler, An Appreciation by Friends* 1899, *College Administration* 1900, *The Youth's Dream of Life* 1900, *God in His World* 1900, *A Liberal Education and a Liberal Faith: A Series of Baccalaureate Addresses* 1903, *A History of Education in the United States Since the Civil War* 1910, *Letters from a Father To His Son Entering College* 1912, *Letters from a Father to His Daughter Entering College* 1913, *The Family; An Historical and Social Study* 1913, *Notes on the History of the College for Women of Western Reserve University for its First Twenty-Five Years 1888–1913* 1913, *The American College: What It Is, and What It May Become* 1914, *The Ministry: An Appeal to College Men* 1916, *The College Gateway* 1918, *The American Colleges and Universities in the Great War, 1914–1919; A History* 1920, *Higher Education in Australia and New Zealand* 1922, *Human Australasia: Studies of Society and of Education in Australia and New Zealand* 1923, *What Education Has the Most Worth?: A Study in Educational Values, Conditions, Methods, Force, and Results* 1924, *The College President* 1926, *Guides, Philosophers, and Friends: Studies of College Men* 1927, *The American and German University: One Hundred Years of History* 1928, *Education and Religion: The Bedell Lectures for 1926–27, and Other Addresses on Construction and Reconstruction in Education* 1929, *American Society; Interpretations of Educational and Other Forces* 1931, *Friends of Men: Being a Second Series of Guides, Philosophers, and Friends* 1933, *The American College and University: A Human Fellowship* 1935.

Tibbetts, Luther Calvin 1820–1902, born: South Berwick; at age of fifty removed to Riverside, California, for his health; discovered and propagated the first seedless orange which he named Washington Seedless Orange 1874; Tibbetts is regarded as the father of the modern orange industry, his wife Eliza started what is generally regarded as the first cult in California, by delivering messages from the other side in a gauze-lined room; one of the original Washington Seedless Orange trees is still alive, at this date.

Tibbetts, Margaret Joy 1919– ?, born: Bethel; A.B. Wheaton College, M.A. Bryn Mawr College; began work for the Office of Strategic Services, Washington 1944, later served with the Department of State in Washington, the American Embassy in London, the International Cooperation Administration and the American

Embassy in Brussels, ambassador of the United States to Norway 1964–69, as such: ranking female foreign service officer, deputy assistant secretary of state for European affairs 1969–71; awarded the Distinguished Honor Award, the highest decoration of the U.S. State Department 1971; retired to Bethel, where she served as president of the Bethel Historical Society.

Tillson, Davis 1830–95, born: Rockland; attended U.S. Military Academy 1849–51, compelled to resign when an accident required the amputation of one of his legs; member: Maine House of Representatives 1857, Maine adjutant general 1858, collector of U.S. customs for Waldoboro District 1861; in the Civil War: commissioned captain of the 2nd Maine Battery, a unit of the 1st Mounted Artillery Regiment 1861, promoted to major, USV, May 1862, lieutenant colonel, USV, December 1862; chief of artillery to various commanders, distinguished himself at Cedar Mountain and 2nd Manassas; commissioned brigadier general, USV, 1863, ordered to Cincinnati as chief of artillery in the Department of the Ohio, commanding officer: defensive works at Knoxville, commanding officer: a brigade of infantry in Ammens division of the XXIII Corps; commanding officer: District of East Tennessee, commanding officer: 4th Division, XXIII Corps 1865, commanding officer: a division of the Army of the Cumberland to the end of the war; prominent in the recruitment of Negro troops; directed branches of the Freedman's Bureau in Tennessee and Georgia 1866–67; became a cotton planter in Georgia for a year before returning to Rockland 1868; became a key figure in the development of the granite and lime trade on the western shores of Penobscot Bay; buried in Achorn Cemetery.

Tinker, Chauncey Brewster 1876–1963, born: Auburn; A.B. Yale College 1899, A.M. 1900, Ph.D. 1902, Litt.D. 1946, Litt.D. Wooster College 1919, Hobart College 1933, University of Rochester 1934, Princeton University 1934; associate professor of English: Bryn Mawr College 1902–03, instructor in English: Yale University 1903–08, assistant professor 1908–13, professor of English literature 1913–45; keeper of rare books, Yale University library from 1931; public orator 1946; professor of poetry, Norton Foundation, Harvard University 1938–39; chancellor: American Academy of Arts and Sciences 1949–51.

Toppan, Christopher 1671–1747, born: Newbury, Massachusetts; son of a physician; A.B. Harvard College 1691, A.M. 1693; as an undergraduate, known as the most industrious of his class; preached, as well as taught school in Newbury from 1694; purchased a parcel of land in Damariscotta 1702, later made purchases in Pemaquid and Sheepscot, eventually acquired most of the present towns of Newcastle and Damariscotta; came into conflict with the descendants of settlers driven from their respective homes in the Indian wars, who refused giving quit claims to their lands; Queen Ann's War put any plans for redevelopment on hold for twenty years; in 1720, began a fort on Mason's Neck and the recultivation of the Sheepscot area, cut a road to what is now Damariscotta Mills and built a mill in that place, found a minister and physician for the area between the Sheepscot and Damaricotta Rivers, on occasion, practiced medicine and preached himself, came into severe conflict with timber thieves; fought the pretensions of David Dunbar, who was authorized by the Board of Trade to establish the Province of Georgia with settlers drawn primarily from Ulster; with the resolution of his conflict with Dunbar finalized, he began the process of surveying his land into lots, specifying parsonage and school locations, room for burying grounds. &c.; acquired considerable fame for his examination and disquistion on an amphisbaena, a two-headed snake, later immortalized by John Greenleaf Whittier in his poem *The Two-Headed Snake of Newbury*; distinctly Old Lights in his theology, fought the wild forces of the Great Awakening when they invaded Newbury; attempted to whip George Whitefield with a bullwhip and denounced his revival as the delusion of Satan; eventually, he was displaced from his pulpit and replaced by a Presbyterian graduate of Yale College; despite these tribulations, continued to be respected for his skill as a physician.

Torrey, Joseph William 1828–84, born: Bath; attended school in Roxbury, Massachusetts; reporter for the Boston *Times*, associated with Benjamin Shillaber in the publication of the *Carpet Bag*; removed to Melbourne, Australia, where he clerked in a commercial house 1853, removed to Hong Kong, where he was partner in the firm of Montgomery, Parker & Co. 1857; editor and publisher of the *China Mail* and *Hong Kong Times*; appointed U.S. consul in Siam and practiced law; founded the American Trading Co. in Borneo 1864, which came to hold 20,000 square miles in the provinces of Amboy and Mavoodu, Torrey was recognized as rajah by the sultan and exercised absolute sovereignty 1865–79; secretary of the U.S. legation in Siam 1879–83; after his return to the United States, Torrey was appointed chief adviser to the sultan of Borneo, but died before he could assume office.

Townsend, Luther Tracy 1838–1922, born: Orono; from the age of thirteen worked as a fireman on the Boston, Concord & Montréal Railroad, studied Latin and Shakespeare in odd moments, studied for a time at the New Hampshire Conference Seminary, A.B. Dartmouth College ΦBK 1859, D.D. 1871, A.M. Wesleyan University 1871, graduate: Andover Theological Seminary 1862; in the Civil War: enlisted in the 16th Regiment, New Hampshire Volunteers, served as ordnance officer, surgeon, commissary officer, nurse, and chaplain, urged to take a colonelcy of a regiment then recruiting, declined; ordained Methodist Episcopal ministry 1864; professor of Hebrew, Chaldee, and New Testament Greek: Boston University 1868–70, professor of historical theology 1872, professor of practical theology and sacred rhetoric 1872–93; author: *Credo* 1869, *Sword and Garment* 1871, *Godman* 1872, *Lost Forever* 1873, *Arena and Throne* 1874, *Supernatural Factor in Revivals* 1877, *Intermediate World* 1878, *Fate of Republics* 1880, *Art of Speech* (two volumes) 1880, *Mosaic Record and Modern Science* 1881, *Collapse of Evolution* 1905, *God and the Nation* 1905, *Bible Stud-*

ies: Rules of Interpretation and Current Difficulties and Objections 1913, *The Stars Are Not Inhabited* 1914, *God and War* 1915, *Hell and Demons—Are They Myths or Realities?* 1921, *The Riddle of Spiritualism* 1921; member: Victoria Institute, London.

Tozier, Andrew Jackson 1838–1910, born: Monmouth; sergeant, Company I, 20th Maine Infantry, recipient: Medal of Honor, at Gettysburg, Pennsylvania, 2 July 1863, "At the crisis of the engagement this soldier...stood alone in an advanced position, the regiment having been borne back, and defended his colors with musket and ammunition picked up at his feet." Buried in Litchfield Plains Cemetery.

Tracy, Merle Elliott 1879–1945, born: Tremont; son of a general contractor and dealer in lumber and ice; blind from birth, student: Perkins Institution for the Blind, Boston, 1891–96; entered the general contracting business with his father, also Tremont superintendent of schools 1904–05, moderator: Tremont town meeting 1900–05, associated with the *Cambridge* (Massachusetts) *Chronicle* 1906–09, after this brief encounter with journalism, returned to contracting, building residences and office buildings in New Hampshire and Texas, where he removed in 1912; chief editorial writer, editorial director: *Houston* (Texas) *Chronicle* 1913–26; his articles on the Ku Klux Klan attracted national attention; vice president: Rein Printing Company; member, chairman: Houston city planning commission 1924–26; editorial columnist: Scripps-Howard Newspapers 1926–36; his column "M. E. Tracy Says" appeared in the *New York World-Telegram* and in twenty-six other Scripps-Howard newspapers; editor and publisher: *Current History* (purchased from the New York Times Company) 1936–39; author: *Our Country, Our People and Theirs* 1938, *New World Challenge to Democracy* 1940, several novels, short stories, and a biography *Life of Captain Kidd*; first blind newspaper reporter, publisher.

Trathen, James 1811–74, born: aboard a vessel off the coast of Maine; went to sea at an early age, served as commander of various merchant vessels; in the Civil War: volunteered and was commissioned acting volunteer lieutenant August 1861, initially assigned to the command of the bark *Midnight* in the Gulf Patrolling Squadron, cruised independently off the coast of Texas, occasionally bombarding coastal positions of the Confederate Army; assumed command of the steam vessel USS *Mount Vernon* and joined the North Atlantic Blockading Squadron October 1862, patrolling off Wilmington, North Carolina; his vessel captured eight merchantmen trying to run the blockade; on 31 July 1863, his command daringly captured the steamer *Kate*, which was protected by the heavy guns of Fort Fisher; promoted to lieutenant commander, USN, 16 May 1865; died at the Washington Navy Yard; the navy honored Trathen by naming a Fletcher-class destroyer (DD-530) for him, launched in 1942, she was accorded eight battle stars for World War II and one for Korea.

Treat, Charles Gould 1859–1941, born: Dexter, attended public schools in Monroe, Wisconsin, B.S. U.S. Military Academy 1882, commissioned second lieutenant, USA, promoted through the ranks to brigadier general, USA, 1922, major general, USA, on the retired list 1930; assigned to the 5th Artillery 1882, received instruction at the Torpedo School, Willets Point, New York, 1885, attended Artillery School, Fortress Monroe, Virginia, 1886–88, aide-de-camp General Oliver O. Howard, commanding officer: Atlantic Division, USA, Governor's Island, New York, 1889–94, adjutant: Light Artillery School, Fort Riley, Kansas, 1894–96; in the Spanish-American War: adjutant: Light Artillery Brigade, 5th Army Corps, took this brigade to Santiago, Cuba; on duty mustering out New York volunteers; assistant adjutant general: U.S. military governor, Havana, Cuba, 1898–1900; senior artillery instructor, commandant of cadets: U.S. Military Academy 1901–05; inspector general, Army of Pacification, Cuba 1906–08; assigned to the 4th Field Artillery, Fort Myers, Virginia, graduate: Army War College, Washington 1911, commanding officer: 3rd Field Artillery, Fort Sam Houston, Texas, 1911–14; member: General Staff Corps, Washington, 1914–16, commanding officer: Hawaiian Brigade, Honolulu, 1916–17; in World War I: commanding officer: 37th Ohio Division, Camp Sheridan, Alabama, 1917–18, assigned to the Western Department, San Francisco, 1918; chief of American Military Mission to Italy, commanding Base Section 8 and the American Expeditionary Forces in Italy 1918–19; following the armistice, appointed by the Supreme War Council to a committee investigating incidents between Italians and Yugoslavs at Laiback, Yugoslavia; assigned to Camp Stevens, Ohio, 1919; commandant: Fort Sam Houston, Texas, 1920; assigned to the Philippine Department, commanding officer: Fort Stotsenberg to his retirement in 1922; awarded the Distinguished Service Medal 1918, decorated: Serbian Order of the White Eagle with swords, Italian Order of St. Maurice and St. Lazarus 1920; organized and played on the first army polo team at Fort Riley, Kansas, 1895, continued as a leader in the development of army polo, thereafter, while at West Point, he was instrumental in making polo one of its organized sports, army polo representative until his retirement.

Tripp, Bartlett 1842–1911, born: Harmony; attended local circuit school, Hartland Academy, Corinna Academy, began teaching at age fourteen, graduate: Coburn Classical Institute, attended Waterville College 1857–60, paying tuition by teaching in Bucksport and Old Town; after leaving college, journeyed to California where he was assistant engineer in laying out the line for the Central Pacific Railroad; taught school in Utah 1862–64, where his students included future U.S. Senator Frank Cannon and future Governor Heber Wells; L.L. B. Albany (New York) Law School 1867, practiced law in Augusta in partnership with Eben Pillsbury 1867–69; elected alderman 1868; removed to Yankton, Dakota Territory, 1869; president: Yankton school board 1875–85; one of the incorporators of Yankton College 1881; member, first board of regents: University of South Dakota; chairman: commission for codifying laws of South Dakota 1875; unsuccessful Democrat candidate for delegate to the U.S.

House of Representatives 1878; president: South Dakota Constitutional Convention 1883; chief justice: South Dakota Supreme Court 1885–89; president: Dakota Territorial Bar Association, South Dakota Bar Association; envoy extraordinary and minister plenipotentiary to Austria-Hungary 1893–97; member and chairman: Samoan Commission, which settled the dispute between the United States, Germany, and Great Britain 1899; lecturer on constitutional law: University of South Dakota from 1901; Bartlett County, South Dakota, was named in his honor.

Tuck, Amos 1810–79, born: Parsonsfield; graduate: Effingham (New Hampshire) Academy, A.B. Dartmouth College 1835; member: New Hampshire bar 1835, practiced in Exeter; member: New Hampshire House of Representatives 1842, broke with Democrats over Texas; elected to U.S. House of Representatives by a fusion of independent Democrats and Whigs (first term: Independent, second term: Free Soil, third term: Whig), served 1843–53, unsuccessful candidate for reelection 1852; prominently held antislavery, anti Mexican War views, prominent in the establishment of Republican party; vice president: first Republican National Convention, Cincinnati 1856; delegate: peace convention 1861; appointed naval officer: Boston and Charlestown 1861–65; had a national reputation as a lawyer, often hired by western railroads; trustee: Phillips Academy, Exeter 1853–79; his son Edward established the Amos Tuck School of Administration and Finance at Dartmouth College; buried in Exeter Cemetery.

Tucker, Richard Hawley 1859–1952, born: Wiscasset; son of a ship captain; B.S. Lehigh University 1879, Sc.D. 1922; assistant astronomer: Dudley Observatory, Albany, New York 1879-83, instructor in mathematics and astronomy: Lehigh University 1883–84, assistant: Argentine National Observatory, Cordoba, 1884–93, astronomer, senior astronomer: Lick Observatory, University of California, 1893–1908, director: Southern Observatory, Carnegie Institution, San Luis, Argentina, 1908–11, while there, constructed an observatory and charted 87,000 stars filling in the southern sky, senior astronomer: Lick Observatory 1911–26; his specialty was the precise determination of positions and motions of stars observed with the meridian circle; his observations of the transit of Venus 1882, in particular, drew international comment and approval; author: *Volume IV* 1900, *Volume VI* 1903, *Volume X* 1907, *Volume XV* 1925, of the Lick Observatory Publications, numerous contributions to astronomical journals, member of numerous honorific organizations, subsequent to his death, a crater on the moon was named in his honor; member: Wiscasset Fire Society.

Tucker, Samuel 1747–1833, born: Marblehead, Massachusetts; shipped out on the HMS *Royal George* at age eleven, advanced rapidly, commanded a merchantman at age twenty, narrowly averted service in the Royal Navy, during the Revolution, returned to America, taking charge of the vessel on which he was embarked during a storm, this led to his introduction to George Washington by Robert Morris, the owner of the vessel; commissioned captain in the Continental Navy, 20 January 1776, assigned to the command of the armed schooner *Franklin*, the vessel had to be fitted out and, in the meantime, Tucker commanded a small schooner *Young Phoenix*, with which he captured a British transport, for which he received the thanks of Washington and the army, made commander of the schooner *Hancock*, March 1776, captured more than thirty vessels in the year; commanding officer: frigate *Boston*, 15 March 1777, conveyed John Adams to France as minister, captured five vessels on the way home, convoyed a fleet of merchantmen from the West Indies to Philadelphia, with supplies for the Continental Army 1779; captured the British frigate HMS *Pole* without firing a gun; along with his command of the *Boston*, took on command of the *Confederacy*; designated commodore; captured several privateers, took part in the disastrous defense of Charleston, captured, along with the rest of the American squadron, paroled, went to Boston, effected an exchange with Captain Wardlaw, Royal Navy, who had been captured aboard the British frigate *Thorn*, by Tucker; assuming command of his former prize, captured seven prizes before being taken by the British frigate HMS *Hind*, July 1781, carried off to Prince Edward Island, managed to escape in an open boat to Boston; after the war, commanded several packets, settled in on a farm in Bremen 1792; in the War of 1812: recalled and given the command of a schooner, which he armed with two cannon borrowed from the fort at Edgecomb, took the privateer *Crown*, the valuable stores of which he distributed to the poor of Lincoln County; member: Bristol Board of Selectmen, member: Massachusetts House of Representatives 1814–18, delegate: Maine Constitutional Convention 1819, presidential elector 1820, member: Maine House of Representatives 1820–21; buried in Bremen; the U.S. Navy has named two destroyers in his honor, the first was launched in 1915, the second was launched in 1936 and received one battle star for World War II.

Tuttle, Charles Wesley 1829–81; born: Newfield; attended public school in Newfield and in Dover, New Hampshire, apprenticed to his uncle, a carpenter; constructed a telescope, removed to Cambridge, Massachusetts, 1849, became a student at the Harvard University Observatory, under William Cranch Bond 1850, appointed assistant observer 1851, sent to England in charge of a chronometric expedition of the U.S. Coast Survey for the determination of the difference in longitude between Liverpool and Cambridge; Harvard University conferred upon him a degree of A.M. in 1854, Dartmouth College awarded him an honorary Ph.D. in 1880; failing eyesight compelled him to yield this position, studied law at the Harvard University Law School, member: Massachusetts bar 1856, practiced in Newburyport and later in Boston until the time of his death; in his leisure time devoted to historical research, with a reputation as an original investigator; a founder, treasurer, and corresponding secretary of the Prince Society, before which he read many papers, also lectured on astronomical matters and published frequently in astronomical journals, his monograph *Captain John Mason, the Founder of New Hampshire* was later published in 1887.

Tuttle, Horace Parnell 1839–1923, born: Newfield; brother of Charles Wesley Tuttle; removed to Cambridge with his brother, where he received his education; entered the U.S. Navy as acting assistant paymaster, served aboard USS *Catskill* 1864, promoted to paymaster 1866, discharged 1875; invented the process for inserting a rifled steel core into a brass or iron cannon, while denied a patent by the U.S. Patent Office, the process was quickly adopted by the English and Germans 1857; devised a method of long-distance communication by use of a Drummond (or lime) light, this was quickly adopted by the U.S. Navy; discovered thirteen comets between 1857 and 1866, including the Swift-Tuttle, the source of the annual Perseid meteor shower 1862, and the Tempel-Tuttle Comet, source of the annual Leonid meteor shower 1866; also discovered the asteroids Maïa and Clytie 1861–62; assistant computer at the U.S. Naval Observatory; author: *Pay Tables of the United States Navy* 1872.

Tyler, Carroll Leslie 1898– ?, born: Waterville; graduate: Phillips Academy, Exeter 1916, B.S. U.S. Naval Academy 1920; commissioned ensign, USN, 1920; advanced through the ranks to captain, USN, 1947; assistant director, director: Research & Development Division, Bureau of Ordnance, USN, 1942–45, special assistant to Vannevar Bush, chairman: Office of Science Research and Development; in charge of project that developed the proximity fuse, thought by many to be one of the three most important scientific developments of World War II, the others being the atomic bomb and radar; manager, Santa Fe operations office: Atomic Energy Commission 1947–54, oversaw several atomic tests; general manager, U.S. Air Force Academy project for Skidmore, Owings, and Merrill, architects 1954–58; vice president, project manager: Reynolds Electrical and Engineering Co. from 1958; decorated: Legion of Merit, member: Order of the British Empire.

Upham, Thomas Cogswell 1799–1872, born: Deerfield, New Hampshire; A.B. Dartmouth College 1818, graduate: Andover Theological Seminary 1821; associate pastor: Rochester, New Hampshire, 1823–24; professor of mental and moral philosophy: Bowdoin College 1824–67; patron of colonization of freed Negro slaves in Africa (had an enormous effect on many, including John Russwurm), outspoken supporter of temperance movement, translator: Jahn's *Biblical Archaeology* 1833, author: *Outline of Imperfect and Disordered Mental Action* (precursor of modern psychiatric diagnosis and treatment) 1834, *Principles of the Interior or Hidden Life* (best-selling classic) 1843, *American Cottage Life* 1851, *A Philosophical and Practical Treatise on the Will* 1834, *Letters Aesthetic, Social, and Moral, Written from Europe, Egypt, and Palestine* 1855, won a prize for writing an essay calling for the creation of a congress of nations.

Upton, Benjamin Franklin 1818– after 1899, born: Dixmont; daguerreotyper in Brunswick 1847, removed to Bath 1851, established gallery, invented and patented daguerreotype apparatus: a mercury bath for plates and a method of polishing plates; removed to St. Anthony, Minnesota, settled in Big Lake 1856; pioneer photographer

Eminent Mainers

of the West, specializing in landscape scenes and stereographs, Indian portraits in the Sioux, Chippewa, and Winnebago tribes, his photographs are widely collected and some of the images are quite famous; removed to St, Augustine, Florida, 1875, practiced until well past eighty, a familiar figure traveling on his bicycle with a large camera balanced on behind.

Upton, George Bruce 1804–74, born: Eastport; after apprenticing with several businesses in Boston, became confidential clerk for Baker and Barrett, Nantucket, 1821, formed partnership with Barrett and engaged in sperm whaling, shipbuilding, and the manufacture of a vast number of candles 1825; member: Massachusetts House of Representatives 1837–41, Massachusetts Senate 1839, 1840, 1843; delegate: Whig National Convention 1844; removed to Boston, treasurer: Michigan Central Railroad 1848–54; engaged in shipping and the management of several famous clipper ships; member: Massachusetts Executive Council 1853, delegate: Massachusetts Constitutional Convention 1853; outspoken in his views about his concern for the safety of sailors and the sanctity of property during war, his protests on the *Alabama* claims and settlement for his ship *Nora* elicited the disparagement of the British prime minister, Lord John Russell, which resulted in a published response in the London papers, wherein Upton blamed the British for the construction of the raiders and having operated them, attracting international attention; promoted the Sailors' Snug Harbor and several, then radical, suggestions about life-saving equipment for ships.

Urann, Marcus Libby 1873–1963, born: Sullivan; B.S. University of Maine 1897, L.L.D., member: Maine bar 1897, member: Massachusetts bar 1898; practiced in Boston, South Hanson, Massachusetts; treasurer: United Cape Cod Cranberry Co., president: Cascade Foods, Ltd., president: National Cranberry Association, devised the Ocean Spray name and line; director: National Canners Association.

Vachon, Joseph Peter 1887–1961, born: Westbrook; enlisted in U.S. Army, coastal artillery as private, promoted through the ranks to sergeant, commissioned second lieutenant, USA, Philippine Scouts 1912, second lieutenant, USA, 1916, promoted through the ranks to brigadier general, USA, 1941; served in the Philippines, China, and Hawaii; instructor with Illinois National Guard, Connecticut National Guard, Organized Reserve District, Englewood, New Jersey; graduate: advanced course, Infantry School, command and staff schools; posted to the Philippines 1 November 1941, commanding general: 43rd Infantry Division, given command of 101st Division, Philippine Army by General MacArthur; organized the Mindinao Force; prisoner of war from 10 May 1942 to August 1945, retired 1946; decorations include: Distinguished Service Medal for exceptionally meritorious service, Silver Star for gallantry in action.

Valesh, Eva McDonald 1866–1956, born: Orono; apprentice printer: *Spectator*, Minneapolis, protégé of labor leader John McGaughey, recruited to write a series of articles on Minneapolis working women for the *St. Paul Globe*, accused of fomenting a strike in a local garment factory 1888, organizer for the Knights of Labor and the Eight-Hour League; author: *A Tale of the Twin Cities* about a Maine family's entanglement in the politics of a streetcar strike 1889, drew the attention of Ignatius Donnelly, president: Minnesota Farmers' Alliance; national lecturer for the Farmers' Alliance, wrote extensively for labor and reform journals; removed to New York where she was employed by William Randolph Hearst's *New York Journal American* 1897–98, as reporter, sent to Cuba, covered the sex and crime beat for the city desk and worked as a political reporter; removed to Washington, D.C., created her own syndicated political letter; assistant editor: *American Federationist* with Samuel Gompers, president: American Federation of Labor; wrote articles on working women, child labor, and education 1900–09; member: National Civic Federation and its women's department, organized welfare work for government employees, publicized work of National Civic Federation women; president: Women's Committee on National Industrial Problems; charter member: National Committee on Prison Labor; member: New York Civic Forum, Federation of Women's Clubs; active in Democratic party politics; member: Women's Trade Union League, involved in shirtwaist-makers strike 1910; founder and editor: *American Club Woman* magazine 1911–20; in World War I: organized the War Children's Relief Fund and War Children's Christmas Fund; known by some as the "Joan of Arc of the Labor Women" of this country.

Vallée, Hubert Prior Rudy 1891–1986, born: Island Pond, Vermont, raised in Westbrook, son of a druggist; played saxophone in a pierside band, Portland, attended University of Maine, Ph.B. Yale University 1927; president: American Federation of Actors 1937; played with the Savoy Havana Band at Hotel Savoy, London, 1924–25, broadcast and recorded in London, led Yale football band in his senior year, toured the United States with college band called the Connecticut Yankees 1928, made first U.S. radio broadcasts 1928, played with orchestra for ten years on National Broadcasting Co.'s *Fleischmann Variety Hour*, later *The Royal Gelatin Hour*, which quickly became the second most popular radio program (the first being *Amos 'n Andy*); appeared at the Paramount theatres, New York and Brooklyn, for ten weeks, spring of 1929, returning in October for a run of nearly two years; in an act of clear desperation, President Hoover offered to him a medal if he could sing a song that would make people forget their troubles and the Great Depression; starred in motion picture *Vagabond Lover* 1929, *George White's Scandals* 1934, *Sweet Music* 1935, *Gold Diggers in Paris* 1938, *Second Fiddle* 1939, *Time Out for Rhythm, Too Many Blondes* 1941; appeared in: *Man Alive, People Are Funny, It's In the Bag, The Fabulous Suzanne, I Remember Mamma, The Bachelor and Bobby Soxer, Beautiful Blonde from Bashful Bend, Father Was a Fullback, Mother Is a Freshman, The Admiral Was A Lady, The Palm Beach Story, Mad Wednesday, Ricochet Romance, Gentleman Marry Brunettes, How to Succeed in Business*

Without Really Trying, Live a Little, Love a Little; appeared on Broadway in stage show of *George White's Scandals* 1931, played stage show in London during Coronation Week 1937, played the Cocoanut Grove nightclub, Los Angeles, 1937, 1938; weekly radio broadcast for Standard Brands 1929–39, National Dairies, Sealtest 1940–41, *Drene Show* 1944-46, *Philip Morris* 1946-47, *Rudy Vallée Show* 1950; frequent nightclub appearances; composer of songs, arranged the *Maine Stein Song;* in World War I: served in USN, in World War II: served in USCG; recipient: New York Critics' Award 1962; member: American Federation of Musicians, American Society of Authors and Composers, Academy of Motion Picture Arts and Sciences, Screen Actors Guild, American Arbitration Association, *La Société des 40 Hommes et 8 Chevaux;* author: *Vagabond Dreams Come True* 1930, *My Time Is Your Time: The Story of Rudy Vallée* 1962, *Let the Chips Fall* 1975; buried in Saint Hyacinth's Cemetery, Westbrook.

Vannah, Letitia Katherine Kate 1855–1933, born: Gardiner; daughter of a hardware merchant; graduate: Gardiner High School, St. Joseph's College, Emmitsburg, Maryland; a devout Catholic, she lived with her widowed mother in Gardiner until her mother's death, after which melancholy event she divided her time between New York, London, and Boston; had installed in that home a pipe organ, with which she accompanied visiting singers, such as Madame Schumann-Heinck, Madame Blauvelt, and Madame Emma Calvé; she was engaged to a son of James G. Blaine previous to his early death; as a journalist, she wrote under the pen name Kate Van Twinkle; as a poetess, she published one volume of verse; as a writer of numerous songs, she is best remembered for *Come — The Sun is Going Down, Three Roses, Parting, O Salutaris, Veni Creator,* and the Eucharist hymn written for the Twentieth Eucharist Congress in Chicago, 1926; her *Goodbye, Sweet Day* (words by Celia Thaxter) achieved greatest fame; she is known to have written one opera.

Vaughan, Benjamin 1751–1835, born: Jamaica; grandson of Benjamin Hallowell, Boston merchant and proprietor of Hallowell, cousin of Robert Hallowell Gardiner; after attending Cambridge University, where he was a student of Joseph Priestly, he received his M.D. from the University of Edinburgh; propagandized for the colonial cause during the American Revolution, supported free trade and the French Revolution; because of his friendship with Benjamin Franklin and his family relationship with Henry Laurens, who along with Franklin was an American peace delegate, Vaughan was chosen by the Rockingham government as an unofficial conduit between British authorities and the Americans, made several trips between London and Paris communicating proposals and counterproposals, in particular his influence was most important in the final and almost-fatal sticking point: the right of return and property rights of refugee Tories, which was settled, despite much American opposition, in the Tories' favor (it should be noted that Vaughan, his brother, his Gardiner kin, and the Waldo heirs profited mightily from this); member of Parliament from Calne 1792–94, fled to France to avoid arrest only to be imprisoned in France as a suspected spy 1794, released to Switzerland, thence Hallowell, where his brother Charles had settled; maintained a wide correspondence with American political and scientific leaders, engaged in scientific farming, practiced medicine among the poor and supplied them with medicines, often for free; recipient of an honorary L.L.D. from Harvard College 1807, Bowdoin College 1812; a founder: Maine Historical Society; owned the largest individually owned library in New England; author of many papers, some of which were collected and published under the signature of Calm Observer in 1783, later translated into French and German, a life of James Gouyer entitled *Klyogg, or the Rural Socrates* 1806, two state papers, one concerning the northeast boundary, at the request of President John Adams, editor of the first compilation of Franklin's writing in England; designed the Maine state seal.

Vaughan, Charles 1759–1839, born: London, brother of Benjamin Vaughan; raised in Jamaica; removed to Hallowell 1785, went to England to publicize speculations 1790–91, merchant in Boston 1791–96, carried on an extensive trade with the West Indies and England, declared bankruptcy 1798; an incorporator of the Boston Library Society, Massachusetts Society for the Promotion of Agriculture, Massachusetts Society for the Aid of Immigrants, Hallowell Academy; brother-in-law to the architect Charles Bulfinch, with whom he constructed a block in Boston known as the Franklin Crescent, in Hallowell he constructed a brewery and distillery, wharves, and commercial buildings, private houses, a printing shop, and a wet-dock for ship timbers; acted as agent for nonresident landowners; active, along with his brother, Benjamin, in scientific farming, imported numerous cattle, sheep, and swine of improved breed as well as seeds; Bowdoin College overseer 1811–39.

Vaughan, William 1703–46; born: Portsmouth, New Hampshire; son of Lieutenant Governor George Vaughan; A.B. Harvard College 1722, A.M. 1725; busied himself settling his father's estate; initially was a merchant in Portsmouth but soon turned his attention to fishing at Matinicus Island, where he based a fishing operation that extended as far as Newfoundland; in 1732 shifted his attention to lumbering; in a cooperative deal with David Dunbar, surveyor of the king's woods, acquired title to most of the land in Bristol, Bremen, Damariscotta, Nobleboro, Newcastle, Jefferson, and Waldoboro, which involved him in a bitter and protracted series of lawsuits with Christopher Toppan; at Damariscotta Falls (now Damariscotta Mills), cleared fifty acres, constructed dams, two double sawmills, and a gristmill, as well as houses and a fine mansion, all protected by a fort 100 feet square; provided lumber for the Boston market, including the oak timbers for Governor Belcher's mansion at Milton; experienced considerable trouble with the local Indians, who ambushed his log rafts on Damariscotta Lake and wounded his Negro slave Plato; authorized to raise a militia company to patrol the woods; made at least one voyage to England to attend meetings of the Board of Trade; with the rise of international tensions, and the likelihood of renewed warfare on the frontier, Vaughan conceived of a plan to seize Louisbourg citadel, which he carried to Boston and New Hampshire, whipping up support and raising militia companies, so much so that Governors Belcher and Wentworth cautioned him not to raise too many men; general enthusiasm was so great that, despite great pessimism on the part of high officials, funds were quickly raised for what became the Pepperrell Expedition; serving as a civilian participant, Vaughan was given command of the first 400 men landed to feel out the fortifications and burn outlying buildings, warehouses, and stores; the smoke of the fires having frightened the French garrison out of the Grand Battery, Vaughan paid a Cape Cod Indian to squeeze through an embrasure and open the gate; signaling Pepperrell that the battery had been taken, Vaughan had to repel a French counterattack before additional troops could arrive; worked ceaselessly to prepare for an assault on the Island Battery, as well as destroy French shipping, by means of a fireship; subsequent to the surrender of Louisbourg, Vaughan, feeling that he was not receiving proper acknowledgment, departed for London, where he originally demanded appointment as governor of Nova Scotia; before this or any other reward could be bestowed, Vaughan died of smallpox in Bagshot, England; in 1812, the Commonwealth of Massachusetts finally compensated his heirs with one-half of a township.

Veazie, Samuel 1787–1868, born: Portland; settled in Topsham, where he engaged in lumbering and shipbuilding, traded with the West Indies; in the War of 1812, became general of militia; purchased the Davis mills in Old Town and all the waterpower rights on the west side of Old Town Falls 1826, removed to Bangor; sole owner of the Penobscot boom, sole owner of the Veazie bank; with the encouragement of John A. Poor, purchased the Bangor & Piscataquis Canal & Railroad Co. (which saw the first use of steam traction in northern New England in 1836) in 1854, reorganized it as the Bangor, Old Town & Milford Railroad Co. (although it was known locally as the Veazie Railroad), connecting his mills in Old Town and the Bangor waterfront; at considerable expense built the two railroad bridges necessary to cross the Penobscot River; member: Maine Executive Council 1837, Bangor alderman; removed to Veazie, which was named in his honor.

Verrill, Addison Emery 1839–1926, born: Greenwood; cousin of C. A. Stephens; in boyhood, collected plants, mammals, birds, insects and discovered several rare minerals, not before known in Maine; B.S. Lawrence Scientific School, Harvard University 1862, A.M. Yale University 1867; professor of zoology at Yale College 1864–1907, first professor of zoology in the United States; curator: zoological section of the Peabody Museum 1865–1901; instructor in geology: Sheffield School, Yale University 1874–94; curator: Boston Society of Natural History 1864–74; professor of comparative anatomy and entomology: University of Wisconsin 1868–70; associate editor: *American Journal of Science* 1869–1920; assistant in charge of scientific explorations by the U.S. Fish Commission 1871–87, identified over 1,000 new forms, ichthyologist and authority on invertebrates, author of over 350 papers on zoology and geology, as mining and geological expert investigated coal and iron properties in New York, Vermont, Pennsylvania, Virginia, North Carolina, and Alabama; author, his works include: *Report upon the Invertebrate Animals of Vineyard Sound and Adjacent Waters* 1873, *The Bermuda Islands* 1903, *Zoology of the Bermuda Islands*, vol. 1, 1903, *Geology and Paleonotology of the Bermudas* 1906, *Coral Reefs of the Bermudas* 1907, *Monograph of the Shallow Water Starfishes of the North Pacific Coast* 1914, *Report on West Indian Starfishes* 1915, *Report on Alcyonaria and Actinaria of Canadian Arctic Expedition* 1921, *Crustacea of Bermuda,* three parts, 1923, *Alcyonaria of the Blake Expedition* 1925; member: National Academy of Science; uncle of Harry M. Verrill, close friend and associate of E. S. Morse.

Very, Edward Wilson 1847–1910, born: Belfast; graduate: U.S. Naval Academy 1871; while stationed at Washington Navy Yard, invented eponymous Very Pistol flare gun, still in worldwide use; after resignation from navy employed by the Hotchkiss Ordnance Co., later by the American Ordnance Co.

Vinal, Harold 1891–1965, born: Vinalhaven; dropped out of high school, removed to Boston, managed a bookstore on Beacon Hill 1910–15, piano teacher to 1921; founded *Voices* magazine, subtitled "An Open Forum for the Poets," later "A Journal of Verse" 1921; first to publish Allen Tate, Robert Penn Warren, Mark Van Doren, Kenneth Fearing, Genevieve Taggard, Kenneth Patchen; published a 46-page volume of his own poetry *White April* as number eleven in the Yale Series of Younger Poets 1922, removed to New York 1923, published a second volume *Voyage*, published Archibald MacLeish, Edgar Lee Masters, Carl Sandburg, Katherine Mansfield, Wallace Stevens, and others; Vinal's poetry appeared in *The Nation, The Century, New Republic, Harper's Poetry, New York Sun*; his essays appeared in the *Christian Science Monitor*, produced a total of eight volumes of poetry between 1922 and 1944, including *Selected Poems* 1948, *Hurricane* 1936, a book-length chronicle of the Maine Coast in blank verse, *Attic for the Nightingale: A Sheaf of Informal Essays* 1934; executive secretary: Poetry Society of America 1938–49.

Vinton, Francis Laurens 1835–79, born: Fort Preble, South Portland; son of an regular army officer who was killed in the Mexican War at Vera Cruz; graduate: U.S. Military Academy 1856 (10/49); assigned to the cavalry/infantry, resigned 1856 to attend École des Mines in Paris 1856–60, taught at the Cooper Union, headed a minerals expedition to Honduras 1861; returned to be commissioned captain, USA, assigned to the 16th U.S. Infantry; colonel, USV, commanding officer: 43rd New York; commanding officer: 3rd Brigade, 2nd Division VI Corps: led his regiment at Williamsburg, Gaines Mill, promoted to brigadier general, USV, severely wounded at Fredericksburg, resigned; first professor of mining engineering: Columbia University, School of Mines 1864–77, professor of civil engineering 1864–70; published numerous articles in *Engineering and Mining Journal*; author: *The Guardian, A Diversion* 1869, *Lectures on Machines* 1869, *Theory of the Strength of Materials* 1874; consulting engineer in Denver, died in Leadville, Colorado, eventually buried in Swan Point Cemetery, Providence, Rhode Island.

Vinton, Frederick Porter 1846–1911, born: Bangor; removed with his family at age ten to Chicago, returned East 1860, while working as a clerk and bookkeeper, studied art at Lowell Institute, Boston, received encouragement from Wílliam Morris Hunt, studied art anatomy with Dr. William Rimmer, studied in Paris, with Léon Bonnat and in Munich with Ferdinand Wagner and Wilhelm Dietz, exhibited his *Italian Girl* at the Paris Salon 1878; opened studio in Boston 1878, painted portraits of Sir Lyon Playfair, Alexander Vinton 1880, Wendell Phillips 1881, William Warren 1882, Francis Parkman 1883, Andrew P. Peabody and General Charles Devens 1884, George Choate and George F. Hoare 1885; received much recognition; member: National Institute of Arts and Letters, academician: National Academy of Art, recipient: Gold Medal, Columbian Exposition, Chicago, 1893.

Vose, George Leonard 1831–1910, born: Augusta; attended school in Augusta and Salem, Massachusetts; attended the Lawrence Scientific School at Harvard University 1849–50; began as assistant engineer on the Kennebec and Portland Railroad, later engaged on other roads to 1859, associate editor: *American Railway Times*, Boston 1859–63, removed to Paris where he was occupied with sundry railway projects in Maine and New Hampshire 1866–72, professor of civil engineering: Bowdoin College 1872–81, Massachusetts Institute of Technology 1881–86; father-in-law of Arlo Bates; author: *Handbook of Railroad Construction* 1857, *Orographic Geology, or the Origin and Structure of Mountains* 1866, *Manual for Railroad Engineers and Engineering Students* 1873, *A Graphic Method for Solving Algebraic Problems* 1875, *Elementary Course of Geometric Drawing* 1878.

Wadsworth, Alexander Scammel 1790–1851, born: Portland; son of Peleg Wadsworth; appointed midshipman, USN, 1804, promoted to lieutenant, USN, 1810, first lieutenant aboard USS *Constitution* during that vessel's fight with HMS *Guerrière*, recipient of a silver medal and included in the vote of thanks received by the commanding officer, Isaac Hull, and his officers; first lieutenant aboard corvette USS *Adams*, on her cruise of 1814, where she captured ten prizes, subsequently, she was chased up the Penobscot River by a British squadron, after mounting a gallant and inspired defense, she was intentionally burned, and the officers and men made their way overland to Portland; promoted to master commandant, USN, 1816; commanding officer: USS *Prometheus* in the Mediterranean squadron 1816–17, commanding officer: sloop USS *John Adams* cruised the West Indies, suppressing piracy 1818–22, promoted to captain, USN, 1825, surveyed Narragansett Bay, commanding officer: USS *Constellation* in the Mediterranean squadron 1829–32, commodore USN, commanding the Pacific squadron 1834–36, member of the Board of Navy Commissioners 1837–40, inspector of ordnance 1841–50, died at Washington; uncle of H. W. Longfellow; three U.S. naval vessels have been named in his honor, the first USS *Wadsworth* (DD-60), the first American warship to be driven by a geared turbine, was launched at Bath Iron Works 1915, was the flagship of the first squadron of U.S. naval vessels dispatched to Great Britain, after the declaration of war in World War I, 6 April 1917, saw hard service in the Western Approaches, participated as a picket in the transatlantic flight of four Navy-Curtiss flying boats, May 1919, the second USS *Wadsworth* (DD-516), was launched at Bath Iron Works 1942, earned seven battle stars and a Presidential Unit Citation for her distinguished conduct at Okinawa, the third USS *Wadsworth* (FFG-9), was launched 1978.

Wadsworth, Henry 1783–1804, born: Portland; son of Peleg Wadsworth; entered the U.S. Navy as midshipman 1799; spent his leisure time writing; attached to the USS *Constitution*, commanded by his neighbor Edward Preble in the Tripoli War, appointed acting lieutenant, volunteered to help sail the bomb ship *Intrepid* into Tripoli Harbor and was killed, along with the rest of the company, when it prematurely detonated; his nephew Henry Wadsworth Longfellow was named in his honor.

Wadsworth, Marshman Edward 1847–1921, born: Livermore Falls; son of a farmer, brother of Harrison Wadsworth; A.B. Bowdoin College ΦBK 1869, A.M. 1872, A.B. Harvard College 1874, A.M., Ph.D. 1879, M.D. National Medical College 1894; principal and school superintendent in Maine, New Hampshire, Minnesota, and Wisconsin 1863–73; professor of chemistry: Boston Dental College 1873–74, instructor in mathematics and mineralogy: Harvard University 1874–77, assistant in geology: Museum of Comparative Zoology, Harvard University, 1877–87, professor of mineralogy and geology: Colby College 1885–87; assistant geologist: Minnesota Geological Survey 1886–87; director and professor of mining geology and petrography, founding president: Michigan College of Mining 1887–97, Michigan state geologist 1888–93, professor of mining and geology, dean: School of Mines and Mineralogy, Pennsylvania State College; a pioneer in microscopic petrography, taught first course in United States, applied to meteorites, Precambrian geology, &c.; author: *Geology of Iron and Copper Districts of Lake Superior* 1880, *Lithogical Studies* 1884, with Josiah Whitney: *The Azoid System and Its Proposed Subdivisions* 1884, *Preliminary Description of the Peridoltes, Gabbros, Diabases, and Audisites of Minnesota* 1885, *Crystallography* 1909.

Wadsworth, Peleg 1748–1829, born: Duxbury, Massachusetts; A.B. Harvard College 1769, A.M. 1772; after teaching for a short time, engaged in mercantile pursuits; at the outbreak of the American Revolution, made captain of a company of minutemen from Roxbury, rose rapidly in rank, become adjutant general of Massachusetts 1776, participated in the battle of Long Island 1776, promoted to brigadier general 1777, second officer in command in the Penobscot Expedition, where he was captured and, later, escaped; appointed military commander of District of Maine, captured by the British at his headquarters in Thomaston, once again escaped; settled in Portland; member: U.S. House of Representatives (Federalist) 1792–1806; removed to Hiram, where he had been granted a large parcel of land for his service in the Revolution; Bowdoin College overseer 1794–1800; father of A. S. Wadsworth, Henry Wadsworth, grandfather of H. W. Longfellow; buried in Hiram.

Waldo, Francis 1723–84, born: Falmouth (that part that was later Portland), son of Samuel Waldo I, brother of Samuel Waldo II; graduate: Boston Latin School; A.B. Harvard College 1747, A.M. 1750; when his father's regiment was sent to Canada, his name was carried on the rolls as lieutenant; subsequent to the war, he and his father went to Europe, but rather than enter the University of Paris, he returned to Falmouth where he busied himself in his father's financial affairs, attempted to secure a position in Nathaniel Sparhawk's warehouse in Kittery, ended up gathering lumber on Casco Bay, appointed first collector of customs for the district from Cape Porpoise to the Kennebec 1758–70, issued in pursuance of strict orders from the surveyor general, a proclamation against smuggling rum, sugar, and molasses, which had previously been winked at, and the officers were directed to execute the law with rigor, a highly unpopular move 1763; along with Stephen Longfellow I, Waldo was appointed by the general court, to farm out the excise on tea, coffee, and pottery for Cumberland County; as member of St. Paul's parish, he was a warm supporter of its controversial pastor, John Wiswall; elected representative to the general court from Falmouth 1762–63, where he generally voted with the conservatives, particularly when they attempted to change significantly the relations between militia and royal military officers; failed in reelection, immediately appointed justice of the peace for Cumberland County by governor in council; in this capacity he became involved in what became the first riot of the American Revolution in Maine, when he busted a smuggler and found smuggled goods, attempted to remove the goods, got as far as the house of the comptroller, Arthur Savage, where a mob assembled and stormed the house with clubs and stones, the next morning the goods were gone and a deputy sheriff left to guard had been kidnapped 1766; came into severe straits with the new comptroller of customs, John Malcom, an ardent patriot; left Falmouth permanently shortly before the great fire, in which his home, distillery, and the customs house, his personal property, were destroyed 1775; proscribed as Tory and his property confiscated, particularly troublesome to the authorities was Waldo's old, lame, offensive Negro man named Scipio 1778; taking up residence in Pall Mall, London, he became a member of the New England Club and the Brompton Row Tory Club; when he died in Tunbridge, his remaining property was sold, some going to his niece, Lucy Flucker Knox, wife of Henry Knox.

Waldo, Samuel II 1723–70, born: Falmouth (that portion that is now Portland), son of Samuel Waldo I, brother of Francis Waldo; A.B. Harvard College 1743, A.M.

1746; upon receiving his undergraduate degree, built a mansion on Middle Street, opposite the Second Parish Church, devoted himself to the management of family property and mills in the vicinity; elected member of the Massachusetts House of Representatives from Falmouth 1744, became closely involved in preparations for the Louisbourg campaign, appointed aide-de-camp and commissary of the artillery train, because of his business connections, was uncommonly successful in providing proper supplies; commissioned by Governor Shirley captain of the 2nd Massachusetts Regiment 1745; went to Frankfort, Germany, to recruit immigrants for the Waldo patent 1753, collected sixty families, took them down the Rhine to Amsterdam, where they embarked; arriving late at Broad Bay, they were herded into sheds, where many froze to death the first winter; during the French and Indian War, busied himself hiring and impressing vessels to take supplies and men to various Maine forts as they came under attack; financed a scalping expedition; after his father's death, succeeded to his colonelcy of the York regiment 1759; appointed judge of probate for Cumberland County 1760–70; became involved in a furious dispute with the Reverend Thomas Smith, wherein Waldo promoted schisms that produced the New Casco and Stroudwater parishes, as well as the creation of St. Paul's Episcopal Church in Falmouth; Waldo remained popular and was sent to the Massachusetts House of Representatives for several terms 1757–62; when reelected in 1764, he supported Governor Hutchinson (who would eventually go into exile because of his Toryism); instructed by the town to do his best to secure the repeal of the Stamp Act, he failed and was subsequently dropped by the voters, nonetheless, he gave a party that verged on riot to celebrate the ultimate repeal of the act; as judge, became very unpopular in his attempt to bring to justice debtor rioters, compounded this by attending St. Paul's church; died before the outbreak of the Revolution and was buried in great pomp beneath St. Paul's church; after the burning of Falmouth, his remains were removed to the family tomb at King's Chapel, Boston; subsequent to the Revolution, most of his property was confiscated as Loyalist property.

Walker, Clement Adams 1820–83, born: Fryeburg; graduate: Fryeburg Academy, A.B. Dartmouth College ΦΒΚ 1842, while an undergraduate, an uncle refused to continue paying his tuition because he refused to enter the ministry, spent some time in the South as a tutor, studied medicine in Fryeburg with Dr. Israel Bradley and in Boston with Charles Harrison Stedman; M.D. Harvard University Medical School 1850, during 1847–48, an epidemic of cholera and ship's fever broke out among immigrants at the Deer Isle quarantine station, Walker volunteered his help treating these then unfamiliar and fearsome diseases; appointed assistant superintendent 1849–51; following his graduation, he practiced in South Boston with Dr. Stedman, then the physician to all city institutions, including the Boston Lunatic Hospital; became superintendent of this institution 1851, served to 1881; a pioneer in the humane treatment of mental patients, abandoned the use of isolated cells for the violent, invented a camisole to replace the straitjacket, battled public and political indifference and hostility to establish the State Hospital for the Insane at Danvers; a frequent witness in legal cases, retained by the federal government to examine Charles Guiteau after Guiteau assassinated President Garfield; even attempted to save the life of the prisoner who had murdered his brother, Galen C. Walker, deputy warden of the Charlestown prison; for his treatment of insane German citizens, was decorated by the German government.

Walker, Cyrus 1827–1913, born: Madison; attended local public school, taught school, sawyer, log driver on the Kennebec River, manager of a starch factory, removed to Wisconsin, where he was a surveyor, sailed from New York to San Francisco, via Panama 1853, originally intending to continue to Australia, but was induced by William Chaloner Talbot, formerly of Machias, to join a party sailing for Puget Sound, Washington, to find a site and build a sawmill for the lumber manufacturing firm of W. C. Talbot & Co., later Pope & Talbot; a suitable site was found in Port Gamble, initially employed as a timekeeper, accountant, and general utility man, promoted to general manager 1861, in charge of the mills, the fleet of ships that carried lumber to all parts of the world, and other properties, acquired an interest in the company, became a stockholder when Puget Mill Co. was incorporated in 1874, became one of the largest landholders in the Northwest, including large tracts in what became Seattle; declined nominations for the U.S. Senate from both parties; son-in-law of William Chaloner Talbot.

Walker, Fred Allan 1867–1947, born: South Berwick; B.L. Dartmouth College Law School 1888, A.M. 1925; managing editor: *Springfield Republican* 1893–96, *Boston Journal* 1896–1909, *Baltimore News* 1909–11; publisher: *Washington Times* 1911–19; editorial assistant to Arthur Brisbane on Hearst publications 1919–20; publisher: *New York Evening Telegram* 1920-25; chairman: executive board: *New York Sun* 1925–34; chairman: Publishers' Association of New York 1923–33.

Walker, Perley 1875–1927, born: Embden; B.M.E. University of Maine 1896, M.E. 1900, M.M.E. Cornell University 1901; instructor in mechanical engineering: University of Maine 1896–1900; draftsman in estimation and design: Newport News Shipbuilding Co. 1901–02; professor of mechanical engineering: University of Maine 1902–05; dean: school of engineering and professor of industrial design, University of Kansas from 1913; consulting engineer: petroleum and power engineering lines; in World War I: colonel of Engineers and commanding officer 314th Engineers Reserve; author: *Management Engineering* 1923, *Industrial Coal* 1924.

Wallis, Frank E. 1862–1929, born: Eastport; educated privately in Boston, began the study of architecture at an early age in the office of Cabot and Chandler, Boston, 1876–85; spent the year of 1885–86 in travel and study in Europe, on his return, traveled from Massachusetts to Georgia sketching and measuring colonial architecture and furniture, published in the form of a book: *Old Colonial Architecture and Furniture* 1887, the first such collection to appear in the United States, received with enthusiasm and formed a part of nearly every architectural library; associated with Richard Morris Hunt from 1888, practiced together until Hunt's death 1895; during this period he worked on the Astor, Gerry, and Vanderbilt homes, the Marble House, Biltmore, and many other famous houses; opened his own office in New York; although he established the perpendicular style of Gothic architecture as the predominant style in cities, his real love was for Georgian colonial architecture, a revival of which was largely his doing; known as Colonial Wallis; after his retirement in 1922, removed to France where he devoted much of his time translating histories of the French guilds of the thirteenth century from original sources, delving into monastic records and chronicles, published after his death as *History and Influence of the French Guilds of the 13th Century*, also the author of: *American Architecture, Decoration, and Furniture* 1890, *How to Know Architecture* 1910; received a gold medal from the French government for his Colonial exhibit at the Paris Exposition, also received a diploma for his work on the administration building at the Columbian Exposition, Chicago, 1893; U.S. delegate to the Tenth Annual Housing Conference, the Hague, 1913, Eleventh International Congress of Architects, also in the Hague, 1927; he wanted his epitaph to read "An Honest Architect."

Walton, James Henry 1878–1947, born: Deer Isle; B.S. Massachusetts Institute of Technology 1899, Austin Traveling Fellow: Massachusetts Institute of Technology 1901–03, Ph.D. University of Heidelberg 1903; assistant in chemistry: University of Illinois 1899–1900, Massachusetts Institute of Technology 1900–01, instructor in chemistry: University of Illinois 1903–06, associate professor 1906–07; assistant professor of chemistry: University of Wisconsin 1907–12, associate professor 1912–19, professor from 1919; in World War I: major, Engineers USA, in charge of training in gas defense in the United States, 1st Army gas officer, American Expeditionary Forces 1918–19; author: *Elementary Quantitative Analysis* 1907, *Qualitative Chemical Analysis* 1911, *A Laboratory Manual of General Chemistry* 1921, *Introduction to Qualitative Analysis* 1937, *An Introduction to General Chemistry* 1943, numerous papers in scientific journals, prepared four monographs on gas warfare used in training troops in the United States and in the American Expeditionary Forces.

Warren, Frederick Morris 1859–1931, born: Durham; graduate: Phillips Academy, Andover 1875; spent two years in Paris and Hanover, Germany; A.B. Amherst College 1880, studied at the Sorbonne 1884–86, Ph.D. Johns Hopkins University 1887; instructor of modern languages: Western Reserve College 1881–83, instructor and associate professor of modern languages: Johns Hopkins University 1886–91, professor of romance languages: Adelbert College (Western Reserve) 1891–1901, Street professor of modern languages: Yale University 1900–26; author: *A Primer of French Literature* 1889, *A History of the Novel Previous to the Seventeenth Century* 1895, *Ten*

Frenchmen of the Nineteenth Century 1904, contributor to *Modern Language Notes,*
American Journal of Philogy, The Chautauquan, editor of various French texts; associate
editor: *Modern Philology;* president: Modern Language Association of America 1908.

Washburn, Cadwallader Colden 1818–82, born: Livermore; son of a farmer,

brother of William Drew, Charles Ames, Israel
Washburn, Jr., Elihu Washburne; brought up on his
father's farm, attended public school in winter;
L.L.D. (Hon.) University of Wisconsin 1873;
clerked in a store in Hallowell; joined the geological survey of Iowa under David Dale Owen 1839;
studied law in the office of his uncle, Reuel Washburn, Livermore, continued with Joseph B. Wells;
Rock Island County (Illinois) surveyor; member:
Wisconsin bar 1842, practiced at Mineral Point
1844–55, entered into a partnership with Cyrus
Woodman, agent of the New England Land Co.;
established the Mineral Point Bank 1852; member:
U.S. House of Representatives (originally as a Whig, later Republican) 1854–61,
1867–71 (first term: chairman, Committee on Private Land Claims, second term:
chairman, Committee on Expenditures on Public Buildings and Grounds); served
simultaneously with his brother Elihu and Israel Jr.; unsuccessful candidate for the
U.S. Senate, a seat ultimately won by Timothy Howe, who was also born in Liver-
more; participant in the Peace Convention just prior to the outbreak of the Civil
War; while in fistfight on the floor of Congress scalped Barksdale of his wig; in the
Civil War: raised the 2nd Wisconsin Cavalry, served under General Curtis in
Arkansas, conspicuous in the battle of Grand Coteau, promoted brigadier general,
USV, and major general, USV, commanded the 13th Corps at Vicksburg, captured
Fort Esperanza, on Matagorda Bay 1863, commanded the district of west Tennessee
1864–65; elected tenth governor of Wisconsin 1872–74, despite his great wealth and
the fact that he, himself, was a railroad owner, blamed much of the graft and corruption in the federal government on the influence of the railroads; urged the passage of
the Graham Law, which required a large cash bond from any liquor seller and respon-
sibility for any illegal actions committed by the purchaser; unsuccessful candidate for
reelection 1873, and for the U.S. Senate 1875; perfected method of grinding hard red
winter wheat, established mills in Minneapolis and co-founded Pillsbury and Washburn, largest manufacturer of flour in the world, which produced Gold Medal Flour
and became the basis of General Mills, Inc.; owner of very extensive timberlands
in Wisconsin and Minnesota; founder: Washburn Observatory, University of Wisconsin, of which he was named regent for life 1879; buried in Oak Grove Cemetery,
La Crosse, Wisconsin.

Washburn, Cadwallader Lincoln 1866–1965, born: Brunswick; son of William Drew Washburn, brother of Stanley Washburn, Elizabeth Washburn Wright; deaf from an early age, A.B. Gallaudet College 1890, D.Sc. 1924, L.H.D. Bowdoin College 1947; student of architecture: Massachusetts Institute of Technology, Art Students League, pupil of H. Siddons Mowbray, William Merrit Chase; spy in Japan and Manchuria during the Russo-Japanese War 1904–05, war correspondent during the Chinese Revolution, correspondent: *Chicago Daily News* in Mexico 1910–12, in Marquesas Islands collecting bird eggs and nests for Museum of Comparative Oology; director: Washburn Coal Company of North Dakota; his paintings and dry points hang in the British Museum, Victoria and Albert Museum, Musée du Luxembourg, Bibliothèque National, Paris, Rijks Museum, Amsterdam, Honolulu Academy of Arts, Houston Art Institute, Philadelphia Museum of Art, Minneapolis Institute of Art, Library of Congress, Corcoran Art Gallery, Metropolitan Museum of Art, New York.

Washburn, Charles Ames 1822–89, born: Livermore; brother of Cadwallader Colden Washburn, and others; A.B. Bowdoin College 1848; migrated to Mineral Point, Wisconsin; member: Wisconsin bar, removed to San Francisco 1850; editor: *Alta California* 1853–58, editor: *San Francisco Daily Times* 1858–60; Republican presidential elector 1860; U.S. commissioner to Paraguay 1861–63, U.S. minister to Paraguay 1863–68; was a direct observer of the war between Paraguay and Brazil, when foreign residents were accused of conspiring against the dictator Lopez and when the United States was accused of giving aid to Brazil during Paraguay's war with that country, had to escape by canoe, making his way thence to the USS *Wasp*; later cleared of any wrongdoing by a congressional committee; inventor of the typograph; author: *Philip Thaxter* 1861, *Gomery of Montgomery* 1865, *Political Evolution* 1877, *From Poverty to Competence* 1877, *History of Paraguay* (two volumes) 1879; buried in Livermore.

Washburn, Israel, Jr. 1813–83, born: Livermore; brother of Cadwallader Colden Washburn, and others; L.L.D. (Hon.) Tufts University 1872; member: Maine bar 1834, practiced in Orono; member: Maine House of Representatives 1842–43; member: U.S. House of Representatives (first term: Whig, subsequent terms: Republican) 1851–61, chairman: Committee on Elections; a founder of the Republican party in Maine, first to propose the name Republican; elected twenty-third governor of Maine 1861–62; collector of customs, Portland 1863–77; president of the Tufts University Board of Trustees, refused the presidency of Tufts University 1875; president: Rumford Falls & Buckfield Railroad Co. 1878–83; author: *Notes, Historical, Descriptive, and Personal, of Livermore, Maine* 1874, frequent contributor to *Universalist Quarterly*; buried in Mt. Hope Cemetery, Bangor.

Washburn, Stanley 1878–1950, born: Livermore; son of William Drew Washburn, brother of Cadwallader L. Washburn, Elizabeth Washburn Wright; graduate:

Hill School, Pottstown, Pennsylvania, A.B. Williams College 1901, D.H.L. 1921; student: Harvard University Law School 1901–02; police reporter: *Minneapolis Journal* 1902, staff writer, market editor: *Minneapolis Times* 1902–04, war correspondent: *Chicago Daily News* 1904–06, covered the Russo-Japanese War, finding that reporters were barred from the frontlines, operated the dispatch boat *Fawan* for four months from a base in Cheefoo, China, and a secret base near Port Arthur, Manchuria, and by running through uncharted mine fields at night, was able to transmit the only dispatches that didn't originate from hotel lobbies in Tokyo, with Nogi's army before fall of Port Arthur, with 3rd Japanese Army until the end of the war, organized a news service for the *Chicago Daily News* in the Far East and India, organized a news service in the Black Sea, 1905, covering the Russian Revolution of that year and the Odessa mutiny, carried British and United States government dispatches, mail, and refugees, during one of the worst storms in the history of the Black Sea, when all other vessels sought shelter, he left Constantinople for Odessa and the Caucasus, returned with his mission accomplished and a load of refugees, as well; headed an expedition in British Columbia 1909–10 to survey sources of waterpower from rivers arising in Alberta, traveling with pack animals across 1,000 miles of uncharted territory, surveying the route for the Grand Trunk Railroad; with the outbreak of World War I, went to Europe for Collier's *Weekly Magazine* 1914, to Russia as special correspondent for *London Times*, attached to Russian Army for twenty-six months, only American on Russian front 1914–16, attached to Romanian Army, engaged to write foreign policy of Russia for Russian government 1916; with French Army at Verdun, April 1916; with the entry of the United States in World War I, resigned from the *London Times* and entered the Officer Reserve Corps, USA, 1917, with rank of major, attached to Secretary of State Lansing as military adviser, military aide to John F. Stevens, director of the Trans-Siberian Railroad during the Russian Revolution 1917–18, transferred at Vladivostok to Elihu Root's diplomatic mission to Russia as military aide and assistant secretary of mission, G2 of 26th Division USA in France 1918, served in Toul and Château-Thierry sectors, invalided home, September 1918; lieutenant Military Intelligence 1931, military aide to Queen Marie of Romania during her visit to the United States 1926; decorated by Emperor of Japan: Order of Imperial Crown 1907, by the czar: Order of St. Anna 1915, by General Brossilov: Order of St. George 1916, by King of Roumania: commander, Order of the Crown; delegate: Republican National Convention 1912; member: secretariat of American delegation to Disarmament Conference to liaison between American and Japanese delegations, Washington, 1921; president: Washburn Lignite Coal Co., Wilton, North Dakota, 1926–29; director: National Security League, made some 1,000 speeches in 42 states; war correspondent or soldier with 20 armies, covered some 100 battles from 1904; author: *The Cable Game* 1912, *The Man in Hiding* (a play) 1912, *Trails, Trappers, and Tenderfeet in Western Canada* 1912, *Nogi—The Study of a Man Against the Background of a Great War* 1913, *Two in the Wilderness* 1914, *Field Notes from the Russian Front* 1915, *The Russian Campaign, April to August 1915, Victory in Defeat* 1916, *The Russian Offensive* 1916, writer of propaganda for the British, Russian, and French 1939–40, speaker and broadcaster on morale, military and naval intelligence; buried in Arlington National Cemetery.

Washburn, William Drew 1827–1912, born: Livermore; son of Israel Washburn, Sr.; attended Gorham and Farmington academies, A.B. Bowdoin College 1854; read law with his brother, Israel Washburn, Jr., then a member of Congress and later governor of Maine, and John Peters, later chief justice: Maine Supreme Judicial Court; member: Maine bar 1857, removed to Minneapolis, practiced law; agent of the Minneapolis Mill Co., later stockholder and director, built at St. Anthony's Falls the Lincoln Sawmill, erected at Anoka, Minnesota, the largest lumber mill in the state 1872; principal projector and vice president, later president, of the Minneapolis & St. Louis Railroad 1870; director: Sioux City Railroad Co., instrumental in the building of the Sault Ste. Marie Railroad 1888, built the Minneapolis & Pacific Railroad, afterwards united with the Sault Ste. Marie line as the Minneapolis, St. Paul & Sault Ste. Marie Railroad; part-owner of the Minneapolis Harvester Works; a principal owner: Washburn and Crosby Flouring Mills (later General Foods, Inc.), stockholder and director: Pillsbury and Washburn Co., the largest flour mill in the world; member: Minnesota House of Representatives 1858, 1871; surveyor general of Minnesota 1861–65; candidate for governor 1873; member: U.S. House of Representatives (Republican) 1879–85, chairman: Committee on Improvement of the Mississippi River and Its Tributaries, member: U.S. Senate 1889–95, member of committees on commerce, post offices, and post roads and agriculture, took a prominent part in the restriction of Chinese immigration, initiated legislation for the construction of reservoirs at the head of the Mississippi River; an early proponent of irrigation and the construction of dams for that purpose; introduced a bill ending the trading in options and futures in agricultural products; father of Cadwallader A. and Stanley Washburn, Elizabeth Washburn Wright, his wife was the sister of John Crosby, his partner in Washburn and Crosby; buried in Lakewood Cemetery, Minneapolis.

Washburne, Elihu Benjamin 1816–87, born: Livermore; brother of Cadwallader Washburn, and others; printer's assistant in Augusta, assistant editor of the *Kennebec Journal*; student: Harvard University Law School 1839–40; settled in Galena, Illinois; delegate: Whig National Convention 1844, 1852, nominated Henry Clay for president, National Whig Convention, Baltimore 1844; member: U.S. House of Representatives 1853–69, (first term: Whig, subsequently: Republican), chairman: Committee on Commerce, member: Committee on Appropriations; an old friend and political ally of Abraham Lincoln, served as Lin-

coln's unofficial representative in Washington between the time of his election and inauguration, only man to greet Lincoln on his arrival in Washington prior to his inauguration 1861; put his fellow townsman, Ulysses S. Grant, forward for his commission as colonel, sponsored his advance to major general; Grant received the returns of the presidential election of 1868 at Washburne's home in Galena, later, gave him a courtesy appointment as U.S. secretary of state 1869, after service, in that position, for a few days, Grant then appointed him minister to France 1869–77, his service of eight and one half years remains a record of duration for any U.S. minister to a foreign country; Washburne was the only representative of a foreign nation to remain in Paris during the siege of Paris and the Commune, gave sanctuary and sustenance to as many as 4,000 people, during the siege; equally esteemed by the Germans, Washburne declined the reception of the highest German honor given to civilians, the emperor, Wilhelm I, had his portrait painted and given to Washburne; subsequent to the siege, Washburne was, by common consent, the dean of the diplomatic corps in Paris, declined appointment as secretary of the U.S. Treasury 1874; author: *Reflections of a Minister to France 1869–1877*; nominated for president of the United States 1880; buried in Greenwood Cemetery, Galena, Illinois.

Wasson, David Atwood 1823–87, born: West Brooksville; son of a farmer and owner of several coasting vessels; champion wrestler of his village but injured himself so severely that he spent his last thirty years a cripple; attended public school in Brooksville, North Yarmouth Academy, graduate: Phillips Academy, Andover, dismissed from Bowdoin College in his junior year for involvement in a student disturbance 1848; studied law in Belfast, after practicing for a short time, entered Bangor Theological Seminary, although ordained, his heterodox opinions, freely given, caused him to be without a church; established an independent society at Groveland, Massachusetts, which attracted the attention of leading theologians; in the absence of the Reverend Thomas Wentworth Higginson, officiated at Higginson's church in Worcester 1855, later, ill-health forced him to resign as Higginson's associate; settled in Medford, where he wrote some of his best literary efforts, notably: "The New World and the New Man," "Ease in Work," "Individuality, Hinderance, Originality," all published in the *Atlantic Monthly*, and which received wide attention, also wrote for *The Radical*, *North American Review*; spoke before the Concord Club, the Free Religious Association, helped found the Radical Club; accompanied the artist Bradford on a voyage to Labrador, which he described in the *Atlantic Monthly*; resuming preaching, officiated at Theodore Parker's society in Boston 1856–57; although he was recommended for a consulship abroad by Ralph Waldo Emerson, he became, instead, storekeeper: U.S. customs house, West Medford, 1857–60; spent the next three years in Stuttgart, Germany, wrote an article "Church and State in Germany," which was published in the *Unitarian Monthly*; his ministry of the Twenty-Eighth Congregational Society in Boston, where he succeeded Theodore Parker, was cut short by illness; known as a brilliant conversationalist and a moving preacher, his later years were spent in Medford, crippled and blind; author: *Poems* 1888, *Essays: Religious, Social, Political* 1889.

Waters, William Everett 1856–1924, born: Winthrop; A.B. Yale College 1878, Ph.D. Yale University 1887; tutor in classics: Yale University 1883-87, professor of Greek and comparative philology: University of Cincinnati 1890–94, professor and president: Wells College 1894–1900, professor of Greek language and literature: New York University 1902–23; author: *Inductive Greek Method* 1888, *Cane Trimelchionis of Petronius* 1902.

Waxaway fl.1694–1710, born: Maine; resided at Amassokanty (Farmington Falls), participated in the dog feast of war 1694, enlisted with Bomoseen and Claude-Sébastien de Villieu in their furious attack on Oyster River (Durham, New Hampshire) 1694, deeply affected by the slaughter, ransomed one of Bomoseen's captives, Mrs. Ann Jenkins, helped several other prisoners and was thereafter inclined to pacifism; *dogique* or religious assistant to Father Vincent Bigot at Amassokanty 1694–1701; spoke good English and was known to English prisoners as the Indian minister and Prince Waxaway; accompanied Bigot to Canada 1701; was probably the English-speaking chief at a conference of New England deputies at Falmouth (Portland) 1701; he and several other Abenaki chiefs signed a peace treaty with Massachusetts at Falmouth 1703; did much to alleviate the suffering of English captives; removed to Norridgewock (Madison) 1704; purchased the captive Lieutenant Josiah Littlefield of Wells from his Abenaki master and nursed him back to health before conducting him to Falmouth 1710.

Webster, Harrie 1843–1921, born: Farmington; graduate: Farmington Academy; in the Civil War: 3rd assistant engineer, USN, 1862, served under Farragut on Mississippi, Mobile Bay; wrecked on USS *Vandalia*, Samoa 1892; chief engineer on several naval vessels; chief engineer: bureau of steam engineering, captain, USN, 1903, retired as rear admiral, USN, 1903; his article "Korea, the Hermit Kingdom" appeared in the March 1900 issue of *National Geographic Magazine*.

Weeks, Edward Henry 1871–1962, born: Vassalboro, son of a farmer and later superintendent of buildings at the Friends School (later Moses Brown School), Providence, Rhode Island, where Weeks received his preliminary education; Ph.B. Brown University 1893, Sc.M. Bryant College 1939; governor of boys and instructor in mathematics and Latin: Friends School 1893–95; salesman: Old Colony Cooperative Bank, Providence, general manager 1897, president 1928, chairman of the board 1945–62; under his direction Old Colony became the largest savings and loan association in Rhode Island and one of the largest in the country, with assets of over $180 million in 1945; at his own initiative and expense, made a tour of European methods in slum clearance and low-cost housing, attended an international congress of building societies, building and loan associations, and homestead associations 1935; director: Federal Home Loan Association, Boston 1932–52; member: Providence Planning Board, chairman: Providence Safety Council; in 1946, the Rhode Island General Assembly passed a joint resolution commending him for his fifty years of work in banking; while an undergraduate at Brown, lettered in football, baseball, and track, in baseball, he is credited with revolutionizing the style of play at first base by taking his position off the base, set a Brown University record for the 100-yard dash at 10.1 seconds that stood for many years.

Weinstein (born Sklarsky), Lewis H. 1905–95, born: Aran, Lithuania; emigrated to Portland with parents 1906; bill collector, violinist with pierside band (with Rudy Vallée), graduate: Portland High School, barker and cashier: Riverton Park, Portland, college summers, A.B. *magna cum laude* Harvard College ΦBK 1927, L.L.B. Harvard University Law School 1930; member: Massachusetts bar 1930, member: law firm of Rome and Israel, Boston; librettist: *So Let 'Um Foreclose*, published by William H. Barker & Company, sold over 25,000 copies 1934; in World War II: graduate: School of Military Government, Charlottesville, Virginia, graduate: Command and General Staff School, Fort Leavenworth, Kansas; lieutenant, USA, chief: liaison section, European Theatre of Operations, USA (on staff of General Eisenhower), as such, liaison officer between General Eisenhower and General Charles De Gaulle during the liberation of Paris 1944; adjudicated the case of Maurice Chevalier, who had been accused of collaboration, made it possible for Chevalier to return to his career; prevailed upon Eisenhower to visit Nazi death camps; decorated by the French: Légion d'Honneur, croix de guerre; partner: law firm of Foley, Hoag, and Eliot from 1947, instrumental in obtaining a favorable vote in the United Nations for the partition of Palestine 1947, deeply involved in the diplomatic negotiations over Israel's withdrawal from the Sinai 1956; chairman: Massachusetts State Housing Authority from 1946; responsible for changing the mind and subsequent policies of Congressman John F. Kennedy on Israel, speechwriter for Senator John F. Kennedy on Middle Eastern affairs, compiled data for President Kennedy on: Soviet treatment of Jews 1963, participant in numerous international conferences on human rights; chairman: Overseas Committee, Council of Jewish Federations; professor of trial practice: Harvard University Law School, land planning and development: Massachusetts Institute of Technology; author: *Masa, Odyssey of an American Jew* 1989, *Odyssey of a Boston Lawyer.*

Wells, Daniel, Jr. 1808–1902, born: West Waterville; attended public schools, taught school, engaged in mercantile business at Palmyra, removed to Milwaukee, Wisconsin, 1838, engaged in lumbering and banking, appointed probate judge of Milwaukee 1838; member: Territorial Council 1838–40; member: U.S. House of Representatives 1853–57 (Democrat), chairman: Committee on Expenditures in the Department of State; while in Congress, secured government monies to build the harbors of Milwaukee, Racine, and Kenosha; engaged in the development of railroads, director: Chicago, Milwaukee & St. Paul Railroad 1865–66, president: LaCrosse & Milwaukee Railroad, Southern Minnesota Railroad, St. Paul & Minnesota Valley Railroad; known generally as Uncle Daniel, left an estate of $20,000,000, achieved considerable notoriety when he attempted to corner the lard market 1883; buried in Forest Home Cemetery, Milwaukee.

Wenemouet ?–1730; a chief of the Penobscots; along with thirteen other chiefs, signed a peace treaty with the English at Mere Point 1699; at the end of Queen Ann's War, along with eighteen other chiefs, signed a peace treaty with the English at the second Conference of Portsmouth 1714; as head chief of the Penobscots was unenthusiastic about resuming hostilities, welcomed English overtures for peace 1724, sent wampum belts to the Canadian Abenakis and Hurons proposing peace with the English, which they refused, thus driving a wedge between the Penobscots and the rest of the Abenakis; in negotiations with Governor Dummer, agreed to a cease-fire east of the Kennebec and attempted to urge other tribes to join, Dummer agreed to respect land titles and guaranteed their privileges as English subjects; managed to overcome fierce French opposition and persuaded most of the Canadian Abenakis and mission Iroquois to join in a peace, sent messengers to the Malecites and the Micmacs asking them to attend the Penobscot annual meeting and discuss peace, a satisfactory peace was established with all divisions of the Abenakis and Massachusetts authorities at Falmouth (Portland) 1727; by freeing the Penobscots from French ties and seeking accommodation with the English, he enabled his people to avoid defeat and retain at least a part of their ancient territory into modern times.

Westbrook, Thomas 1674–1744, born: Portsmouth, New Hampshire; son of an English immigrant farmer; in 1704 offered his services to the province as Indian scout and provider of firewood to isolated forts; by 1712 Westbrook had risen in rank to captain, elected selectman of Portsmouth; appointed to the New Hampshire Provincial Council 1716; granted the right to maintain a public house next to the militia parade ground in Portsmouth 1719, this structure is extant and is known as Waldron House; dispatched to Casco Bay by the provincial council to inquire into what conditions were producing so much conflict between settlers and local tribes 1719, led a party of 200 men, in the depth of winter, to arrest Father Sebastien Râle at Norridgewock; failing that, they sacked the settlement and seized Râle's strongbox containing letters from the governor of New France, that, when read, confirmed British suspicions that Râle was instigating Indian raids; subsequent to the destruction of Norridgewock, several tribes began raiding English settlements; in retaliation, English forces (not under the command of Westbrook) returned to Norridgewock, killed Râle, and sent his scalp, along with those of twenty seven of his followers, to the general court in Boston 1724; Westbrook was made commandant of all eastern military forces 1723, with headquarters in Falmouth; erecting a house in Stroudwater, he entered the mast trade, built mills on Stroudwater Creek; appointed mast agent for the Royal

Navy; became associated with Samuel Waldo, who later brought successful suits against Westbrook that stripped him of his extensive lands; subsequent to his death, he was buried in a grave marked only by a pile of rocks, an archaeological excavation in 1976, found what was conclusively proved to be Westbrook's remains, which were reburied; father-in-law of Richard Waldron; the city of Westbrook was named in his honor.

Weston, Samuel Burns 1855–1936, born: Madison; twin brother of Stephen Francis Weston; A.B. Antioch College 1876, Hum.D. 1931, S.T.D. Harvard University Divinity School 1879; Unitarian minister: Leicester, Massachusetts 1879–81, student at the universities of Berlin, Leipzig, and Geneva 1882–83; while at Harvard College, was deeply influenced by the thinking of Ralph Waldo Emerson, particularly that, in the future, religion would primarily concern itself with relations among humans; founder, lecturer, director: the Society for Ethical Culture, Philadelphia, 1885–90, 1897–1935, editor and publisher: *Ethical Record*, *International Journal of Ethics* 1890–1914; founded the Contemporary Club, Philadelphia, the first such organization in Philadelphia to offer membership to men and women on an equal basis 1885, founded the Philadelphia Forum, organized the Working Boys' Club, which later became the Southwark Neighborhood House; author: *Six Discourses* 1880; a founder: the Ausable Club, St. Huberts, New York, founder: Adirondack Trail Association, Keene Heights Library.

Weymouth, Frank Elwyn 1874–1941, born: Medford; B.S. University of Maine 1896; city engineer: Malden, Massachusetts, with Metropolitan Water District, Boston, assistant city engineer: Winnipeg, Manitoba, 1899; surveyor: Panama Canal 1899-1903; civil engineer: U.S. Reclamation Service, supervisor: Arrowrock Dam, Idaho, then the world's tallest dam 1908; chief of construction: U.S. Reclamation Service 1916, chief engineer 1920, directed feasibility studies for Hoover Dam, resigned 1924; president: Brock & Davis, engineers 1924–26; consultant to Mexican government; with authorization of Hoover Dam, was hired by the Metropolitan Water District of Southern California to construct the Colorado aqueduct from 1928; died soon after completion; buried in Calvary Cemetery, Los Angeles.

Wheelwright, Esther 1695–1780, born: Wells; carried off to captivity by the Abenakis, subsequent to the raid on Wells 1703 lived among the Abenakis to 1709, ward of French governor the Marquis de Vaudreuil, sent to the Ursuline convent 1709, probationary nun 1713, refused to return home subsequent to the Treaty of Utrecht, became Sister Esther Marie Joseph de l'Enfant Jesu 1714, during the siege of Québec remained in the convent with a few others, elected mother superior of the Ursulines in Québec 1760.

Whipple, William 1730–85, born: Kittery; son of a maltster and shipmaster; attended school in Kittery, master of a vessel before the age of twenty-one; mariner in slave trade 1752–60, later freed his own slaves; entered business in Portsmouth with his brother Joseph 1759–74; member: New Hampshire Provincial Congress 1775; delegate to Continental Congress 1775, 1776, 1778, signer of the Declaration of Independence 1776; commissioned commanding brigadier general: New Hampshire militia 1777, present at the battles of Saratoga and Stillwater, signed the articles of capitulation on behalf of General Horatio Gates at General Burgoyne's surrender, put in charge of British prisoners of war at their camp near Boston; participated in General John Sullivan's Rhode Island Expedition; declined appointment to the board of admiralty; member: New Hampshire Assembly 1780–84; judge: New Hampshire Supreme Court 1782; financial receiver for New Hampshire 1782–84; buried in Old North Burial Ground, Portsmouth.

White, Clarence J. 1944–73, born: Lewiston; removed with his family to Burbank, California, 1954; with brothers Roland and Eric formed a band called the Country Boys, appeared on television and radio, played at fairs, dances, bars, and clubs; by 1960 group was called Kentucky Colonels, one of the first bluegrass revival groups, played a major role in sparking an interest in country music in Los Angeles, greatly influenced by Doc Watson, adopted Watson's style of flat-picking fiddle tunes on the guitar; recorded several albums on the World Pacific label, including the influential *Appalachin Swing* 1964; formed a group called Nashville West 1967; invited to play on the Byrds' influential country-rock album *Sweetheart of the Rodeo* 1968, joined the Byrds full time 1969–72; demonstrated his prowess on electric guitar in double album *untitled* 1970; influenced the Eagles, Poco, and Manassas; revitalized the Kentucky Colonels 1972, formed a group Muleskinner with David Grisman, recorded a single album *Muleskinner* that spurred the bluegrass revival and inspired Jerry Garcia and Grisman to form a bluegrass band Old and in the Way; run down and killed by a drunken motorist outside a bluegrass club near Palmdale, California; a retrospective volume, entitled *Clarence White: Bluegrass Guitar* was published 1980, with transcriptions of many of his famous guitar solos.

White, Ellen Gould Harmon 1827–1915, born: Gorham; converted to Millerism by William Miller (who predicted the second coming of Christ and the end of the world would arrive on 22 October, 1844), after the great disappointment, White had a vision that she had been transported to heaven, December 1844; organized the General Conference of Adventist Churches 1863; a founder of the Western Health Reform Institution, Battle Creek, Michigan 1866, Battle Creek College (first Seventh Day Adventist school) 1874, an organizer: South Publishing Association 1901, a founder: College of Evangelists, Loma Linda, California, 1909; author: *Life Sketches… of Elder James White and His Wife, Mrs. Ellen G. White* 1880, *Life Sketches of Ellen G. White* 1915.

White, Elwyn Brooks 1899–1985, born: Mount Vernon, New York; A.B. Cornell University 1921; writer and contributing editor: *The New Yorker*, contributing editor: *Harper's* 1938–43; settled in Brooklin, farmer; recipient: Gold Medal, American Academy of Arts and Letters, Presidential Medal of Freedom, Pulitzer Prize, special citation 1978; his works include: *The Lady Is Cold* 1923, *Is Sex Necessary?* (with James Thurber) 1929, *Quo Vadimus* 1939, *A Subtreasury of American Humor* (with his wife, Katherine White) 1941, *One Man's Meat* 1942, *Stuart Little* 1945, *The Wild Flag* 1946, *Charlotte's Web* 1952, *The Second Tree from the Corner* 1954, *The Trumpet of the Swan* 1970; buried in Brooklin Cemetery.

White, Florence Donnell 1882–1950, born: Alna; A.B. Mt. Holyoke College ΦBK 1903, A.M. 1907, Ph.D. Bryn Mawr College 1915, student at University of Paris 1903-04; teacher of French: Springfield (Massachusetts) Classical High School 1904–06, instructor in French: Vassar College, assistant professor, associate professor, professor from 1921, chairman: Department of French from 1918; decorated: chevalier de la Légion d'Honneur 1934; author: *Voltaire's Essay on Epic Poetry, A Study and an Edition* 1915; buried in Sheepscot.

White, Katherine Sergeant Angell 1892–1977, born: Winchester, Massachusetts; A.B. Bryn Mawr College 1914; associate editor: *The New Yorker* magazine from 1925; settled in Brooklin; author: *Onward and Upward in the Garden* 1979, coauthor: *A Subtreasury of American Humor* 1941; wife of E. B. White; buried in Brooklin Cemetery.

White, Wallace Humphrey, Jr. 1877–1952, born: Lewiston; son of a lawyer; A.B. Bowdoin College 1899, L.L.D. 1928, Bates College 1938, studied law at Columbian University Law School (later George Washington University) 1900–02; private secretary to his grandfather, Senator William Frye; member: District of Columbia bar 1902, member: Maine bar 1903; practiced in Lewiston; member: U.S. House of Representatives (Republican), Second District 1916–30, member: Committees on the Merchant Marine and Fisheries, chairman 1927–31, Education and Pensions, member: U.S. Senate 1930–49, chairman: Committee on Expenditures in the Department of Justice, Committee on Interstate and Foreign Commerce, member: Committee on Woman Suffrage, Committee on Merchant Marine and Fisheries; minority leader 1944–47, majority leader 1947–49; member, Board of Visitors: U.S. Coast Guard Academy, regent: Smithsonian Institution; coauthor: Radio Control Act, which set up the Federal Radio Commission 1927, coauthor: Jones-White Merchant Marine Act 1928; U.S. Commissioner: New York World's Fair 1939–40, Bowdoin College overseer from 1927; buried in Mt. Auburn Cemetery, Auburn.

Whitman, Charles Otis 1842–1910, born: Woodstock; attended high school in Norway with Addison Verrill and Sidney Smith, A.B. Bowdoin College 1868,

A.M. 1871, Ph.D. University of Leipzig 1878, fellow: Johns Hopkins University 1879, L.L.D. University of Nebraska 1894, Sc.D. Bowdoin College 1909; principal: Westford (Massachusetts) Academy 1868–72, master in English: Boston High School 1872–74, professor of zoology: Imperial University of Japan 1880–81, Naples zoological station 1882, assistant in zoology: Harvard University 1883–85, professor of zoology: Clark University 1885–92, professor and head of Department of Zoology and curator of zoological museum: University of Chicago from 1892; founding director: Woods Hole Biological Laboratory 1883–1908; editor: *Journal of Morphology* from 1887, *Biological Bulletin* from 1897; author: *Methods of Research in Microscopical Anatomy and Embryology.*

Whitman, Royal 1857–1946, born: Portland; M.D. Harvard University Medical School 1882; specialist in surgery of deformities and diseases of the joints, professor of orthopedic surgery: Columbia University College of Physicians and Surgeons; originated abduction treatment for treating fracture of neck of femurs, operations for paralytic deformities.

Whitman, Royal Emerson 1833–1913, born: Turner; cousin of Royal Bird Bradford, Oliver Otis Howard; book peddler; in the Civil War: enlisted in the 23rd Maine Volunteers, sergeant-major, USV, rose in rank to captain, USV, in seven months; as major, USV, 30th Maine Volunteer Infantry, wounded at Sabine Crossroads, Louisiana, rose in rank to lieutenant colonel, USV, and colonel, USV, commanding officer: 30th Maine Volunteer Infantry 1865; reenlisted after the war, appointed first lieutenant, USA, from Maine 1867, attached to the Troop I, 3rd Cavalry, commander of the garrison at Camp Grant, Arizona; closely aligned with the thinking of his cousin, General O. O. Howard, took it upon himself to offer sanctuary at Camp Grant to a number of Apaches, who were later brutally attacked by a force composed of Anglo settlers, Pinal Indians, and Mexicans; although Whitman's actions were sanctioned by General William T. Sherman, he was court-martialed on a variety of charges; eventually, all charges were dropped, and he was allowed to retire for disability; removing to Washington, D.C., he designed the Whitman saddle and started a company for its production.

Whitney, Amos 1832–1920, born: Biddeford; son of a machinist; attended school in Biddeford and Saccarappa (now Westbrook); at age thirteen, apprenticed to the Essex Machine Co., Lawrence, Massachusetts, manufacturers of machinery used in the production of locomotives, cotton gins, and machinists tools; after three years as an apprentice and one year as a journeyman, entered the employ of the Colt Firearms Co., Hartford, Connecticut; became a contractor for the Phoenix Iron Works, Hartford, 1854; soon after Hezekiah Conant invented a machine for winding thread, known as a spooler, the patent for which was purchased by the Willimantic Linen Co. and invited bids for its manufacture, Whitney, with a fellow employee Francis A.

Pratt, secured the contract for its production and organized the firm of Pratt & Whitney 1860, by 1869 it had become the largest manufacturer in the world of certain types of machinery, originated several types of machinery, firearms, typesetters, sewing machines, &c.; employed William Augustus Rogers, professor of astronomy at Harvard University, and George Bond (son of William Cranch Bond) of Stevens Institute of Technology to conduct experiments with a view to the construction of an apparatus for exact and uniform measurement, as a result, Pratt & Whitney was able to develop an absolutely reliable set of standards which were adopted, worldwide 1879; selected by Hotchkiss Ordnance as contractors for the U.S. Navy to make the Hotchkiss revolving three- and six-pound rapid-fire gun 1888; due, in part, to Whitney's concern for the welfare and further education of his operatives, Pratt & Whitney became one of the most successful mechanical colleges in the world, educated hundreds of apprentices, many of whom rose to the top of their profession, the waiting list sometimes extended for many years; president: Gray Pay Station Telephone Co., secretary, treasurer: Whitney Manufacturing Co., director: Hartford Faience Co.; his chief hobby was collecting ivory; retired to South Poland.

Whitney, Henry Clay 1831–1905, born: Detroit; student: Augusta College, Kentucky, Farmers College, Ohio; member: Illinois bar, intimate friend of Abraham Lincoln from 1854; paymaster, USA, 1861–65; member: Kansas Senate 1871–72; attorney for Illinois Central Railroad 1855–61, Florida Southern Railroad 1881–82; author: *Life on the Circuit with Lincoln* 1892, *Marriage and Divorce* 1894, *Lincoln's Last Speech* 1896, *Lincoln in Reminiscent and Colloquial Moods*, also many essays on Lincoln.

Whitney, John Hay 1904–82, born: Ellsworth; brother of Joan Whitney Payson; A.B. Yale College 1926, student at Oxford University 1926-27, L.H.D. (Hon.) Kenyon College, L.L.D. Colgate University, Brown University 1958, Exeter University 1959, Colby College, Columbia University; senior partner: J. H. Whitney & Co., New York, chairman: Whitney Communications; during World War II: USAAF; U.S. ambassador to Great Britain 1956–61; publisher: *New York Herald-Tribune* 1957–61, president, publisher: World Journal Tribune, Inc. 1961, editor in chief, publisher 1961–66, director, member: Editorial Committee 1966–67, chairman: International Herald Tribune, Paris, president: Whitcom Investment Co., past director: Dun & Bradstreet, Inc.; chairman: John Hay Whitney Foundation; member: President's Commission on Education Beyond High School, special adviser and consultant on public affairs: U.S. Department of State; trustee: National Gallery of Art, fellow: Yale Corporation 1956–70; decorated: Bronze Star, chevalier de la Légion d'Honneur, commander: Order of the British Empire, Knight of St. John of Jerusalem.

Whittier, Charles Comfort 1870–1950, born: Somerset County; son of a farmer; B.C.E. University of Maine 1899; assistant engineer, maintenance of way: Boston & Maine Railroad 1899–1900, assistant engineer: Southwestern Railroad, Bisbee, Arizona; mining engineer with Robert W. Hunt Co., Chicago, 1901–03, chief engineer and general manager: Zeigler Coal Co., Zeigler, Illinois, 1904–07, inspecting and reporting engineer: Robert W. Hunt Co., Ltd., Montréal, 1913–15, chief engineer and managing director: Field Mining and Milling Co. 1915–19, vice president and chief engineer: Robert W. Hunt Co. 1923–32; partner: Nutrition Research Laboratories (later renamed Whittier Laboratories, in his honor); secretary: Illinois Industries Commission; inventor of mineral materials, vitamins (most importantly: vitamin D, in a nonpoisonous form), and foods, specialist in value and use of industrial plants and processing of mineral deposits, development of new and improved mineral combinations.

Whittier, Frank Nathaniel 1861–1924, born: Farmington Falls; son of a farmer; graduate: Wilton Academy, A.B. Bowdoin College φBK 1885, champion rower, A.M. 1888, Sc.D. 1924, M.D. Medical School of Maine 1889; director: Sargent Gymnasium, Bowdoin College, 1886, Bowdoin College physician 1890, lecturer on hygiene: Medical School of Maine 1891, instructor in pathology and bacteriology 1897, professor 1901–24; Brunswick milk inspector; as forensic pathologist, the first in the nation to develop a blood serum test to compare blood samples and also to develop a method to match bullets and weapons through microscopic analysis of markings, both came to be universally adopted, expert witness in many criminal cases; chairman of the Committee on Venereal Diseases for the Maine Medical Association; mainly responsible for the acquisition and development of the Whittier Athletic Field, named in his honor as well as the equipment and arrangement of the Sargent Gymnasium and the Hyde Athletic Building at Bowdoin; it was his suggestion that Bowdoin adopt the polar bear as mascot on account of the pioneer work done in the Arctic by Bowdoin alumni Robert E. Peary and Donald MacMillan; coauthor: *Brunswick: An Historical Play* 1912; Cumberland County medical examiner 1909–17, 1919–24; father of Dr. Alice Whittier, first female pediatrician practicing in Maine.

Wiggin, Kate Douglas Smith 1856–1923, born: Philadelphia, Pennsylvania; removed, with her parents to Hollis, as an infant, attended Abbott Academy, Andover, Massachusetts, removed to California 1876, studied kindergarten methods in Los Angeles under Emma Marwedel; taught for a year at Santa Barbara College, called upon to organize the Silver Street Kindergarten, San Francisco, the first free kindergarten in the West; organized the California Training School 1880, led to the establishment of some sixty kindergartens on the West Coast; married Samuel Bradley Wiggin 1880, who died 1889, later married George Christopher Riggs; first published in *St. Nicholas* 1878, removed to New York 1888, summered in Hollis to the end of her life; author: *Kindergarten Chimes: A Collection of Songs and Games Composed and Arranged for Kindergartens and Primary Schools* 1887, *The Bird's Christmas Carol* 1887, *The Story of Patsy* 1889, *A Summer in a Cañon: A California Story* 1889, *Children's Rights: A Book of Nursery Logic* 1892, *The Village Watch-Tower* 1895, *Froebel's Gifts*

1895, *Froebel's Occupations* 1896, *Marm Lisa* 1896, *Penelope's English Experiences* 1900, *Penelope's Progress* 1900, *Penelope's Experiences in Scotland: Being Extracts from the Commonplace Book of Penelope Hamilton* 1900, *Penelope's Irish Experiences* 1901, *A Cathedral Courtship* 1901, *Golden Numbers: A Book of Verse for Youth* 1902, *The Diary of a Goose Girl* 1902, *Half-a-Dozen Housekeepers: A Story for Girls, In Half-a-Dozen Chapters* 1903, *Rebecca of Sunnybrook Farm* 1903, *The Affair at the Inn* 1904, *A Thanksgiving Retrospective: or, Simplicity of Life in Old New England* 1906, *Homespun Tales: Rose 'o the River, The Old Peabody Pew and Susanna and Sue* 1907, *Pinafore Palace* 1907, *New Chronicles of Rebecca* 1907, *Magic Casements: A Second Fairy Book* 1907, *The Arabian Nights, Their Best-Known Works* 1909, *A Book of Dorcas Dishes: Family Recipes* 1911, *The Talking Beasts: A Book of Fable Wisdom* 1911, *Mother Carey's Chickens* 1911, *Robinetta* 1911, *The Story of Waitstill Baxter* 1913, *Bluebeard; A Musical Fantasy* 1914, *Penelope's Postscripts: Switzerland, Venice, Wales, Devon, Home* 1915, *The Girl and the Kingdom: Learning to Teach* 1915, *The Romance of the Christmas Card* 1916, *My Books That You Know: How I Wrote Them, Where, and Something About Their Character* 1917–18, *The Story Hour; A Book for the Home and the Kindergarten* 1918, *Ladies in Waiting* 1919, *Timothy's Quest: A Story for Anybody, Young or Old Who Cares to Read It* 1921, *My Garden of Memory* (autobiography) 1923, *Love by Express: A Novel of California* 1924, *Creeping Jenny and Other New England Stories* 1924, *Quilt of Happiness: and Other New England Stories* 1924; buried in Tory Hill Cemetery, Buxton.

Wilder, Amos Parker 1862–1936, born: Calais; son of a manufacturer; attended public schools in Augusta, graduate: Worcester (Massachusetts) Military Academy, A.B. Yale College 1884 (member: Skull and Bones), Ph.D. Yale University 1892; taught for a year at Bartlett's School, Old Lyme, Connecticut, at a preparatory school in Faribault, Minnesota; member: editorial staff: *Philadelphia Press* 1886–88, editor: *New Haven Palladium* 1888–92, immediately began a campaign to reform New Haven city government; editorial writer for the *New York Mail and Express*, *New York Commercial Advertiser* 1892–94; part-owner and editor: *Wisconsin State Journal* 1894–1906, supported the policies of Robert M. La Follette, Sr., gained a reputation as a fearless editor and lecturer on municipal and state government reform; appointed by Theodore Roosevelt: U.S. consul general, Hong Kong 1906–09, Shanghai 1909–14; executive secretary: Yale-in-China Association, New Haven 1914–20, which maintained a humanitarian and medical project in Hunan Province, China, lectured across the country and raised significant funds; associate editor: *New Haven Journal Courier* 1920–29, an interesting aspect of the newspaper's editorial policy was the alternation between the militantly anti-prohibitionist editorials of Norris Osbourn with Wilder's own bone-dry statements, many of which were reprinted in national magazines; decorated by the Chinese government for his work in connection with the American Red Cross during a plague in 1911.

Wildes, William Henry 1893– ?, born: Skowhegan; son of a merchant and civil engineer; attended public schools in Skowhegan; associated with E. H. Rollins & Sons, investment bankers, Boston, as a clerk in their Chicago office 1916, vice president and director 1924; executive vice president and director: Central Public Service Corp. 1930, executive vice president and director: Consolidated Electric & Gas Co., Chicago 1932, president: Republic Natural Gas Co., Dallas, Texas, and its subsidiary Texas Coast Oil Co., Corpus Christi, Texas, from 1935; Republic Natural Gas Co. was a gas producer selling its gas to pipeline companies for distribution in Iowa, Nebraska, and Minnesota, principal developers of the Hugoton gas field, located in Texas, Oklahoma, and Kansas, the largest gas field in the world, to that date; in World War I: captain, USA, 33rd Division, participated in the St. Mihiel, Argonne, and Cambrai offensives; director: Republic National Bank of Dallas, Independent Natural Gas Association of America, the Texas Mid-Continent Oil and Gas Association, Independent Petroleum Association; son-in-law of Arthur Robinson Gould.

Wilkes, Eliza Tupper 1844–1917, born: Houlton; daughter of a Congregational minister; attended Calais Academy, A.B. Central University, Pella, Pennsylvania, 1866; first female Unitarian minister, pastor: Menasha, Wisconsin, Rochester, Minnesota, LuVerne, Minnesota, Oakland, California, Santa Barbara; dedicated suffragist, spoke before the California legislature and large public meetings in favor of the proposed 19th Amendment (often juxtaposed with Mary Deering Caswell); appointed to represent California by Governor Hiram Johnson at the International Suffrage Association meeting in Budapest 1913.

Willard, Joseph 1738–1804, born: Biddeford; son of Samuel Willard, left fatherless at age three; proficient in mathematics and navigation from an early age, kept a school for navigation in Scarborough, made several coasting voyages before college; determining that he wished to become a physician, he was informed by Samuel Moody, that to become a doctor he must have Latin and to do so, he must attend Harvard College, Moody took up a subscription for Willard's tuition and arranged for him to be a waiter and scholar of the house; A.B. *cum laude* Harvard College 1765, S.T.D. 1785, L.L.D. Yale College 1790; as an undergraduate, roomed with William Pepperrell; the balance of his college bills were picked up by the father of his classmate, Nathaniel Sparhawk, who along with others, was very proud of this representative of the district, describing him as unquestionably the best geometrician, the best astronomer, and the best classical scholar in his class; like his father, kept school in Lancaster, while bringing out *Ames's Almanack Revived and Improved for 1766*; tutor in Greek: Harvard College, 1765–72, while serving in this position, undergraduate complaints of his autocratic behavior rose to the level of riot, where his quarters were vandalized and he was hung in effigy; appointed senior tutor and member of the Harvard Corporation 1768; issued a pass by General Thomas Gage to travel to Lake Superior to observe a transit of Venus 1769; ordained Congregational minister 1770, minister:

First Congregational Church, Beverly, Massachusetts, 1772–81, on the Dark Day (actually the result of a very large forest fire in the west), 19 May 1780, calmed the excited populace by setting up his astronomical instruments to record the phenomenon; as founding member, vice president, and recording secretary of the American Academy of Arts and Sciences, long served as the voice and pen of that organization, the first two volumes of its *Memoirs* contain several long articles on such matters as "A Method of Finding the Altitude and Longitude of the Nonagesmial Degree of the Ecliptic," "A Table of the Equations to Equal Altitudes, for the Latitude of the University of Cambridge," "A Memoir, Concerning Observations of a Solar Eclipse, October 27, 1780, made at Beverly," "Observations made at Beverly to Determine the Variations of the Magnetic Needle," "Observations of the Transit of Mercury over the Sun's Disk, November 5th., 1789," &c.; as recording secretary, his correspondence ranged as far as St. Petersburg, Russia, resulted in his election to the Royal Society of England, the Medical Society of London, the Royal Society of Göttingen, the American Philosophical Society, &c.; elected thirteenth president of Harvard College 1781–84, his salary was paid from the toll receipts of Harvard's Charles River Bridge, his children long remembered sitting around the table counting the contents of bags of small coins of various nations; kept Harvard College operating during a very difficult period; established Harvard University Medical School; an incorporator and president of the Massachusetts Congregational Charitable Society, charter member of the Society for the Propagating of the Gospel among the Indians and Others in North America; after his sudden death in New Bedford, buried in Cambridge burying ground.

Williams, Ben Ames 1889–1953, born: Macon, Mississippi; A.B. Dartmouth College 1910, Litt.D. Colby College 1942, Dartmouth College 1946; settled in Searsmont; author: *All the Brothers Were Valiant* 1919, *The Sea Bride* 1919, *The Great Accident* 1920, *Evere* 1921, *Black Pearl* 1922, *Thrifty Stock* 1923, *Audacity* 1924, *The Rational Hind* 1925, *The Silver Forest* 1926, *Immortal Longings* 1927, *Splendor* 1927, *Death on Scurvy Street* 1929, *Touchstone* 1930, *Great Oaks* 1930, *An End to Mirth* 1931, *Pirate's Purchase* 1931, *Honey Flow* 1932, *Money Musk* 1932, *Pascal's Mill* 1933, *Mischief* 1933, *Hostile Valley* 1934, *Small Town Girl* 1935, *Crucible* 1937, *The Strumpet Sea* 1938, *Thread of Scarlet* 1939, *The Happy End* 1939, *Come Spring* 1940, *The Strange Woman* 1941, *Time of Peace* 1942, *Amateurs at War* 1943, *Leave Her to Heaven* (later made into a movie) 1944, *It's A Free Country* 1945, *Honor Divided* 1947, *Fraternity Village* 1949, *Over Glen* 1950, *The Unconquered* 1953.

Williams, Edward Patterson 1833–70, born: Castine; son of Hezekiah Williams; graduate: U.S. Naval Academy 1853, commissioned lieutenant, USN, 1855; in the Civil War: served aboard USS *Paul Jones* in the South Atlantic squadron, executive officer aboard USS *Powhatan*, promoted to lieutenant commander, USN, 1862; volunteered to assist in the storming of Fort Sumter 1863, commanded the first division of boats and marines, taken prisoner and held in Columbia, South Carolina, until exchanged; promoted to commander, USN, 1866; served on ordnance duty in Boston and New York; took command of the USS *Oneida* on the Asiatic station 1869; sailing from Yokohama, Japan, *Oneida* was run down and sunk by the English steamer *Bombay*, which, after having extricated her bow from *Oneida*, steamed away without rendering assistance, 22 officers and 115 enlisted men were lost, including Williams, who refused to leave the bridge; his two younger brothers, Henry and Charles, both served with the 10th Missouri Cavalry, CSA, during the Civil War.

Williams, James Leon 1852–1932, born: Embden; attended public school in Emden, Solon, Skowhegan, Oak Grove Seminary, Vassalboro; studied dentistry with Dr. E. J. Roberts, North Vassalboro, practiced in North Vassalboro, New York, New Haven, Connecticut, and Philadelphia; D.D.S. Royal College of Surgeons of Ireland 1879; removed to London, where he practiced from 1887, returned to United States 1915; associated with Dentists' Supply Co., New York, in production of his invention, the Trubyte system of artificial teeth; discovered that there are three distinct types of teeth in all races of men and that these three types are strongly marked in anthropoid apes, apparently proving a near relationship between man and the anthropoid apes; while in Britain, was, by appointment, dentist and purveyor of dentures to the British royal family; fellow: American College of Dentists, American Academy of Dental Science, Royal Anthropological Institute of Great Britain and Ireland; presented to the American Museum of Natural History a collection of pre-historic human teeth that forms the nucleus of the display on teeth in the Hall of Man; it was his examination of molar wear of the Piltdown man that originated the questions which caused it to be found a fraud; a photographer of note, his photogravures continue to fetch high prices; author: *Studies in the Histo-Genesis of the Teeth and Contiguous Parts* 1882, *On the Formation and Structure of Dental Enamel* 1895, *A Contribution to the Study of Pathology of Enamel* 1897; advanced the theory that bacteria was not only present at the formation of caries, but also that bacteria was acid producing; author: *The Home and Haunts of Shakespeare, Gray and the Elegy, The Land of Sleepy Hollow*; retired to Emden; buried in Bingham Village Cemetery.

Williams, Joseph Hartwell 1814–96, born: Augusta; son of Reuel Williams, son-in-law of Lot Morrill, cousin of Seth Williams, grandson of Daniel Cony; attended public school in Augusta and Wiscasset Academy, A.B. Harvard College 1834, student for two years at Dane Law School, Cambridge, Massachusetts, practiced law in Augusta from 1837; broke with the Democratic party over slavery; nominated without his knowledge by the Republicans and was elected member: Maine Senate 1856, president 1857, became acting governor of Maine (Republican) following the resignation of Hannibal Hamlin to accept a seat in the U.S. Senate, served 1857–58, refused renomination because he differed with the Prohibition plank of the Republican platform; member: Maine House of Representatives 1864, 1865, 1866, chairman:

Committee on Finance; member: Maine House of Representatives (Independent) 1874–76; unsuccessful Democratic candidate for governor 1877; author: *A Brief Study in Genealogy* 1885; a founder, along with his father and Lot Morrill, of the Union Mutual Insurance Co. 1848; buried in Riverside Cemetery.

Williams, Reuel 1783–1862, born Hallowell; graduate: Hallowell Academy, although qualified for college entrance at age fifteen, obliged by family circumstance to become a toll collector on the Augusta bridge; A.M. (Hon.) Harvard College 1815, L.L.D. Bowdoin College 1855; attracted the attention of James Bridge, who invited him to enter his law firm in Augusta; member: Massachusetts bar 1804, engaged as junior counsel, with Nathan Dane of Boston, for the Kennebec proprietors, whose agent and attorney was James Bridge 1807; took over the interests of the firm, with the retirement of James Bridge 1812; in 1816, Williams, along with James Bridge and Thomas Winthrop, purchased the remaining lands, property, and interests of the Kennebec proprietors; administrator of Bowdoin College timberlands; a founder of the Maine Historical Society 1822; member: Maine House of Representatives 1822–26, 1829, 1832, 1848, Maine Senate 1827–28; commissioner to divide public lands held in common between Maine and Massachusetts 1825, commissioner of public buildings 1831, oversaw the completion of the Maine statehouse; appointed commissioner, with William Pitt Fessenden and Nicholas Emery, to attempt to settle the boundary dispute with Canada 1832; member: U.S. Senate (Democrat) 1837–43, chairman: Committee on Naval Affairs; while in the Senate, delivered a number of powerful speeches on the boundary dispute with Canada; a key figure in moving state capital to Augusta, in the establishment of Maine Insane Hospital, and the boundary dispute that led to the Aroostook War; Bowdoin College trustee 1822–60; commissioner to plan coastal defenses for the Northern states 1861; Bowdoin College trustee 1822–60; son-in-law to Daniel Cony, uncle of Seth Williams, father of Joseph Hartwell Williams, father-in-law of Sylvester Judd; buried in Riverside Cemetery.

Williams, Seth 1822–66, born: Augusta; nephew of Reuel Williams; attended public schools in Augusta, graduate: U.S. Military Academy 1842; commissioned second lieutenant, USA, assigned to artillery, promoted to first lieutenant, USA, 1847; in the war with Mexican: aide to General Robert Patterson, took part in all the important battles, brevetted captain, USA, for gallantry at Cerro Gordo; adjutant to Robert E. Lee, USA, commandant: U.S. Military Academy 1850–53; in the Civil War: brigadier general, USV, 1861, adjutant general of the Army of the Potomac under Generals McClellan, Burnside, Hooker, and Meade; appointed by General Grant inspector general 1864–66; brevetted major general, USV, for brave conduct in the field from Gettysburg to Petersburg, brevetted brigadier general, USA, 1865 for gallant conduct in the final campaign from Richmond to Appomottax; personally carried General Grant's message to General Lee, requesting the latter's surrender, present at General Lee's surrender (along with Rufus Ingalls), in Wilmer McLean's parlor;

adjutant general of the military district of the Atlantic, headquartered in Philadelphia; buried in Forest Grove Cemetery, Augusta.

Williamson, William Durkee 1779–1846, born: Canterbury, Connecticut; son of a farmer, with whom, he, as a child, removed to Amherst, Massachusetts; taught school for two terms, student at Williams College 1800–02, A.B. Brown University ΦBK 1804, A.M. 1804, Harvard College 1820; studied law in Amherst, Massachusetts, with Warren and Fryeburg; member: Massachusetts bar 1807, practiced in Bangor; Penobscot County attorney 1811–18, member: Massachusetts Senate 1816, 1820, member and president, subsequent to the resignation of William Moody: Maine Senate 1820, 1821, became acting governor of Maine, subsequent to the resignation of William King 28 May 1821, resigned governorship 25 December 1821; member- at-large: U.S. House of Representatives (Democrat) 1821–23; Penobscot County judge of probate 1824–40; Bowdoin College overseer 1821–31, Bangor Theological Seminary; president: Bangor Bank; an original member: Maine Historical Society; contributor: *American Quarterly Register, Collections of the Massachusetts Historical Society,* author: *The History of Maine from Its First Discovery in 1602 to the Separation, A.D. 1820, Inclusive* (two olumes) 1832; buried in Mt. Hope Cemetery, Bangor.

Willis, Nathaniel Parker 1806–72, born: Portland; son of Nathaniel Willis, founder of the *Eastern Argus* and *Youth's Companion*, brother of Sara Willis Payson and Richard Willis, composer of *It Came Upon a Midnight Clear*; graduate: Phillips Academy, Andover, A.B. Yale College 1827; owner and editor: *American Monthly Magazine* 1829–31; co-editor: *New York Mirror* 1831–33, foreign correspondent: *New York Mirror* 1833–44; attaché: U.S. State Department; met with great acclaim in Great Britain as a commentator on British social intricacies, returning to New York, Willis was the highest-paid journalist in the United States; as owner of the *Evening Mirror*, employed Edgar Allan Poe, among others; later began the *National Press*, later *Home Journal*; during Civil War, removed to Washington, D.C., where he was on close terms with Lincoln; although not a member of the Transcendental school, introduced American readers to orientalism, ancient Chinese poetry, and even the work of Sardinian gypsies, made use of the concept of "noble savage" to illustrate the deficiencies of modern life; at his funeral, his pallbearers included: Richard Henry Dana, Oliver Wendell Holmes, Sr., James Russell Lowell, and Henry Wadsworth Longfellow; author: *Scripture Sketches* 1827, *Fugitive Poetry* 1829, *Poem Delivered before the Society of the United Brethren* 1831, *Melanie, and Other Poems* 1835, *The Lady Jane and Other Poems* 1835, *Penciling by the Way* 1835, *Inklings of Adventure* 1836, *Bianca Visconti*, a drama 1839, *Tortesa, the Usurer*, a drama 1839, *Loiterings of Travel* 1839, *l'Abri, or the Tent Pitched* 1839, *Letters from Under a Bridge* 1840, *Poems of Passion* 1843, *Lady Jane, and Other Poems* 1844, *Dashes at Life with a Free Pencil* 1845, *Rural Letters* 1849, *Life Here and There* 1850, *People I Have Met* 1850, *Hurrygraphs* 1851, *Fun Jottings* 1853, *A Summer Cruise in the Mediterranean* 1853, *A Health Trip in the Tropics* 1854, *Out Doors at*

Idlewild 1854, *Famous Persons and Places* 1854, *The Rag Bag* 1855, *Paul Fane*, a novel 1857, *Poems* 1858, *The Convalescent* 1859, editor: *Scenery of the United States and Canada* 1840, *Scenery and Antiquities of Ireland* 1842, *A Life of Jenny Lind* 1851, *Trenton Falls* 1851, *Outdoors at Idlewild* 1854.

Wilson, Carroll Atwood 1886–1947, born: Benton Falls; son of Charles Branch Wilson; A.B. Williams College ΦBK 1907, L.H.D. 1932, student at Harvard University 1907, Rhodes Scholar, B.C.L. Worcester College, Oxford 1911, A.M. Wesleyan University 1935, L.L.D. Colby College 1940; member: Massachusetts bar 1911, New York bar 1922, U.S. Supreme Court bar 1925; practiced in Boston, member: Hurlburt, Jones, and Hall 1916–19, general counsel: Guggenheim Brothers and allied corporations, from 1919; vice president and director: American Smelting and Refining Co. from 1944; trustee: John Simon Guggenheim Memorial Foundation, Williams College; author: *Descriptive Catalogue of the Works of Thomas Hardy* 1940, *Catalogue of the Collection of Samuel Butler* 1945, *Definitive Bibliography of Gilbert and Sullivan* 1947; editor: first appearance in print of some 400 familiar quotations 1935.

Wilson, Charles Stetson 1873–1947, born: Bangor; grandson of Charles Stetson, grandnephew of Isaiah Stetson; U.S. minister to Bulgaria 1921–28, Romania 1928, Yugoslavia 1933; buried in Mount Hope Cemetery, Bangor

Wilson, Obed J. 1826–1914, born: Bingham; son of a member of the Maine Constitutional Convention 1819 and member of the Maine House of Representatives and Senate, nephew of Robert Gray, discoverer of the Columbia River; attended public schools in Bingham, Bloomfield Academy, Skowhegan, removed to Cincinnati, Ohio, 1846, where he taught school for five years and studied law; traveling agent for Winthrop B. Smith & Co., publishers of school books; later correspondent and literary referee, editor in chief of its publications; member: Sargent, Wilson & Hinkle, senior member: Wilson & Hinkle & Co., later the American Book Co., which became the largest school book publishing company in America.

Wing, Frank Everett 1876–1963, born: Fayette, son of a wholesale fruit dealer; attended public schools in Waterville and the Maine Wesleyan Seminary, Kents Hill, A.B. Wesleyan University, Middletown, Connecticut, 1900, A.M. Tufts University 1949; science teacher in schools in Stamford, Connecticut, Milton, Massachusetts, and Pittsburgh, Pennsylvania, 1900–08, participated in a typhoid examination known as the Pittsburgh Survey; superintendent: Chicago Tuberculosis Institute 1908, general superintendent: Municipal Tuberculosis Sanitarium, Chicago; executive director: Committee of One Hundred of Chicago; general secretary: Social Welfare League, Rochester, New York; director: Boston Dispensary 1920–30, when the Boston Floating Hospital for Infants and Children was transferred from the original ship to a new building adjacent to the Boston Dispensary and merged with it and Tufts Medical

School to form the New England Medical Center, Wing became director of the center to 1950; director: Pratt Diagnostic Hospital 1938–48; author of numerous papers on hospital administration; president: Hospital Council of Metropolitan Boston 1938–41, Massachusetts Hospital Association 1946–48; in World War I: served for a year in France with the Red Cross; a registered Maine Guide, maintained a camp at Kokadjo, where he devoted himself to fishing and philately.

Wing, Simon 1826–1916, born: Saint Albans; daguerreotyper in Waterville, invented a multiplying camera that could produce multiple images of the same picture, revolutionizing the industry, removed to Boston 1861, where he introduced the tintype, patented several other useful advances in photography and the means to display them, owned several studios in the West; spiritualist; an organizer of the Socialist-Labor party and candidate for president of the United States 1892.

Wingate, Joseph Ferdinand 1786– ?, born: Haverhill, Massachusetts; merchant in Bath; member: Massachusetts House of Representatives 1818–19, collector of customs, Bath, 1820–24; member from the Third District: U.S. House of Representatives 1827–31; removed to Windsor; said to be buried in Rest Haven Cemetery, South Windsor, but this writer cannot find any grave marker for him.

Winslow, Edward Francis 1837–1914, born: Augusta; graduate: Augusta High School; removed to Mt. Pleasant, Iowa, 1856, became involved in the construction of railroads; in the Civil War: commissioned captain, USV, in the 4th Iowa Volunteer Cavalry 1861, promoted to major, USV, 3 January 1863, colonel, USV, 4 July 1863; took part in the Vicksburg campaign; the campaign against General Joseph E. Johnson; appointed by General Sherman, chief of cavalry, placed in command of the cavalry forces of the 15th Corps, a post he held until March 1864; in February 1864 commanded the cavalry of General Sherman's army in the campaign against General Leonidas Polk, successfully attacked the Confederate cavalry at Jackson, Mississippi; in command of a brigade of cavalry in the engagement at Guntown, Mississippi, later successfully covered the retreat of Union forces; in October 1864, his command formed a part of General Pleasanton's pursuit of General Sterling Price; severely wounded at Big Blue River, brevetted brigadier general, USV, commanded his brigade in the expedition against Montgomery, Columbus, and Macon, took Columbus by assault; after the war returned to railroad construction; vice president, general manager of the Manhattan Elevated Railway, New York, took control of the property and unified the system of control and management of the line; president: St. Louis & San Francisco Railroad Co., vice president: Atlantic & Pacific Railroad Co. from 1880; also served as president of the New York, Ontario & Western Railroad Co., formed an association for the purpose of building the West Shore Railroad, which he completed in three years; Winslow, Arizona, was named in his honor.

Winslow, Marlon Hamblen 1864–1925, born: Cumberland Mills, Westbrook; removed, with his parents, to Hiawatha, Kansas, 1868, attended district schools and night school in Terre Haute, Indiana; an industrious youth with a crippled father, paid off the mortgage on the family farm by raising forty acres of corn at the age of twelve, began selling scales in Kansas, associated with the United Scales Works of Terre Haute, became an independent manufacturer of scales 1896; president: Winslow Government Scales Works, Inc., manufacturers of the largest scales in the world, on which he held several patents, the last of which was for an extremely simple, yet durable scale capable of weighing one million pounds, made the first scales capable of weighing coal-filled railroad cars, made scales for mine tipples, in use worldwide.

Wiswall, John 1731–1812, born: Boston; son of Peleg Wiswall, a famous Boston schoolmaster; A.B. Harvard College 1749, A.M. 1752, as an undergraduate, Wiswall was degraded for joining in the burning of fences, hogsheads, and an outhouse to celebrate Guy Fawkes; sailed with his classmate, Robert Treat Paine, to Casco Bay but returned to Massachusetts to keep school; in his undergraduate days, harbored visions of a life as an officer in the Royal Navy, pursuant to this, attended a mathematics school in Boston, but, having no sponsor and, therefore, no chance at preferment, returned to schoolkeeping, first in Billerica, then Medford; returned to Falmouth 1752; returned to Boston 1753, to study theology; preached his first sermon in Littleton, New Hampshire, 1754, became an itinerant minister, which brought him to eventually to North Yarmouth; the Reverend Thomas Smith rode in with a call to the pulpit of the Third Church of Falmouth, which at that time held a dangerous position on the frontier, several members of the congregation having been killed by Indians earlier that year; built a house at what is now the corner of Middle and Exchange Streets 1759, married Mercy Minot, daughter of Judge John Minot of Brunswick 1761; shortly after his marriage, became quite deranged and had to be closely confined in a dark chamber, regained his wits after a few months and never suffered a relapse; found himself square in the middle of the fight between the Reverend Smith, his new assistant, Samuel Deane, and the congregation; rumors flowed that the secessionists wanted to raise a new meetinghouse and adopt the Church of England rule, with Wiswall presiding; at one point, the argument led to a fist fight in the street between General Jedidiah Preble and Captain John Waite 1764; later that year, the Episcopalians carried the vote and demanded that the architecture of the new meetinghouse be suitable for worship agreeable to the laws of Great Britain; with Governor Bernard and several other leading Episcopalians of Boston in attendance, the cornerstone of St. Paul's was laid and Wiswall given a formal call and the promise of a salary of £100 per annum; the wardens of St. Paul's immediately wrote to the Society for the Propagation of the Gospel, requesting that Wiswall be given a mission appointment; Wiswall took a mastship to England, where he was ordained deacon and then, priest; Wiswall's conversion was widely reported in colonial newspapers, most commented upon his previous bout with insanity, some even suggested that it was the plan of the

Society for the Propagation of the Gospel to dispatch missionaries to the moon, others more soberly suggested that Wiswall had been irked that Samuel Deane had been chosen Thomas Smith's colleague (in fact, Deane and Wiswall continued to fish together on Casco Bay); after his ordination, the new church could not make good on their salary promise, to augment his income he kept a school; managed to avoid the sectarian arrogance that typified other Church of England preachers (such as Jacob Bailey); local irritation was primarily derived from the attention lavished by officers of the Royal Navy and Royal Army on Wiswall and St. Paul's; Wiswall refused to proclaim a fast day, as ordered by the Massachusetts House of Representatives, nor would he take up a collection for the relief of Bostonians, feeling that would countenance rebellion; subsequent to the battle at Lexington and Concord, temporarily took refuge aboard HMS *Canceaux*, but returned after receiving assurance from the selectmen that he would not be disturbed; a month later, on 9 May 1775, Samuel Thompson and his force intended to capture Captain Mowatt while he worshiped in St. Paul's Church, thwarted by contrary winds, they lay in ambush, and on the next day captured Mowatt and Wiswall while they strolled on Munjoy Hill; the mob, which grew in size to over 300, was undecided as what to do with the captives, particularly since the officer of the deck aboard HMS *Canceaux* threatened to fire on the town if Mowatt was not released; eventually, it was concluded that Mowatt and Wiswall would be paroled, Mowatt almost immediately broke his word and parole by returning to his ship; Wiswall was hauled before a summary court martial, where he defended himself and his word so ably that he was once again released; Wiswall promptly made his way aboard HMS *Canceaux*, on which he made his way to Boston; petitioned General Gage for relief and was appointed chaplain of the 44th and 63rd Regiments; after hearing that his property in Falmouth had been confiscated (it was later destroyed in the fire), he beseeched the Society for the Propagation of the Gospel for assistance; Admiral Graves (who had ordered the burning of Falmouth) appointed Wiswall chaplain aboard HMS *Liverpool*, later HMS *Prescott*, on which he sailed to England 1776; later appointed chaplain aboard HMS *Rainbow*, aboard which he and his sons sailed to Halifax, where he conducted a mathematics school; appointed chaplain aboard HMS *Boyne* 1778, on which he saw several actions against the French fleet in the West Indies, including the battle of the Saints; after the treaty of Paris 1783, served as curate in various small parishes in southeastern England, appointed to succeed Jacob Bailey as missionary in Cornwallis, Nova Scotia, which proved to be a very uncomfortable position given the heterodox nature of the local inhabitants and competition from itinerant revivalists (mostly Tory refugees); eventually settled in the parish of Wilmot and Aylesford where he remained until his death; buried near the Middleton Episcopal Church; his sons eventually left the Royal Navy and founded a distinguished line of magistrates in Nova Scotia.

Wood, Frederick Hill 1877–1943, born: Lebanon; A.B. University of Kansas ΦBK 1897, L.L.B. 1899; member: Kansas and Missouri bars 1899, New York bar 1904;

practiced in Lawrence, Kansas, assistant professor of law: University of Kansas 1899–1901, removed to Kansas City, Missouri 1901–10, general counsel: Saint Louis & San Francisco Railroad 1910–13, Southern Pacific Railroad, New York, 1910–24; partner: Cravath, Henderson, and de Gersdorff, which became Cravath, de Gersdorff, Swaine, and Wood from 1924; as the most prominent and capable anti-New Deal lawyer, argued the O'Fallon test case before the U.S. Supreme Court on principles of railway rate valuation, *Schechter Poultry Corporation* v. *United States* (the so-called sick chicken case) involving the constitutionality of the National Industrial Recovery Act (which resulted in the N.R.I.A. being found to be unconstitutional, a stunning blow to the Roosevelt Administration), the *Carter* v. *Carter Coal Co.* case involving the Guffey Bituminous Coal Conservation Act, and the gold clause case.

Wood, Fremont 1856–1940, born: Winthrop; son of an abolitionist Maine legislator; student: Winthrop Academy, Waterville Classical Academy, Bates College, A.B. 1907, studied law in Winthrop with L. C. Carleton; member: Idaho bar 1881, Boise city attorney, assistant U.S. attorney for territory of Idaho, U.S. attorney for the Territory of Idaho 1889; with Idaho's admission to the Union, became the first federal attorney for the new state 1890–03; prosecuted the Coeur d'Alene miners for conspiracy; elected judge of the third judicial district of Idaho 1906–10, presided over the world-famous trials of William D. Heywood, George A. Pettibone, and Charles Moyer, who were indicted for the murder of former governor Frank Steunenburg; Heywood and Moyer, president and secretary respectively of the Western Federation of Miners, were eventually found not guilty, Harry Orchard confessed to the crime and was sentenced to hang with a recommendation for clemency; Wood was widely applauded for his manifest fairness in his conduction of the trials; an avid fly-fisherman, he took O. K. Davis, the reporter from the *New York Times*, fishing every weekend during the trial; after his term in office, returned to private practice, prepared a legal history of the trial (which still generates considerable debate), and raised fruit on his apple orchard, grew roses; author: *Moyer, Haywood, Pettibone, and Orchard.*

Wood, Henry Clay 1832–1918, born: Winthrop; A.B. Bowdoin College 1854, A.M. 1857, B.S. Norwich College 1874, studied medicine 1854, read law, member: Maine bar 1856; appointed major and aide-de-camp to Major General Samuel Wood, commanding officer: Maine militia 1856; in the Civil War: first lieutenant, 11th U.S. Infantry, recipient: Medal of Honor, at Wilson's Creek, Missouri, 10 August 1861, distinguished gallantry; as major, USA, served as adjutant general to General O. O. Howard in the Nez Perce War, probably saved Howard from removal by inappropriately telegraphing news of Howard's temporary (as it turned out) victory over the hostiles directly to President Rutherford B. Hayes 1877; promoted through the ranks to brigadier general, USA, 1904; author: *The Treaty Status of Young Joseph and His Band of Nez Perce Indians* 1876; buried at Arlington National Cemetery.

Wood, Sarah Barrell Keating 1759–1855, born: York; wife of Abiel Wood; Maine's first novelist, her works include: *Julia and the Illuminated Baron* 1800, *Dorval: or the Speculator, Amelia: or the Influence of Virtue, An Old Man's Story* 1802, *Ferdinand and Elmira: A Russian Story, Tales of the Night* (contains the stories "Storms and Sunshine: or the House on the Hill," "The Hermitage") 1827.

Woodman, Clarence Eugene 1852–1924, born: Saco, A.B. *cum laude* Trinity College φBK 1873, A.M. Amherst College 1877, Ph.D. Manhattan College 1881; converted to Roman Catholicism and ordained priest, pastor: Saint Paul's New York City, lecturer: Newman Hall, University of California, lecturer on electricity: Catholic University 1891–93, astronomer: Smithsonian Eclipse Expedition 1900; author: *Manual of Prayers* 1887, *Bridal Wreath* 1888, *Civil and Religious Liberty* 1890, *Poets and Poetry of Ireland* 1892; knighted by the king of Spain 1894 (Knight Commander, Royal Order of Isabella the Catholic); appointed by the Third Plenary Council of Baltimore to prepare the official manual of prayer for the Roman Catholic Church in the United States.

Woods, Leonard 1807–78, born: Newbury, Massachusetts; son of a clergyman; A.B. Union College 1827 φBK, graduate: Andover Theological Seminary 1831, D.D. Harvard University 1846, L.L.D. Bowdoin College 1866; resident graduate scholar and assistant instructor in Hebrew at Andover Theological Seminary 1831-33, licensed to preach 1833, editor: *Literary and Theological Review*, New York 1834–37; professor of sacred literature: Bangor Theological Seminary 1836–39; fourth president: Bowdoin College, trustee and overseer ex-officio 1839–66; greatly strengthened Bowdoin College financially, built King Chapel, Appleton Hall, Adams Hall (medical school); after his resignation, accepted a commission from the Maine Historical Society to go abroad to gather materials on the early history of the state; translator: George Christian Knapp's *Christian Theology* (two olumes) 1831–33, author: *Discovery of Maine* 1868.

Woods, Solomon Adams 1827–1907, born: Farmington; son of a farmer; attended public school in Farmington and Farmington Academy; manufacturer of doors, sashes, blinds in partnership with Solomon Gray in Boston 1851, bought out Gray's interest 1852, organized the firm of Gray and Woods for the manufacture of the planing machine invented by Gray 1854, later Woods purchased Gray's interest in the machine, which became world famous under the name of Gray and Woods planer; to this other lines of woodworking machines were added, including the Woodworth planer; a larger factory was constructed in South Boston, with branches in Chicago and New York; member: Boston City Council 1869–71, trustee: South Boston Savings Bank.

Woodward, Samuel Walter 1848–1917, born: Damariscotta; graduate: Lincoln Academy; clerked for Cushing & Ames, a clothing and dry goods firm in Boston; with his co-worker, Alvin Lothrop, established Woodward & Lothrop, a drygoods store in Chelsea, Massachusetts, 1873, opened its first store in Washington, D.C., 1880, grew to become one of the largest in the United States; president: Washington Board of Trade, Young Men's Christian Association, American Baptist Missionary Union, director: National City Bank, Union Savings Bank.

Woolson, Abba Louisa Goold 1838–1921, born: Windham; daughter of William Goold, author of *Portland in the Past* and recording secretary of the Maine Historical Society; valedictorian, Girls' High School, Portland, 1856; married the principal, Moses Woolson, 1856; lecturer on literature and history in Boston, New York, Washington, and other cities in the East, her topics were: "English Literature in Connection with English History," "The Influence of Foreign Nations upon English Literature," "Dramas of Shakespeare, as Illustrating English History," "The Historic Cities of Spain"; founder and honorary president: Castilian Club of Boston; founded the Massachusetts Moral Education Association to combat prostitution; served as president of the Massachusetts Society for the University Education of Women; author: *Woman in American Society* (wherein she deplored the hazardous nature of popular fashion, lack of opportunity for female graduates of high school, the need to conform to society's dictates in the display necessary to secure a husband for support) 1873, *Dress Reform* 1874, *Browsing Among Books* 1881, *George Eliot and Her Heroines—A Study* 1886.

Wowurna fl.1670–1738, born: Maine; a leading chief of the Norridgewock division of the Abenakis; an ally of the French, represented twenty leading Norridgewock, Penobscot, Pigwacket, and Androscoggin Indians in a meeting with Governor Shute of Massachusetts at Georgetown on Arrowsic Island 1717, where he denied Shute's right to build forts and new settlements, rejected King George I as the Indians' sovereign and ignored the missionary Joseph Baxter, brought to serve them, insisted that English claims up the Kennebec and east of it were unfounded, "we can't understand how our lands have been purchased, what has been alienated was by our gift," he supported his actions with a letter from Father Râle; as English settlements spread to Merrymeeting Bay, Swan Island, and east of the Kennebec, depredations spread, Wowurna in the van; went to Québec where he informed Governor Rigaud that they were determined to resist the English, the French supplied them with munitions; after an unsatisfactory parley at Georgetown, Father Râle organized a major confrontation at Georgetown 1721; Fathers Râle and LaChasse, Joseph d'Abbadie de Saint-Castin, and Charles Legardeur de Croisil, with 250 Indians and Wowurna marched into Georgetown under French colors; the English refused Wowurna's demands and prepared for war; after an English attempt to seize Râle, Wowurna led a war party that destroyed the settlement on Merrymeeting Bay 1721; Massachusetts declared war

(Dummer's War), destroyed the mission at Norridgewock, and killed Father Râle, after which Wowurna resided in Québec; led a party of warriors in a raid on Damariscove Island 1725; Wowurna and others ratified the peace at Falmouth 1727, as principal of the Norridgewock tribe, visited Boston and drank to the king's health in the council chamber and assured the settlers in Sheepscot of the Indians' peaceful intentions 1738.

Wyman, Walter Scott 1874–1942, born: Oakland; son of a farmer; graduate: Coburn Classical Institute, student of electrical engineering: Tufts University 1893–96; began work as an inspector and assistant superintendent with the Maine Water Co., Waterville 1896; general manager: Waterville and Fairfield Railway & Light Co. 1899–1901, purchased a small hydroelectric plant in Oakland 1899, incorporated as the Messalonskee Electric Co. 1905, subsequently building hydroelectric plants on the Messalonskee and Sebasticook Rivers and a steam plant in Farmingdale, incorporating the above in 1910, as Central Maine Power Co.; by 1924, Wyman had acquired thirty-seven separate electric companies; concerned that drought could threaten the power supply of Maine, envisioned a tremendous floating steam-powered electric station that could be moved anywhere on the coast or up rivers, whenever extra power was required; built the Wyman Dam at Moscow 1929–31; brought in Samuel Insull for capital, CMP was subsumed into New England Public Service Corp.; with Insull's fall and subsequent imprisonment, Wyman salvaged CMP from the wreckage; because of the Fernald Act, which prevented the export of electrical power generated in Maine, Wyman began acquiring positions in many Maine businesses: textiles, shoes, paper, Bath Iron Works, &c.; represented Maine at the World Power Conference, Washington, D.C., 1936; trustee: Colby College; father of William Frizzell Wyman; buried in Forest Grove Cemetery, Augusta, adjacent to his son, William Frizzell Wyman, James G. Blaine, William Howard, and Guy Gannett.

Wyman, Willard Gordon 1898–1969, born: Augusta; attended Lincoln Academy 1912-15, graduate: Coburn Classical Institute, Waterville 1916, attended Bowdoin College 1917, B.S. U.S. Military Academy 1919; graduate: Coastal Artillery School, Fort Monroe, Virginia, Cavalry School, Fort Riley, Kansas; student of Chinese language in Peiping, also attached to mail attachés office, Peiping, 1928–32, member: Central Asiatic Expedition under Roy Chapman Andrews 1930; graduate: Command and General Staff School 1937, aide to commanding general: 1st Cavalry Division, later IX Corps 1940–41, assigned to the Plans Division of the War Department general staff 1941–42, deputy chief of staff for operations: China-Burma-India theater of operations 1942, deputy chief of staff for operations: Allied Force headquarters 1942–43, promoted to brigadier general, USA, 1943, assistant commanding officer: First U.S. Infantry Division 1943–44, promoted to major general, USA, 1944, commanding officer: 71st Infantry Division 1944–45, chief of staff, 1st U.S. Infantry Division 1947–50, during the Korean War, commanding officer: IX Corps 1951–52, commander of Allied Land Forces in Southeastern Europe 1952–54, commanding officer: 6th Army (Presidio) 1954–55, commanding officer: General Continental Army Command, Fort Monroe, Virginia, 1956–58, retired as general, USA, 1958; recipient: Silver Star, croix de guerre with palm (France), Distinguished Service Medal with first oak leaf cluster, two Bronze Stars.

Yeaton, Hopley 1740–1812, born: Portsmouth, New Hampshire; received a land grant in North Lubec, for service in the American Revolution, on which he farmed, while not at sea; commissioned by President Washington 1791, master of the revenue cutter *Scammel*, as such, Yeaton was the first commissioned officer of the Revenue Cutter Service, later merged with the Life Saving Service to become the U.S. Coast Guard; originally buried on his farm in North Lubec, in 1975, the Coast Guard exhumed his body and, in great state, conducted it to New London, Connecticut, aboard the USCGC *Eagle*, where he was reinterred at the U.S. Coast Guard Academy, the USCGC *Yeaton* was named in his honor.

York, Zebulon 1819–1900, born: Avon; attended Maine Wesleyan Seminary, Kents Hill, attended Transylvania University, L.L.B. University of Louisiana (later Tulane University); settled in Vidalia, Louisiana, practiced law, came to own six plantations and 1,700 slaves; was, reportedly, the largest payer of realty tax in Louisiana; in the Civil War: organized the 14th Louisiana Infantry, elected major, lieutenant colonel, and colonel, CSA; commanding officer: 14th Louisiana Infantry; led his regiment in the battles of Williamsburg, Seven Days; colonel, CSA; second Bull Run, Antietam, Fredericksburg, on recruitment duty, so missed Chancellorsville, Gettysburg; brigadier general, CSA; in command of all Louisiana troops in Lee's army, with Early at Lynchburg, Monocacy, and Washington raid; severely wounded at Winchester, losing an arm; attempted to raise troops among foreign-born prisoners; after the war managed the York House, a hotel in Natchez, where he subsequently died and is buried.

Young, Albion Gustavus 1843–1926, born: Lincolneus, graduate: Houlton Academy, M.D. Medical School of Maine 1867, A.M. Bowdoin College 1894, postgraduate work at Harvard University Medical School, University of Berlin; practiced in Houlton 1869, removed to Bridgewater 1870, returned to Houlton 1874, removed to Fort Fairfield 1879–85; secretary: Maine State Board of Health 1885–1917; director: division of communicable diseases, Maine State Department of Health 1917–26; he accepted the post of secretary at a time when there was a smallpox epidemic raging in Québec (one of the worst in the history of the continent), realizing Maine's exposed position, he vaccinated all railroad personnel, warning loggers and residents of border towns of the danger, and thus averted the danger to Maine; secured the appropriation for a state laboratory, wrote the legislation for the Vital Statistics Law 1892, drafted all the earlier health laws of the state; he inspected schoolhouses and exposed their deplorable conditions, wrote a special report on school hygiene, considered the best in the country to that time, requests for which poured in from all sides; after visiting the leading sanatoria in the East and in Canada, he issued a report indicating that a cold northern climate was as favorable to the treatment of tuberculosis as that of the Southwest, which led to the organization of the Maine State Tuberculosis Association and the establishment of the sanitarium in Hebron; through his efforts, Maine was one of the first states to analyze drinking water; he was also a pioneer in the use of disinfectants.

Young, Joshua Moody 1808–66, born: Shapleigh; son of a Harvard graduate, descendent of Samuel Moody, cousin of Ralph Waldo Emerson, Cyrus Hamlin; apprenticed as a printer with the *Portland Eastern Argus*, editor: *Maine Democrat* (Saco); converted to Catholicism, changed name to Josué Maria Young, printer for the *Catholic Telegram* (Cincinnati), trained for the priesthood at Saint Mary's Seminary, Emmitsburg, Maryland, ordained 1838, diocesan missionary, Saint Mary's Church, Lancaster, Ohio, consecrated bishop of Erie (Pennsylvania) 1854, doubled the number of churches in his see, built orphanages, hospitals, and several schools.

Yourcenar, Marguerite 1903–87, born: Brussels, Belgium; settled in Somesville; educated privately by tutors, Litt.D (Hon.) Smith College 1961, Bowdoin College 1968; lecturer at various American and European universities 1940–87; author: novels and short stories, *Nouvelle Eurydice* 1931, *Denier du Rêve* 1934 (English translation: *A Coin in Nine Hands* 1982), *Nouvelles Orientales* 1938, *Le Coup de Grâce* 1939 (English translation 1957), *Mémoires d'Hadrien* 1951 (English translation 1963), *Comme leau qui coule* 1982, *Le Temps ce grand Sculpteur: Essays Pindare* 1932, *Sous Bénéfice d'Inventaire* 1962 (English translation: *The Dark Grain of Piranesi, Anna Soror* 1981), *L'Oeuvre au Noir* 1968, *Mishima ou la Vision du Vide* 1981, *Une Homme Obseur* 1985, *Quoi d'Éternité?*, plays, *Electra ou la Chute des Masques* 1954, *Le Mystère d'Alceste et Qui na pas son Minotaure* 1963, poems and prose poems: *Feux* 1936 (English translation *Fires* 1981), *Les Charites d'Alcippe* 1956 (English translation *The Alms of Alcippe* 1982), articles "The Collegend of Krishna" in *Encounter* 1959, "Humanism in Thomas Mann" in *Partisan Review* 1962, translated into French: *The Waves* by Virginia Woolf 1937, *What Maisie Knew* by Henry James 1947, *Negro Spirituals, Fleuve Profond, Sombre Rivie* 1964, *Poems* by Hortense Flexner 1969, *The Amen Corner* by James Baldwin 1983, *Cinq No Modernes* by Yukio Mishima 1984, *Blues and Gospel* 1984, from modern Greek: *Poemes* by Constantin Cavalfy 1958, from ancient Greek: *La Couronne et la Lyre* 1979; commander of honor, officer, Order of Merit, France, officer, Order of Leopold, Belgium, recipient: Prix Femina Vacaresco 1952, Prix Combat for Sous Benefice d'Inventaire and ensemble of her work 1963, first female to be elected to Academie Française 1980, member: American Academy of Arts and Letters.

Zorach, William 1887–1966, born: Eurburg, Lithuania; brought to America as a child; student at the Cleveland School of Art, National Academy of Design, A.M. Bowdoin College 1958, D.F.A. Colby College 1960, Bates College 1964; settled in Georgetown; prize for sculpture: Chicago Art Institute 1931, Logan Medal for watercolors: Art Institute of Chicago 1932, Gold Medal: National Institute of Arts and Letters 1961, Widener Medal: Pennsylvania Academy of Fine Arts 1963; work in Brooklyn Museum, New York, the Museum of Modern Art, New York, Phillips Gallery, Washington, D.C., sculptor for new post office building, Washington, D.C., four groups of figures for façade of Mayo Clinic, monumental high relief in aluminum: Fairleigh Dickinson University, Klemer Memorial Fountain, Saint Louis; author: *Zorach Explains Sculpture*.